BARRON'S FINANCIAL GUIDES

Barron's Financial
Tables for
Money Management

Adjustable-Rate Mortgages

Third Edition

Jack P. Friedman, Ph.D., CPA, MAI
Jack P. Friedman & Associates
Real Estate Economist and Consultant
Dallas, Texas

Jack C. Harris, Ph.D.
Research Economist
Real Estate Center
Adjunct Professor of Finance
Texas A&M University

BARRON'S

Great effort has been made to develop accurate tables;
however, no warranty of absolute accuracy is given.

All inquiries should be addressed to:
Barron's Educational Series, Inc.
250 Wireless Boulevard
Hauppauge, New York 11788
http://www.barronseduc.com

Library of Congress Catalog Card No. 2003070921

International Standard Book No. 0-7641-2454-4

Library of Congress Cataloging-in-Publication Data
Friedman, Jack P.
    Adjustable-rate mortgages / Jack P. Friedman, Jack C.
Harris.—3rd ed.
        p.   cm.—(Barron's financial tables for better money
management)
        ISBN 0-7641-2454-4
    1. Loan amortization schedules.   2. Adjustable rate
mortgages—Tables. I. Harris, Jack C., 1945–   II. Title.
III. Series.
HG1634.F75   2004
332.8—dc22

                                                        2003070921

PRINTED IN THE UNITED STATES OF AMERICA

9 8 7 6 5 4 3 2 1

Contents

Table 1. Monthly Payments
  Monthly payments necessary to
    amortize a loan
  Interest Rates: 2% to 15% by $\frac{1}{4}$%
  Principal Amounts: $100 to
    $1,000,000
  Amortization Terms: 5 to 20 years
    by five years; 21 to 30 years by
    one year

Table 7. Annual Loan Balance
    Remaining
  Amounts of mortgage principal
    remaining per year
  Interest Rates: 2% to 15% by $1/4$%
  Loan Age: 29 to 20 years by one
    year; 15 to 5 years by five years
  Original Amortization Terms: 15 and
    30 years

ACKNOWLEDGMENTS

Preparing this book would not have been possible without the aid of others. Dr. Mark Rush, visiting scholar at the Federal Reserve Bank in Kansas City, provided a thorough, perceptive review of the work, which improved the text and tables, making them more useful and concise. We are grateful to Tom Hirsch and Don Reis, editors at Barron's Educational Series, who coordinated the earlier editions and offered suggestions that improved the manuscript; to Pat Hunter for this third edition; and especially to Suzanne S. Barnhill, Fairhope, Alabama, for meticulous editing. Despite the assistance received, we remain responsible for any inaccuracies that may exist.

Jack C. Harris
Jack P. Friedman

ABOUT THE AUTHORS

Jack P. Friedman, PhD, CPA, MAI, is a real estate economist and author in Dallas, Texas. Formerly, Friedman was the Julio S. Laguarta Professor of Real Estate in the Department of Finance, and Research Economist in the Real Estate Center, Texas A&M University. Jack C. Harris, PhD, is Research Economist at the Real Estate Center, and Adjunct Professor of Finance, Texas A&M University. The two are the co-authors of Barron's best-selling *Real Estate Dictionary* and *Real Estate Handbook*. Friedman's other books include *The Encyclopedia of Investments*, *The Complete Guide to Investment Opportunities,* and *Income Property Appraisal and Analysis*. The authors have contributed extensively to business and scholarly literature and to the popular media, particularly in the areas of real estate investment and finance. Harris is a recipient of the highly coveted Percy and Betty Wagner Award from the Appraisal Institute.

Preface

In today's mortgage market you will find a variety of types of loans, including adjustable-rate loans, fixed-rate loans, and hybrids that offer some characteristics of both types. The purpose of this book is to familiarize you, the borrower, with the types of loans that are available in the market, so that you can select the most suitable one.

This book will also acquaint you with the fundamentals of the mortgage market. That includes an explanation of who the players are, why there is a choice of mortgage types, and many of the factors you need to consider to select the most suitable loan for your circumstances.

The mortgage originator that you initially borrow from doesn't care which type you select because it expects to earn an origination fee for any type of loan. Behind the mortgage originator is a mortgage investor who wants a rate of return on its investment that is commensurate with the risks for each type of loan. Mortgage investors price their loan offerings so that their interest rates and risk are perceived to bear an appropriate relationship to other investment opportunities they (mortgage investors) have. These include corporate bonds, U.S. Treasury bonds, and mortgage securities.

You should care which loan you get. This includes how much to borrow, how long to repay, and whether it is an adjustable-rate mortgage (ARM), a fixed-rate loan, or a hybrid.

During periods of rising interest rates, mortgage investors prefer adjustable-rate mortgages (ARMs) and price them accordingly, compared with fixed-rate loans. The price relationship is called the "spread" of interest rates. It is obvious why lenders prefer ARMs during rising rates: as rates rise, they get a raise. During periods of declining interest rates, however, lenders want to retain the old (higher) rate for as long as possible. So the "spread" will fluctuate, depending on expectations of future interest rates.

Of course, if market interest rates decline enough, the astute borrower will refinance the entire loan at the new, lower interest rate, defeating the lender's effort to retain a high interest for a long term. The lender's pricing therefore includes market expectations of refinancing as well.

The purpose of this book is to acquaint you with the various types of loans available, to help you decide whether to get a fixed-rate, adjustable-rate, or hybrid mortgage. We hope the increased knowledge you derive from reading this book will allow you to select the type of loan that best suits your expectations of the future, your budget, and your willingness to accept risk.

Glossary

Adjustable-Rate Mortgage. A mortgage loan in which the lender may adjust the rate of interest according to some specific index at periodic intervals during the loan term. Commonly abbreviated *ARM*.

Amortization. The process of retiring the principal balance during the term of the loan. A *self-amortizing* loan is one in which the principal is completely retired at the end of the term.

Annual Adjustment Cap. A limit applied to the change allowed in the interest rate during any one adjustment period; see *Payment Cap*.

Annual Percentage Rate. A measure of the cost of credit expressed as a yearly percentage rate. Includes the contract rate plus discount points amortized over a period of time set by the Truth in Lending law. Commonly abbreviated *APR*.

Contract (Face) Interest Rate. The interest rate on a loan as expressed in the loan agreement. Not the same as the APR. The contract rate does not take into account any discount points charged on the loan.

Discount Points. Charges paid by a borrower to get a mortgage loan. Each discount point equals 1 percent of the amount of the loan and is a onetime charge paid at the time of loan origination.

Effective Interest Rate. The actual cost of credit to the borrower. The effective interest rate takes into account the contract interest rate plus discount points charged at origination, amortized over the actual or estimated life of the loan.

Fixed-Rate Mortgage. A mortgage loan in which the interest rate is constant for the entire term of the loan. Commonly abbreviated *FRM*.

Fully Indexed Rate. The interest rate that can be charged on an ARM based on the current value of the index. The rate is calculated by adding the *margin* to the current value of the index.

Hybrid Mortgage. Combines features of a fixed-rate and an adjustable-rate mortgage. A *step* hybrid offers a fixed rate for 3, 5, 7, or 10 years, then a rate change to the market interest rate, followed by amortization at the new interest rate for the remainder of the term, which totals up to 30 years. A different type of hybrid becomes annually adjustable after the initial fixed period of 3, 5, 7, or 10 years. A *convertible ARM* is a hybrid that acts like an ARM but with opportunities to convert to an FRM at specified times.

Index. The specific indicator of interest rates that governs adjustments in the interest rate on an ARM.

Initial Interest Rate. The interest rate applied to the ARM from the time it is originated until the first adjustment date; see *teaser rate.*

Interest. The cost of borrowed money. Generally expressed as an annual percentage applied to the outstanding principal.

Life-of-Loan Cap. A limitation to the amount an ARM interest rate may change from the initial interest rate over the term of the loan.

Lock-in. An agreement between a loan originator and prospective borrower as to the interest rate and other loan terms that will apply when the loan is closed. The lock-in period is typically 30 to 60 days. There may be a charge to lock in, especially when interest rates are volatile.

Margin. A constant amount added to the value of the index for the purpose of adjusting the interest rate on an ARM. The margin plus the *index* equals the *fully indexed rate.*

Monthly Payment. The periodic payment due on a mortgage loan each month to cover accrued interest and amortize the principal balance.

Negative Amortization. A situation in which the principal balance is increased with each monthly payment because the payment is too small to cover all the interest due on the outstanding principal balance.

Original Principal. The amount of money initially borrowed.

Outstanding Principal. The *principal balance* that remains unpaid at any given time.

Percentage Point. 1 percent of interest. An increase in the interest rate from 9 percent to 10 percent represents a 1 percentage point change.

Permanent Mortgage. A real estate financing arrangement that is expected to remain on the property for a lengthy period, as contrasted with a *construction loan.*

Principal Balance. The amount of principal that has not been repaid or amortized at any one time during the loan term. Same as *outstanding principal.* The amount of interest that accrues over a month is the monthly interest rate multiplied by the principal balance at the beginning of the month.

Rate Adjustment. The process of changing the interest rate on an ARM; consists of reviewing the current interest rate in relation to the current value of the index and adjusting the interest rate accordingly.

Refinance. Replace (pay off) an existing mortgage with a new mortgage, generally to obtain a more favorable interest rate or to extract cash.

Teaser Rate. An interest rate applied to an ARM at origination that is lower than the fully indexed rate at the time. The teaser rate is effective until the first adjustment date on the ARM.

Term. The period of time a loan is scheduled to be in effect. Sometimes referred to as the *maturity* of the loan. A full *amortization* term is the period required to retire the entire debt through systematic installment payments.

How to Find Data on ARM Indexes

Following are the data series commonly used as ARM indexes. You can find current and past values of the series on the Web sites mentioned.

Treasury Yields: Commonly used are the weekly average yields on United States Treasury securities adjusted to a constant maturity of one, three, or ten years, depending on the index used. The maturity usually coincides with the length of the adjustment period. Current values on all maturities can be found on the Federal Reserve site (www.federalreserve.gov/releases/h15/update).
All past values of this index can be found at the same site:

One-year: www.federalreserve.gov/releases/h15/data/wf/tcm1y.txt
Three-year: www.federalreserve.gov/releases/h15/data/wf/tcm3y.txt
Ten-year: www.federalreserve.gov/releases/h15/data/wf/tcm10y.txt.

LIBOR: A commonly used index is the average of London Interbank-offered rates (LIBOR) for six months or one year (depending on adjustment interval) based on U.S. dollar-denominated deposits in the London market. Data for any year from the present back to 1989 can be found at the special Fannie Mae business site (www.efanniemae.com/singlefamily/reference_tools/libor_rates/db_libor_index.jhtml).

Mortgage Rates: One of the oldest indexes is the national average contract interest rate on home mortgage loans closed. The official index is compiled by the Federal Housing Finance Board and can be found at their site (www.fhfb.gov). Current values are reported at www.fhfb.gov/MIRS/MIRS_rates.htm. The entire historical series is available at www.fhfb.gov/MIRS/MIRS_index.htm.

Cost of Funds Index: This slow-moving index is the monthly weighted average cost of savings, borrowings, and advances to members of one of the Federal Home Loan Banks, usually the one covering the home territory of the lender originating the loan. The index for all regional Home Loan Banks is compiled by the Office of Thrift Supervision. Find current values at www.ots.treas.gov/docs/23002.pdf and historical values at www.ots.treas.gov/docs/23001.pdf.

CD Rates: Some six-month adjustable loans are pegged to the weekly average of secondary market interest rates on six-month negotiable certificates of deposit. This average is reported by the Federal Reserve Board at the same site that reports treasury yields (www.federalreserve.gov/releases/h15/update). Historical values are at www.federalreserve.gov/releases/h15/data/wf/cd6m.txt.

Section I
Real Estate Mortgage Selection

Before you buy a house or other real estate, it is appropriate to decide on the type and amount of financing you will use. Although selecting a loan before selecting a home may sound like putting the cart before the horse, consider this: Before you offer a contract on a house, you need to know whether you'll likely qualify to finance the purchase. You'll also need to include in the house contract the type of mortgage loan you'll apply for. This section can help you make these essential decisions. The section that follows provides useful mortgage market considerations, including explanations of the following:

1. Players in the mortgage market
2. Why there are mortgage choices
3. What mortgages are on the menu?
4. When must you decide?
5. Loan applications and processing
6. FRM, ARM, or Hybrid: Which is for you?
7. Amount to borrow
8. Amortization term selection
9. Early mortgage retirement
10. Escrows

Players in the Mortgage Market

The first player you'll likely meet in the loan application process is the loan or mortgage *originator.* The originator may be a commercial bank, a savings bank, or a mortgage banker or broker. Your real estate agent or a friend or business associate may recommend an originator. Perhaps you'll select a likely originator from a newspaper ad, a list of local lenders providing current rates, or the bank that handles your checking account. You may even find an originator through the Internet.

The originator will make an agreement with you, called a *commitment.* Frequently, the originator wants to collect a fee from you, up front, for at least a credit check ($50–$100) and a house appraisal ($300–$500). If things work out as planned, the originator will offer a commitment letter stating the terms of the proposed loan.

The interest rate and/or discount points may be locked in, that is, assured, for the approximate period of time needed to close the purchase, typically 30 to 60 days. Be aware that when interest rates rise sharply, however, originators have been known to devise ways to avoid closing, or to increase interest rates and/or discount points, making the lock-in useless. It is therefore important to check the reputation of the originator and not just pick the one who offers the lowest rate.

Although the originator works with you personally and arranges the loan, the originator does not necessarily provide the money or own the loan. That part is played, behind the scenes, by a *mortgage investor,* often a large institution such as an insurance company. Fannie Mae (FNMA) and Freddie Mac (FHLMC) are the two largest mortgage investors in the United States. Fannie and Freddie tell originators what types of loan they will buy and what prices they are likely to pay at a given interest rate. These are for *conforming loans,* defined as loans that conform to Fannie and Freddie's guidelines as to the property, the income of its owner(s), and the amount of the loan.

Some mortgage investors will offer non-conforming loans. These may allow higher mortgage limits ("jumbo loans") or more liberal credit standards than Fannie or Freddie. They are offered at higher interest rates.

If you don't have a lot of cash to invest in the house, you will need to get an insured loan. Generally, lenders require a minimum cash down payment equal to 20 percent of the cost of the house before they waive the requirement for mortgage insurance. Most home buyers who have little or no equity from a previous sale need mortgage insurance. This type of insurance can be purchased from private companies (hence it is termed private mortgage insurance, or PMI) or from the Federal Housing Administration (FHA), an agency of the federal government. The latter type of loan is an FHA loan and has its own set of standards and guidelines.

At the closing of your home purchase, your mortgage may be funded by the originator (often the originator must borrow from someone else to fund your loan) or by a mortgage investor (your lender). Later—perhaps just hours or possibly years later—another mortgage investor may buy your loan, though you may not be aware of the transaction. Your loan may be sold many times during its life, just like a corporate bond or other debt instrument.

The loan *servicer* is the party you'll send payments to and correspond with. The servicer is paid a monthly fee by the lender. Initially, the originator often serves as the servicer. The servicer's right is often valuable, and the right to service your loan may be sold by one servicer to another. You'll usually know when servicing rights have been sold because you'll be notified of a change in the name and address to which you send your payments.

The ability of servicers to sell rights, and especially of mortgage investors to sell loans, has led to improvements in the availability and interest rates of home mortgages and to a proliferation of types of mortgage loans.

Why There Are Mortgage Choices

As you probably know, investors and borrowers have different preferences. Some mortgage investors prefer the predictability of long-term fixed payments. Others prefer to have investments with interest rates that can change with investment conditions. Some borrowers want stability, whereas others can afford to accept change, for better or worse.

From the late 1940s to the late 1970s, the fixed-payment fully amortizing mortgage was about the only type of permanent mortgage available. However, high interest rates brought about by high inflation in the 1970s caused the demise of many mortgage investors, especially savings institutions. They had only one product to offer: fixed-rate loans. These lost value when market rates increased. Mortgage funds dried up, and home purchases became difficult.

In 1981, Congress allowed savings and loan associations to offer ARMs, to give them a chance to invest in mortgages with interest rates that could rise. For a while, ARMs became very popular, and fixed-rate mortgages were not. In the mid-1980s, ARMs were the dominant, preferred offering. Some said that FRMs were headed for extinction. Fortunately, now most borrowers are offered a choice.

Borrowers often find that the initial rate of an ARM is less than that of an FRM. Lenders offer an incentive to borrowers who give up the safety of an FRM. If interest rates decline, an ARM borrower can soon enjoy the savings automatically, without undergoing the expense and inconvenience of refinancing. Should interest rates rise, the ARM borrower is protected to some extent by *caps*, both annual and life-of-loan, so that interest rate rises are introduced in steps and are limited. Further, ARM rates, over their lifetime, might not rise much above the fixed rate that was available when they first borrowed. Finally, if rates drop significantly, as they did in 2000–2002, the ARM borrower can refinance with an FRM.

Most important, the availability of both types has greatly improved the mortgage market. In the past, rising interest rates were typically accompanied by severe shortages of mortgage money. That no longer seems to occur. Both borrowers and lenders have benefited from the availability of both types of loan.

What Mortgages Are on the Menu?

Numerous types of mortgages have been introduced to U.S. home buyers since 1980. There is hardly a doubt that new types will emerge. The popularity of each type has changed with economic conditions and borrower or lender preferences.

Many mortgages are available with lender insurance from private mortgage insurance companies, the FHA, or the Veterans Administration (VA). Typically, mortgage insurance allows the loan-to-value ratio to exceed 80 percent; often to 95 percent with private mortgage insurance, possibly 97 percent with FHA insurance. Some VA loans require no down payment.

Fixed-Rate Mortgage (FRM)

The traditional mortgage has a fixed rate and a fixed term and is fully amortizing. The

30-year term is the most popular, followed by the 15-year term. The shorter term is preferred by borrowers who wish to pay off the loan in a shorter time and save on interest expense.

Adjustable-Rate Mortgage (ARM)

In an ARM, the interest rate is set for six months, one year, or two years, then periodically adjusted to the fully indexed rate. Typically only a 30-year amortization term is available. Caps on the ARM often limit annual changes of interest rate to 2 percentage points per year and a total of 5 or 6 percentage points over the life of the loan.

Hybrid or Step Mortgage

A type of hybrid mortgage may be designated as 3/27, 5/25, 7/23, or 10/20. The interest rate is fixed initially for three, five, seven, or ten years, with amortization based on 30 years. After the initial period, the interest rate is readjusted once and applies to the balance of the 30-year term. Another type of hybrid is designated 3/1, 5/1, 7/1, or 10/1. These mortgages adjust annually after the initial period of three, five, seven, or ten years.

Balloon Mortgage

This type of mortgage has a fixed term of three, five, seven, or ten years, at which time the entire principal is due. Typically, the borrower pays interest only until maturity. Variations include "guaranteed replacement loan" (rollover), and adjustable interest rates, or some amortization may be provided. A guaranteed replacement loan, also known as a *rollover* provision, is an important feature for a loan with a balloon payment. A rollover assures the borrower of a replacement loan when the balloon payment loan matures. In the absence of a rollover, when the balloon "pops," the borrower must seek replacement financing. If replacement financing is unavailable, whether because of a problem within the property or because of economic conditions, the borrower may face losing the property to foreclosure.

Home Equity Loan or Line of Credit

There are many possible variations on this type of instrument, which is typically a second mortgage. The home equity loan allows a borrower to add on to the initial loan. Generally the interest rate varies frequently, sometimes monthly. Monthly interest can be added to the principal balance until the stated credit limit is reached.

Reverse Mortgage

These loans are available only to home-owners over the age of 55. They allow borrowers to access their home equity without having to sell the home or repay the loan during their lifetime. Borrowers receive a lump sum, a monthly payment, or a line of credit in exchange for the right to proceeds from a future sale of the home (up to the amount outstanding on the loan). Reverse mortgages generally allow for periodic adjustments to the interest rate.

When Must You Decide?

If you are **refinancing** your house, you'll need to tell the loan originator at the time you sign the application, probably on your second visit. The loan originator needs to process paperwork about you and your house to gain approval from the mortgage investor. Part of the process is to determine whether you can afford the payments. To calculate the payments, the originator must know the loan type. If you change your mind after application, but before closing, there may be a charge or delay. The interest rate may be higher than when you first applied. It isn't possible to change your mind after closing; at that point you'd have to refinance again.

When **buying a house initially**, your mortgage selection should come first. When you buy a house or other real property, you ordinarily commit to a "contract for sale." In some places this is called an "agreement of sale"; in Texas it is called an "earnest-money contract." In most Northeastern states, a "binder" precedes the contract for sale.

Regardless of what it is called, that contract describes the conditions required for you to purchase the property. It includes the type of financing you wish to use and normally states, at a minimum, the interest rate, loan type, and loan-to-value ratio or amount. Most residential purchase contracts require you to diligently apply in good faith for the type of loan specified in the contract. If you are unable to obtain a loan with those specifications, you may back out of the contract and, depending on its wording, possibly get a refund of your deposit (earnest money).

If you change your mind about how you want to finance the purchase during the period between the contract signing and the closing (typically two to eight weeks), you may have to go to the seller to renegotiate the house purchase contract. Often, this is awkward. Besides, the seller may not grant your change. Consequently, you ought to decide how to finance your prospective purchase before you sign the house purchase contract. Part of the time spent on the home-shopping process should be used for loan education, including prequalifying yourself (or obtaining preapproval) and selecting the type of loan you prefer.

Loan Applications and Processing

It is a good practice to prequalify or become preapproved when house shopping. Prequalifying means that the real estate agent or loan originator asks you questions about your assets, including your source for a down payment, and your income, expenses, debts, and family size, then applies a few ratios and suggests a maximum house price.

With preapproval, the loan originator does more work, including an investigation to verify the information on your application. At the end of that process, you will be approved to borrow a specific amount of money, provided the house passes its tests (e.g., appraisal, title policy). When you are preapproved, both you and the seller are assured that you have the finances available to complete the purchase.[1]

The loan originator may offer a lock-in for a set period, such as 30 to 60 days. During this time the originator agrees to maintain the rate of interest quoted in the contract. If rates rise, however, many locked-in loans will not close. The originator may have some escape clauses buried in fine print in the contract or drag out the process until the lock-in expires.

A few borrowers may play a game, especially when refinancing. They may lock in a rate but break the lock when interest rates decline, then relock at a lower rate, perhaps with a different loan originator. When interest rates turn up, those borrowers may decide to close on the old lock at a low rate. This practice doesn't always work because originators may find a way out of the agreement when interest rates rise. In addition, the borrower may lose the application fee.

[1] For information about your credit, visit www.myfico.com. You can get your FICO score from the three major credit bureaus for $12 each.

After you apply for a loan, the originator will evaluate your ability to repay the loan. This is called qualifying you for the loan. Assuming that your credit history is adequate, the main constraint is your income. The more you earn, the larger the loan you qualify for. Since ARMs are often originated at payment levels that probably will rise in the future, an ARM would seem to offer a way to qualify for more loan than if you use an FRM. Lenders realize this and, to assure repayment at higher rates, require you to qualify at an interest rate 2 percentage points higher than the initial rate unless the initial rate is locked in for at least three years (as in a three-year hybrid ARM). For conventional ARMs, the qualifying rate is 2 percentage points above the initial rate. FHA ARMs require a rate 1 percentage point above the initial rate.

FRM, ARM, or Hybrid: Which Is for You?

Ordinarily, the interest rates on fixed-rate mortgages (FRMs) are set based on *long-term* bond rates. By contrast, interest rates for adjustable-rate mortgages (ARMs) are most often set by *short-term* interest rates (the index) plus a margin. How ARM rates are set is described later in this book. For now, this process means that most of the time the initial rate of an ARM will be *less* than that of the FRM. When lenders want to push ARMs, they can offer incentives, called *teaser rates*, to make ARMs more attractive at the moment.

Although the ARM will typically bear a lower rate when you apply for a loan, the FRM will retain its rate throughout the life of the loan—15 or 30 years—whereas the ARM rate will fluctuate according to its designated index. The ARM will have adjustment caps to moderate sharp and large fluctuations. These caps typically allow an interest rate fluctuation of 2 percentage points in any year and up to 6 percentage points over the life of the loan.

A **fixed-rate** mortgage is for you if these are important conditions:

1. You prefer the stability of a fixed payment.
2. Your budget can't tolerate much of an increase.
3. You have certain financial goals and need the assurance of a fixed payment to meet them.
4. You believe that interest rates will be higher in the future than they are now.

An **adjustable-rate** mortgage might be for you if

1. You expect interest rates to increase little or not at all, or even decline, during the next decade or more.
2. Your budget can accommodate increased rates and payments.
3. You strive to keep the initial mortgage payments as low as possible.
4. Your income will likely rise with increased interest rates, offsetting higher rates on your debts.

A **hybrid** might be suitable for you if

1. You expect to sell the property within the initial interest rate period (three, five, seven, or ten years).
2. In the event that you don't like the revised interest rate offered at the end of the initial period, you expect to have the financial capability to fully retire the loan.
3. You expect interest rates to fluctuate during the next decade and therefore plan to enjoy a fixed low rate for the initial period and refinance when the opportunity is presented.

A **convertible ARM** would be suitable for you if

1. You believe that interest rates may fluctuate and want an opportunity to lock in at a lower rate.
2. Your ability to refinance in the future may be limited by qualifying criteria.

Amount to Borrow

The standard loan-to-value ratio for FRMs and ARMs is 80 percent. Borrowers with high FICO (Fair Isaac Company) scores can raise that ratio to 90 percent, 95 percent, or 97 percent for many types of loans, though the cost may be high for the increased debt. The added cost is mostly for mortgage insurance, whether offered by a private company or provided by the FHA. Generally there is no added cost for VA mortgages, but only military veterans can qualify for these.

Private mortgage insurance costs may sound reasonable: for FRMs there are often no discount points paid at the front end, but an additional half a percentage point is added to the annual interest rate. For ARMs, the annual fee may be 0.75 percent to 1.25 percent. The cost is really quite expensive, however, because those added amounts apply to the entire loan, not just the 10 percent or 15 percent increment of debt added. FHA mortgage insurance is typically 1.5 discount points plus 0.5 percent added to the interest rate.

Homeowners who want to **borrow extensively** are likely to fit in one of these categories:

1. Don't have the money for a 20 percent down payment (often because this is their first home purchase).
2. Find it cheaper than other financing sources.

3. Can budget for high monthly payments.
4. Enjoy the larger income tax deduction of interest.
5. Need to extract cash from refinancing to use for other (nonhousing) purposes.
6. Have investment opportunities and high earnings expectations.

Homeowners who **borrow less** typically fit in one of these categories:

1. Can afford the 20 percent down payment (e.g., have proceeds from the sale of a previous home).
2. Have other, cheaper sources of credit (e.g., zero-rate loans on cars) or don't need more credit.
3. Don't have investment opportunities that promise a high rate of return.
4. Want low house payments for budgeting purposes.
5. Tend to be financially conservative and dislike being in debt.

You can choose an ARM whether you use PMI or FHA insurance. Even the VA has a hybrid ARM option. There are more varieties of conventional (not FHA or VA) ARMs. Most conventional ARMs carry 2 percent annual caps and 6 percent lifetime caps, whereas FHA ARMs have 1 percent annual and 5 percent lifetime caps.

Amortization Term Selection

Amortization is the process of liquidating a debt (see "How a Loan Is Amortized" for information on the amortization process). ARMs are typically offered only with a 30-year term. The most popular FRMs have 30- and 15-year terms. The 15-year FRMs usually carry a lower interest rate than the 30-year ones.

Generally, one would select a **30-year mortgage** to

1. Minimize the monthly payment.
2. Retain high amounts of principal for income tax deduction purposes.
3. Retain high amounts of principal to make assuming the loan more feasible for a later purchaser of the home.
4. Take advantage of investment opportunities at higher rates than the mortgage rate.

Those who prefer **15-year mortgages** generally

1. Prefer greater ownership security.
2. Can afford higher payments.
3. Want to accelerate the process of owning a debt-free home.

The goals of those who prefer a shorter mortgage life are generally consistent with those who prefer a larger down payment. They are financially more conservative than those who opt for a small down payment and extended payment terms.

Briefly, ARMs are generally available only as 30-year mortgages. Typically, the payment for their initial term (six months or one or two years) will be less than for any type of FRM. Thereafter, interest rates and payments may rise or fall.

Early Mortgage Retirement

Most mortgage loans, whether fixed or adjustable, can be amortized faster than the initial schedule by periodically making payments to principal over and above the regular monthly payment. The increased principal payment can be made systematically or whenever money is available. The borrower should ascertain that the current loan balance is reduced. (Some unfair lenders instead apply your increased principal payment to the last loan payment.) You can monitor the principal by examining the annual statement sent to you by the lender. Ask for an amortization schedule at loan origination. If you have made extra payments, your balance should be lower than the schedule amount.

Biweekly payment plans are convenient for those who are paid every two weeks. There are 26 two-week periods in a year, so when a biweekly-payment loan is arranged at half of the monthly payment of a 30-year fixed-rate loan, the biweekly payment has the effect of making 13 monthly payments in a year. The biweekly-payment loan will therefore be amortized much more quickly than the 30-year monthly-payment loan.

Some companies offer to "convert" your monthly-payment loan to a biweekly loan; the fees they charge, however, may be excessive compared with the benefit they bring. So, if you want a biweekly schedule, arrange it yourself at the outset. You may have to search the nation for lenders to accommodate this, as few lenders offer biweekly loans.

Escrows

Most residential mortgage loans require the establishment of an escrow account for the periodic payment of property taxes and insurance. At closing of the loan, the borrower is required to deposit money in this account for insurance (often for 14 months) and taxes (the prepayment period may vary). The mortgage servicer typically pays no interest to the borrower on these funds. Whenever the escrow fund on a loan declines to the point where it is inadequate to cover expected future needs, with a cushion, the servicer tells the borrower how much the monthly payment must be increased. Should the escrow balance momentarily turn negative, the servicer will seek immediate reimbursement from the borrower.

Typically, the same escrow rules apply to both FRMs and ARMs, so escrows should not be a factor in a borrower's mortgage selection process.

Section II
Welcoming ARMs: How They Work

Background of ARM Development

Adjustable-rate mortgages (ARMs) were introduced into widespread use in 1981, primarily as a way to help mortgage lenders out of a fundamental problem. At the time, most U.S. mortgage lenders were making long-term, fixed-rate loans exclusively. At the same time, most of the funds used to make such loans came from short-term deposits. This mismatch meant that lenders were vulnerable to short-run increases in the cost of deposits while the yield from their portfolios responded relatively slowly to rising interest rates.

At first lenders faced a difficult task in marketing ARMs. Home buyers were accustomed to fixed-rate mortgages (FRMs). They liked the security of locking in a fixed monthly payment. When mortgage interest rates rose to the range of 14 percent to 18 percent, however, FRMs became an unaffordable luxury. Borrowers became more attracted to ARMs, most of which were originated with rates several percentage points below those of fixed-rate loans. Furthermore, many lenders offered even lower rates for the first year of the loan. These "teaser" rates were often discounted down as low as 6 percent, a real bargain in the 1980s. For several years, the majority of new home loans originated were ARMs. By contrast, interest rates at the beginning of the twenty-first century have been extremely low, and ARMs are a very small part of the market. As rates cycle back upward, expect to see renewed interest in ARMs.

Risk

It is undeniable that ARMs involve more risk of higher payments for borrowers than FRMs. However, given that ARMs are generally originated with a lower rate of interest, that most ARMs have some form of protection against rapidly rising interest rates, and the possibility that interest rates may not vary appreciably over the next several years, an ARM loan may be an attractive alternative to fixed-rate financing.

Shopping

Selecting an ARM is more complicated than choosing a fixed-rate loan because there are more factors to consider. No one knows how much monthly payments will change over the life of the loan. Some type of forecast is necessary, based on expectations about how interest rates will change during the next few years. Once such a forecast is made, it is possible to compare several ARMs against each other and to the alternative of an FRM.

Projections

The ease of preparing projections makes this book invaluable. Using the tables and the step-by-step procedures, you will be able to make custom projections, calculating the monthly payments for any year of the loan, how much the payment will change from one year to the next, and how much principal is retired each year. Even without a forecast of interest rates, you can find out how a particular ARM would behave under a "worst case" assumption—that is, if interest rates climb to the ceiling rate allowed every year. The tables also show how discount points add to the real cost of the loan over the first adjustment period. Finally, you are shown how to evaluate the effect of teaser rates on the cost of the loan.

How an ARM Works

FRM Amortizing Payments

Most mortgage loans are *self-amortizing*, which means that the principal is retired as the loan is paid back. Each monthly payment includes a bit of principal in addition to payment of the interest owed on the outstanding principal. Because the principal is reduced with each payment, the amount of interest owed is also reduced. Fixed-payment, fixed-interest loans are arranged so that each total monthly payment—of principal and interest—is the same. As the amount of the payment devoted to interest decreases, the amount used to pay back principal increases. The result is that the reduction in the principal proceeds very slowly during the first several years of the loan term but accelerates rapidly near the end of the term. To see how this works, refer to "How a Loan Is Amortized" (page 37), which shows the amount of principal reduced in each period of a loan (see also Table 7).

Adjustables Amortize

Adjustable-rate loans work the same way. During the period up to the first adjustment, monthly payments are uniform. The amount of the payment is set exactly like that of an FRM at the initial interest rate of the ARM. The likelihood of the initial interest rate changing over the term of the loan does not affect the payments in the first year. In general, the higher the interest rate, the slower the loan is amortized in the early years. When the interest rate is adjusted, the new payment is equivalent to refinancing the loan for the outstanding principal and the remaining term at the new interest rate.

For example, suppose an ARM is originated for 30 years at 6 percent interest. The loan amount is $100,000. The monthly principal and interest payment for the first year is $599.55. At the end of the first year, the interest rate is raised to 7 percent. During the first year, $1,228 of principal was retired, leaving a balance of $98,772. The second-year payments are identical to those for a new loan of $98,772 for 29 years at 7 percent. The payments for each succeeding year are calculated in a similar way—that is, based on the new interest rate, remaining balance, and remaining term.

Index

When an ARM is originated, a particular index is identified for use in adjusting the interest rate. The basic requirements for an index are that it be beyond the direct control of the lender and that it be published regularly in some public document. This tends to protect the borrower from the possibility of the lender manipulating the index. Most indexes relate to the level of interest rates in the market or to the cost of money for lending institutions. The indexes most commonly used are average yields on federal Treasury securities (the maturity of the security generally coincides with the frequency of the ARM adjustment; thus, annually adjusted ARMs are pegged to one-year Treasury security yields), the LIBOR (an indicator of international borrowing), average interest rates on new mortgage loans, and the average cost of funds for mortgage lenders.

Margin

Because the level of the index rarely coincides with the mortgage rate on the loan, the lender will usually add a margin to the value of the index to compute the interest rate on the ARM. For example, if the index is 3 percent, the loan may carry an interest rate of 5 percent, which is a 2-percentage-point margin over the index value. If the index increases to 4 percent, the ARM may be adjusted to 6 percent, keeping the 2-percentage-point margin.

Adjustment Interval

When the ARM is originated, an interval is established for making adjustments. Let's say the ARM is to be adjusted each year. The lender is required to give the borrower notice of any change 30 to 45 days before the rate is adjusted. Therefore, sometime during the eleventh month of the first year, the borrower is informed that the current interest rate is to be adjusted to a specific new interest rate. The notice must give the new rate and the resulting monthly payment. Because the notice must be given in advance, the value of the index used for the adjustment must be available sometime before the adjustment date so that the lender can calculate the new rate and payment. Once this lead time is established at the first adjustment date, it must be consistent in each succeeding year. This prevents the lender from choosing an index value that would maximize the increase in the interest rate.

Fully Indexed Rate

The combination of index value and margin is called the *fully indexed rate*. In most cases, this rate coincides with the interest rate on the loan.

Sometimes, however, the rates are different. Often an ARM is originated at some rate below the fully indexed rate as an inducement to the borrower. These *teaser rates* are applied to the loan until the first adjustment date. When the interest rate is adjusted, it goes to the fully indexed value (unless constrained by a cap). When teaser rates are used, the interest rate may be increased substantially even though the index remains unchanged or possibly has declined.

Caps

Another instance when the ARM interest rate may be different from the fully indexed rate occurs when *adjustment caps* are used. There are several types of caps. All act to limit the change in the monthly payment on the ARM. An *annual cap* sets an upper limit on the amount the interest rate can be changed at the adjustment date. If the annual cap is 2 percentage points, the interest rate cannot be increased or decreased more than 2 percentage points per year. The unused adjustment may be carried over to the next adjustment date.

For example, suppose the fully indexed rate rose by 3 percentage points between adjustments (say, from 5 percent to 8 percent). The lender may increase the interest rate on the ARM by only 2 percentage points (to 7 percent). In the next year, the fully indexed rate remains constant. The lender will then raise the interest rate by 1 percentage point at the next adjustment to set the interest rate on the ARM equal to the fully indexed rate (8 percent). If, however, the fully indexed rate had declined by 1 percentage point, the interest rate on the ARM would not be changed.

A second type of cap is the *life-of-loan cap*. This sets a limit on the maximum change in the interest rate over the loan's life span. For example, if the cap is 5 percentage points and the loan originated at 6 percent interest, the interest rate can never be more than 11 percent, regardless of how much the index changes.

Some ARMs use *payment caps*. These work differently from rate caps. The payment cap sets a limit on the percentage increase in the monthly payment allowed but does not restrict the change in the interest rate. Therefore, the interest rate on the ARM is the same as the fully indexed rate, but the payment may be less than that needed to fully amortize the loan. When the payment is restricted to the point that it does not pay all the interest due on the loan, *negative amortization* will occur. This means that the amount of unpaid interest is added to the principal, and the outstanding principal balance increases each month.

One last thing should be said about interest adjustment caps and teaser rates. In many (but not all) ARMs, the cap applies to all adjustments, including the first adjustment based on the initial teaser rate. In this case, the effect of the teaser rate may extend to the second year. For example, an ARM is originated at 5 percent even though the fully indexed rate is 8 percent. A cap of 2 points per year is offered. If the fully indexed rate stays at 8 percent, the interest rate on the loan will rise to only 7 percent in the second year because of the cap. If the cap does not apply to the initial rate, the interest rate could rise to the full rate of 8 percent. Whether the cap applies in this case or not will be spelled out in the mortgage contract. This can be an important feature to check when considering an ARM with a teaser rate. A *teaser* is defined as a loan offered initially below the fully indexed rate.

Hybrid ARMs

In an effort to appeal to borrowers, lenders have developed new types of loans with features of both fixed-rate loans and ARMs. These variations soften the prospect of increasing the payment burden in several ways. A *hybrid "step" loan* adjusts only once during the loan term, thereby providing a certain predictability to the payment schedule. The same result can be obtained by using a *balloon loan*, which is a fixed-rate loan with a term that is shorter than its amortization schedule—with the loan refinanced at the end of the term. *Convertible ARMs* are regular adjustable loans that include a conversion option. The loan can be converted to a fixed-rate loan at specified periods.

Hybrid Step and Balloon Loans

One type of hybrid is an ARM that adjusts only once during its term. In its most common form, the loan has an amortization term of 30 years, and adjustment commonly occurs at the end of the seventh year (three, five, and ten years are also available). For a borrower who sells the home or refinances before the end of the seven years, the loan is no different from a fixed-rate one. Lenders, however, not wanting to commit to a fixed interest rate for longer than seven years, are willing to offer the loan at a lower contract interest rate than comparable 30-year fixed-rate loans. The discount typically has been about three-eighths of a percentage point (i.e., 6 percent when the going rate is $6^3/_8$ percent for a fixed-rate, 30-year self-amortizing loan).

Borrowers who keep their property and loan until the adjustment of the rate can face a substantial increase in monthly payments. The rate adjusts to the currently prevailing market loan rate, plus a specified margin. If rates have been rising during the seven-year period, the adjustment can be abrupt. Some step loans therefore offer lifetime caps that can place an effective ceiling on the interest rate. The Two-Step Loan offered by Fannie Mae has a 6-percentage-point cap on the interest rate.

Even with this cap, a 6-percentage-point increase in the interest rate can cause a boost in monthly payments of about 50 percent. Increases in interest rates of this magnitude are usually associated with moderate to high inflation rates. Accordingly, possible inflationary increases in the borrower's income should cushion the effect of the higher debt service, and the rising value of the home should lower the risk of default. If the payment is too burdensome, the borrower might try to recover the equity by selling the home at a profit. Nevertheless, the step loan, like most ARMs, is probably not appropriate for anyone on a fixed income.

Hybrid ARM with Extended Initial Fixed Period

Another type of hybrid loan also has an extended initial fixed interest period, typically 3, 5, 7, or 10 years. When that period expires, the loan becomes adjustable annually. These loans will be called 3/1, 5/1, 7/1, or 10/1. The first number represents the fixed interest rate period in years; the second represents the frequency of adjustment thereafter.

A borrower considering a hybrid loan (step or balloon loan) should evaluate the possibility of a substantial increase in monthly payments at the time of adjustment, and whether obtaining a slightly lower initial interest rate is worth this risk.

One can project a worst-case scenario in which the rate is adjusted to its upper limit, as set by the cap. The borrower can then subjectively evaluate the chances of reaching the adjustment period before resale and how such an increase in loan expense will affect the personal budget at that time.

Convertible ARMs

Many borrowers reluctantly accept an ARM because of a lower initial interest rate, in spite of the possibility that loan payments will increase in subsequent years. When interest rates are trending downward, however, borrowers are pleasantly surprised to find that their loan payments are actually decreasing. They are enjoying the benefits of lower interest rates without the expense or inconvenience of refinancing. Nevertheless, it may be advantageous at some point to refinance an ARM with a fixed-rate loan to lock in a relatively low interest rate for the future.

A convertible ARM (CARM) offers this option without the full expense of refinancing the loan. With a typical CARM, the loan may be converted into a fixed-rate one at the borrower's discretion during a designated period after the first year and extending several years into the loan term. The cost of conversion is a nominal fee. The converted loan has a new term and a fixed interest rate that approximates the current rate on comparable fixed-rate loans—or perhaps half a percentage point higher.

When considering whether to take a CARM over a regular ARM, you should assess the value to you of the conversion option. If you decide to convert to a fixed-rate loan, the option saves you the cost of refinancing, but the loan you get will have a higher rate of interest than those available in the market at the time of converting. You must therefore decide whether the savings in conversion costs are worth the extra costs of the new loan. If terms on CARMs are not as good as those on ARMs, you will need to decide whether the benefits are worth the extra costs of the CARM.

Monitoring Your ARM

In 1990, a Federal Savings and Loan Insurance Corporation analysis found errors in more than half of a sample of ARMs involving the interest rate adjustment process. It was not so much that lenders were trying to cheat borrowers as that the adjustment calculations had been delegated to computer programs that were inappropriate, or to hand calculations by inadequately trained personnel. The important lesson is that if you have an ARM, it may pay to check on the lender's calculations rather than merely accept them as accurate.

Most of the mistakes stemmed from using the wrong value for the index on which the interest rate was based. Chances for error were thought to be greatest for older loans (those originated before 1985), loans whose servicing had been sold to an institution other than the originator, and loans pegged to unusual indexes. Although more recent investigations have brought into question the extent of the errors (many estimates center on a 20–30 percent error rate), it seems clear that the chance of errors appearing in your loan are high.

Moreover, if an error is made in the adjustment, the results can be expensive. For example, pegging the interest rate on a $100,000 loan at 7 percent when it should be 6 percent can increase the monthly payment by almost $66. In addition, the principal balance is paid down at a slower rate, and this can mean higher payments in the future. Mistakes can be compounded over time, as future adjustments are affected by the current rate.

This section provides a guide for re-creating the process used to adjust the interest rate. When you receive a notice from the lender that the interest rate is up for adjustment, it will include information on the new interest rate and a corresponding monthly payment amount. It may even include the value of the index on which the adjustment is based. You should be able to verify that the value of the index is correctly stated and that the new interest rate has been calculated according to the rules set forth in your loan contract. With the help of tables in this book, you may calculate the new payment amount. If your calculations do not agree with the lender's, you should ask for an explanation of how the lender arrived at its numbers. In this way, you may catch an error and get it corrected before any damage is done.

Getting Started: Finding the Correct Index Value

Every ARM is tied to a specific index that governs how much the interest rate can be adjusted. Your loan contract will identify the index used for your loan. The first step in monitoring the loan adjustment is finding the appropriate value of the index.

A wide variety of indexes is available. In almost all cases, the index is some measure of market interest rate. Lending institutions are required to use an index that is public information and is general enough that its value does not depend on the individual lending institution's activities. The most widely used indexes are based on a few basic rate series:

- *Mortgage rates.* One of the first indexes used was the average contract rate charged on new (fixed-rate) mortgage loans.
- *Cost-of-funds ratios.* Averages based on interest costs paid by savings and loan associations for deposits and other forms of borrowed funds. This index was also popular in the earliest ARMs. Some loans are pegged to the average rate paid on certificates of deposit (CDs) nationwide.
- *Treasury yields.* The average yield on newly issued federal government bonds. These securities are offered in a variety of maturities, and each has its own yield. Most often, the "constant maturity" measure of yield is used as an index. Treasury yields are the most widely used index in the current market.
- *Other yields.* Some banks use the prime rate to index their ARMs. Another index used by banks is the LIBOR (London Interbank Offered Rate), based on transactions in international markets.

The values of most indexes are reported periodically in readily available sources on the Internet (see "How to Find Data on ARM Indexes," p. xvi). Average contract rates on mortgages and cost-of-funds indexes are printed in the *Wall Street Journal* each Monday and in *Barron's* weekly, in the statistical series. In addition, the Federal Housing Finance Board issues a monthly news release providing current and historical values for the contract rate index.

The value of the index not only depends on the type of security used but may vary as well by the area and time period used to calculate the average. A cost-of-funds ratio can be calculated on one region of the country or nationwide. The index may be based on a weekly average or a semiannual average. These specifics should be detailed in the name of the index; that is why these names tend to be long and complex. It is important that you find the proper index series because the value can vary significantly between series.

The value of an index may remain unchanged for a period of a week up to several months. The value that counts is the one in effect at the time the lender calculates the readjustment. Your loan contract stipulates the amount of advance notice you are to receive before the adjustment of the rate. The lender must complete the calculation before sending you the notice. This means that the value of the index that is used is the one in effect just before you receive the notice. Therefore, if you are to be notified 45 days before the adjustment, look for the index value that was current 45 days before the loan is up for adjustment.

As described earlier, once you have found the index value, compare it with the figure listed in the notification. Small discrepancies may be expected, especially for indexes that change frequently or for those that must be calculated from reported data (such as a six-month average of current Treasury yields). Look for major differences. Document what you have found and ask the lender to explain why there is a difference in the results.

Once you have the current value of the index, you can calculate the interest rate that will be applied to your loan when it is adjusted. First, you have to understand how the interest rate relates to the index value. In general, a "margin" is added to the value of the index that equates to the interest rate. This margin is identified in your mortgage contract. For example, if the value of the index is 4 percent, the lender might add a margin of 2 percentage points to the index value to get the interest rate—in this case, 6 percent.

When you add the margin to the index value, you get a figure referred to as the *fully indexed rate*. This may or may not equate to the interest rate applied to your loan. Often, the interest rate applied when the loan is originated is below the fully indexed rate. This is a *teaser rate*, used to attract borrowers to the ARM. In the absence of any adjustment restrictions, the rate would revert to the fully indexed rate at the time of the first adjustment. If the loan has adjustment caps, however, the rate applied may be somewhat below the fully indexed rate.

There are two types of caps. *Annual caps* apply to each adjustment and tend to limit the amount of change in monthly payments from one year to the next. *Life-of-loan caps* place an overall limit on the amount of adjustment over the life of the loan. In effect, life-of-loan caps place an upper and lower limit on the interest rate, no matter how the index behaves.

Here is how to incorporate caps in your calculations. First, calculate the fully indexed rate based on the value of the index plus the margin. Second, compare this rate to the rate currently in effect on your mortgage. If the fully indexed rate differs from your current rate by more than the annual cap, the new interest rate will equal the old rate plus or minus the cap. Finally, compare the fully indexed rate with the interest rate charged on your loan when it was first made plus the life-of-loan cap. If the fully indexed rate is higher, the new interest rate will be your initial rate plus the life-of-loan cap. Your interest rate can never be higher than this rate.

Here's an example. Suppose the ARM was originated with an interest rate of $3\frac{1}{2}$ percent. The margin is $2\frac{1}{2}$ percentage points. The annual cap is 2 percentage points, and the life-of-loan cap is 6 percentage points. The first adjustment date is impending. The current value of the index is $4^1/_2$ percent. Accordingly, the fully indexed rate is $4^1/_2$ plus $2^1/_2$ equals 7 percent. Because of the annual cap, the rate can be raised to no more than $5^1/_2$ percent in this period ($3^1/_2$ percent plus 2 percentage points). The interest rate for the second year will therefore be $5^1/_2$ percent. If the index stays at $4^1/_2$ percent at the end of the second year, the interest rate can be adjusted up to the fully indexed rate of 7 percent in the third year. That is because the amount of adjustment is less than the annual cap. The life-of-loan cap places a maximum on the interest rate of $3^1/_2$ percent plus 6 percentage points, or $9^1/_2$ percent. Since the rate for the second year is $5^1/_2$ percent, the life-of-loan cap does not affect this adjustment, nor would it affect the 7 percent rate that might result in the third year.

As you did with the index value, compare your calculations with the rate indicated on the lender's notification. It is common practice to round off rates to the nearest eighth of a percentage point. Once again, look for substantial errors and bring them to the attention of the lender.

There is a high probability that if the lender has made an error in the adjustment, you will have caught it by verifying the value of the index or calculating the proper interest rate. However, you may want to satisfy yourself that the new payment amount (for principal and interest) is correct. Once you have the new interest rate, you can estimate the new payment by following Table 2 in this book. You will need the old payment amount, the old interest rate, the new interest rate, and the number of years remaining in the loan term at the time of adjustment. Once again, when you have an estimate, compare it with the lender's statement for agreement, allowing some discrepancy for differences in mathematical precision or rounding off.

In general, the estimates should be within a few dollars of each other.

After you have organized your documents and information sources to check the lender's notification, it is an easy matter to monitor your loan in succeeding years. Also, it is a good idea to keep a running tab on how much you owe on the loan. You can do this easily by subtracting the amount of principal paid each month from your old balance. To calculate the amount of principal payment, start with the total payment and subtract every other payment that is due. The difference reduces principal. Specifically, from the total payment, subtract taxes and insurance that are put into escrow, mortgage insurance, and interest expense. The remainder should be the payment applied toward principal. This principal payment is subtracted from the principal balance owed at the end of the prior month to derive the principal balance at the end of the current month.

To find the interest paid, multiply the principal balance at the beginning of the month by the annual interest rate (expressed as a decimal or common fraction) and divide by 12 to derive the monthly amount.

Characteristics of Fixed-Rate Self-Amortizing Mortgages

A fully amortizing fixed-rate, fixed-payment mortgage (these are common characteristics) is one in which the balance will be exactly paid off at the end of the term, provided all payments are made on schedule. Borrowers should be aware of the following points:

1. *Payments must exceed interest for amortization to occur.* The total payments in a year must exceed the interest for the principal to be paid

down. As a simplified example, if a $100,000 loan is originated at 6 percent interest, the interest will be $6,000 in the first year. Consequently, if total payments in that year do not exceed $6,000, then no part of the payment has been applied to amortize the principal. If $7,000 is paid, then $6,000 is interest, and $1,000 reduces principal.

A more complex, but common, example is when monthly payments are used. The monthly interest rate is ordinarily $\frac{1}{12}$ of the stated rate. So a 6 percent monthly payment mortgage is really $\frac{1}{2}$ percent per month. For amortization to occur, payments must exceed the interest, which begins at $500 per month.

2. *Linearity exists across payment requirements.* Payment requirements are linear per dollar borrowed, given the same interest rate and amortization term. For example, a $200,000 loan requires exactly twice the payment of a $100,000 loan.

3. *Payments are not linear across the term spectrum.* Payment requirements are *not* linear across the term spectrum. The required monthly payment on a 15-year mortgage is not double that on a 30-year mortgage. Total payments on a 30-year loan are not twice those on a 15-year loan.

4. *Payments are not linear across interest rates.* Payment requirements are *not* linear across the interest rate spectrum. For example, the required monthly payment on a loan at 10 percent is not double that of a 5 percent interest rate loan. (Although the interest rate is double, the principal is retired only once.)

5. *Tables provide for principal and interest only.* These tables show principal and interest only. They do not include hazard insurance, mortgage insurance, or real estate taxes. Taxes and insurance cannot be included in any tables because

they vary by property, location, insurance carrier, and coverage. Most residential loans include monthly escrows for these expenses, so when you prepare a budget, consider insurance and real estate tax expenses in budgeting for the monthly house payment.

6. *Tables reflect rounding and truncation effects.* The amounts shown in these tables should exactly equal your lender calculations, with the possibility of a monthly variation of a few cents caused by rounding or truncating interest rates. Rounding to a monthly interest rate may involve a repeating decimal, such as .0066666 . . . , which may be truncated (cut off) at a set number of decimal places or rounded to .006667. This may cause a variation of a few cents in the payment.

Instead of rounding down when the fraction is less than half a cent, many lenders round any fraction of a cent in the payment *up to* the next cent to assure amortization within the term.

7. *Interpolation and extrapolation of principal amounts is possible.* If the precise amount you borrow is not on the tables, you can total the payments or find a ratio. Do both computations for assurance.

For example, suppose you borrow $54,800 for 30 years at 8 percent interest. You can do the following:

(*a*) Add the amounts of loan on the tables and corresponding payments to equal your loan amount and derive your payment amount:

Loan	Payments
$50,000	$366.88
4,000	29.35
800	5.87
$54,800	$402.10

(b) Find the ratio of the loan to a $100,000 loan (0.548 in this case) and multiply that ratio by the payment for a $100,000 loan:

$$0.548 \times \$733.76 = \$402.10$$

8. *Final payment of the loan may differ.* The final loan payment (that is, the 360th payment of a 30-year loan) may be slightly different from previous payments because of rounding or truncating.

How ARMs Compare with FRMs

1. *The mortgage interest rate will fluctuate.* The adjustable-rate mortgage provides for an interest rate that will fluctuate depending on current interest rates, specifically the security that the mortgage is indexed to.
2. *Changes in rate will occur periodically.* Most adjustable-rate mortgages call for interest rate changes every six months or year. The "hybrid" step mortgage, may have only one change during its life.
3. *New payment.* The new payment on an ARM is typically calculated based on the new interest rate, new principal balance, and remaining amortization term.
4. *Example of new payment calculation for ARM.*
   (a) Given: An adjustable-rate mortgage loan is originated for $100,000. The initial rate is 6 percent; the initial term is 30 years. The rate is adjustable annually and has an annual cap of 2 percentage points and a life-of-loan cap of 5 percentage points.
   (b) The initial monthly principal and interest payment is $599.55 (see Table 1, page 76).
   (c) After one year, the balance has been reduced to $98,770 (see Table 7, page 277).

(d) Interest rates rose sharply during the first year—by more than 2 percentage points. The 2 percent annual cap sets the limit on rate increases for year 2.

(e) The principal and interest payment for year 2 is based on the new interest rate, the principal at the end of the first year (the remaining balance), and the remaining term.

(f) The remaining balance approximates $98,770 (see Table 7, page 277, 98.77%), the remaining term is 29 years, and the new interest rate is 8 percent.

8% Interest, 29 Years Remain

Loan Principal	Required Payment
$95,000	$702.95
3,000	22.20
700	5.18
70	.52
$98,770	$730.85

(g) Calculate the payment for year 2 in Table 1: $730.85. Table 2 will show the percentage increase: from $599.55 to $730.85 = 21.90 percent. (See page 184.)

(h) During the second year, the $98,770 principal will be amortized like an 8 percent loan with a 29-year term.

(i) The loan's interest rate will readjust at the end of every year, but the new payment can be calculated in the same way each year.

How a Loan Is Amortized

Most real estate mortgage loans are self-amortizing; the vast majority are set up to fully pay off the principal over a set time, such as 15 or 30 years. Monthly payments are precisely calculated at the start of the loan, to include enough principal and interest to retire the loan at the end of the full amortization term. Normally the total principal and interest payment on a fixed-rate loan is the same each month. Payments on an adjustable-rate mortgage (ARM) will fluctuate based on changing interest rates. Still, each time the new payment on an ARM is calculated, it is sufficient to retire exactly the remaining principal over the remaining term at the new rate of interest. Payments must always exceed interest to provide amortization.

For purposes of this illustration, assume a $100,000 mortgage loan at a stated annual rate of 6 percent, with a 30-year amortization term, requiring monthly payments. The monthly payment is set at $599.55 (see Table 1). The stated *monthly* interest rate is $1/_{12}$ of 6 percent, which is $1/_2$ percent or 0.005.

The table below demonstrates amortization for the first three months and last two months of a 30-year loan.

Column 1 offers the month from 1 to 360 (30 years).

Column 2 offers the principal balance at the beginning of that month, which is the same as the balance at the end of the previous month.

Column 3 is the constant payment of principal and interest.

Column 4 is the amount of interest each month. It is derived by multiplying the monthly interest rate by the principal at the beginning of each month (Column 2).

Column 5 is the amount of principal paid each month. It is found by subtracting the interest (Column 4) from the monthly payment (Column 3).

Column 6 is the remaining balance at the end of the month. It is found by subtracting the principal paid that month (Column 5) from the balance at the end of the previous month (Column 2).

Amortization occurs slowly during the early years, then more rapidly as the loan balance declines in the later years. At the end of the full amortization term, the balance in Column 6 will be zero; the sum of amounts in Column 5 will then equal the initial principal.

(1) Month	(2) Balance Beginning of Month	(3) Payment of P&I, End of Month	(4) Monthly Interest at 5% of Principal at Beginning of Month	(5) Principal Payment	(6) Remaining Balance at End of Month
1	$100,000.00	$599.55	$500.00	$99.55	$99,900.45
2	$99,900.45	$599.55	$499.50	$100.05	$99,800.40
3	$99,800.40	$599.55	$499.00	$100.55	$99,699.85
359	$1,190.17	$599.55	$5.95	$593.60	$596.57
360	$596.57	$599.55	$2.98	$596.57	0

Total principal paid $100,000.00

Section III
Tables Provided

Seven different tables are provided to facilitate mortgage loan computations. An explanation of each table and example of use is shown on the pages that precede each table. A brief explanation follows.

Table 1, **Monthly Payments**, offers the monthly payment on a mortgage loan. Use for fixed-rate loans or the initial and subsequent periods of an adjustable-rate loan.

Table 2, **Payment Adjustments**, offers the percentage change in payments, given an interest rate change.

Table 3, **Borrower's Worst-Case APR**, offers the annual percentage rate, which is the effective interest rate over the loan term, given maximum interest rate increases for an ARM with caps.

Table 4, **Borrower's Worst-Case Monthly Payments**, offers payments per $100,000 loan given maximum interest rate increases for an ARM with caps.

Table 5, **APR for First Year**, offers the effective interest rate for the first year given a mortgage loan with discount points.

Table 6, **Value of Below-Market Initial Rate**, offers the current value of teaser rates, given one- or two-year renewal terms.

Table 7, **Annual Loan Balance Remaining**, offers the percentage remaining of the original loan. Use for fixed-rate mortgages and initial term of ARMs.

Table 1
Monthly Payments Necessary to Amortize a Loan

The purpose of this table is to provide the monthly payment of principal and interest required to amortize a mortgage loan. This table can be used for both fixed-payment and adjustable-rate mortgages.

How to Use Tables

1. Select the appropriate interest rate page. Interest rates are shown in the upper outside corner of the page.
2. Select the number of "Years Remaining in Term." Initially, this will be the loan term chosen by the borrower, frequently 30 years, though 15-year terms are also popular.
3. Select the "Amount Borrowed."
4. The monthly payment of principal and interest required is found at the intersection of "Amount Borrowed" and "Years Remaining in Term."

Example 1

Connie borrows $100,000 at 6 percent interest for a 30-year term. To find the monthly payment, go to the page in Table 1 for 6 percent loans. Go down the 30-year column to the row for $100,000. The payment shown is $599.55.

Example 2

Elaine borrows $300,000 for a 15-year monthly-payment loan at an 8 percent interest rate. The monthly payment is $2,866.96 (see page 93). This is the constant principal and interest requirement on a fixed-rate mortgage over its entire life or the initial period of an adjustable-rate mortgage.

Example 3

Jeanie has an ARM with 25 years remaining in the term. The lender reports the principal balance as $48,000 and says the new rate will be $6\frac{1}{2}$ percent. To find her new payment, she would go to the $6\frac{1}{2}$ percent page in Table 1, look in the 25-year column for $45,000, and get a payment of $303.84. Next she would find the payment for $3,000 in the same column—$20.26. The new payment is the sum of these two: $324.10.

Monthly Payments
Necessary to Amortize a Loan

YEARS REMAINING IN TERM

AMOUNT BORROWED	30	29	28	27	26	25	24
100	0.37	0.38	0.39	0.40	0.41	0.42	0.44
200	0.74	0.76	0.78	0.80	0.82	0.85	0.87
300	1.11	1.14	1.17	1.20	1.23	1.27	1.31
400	1.48	1.52	1.56	1.60	1.65	1.70	1.75
500	1.85	1.89	1.94	2.00	2.06	2.12	2.19
600	2.22	2.27	2.33	2.40	2.47	2.54	2.62
700	2.59	2.65	2.72	2.80	2.88	2.97	3.06
800	2.96	3.03	3.11	3.20	3.29	3.39	3.50
900	3.33	3.41	3.50	3.60	3.70	3.81	3.94
1,000	3.70	3.79	3.89	4.00	4.11	4.24	4.37
2,000	7.39	7.58	7.78	7.99	8.23	8.48	8.75
3,000	11.09	11.37	11.67	11.99	12.34	12.72	13.12
4,000	14.78	15.16	15.56	15.99	16.45	16.95	17.50
5,000	18.48	18.95	19.45	19.98	20.56	21.19	21.87
6,000	22.18	22.74	23.34	23.98	24.68	25.43	26.25
7,000	25.87	26.53	27.23	27.98	28.79	29.67	30.62
8,000	29.57	30.31	31.11	31.98	32.90	33.91	35.00
9,000	33.27	34.10	35.00	35.97	37.02	38.15	39.37
10,000	36.96	37.89	38.89	39.97	41.13	42.39	43.75
15,000	55.44	56.84	58.34	59.95	61.69	63.58	65.62
20,000	73.92	75.79	77.79	79.94	82.26	84.77	87.50
25,000	92.40	94.73	97.23	99.92	102.82	105.96	109.37
30,000	110.89	113.68	116.68	119.91	123.39	127.16	131.24
35,000	129.37	132.63	136.13	139.89	143.95	148.35	153.12
40,000	147.85	151.57	155.57	159.88	164.52	169.54	174.99
45,000	166.33	170.52	175.02	179.86	185.08	190.73	196.87
50,000	184.81	189.47	194.47	199.85	205.65	211.93	218.74
55,000	203.29	208.41	213.91	219.83	226.21	233.12	240.61
60,000	221.77	227.36	233.36	239.81	246.78	254.31	262.49
65,000	240.25	246.31	252.81	259.80	267.34	275.51	284.36
70,000	258.73	265.25	272.25	279.78	287.91	296.70	306.24
75,000	277.21	284.20	291.70	299.77	308.47	317.89	328.11
80,000	295.70	303.15	311.15	319.75	329.04	339.08	349.98
85,000	314.18	322.09	330.59	339.74	349.60	360.28	371.86
90,000	332.66	341.04	350.04	359.72	370.17	381.47	393.73
95,000	351.14	359.99	369.48	379.71	390.73	402.66	415.61
100,000	369.62	378.93	388.93	399.69	411.30	423.85	437.48
110,000	406.58	416.83	427.82	439.66	452.43	466.24	481.23
120,000	443.54	454.72	466.72	479.63	493.56	508.63	524.98
130,000	480.51	492.61	505.61	519.60	534.69	551.01	568.72
140,000	517.47	530.51	544.50	559.57	575.82	593.40	612.47
150,000	554.43	568.40	583.40	599.54	616.95	635.78	656.22
200,000	739.24	757.87	777.86	799.38	822.59	847.71	874.96
250,000	924.05	947.33	972.33	999.23	1028.24	1059.64	1093.70
300,000	1108.86	1136.80	1166.79	1199.07	1233.89	1271.56	1312.44
350,000	1293.67	1326.27	1361.26	1398.92	1439.54	1483.49	1531.18
400,000	1478.48	1515.73	1555.73	1598.76	1645.19	1695.42	1749.92
450,000	1663.29	1705.20	1750.19	1798.61	1850.84	1907.34	1968.66
500,000	1848.10	1894.67	1944.66	1998.45	2056.49	2119.27	2187.40
550,000	2032.91	2084.13	2139.12	2198.30	2262.13	2331.20	2406.14
600,000	2217.72	2273.60	2333.59	2398.14	2467.78	2543.13	2624.88
650,000	2402.53	2463.07	2528.05	2597.99	2673.43	2755.05	2843.62
700,000	2587.34	2652.53	2722.52	2797.83	2879.08	2966.98	3062.36
750,000	2772.15	2842.00	2916.99	2997.68	3084.73	3178.91	3281.10
800,000	2956.96	3031.47	3111.45	3197.52	3290.38	3390.83	3499.84
850,000	3141.77	3220.93	3305.92	3397.37	3496.03	3602.76	3718.58
900,000	3326.58	3410.40	3500.38	3597.21	3701.67	3814.69	3937.32
950,000	3511.38	3599.87	3694.85	3797.06	3907.32	4026.62	4156.07
1,000,000	3696.19	3789.33	3889.31	3996.90	4112.97	4238.54	4374.81

Monthly Payments **2%**
Necessary to Amortize a Loan

AMOUNT BORROWED	YEARS REMAINING IN TERM						
	23	22	21	20	15	10	5
100	0.45	0.47	0.49	0.51	0.64	0.92	1.75
200	0.90	0.94	0.97	1.01	1.29	1.84	3.51
300	1.36	1.41	1.46	1.52	1.93	2.76	5.26
400	1.81	1.87	1.95	2.02	2.57	3.68	7.01
500	2.26	2.34	2.43	2.53	3.22	4.60	8.76
600	2.71	2.81	2.92	3.04	3.86	5.52	10.52
700	3.17	3.28	3.40	3.54	4.50	6.44	12.27
800	3.62	3.75	3.89	4.05	5.15	7.36	14.02
900	4.07	4.22	4.38	4.55	5.79	8.28	15.77
1,000	4.52	4.69	4.86	5.06	6.44	9.20	17.53
2,000	9.05	9.37	9.73	10.12	12.87	18.40	35.06
3,000	13.57	14.06	14.59	15.18	19.31	27.60	52.58
4,000	18.09	18.74	19.45	20.24	25.74	36.81	70.11
5,000	22.62	23.43	24.32	25.29	32.18	46.01	87.64
6,000	27.14	28.11	29.18	30.35	38.61	55.21	105.17
7,000	31.66	32.80	34.04	35.41	45.05	64.41	122.69
8,000	36.19	37.48	38.90	40.47	51.48	73.61	140.22
9,000	40.71	42.17	43.77	45.53	57.92	82.81	157.75
10,000	45.23	46.85	48.63	50.59	64.35	92.01	175.28
15,000	67.85	70.28	72.95	75.88	96.53	138.02	262.92
20,000	90.46	93.70	97.26	101.18	128.70	184.03	350.56
25,000	113.08	117.13	121.58	126.47	160.88	230.03	438.19
30,000	135.69	140.56	145.89	151.77	193.05	276.04	525.83
35,000	158.31	163.98	170.21	177.06	225.23	322.05	613.47
40,000	180.93	187.41	194.52	202.35	257.40	368.05	701.11
45,000	203.54	210.84	218.84	227.65	289.58	414.06	788.75
50,000	226.16	234.26	243.15	252.94	321.75	460.07	876.39
55,000	248.77	257.69	267.47	278.24	353.93	506.07	964.03
60,000	271.39	281.11	291.78	303.53	386.11	552.08	1051.67
65,000	294.00	304.54	316.10	328.82	418.28	598.09	1139.30
70,000	316.62	327.97	340.41	354.12	450.46	644.09	1226.94
75,000	339.24	351.39	364.73	379.41	482.63	690.10	1314.58
80,000	361.85	374.82	389.04	404.71	514.81	736.11	1402.22
85,000	384.47	398.24	413.36	430.00	546.98	782.11	1489.86
90,000	407.08	421.67	437.67	455.30	579.16	828.12	1577.50
95,000	429.70	445.10	461.99	480.59	611.33	874.13	1665.14
100,000	452.32	468.52	486.30	505.88	643.51	920.13	1752.78
110,000	497.55	515.38	534.93	556.47	707.86	1012.15	1928.05
120,000	542.78	562.23	583.56	607.06	772.21	1104.16	2103.33
130,000	588.01	609.08	632.19	657.65	836.56	1196.17	2278.61
140,000	633.24	655.93	680.82	708.24	900.91	1288.19	2453.89
150,000	678.47	702.78	729.45	758.83	965.26	1380.20	2629.16
200,000	904.63	937.05	972.60	1011.77	1287.02	1840.27	3505.55
250,000	1130.79	1171.31	1215.75	1264.71	1608.77	2300.34	4381.94
300,000	1356.95	1405.57	1458.90	1517.65	1930.53	2760.40	5258.33
350,000	1583.10	1639.83	1702.05	1770.59	2252.28	3220.47	6134.72
400,000	1809.26	1874.09	1945.20	2023.53	2574.03	3680.54	7011.10
450,000	2035.42	2108.35	2188.35	2276.48	2895.79	4140.61	7887.49
500,000	2261.58	2342.62	2431.50	2529.42	3217.54	4600.67	8763.88
550,000	2487.73	2576.88	2674.65	2782.36	3539.30	5060.74	9640.27
600,000	2713.89	2811.14	2917.80	3035.30	3861.05	5520.81	10516.66
650,000	2940.05	3045.40	3160.95	3288.24	4182.81	5980.87	11393.04
700,000	3166.21	3279.66	3404.11	3541.18	4504.56	6440.94	12269.43
750,000	3392.36	3513.92	3647.26	3794.13	4826.32	6901.01	13145.82
800,000	3618.52	3748.19	3890.41	4047.07	5148.07	7361.08	14022.21
850,000	3844.68	3982.45	4133.56	4300.01	5469.82	7821.14	14898.60
900,000	4070.84	4216.71	4376.71	4552.95	5791.58	8281.21	15774.98
950,000	4296.99	4450.97	4619.86	4805.89	6113.33	8741.28	16651.37
1,000,000	4523.15	4685.23	4863.01	5058.83	6435.09	9201.35	17527.76

2¼%   Monthly Payments
Necessary to Amortize a Loan

AMOUNT BORROWED	\n YEARS REMAINING IN TERM						
	30	29	28	27	26	25	24
100	0.38	0.39	0.40	0.41	0.42	0.44	0.45
200	0.76	0.78	0.80	0.82	0.85	0.87	0.90
300	1.15	1.17	1.20	1.24	1.27	1.31	1.35
400	1.53	1.57	1.61	1.65	1.69	1.74	1.80
500	1.91	1.96	2.01	2.06	2.12	2.18	2.25
600	2.29	2.35	2.41	2.47	2.54	2.62	2.70
700	2.68	2.74	2.81	2.88	2.97	3.05	3.15
800	3.06	3.13	3.21	3.30	3.39	3.49	3.60
900	3.44	3.52	3.61	3.71	3.81	3.93	4.05
1,000	3.82	3.91	4.01	4.12	4.24	4.36	4.50
2,000	7.64	7.83	8.03	8.24	8.47	8.72	8.99
3,000	11.47	11.74	12.04	12.36	12.71	13.08	13.49
4,000	15.29	15.66	16.06	16.48	16.95	17.45	17.99
5,000	19.11	19.57	20.07	20.61	21.18	21.81	22.48
6,000	22.93	23.49	24.09	24.73	25.42	26.17	26.98
7,000	26.76	27.40	28.10	28.85	29.66	30.53	31.48
8,000	30.58	31.32	32.11	32.97	33.89	34.89	35.97
9,000	34.40	35.23	36.13	37.09	38.13	39.25	40.47
10,000	38.22	39.15	40.14	41.21	42.36	43.61	44.97
15,000	57.34	58.72	60.21	61.82	63.55	65.42	67.45
20,000	76.45	78.30	80.28	82.42	84.73	87.23	89.94
25,000	95.56	97.87	100.35	103.03	105.91	109.03	112.42
30,000	114.67	117.45	120.43	123.63	127.09	130.84	134.91
35,000	133.79	137.02	140.50	144.24	148.28	152.65	157.39
40,000	152.90	156.60	160.57	164.84	169.46	174.45	179.87
45,000	172.01	176.17	180.64	185.45	190.64	196.26	202.36
50,000	191.12	195.74	200.71	206.05	211.82	218.07	224.84
55,000	210.24	215.32	220.78	226.66	233.00	239.87	247.33
60,000	229.35	234.89	240.85	247.26	254.19	261.68	269.81
65,000	248.46	254.47	260.92	267.87	275.37	283.48	292.30
70,000	267.57	274.04	280.99	288.47	296.55	305.29	314.78
75,000	286.68	293.62	301.06	309.08	317.73	327.10	337.26
80,000	305.80	313.19	321.13	329.69	338.91	348.90	359.75
85,000	324.91	332.77	341.21	350.29	360.10	370.71	382.23
90,000	344.02	352.34	361.28	370.90	381.28	392.52	404.72
95,000	363.13	371.92	381.35	391.50	402.46	414.32	427.20
100,000	382.25	391.49	401.42	412.11	423.64	436.13	449.69
110,000	420.47	430.64	441.56	453.32	466.01	479.74	494.66
120,000	458.70	469.79	481.70	494.53	508.37	523.36	539.62
130,000	496.92	508.94	521.84	535.74	550.74	566.97	584.59
140,000	535.14	548.09	561.99	576.95	593.10	610.58	629.56
150,000	573.37	587.23	602.13	618.16	635.47	654.20	674.53
200,000	764.49	782.98	802.84	824.21	847.29	872.26	899.37
250,000	955.62	978.72	1003.55	1030.27	1059.11	1090.33	1124.22
300,000	1146.74	1174.47	1204.25	1236.32	1270.93	1308.39	1349.06
350,000	1337.86	1370.21	1404.96	1442.37	1482.75	1526.46	1573.90
400,000	1528.98	1565.96	1605.67	1648.43	1694.57	1744.52	1798.75
450,000	1720.11	1761.70	1806.38	1854.48	1906.40	1962.59	2023.59
500,000	1911.23	1957.45	2007.09	2060.53	2118.22	2180.65	2248.43
550,000	2102.35	2153.19	2207.80	2266.59	2330.04	2398.72	2473.28
600,000	2293.48	2348.94	2408.51	2472.64	2541.86	2616.78	2698.12
650,000	2484.60	2544.68	2609.22	2678.69	2753.68	2834.85	2922.96
700,000	2675.72	2740.43	2809.93	2884.75	2965.51	3052.91	3147.81
750,000	2866.85	2936.17	3010.64	3090.80	3177.33	3270.98	3372.65
800,000	3057.97	3131.92	3211.35	3296.85	3389.15	3489.05	3597.49
850,000	3249.09	3327.66	3412.05	3502.91	3600.97	3707.11	3822.34
900,000	3440.21	3523.41	3612.76	3708.96	3812.79	3925.18	4047.18
950,000	3631.34	3719.15	3813.47	3915.01	4024.62	4143.24	4272.02
1,000,000	3822.46	3914.90	4014.18	4121.07	4236.44	4361.31	4496.87

Monthly Payments

Necessary to Amortize a Loan

2¹/₄%

AMOUNT BORROWED	YEARS REMAINING IN TERM						
	23	22	21	20	15	10	5
100	0.46	0.48	0.50	0.52	0.66	0.93	1.76
200	0.93	0.96	1.00	1.04	1.31	1.86	3.53
300	1.39	1.44	1.49	1.55	1.97	2.79	5.29
400	1.86	1.92	1.99	2.07	2.62	3.73	7.05
500	2.32	2.40	2.49	2.59	3.28	4.66	8.82
600	2.79	2.88	2.99	3.11	3.93	5.59	10.58
700	3.25	3.36	3.49	3.62	4.59	6.52	12.35
800	3.72	3.84	3.99	4.14	5.24	7.45	14.11
900	4.18	4.33	4.48	4.66	5.90	8.38	15.87
1,000	4.64	4.81	4.98	5.18	6.55	9.31	17.64
2,000	9.29	9.61	9.97	10.36	13.10	18.63	35.27
3,000	13.93	14.42	14.95	15.53	19.65	27.94	52.91
4,000	18.58	19.22	19.93	20.71	26.20	37.25	70.55
5,000	23.22	24.03	24.91	25.89	32.75	46.57	88.19
6,000	27.87	28.84	29.90	31.07	39.31	55.88	105.82
7,000	32.51	33.64	34.88	36.25	45.86	65.20	123.46
8,000	37.16	38.45	39.86	41.42	52.41	74.51	141.10
9,000	41.80	43.25	44.85	46.60	58.96	83.82	158.74
10,000	46.45	48.06	49.83	51.78	65.51	93.14	176.37
15,000	69.67	72.09	74.74	77.67	98.26	139.71	264.56
20,000	92.89	96.12	99.66	103.56	131.02	186.27	352.75
25,000	116.11	120.15	124.57	129.45	163.77	232.84	440.93
30,000	139.34	144.18	149.49	155.34	196.53	279.41	529.12
35,000	162.56	168.21	174.40	181.23	229.28	325.98	617.31
40,000	185.78	192.24	199.32	207.12	262.03	372.55	705.49
45,000	209.00	216.26	224.23	233.01	294.79	419.12	793.68
50,000	232.23	240.29	249.15	258.90	327.54	465.69	881.87
55,000	255.45	264.32	274.06	284.79	360.30	512.26	970.05
60,000	278.67	288.35	298.98	310.68	393.05	558.82	1058.24
65,000	301.89	312.38	323.89	336.58	425.81	605.39	1146.43
70,000	325.12	336.41	348.81	362.47	458.56	651.96	1234.61
75,000	348.34	360.44	373.72	388.36	491.31	698.53	1322.80
80,000	371.56	384.47	398.64	414.25	524.07	745.10	1410.99
85,000	394.78	408.50	423.55	440.14	556.82	791.67	1499.17
90,000	418.01	432.53	448.47	466.03	589.58	838.24	1587.36
95,000	441.23	456.56	473.38	491.92	622.33	884.81	1675.55
100,000	464.45	480.59	498.30	517.81	655.08	931.37	1763.73
110,000	510.90	528.65	548.13	569.59	720.59	1024.51	1940.11
120,000	557.34	576.71	597.96	621.37	786.10	1117.65	2116.48
130,000	603.79	624.77	647.78	673.15	851.61	1210.79	2292.85
140,000	650.23	672.82	697.61	724.93	917.12	1303.92	2469.23
150,000	696.68	720.88	747.44	776.71	982.63	1397.06	2645.60
200,000	928.90	961.18	996.59	1035.62	1310.17	1862.75	3527.47
250,000	1161.13	1201.47	1245.74	1294.52	1637.71	2328.43	4409.34
300,000	1393.35	1441.77	1494.89	1553.42	1965.25	2794.12	5291.20
350,000	1625.58	1682.06	1744.04	1812.33	2292.80	3259.81	6173.07
400,000	1857.80	1922.35	1993.18	2071.23	2620.34	3725.49	7054.94
450,000	2090.03	2162.65	2242.33	2330.14	2947.88	4191.18	7936.81
500,000	2322.26	2402.94	2491.48	2589.04	3275.42	4656.87	8818.67
550,000	2554.48	2643.24	2740.63	2847.95	3602.97	5122.56	9700.54
600,000	2786.71	2883.53	2989.78	3106.85	3930.51	5588.24	10582.41
650,000	3018.93	3123.83	3238.92	3365.75	4258.05	6053.93	11464.27
700,000	3251.16	3364.12	3488.07	3624.66	4585.59	6519.62	12346.14
750,000	3483.38	3604.42	3737.22	3883.56	4913.14	6985.30	13228.01
800,000	3715.61	3844.71	3986.37	4142.47	5240.68	7450.99	14109.88
850,000	3947.83	4085.00	4235.52	4401.37	5568.22	7916.68	14991.74
900,000	4180.06	4325.30	4484.66	4660.27	5895.76	8382.36	15873.61
950,000	4412.28	4565.59	4733.81	4919.18	6223.31	8848.05	16755.48
1,000,000	4644.51	4805.89	4982.96	5178.08	6550.85	9313.74	17637.34

2¹/₂%

Monthly Payments
Necessary to Amortize a Loan

YEARS REMAINING IN TERM

AMOUNT BORROWED	30	29	28	27	26	25	24
100	0.40	0.40	0.41	0.42	0.44	0.45	0.46
200	0.79	0.81	0.83	0.85	0.87	0.90	0.92
300	1.19	1.21	1.24	1.27	1.31	1.35	1.39
400	1.58	1.62	1.66	1.70	1.74	1.79	1.85
500	1.98	2.02	2.07	2.12	2.18	2.24	2.31
600	2.37	2.43	2.48	2.55	2.62	2.69	2.77
700	2.77	2.83	2.90	2.97	3.05	3.14	3.23
800	3.16	3.23	3.31	3.40	3.49	3.59	3.70
900	3.56	3.64	3.73	3.82	3.93	4.04	4.16
1,000	3.95	4.04	4.14	4.25	4.36	4.49	4.62
2,000	7.90	8.09	8.28	8.49	8.72	8.97	9.24
3,000	11.85	12.13	12.42	12.74	13.09	13.46	13.86
4,000	15.80	16.17	16.57	16.99	17.45	17.94	18.48
5,000	19.76	20.21	20.71	21.24	21.81	22.43	23.10
6,000	23.71	24.26	24.85	25.48	26.17	26.92	27.73
7,000	27.66	28.30	28.99	29.73	30.53	31.40	32.35
8,000	31.61	32.34	33.13	33.98	34.90	35.89	36.97
9,000	35.56	36.39	37.27	38.23	39.26	40.38	41.59
10,000	39.51	40.43	41.41	42.47	43.62	44.86	46.21
15,000	59.27	60.64	62.12	63.71	65.43	67.29	69.31
20,000	79.02	80.86	82.83	84.95	87.24	89.72	92.42
25,000	98.78	101.07	103.53	106.19	109.05	112.15	115.52
30,000	118.54	121.29	124.24	127.42	130.86	134.59	138.63
35,000	138.29	141.50	144.95	148.66	152.67	157.02	161.73
40,000	158.05	161.71	165.66	169.90	174.48	179.45	184.84
45,000	177.80	181.93	186.36	191.14	196.29	201.88	207.94
50,000	197.56	202.14	207.07	212.37	218.10	224.31	231.05
55,000	217.32	222.36	227.78	233.61	239.91	246.74	254.15
60,000	237.07	242.57	248.48	254.85	261.72	269.17	277.26
65,000	256.83	262.79	269.19	276.09	283.54	291.60	300.36
70,000	276.58	283.00	289.90	297.32	305.35	314.03	323.47
75,000	296.34	303.22	310.60	318.56	327.16	336.46	346.57
80,000	316.10	323.43	331.31	339.80	348.97	358.89	369.68
85,000	335.85	343.64	352.02	361.04	370.78	381.32	392.78
90,000	355.61	363.86	372.72	382.27	392.59	403.76	415.89
95,000	375.36	384.07	393.43	403.51	414.40	426.19	438.99
100,000	395.12	404.29	414.14	424.75	436.21	448.62	462.09
110,000	434.63	444.72	455.55	467.22	479.83	493.48	508.30
120,000	474.15	485.14	496.97	509.70	523.45	538.34	554.51
130,000	513.66	525.57	538.38	552.17	567.07	583.20	600.72
140,000	553.17	566.00	579.79	594.65	610.69	628.06	646.93
150,000	592.68	606.43	621.21	637.12	654.31	672.93	693.14
200,000	790.24	808.57	828.28	849.50	872.42	897.23	924.19
250,000	987.80	1010.72	1035.34	1061.87	1090.52	1121.54	1155.24
300,000	1185.36	1212.86	1242.41	1274.25	1308.62	1345.85	1386.28
350,000	1382.92	1415.01	1449.48	1486.62	1526.73	1570.16	1617.33
400,000	1580.48	1617.15	1656.55	1699.00	1744.83	1794.47	1848.38
450,000	1778.04	1819.29	1863.62	1911.37	1962.94	2018.78	2079.43
500,000	1975.60	2021.44	2070.69	2123.74	2181.04	2243.08	2310.47
550,000	2173.16	2223.58	2277.76	2336.12	2399.14	2467.39	2541.52
600,000	2370.73	2425.72	2484.83	2548.49	2617.25	2691.70	2772.57
650,000	2568.29	2627.87	2691.90	2760.87	2835.35	2916.01	3003.61
700,000	2765.85	2830.01	2898.97	2973.24	3053.45	3140.32	3234.66
750,000	2963.41	3032.16	3106.03	3185.62	3271.56	3364.63	3465.71
800,000	3160.97	3234.30	3313.10	3397.99	3489.66	3588.93	3696.76
850,000	3358.53	3436.44	3520.17	3610.37	3707.77	3813.24	3927.80
900,000	3556.09	3638.59	3727.24	3822.74	3925.87	4037.55	4158.85
950,000	3753.65	3840.73	3934.31	4035.11	4143.97	4261.86	4389.90
1,000,000	3951.21	4042.87	4141.38	4247.49	4362.08	4486.17	4620.95

Monthly Payments
Necessary to Amortize a Loan

2¹/₂%

YEARS REMAINING IN TERM

AMOUNT BORROWED	23	22	21	20	15	10	5
100	0.48	0.49	0.51	0.53	0.67	0.94	1.77
200	0.95	0.99	1.02	1.06	1.33	1.89	3.55
300	1.43	1.48	1.53	1.59	2.00	2.83	5.32
400	1.91	1.97	2.04	2.12	2.67	3.77	7.10
500	2.38	2.46	2.55	2.65	3.33	4.71	8.87
600	2.86	2.96	3.06	3.18	4.00	5.66	10.65
700	3.34	3.45	3.57	3.71	4.67	6.60	12.42
800	3.81	3.94	4.08	4.24	5.33	7.54	14.20
900	4.29	4.44	4.59	4.77	6.00	8.48	15.97
1,000	4.77	4.93	5.10	5.30	6.67	9.43	17.75
2,000	9.54	9.86	10.21	10.60	13.34	18.85	35.49
3,000	14.30	14.79	15.31	15.90	20.00	28.28	53.24
4,000	19.07	19.71	20.42	21.20	26.67	37.71	70.99
5,000	23.84	24.64	25.52	26.50	33.34	47.13	88.74
6,000	28.61	29.57	30.63	31.79	40.01	56.56	106.48
7,000	33.37	34.50	35.73	37.09	46.68	65.99	124.23
8,000	38.14	39.43	40.84	42.39	53.34	75.42	141.98
9,000	42.91	44.36	45.94	47.69	60.01	84.84	159.73
10,000	47.68	49.28	51.05	52.99	66.68	94.27	177.47
15,000	71.52	73.93	76.57	79.49	100.02	141.40	266.21
20,000	95.36	98.57	102.09	105.98	133.36	188.54	354.95
25,000	119.20	123.21	127.62	132.48	166.70	235.67	443.68
30,000	143.03	147.85	153.14	158.97	200.04	282.81	532.42
35,000	166.87	172.49	178.66	185.47	233.38	329.94	621.16
40,000	190.71	197.14	204.19	211.96	266.72	377.08	709.89
45,000	214.55	221.78	229.71	238.46	300.06	424.21	798.63
50,000	238.39	246.42	255.23	264.95	333.39	471.35	887.37
55,000	262.23	271.06	280.76	291.45	366.73	518.48	976.10
60,000	286.07	295.70	306.28	317.94	400.07	565.62	1064.84
65,000	309.91	320.35	331.80	344.44	433.41	612.75	1153.58
70,000	333.75	344.99	357.33	370.93	466.75	659.89	1242.32
75,000	357.59	369.63	382.85	397.43	500.09	707.02	1331.05
80,000	381.42	394.27	408.38	423.92	533.43	754.16	1419.79
85,000	405.26	418.91	433.90	450.42	566.77	801.29	1508.53
90,000	429.10	443.56	459.42	476.91	600.11	848.43	1597.26
95,000	452.94	468.20	484.95	503.41	633.45	895.56	1686.00
100,000	476.78	492.84	510.47	529.90	666.79	942.70	1774.74
110,000	524.46	542.12	561.52	582.89	733.47	1036.97	1952.21
120,000	572.14	591.41	612.56	635.88	800.15	1131.24	2129.68
130,000	619.81	640.69	663.61	688.87	866.83	1225.51	2307.16
140,000	667.49	689.98	714.66	741.86	933.50	1319.78	2484.63
150,000	715.17	739.26	765.70	794.85	1000.18	1414.05	2662.10
200,000	953.56	985.68	1020.94	1059.81	1333.58	1885.40	3549.47
250,000	1191.95	1232.10	1276.17	1324.76	1666.97	2356.75	4436.84
300,000	1430.34	1478.52	1531.41	1589.71	2000.37	2828.10	5324.21
350,000	1668.73	1724.94	1786.64	1854.66	2333.76	3299.45	6211.58
400,000	1907.12	1971.36	2041.88	2119.61	2667.16	3770.80	7098.94
450,000	2145.51	2217.78	2297.11	2384.56	3000.55	4242.15	7986.31
500,000	2383.90	2464.20	2552.34	2649.51	3333.95	4713.50	8873.68
550,000	2622.29	2710.62	2807.58	2914.47	3667.34	5184.84	9761.05
600,000	2860.68	2957.04	3062.81	3179.42	4000.74	5656.19	10648.42
650,000	3099.07	3203.46	3318.05	3444.37	4334.13	6127.54	11535.79
700,000	3337.46	3449.88	3573.28	3709.32	4667.52	6598.89	12423.15
750,000	3575.85	3696.30	3828.52	3974.27	5000.92	7070.24	13310.52
800,000	3814.25	3942.72	4083.75	4239.22	5334.31	7541.59	14197.89
850,000	4052.64	4189.14	4338.99	4504.17	5667.71	8012.94	15085.26
900,000	4291.03	4435.56	4594.22	4769.13	6001.10	8484.29	15972.63
950,000	4529.42	4681.98	4849.45	5034.08	6334.50	8955.64	16859.99
1,000,000	4767.81	4928.40	5104.69	5299.03	6667.89	9426.99	17747.36

Monthly Payments
Necessary to Amortize a Loan

YEARS REMAINING IN TERM

AMOUNT BORROWED	30	29	28	27	26	25	24
100	0.41	0.42	0.43	0.44	0.45	0.46	0.47
200	0.82	0.83	0.85	0.88	0.90	0.92	0.95
300	1.22	1.25	1.28	1.31	1.35	1.38	1.42
400	1.63	1.67	1.71	1.75	1.80	1.85	1.90
500	2.04	2.09	2.14	2.19	2.24	2.31	2.37
600	2.45	2.50	2.56	2.63	2.69	2.77	2.85
700	2.86	2.92	2.99	3.06	3.14	3.23	3.32
800	3.27	3.34	3.42	3.50	3.59	3.69	3.80
900	3.67	3.76	3.84	3.94	4.04	4.15	4.27
1,000	4.08	4.17	4.27	4.38	4.49	4.61	4.75
2,000	8.16	8.35	8.54	8.75	8.98	9.23	9.49
3,000	12.25	12.52	12.81	13.13	13.47	13.84	14.24
4,000	16.33	16.69	17.08	17.50	17.96	18.45	18.99
5,000	20.41	20.87	21.35	21.88	22.45	23.07	23.74
6,000	24.49	25.04	25.63	26.26	26.94	27.68	28.48
7,000	28.58	29.21	29.90	30.63	31.43	32.29	33.23
8,000	32.66	33.39	34.17	35.01	35.92	36.90	37.98
9,000	36.74	37.56	38.44	39.39	40.41	41.52	42.72
10,000	40.82	41.73	42.71	43.76	44.90	46.13	47.47
15,000	61.24	62.60	64.06	65.64	67.35	69.20	71.21
20,000	81.65	83.46	85.42	87.52	89.80	92.26	94.94
25,000	102.06	104.33	106.77	109.40	112.25	115.33	118.68
30,000	122.47	125.20	128.13	131.28	134.70	138.39	142.41
35,000	142.88	146.06	149.48	153.16	157.15	161.46	166.15
40,000	163.30	166.93	170.84	175.05	179.60	184.52	189.88
45,000	183.71	187.80	192.19	196.93	202.04	207.59	213.62
50,000	204.12	208.66	213.54	218.81	224.49	230.66	237.35
55,000	224.53	229.53	234.90	240.69	246.94	253.72	261.09
60,000	244.94	250.39	256.25	262.57	269.39	276.79	284.82
65,000	265.36	271.26	277.61	284.45	291.84	299.85	308.56
70,000	285.77	292.13	298.96	306.33	314.29	322.92	332.29
75,000	306.18	312.99	320.32	328.21	336.74	345.98	356.03
80,000	326.59	333.86	341.67	350.09	359.19	369.05	379.76
85,000	347.01	354.72	363.03	371.97	381.64	392.11	403.50
90,000	367.42	375.59	384.38	393.85	404.09	415.18	427.23
95,000	387.83	396.46	405.73	415.73	426.54	438.25	450.97
100,000	408.24	417.32	427.09	437.61	448.99	461.31	474.70
110,000	449.07	459.06	469.80	481.38	493.89	507.44	522.17
120,000	489.89	500.79	512.51	525.14	538.79	553.57	569.64
130,000	530.71	542.52	555.22	568.90	583.68	599.70	617.11
140,000	571.54	584.25	597.92	612.66	628.58	645.84	664.58
150,000	612.36	625.98	640.63	656.42	673.48	691.97	712.05
200,000	816.48	834.65	854.18	875.23	897.98	922.62	949.41
250,000	1020.61	1043.31	1067.72	1094.04	1122.47	1153.28	1186.76
300,000	1224.72	1251.97	1281.27	1312.84	1346.96	1383.93	1424.11
350,000	1428.84	1460.63	1494.81	1531.65	1571.46	1614.59	1661.46
400,000	1632.96	1669.29	1708.35	1750.46	1795.95	1845.24	1898.81
450,000	1837.09	1877.95	1921.90	1969.26	2020.44	2075.90	2136.16
500,000	2041.21	2086.61	2135.44	2188.07	2244.94	2306.55	2373.51
550,000	2245.33	2295.28	2348.99	2406.88	2469.43	2537.21	2610.87
600,000	2449.45	2503.94	2562.53	2625.68	2693.93	2767.87	2848.22
650,000	2653.57	2712.60	2776.08	2844.49	2918.42	2998.52	3085.57
700,000	2857.69	2921.26	2989.62	3063.30	3142.91	3229.18	3322.92
750,000	3061.81	3129.92	3203.16	3282.11	3367.41	3459.83	3560.27
800,000	3265.93	3338.58	3416.71	3500.91	3591.90	3690.49	3797.62
850,000	3470.05	3547.24	3630.25	3719.72	3816.39	3921.14	4034.97
900,000	3674.17	3755.91	3843.80	3938.53	4040.89	4151.80	4272.32
950,000	3878.29	3964.57	4057.34	4157.33	4265.38	4382.45	4509.68
1,000,000	4082.41	4173.23	4270.89	4376.14	4489.88	4613.11	4747.03

Monthly Payments $2^3/_4\%$
Necessary to Amortize a Loan

AMOUNT BORROWED	YEARS REMAINING IN TERM						
	23	22	21	20	15	10	5
100	0.49	0.51	0.52	0.54	0.68	0.95	1.79
200	0.98	1.01	1.05	1.08	1.36	1.91	3.57
300	1.47	1.52	1.57	1.63	2.04	2.86	5.36
400	1.96	2.02	2.09	2.17	2.71	3.82	7.14
500	2.45	2.53	2.61	2.71	3.39	4.77	8.93
600	2.94	3.03	3.14	3.25	4.07	5.72	10.71
700	3.43	3.54	3.66	3.80	4.75	6.68	12.50
800	3.91	4.04	4.18	4.34	5.43	7.63	14.29
900	4.40	4.55	4.71	4.88	6.11	8.59	16.07
1,000	4.89	5.05	5.23	5.42	6.79	9.54	17.86
2,000	9.79	10.11	10.46	10.84	13.57	19.08	35.72
3,000	14.68	15.16	15.68	16.26	20.36	28.62	53.57
4,000	19.57	20.21	20.91	21.69	27.14	38.16	71.43
5,000	24.47	25.26	26.14	27.11	33.93	47.71	89.29
6,000	29.36	30.32	31.37	32.53	40.72	57.25	107.15
7,000	34.25	35.37	36.60	37.95	47.50	66.79	125.00
8,000	39.14	40.42	41.83	43.37	54.29	76.33	142.86
9,000	44.04	45.47	47.05	48.79	61.08	85.87	160.72
10,000	48.93	50.53	52.28	54.22	67.86	95.41	178.58
15,000	73.40	75.79	78.42	81.32	101.79	143.12	267.87
20,000	97.86	101.06	104.56	108.43	135.72	190.82	357.16
25,000	122.33	126.32	130.70	135.54	169.66	238.53	446.45
30,000	146.79	151.58	156.85	162.65	203.59	286.23	535.73
35,000	171.26	176.85	182.99	189.76	237.52	333.94	625.02
40,000	195.72	202.11	209.13	216.87	271.45	381.64	714.31
45,000	220.19	227.37	235.27	243.97	305.38	429.35	803.60
50,000	244.65	252.64	261.41	271.08	339.31	477.06	892.89
55,000	269.12	277.90	287.55	298.19	373.24	524.76	982.18
60,000	293.58	303.17	313.69	325.30	407.17	572.47	1071.47
65,000	318.05	328.43	339.83	352.41	441.10	620.17	1160.76
70,000	342.51	353.69	365.97	379.52	475.04	667.88	1250.05
75,000	366.98	378.96	392.11	406.62	508.97	715.58	1339.34
80,000	391.44	404.22	418.25	433.73	542.90	763.29	1428.62
85,000	415.91	429.48	444.40	460.84	576.83	810.99	1517.91
90,000	440.37	454.75	470.54	487.95	610.76	858.70	1607.20
95,000	464.84	480.01	496.68	515.06	644.69	906.40	1696.49
100,000	489.30	505.28	522.82	542.17	678.62	954.11	1785.78
110,000	538.23	555.80	575.10	596.38	746.48	1049.52	1964.36
120,000	587.16	606.33	627.38	650.60	814.35	1144.93	2142.94
130,000	636.09	656.86	679.66	704.82	882.21	1240.34	2321.52
140,000	685.02	707.39	731.95	759.03	950.07	1335.75	2500.09
150,000	733.95	757.91	784.23	813.25	1017.93	1431.17	2678.67
200,000	978.61	1010.55	1045.64	1084.33	1357.24	1908.22	3571.56
250,000	1223.26	1263.19	1307.05	1355.42	1696.55	2385.28	4464.45
300,000	1467.91	1515.83	1568.46	1626.50	2035.86	2862.33	5357.34
350,000	1712.56	1768.47	1829.87	1897.58	2375.18	3339.39	6250.23
400,000	1957.21	2021.10	2091.27	2168.67	2714.49	3816.44	7143.12
450,000	2201.86	2273.74	2352.68	2439.75	3053.80	4293.50	8036.01
500,000	2446.51	2526.38	2614.09	2710.83	3393.11	4770.55	8928.91
550,000	2691.17	2779.02	2875.50	2981.91	3732.42	5247.61	9821.80
600,000	2935.82	3031.66	3136.91	3253.00	4071.73	5724.66	10714.69
650,000	3180.47	3284.29	3398.32	3524.08	4411.04	6201.72	11607.58
700,000	3425.12	3536.93	3659.73	3795.16	4750.35	6678.77	12500.47
750,000	3669.77	3789.57	3921.14	4066.25	5089.66	7155.83	13393.36
800,000	3914.42	4042.21	4182.56	4337.33	5428.97	7632.88	14286.25
850,000	4159.07	4294.85	4443.96	4608.41	5768.28	8109.94	15179.14
900,000	4403.73	4547.48	4705.37	4879.50	6107.59	8586.99	16072.03
950,000	4648.38	4800.12	4966.78	5150.58	6446.91	9064.05	16964.92
1,000,000	4893.03	5052.76	5228.19	5421.66	6786.22	9541.10	17857.81

3%   Monthly Payments
Necessary to Amortize a Loan

AMOUNT BORROWED	YEARS REMAINING IN TERM						
	30	29	28	27	26	25	24
100	0.42	0.43	0.44	0.45	0.46	0.47	0.49
200	0.84	0.86	0.88	0.90	0.92	0.95	0.98
300	1.26	1.29	1.32	1.35	1.39	1.42	1.46
400	1.69	1.72	1.76	1.80	1.85	1.90	1.95
500	2.11	2.15	2.20	2.25	2.31	2.37	2.44
600	2.53	2.58	2.64	2.70	2.77	2.85	2.93
700	2.95	3.01	3.08	3.15	3.23	3.32	3.41
800	3.37	3.44	3.52	3.61	3.70	3.79	3.90
900	3.79	3.88	3.96	4.06	4.16	4.27	4.39
1,000	4.22	4.31	4.40	4.51	4.62	4.74	4.88
2,000	8.43	8.61	8.81	9.01	9.24	9.48	9.75
3,000	12.65	12.92	13.21	13.52	13.86	14.23	14.63
4,000	16.86	17.22	17.61	18.03	18.48	18.97	19.50
5,000	21.08	21.53	22.01	22.54	23.10	23.71	24.38
6,000	25.30	25.84	26.42	27.04	27.72	28.45	29.25
7,000	29.51	30.14	30.82	31.55	32.34	33.19	34.13
8,000	33.73	34.45	35.22	36.06	36.96	37.94	39.00
9,000	37.94	38.75	39.62	40.56	41.58	42.68	43.88
10,000	42.16	43.06	44.03	45.07	46.20	47.42	48.75
15,000	63.24	64.59	66.04	67.61	69.30	71.13	73.13
20,000	84.32	86.12	88.05	90.14	92.40	94.84	97.50
25,000	105.40	107.65	110.07	112.68	115.50	118.55	121.88
30,000	126.48	129.18	132.08	135.21	138.59	142.26	146.25
35,000	147.56	150.71	154.09	157.75	161.69	165.97	170.63
40,000	168.64	172.24	176.11	180.28	184.79	189.68	195.00
45,000	189.72	193.77	198.12	202.82	207.89	213.40	219.38
50,000	210.80	215.30	220.13	225.35	230.99	237.11	243.75
55,000	231.88	236.83	242.15	247.89	254.09	260.82	268.13
60,000	252.96	258.36	264.16	270.42	277.19	284.53	292.51
65,000	274.04	279.89	286.17	292.96	300.29	308.24	316.88
70,000	295.12	301.42	308.19	315.49	323.39	331.95	341.26
75,000	316.20	322.95	330.20	338.03	346.49	355.66	365.63
80,000	337.28	344.48	352.21	360.56	369.58	379.37	390.01
85,000	358.36	366.00	374.23	383.10	392.68	403.08	414.38
90,000	379.44	387.53	396.24	405.63	415.78	426.79	438.76
95,000	400.52	409.06	418.25	428.17	438.88	450.50	463.13
100,000	421.60	430.59	440.27	450.70	461.98	474.21	487.51
110,000	463.76	473.65	484.29	495.77	508.18	521.63	536.26
120,000	505.92	516.71	528.32	540.84	554.38	569.05	585.01
130,000	548.09	559.77	572.35	585.91	600.58	616.47	633.76
140,000	590.25	602.83	616.37	630.98	646.77	663.90	682.51
150,000	632.41	645.89	660.40	676.05	692.97	711.32	731.26
200,000	843.21	861.19	880.53	901.40	923.96	948.42	975.02
250,000	1054.01	1076.48	1100.67	1126.75	1154.95	1185.53	1218.77
300,000	1264.81	1291.78	1320.80	1352.10	1385.94	1422.63	1462.53
350,000	1475.61	1507.08	1540.94	1577.45	1616.93	1659.74	1706.28
400,000	1686.42	1722.38	1761.07	1802.80	1847.92	1896.85	1950.04
450,000	1897.22	1937.67	1981.20	2028.15	2078.92	2133.95	2193.79
500,000	2108.02	2152.97	2201.34	2253.50	2309.91	2371.06	2437.55
550,000	2318.82	2368.27	2421.47	2478.85	2540.90	2608.16	2681.30
600,000	2529.62	2583.56	2641.60	2704.20	2771.89	2845.27	2925.06
650,000	2740.43	2798.86	2861.74	2929.55	3002.88	3082.37	3168.81
700,000	2951.23	3014.16	3081.87	3154.90	3233.87	3319.48	3412.57
750,000	3162.03	3229.45	3302.01	3380.25	3464.86	3556.58	3656.32
800,000	3372.83	3444.75	3522.14	3605.60	3695.85	3793.69	3900.08
850,000	3583.63	3660.05	3742.27	3830.95	3926.84	4030.80	4143.83
900,000	3794.44	3875.35	3962.41	4056.30	4157.83	4267.90	4387.59
950,000	4005.24	4090.64	4182.54	4281.66	4388.82	4505.01	4631.34
1,000,000	4216.04	4305.94	4402.67	4507.01	4619.81	4742.11	4875.10

Monthly Payments 3%

Necessary to Amortize a Loan

AMOUNT BORROWED	YEARS REMAINING IN TERM						
	23	22	21	20	15	10	5
100	0.50	0.52	0.54	0.55	0.69	0.97	1.80
200	1.00	1.04	1.07	1.11	1.38	1.93	3.59
300	1.51	1.55	1.61	1.66	2.07	2.90	5.39
400	2.01	2.07	2.14	2.22	2.76	3.86	7.19
500	2.51	2.59	2.68	2.77	3.45	4.83	8.98
600	3.01	3.11	3.21	3.33	4.14	5.79	10.78
700	3.51	3.63	3.75	3.88	4.83	6.76	12.58
800	4.02	4.14	4.28	4.44	5.52	7.72	14.37
900	4.52	4.66	4.82	4.99	6.22	8.69	16.17
1,000	5.02	5.18	5.35	5.55	6.91	9.66	17.97
2,000	10.04	10.36	10.71	11.09	13.81	19.31	35.94
3,000	15.06	15.54	16.06	16.64	20.72	28.97	53.91
4,000	20.08	20.72	21.41	22.18	27.62	38.62	71.87
5,000	25.10	25.89	26.77	27.73	34.53	48.28	89.84
6,000	30.12	31.07	32.12	33.28	41.43	57.94	107.81
7,000	35.14	36.25	37.47	38.82	48.34	67.59	125.78
8,000	40.16	41.43	42.83	44.37	55.25	77.25	143.75
9,000	45.18	46.61	48.18	49.91	62.15	86.90	161.72
10,000	50.20	51.79	53.53	55.46	69.06	96.56	179.69
15,000	75.30	77.68	80.30	83.19	103.59	144.84	269.53
20,000	100.40	103.58	107.07	110.92	138.12	193.12	359.37
25,000	125.50	129.47	133.84	138.65	172.65	241.40	449.22
30,000	150.60	155.37	160.60	166.38	207.17	289.68	539.06
35,000	175.71	181.26	187.37	194.11	241.70	337.96	628.90
40,000	200.81	207.16	214.14	221.84	276.23	386.24	718.75
45,000	225.91	233.05	240.90	249.57	310.76	434.52	808.59
50,000	251.01	258.95	267.67	277.30	345.29	482.80	898.43
55,000	276.11	284.84	294.44	305.03	379.82	531.08	988.28
60,000	301.21	310.74	321.21	332.76	414.35	579.36	1078.12
65,000	326.31	336.63	347.97	360.49	448.88	627.64	1167.96
70,000	351.41	362.53	374.74	388.22	483.41	675.93	1257.81
75,000	376.51	388.42	401.51	415.95	517.94	724.21	1347.65
80,000	401.61	414.32	428.28	443.68	552.47	772.49	1437.50
85,000	426.71	440.21	455.04	471.41	586.99	820.77	1527.34
90,000	451.81	466.11	481.81	499.14	621.52	869.05	1617.18
95,000	476.92	492.00	508.58	526.87	656.05	917.33	1707.03
100,000	502.02	517.90	535.34	554.60	690.58	965.61	1796.87
110,000	552.22	569.69	588.88	610.06	759.64	1062.17	1976.56
120,000	602.42	621.47	642.41	665.52	828.70	1158.73	2156.24
130,000	652.62	673.26	695.95	720.98	897.76	1255.29	2335.93
140,000	702.82	725.05	749.48	776.44	966.81	1351.85	2515.62
150,000	753.02	776.84	803.02	831.90	1035.87	1448.41	2695.30
200,000	1004.03	1035.79	1070.69	1109.20	1381.16	1931.21	3593.74
250,000	1255.04	1294.74	1338.36	1386.49	1726.45	2414.02	4492.17
300,000	1506.05	1553.69	1606.03	1663.79	2071.74	2896.82	5390.61
350,000	1757.06	1812.63	1873.70	1941.09	2417.04	3379.63	6289.04
400,000	2008.06	2071.58	2141.38	2218.39	2762.33	3862.43	7187.48
450,000	2259.07	2330.53	2409.05	2495.69	3107.62	4345.23	8085.91
500,000	2510.08	2589.48	2676.72	2772.99	3452.91	4828.04	8984.35
550,000	2761.09	2848.43	2944.39	3050.29	3798.20	5310.84	9882.78
600,000	3012.10	3107.37	3212.06	3327.59	4143.49	5793.64	10781.21
650,000	3263.11	3366.32	3479.74	3604.88	4488.78	6276.45	11679.65
700,000	3514.11	3625.27	3747.41	3882.18	4834.07	6759.25	12578.08
750,000	3765.12	3884.22	4015.08	4159.48	5179.36	7242.06	13476.52
800,000	4016.13	4143.16	4282.75	4436.78	5524.65	7724.86	14374.95
850,000	4267.14	4402.11	4550.43	4714.08	5869.94	8207.66	15273.39
900,000	4518.15	4661.06	4818.10	4991.38	6215.23	8690.47	16171.82
950,000	4769.15	4920.01	5085.77	5268.68	6560.53	9173.27	17070.26
1,000,000	5020.16	5178.96	5353.44	5545.98	6905.82	9656.07	17968.69

3¼%

Monthly Payments
Necessary to Amortize a Loan

AMOUNT BORROWED	YEARS REMAINING IN TERM						
	30	29	28	27	26	25	24
100	0.44	0.44	0.45	0.46	0.48	0.49	0.50
200	0.87	0.89	0.91	0.93	0.95	0.97	1.00
300	1.31	1.33	1.36	1.39	1.43	1.46	1.50
400	1.74	1.78	1.81	1.86	1.90	1.95	2.00
500	2.18	2.22	2.27	2.32	2.38	2.44	2.50
600	2.61	2.66	2.72	2.78	2.85	2.92	3.00
700	3.05	3.11	3.18	3.25	3.33	3.41	3.50
800	3.48	3.55	3.63	3.71	3.80	3.90	4.00
900	3.92	4.00	4.08	4.18	4.28	4.39	4.50
1,000	4.35	4.44	4.54	4.64	4.75	4.87	5.01
2,000	8.70	8.88	9.07	9.28	9.50	9.75	10.01
3,000	13.06	13.32	13.61	13.92	14.26	14.62	15.02
4,000	17.41	17.76	18.15	18.56	19.01	19.49	20.02
5,000	21.76	22.20	22.68	23.20	23.76	24.37	25.03
6,000	26.11	26.65	27.22	27.84	28.51	29.24	30.03
7,000	30.46	31.09	31.76	32.48	33.26	34.11	35.04
8,000	34.82	35.53	36.29	37.12	38.01	38.99	40.04
9,000	39.17	39.97	40.83	41.76	42.77	43.86	45.05
10,000	43.52	44.41	45.37	46.40	47.52	48.73	50.05
15,000	65.28	66.61	68.05	69.60	71.28	73.10	75.08
20,000	87.04	88.82	90.73	92.80	95.04	97.46	100.10
25,000	108.80	111.02	113.42	116.00	118.80	121.83	125.13
30,000	130.56	133.23	136.10	139.20	142.56	146.19	150.15
35,000	152.32	155.43	158.79	162.40	166.32	170.56	175.18
40,000	174.08	177.64	181.47	185.60	190.07	194.93	200.21
45,000	195.84	199.84	204.15	208.80	213.83	219.29	225.23
50,000	217.60	222.05	226.84	232.00	237.59	243.66	250.26
55,000	239.36	244.25	249.52	255.20	261.35	268.02	275.28
60,000	261.12	266.46	272.20	278.40	285.11	292.39	300.31
65,000	282.88	288.66	294.89	301.60	308.87	316.76	325.33
70,000	304.64	310.87	317.57	324.80	332.63	341.12	350.36
75,000	326.40	333.07	340.25	348.00	356.39	365.49	375.39
80,000	348.17	355.28	362.94	371.20	380.15	389.85	400.41
85,000	369.93	377.48	385.62	394.40	403.91	414.22	425.44
90,000	391.69	399.69	408.30	417.61	427.67	438.58	450.46
95,000	413.45	421.89	430.99	440.81	451.43	462.95	475.49
100,000	435.21	444.10	453.67	464.01	475.19	487.32	500.51
110,000	478.73	488.51	499.04	510.41	522.71	536.05	550.57
120,000	522.25	532.92	544.41	556.81	570.22	584.78	600.62
130,000	565.77	577.33	589.77	603.21	617.74	633.51	650.67
140,000	609.29	621.74	635.14	649.61	665.26	682.24	700.72
150,000	652.81	666.15	680.51	696.01	712.78	730.97	750.77
200,000	870.41	888.20	907.34	928.01	950.37	974.63	1001.03
250,000	1088.02	1110.24	1134.18	1160.01	1187.97	1218.29	1251.28
300,000	1305.62	1332.29	1361.02	1392.02	1425.56	1461.95	1501.54
350,000	1523.22	1554.34	1587.85	1624.02	1663.15	1705.61	1751.80
400,000	1740.83	1776.39	1814.69	1856.02	1900.75	1949.26	2002.06
450,000	1958.43	1998.44	2041.52	2088.03	2138.34	2192.92	2252.31
500,000	2176.03	2220.49	2268.36	2320.03	2375.93	2436.58	2502.57
550,000	2393.63	2442.54	2495.20	2552.03	2613.53	2680.24	2752.83
600,000	2611.24	2664.59	2722.03	2784.03	2851.12	2923.90	3003.08
650,000	2828.84	2886.64	2948.87	3016.04	3088.71	3167.56	3253.34
700,000	3046.44	3108.68	3175.70	3248.04	3326.31	3411.21	3503.60
750,000	3264.05	3330.73	3402.54	3480.04	3563.90	3654.87	3753.85
800,000	3481.65	3552.78	3629.38	3712.05	3801.49	3898.53	4004.11
850,000	3699.25	3774.83	3856.21	3944.05	4039.08	4142.19	4254.37
900,000	3916.86	3996.88	4083.05	4176.05	4276.68	4385.85	4504.63
950,000	4134.46	4218.93	4309.89	4408.05	4514.27	4629.50	4754.88
1,000,000	4352.06	4440.98	4536.72	4640.06	4751.86	4873.16	5015.14

Monthly Payments $3^1/4\%$

Necessary to Amortize a Loan

AMOUNT BORROWED	YEARS REMAINING IN TERM						
	23	22	21	20	15	10	5
100	0.51	0.53	0.55	0.57	0.70	0.98	1.81
200	1.03	1.06	1.10	1.13	1.41	1.95	3.62
300	1.54	1.59	1.64	1.70	2.11	2.93	5.42
400	2.06	2.12	2.19	2.27	2.81	3.91	7.23
500	2.57	2.65	2.74	2.84	3.51	4.89	9.04
600	3.09	3.18	3.29	3.40	4.22	5.86	10.85
700	3.60	3.71	3.84	3.97	4.92	6.84	12.66
800	4.12	4.25	4.38	4.54	5.62	7.82	14.46
900	4.63	4.78	4.93	5.10	6.32	8.79	16.27
1,000	5.15	5.31	5.48	5.67	7.03	9.77	18.08
2,000	10.30	10.61	10.96	11.34	14.05	19.54	36.16
3,000	15.45	15.92	16.44	17.02	21.08	29.32	54.24
4,000	20.60	21.23	21.92	22.69	28.11	39.09	72.32
5,000	25.75	26.53	27.40	28.36	35.13	48.86	90.40
6,000	30.90	31.84	32.88	34.03	42.16	58.63	108.48
7,000	36.04	37.15	38.36	39.70	49.19	68.40	126.56
8,000	41.19	42.46	43.84	45.38	56.21	78.18	144.64
9,000	46.34	47.76	49.32	51.05	63.24	87.95	162.72
10,000	51.49	53.07	54.80	56.72	70.27	97.72	180.80
15,000	77.24	79.60	82.21	85.08	105.40	146.58	271.20
20,000	102.98	106.14	109.61	113.44	140.53	195.44	361.60
25,000	128.73	132.67	137.01	141.80	175.67	244.30	452.00
30,000	154.48	159.21	164.41	170.16	210.80	293.16	542.40
35,000	180.22	185.74	191.82	198.52	245.93	342.02	632.80
40,000	205.97	212.28	219.22	226.88	281.07	390.88	723.20
45,000	231.71	238.81	246.62	255.24	316.20	439.74	813.60
50,000	257.46	265.35	274.02	283.60	351.33	488.60	904.00
55,000	283.21	291.88	301.42	311.96	386.47	537.45	994.40
60,000	308.95	318.42	328.83	340.32	421.60	586.31	1084.80
65,000	334.70	344.95	356.23	368.68	456.73	635.17	1175.20
70,000	360.44	371.49	383.63	397.04	491.87	684.03	1265.60
75,000	386.19	398.02	411.03	425.40	527.00	732.89	1356.00
80,000	411.94	424.56	438.44	453.76	562.14	781.75	1446.40
85,000	437.68	451.09	465.84	482.12	597.27	830.61	1536.80
90,000	463.43	477.63	493.24	510.48	632.40	879.47	1627.20
95,000	489.17	504.16	520.64	538.84	667.54	928.33	1717.60
100,000	514.92	530.70	548.04	567.20	702.67	977.19	1808.00
110,000	566.41	583.77	602.85	623.92	772.94	1074.91	1988.80
120,000	617.90	636.84	657.65	680.63	843.20	1172.63	2169.60
130,000	669.40	689.91	712.46	737.35	913.47	1270.35	2350.40
140,000	720.89	742.98	767.26	794.07	983.74	1368.07	2531.20
150,000	772.38	796.05	822.07	850.79	1054.00	1465.79	2712.00
200,000	1029.84	1061.39	1096.09	1134.39	1405.34	1954.38	3616.00
250,000	1287.30	1326.74	1370.11	1417.99	1756.67	2442.98	4520.00
300,000	1544.76	1592.09	1644.13	1701.59	2108.01	2931.57	5424.00
350,000	1802.22	1857.44	1918.15	1985.19	2459.34	3420.17	6328.00
400,000	2059.68	2122.79	2192.18	2268.78	2810.68	3908.76	7232.00
450,000	2317.14	2388.14	2466.20	2552.38	3162.01	4397.36	8136.00
500,000	2574.60	2653.49	2740.22	2835.98	3513.34	4885.95	9040.00
550,000	2832.06	2918.84	3014.24	3119.58	3864.68	5374.55	9944.00
600,000	3089.52	3184.03	3288.27	3403.17	4216.01	5863.14	10848.00
650,000	3346.98	3449.53	3562.29	3686.77	4567.35	6351.74	11752.00
700,000	3604.44	3714.88	3836.31	3970.37	4918.68	6840.33	12656.00
750,000	3861.90	3980.23	4110.33	4253.97	5270.02	7328.93	13560.00
800,000	4119.35	4245.58	4384.35	4537.57	5621.35	7817.52	14464.00
850,000	4376.81	4510.93	4658.38	4821.16	5972.68	8306.12	15368.00
900,000	4634.27	4776.28	4932.40	5104.76	6324.02	8794.71	16272.00
950,000	4891.73	5041.62	5206.42	5388.36	6675.35	9283.31	17176.00
1,000,000	5149.19	5306.97	5480.44	5671.96	7026.69	9771.90	18080.00

3¹/2%   Monthly Payments
Necessary to Amortize a Loan

YEARS REMAINING IN TERM

AMOUNT BORROWED	30	29	28	27	26	25	24
100	0.45	0.46	0.47	0.48	0.49	0.50	0.51
200	0.90	0.92	0.93	0.96	0.98	1.00	1.03
300	1.35	1.37	1.40	1.43	1.47	1.50	1.54
400	1.80	1.83	1.87	1.91	1.95	2.00	2.05
500	2.25	2.29	2.34	2.39	2.44	2.50	2.57
600	2.69	2.75	2.80	2.87	2.93	3.00	3.08
700	3.14	3.20	3.27	3.34	3.42	3.50	3.60
800	3.59	3.66	3.74	3.82	3.91	4.00	4.11
900	4.04	4.12	4.21	4.30	4.40	4.51	4.62
1,000	4.49	4.58	4.67	4.78	4.89	5.01	5.14
2,000	8.98	9.16	9.35	9.55	9.77	10.01	10.27
3,000	13.47	13.73	14.02	14.33	14.66	15.02	15.41
4,000	17.96	18.31	18.69	19.10	19.54	20.02	20.55
5,000	22.45	22.89	23.36	23.88	24.43	25.03	25.69
6,000	26.94	27.47	28.04	28.65	29.32	30.04	30.82
7,000	31.43	32.05	32.71	33.43	34.20	35.04	35.96
8,000	35.92	36.63	37.38	38.20	39.09	40.05	41.10
9,000	40.41	41.20	42.06	42.98	43.97	45.06	46.23
10,000	44.90	45.78	46.73	47.75	48.86	50.06	51.37
15,000	67.36	68.67	70.09	71.63	73.29	75.09	77.06
20,000	89.81	91.57	93.46	95.51	97.72	100.12	102.74
25,000	112.26	114.46	116.82	119.38	122.15	125.16	128.43
30,000	134.71	137.35	140.19	143.26	146.58	150.19	154.11
35,000	157.17	160.24	163.55	167.13	171.01	175.22	179.80
40,000	179.62	183.13	186.92	191.01	195.44	200.25	205.49
45,000	202.07	206.02	210.28	214.89	219.87	225.28	231.17
50,000	224.52	228.92	233.65	238.76	244.30	250.31	256.86
55,000	246.97	251.81	257.01	262.64	268.73	275.34	282.54
60,000	269.43	274.70	280.38	286.52	293.16	300.37	308.23
65,000	291.88	297.59	303.74	310.39	317.59	325.41	333.91
70,000	314.33	320.48	327.11	334.27	342.02	350.44	359.60
75,000	336.78	343.37	350.47	358.15	366.45	375.47	385.29
80,000	359.24	366.26	373.84	382.02	390.88	400.50	410.97
85,000	381.69	389.16	397.20	405.90	415.31	425.53	436.66
90,000	404.14	412.05	420.57	429.77	439.74	450.56	462.34
95,000	426.59	434.94	443.93	453.65	464.17	475.59	488.03
100,000	449.04	457.83	467.30	477.53	488.60	500.62	513.71
110,000	493.95	503.61	514.03	525.28	537.46	550.69	565.08
120,000	538.85	549.40	560.76	573.03	586.32	600.75	616.46
130,000	583.76	595.18	607.49	620.79	635.18	650.81	667.83
140,000	628.66	640.96	654.22	668.54	684.04	700.87	719.20
150,000	673.57	686.75	700.95	716.29	732.90	750.94	770.57
200,000	898.09	915.66	934.60	955.05	977.20	1001.25	1027.43
250,000	1122.61	1144.58	1168.25	1193.82	1221.50	1251.56	1284.28
300,000	1347.13	1373.49	1401.90	1432.58	1465.80	1501.87	1541.14
350,000	1571.66	1602.41	1635.55	1671.35	1710.10	1752.18	1798.00
400,000	1796.18	1831.32	1869.20	1910.11	1954.40	2002.49	2054.85
450,000	2020.70	2060.24	2102.85	2148.87	2198.71	2252.81	2311.71
500,000	2245.22	2289.16	2336.50	2387.64	2443.01	2503.12	2568.57
550,000	2469.75	2518.07	2570.15	2626.40	2687.31	2753.43	2825.42
600,000	2694.27	2746.99	2803.80	2865.16	2931.61	3003.74	3082.28
650,000	2918.79	2975.90	3037.45	3103.93	3175.91	3254.05	3339.14
700,000	3143.31	3204.82	3271.10	3342.69	3420.21	3504.36	3595.99
750,000	3367.84	3433.73	3504.75	3581.45	3664.51	3754.68	3852.85
800,000	3592.36	3662.65	3738.40	3820.22	3908.81	4004.99	4109.71
850,000	3816.88	3891.56	3972.05	4058.98	4153.11	4255.30	4366.56
900,000	4041.40	4120.48	4205.70	4297.74	4397.41	4505.61	4623.42
950,000	4265.92	4349.39	4439.35	4536.51	4641.71	4755.92	4880.28
1,000,000	4490.45	4578.31	4673.00	4775.27	4886.01	5006.24	5137.14

Monthly Payments
Necessary to Amortize a Loan

3¹/₂%

AMOUNT BORROWED	YEARS REMAINING IN TERM						
	23	22	21	20	15	10	5
100	0.53	0.54	0.56	0.58	0.71	0.99	1.82
200	1.06	1.09	1.12	1.16	1.43	1.98	3.64
300	1.58	1.63	1.68	1.74	2.14	2.97	5.46
400	2.11	2.17	2.24	2.32	2.86	3.96	7.28
500	2.64	2.72	2.80	2.90	3.57	4.94	9.10
600	3.17	3.26	3.37	3.48	4.29	5.93	10.92
700	3.70	3.81	3.93	4.06	5.00	6.92	12.73
800	4.22	4.35	4.49	4.64	5.72	7.91	14.55
900	4.75	4.89	5.05	5.22	6.43	8.90	16.37
1,000	5.28	5.44	5.61	5.80	7.15	9.89	18.19
2,000	10.56	10.87	11.22	11.60	14.30	19.78	36.38
3,000	15.84	16.31	16.83	17.40	21.45	29.67	54.58
4,000	21.12	21.75	22.44	23.20	28.60	39.55	72.77
5,000	26.40	27.18	28.05	29.00	35.74	49.44	90.96
6,000	31.68	32.62	33.66	34.80	42.89	59.33	109.15
7,000	36.96	38.06	39.26	40.60	50.04	69.22	127.34
8,000	42.24	43.49	44.87	46.40	57.19	79.11	145.53
9,000	47.52	48.93	50.48	52.20	64.34	89.00	163.73
10,000	52.80	54.37	56.09	58.00	71.49	98.89	181.92
15,000	79.20	81.55	84.14	86.99	107.23	148.33	272.88
20,000	105.60	108.74	112.18	115.99	142.98	197.77	363.83
25,000	132.00	135.92	140.23	144.99	178.72	247.21	454.79
30,000	158.40	163.10	168.28	173.99	214.46	296.66	545.75
35,000	184.80	190.29	196.32	202.99	250.21	346.10	636.71
40,000	211.20	217.47	224.37	231.98	285.95	395.54	727.67
45,000	237.60	244.66	252.41	260.98	321.70	444.99	818.63
50,000	264.01	271.84	280.46	289.98	357.44	494.43	909.59
55,000	290.41	299.02	308.50	318.98	393.19	543.87	1000.55
60,000	316.81	326.21	336.55	347.98	428.93	593.32	1091.50
65,000	343.21	353.39	364.60	376.97	464.67	642.76	1182.46
70,000	369.61	380.58	392.64	405.97	500.42	692.20	1273.42
75,000	396.01	407.76	420.69	434.97	536.16	741.64	1364.38
80,000	422.41	434.94	448.73	463.97	571.91	791.09	1455.34
85,000	448.81	462.13	476.78	492.97	607.65	840.53	1546.30
90,000	475.21	489.31	504.83	521.96	643.39	889.97	1637.26
95,000	501.61	516.50	532.87	550.96	679.14	939.42	1728.22
100,000	528.01	543.68	560.92	579.96	714.88	988.86	1819.17
110,000	580.81	598.05	617.01	637.96	786.37	1087.74	2001.09
120,000	633.61	652.42	673.10	695.95	857.86	1186.63	2183.01
130,000	686.41	706.78	729.19	753.95	929.35	1285.52	2364.93
140,000	739.21	761.15	785.28	811.94	1000.84	1384.40	2546.84
150,000	792.02	815.52	841.38	869.94	1072.32	1483.29	2728.76
200,000	1056.02	1087.36	1121.84	1159.92	1429.77	1977.72	3638.35
250,000	1320.03	1359.20	1402.29	1449.90	1787.21	2472.15	4547.94
300,000	1584.03	1631.04	1682.75	1739.88	2144.65	2966.58	5457.52
350,000	1848.04	1902.88	1963.21	2029.86	2502.09	3461.01	6367.11
400,000	2112.04	2174.72	2243.67	2319.84	2859.53	3955.43	7276.70
450,000	2376.05	2446.56	2524.13	2609.82	3216.97	4449.86	8186.29
500,000	2640.05	2718.40	2804.59	2899.80	3574.41	4944.29	9095.87
550,000	2904.06	2990.24	3085.05	3189.78	3931.85	5438.72	10005.46
600,000	3168.06	3262.08	3365.51	3479.76	4289.30	5933.15	10915.05
650,000	3432.07	3533.92	3645.96	3769.74	4646.74	6427.58	11824.63
700,000	3696.07	3805.76	3926.42	4059.72	5004.18	6922.01	12734.22
750,000	3960.08	4077.60	4206.88	4349.70	5361.62	7416.44	13643.81
800,000	4224.08	4349.44	4487.34	4639.68	5719.06	7910.87	14553.40
850,000	4488.09	4621.28	4767.80	4929.66	6076.50	8405.30	15462.98
900,000	4752.10	4893.12	5048.26	5219.64	6433.94	8899.73	16372.57
950,000	5016.10	5164.96	5328.72	5509.62	6791.38	9394.16	17282.16
1,000,000	5280.11	5436.80	5609.18	5799.60	7148.83	9888.59	18191.74

Monthly Payments
Necessary to Amortize a Loan

YEARS REMAINING IN TERM

AMOUNT BORROWED	30	29	28	27	26	25	24
100	0.46	0.47	0.48	0.49	0.50	0.51	0.53
200	0.93	0.94	0.96	0.98	1.00	1.03	1.05
300	1.39	1.42	1.44	1.47	1.51	1.54	1.58
400	1.85	1.89	1.92	1.97	2.01	2.06	2.11
500	2.32	2.36	2.41	2.46	2.51	2.57	2.64
600	2.78	2.83	2.89	2.95	3.01	3.08	3.16
700	3.24	3.30	3.37	3.44	3.52	3.60	3.69
800	3.70	3.77	3.85	3.93	4.02	4.11	4.22
900	4.17	4.25	4.33	4.42	4.52	4.63	4.74
1,000	4.63	4.72	4.81	4.91	5.02	5.14	5.27
2,000	9.26	9.44	9.62	9.83	10.04	10.28	10.54
3,000	13.89	14.15	14.43	14.74	15.07	15.42	15.81
4,000	18.52	18.87	19.25	19.65	20.09	20.57	21.08
5,000	23.16	23.59	24.06	24.56	25.11	25.71	26.36
6,000	27.79	28.31	28.87	29.48	30.13	30.85	31.63
7,000	32.42	33.03	33.68	34.39	35.16	35.99	36.90
8,000	37.05	37.74	38.49	39.30	40.18	41.13	42.17
9,000	41.68	42.46	43.30	44.21	45.20	46.27	47.44
10,000	46.31	47.18	48.11	49.13	50.22	51.41	52.71
15,000	69.47	70.77	72.17	73.69	75.33	77.12	79.07
20,000	92.62	94.36	96.23	98.25	100.44	102.83	105.42
25,000	115.78	117.95	120.29	122.82	125.56	128.53	131.78
30,000	138.93	141.54	144.34	147.38	150.67	154.24	158.13
35,000	162.09	165.13	168.40	171.94	175.78	179.95	184.49
40,000	185.25	188.72	192.46	196.50	200.89	205.65	210.84
45,000	208.40	212.31	216.52	221.07	226.00	231.36	237.20
50,000	231.56	235.90	240.57	245.63	251.11	257.07	263.55
55,000	254.71	259.48	264.63	270.19	276.22	282.77	289.91
60,000	277.87	283.07	288.69	294.76	301.33	308.48	316.26
65,000	301.03	306.66	312.75	319.32	326.44	334.19	342.62
70,000	324.18	330.25	336.80	343.88	351.56	359.89	368.97
75,000	347.34	353.84	360.86	368.45	376.67	385.60	395.33
80,000	370.49	377.43	384.92	393.01	401.78	411.30	421.69
85,000	393.65	401.02	408.98	417.57	426.89	437.01	448.04
90,000	416.80	424.61	433.03	442.14	452.00	462.72	474.40
95,000	439.96	448.20	457.09	466.70	477.11	488.42	500.75
100,000	463.12	471.79	481.15	491.26	502.22	514.13	527.11
110,000	509.43	518.97	529.26	540.39	552.45	565.54	579.82
120,000	555.74	566.15	577.38	589.51	602.67	616.96	632.53
130,000	602.05	613.33	625.49	638.64	652.89	668.37	685.24
140,000	648.36	660.51	673.61	687.77	703.11	719.78	737.95
150,000	694.67	707.69	721.72	736.89	753.33	771.20	790.66
200,000	926.23	943.58	962.30	982.52	1004.45	1028.26	1054.21
250,000	1157.79	1179.48	1202.87	1228.16	1255.56	1285.33	1317.77
300,000	1389.35	1415.37	1443.44	1473.79	1506.67	1542.39	1581.32
350,000	1620.90	1651.27	1684.02	1719.42	1757.79	1799.46	1844.87
400,000	1852.46	1887.16	1924.59	1965.05	2008.89	2056.52	2108.43
450,000	2084.02	2123.06	2165.16	2210.68	2260.00	2313.59	2371.98
500,000	2315.58	2358.95	2405.74	2456.31	2511.11	2570.66	2635.53
550,000	2547.14	2594.85	2646.31	2701.94	2762.23	2827.72	2899.09
600,000	2778.69	2830.74	2886.89	2947.57	3013.34	3084.79	3162.64
650,000	3010.25	3066.64	3127.46	3193.20	3264.45	3341.85	3426.19
700,000	3241.81	3302.54	3368.03	3438.84	3515.56	3598.92	3689.75
750,000	3473.37	3538.43	3608.61	3684.47	3766.67	3855.98	3953.30
800,000	3704.92	3774.33	3849.18	3930.10	4017.78	4113.05	4216.85
850,000	3936.48	4010.22	4089.75	4175.73	4268.89	4370.12	4480.40
900,000	4168.04	4246.12	4330.33	4421.36	4520.01	4627.18	4743.96
950,000	4399.60	4482.01	4570.90	4666.99	4771.12	4884.25	5007.51
1,000,000	4631.16	4717.91	4811.48	4912.62	5022.23	5141.31	5271.06

Monthly Payments $3\frac{3}{4}\%$

Necessary to Amortize a Loan

AMOUNT BORROWED	YEARS REMAINING IN TERM						
	23	22	21	20	15	10	5
100	0.54	0.56	0.57	0.59	0.73	1.00	1.83
200	1.08	1.11	1.15	1.19	1.45	2.00	3.66
300	1.62	1.67	1.72	1.78	2.18	3.00	5.49
400	2.17	2.23	2.30	2.37	2.91	4.00	7.32
500	2.71	2.78	2.87	2.96	3.64	5.00	9.15
600	3.25	3.34	3.44	3.56	4.36	6.00	10.98
700	3.79	3.90	4.02	4.15	5.09	7.00	12.81
800	4.33	4.45	4.59	4.74	5.82	8.00	14.64
900	4.87	5.01	5.17	5.34	6.55	9.01	16.47
1,000	5.41	5.57	5.74	5.93	7.27	10.01	18.30
2,000	10.83	11.14	11.48	11.86	14.54	20.01	36.61
3,000	16.24	16.71	17.22	17.79	21.82	30.02	54.91
4,000	21.65	22.27	22.96	23.72	29.09	40.02	73.22
5,000	27.06	27.84	28.70	29.64	36.36	50.03	91.52
6,000	32.48	33.41	34.44	35.57	43.63	60.04	109.82
7,000	37.89	38.98	40.18	41.50	50.91	70.04	128.13
8,000	43.30	44.55	45.92	47.43	58.18	80.05	146.43
9,000	48.72	50.12	51.66	53.36	65.45	90.06	164.74
10,000	54.13	55.68	57.40	59.29	72.72	100.06	183.04
15,000	81.19	83.53	86.09	88.93	109.08	150.09	274.56
20,000	108.26	111.37	114.79	118.58	145.44	200.12	366.08
25,000	135.32	139.21	143.49	148.22	181.81	250.15	457.60
30,000	162.39	167.05	172.19	177.87	218.17	300.18	549.12
35,000	189.45	194.89	200.89	207.51	254.53	350.21	640.64
40,000	216.52	222.74	229.59	237.16	290.89	400.24	732.16
45,000	243.58	250.58	258.28	266.80	327.25	450.28	823.68
50,000	270.64	278.42	286.98	296.44	363.61	500.31	915.20
55,000	297.71	306.26	315.68	326.09	399.97	550.34	1006.72
60,000	324.77	334.10	344.38	355.73	436.33	600.37	1098.24
65,000	351.84	361.95	373.08	385.38	472.69	650.40	1189.75
70,000	378.90	389.79	401.77	415.02	509.06	700.43	1281.27
75,000	405.97	417.63	430.47	444.67	545.42	750.46	1372.79
80,000	433.03	445.47	459.17	474.31	581.78	800.49	1464.31
85,000	460.09	473.32	487.87	503.96	618.14	850.52	1555.83
90,000	487.16	501.16	516.57	533.60	654.50	900.55	1647.35
95,000	514.22	529.00	545.26	563.24	690.86	950.58	1738.87
100,000	541.29	556.84	573.96	592.89	727.22	1000.61	1830.39
110,000	595.42	612.53	631.36	652.18	799.94	1100.67	2013.43
120,000	649.55	668.21	688.76	711.47	872.67	1200.73	2196.47
130,000	703.67	723.89	746.15	770.75	945.39	1300.80	2379.51
140,000	757.80	779.58	803.55	830.04	1018.11	1400.86	2562.55
150,000	811.93	835.26	860.94	889.33	1090.83	1500.92	2745.59
200,000	1082.58	1113.68	1147.93	1185.78	1454.44	2001.22	3660.78
250,000	1353.22	1392.10	1434.91	1482.22	1818.06	2501.53	4575.98
300,000	1623.86	1670.52	1721.89	1778.66	2181.67	3001.84	5491.18
350,000	1894.51	1948.95	2008.87	2075.11	2545.28	3502.14	6406.37
400,000	2165.15	2227.37	2295.85	2371.55	2908.89	4002.45	7321.57
450,000	2435.80	2505.79	2582.83	2668.00	3272.50	4502.76	8236.76
500,000	2706.44	2784.21	2869.82	2964.44	3636.11	5003.06	9151.96
550,000	2977.09	3062.63	3156.80	3260.89	3999.72	5503.37	10067.16
600,000	3247.73	3341.05	3443.78	3557.33	4363.33	6003.67	10982.35
650,000	3518.37	3619.47	3730.76	3853.77	4726.95	6503.98	11897.55
700,000	3789.02	3897.89	4017.74	4150.22	5090.56	7004.29	12812.74
750,000	4059.66	4176.31	4304.72	4446.66	5454.17	7504.59	13727.94
800,000	4330.31	4454.73	4591.70	4743.11	5817.78	8004.90	14643.13
850,000	4600.95	4733.15	4878.69	5039.55	6181.39	8505.21	15558.33
900,000	4871.59	5011.57	5165.67	5335.99	6545.00	9005.51	16473.53
950,000	5142.24	5290.00	5452.65	5632.44	6908.61	9505.82	17388.72
1,000,000	5412.88	5568.42	5739.63	5928.88	7272.22	10006.12	18303.92

Monthly Payments
Necessary to Amortize a Loan

AMOUNT BORROWED	30	29	28	27	26	25	24
			YEARS REMAINING IN TERM				
100	0.48	0.49	0.50	0.51	0.52	0.53	0.54
200	0.95	0.97	0.99	1.01	1.03	1.06	1.08
300	1.43	1.46	1.49	1.52	1.55	1.58	1.62
400	1.91	1.94	1.98	2.02	2.06	2.11	2.16
500	2.39	2.43	2.48	2.53	2.58	2.64	2.70
600	2.86	2.92	2.97	3.03	3.10	3.17	3.24
700	3.34	3.40	3.47	3.54	3.61	3.69	3.78
800	3.82	3.89	3.96	4.04	4.13	4.22	4.33
900	4.30	4.37	4.46	4.55	4.64	4.75	4.87
1,000	4.77	4.86	4.95	5.05	5.16	5.28	5.41
2,000	9.55	9.72	9.90	10.10	10.32	10.56	10.81
3,000	14.32	14.58	14.86	15.16	15.48	15.84	16.22
4,000	19.10	19.44	19.81	20.21	20.64	21.11	21.63
5,000	23.87	24.30	24.76	25.26	25.80	26.39	27.03
6,000	28.64	29.16	29.71	30.31	30.96	31.67	32.44
7,000	33.42	34.02	34.66	35.36	36.12	36.95	37.85
8,000	38.19	38.88	39.62	40.42	41.28	42.23	43.26
9,000	42.97	43.74	44.57	45.47	46.44	47.51	48.66
10,000	47.74	48.60	49.52	50.52	51.60	52.78	54.07
15,000	71.61	72.90	74.28	75.78	77.41	79.18	81.10
20,000	95.48	97.19	99.04	101.04	103.21	105.57	108.14
25,000	119.35	121.49	123.80	126.30	129.01	131.96	135.17
30,000	143.22	145.79	148.56	151.56	154.81	158.35	162.21
35,000	167.10	170.09	173.32	176.82	180.62	184.74	189.24
40,000	190.97	194.39	198.08	202.08	206.42	211.13	216.28
45,000	214.84	218.69	222.85	227.34	232.22	237.53	243.31
50,000	238.71	242.99	247.61	252.60	258.02	263.92	270.35
55,000	262.58	267.29	272.37	277.86	283.83	290.31	297.38
60,000	286.45	291.58	297.13	303.12	309.63	316.70	324.41
65,000	310.32	315.88	321.89	328.39	335.43	343.09	351.45
70,000	334.19	340.18	346.65	353.65	361.23	369.49	378.48
75,000	358.06	364.48	371.41	378.91	387.04	395.88	405.52
80,000	381.93	388.78	396.17	404.17	412.84	422.27	432.55
85,000	405.80	413.08	420.93	429.43	438.64	448.66	459.59
90,000	429.67	437.38	445.69	454.69	464.44	475.05	486.62
95,000	453.54	461.67	470.45	479.95	490.25	501.44	513.66
100,000	477.42	485.97	495.21	505.21	516.05	527.84	540.69
110,000	525.16	534.57	544.73	555.73	567.65	580.62	594.76
120,000	572.90	583.17	594.25	606.25	619.26	633.40	648.83
130,000	620.64	631.77	643.78	656.77	670.86	686.19	702.90
140,000	668.38	680.36	693.30	707.29	722.47	738.97	756.97
150,000	716.12	728.96	742.82	757.81	774.07	791.76	811.04
200,000	954.83	971.95	990.42	1010.42	1032.10	1055.67	1081.38
250,000	1193.54	1214.93	1238.03	1263.02	1290.12	1319.59	1351.73
300,000	1432.25	1457.92	1485.64	1515.62	1548.15	1583.51	1622.07
350,000	1670.95	1700.91	1733.24	1768.23	1806.17	1847.43	1892.42
400,000	1909.66	1943.89	1980.85	2020.83	2064.20	2111.35	2162.76
450,000	2148.37	2186.88	2228.46	2273.44	2322.22	2375.27	2433.11
500,000	2387.08	2429.87	2476.06	2526.04	2580.25	2639.18	2703.45
550,000	2625.78	2672.85	2723.67	2778.65	2838.27	2903.10	2973.80
600,000	2864.49	2915.84	2971.27	3031.25	3096.29	3167.02	3244.14
650,000	3103.20	3158.83	3218.88	3283.85	3354.32	3430.94	3514.49
700,000	3341.91	3401.81	3466.49	3536.46	3612.34	3694.86	3784.84
750,000	3580.61	3644.80	3714.09	3789.06	3870.37	3958.78	4055.18
800,000	3819.32	3887.79	3961.70	4041.67	4128.39	4222.69	4325.53
850,000	4058.03	4130.77	4209.30	4294.27	4386.42	4486.61	4595.87
900,000	4296.74	4373.76	4456.91	4546.87	4644.44	4750.53	4866.22
950,000	4535.45	4616.75	4704.52	4799.48	4902.47	5014.45	5136.56
1,000,000	4774.15	4859.73	4952.12	5052.08	5160.49	5278.37	5406.91

Monthly Payments 4%
Necessary to Amortize a Loan

AMOUNT BORROWED	YEARS REMAINING IN TERM						
	23	22	21	20	15	10	5
100	0.55	0.57	0.59	0.61	0.74	1.01	1.84
200	1.11	1.14	1.17	1.21	1.48	2.02	3.68
300	1.66	1.71	1.76	1.82	2.22	3.04	5.52
400	2.22	2.28	2.35	2.42	2.96	4.05	7.37
500	2.77	2.85	2.94	3.03	3.70	5.06	9.21
600	3.33	3.42	3.52	3.64	4.44	6.07	11.05
700	3.88	3.99	4.11	4.24	5.18	7.09	12.89
800	4.44	4.56	4.70	4.85	5.92	8.10	14.73
900	4.99	5.13	5.28	5.45	6.66	9.11	16.57
1,000	5.55	5.70	5.87	6.06	7.40	10.12	18.42
2,000	11.10	11.40	11.74	12.12	14.79	20.25	36.83
3,000	16.64	17.11	17.62	18.18	22.19	30.37	55.25
4,000	22.19	22.81	23.49	24.24	29.59	40.50	73.67
5,000	27.74	28.51	29.36	30.30	36.98	50.62	92.08
6,000	33.29	34.21	35.23	36.36	44.38	60.75	110.50
7,000	38.83	39.91	41.10	42.42	51.78	70.87	128.92
8,000	44.38	45.61	46.97	48.48	59.18	81.00	147.33
9,000	49.93	51.32	52.85	54.54	66.57	91.12	165.75
10,000	55.48	57.02	58.72	60.60	73.97	101.25	184.17
15,000	83.21	85.53	88.08	90.90	110.95	151.87	276.25
20,000	110.95	114.04	117.44	121.20	147.94	202.49	368.33
25,000	138.69	142.55	146.79	151.50	184.92	253.11	460.41
30,000	166.43	171.05	176.15	181.79	221.91	303.74	552.50
35,000	194.16	199.56	205.51	212.09	258.89	354.36	644.58
40,000	221.90	228.07	234.87	242.39	295.88	404.98	736.66
45,000	249.64	256.58	264.23	272.69	332.86	455.60	828.74
50,000	277.38	285.09	293.59	302.99	369.84	506.23	920.83
55,000	305.11	313.60	322.95	333.29	406.83	556.85	1012.91
60,000	332.85	342.11	352.31	363.59	443.81	607.47	1104.99
65,000	360.59	370.62	381.67	393.89	480.80	658.09	1197.07
70,000	388.33	399.13	411.03	424.19	517.78	708.72	1289.16
75,000	416.06	427.64	440.38	454.49	554.77	759.34	1381.24
80,000	443.80	456.14	469.74	484.78	591.75	809.96	1473.32
85,000	471.54	484.65	499.10	515.08	628.73	860.58	1565.40
90,000	499.28	513.16	528.46	545.38	665.72	911.21	1657.49
95,000	527.01	541.67	557.82	575.68	702.70	961.83	1749.57
100,000	554.75	570.18	587.18	605.98	739.69	1012.45	1841.65
110,000	610.23	627.20	645.90	666.58	813.66	1113.70	2025.82
120,000	665.70	684.22	704.61	727.18	887.63	1214.94	2209.98
130,000	721.18	741.24	763.33	787.77	961.59	1316.19	2394.15
140,000	776.65	798.25	822.05	848.37	1035.56	1417.43	2578.31
150,000	832.13	855.27	880.77	908.97	1109.53	1518.68	2762.48
200,000	1109.50	1140.36	1174.36	1211.96	1479.38	2024.90	3683.30
250,000	1386.88	1425.45	1467.95	1514.95	1849.22	2531.13	4604.13
300,000	1664.25	1710.54	1761.54	1817.94	2219.06	3037.35	5524.96
350,000	1941.63	1995.63	2055.13	2120.93	2588.91	3543.58	6445.78
400,000	2219.00	2280.72	2348.72	2423.92	2958.75	4049.81	7366.61
450,000	2496.38	2565.81	2642.31	2726.91	3328.60	4556.03	8287.43
500,000	2773.75	2850.91	2935.90	3029.90	3698.44	5062.26	9208.26
550,000	3051.13	3136.00	3229.48	3332.89	4068.28	5568.48	10129.09
600,000	3328.50	3421.09	3523.07	3635.88	4438.13	6074.71	11049.91
650,000	3605.88	3706.18	3816.66	3938.87	4807.97	6580.93	11970.74
700,000	3883.25	3991.27	4110.25	4241.86	5177.82	7087.16	12891.57
750,000	4160.63	4276.36	4403.84	4544.85	5547.66	7593.39	13812.39
800,000	4438.00	4561.45	4697.43	4847.84	5917.50	8099.61	14733.22
850,000	4715.38	4846.54	4991.02	5150.83	6287.35	8605.84	15654.04
900,000	4992.75	5131.63	5284.61	5453.82	6657.19	9112.06	16574.87
950,000	5270.13	5416.72	5578.20	5756.81	7027.04	9618.29	17495.70
1,000,000	5547.50	5701.81	5871.79	6059.80	7396.88	10124.51	18416.52

Monthly Payments
Necessary to Amortize a Loan

AMOUNT BORROWED	YEARS REMAINING IN TERM						
	30	29	28	27	26	25	24
100	0.49	0.50	0.51	0.52	0.53	0.54	0.55
200	0.98	1.00	1.02	1.04	1.06	1.08	1.11
300	1.48	1.50	1.53	1.56	1.59	1.63	1.66
400	1.97	2.00	2.04	2.08	2.12	2.17	2.22
500	2.46	2.50	2.55	2.60	2.65	2.71	2.77
600	2.95	3.00	3.06	3.12	3.18	3.25	3.33
700	3.44	3.50	3.57	3.64	3.71	3.79	3.88
800	3.94	4.00	4.08	4.15	4.24	4.33	4.44
900	4.43	4.50	4.59	4.67	4.77	4.88	4.99
1,000	4.92	5.00	5.09	5.19	5.30	5.42	5.54
2,000	9.84	10.01	10.19	10.39	10.60	10.83	11.09
3,000	14.76	15.01	15.28	15.58	15.90	16.25	16.63
4,000	19.68	20.02	20.38	20.77	21.20	21.67	22.18
5,000	24.60	25.02	25.47	25.97	26.50	27.09	27.72
6,000	29.52	30.02	30.57	31.16	31.80	32.50	33.27
7,000	34.44	35.03	35.66	36.36	37.11	37.92	38.81
8,000	39.36	40.03	40.76	41.55	42.41	43.34	44.36
9,000	44.27	45.03	45.85	46.74	47.71	48.76	49.90
10,000	49.19	50.04	50.95	51.94	53.01	54.17	55.45
15,000	73.79	75.06	76.42	77.90	79.51	81.26	83.17
20,000	98.39	100.08	101.90	103.87	106.02	108.35	110.89
25,000	122.98	125.09	127.37	129.84	132.52	135.43	138.62
30,000	147.58	150.11	152.85	155.81	159.02	162.52	166.34
35,000	172.18	175.13	178.32	181.78	185.53	189.61	194.06
40,000	196.78	200.15	203.80	207.74	212.03	216.70	221.79
45,000	221.37	225.17	229.27	233.71	238.53	243.78	249.51
50,000	245.97	250.19	254.75	259.68	265.04	270.87	277.23
55,000	270.57	275.21	280.22	285.65	291.54	297.96	304.96
60,000	295.16	300.23	305.69	311.62	318.05	325.04	332.68
65,000	319.76	325.24	331.17	337.59	344.55	352.13	360.40
70,000	344.36	350.26	356.64	363.55	371.05	379.22	388.13
75,000	368.95	375.28	382.12	389.52	397.56	406.30	415.85
80,000	393.55	400.30	407.59	415.49	424.06	433.39	443.57
85,000	418.15	425.32	433.07	441.46	450.57	460.48	471.29
90,000	442.75	450.34	458.54	467.43	477.07	487.56	499.02
95,000	467.34	475.36	484.02	493.39	503.57	514.65	526.74
100,000	491.94	500.38	509.49	519.36	530.08	541.74	554.46
110,000	541.13	550.41	560.44	571.30	583.08	595.91	609.91
120,000	590.33	600.45	611.39	623.23	636.09	650.09	665.36
130,000	639.52	650.49	662.34	675.17	689.10	704.26	720.80
140,000	688.72	700.53	713.29	727.11	742.11	758.43	776.25
150,000	737.91	750.56	764.24	779.04	795.12	812.61	831.70
200,000	983.88	1000.75	1018.98	1038.72	1060.15	1083.48	1108.93
250,000	1229.85	1250.94	1273.73	1298.40	1325.19	1354.35	1386.16
300,000	1475.82	1501.13	1528.47	1558.09	1590.23	1625.21	1663.39
350,000	1721.79	1751.31	1783.22	1817.77	1855.27	1896.08	1940.63
400,000	1967.76	2001.50	2037.96	2077.45	2120.31	2166.95	2217.86
450,000	2213.73	2251.69	2292.71	2337.13	2385.35	2437.82	2495.09
500,000	2459.70	2501.88	2547.45	2596.81	2650.39	2708.69	2772.32
550,000	2705.67	2752.07	2802.20	2856.49	2915.42	2979.56	3049.55
600,000	2951.64	3002.25	3056.94	3116.17	3180.46	3250.43	3326.79
650,000	3197.61	3252.44	3311.69	3375.85	3445.50	3521.30	3604.02
700,000	3443.58	3502.63	3566.44	3635.53	3710.54	3792.17	3881.25
750,000	3689.55	3752.82	3821.18	3895.21	3975.58	4063.04	4158.48
800,000	3935.52	4003.00	4075.93	4154.90	4240.62	4333.90	4435.71
850,000	4181.49	4253.19	4330.67	4414.58	4505.65	4604.77	4712.95
900,000	4427.46	4503.38	4585.42	4674.26	4770.69	4875.64	4990.18
950,000	4673.43	4753.57	4840.16	4933.94	5035.73	5146.51	5267.41
1,000,000	4919.40	5003.76	5094.91	5193.62	5300.77	5417.38	5544.64

Monthly Payments
Necessary to Amortize a Loan

4¹/₄%

AMOUNT BORROWED	\multicolumn{7}{c}{YEARS REMAINING IN TERM}
	23	22	21	20	15	10	5
100	0.57	0.58	0.60	0.62	0.75	1.02	1.85
200	1.14	1.17	1.20	1.24	1.50	2.05	3.71
300	1.71	1.75	1.80	1.86	2.26	3.07	5.56
400	2.27	2.33	2.40	2.48	3.01	4.10	7.41
500	2.84	2.92	3.00	3.10	3.76	5.12	9.26
600	3.41	3.50	3.60	3.72	4.51	6.15	11.12
700	3.98	4.09	4.20	4.33	5.27	7.17	12.97
800	4.55	4.67	4.80	4.95	6.02	8.20	14.82
900	5.12	5.25	5.41	5.57	6.77	9.22	16.68
1,000	5.68	5.84	6.01	6.19	7.52	10.24	18.53
2,000	11.37	11.67	12.01	12.38	15.05	20.49	37.06
3,000	17.05	17.51	18.02	18.58	22.57	30.73	55.59
4,000	22.74	23.35	24.02	24.77	30.09	40.98	74.12
5,000	28.42	29.18	30.03	30.96	37.61	51.22	92.65
6,000	34.10	35.02	36.03	37.15	45.14	61.46	111.18
7,000	39.79	40.86	42.04	43.35	52.66	71.71	129.71
8,000	45.47	46.70	48.05	49.54	60.18	81.95	148.24
9,000	51.16	52.53	54.05	55.73	67.71	92.19	166.77
10,000	56.84	58.37	60.06	61.92	75.23	102.44	185.30
15,000	85.26	87.55	90.08	92.89	112.84	153.66	277.94
20,000	113.68	116.74	120.11	123.85	150.46	204.88	370.59
25,000	142.10	145.92	150.14	154.81	188.07	256.09	463.24
30,000	170.52	175.11	180.17	185.77	225.68	307.31	555.89
35,000	198.94	204.29	210.20	216.73	263.30	358.53	648.53
40,000	227.36	233.48	240.23	247.69	300.91	409.75	741.18
45,000	255.78	262.66	270.25	278.66	338.53	460.97	833.83
50,000	284.20	291.85	300.28	309.62	376.14	512.19	926.48
55,000	312.62	321.03	330.31	340.58	413.75	563.41	1019.13
60,000	341.04	350.22	360.34	371.54	451.37	614.63	1111.77
65,000	369.46	379.40	390.37	402.50	488.98	665.84	1204.42
70,000	397.88	408.59	420.39	433.46	526.59	717.06	1297.07
75,000	426.30	437.77	450.42	464.43	564.21	768.28	1389.72
80,000	454.72	466.96	480.45	495.39	601.82	819.50	1482.36
85,000	483.14	496.14	510.48	526.35	639.44	870.72	1575.01
90,000	511.56	525.33	540.51	557.31	677.05	921.94	1667.66
95,000	539.98	554.51	570.54	588.27	714.66	973.16	1760.31
100,000	568.40	583.70	600.56	619.23	752.28	1024.38	1852.96
110,000	625.23	642.07	660.62	681.16	827.51	1126.81	2038.25
120,000	682.07	700.44	720.68	743.08	902.73	1229.25	2223.55
130,000	738.91	758.81	780.73	805.00	977.96	1331.69	2408.84
140,000	795.75	817.18	840.79	866.93	1053.19	1434.13	2594.14
150,000	852.59	875.54	900.85	928.85	1128.42	1536.56	2779.43
200,000	1136.79	1167.39	1201.13	1238.47	1504.56	2048.75	3705.91
250,000	1420.99	1459.24	1501.41	1548.09	1880.70	2560.94	4632.39
300,000	1705.19	1751.09	1801.69	1857.70	2256.84	3073.13	5558.87
350,000	1989.38	2042.94	2101.97	2167.32	2632.97	3585.31	6485.34
400,000	2273.58	2334.79	2402.26	2476.94	3009.11	4097.50	7411.82
450,000	2557.78	2626.63	2702.54	2786.56	3385.25	4609.69	8338.30
500,000	2841.98	2918.48	3002.82	3096.17	3761.39	5121.88	9264.78
550,000	3126.17	3210.33	3303.10	3405.79	4137.53	5634.06	10191.26
600,000	3410.37	3502.18	3603.39	3715.41	4513.67	6146.25	11117.73
650,000	3694.57	3794.03	3903.67	4025.02	4889.81	6658.44	12044.21
700,000	3978.77	4085.88	4203.95	4334.64	5265.95	7170.63	12970.69
750,000	4262.97	4377.72	4504.23	4644.26	5642.09	7682.82	13897.17
800,000	4547.16	4669.57	4804.51	4953.88	6018.23	8195.00	14823.64
850,000	4831.36	4961.42	5104.80	5263.49	6394.37	8707.19	15750.12
900,000	5115.56	5253.27	5405.08	5573.11	6770.51	9219.38	16676.60
950,000	5399.76	5545.12	5705.36	5882.73	7146.64	9731.57	17603.08
1,000,000	5683.95	5836.96	6005.64	6192.34	7522.78	10243.75	18529.56

4¹/₂%

Monthly Payments
Necessary to Amortize a Loan

YEARS REMAINING IN TERM

AMOUNT BORROWED	30	29	28	27	26	25	24
100	0.51	0.51	0.52	0.53	0.54	0.56	0.57
200	1.01	1.03	1.05	1.07	1.09	1.11	1.14
300	1.52	1.54	1.57	1.60	1.63	1.67	1.71
400	2.03	2.06	2.10	2.13	2.18	2.22	2.27
500	2.53	2.57	2.62	2.67	2.72	2.78	2.84
600	3.04	3.09	3.14	3.20	3.27	3.33	3.41
700	3.55	3.60	3.67	3.74	3.81	3.89	3.98
800	4.05	4.12	4.19	4.27	4.35	4.45	4.55
900	4.56	4.63	4.72	4.80	4.90	5.00	5.12
1,000	5.07	5.15	5.24	5.34	5.44	5.56	5.68
2,000	10.13	10.30	10.48	10.67	10.89	11.12	11.37
3,000	15.20	15.45	15.72	16.01	16.33	16.67	17.05
4,000	20.27	20.60	20.96	21.35	21.77	22.23	22.74
5,000	25.33	25.75	26.20	26.69	27.22	27.79	28.42
6,000	30.40	30.90	31.44	32.02	32.66	33.35	34.11
7,000	35.47	36.05	36.68	37.36	38.10	38.91	39.79
8,000	40.53	41.20	41.92	42.70	43.54	44.47	45.47
9,000	45.60	46.35	47.16	48.03	48.99	50.02	51.16
10,000	50.67	51.50	52.40	53.37	54.43	55.58	56.84
15,000	76.00	77.25	78.60	80.06	81.65	83.37	85.26
20,000	101.34	103.00	104.80	106.74	108.86	111.17	113.68
25,000	126.67	128.75	130.99	133.43	136.08	138.96	142.11
30,000	152.01	154.50	157.19	160.12	163.29	166.75	170.53
35,000	177.34	180.25	183.39	186.80	190.51	194.54	198.95
40,000	202.67	206.00	209.59	213.49	217.72	222.33	227.37
45,000	228.01	231.75	235.79	240.17	244.94	250.12	255.79
50,000	253.34	257.50	261.99	266.86	272.15	277.92	284.21
55,000	278.68	283.25	288.19	293.55	299.37	305.71	312.63
60,000	304.01	309.00	314.39	320.23	326.58	333.50	341.05
65,000	329.35	334.75	340.59	346.92	353.80	361.29	369.48
70,000	354.68	360.50	366.79	373.60	381.01	389.08	397.90
75,000	380.01	386.24	392.98	400.29	408.23	416.87	426.32
80,000	405.35	411.99	419.18	426.98	435.44	444.67	454.74
85,000	430.68	437.74	445.38	453.66	462.66	472.46	483.16
90,000	456.02	463.49	471.58	480.35	489.87	500.25	511.58
95,000	481.35	489.24	497.78	507.03	517.09	528.04	540.00
100,000	506.69	514.99	523.98	533.72	544.30	555.83	568.42
110,000	557.35	566.49	576.38	587.09	598.73	611.42	625.27
120,000	608.02	617.99	628.78	640.46	653.16	667.00	682.11
130,000	658.69	669.49	681.17	693.84	707.60	722.58	738.95
140,000	709.36	720.99	733.57	747.21	762.03	778.17	795.79
150,000	760.03	772.49	785.97	800.58	816.46	833.75	852.64
200,000	1013.37	1029.99	1047.96	1067.44	1088.61	1111.66	1136.85
250,000	1266.71	1287.48	1309.95	1334.30	1360.76	1389.58	1421.06
300,000	1520.06	1544.98	1571.94	1601.16	1632.91	1667.50	1705.27
350,000	1773.40	1802.48	1833.93	1868.02	1905.06	1945.41	1989.49
400,000	2026.74	2059.97	2095.92	2134.88	2177.22	2223.33	2273.70
450,000	2280.08	2317.47	2357.91	2401.74	2449.37	2501.25	2557.91
500,000	2533.43	2574.97	2619.90	2668.60	2721.52	2779.16	2842.12
550,000	2786.77	2832.46	2881.89	2935.46	2993.67	3057.08	3126.34
600,000	3040.11	3089.96	3143.88	3202.32	3265.82	3334.99	3410.55
650,000	3293.45	3347.46	3405.87	3469.18	3537.98	3612.91	3694.76
700,000	3546.80	3604.95	3667.86	3736.04	3810.13	3890.83	3978.97
750,000	3800.14	3862.45	3929.85	4002.90	4082.28	4168.74	4263.19
800,000	4053.48	4119.95	4191.84	4269.76	4354.43	4446.66	4547.40
850,000	4306.83	4377.44	4453.83	4536.62	4626.58	4724.58	4831.61
900,000	4560.17	4634.94	4715.82	4803.48	4898.74	5002.49	5115.82
950,000	4813.51	4892.44	4977.81	5070.34	5170.89	5280.41	5400.04
1,000,000	5066.85	5149.93	5239.80	5337.20	5443.04	5558.32	5684.25

Monthly Payments 4½%
Necessary to Amortize a Loan

AMOUNT BORROWED	YEARS REMAINING IN TERM						
	23	22	21	20	15	10	5
100	0.58	0.60	0.61	0.63	0.76	1.04	1.86
200	1.16	1.19	1.23	1.27	1.53	2.07	3.73
300	1.75	1.79	1.84	1.90	2.29	3.11	5.59
400	2.33	2.39	2.46	2.53	3.06	4.15	7.46
500	2.91	2.99	3.07	3.16	3.82	5.18	9.32
600	3.49	3.58	3.68	3.80	4.59	6.22	11.19
700	4.08	4.18	4.30	4.43	5.35	7.25	13.05
800	4.66	4.78	4.91	5.06	6.12	8.29	14.91
900	5.24	5.38	5.53	5.69	6.88	9.33	16.78
1,000	5.82	5.97	6.14	6.33	7.65	10.36	18.64
2,000	11.64	11.95	12.28	12.65	15.30	20.73	37.29
3,000	17.47	17.92	18.42	18.98	22.95	31.09	55.93
4,000	23.29	23.90	24.56	25.31	30.60	41.46	74.57
5,000	29.11	29.87	30.71	31.63	38.25	51.82	93.22
6,000	34.93	35.84	36.85	37.96	45.90	62.18	111.86
7,000	40.76	41.82	42.99	44.29	53.55	72.55	130.50
8,000	46.58	47.79	49.13	50.61	61.20	82.91	149.14
9,000	52.40	53.76	55.27	56.94	68.85	93.27	167.79
10,000	58.22	59.74	61.41	63.26	76.50	103.64	186.43
15,000	87.33	89.61	92.12	94.90	114.75	155.46	279.65
20,000	116.44	119.48	122.82	126.53	153.00	207.28	372.86
25,000	145.56	149.35	153.53	158.16	191.25	259.10	466.08
30,000	174.67	179.22	184.24	189.79	229.50	310.92	559.29
35,000	203.78	209.09	214.94	221.43	267.75	362.73	652.51
40,000	232.89	238.95	245.65	253.06	306.00	414.55	745.72
45,000	262.00	268.82	276.35	284.69	344.25	466.37	838.94
50,000	291.11	298.69	307.06	316.32	382.50	518.19	932.15
55,000	320.22	328.56	337.76	347.96	420.75	570.01	1025.37
60,000	349.33	358.43	368.47	379.59	459.00	621.83	1118.58
65,000	378.44	388.30	399.18	411.22	497.25	673.65	1211.80
70,000	407.55	418.17	429.88	442.85	535.50	725.47	1305.01
75,000	436.67	448.04	460.59	474.49	573.74	777.29	1398.23
80,000	465.78	477.91	491.29	506.12	611.99	829.11	1491.44
85,000	494.89	507.78	522.00	537.75	650.24	880.93	1584.66
90,000	524.00	537.65	552.71	569.38	688.49	932.75	1677.87
95,000	553.11	567.52	583.41	601.02	726.74	984.56	1771.09
100,000	582.22	597.39	614.12	632.65	764.99	1036.38	1864.30
110,000	640.44	657.12	675.53	695.91	841.49	1140.02	2050.73
120,000	698.67	716.86	736.94	759.18	917.99	1243.66	2237.16
130,000	756.89	776.60	798.35	822.44	994.49	1347.30	2423.59
140,000	815.11	836.34	859.76	885.71	1070.99	1450.94	2610.02
150,000	873.33	896.08	921.18	948.97	1147.49	1554.58	2796.45
200,000	1164.44	1194.77	1228.23	1265.30	1529.99	2072.77	3728.60
250,000	1455.55	1493.47	1535.29	1581.62	1912.48	2590.96	4660.75
300,000	1746.66	1792.16	1842.35	1897.95	2294.98	3109.15	5592.91
350,000	2037.77	2090.85	2149.41	2214.27	2677.48	3627.34	6525.06
400,000	2328.88	2389.54	2456.47	2530.60	3059.97	4145.54	7457.21
450,000	2619.99	2688.24	2763.53	2846.92	3442.47	4663.73	8389.36
500,000	2911.11	2986.93	3070.58	3163.25	3824.97	5181.92	9321.51
550,000	3202.22	3285.62	3377.64	3479.57	4207.46	5700.11	10253.66
600,000	3493.33	3584.32	3684.70	3795.90	4589.96	6218.30	11185.81
650,000	3784.44	3883.01	3991.76	4112.22	4972.46	6736.50	12117.96
700,000	4075.55	4181.70	4298.82	4428.55	5354.95	7254.69	13050.11
750,000	4366.66	4480.40	4605.88	4744.87	5737.45	7772.88	13982.26
800,000	4657.77	4779.09	4912.94	5061.20	6119.95	8291.07	14914.42
850,000	4948.88	5077.78	5219.99	5377.52	6502.44	8809.26	15846.57
900,000	5239.99	5376.48	5527.05	5693.84	6884.94	9327.46	16778.72
950,000	5531.10	5675.17	5834.11	6010.17	7267.44	9845.65	17710.87
1,000,000	5822.21	5973.86	6141.17	6326.49	7649.93	10363.84	18643.02

4³/₄% Monthly Payments
Necessary to Amortize a Loan

AMOUNT BORROWED	YEARS REMAINING IN TERM						
	30	29	28	27	26	25	24
100	0.52	0.53	0.54	0.55	0.56	0.57	0.58
200	1.04	1.06	1.08	1.10	1.12	1.14	1.17
300	1.56	1.59	1.62	1.64	1.68	1.71	1.75
400	2.09	2.12	2.15	2.19	2.23	2.28	2.33
500	2.61	2.65	2.69	2.74	2.79	2.85	2.91
600	3.13	3.18	3.23	3.29	3.35	3.42	3.50
700	3.65	3.71	3.77	3.84	3.91	3.99	4.08
800	4.17	4.24	4.31	4.39	4.47	4.56	4.66
900	4.69	4.77	4.85	4.93	5.03	5.13	5.24
1,000	5.22	5.30	5.39	5.48	5.59	5.59	5.83
2,000	10.43	10.60	10.77	10.97	11.17	11.40	11.65
3,000	15.65	15.89	16.16	16.45	16.76	17.10	17.48
4,000	20.87	21.19	21.55	21.93	22.35	22.80	23.30
5,000	26.08	26.49	26.93	27.41	27.94	28.51	29.13
6,000	31.30	31.79	32.32	32.90	33.52	34.21	34.95
7,000	36.52	37.09	37.71	38.38	39.11	39.91	40.78
8,000	41.73	42.39	43.09	43.86	44.70	45.61	46.61
9,000	46.95	47.68	48.48	49.35	50.29	51.31	52.43
10,000	52.16	52.98	53.87	54.83	55.87	57.01	58.26
15,000	78.25	79.47	80.80	82.24	83.81	85.52	87.39
20,000	104.33	105.96	107.74	109.66	111.75	114.02	116.51
25,000	130.41	132.46	134.67	137.07	139.68	142.53	145.64
30,000	156.49	158.95	161.60	164.48	167.62	171.04	174.77
35,000	182.58	185.44	188.54	191.90	195.55	199.54	203.90
40,000	208.66	211.93	215.47	219.31	223.49	228.05	233.03
45,000	234.74	238.42	242.40	246.73	251.43	256.55	262.16
50,000	260.82	264.91	269.34	274.14	279.36	285.06	291.29
55,000	286.91	291.40	296.27	301.55	307.30	313.56	320.41
60,000	312.99	317.89	323.21	328.97	335.24	342.07	349.54
65,000	339.07	344.38	350.14	356.38	363.17	370.58	378.67
70,000	365.15	370.88	377.07	383.80	391.11	399.08	407.80
75,000	391.24	397.37	404.01	411.21	419.05	427.59	436.93
80,000	417.32	423.86	430.94	438.62	446.98	456.09	466.06
85,000	443.40	450.35	457.87	466.04	474.92	484.60	495.18
90,000	469.48	476.84	484.81	493.45	502.85	513.11	524.31
95,000	495.56	503.33	511.74	520.87	530.79	541.61	553.44
100,000	521.65	529.82	538.68	548.28	558.73	570.12	582.57
110,000	573.81	582.81	592.54	603.11	614.60	627.13	640.83
120,000	625.98	635.79	646.41	657.94	670.47	684.14	699.08
130,000	678.14	688.77	700.28	712.76	726.35	741.15	757.34
140,000	730.31	741.75	754.15	767.59	782.22	798.16	815.60
150,000	782.47	794.73	808.01	822.42	838.09	855.18	873.86
200,000	1043.29	1059.65	1077.35	1096.56	1117.45	1140.23	1165.14
250,000	1304.12	1324.56	1346.69	1370.70	1396.82	1425.29	1456.43
300,000	1564.94	1589.47	1616.03	1644.84	1676.18	1710.35	1747.71
350,000	1825.77	1854.38	1885.36	1918.98	1955.55	1995.41	2039.00
400,000	2086.59	2119.29	2154.70	2193.12	2234.91	2280.47	2330.28
450,000	2347.41	2384.20	2424.04	2467.26	2514.27	2565.53	2621.57
500,000	2608.24	2649.11	2693.38	2741.40	2793.64	2850.59	2912.85
550,000	2869.06	2914.02	2962.71	3015.54	3073.00	3135.65	3204.14
600,000	3129.88	3178.94	3232.05	3289.68	3352.36	3420.70	3495.42
650,000	3390.71	3443.85	3501.39	3563.82	3631.73	3705.76	3786.71
700,000	3651.53	3708.76	3770.73	3837.96	3911.09	3990.82	4077.99
750,000	3912.36	3973.67	4040.06	4112.10	4190.45	4275.88	4369.28
800,000	4173.18	4238.58	4309.40	4386.24	4469.82	4560.94	4660.56
850,000	4434.00	4503.49	4578.74	4660.39	4749.18	4846.00	4951.85
900,000	4694.83	4768.41	4848.08	4934.53	5028.55	5131.06	5243.13
950,000	4955.65	5033.32	5117.41	5208.67	5307.91	5416.11	5534.42
1,000,000	5216.47	5298.23	5386.75	5482.81	5587.27	5701.17	5825.70

Monthly Payments 4³/₄%
Necessary to Amortize a Loan

AMOUNT BORROWED	YEARS REMAINING IN TERM						
	23	22	21	20	15	10	5
100	0.60	0.61	0.63	0.65	0.78	1.05	1.88
200	1.19	1.22	1.26	1.29	1.56	2.10	3.75
300	1.79	1.83	1.88	1.94	2.33	3.15	5.63
400	2.38	2.44	2.51	2.58	3.11	4.19	7.50
500	2.98	3.06	3.14	3.23	3.89	5.24	9.38
600	3.58	3.67	3.77	3.88	4.67	6.29	11.25
700	4.17	4.28	4.39	4.52	5.44	7.34	13.13
800	4.77	4.89	5.02	5.17	6.22	8.39	15.01
900	5.37	5.50	5.65	5.82	7.00	9.44	16.88
1,000	5.96	6.11	6.28	6.46	7.78	10.48	18.76
2,000	11.92	12.22	12.56	12.92	15.56	20.97	37.51
3,000	17.89	18.34	18.84	19.39	23.33	31.45	56.27
4,000	23.85	24.45	25.11	25.85	31.11	41.94	75.03
5,000	29.81	30.56	31.39	32.31	38.89	52.42	93.78
6,000	35.77	36.67	37.67	38.77	46.67	62.91	112.54
7,000	41.74	42.79	43.95	45.24	54.45	73.39	131.30
8,000	47.70	48.90	50.23	51.70	62.23	83.88	150.06
9,000	53.66	55.01	56.51	58.16	70.00	94.36	168.81
10,000	59.62	61.12	62.78	64.62	77.78	104.85	187.57
15,000	89.43	91.69	94.18	96.93	116.67	157.27	281.35
20,000	119.25	122.25	125.57	129.24	155.57	209.70	375.14
25,000	149.06	152.81	156.96	161.56	194.46	262.12	468.92
30,000	178.87	183.37	188.35	193.87	233.35	314.54	562.71
35,000	208.68	213.94	219.74	226.18	272.24	366.97	656.49
40,000	238.49	244.50	251.13	258.49	311.13	419.39	750.28
45,000	268.30	275.06	282.53	290.80	350.02	471.81	844.06
50,000	298.11	305.62	313.92	323.11	388.92	524.24	937.85
55,000	327.92	336.19	345.31	355.42	427.81	576.66	1031.63
60,000	357.74	366.75	376.70	387.73	466.70	629.09	1125.41
65,000	387.55	397.31	408.09	420.05	505.59	681.51	1219.20
70,000	417.36	427.87	439.48	452.36	544.48	733.93	1312.98
75,000	447.17	458.44	470.88	484.67	583.37	786.36	1406.77
80,000	476.98	489.00	502.27	516.98	622.27	838.78	1500.55
85,000	506.79	519.56	533.66	549.29	661.16	891.21	1594.34
90,000	536.60	550.12	565.05	581.60	700.05	943.63	1688.12
95,000	566.41	580.69	596.44	613.91	738.94	996.05	1781.91
100,000	596.23	611.25	627.84	646.22	777.83	1048.48	1875.69
110,000	655.85	672.37	690.62	710.85	855.62	1153.33	2063.26
120,000	715.47	733.50	753.40	775.47	933.40	1258.17	2250.83
130,000	775.09	794.62	816.19	840.09	1011.18	1363.02	2438.40
140,000	834.72	855.75	878.97	904.71	1088.96	1467.87	2625.97
150,000	894.34	916.87	941.75	969.34	1166.75	1572.72	2813.54
200,000	1192.45	1222.50	1255.67	1292.45	1555.66	2096.95	3751.38
250,000	1490.56	1528.12	1569.59	1615.56	1944.58	2621.19	4689.23
300,000	1788.68	1833.74	1883.51	1938.67	2333.50	3145.43	5627.07
350,000	2086.79	2139.37	2197.42	2261.78	2722.41	3669.67	6564.92
400,000	2384.90	2444.99	2511.34	2584.89	3111.33	4193.91	7502.76
450,000	2683.01	2750.62	2825.26	2908.01	3500.24	4718.15	8440.61
500,000	2981.13	3056.24	3139.18	3231.12	3889.16	5242.39	9378.46
550,000	3279.24	3361.87	3453.10	3554.23	4278.08	5766.63	10316.30
600,000	3577.35	3667.49	3767.01	3877.34	4666.99	6290.86	11254.15
650,000	3875.46	3973.11	4080.93	4200.45	5055.91	6815.10	12191.99
700,000	4173.58	4278.74	4394.85	4523.57	5444.82	7339.34	13129.84
750,000	4471.69	4584.36	4708.77	4846.68	5833.74	7863.58	14067.68
800,000	4769.80	4889.99	5022.69	5169.79	6222.66	8387.82	15005.53
850,000	5067.91	5195.61	5336.60	5492.90	6611.57	8912.06	15943.38
900,000	5366.03	5501.23	5650.52	5816.01	7000.49	9436.30	16881.22
950,000	5664.14	5806.86	5964.44	6139.12	7389.40	9960.54	17819.07
1,000,000	5962.25	6112.48	6278.36	6462.24	7778.32	10484.77	18756.91

Monthly Payments
Necessary to Amortize a Loan

AMOUNT BORROWED	YEARS REMAINING IN TERM						
	30	29	28	27	26	25	24
100	0.54	0.54	0.55	0.56	0.57	0.58	0.60
200	1.07	1.09	1.11	1.13	1.15	1.17	1.19
300	1.61	1.63	1.66	1.69	1.72	1.75	1.79
400	2.15	2.18	2.21	2.25	2.29	2.34	2.39
500	2.68	2.72	2.77	2.82	2.87	2.92	2.98
600	3.22	3.27	3.32	3.38	3.44	3.51	3.58
700	3.76	3.81	3.88	3.94	4.01	4.09	4.18
800	4.29	4.36	4.43	4.50	4.59	4.68	4.78
900	4.83	4.90	4.98	5.07	5.16	5.26	5.37
1,000	5.37	5.45	5.54	5.63	5.73	5.85	5.97
2,000	10.74	10.90	11.07	11.26	11.47	11.69	11.94
3,000	16.10	16.35	16.61	16.89	17.20	17.54	17.91
4,000	21.47	21.79	22.14	22.52	22.93	23.38	23.88
5,000	26.84	27.24	27.68	28.15	28.67	29.23	29.84
6,000	32.21	32.69	33.21	33.78	34.40	35.08	35.81
7,000	37.58	38.14	38.75	39.41	40.13	40.92	41.78
8,000	42.95	43.59	44.29	45.04	45.87	46.77	47.75
9,000	48.31	49.04	49.82	50.67	51.60	52.61	53.72
10,000	53.68	54.49	55.36	56.30	57.33	58.46	59.69
15,000	80.52	81.73	83.04	84.46	86.00	87.69	89.53
20,000	107.36	108.97	110.71	112.61	114.67	116.92	119.38
25,000	134.21	136.22	138.39	140.76	143.34	146.15	149.22
30,000	161.05	163.46	166.07	168.91	172.00	175.38	179.07
35,000	187.89	190.70	193.75	197.06	200.67	204.61	208.91
40,000	214.73	217.94	221.43	225.22	229.34	233.84	238.76
45,000	241.57	245.19	249.11	253.37	258.00	263.07	268.60
50,000	268.41	272.43	276.79	281.52	286.67	292.30	298.45
55,000	295.25	299.67	304.47	309.67	315.34	321.52	328.29
60,000	322.09	326.92	332.14	337.82	344.01	350.75	358.14
65,000	348.93	354.16	359.82	365.98	372.67	379.98	387.98
70,000	375.78	381.40	387.50	394.13	401.34	409.21	417.83
75,000	402.62	408.65	415.18	422.28	430.01	438.44	447.67
80,000	429.46	435.89	442.86	450.43	458.67	467.67	477.52
85,000	456.30	463.13	470.54	478.58	487.34	496.90	507.36
90,000	483.14	490.37	498.22	506.74	516.01	526.13	537.21
95,000	509.98	517.62	525.90	534.89	544.68	555.36	567.05
100,000	536.82	544.86	553.57	563.04	573.34	584.59	596.90
110,000	590.50	599.35	608.93	619.34	630.68	643.05	656.59
120,000	644.19	653.83	664.29	675.65	688.01	701.51	716.28
130,000	697.87	708.32	719.65	731.95	745.35	759.97	775.97
140,000	751.55	762.80	775.00	788.25	802.68	818.43	835.66
150,000	805.23	817.29	830.36	844.56	860.02	876.89	895.35
200,000	1073.64	1089.72	1107.15	1126.08	1146.69	1169.18	1193.80
250,000	1342.05	1362.15	1383.93	1407.60	1433.36	1461.48	1492.24
300,000	1610.46	1634.58	1660.72	1689.12	1720.03	1753.77	1790.69
350,000	1878.88	1907.01	1937.51	1970.64	2006.70	2046.07	2089.14
400,000	2147.29	2179.44	2214.30	2252.16	2293.37	2338.36	2387.59
450,000	2415.70	2451.87	2491.08	2533.68	2580.05	2630.66	2686.04
500,000	2684.11	2724.30	2767.87	2815.20	2866.72	2922.95	2984.49
550,000	2952.52	2996.73	3044.66	3096.71	3153.39	3215.25	3282.94
600,000	3220.93	3269.16	3321.44	3378.23	3440.06	3507.54	3581.39
650,000	3489.34	3541.59	3598.23	3659.75	3726.73	3799.84	3879.83
700,000	3757.75	3814.02	3875.02	3941.27	4013.41	4092.13	4178.28
750,000	4026.16	4086.45	4151.80	4222.79	4300.08	4384.43	4476.73
800,000	4294.57	4358.88	4428.59	4504.31	4586.75	4676.72	4775.18
850,000	4562.98	4631.31	4705.38	4785.83	4873.42	4969.02	5073.63
900,000	4831.39	4903.74	4982.17	5067.35	5160.09	5261.31	5372.08
950,000	5099.81	5176.17	5258.95	5348.87	5446.76	5553.61	5670.53
1,000,000	5368.22	5448.60	5535.74	5630.39	5733.44	5845.90	5968.98

Monthly Payments 5%
Necessary to Amortize a Loan

AMOUNT BORROWED	YEARS REMAINING IN TERM						
	23	22	21	20	15	10	5
100	0.61	0.63	0.64	0.66	0.79	1.06	1.89
200	1.22	1.25	1.28	1.32	1.58	2.12	3.77
300	1.83	1.88	1.93	1.98	2.37	3.18	5.66
400	2.44	2.50	2.57	2.64	3.16	4.24	7.55
500	3.05	3.13	3.21	3.30	3.95	5.30	9.44
600	3.66	3.75	3.85	3.96	4.74	6.36	11.32
700	4.27	4.38	4.49	4.62	5.54	7.42	13.21
800	4.88	5.00	5.13	5.28	6.33	8.49	15.10
900	5.49	5.63	5.78	5.94	7.12	9.55	16.98
1,000	6.10	6.25	6.42	6.60	7.91	10.61	18.87
2,000	12.21	12.51	12.83	13.20	15.82	21.21	37.74
3,000	18.31	18.76	19.25	19.80	23.72	31.82	56.61
4,000	24.42	25.01	25.67	26.40	31.63	42.43	75.48
5,000	30.52	31.26	32.09	33.00	39.54	53.03	94.36
6,000	36.62	37.52	38.50	39.60	47.45	63.64	113.23
7,000	42.73	43.77	44.92	46.20	55.36	74.25	132.10
8,000	48.83	50.02	51.34	52.80	63.26	84.85	150.97
9,000	54.94	56.28	57.75	59.40	71.17	95.46	169.84
10,000	61.04	62.53	64.17	66.00	79.08	106.07	188.71
15,000	91.56	93.79	96.26	98.99	118.62	159.10	283.07
20,000	122.08	125.06	128.34	131.99	158.16	212.13	377.42
25,000	152.60	156.32	160.43	164.99	197.70	265.16	471.78
30,000	183.12	187.58	192.52	197.99	237.24	318.20	566.14
35,000	213.64	218.85	224.60	230.98	276.78	371.23	660.49
40,000	244.16	250.11	256.69	263.98	316.32	424.26	754.85
45,000	274.68	281.38	288.77	296.98	355.86	477.29	849.21
50,000	305.20	312.64	320.86	329.98	395.40	530.33	943.56
55,000	335.72	343.90	352.95	362.98	434.94	583.36	1037.92
60,000	366.24	375.17	385.03	395.97	474.48	636.39	1132.27
65,000	396.76	406.43	417.12	428.97	514.02	689.43	1226.63
70,000	427.28	437.70	449.20	461.97	553.56	742.46	1320.99
75,000	457.80	468.96	481.29	494.97	593.10	795.49	1415.34
80,000	488.32	500.22	513.37	527.96	632.63	848.52	1509.70
85,000	518.85	531.49	545.46	560.96	672.17	901.56	1604.05
90,000	549.37	562.75	577.55	593.96	711.71	954.59	1698.41
95,000	579.89	594.02	609.63	626.96	751.25	1007.62	1792.77
100,000	610.41	625.28	641.72	659.96	790.79	1060.66	1887.12
110,000	671.45	687.81	705.89	725.95	869.87	1166.72	2075.84
120,000	732.49	750.34	770.06	791.95	948.95	1272.79	2264.55
130,000	793.53	812.86	834.23	857.94	1028.03	1378.85	2453.26
140,000	854.57	875.39	898.41	923.94	1107.11	1484.92	2641.97
150,000	915.61	937.92	962.58	989.93	1186.19	1590.98	2830.69
200,000	1220.81	1250.56	1283.44	1319.91	1581.59	2121.31	3774.25
250,000	1526.01	1563.20	1604.30	1649.89	1976.98	2651.64	4717.81
300,000	1831.22	1875.84	1925.16	1979.87	2372.38	3181.97	5661.37
350,000	2136.42	2188.48	2246.02	2309.85	2767.78	3712.29	6604.93
400,000	2441.62	2501.12	2566.87	2639.82	3163.17	4242.62	7548.49
450,000	2746.83	2813.76	2887.73	2969.80	3558.57	4772.95	8492.06
500,000	3052.03	3126.40	3208.59	3299.78	3953.97	5303.28	9435.62
550,000	3357.23	3439.04	3529.45	3629.76	4349.36	5833.60	10379.18
600,000	3662.44	3751.68	3850.31	3959.73	4744.76	6363.93	11322.74
650,000	3967.64	4064.32	4171.17	4289.71	5140.16	6894.26	12266.30
700,000	4272.84	4376.97	4492.03	4619.69	5535.56	7424.59	13209.86
750,000	4578.04	4689.61	4812.89	4949.67	5930.95	7954.91	14153.43
800,000	4883.25	5002.25	5133.75	5279.65	6326.35	8485.24	15096.99
850,000	5188.45	5314.89	5454.61	5609.60	6721.75	9015.57	16040.55
900,000	5493.65	5627.53	5775.47	5939.60	7117.14	9545.90	16984.11
950,000	5798.86	5940.17	6096.33	6269.58	7512.54	10076.22	17927.67
1,000,000	6104.06	6252.81	6417.19	6599.56	7907.94	10606.55	18871.23

5¼%

Monthly Payments
Necessary to Amortize a Loan

YEARS REMAINING IN TERM

AMOUNT BORROWED	30	29	28	27	26	25	24
100	0.55	0.56	0.57	0.58	0.59	0.60	0.61
200	1.10	1.12	1.14	1.16	1.18	1.20	1.22
300	1.66	1.68	1.71	1.73	1.76	1.80	1.83
400	2.21	2.24	2.27	2.31	2.35	2.40	2.45
500	2.76	2.80	2.84	2.89	2.94	3.00	3.06
600	3.31	3.36	3.41	3.47	3.53	3.60	3.67
700	3.87	3.92	3.98	4.05	4.12	4.19	4.28
800	4.42	4.48	4.55	4.62	4.71	4.79	4.89
900	4.97	5.04	5.12	5.20	5.29	5.39	5.50
1,000	5.52	5.60	5.69	5.78	5.88	5.99	6.11
2,000	11.04	11.20	11.37	11.56	11.76	11.98	12.23
3,000	16.57	16.80	17.06	17.34	17.64	17.98	18.34
4,000	22.09	22.40	22.75	23.12	23.53	23.97	24.46
5,000	27.61	28.01	28.43	28.90	29.41	29.96	30.57
6,000	33.13	33.61	34.12	34.68	35.29	35.95	36.68
7,000	38.65	39.21	39.81	40.46	41.17	41.95	42.80
8,000	44.18	44.81	45.49	46.24	47.05	47.94	48.91
9,000	49.70	50.41	51.18	52.02	52.93	53.93	55.03
10,000	55.22	56.01	56.87	57.80	58.82	59.92	61.14
15,000	82.83	84.02	85.30	86.70	88.22	89.89	91.71
20,000	110.44	112.02	113.73	115.60	117.63	119.85	122.28
25,000	138.05	140.03	142.17	144.50	147.04	149.81	152.85
30,000	165.66	168.03	170.60	173.40	176.45	179.77	183.42
35,000	193.27	196.04	199.04	202.30	205.85	209.74	213.99
40,000	220.88	224.04	227.47	231.20	235.26	239.70	244.56
45,000	248.49	252.05	255.90	260.10	264.67	269.66	275.13
50,000	276.10	280.05	284.34	289.00	294.08	299.62	305.70
55,000	303.71	308.06	312.77	317.90	323.48	329.59	336.27
60,000	331.32	336.06	341.20	346.80	352.89	359.55	366.84
65,000	358.93	364.07	369.64	375.69	382.30	389.51	397.41
70,000	386.54	392.07	398.07	404.59	411.71	419.47	427.98
75,000	414.15	420.08	426.50	433.49	441.11	449.44	458.55
80,000	441.76	448.08	454.94	462.39	470.52	479.40	489.12
85,000	469.37	476.09	483.37	491.29	499.93	509.36	519.69
90,000	496.98	504.09	511.80	520.19	529.34	539.32	550.26
95,000	524.59	532.10	540.24	549.09	558.74	569.29	580.83
100,000	552.20	560.10	568.67	577.99	588.15	599.25	611.40
110,000	607.42	616.11	625.54	635.79	646.97	659.17	672.55
120,000	662.64	672.12	682.41	693.59	705.78	719.10	733.69
130,000	717.86	728.13	739.27	751.39	764.60	779.02	794.83
140,000	773.09	784.14	796.14	809.19	823.41	838.95	855.97
150,000	828.31	840.15	853.01	866.99	882.23	898.87	917.11
200,000	1104.41	1120.20	1137.34	1155.98	1176.30	1198.50	1222.81
250,000	1380.51	1400.25	1421.68	1444.98	1470.38	1498.12	1528.51
300,000	1656.61	1680.30	1706.02	1733.98	1764.45	1797.74	1834.21
350,000	1932.71	1960.36	1990.35	2022.97	2058.53	2097.37	2139.92
400,000	2208.81	2240.41	2274.69	2311.97	2352.60	2396.99	2445.62
450,000	2484.92	2520.46	2559.02	2600.97	2646.68	2696.61	2751.32
500,000	2761.02	2800.51	2843.36	2889.96	2940.75	2996.24	3057.02
550,000	3037.12	3080.56	3127.70	3178.96	3234.83	3295.86	3362.73
600,000	3313.22	3360.61	3412.03	3467.95	3528.90	3595.49	3668.43
650,000	3589.32	3640.66	3696.37	3756.95	3822.98	3895.11	3974.13
700,000	3865.43	3920.71	3980.70	4045.95	4117.05	4194.73	4279.83
750,000	4141.53	4200.76	4265.04	4334.94	4411.13	4494.36	4585.54
800,000	4417.63	4480.81	4549.38	4623.94	4705.20	4793.98	4891.24
850,000	4693.73	4760.86	4833.71	4912.93	4999.28	5093.61	5196.94
900,000	4969.83	5040.91	5118.05	5201.93	5293.35	5393.23	5502.64
950,000	5245.94	5320.96	5402.39	5490.93	5587.43	5692.85	5808.34
1,000,000	5522.04	5601.01	5686.72	5779.92	5881.50	5992.48	6114.05

Monthly Payments 5¼%
Necessary to Amortize a Loan

AMOUNT BORROWED	YEARS REMAINING IN TERM						
	23	22	21	20	15	10	5
100	0.62	0.64	0.66	0.67	0.80	1.07	1.90
200	1.25	1.28	1.31	1.35	1.61	2.15	3.80
300	1.87	1.92	1.97	2.02	2.41	3.22	5.70
400	2.50	2.56	2.62	2.70	3.22	4.29	7.59
500	3.12	3.20	3.28	3.37	4.02	5.36	9.49
600	3.75	3.84	3.93	4.04	4.82	6.44	11.39
700	4.37	4.48	4.59	4.72	5.63	7.51	13.29
800	5.00	5.12	5.25	5.39	6.43	8.58	15.19
900	5.62	5.76	5.90	6.06	7.23	9.66	17.09
1,000	6.25	6.39	6.56	6.74	8.04	10.73	18.99
2,000	12.50	12.79	13.12	13.48	16.08	21.46	37.97
3,000	18.74	19.18	19.67	20.22	24.12	32.19	56.96
4,000	24.99	25.58	26.23	26.95	32.16	42.92	75.94
5,000	31.24	31.97	32.79	33.69	40.19	53.65	94.93
6,000	37.49	38.37	39.35	40.43	48.23	64.38	113.92
7,000	43.73	44.76	45.90	47.17	56.27	75.10	132.90
8,000	49.98	51.16	52.46	53.91	64.31	85.83	151.89
9,000	56.23	57.55	59.02	60.65	72.35	96.56	170.87
10,000	62.48	63.95	65.58	67.38	80.39	107.29	189.86
15,000	93.71	95.92	98.36	101.08	120.58	160.94	284.79
20,000	124.95	127.90	131.15	134.77	160.78	214.58	379.72
25,000	156.19	159.87	163.94	168.46	200.97	268.23	474.65
30,000	187.43	191.84	196.73	202.15	241.16	321.88	569.58
35,000	218.67	223.82	229.52	235.85	281.36	375.52	664.51
40,000	249.90	255.79	262.31	269.54	321.55	429.17	759.44
45,000	281.14	287.77	295.09	303.23	361.74	482.81	854.37
50,000	312.38	319.74	327.88	336.92	401.94	536.46	949.30
55,000	343.62	351.71	360.67	370.61	442.13	590.10	1044.23
60,000	374.86	383.69	393.46	404.31	482.33	643.75	1139.16
65,000	406.09	415.66	426.25	438.00	522.52	697.40	1234.09
70,000	437.33	447.64	459.03	471.69	562.71	751.04	1329.02
75,000	468.57	479.61	491.82	505.38	602.91	804.69	1423.95
80,000	499.81	511.59	524.61	539.08	643.10	858.33	1518.88
85,000	531.05	543.56	557.40	572.77	683.30	911.98	1613.81
90,000	562.28	575.53	590.19	606.46	723.49	965.63	1708.74
95,000	593.52	607.51	622.98	640.15	763.68	1019.27	1803.67
100,000	624.76	639.48	655.76	673.84	803.88	1072.92	1898.60
110,000	687.24	703.43	721.34	741.23	884.27	1180.21	2088.46
120,000	749.71	767.38	786.92	808.61	964.65	1287.50	2278.32
130,000	812.19	831.33	852.49	876.00	1045.04	1394.79	2468.18
140,000	874.67	895.27	918.07	943.38	1125.43	1502.08	2658.04
150,000	937.14	959.22	983.65	1010.77	1205.82	1609.38	2847.90
200,000	1249.52	1278.96	1311.53	1347.69	1607.76	2145.83	3797.20
250,000	1561.90	1598.70	1639.41	1684.61	2009.69	2682.29	4746.50
300,000	1874.28	1918.45	1967.29	2021.53	2411.63	3218.75	5695.80
350,000	2186.66	2238.19	2295.17	2358.45	2813.57	3755.21	6645.09
400,000	2499.04	2557.93	2623.06	2695.38	3215.51	4291.67	7594.39
450,000	2811.42	2877.67	2950.94	3032.30	3617.45	4828.13	8543.69
500,000	3123.80	3197.41	3278.82	3369.22	4019.39	5364.59	9492.99
550,000	3436.18	3517.15	3606.70	3706.14	4421.33	5901.04	10442.29
600,000	3748.57	3836.89	3934.58	4043.06	4823.27	6437.50	11391.59
650,000	4060.95	4156.63	4262.47	4379.99	5225.21	6973.96	12340.89
700,000	4373.33	4476.37	4590.35	4716.91	5627.14	7510.42	13290.19
750,000	4685.71	4796.11	4918.23	5053.83	6029.08	8046.88	14239.49
800,000	4998.09	5115.85	5246.11	5390.75	6431.02	8583.34	15188.79
850,000	5310.47	5435.59	5573.99	5727.68	6832.96	9119.79	16138.09
900,000	5622.85	5755.34	5901.88	6064.60	7234.90	9656.25	17087.39
950,000	5935.23	6075.08	6229.76	6401.52	7636.84	10192.71	18036.68
1,000,000	6247.61	6394.82	6557.64	6738.44	8038.78	10729.17	18985.98

5¹/₂%

Monthly Payments
Necessary to Amortize a Loan

AMOUNT BORROWED	YEARS REMAINING IN TERM						
	30	29	28	27	26	25	24
100	0.57	0.58	0.58	0.59	0.60	0.61	0.63
200	1.14	1.15	1.17	1.19	1.21	1.23	1.25
300	1.70	1.73	1.75	1.78	1.81	1.84	1.88
400	2.27	2.30	2.34	2.37	2.41	2.46	2.50
500	2.84	2.88	2.92	2.97	3.02	3.07	3.13
600	3.41	3.45	3.50	3.56	3.62	3.68	3.76
700	3.97	4.03	4.09	4.15	4.22	4.30	4.38
800	4.54	4.60	4.67	4.75	4.83	4.91	5.01
900	5.11	5.18	5.26	5.34	5.43	5.53	5.63
1,000	5.68	5.76	5.84	5.93	6.03	6.14	6.26
2,000	11.36	11.51	11.68	11.86	12.06	12.28	12.52
3,000	17.03	17.27	17.52	17.79	18.09	18.42	18.78
4,000	22.71	23.02	23.36	23.73	24.13	24.56	25.04
5,000	28.39	28.78	29.20	29.66	30.16	30.70	31.30
6,000	34.07	34.53	35.04	35.59	36.19	36.85	37.57
7,000	39.75	40.29	40.88	41.52	42.22	42.99	43.83
8,000	45.42	46.04	46.72	47.45	48.25	49.13	50.09
9,000	51.10	51.80	52.56	53.38	54.28	55.27	56.35
10,000	56.78	57.55	58.40	59.31	60.31	61.41	62.61
15,000	85.17	86.33	87.59	88.97	90.47	92.11	93.91
20,000	113.56	115.11	116.79	118.63	120.63	122.82	125.22
25,000	141.95	143.89	145.99	148.28	150.79	153.52	156.52
30,000	170.34	172.66	175.19	177.94	180.94	184.23	187.83
35,000	198.73	201.44	204.39	207.60	211.10	214.93	219.13
40,000	227.12	230.22	233.59	237.25	241.26	245.63	250.44
45,000	255.51	258.99	262.78	266.91	271.41	276.34	281.74
50,000	283.89	287.77	291.98	296.57	301.57	307.04	313.04
55,000	312.28	316.55	321.18	326.23	331.73	337.75	344.35
60,000	340.67	345.33	350.38	355.88	361.89	368.45	375.65
65,000	369.06	374.10	379.58	385.54	392.04	399.16	406.96
70,000	397.45	402.88	408.78	415.20	422.20	429.86	438.26
75,000	425.84	431.66	437.97	444.85	452.36	460.57	469.57
80,000	454.23	460.43	467.17	474.51	482.51	491.27	500.87
85,000	482.62	489.21	496.37	504.17	512.67	521.97	532.18
90,000	511.01	517.99	525.57	533.82	542.83	552.68	563.48
95,000	539.40	546.76	554.77	563.48	572.99	583.38	594.78
100,000	567.79	575.54	583.97	593.14	603.14	614.09	626.09
110,000	624.57	633.10	642.36	652.45	663.46	675.50	688.70
120,000	681.35	690.65	700.76	711.76	723.77	736.90	751.31
130,000	738.13	748.20	759.16	771.08	784.09	798.31	813.92
140,000	794.90	805.76	817.55	830.39	844.40	859.72	876.52
150,000	851.68	863.31	875.95	889.71	904.71	921.13	939.13
200,000	1135.58	1151.08	1167.93	1186.27	1206.29	1228.17	1252.18
250,000	1419.47	1438.86	1459.91	1482.84	1507.86	1535.22	1565.23
300,000	1703.37	1726.63	1751.90	1779.41	1809.43	1842.26	1878.27
350,000	1987.26	2014.40	2043.88	2075.98	2111.00	2149.31	2191.31
400,000	2271.16	2302.17	2335.86	2372.55	2412.57	2456.35	2504.36
450,000	2555.05	2589.94	2627.85	2669.12	2714.14	2763.39	2817.40
500,000	2838.95	2877.71	2919.83	2965.68	3015.72	3070.44	3130.44
550,000	3122.84	3165.48	3211.81	3262.25	3317.29	3377.48	3443.49
600,000	3406.73	3453.25	3503.79	3558.82	3618.86	3684.52	3756.53
650,000	3690.63	3741.02	3795.78	3855.39	3920.43	3991.57	4069.58
700,000	3974.52	4028.79	4087.76	4151.96	4222.00	4298.61	4382.62
750,000	4258.42	4316.57	4379.74	4448.53	4523.57	4605.66	4695.67
800,000	4542.31	4604.34	4671.73	4745.09	4825.15	4912.70	5008.71
850,000	4826.21	4892.11	4963.71	5041.66	5126.72	5219.74	5321.76
900,000	5110.10	5179.88	5255.69	5338.23	5428.29	5526.79	5634.80
950,000	5394.00	5467.65	5547.68	5634.80	5729.86	5833.83	5947.84
1,000,000	5677.89	5755.42	5839.66	5931.37	6031.43	6140.87	6260.89

Monthly Payments

Necessary to Amortize a Loan

5¹/₂%

AMOUNT BORROWED	YEARS REMAINING IN TERM						
	23	22	21	20	15	10	5
100	0.64	0.65	0.67	0.69	0.82	1.09	1.91
200	1.28	1.31	1.34	1.38	1.63	2.17	3.82
300	1.92	1.96	2.01	2.06	2.45	3.26	5.73
400	2.56	2.62	2.68	2.75	3.27	4.34	7.64
500	3.20	3.27	3.35	3.44	4.09	5.43	9.55
600	3.84	3.92	4.02	4.13	4.90	6.51	11.46
700	4.48	4.58	4.69	4.82	5.72	7.60	13.37
800	5.11	5.23	5.36	5.50	6.54	8.68	15.28
900	5.75	5.88	6.03	6.19	7.35	9.77	17.19
1,000	6.39	6.54	6.70	6.88	8.17	10.85	19.10
2,000	12.79	13.08	13.40	13.76	16.34	21.71	38.20
3,000	19.18	19.62	20.10	20.64	24.51	32.56	57.30
4,000	25.57	26.15	26.80	27.52	32.68	43.41	76.40
5,000	31.96	32.69	33.50	34.39	40.85	54.26	95.51
6,000	38.36	39.23	40.20	41.27	49.03	65.12	114.61
7,000	44.75	45.77	46.90	48.15	57.20	75.97	133.71
8,000	51.14	52.31	53.60	55.03	65.37	86.82	152.81
9,000	57.54	58.85	60.30	61.91	73.54	97.67	171.91
10,000	63.93	65.38	67.00	68.79	81.71	108.53	191.01
15,000	95.89	98.08	100.50	103.18	122.56	162.79	286.52
20,000	127.86	130.77	133.99	137.58	163.42	217.05	382.02
25,000	159.82	163.46	167.49	171.97	204.27	271.32	477.53
30,000	191.79	196.15	200.99	206.37	245.13	325.58	573.03
35,000	223.75	228.85	234.49	240.76	285.98	379.84	668.54
40,000	255.72	261.54	267.99	275.15	326.83	434.11	764.05
45,000	287.68	294.23	301.49	309.55	367.69	488.37	859.55
50,000	319.64	326.92	334.99	343.94	408.54	542.63	955.06
55,000	351.61	359.62	368.48	378.34	449.40	596.89	1050.56
60,000	383.57	392.31	401.98	412.73	490.25	651.16	1146.07
65,000	415.54	425.00	435.48	447.13	531.10	705.42	1241.58
70,000	447.50	457.69	468.98	481.52	571.96	759.68	1337.08
75,000	479.47	490.39	502.48	515.92	612.81	813.95	1432.59
80,000	511.43	523.08	535.98	550.31	653.67	868.21	1528.09
85,000	543.39	555.77	569.47	584.70	694.52	922.47	1623.60
90,000	575.36	588.46	602.97	619.10	735.38	976.74	1719.10
95,000	607.32	621.16	636.47	653.49	776.23	1031.00	1814.61
100,000	639.29	653.85	669.97	687.89	817.08	1085.26	1910.12
110,000	703.22	719.23	736.97	756.68	898.79	1193.79	2101.13
120,000	767.15	784.62	803.96	825.46	980.50	1302.32	2292.14
130,000	831.07	850.00	870.96	894.25	1062.21	1410.84	2483.15
140,000	895.00	915.39	937.96	963.04	1143.92	1519.37	2674.16
150,000	958.93	980.77	1004.96	1031.83	1225.63	1627.89	2865.17
200,000	1278.58	1307.70	1339.94	1375.77	1634.17	2170.53	3820.23
250,000	1598.22	1634.62	1674.93	1719.72	2042.71	2713.16	4775.29
300,000	1917.86	1961.55	2009.91	2063.66	2451.25	3255.79	5730.35
350,000	2237.51	2288.47	2344.90	2407.61	2859.79	3798.42	6685.41
400,000	2557.15	2615.40	2679.88	2751.55	3268.33	4341.05	7640.46
450,000	2876.79	2942.32	3014.87	3095.49	3676.88	4883.68	8595.52
500,000	3196.44	3269.25	3349.85	3439.44	4085.42	5426.31	9550.58
550,000	3516.08	3596.17	3684.84	3783.38	4493.96	5968.95	10505.64
600,000	3835.73	3923.09	4019.82	4127.32	4902.50	6511.58	11460.70
650,000	4155.37	4250.02	4354.81	4471.27	5311.04	7054.21	12415.76
700,000	4475.01	4576.94	4689.79	4815.21	5719.58	7596.84	13370.81
750,000	4794.66	4903.87	5024.78	5159.15	6128.13	8139.47	14325.87
800,000	5114.30	5230.79	5359.76	5503.10	6536.67	8682.10	15280.93
850,000	5433.95	5557.72	5694.75	5847.04	6945.21	9224.73	16235.99
900,000	5753.59	5884.64	6029.73	6190.99	7353.75	9767.37	17191.05
950,000	6073.23	6211.57	6364.72	6534.93	7762.29	10310.00	18146.10
1,000,000	6392.88	6538.49	6699.70	6878.87	8170.83	10852.63	19101.16

5³/₄% Monthly Payments
Necessary to Amortize a Loan

AMOUNT BORROWED	YEARS REMAINING IN TERM						
	30	29	28	27	26	25	24
100	0.58	0.59	0.60	0.61	0.62	0.63	0.64
200	1.17	1.18	1.20	1.22	1.24	1.26	1.28
300	1.75	1.77	1.80	1.83	1.85	1.89	1.92
400	2.33	2.36	2.40	2.43	2.47	2.52	2.56
500	2.92	2.96	3.00	3.04	3.09	3.15	3.20
600	3.50	3.55	3.60	3.65	3.71	3.77	3.85
700	4.09	4.14	4.20	4.26	4.33	4.40	4.49
800	4.67	4.73	4.80	4.87	4.95	5.03	5.13
900	5.25	5.32	5.40	5.48	5.56	5.66	5.77
1,000	5.84	5.91	5.99	6.08	6.18	6.29	6.41
2,000	11.67	11.82	11.99	12.17	12.37	12.58	12.82
3,000	17.51	17.74	17.98	18.25	18.55	18.87	19.23
4,000	23.34	23.65	23.98	24.34	24.73	25.16	25.64
5,000	29.18	29.56	29.97	30.42	30.92	31.46	32.05
6,000	35.01	35.47	35.97	36.51	37.10	37.75	38.46
7,000	40.85	41.38	41.96	42.59	43.28	44.04	44.87
8,000	46.69	47.29	47.96	48.68	49.47	50.33	51.28
9,000	52.52	53.21	53.95	54.76	55.65	56.62	57.69
10,000	58.36	59.12	59.95	60.85	61.83	62.91	64.09
15,000	87.54	88.68	89.92	91.27	92.75	94.37	96.14
20,000	116.71	118.24	119.89	121.69	123.66	125.82	128.19
25,000	145.89	147.79	149.86	152.12	154.58	157.28	160.24
30,000	175.07	177.35	179.84	182.54	185.50	188.73	192.28
35,000	204.25	206.91	209.81	212.96	216.41	220.19	224.33
40,000	233.43	236.47	239.78	243.39	247.33	251.64	256.38
45,000	262.61	266.03	269.75	273.81	278.24	283.10	288.43
50,000	291.79	295.59	299.73	304.23	309.16	314.55	320.47
55,000	320.97	325.15	329.70	334.66	340.08	346.01	352.52
60,000	350.14	354.71	359.67	365.08	370.99	377.46	384.57
65,000	379.32	384.27	389.64	395.50	401.91	408.92	416.62
70,000	408.50	413.82	419.62	425.93	432.82	440.37	448.66
75,000	437.68	443.38	449.59	456.35	463.74	471.83	480.71
80,000	466.86	472.94	479.56	486.78	494.66	503.29	512.76
85,000	496.04	502.50	509.53	517.20	525.57	534.74	544.81
90,000	525.22	532.06	539.51	547.62	556.49	566.20	576.85
95,000	554.39	561.62	569.48	578.05	587.40	597.65	608.90
100,000	583.57	591.18	599.45	608.47	618.32	629.11	640.95
110,000	641.93	650.30	659.40	669.32	680.15	692.02	705.04
120,000	700.29	709.41	719.34	730.16	741.98	754.93	769.14
130,000	758.64	768.53	779.29	791.01	803.82	817.84	833.23
140,000	817.00	827.65	839.23	851.86	865.65	880.75	897.33
150,000	875.36	886.77	899.18	912.70	927.48	943.66	961.42
200,000	1167.15	1182.36	1198.90	1216.94	1236.64	1258.21	1281.90
250,000	1458.93	1477.94	1498.63	1521.17	1545.80	1572.77	1602.37
300,000	1750.72	1773.53	1798.35	1825.41	1854.96	1887.32	1922.84
350,000	2042.50	2069.12	2098.08	2129.64	2164.12	2201.87	2243.32
400,000	2334.29	2364.71	2397.80	2433.88	2473.28	2516.43	2563.79
450,000	2626.08	2660.30	2697.53	2738.11	2782.44	2830.98	2884.26
500,000	2917.86	2955.89	2997.26	3042.35	3091.60	3145.53	3204.74
550,000	3209.65	3251.48	3296.98	3346.58	3400.76	3460.09	3525.21
600,000	3501.44	3547.07	3596.71	3650.81	3709.92	3774.64	3845.69
650,000	3793.22	3842.66	3896.43	3955.05	4019.08	4089.19	4166.16
700,000	4085.01	4138.25	4196.16	4259.28	4328.24	4403.74	4486.63
750,000	4376.80	4433.83	4495.88	4563.52	4637.40	4718.30	4807.11
800,000	4668.58	4729.42	4795.61	4867.75	4946.56	5032.85	5127.58
850,000	4960.37	5025.01	5095.33	5171.99	5255.72	5347.40	5448.06
900,000	5252.16	5320.60	5395.06	5476.22	5564.88	5661.96	5768.53
950,000	5543.94	5616.19	5694.79	5780.46	5874.04	5976.51	6089.00
1,000,000	5835.73	5911.78	5994.51	6084.69	6183.20	6291.06	6409.48

Monthly Payments 5¾%
Necessary to Amortize a Loan

AMOUNT BORROWED	YEARS REMAINING IN TERM						
	23	22	21	20	15	10	5
100	0.65	0.67	0.68	0.70	0.83	1.10	1.92
200	1.31	1.34	1.37	1.40	1.66	2.20	3.84
300	1.96	2.01	2.05	2.11	2.49	3.29	5.77
400	2.62	2.67	2.74	2.81	3.32	4.39	7.69
500	3.27	3.34	3.42	3.51	4.15	5.49	9.61
600	3.92	4.01	4.11	4.21	4.98	6.59	11.53
700	4.58	4.68	4.79	4.91	5.81	7.68	13.45
800	5.23	5.35	5.47	5.62	6.64	8.78	15.37
900	5.89	6.02	6.16	6.32	7.47	9.88	17.30
1,000	6.54	6.68	6.84	7.02	8.30	10.98	19.22
2,000	13.08	13.37	13.69	14.04	16.61	21.95	38.43
3,000	19.62	20.05	20.53	21.06	24.91	32.93	57.65
4,000	26.16	26.74	27.37	28.08	33.22	43.91	76.87
5,000	32.70	33.42	34.22	35.10	41.52	54.88	96.08
6,000	39.24	40.10	41.06	42.13	49.82	65.86	115.30
7,000	45.78	46.79	47.90	49.15	58.13	76.84	134.52
8,000	52.32	53.47	54.75	56.17	66.43	87.82	153.73
9,000	58.86	60.15	61.59	63.19	74.74	98.79	172.95
10,000	65.40	66.84	68.43	70.21	83.04	109.77	192.17
15,000	98.10	100.26	102.65	105.31	124.56	164.65	288.25
20,000	130.80	133.68	136.87	140.42	166.08	219.54	384.34
25,000	163.50	167.10	171.08	175.52	207.60	274.42	480.42
30,000	196.20	200.51	205.30	210.63	249.12	329.31	576.50
35,000	228.89	233.93	239.52	245.73	290.64	384.19	672.59
40,000	261.59	267.35	273.73	280.83	332.16	439.08	768.67
45,000	294.29	300.77	307.95	315.94	373.68	493.96	864.75
50,000	326.99	334.19	342.17	351.04	415.21	548.85	960.84
55,000	359.69	367.61	376.38	386.15	456.73	603.73	1056.92
60,000	392.39	401.03	410.60	421.25	498.25	658.62	1153.01
65,000	425.09	434.45	444.82	456.35	539.77	713.50	1249.09
70,000	457.79	467.87	479.03	491.46	581.29	768.38	1345.17
75,000	490.49	501.29	513.25	526.56	622.81	823.27	1441.26
80,000	523.19	534.70	547.47	561.67	664.33	878.15	1537.34
85,000	555.89	568.12	581.68	596.77	705.85	933.04	1633.43
90,000	588.59	601.54	615.90	631.88	747.37	987.92	1729.51
95,000	621.28	634.96	650.12	666.98	788.89	1042.81	1825.59
100,000	653.98	668.38	684.34	702.08	830.41	1097.69	1921.68
110,000	719.38	735.22	752.77	772.29	913.45	1207.46	2113.84
120,000	784.78	802.06	821.20	842.50	996.49	1317.23	2306.01
130,000	850.18	868.89	889.64	912.71	1079.53	1427.00	2498.18
140,000	915.58	935.73	958.07	982.92	1162.57	1536.77	2690.35
150,000	980.98	1002.57	1026.50	1053.13	1245.62	1646.54	2882.52
200,000	1307.97	1336.76	1368.67	1404.17	1660.82	2195.38	3843.35
250,000	1634.96	1670.95	1710.84	1755.21	2076.03	2744.23	4804.19
300,000	1961.95	2005.14	2053.01	2106.25	2491.23	3293.08	5765.03
350,000	2288.94	2339.33	2395.17	2457.29	2906.44	3841.92	6725.87
400,000	2615.94	2673.52	2737.34	2808.33	3321.64	4390.77	7686.71
450,000	2942.93	3007.71	3079.51	3159.38	3736.85	4939.61	8647.55
500,000	3269.92	3341.90	3421.68	3510.42	4152.05	5488.46	9608.38
550,000	3596.91	3676.09	3763.84	3861.46	4567.26	6037.31	10569.22
600,000	3923.90	4010.28	4106.01	4212.50	4982.46	6586.15	11530.06
650,000	4250.90	4344.47	4448.18	4563.54	5397.67	7135.00	12490.90
700,000	4577.89	4678.67	4790.35	4914.58	5812.87	7683.85	13451.74
750,000	4904.88	5012.86	5132.51	5265.63	6228.08	8232.69	14412.58
800,000	5231.87	5347.05	5474.68	5616.67	6643.28	8781.54	15373.41
850,000	5558.86	5681.24	5816.85	5967.71	7058.49	9330.38	16334.25
900,000	5885.86	6015.43	6159.02	6318.75	7473.69	9879.23	17295.09
950,000	6212.85	6349.62	6501.18	6669.79	7888.90	10428.08	18255.93
1,000,000	6539.84	6683.81	6843.35	7020.84	8304.10	10976.92	19216.77

Monthly Payments
Necessary to Amortize a Loan

AMOUNT BORROWED	YEARS REMAINING IN TERM						
	30	29	28	27	26	25	24
100	0.60	0.61	0.62	0.62	0.63	0.64	0.66
200	1.20	1.21	1.23	1.25	1.27	1.29	1.31
300	1.80	1.82	1.85	1.87	1.90	1.93	1.97
400	2.40	2.43	2.46	2.50	2.53	2.58	2.62
500	3.00	3.04	3.08	3.12	3.17	3.22	3.28
600	3.60	3.64	3.69	3.74	3.80	3.87	3.94
700	4.20	4.25	4.31	4.37	4.44	4.51	4.59
800	4.80	4.86	4.92	4.99	5.07	5.15	5.25
900	5.40	5.46	5.54	5.62	5.70	5.80	5.90
1,000	6.00	6.07	6.15	6.24	6.34	6.44	6.56
2,000	11.99	12.14	12.30	12.48	12.67	12.89	13.12
3,000	17.99	18.21	18.45	18.72	19.01	19.33	19.68
4,000	23.98	24.28	24.60	24.96	25.35	25.77	26.24
5,000	29.98	30.35	30.76	31.20	31.68	32.22	32.80
6,000	35.97	36.42	36.91	37.44	38.02	38.66	39.36
7,000	41.97	42.49	43.06	43.68	44.36	45.10	45.92
8,000	47.96	48.56	49.21	49.92	50.69	51.54	52.48
9,000	53.96	54.63	55.36	56.16	57.03	57.99	59.04
10,000	59.96	60.70	61.51	62.40	63.37	64.43	65.60
15,000	89.93	91.05	92.27	93.60	95.05	96.65	98.40
20,000	119.91	121.40	123.02	124.80	126.74	128.86	131.20
25,000	149.89	151.75	153.78	156.00	158.42	161.08	163.99
30,000	179.87	182.10	184.54	187.20	190.10	193.29	196.79
35,000	209.84	212.45	215.29	218.39	221.79	225.51	229.59
40,000	239.82	242.80	246.05	249.59	253.47	257.72	262.39
45,000	269.80	273.15	276.81	280.79	285.15	289.94	295.19
50,000	299.78	303.50	307.56	311.99	316.84	322.15	327.99
55,000	329.75	333.85	338.32	343.19	348.52	354.37	360.79
60,000	359.73	364.20	369.07	374.39	380.21	386.58	393.59
65,000	389.71	394.55	399.83	405.59	411.89	418.80	426.39
70,000	419.69	424.90	430.59	436.79	443.57	451.01	459.18
75,000	449.66	455.25	461.34	467.99	475.26	483.23	491.98
80,000	479.64	485.60	492.10	499.19	506.94	515.44	524.78
85,000	509.62	515.95	522.86	530.39	538.63	547.66	557.58
90,000	539.60	546.30	553.61	561.59	570.31	579.87	590.38
95,000	569.57	576.65	584.37	592.79	601.99	612.09	623.18
100,000	599.55	607.00	615.12	623.99	633.68	644.30	655.98
110,000	659.51	667.71	676.64	686.38	697.04	708.73	721.58
120,000	719.46	728.41	738.15	748.78	760.41	773.16	787.17
130,000	779.42	789.11	799.66	811.18	823.78	837.59	852.77
140,000	839.37	849.81	861.17	873.58	887.15	902.02	918.37
150,000	899.33	910.51	922.69	935.98	950.52	966.45	983.97
200,000	1199.10	1214.01	1230.25	1247.97	1267.35	1288.60	1311.96
250,000	1498.88	1517.51	1537.81	1559.96	1584.19	1610.75	1639.95
300,000	1798.65	1821.01	1845.37	1871.96	1901.03	1932.90	1967.93
350,000	2098.43	2124.52	2152.93	2183.95	2217.87	2255.05	2295.92
400,000	2398.20	2428.02	2460.50	2495.94	2534.71	2577.21	2623.91
450,000	2697.98	2731.52	2768.06	2807.93	2851.55	2899.36	2951.90
500,000	2997.75	3035.02	3075.62	3119.93	3168.38	3221.51	3279.89
550,000	3297.53	3338.53	3383.18	3431.92	3485.22	3543.66	3607.88
600,000	3597.30	3642.03	3690.74	3743.91	3802.06	3865.81	3935.87
650,000	3897.08	3945.53	3998.31	4055.90	4118.90	4187.96	4263.86
700,000	4196.85	4249.03	4305.87	4367.90	4435.74	4510.11	4591.85
750,000	4496.63	4552.53	4613.43	4679.89	4752.58	4832.26	4919.84
800,000	4796.40	4856.04	4920.99	4991.88	5069.42	5154.41	5247.82
850,000	5096.18	5159.54	5228.55	5303.88	5386.25	5476.56	5575.81
900,000	5395.95	5463.04	5536.12	5615.87	5703.09	5798.71	5903.80
950,000	5695.73	5766.54	5843.68	5927.86	6019.93	6120.86	6231.79
1,000,000	5995.51	6070.05	6151.24	6239.85	6336.77	6443.01	6559.78

Monthly Payments 6%
Necessary to Amortize a Loan

AMOUNT BORROWED	YEARS REMAINING IN TERM						
	23	22	21	20	15	10	5
100	0.67	0.68	0.70	0.72	0.84	1.11	1.93
200	1.34	1.37	1.40	1.43	1.69	2.22	3.87
300	2.01	2.05	2.10	2.15	2.53	3.33	5.80
400	2.68	2.73	2.80	2.87	3.38	4.44	7.73
500	3.34	3.42	3.49	3.58	4.22	5.55	9.67
600	4.01	4.10	4.19	4.30	5.06	6.66	11.60
700	4.68	4.78	4.89	5.02	5.91	7.77	13.53
800	5.35	5.46	5.59	5.73	6.75	8.88	15.47
900	6.02	6.15	6.29	6.45	7.59	9.99	17.40
1,000	6.69	6.83	6.99	7.16	8.44	11.10	19.33
2,000	13.38	13.66	13.98	14.33	16.88	22.20	38.67
3,000	20.07	20.49	20.97	21.49	25.32	33.31	58.00
4,000	26.75	27.32	27.95	28.66	33.75	44.41	77.33
5,000	33.44	34.15	34.94	35.82	42.19	55.51	96.66
6,000	40.13	40.98	41.93	42.99	50.63	66.61	116.00
7,000	46.82	47.82	48.92	50.15	59.07	77.71	135.33
8,000	53.51	54.65	55.91	57.31	67.51	88.82	154.66
9,000	60.20	61.48	62.90	64.48	75.95	99.92	174.00
10,000	66.88	68.31	69.89	71.64	84.39	111.02	193.33
15,000	100.33	102.46	104.83	107.46	126.58	166.53	289.99
20,000	133.77	136.61	139.77	143.29	168.77	222.04	386.66
25,000	167.21	170.77	174.71	179.11	210.96	277.55	483.32
30,000	200.65	204.92	209.66	214.93	253.16	333.06	579.98
35,000	234.10	239.08	244.60	250.75	295.35	388.57	676.65
40,000	267.54	273.23	279.54	286.57	337.54	444.08	773.31
45,000	300.98	307.38	314.49	322.39	379.74	499.59	869.98
50,000	334.42	341.54	349.43	358.22	421.93	555.10	966.64
55,000	367.87	375.69	384.37	394.04	464.12	610.61	1063.30
60,000	401.31	409.84	419.31	429.86	506.31	666.12	1159.97
65,000	434.75	444.00	454.26	465.68	548.51	721.63	1256.63
70,000	468.19	478.15	489.20	501.50	590.70	777.14	1353.30
75,000	501.64	512.31	524.14	537.32	632.89	832.65	1449.96
80,000	535.08	546.46	559.09	573.14	675.09	888.16	1546.62
85,000	568.52	580.61	594.03	608.97	717.28	943.67	1643.29
90,000	601.96	614.77	628.97	644.79	759.47	999.18	1739.95
95,000	635.40	648.92	663.91	680.61	801.66	1054.69	1836.62
100,000	668.85	683.07	698.86	716.43	843.86	1110.21	1933.28
110,000	735.73	751.38	768.74	788.07	928.24	1221.23	2126.61
120,000	802.62	819.69	838.63	859.72	1012.63	1332.25	2319.94
130,000	869.50	888.00	908.51	931.36	1097.01	1443.27	2513.26
140,000	936.39	956.30	978.40	1003.00	1181.40	1554.29	2706.59
150,000	1003.27	1024.61	1048.29	1074.65	1265.79	1665.31	2899.92
200,000	1337.69	1366.15	1397.71	1432.86	1687.71	2220.41	3866.56
250,000	1672.12	1707.69	1747.14	1791.08	2109.64	2775.51	4833.20
300,000	2006.54	2049.22	2096.57	2149.29	2531.57	3330.62	5799.84
350,000	2340.97	2390.76	2446.00	2507.51	2953.50	3885.72	6766.48
400,000	2675.39	2732.30	2795.43	2865.72	3375.43	4440.82	7733.12
450,000	3009.81	3073.84	3144.86	3223.94	3797.36	4995.92	8699.76
500,000	3344.24	3415.37	3494.28	3582.16	4219.28	5551.03	9666.40
550,000	3678.66	3756.91	3843.71	3940.37	4641.21	6106.13	10633.04
600,000	4013.08	4098.45	4193.14	4298.59	5063.14	6661.23	11599.68
650,000	4347.51	4439.98	4542.57	4656.80	5485.07	7216.33	12566.32
700,000	4681.93	4781.52	4892.00	5015.02	5907.00	7771.44	13532.96
750,000	5016.35	5123.06	5241.43	5373.23	6328.93	8326.54	14499.60
800,000	5350.78	5464.60	5590.86	5731.45	6750.85	8881.64	15466.24
850,000	5685.20	5806.13	5940.28	6089.66	7172.78	9436.74	16432.88
900,000	6019.62	6147.67	6289.71	6447.88	7594.71	9991.85	17399.52
950,000	6354.05	6489.21	6639.14	6806.10	8016.64	10546.95	18366.16
1,000,000	6688.47	6830.74	6988.57	7164.31	8438.57	11102.05	19332.80

6¼%

Monthly Payments
Necessary to Amortize a Loan

AMOUNT BORROWED	YEARS REMAINING IN TERM						
	30	29	28	27	26	25	24
100	0.62	0.62	0.63	0.64	0.65	0.66	0.67
200	1.23	1.25	1.26	1.28	1.30	1.32	1.34
300	1.85	1.87	1.89	1.92	1.95	1.98	2.01
400	2.46	2.49	2.52	2.56	2.60	2.64	2.68
500	3.08	3.12	3.15	3.20	3.25	3.30	3.36
600	3.69	3.74	3.79	3.84	3.90	3.96	4.03
700	4.31	4.36	4.42	4.48	4.54	4.62	4.70
800	4.93	4.98	5.05	5.12	5.19	5.28	5.37
900	5.54	5.61	5.68	5.76	5.84	5.94	6.04
1,000	6.16	6.23	6.31	6.40	6.49	6.60	6.71
2,000	12.31	12.46	12.62	12.79	12.98	13.19	13.42
3,000	18.47	18.69	18.93	19.19	19.48	19.79	20.14
4,000	24.63	24.92	25.24	25.59	25.97	26.39	26.85
5,000	30.79	31.15	31.55	31.98	32.46	32.98	33.56
6,000	36.94	37.38	37.86	38.38	38.95	39.58	40.27
7,000	43.10	43.61	44.17	44.78	45.44	46.18	46.98
8,000	49.26	49.84	50.48	51.17	51.94	52.77	53.69
9,000	55.41	56.07	56.79	57.57	58.43	59.37	60.41
10,000	61.57	62.30	63.10	63.97	64.92	65.97	67.12
15,000	92.36	93.45	94.65	95.95	97.38	98.95	100.68
20,000	123.14	124.60	126.20	127.94	129.84	131.93	134.24
25,000	153.93	155.75	157.75	159.92	162.30	164.92	167.79
30,000	184.72	186.91	189.29	191.90	194.76	197.90	201.35
35,000	215.50	218.06	220.84	223.89	227.22	230.88	234.91
40,000	246.29	249.21	252.39	255.87	259.68	263.87	268.47
45,000	277.07	280.36	283.94	287.86	292.14	296.85	302.03
50,000	307.86	311.51	315.49	319.84	324.61	329.83	335.59
55,000	338.64	342.66	347.04	351.83	357.07	362.82	369.15
60,000	369.43	373.81	378.59	383.81	389.53	395.80	402.71
65,000	400.22	404.96	410.14	415.79	421.99	428.79	436.27
70,000	431.00	436.11	441.69	447.78	454.45	461.77	469.82
75,000	461.79	467.26	473.24	479.76	486.91	494.75	503.38
80,000	492.57	498.41	504.78	511.75	519.37	527.74	536.94
85,000	523.36	529.57	536.33	543.73	551.83	560.72	570.50
90,000	554.15	560.72	567.88	575.71	584.29	593.70	604.06
95,000	584.93	591.87	599.43	607.70	616.75	626.69	637.62
100,000	615.72	623.02	630.98	639.68	649.21	659.67	671.18
110,000	677.29	685.32	694.08	703.65	714.13	725.64	738.30
120,000	738.86	747.62	757.18	767.62	779.05	791.60	805.41
130,000	800.43	809.92	820.27	831.59	843.97	857.57	872.53
140,000	862.00	872.22	883.37	895.55	908.90	923.54	939.65
150,000	923.58	934.53	946.47	959.52	973.82	989.50	1006.77
200,000	1231.43	1246.04	1261.96	1279.36	1298.42	1319.34	1342.35
250,000	1539.29	1557.54	1577.45	1599.20	1623.03	1649.17	1677.94
300,000	1847.15	1869.05	1892.94	1919.05	1947.63	1979.00	2013.53
350,000	2155.01	2180.56	2208.43	2238.89	2272.24	2308.84	2349.12
400,000	2462.87	2492.07	2523.92	2558.73	2596.84	2638.68	2684.71
450,000	2770.73	2803.58	2839.41	2878.57	2921.45	2968.51	3020.30
500,000	3078.59	3115.09	3154.90	3198.41	3246.05	3298.35	3355.89
550,000	3386.44	3426.60	3470.33	3518.25	3570.66	3628.18	3691.48
600,000	3694.30	3738.11	3785.88	3838.09	3895.26	3958.02	4027.06
650,000	4002.16	4049.62	4101.37	4157.93	4219.87	4287.85	4362.65
700,000	4310.02	4361.12	4416.86	4477.77	4544.48	4617.69	4698.24
750,000	4617.88	4672.63	4732.35	4797.61	4869.08	4947.52	5033.83
800,000	4925.74	4984.14	5047.84	5117.46	5193.69	5277.36	5369.42
850,000	5233.60	5295.65	5363.33	5437.30	5518.29	5607.19	5705.01
900,000	5541.45	5607.16	5678.82	5757.14	5842.90	5937.02	6040.60
950,000	5849.31	5918.67	5994.31	6076.98	6167.50	6266.86	6376.18
1,000,000	6157.17	6230.18	6309.80	6396.82	6492.11	6596.69	6711.77

Monthly Payments 6¼%
Necessary to Amortize a Loan

AMOUNT BORROWED	YEARS REMAINING IN TERM						
	23	22	21	20	15	10	5
100	0.68	0.70	0.71	0.73	0.86	1.12	1.94
200	1.37	1.40	1.43	1.46	1.71	2.25	3.89
300	2.05	2.09	2.14	2.19	2.57	3.37	5.83
400	2.74	2.79	2.85	2.92	3.43	4.49	7.78
500	3.42	3.49	3.57	3.65	4.29	5.61	9.72
600	4.10	4.19	4.28	4.39	5.14	6.74	11.67
700	4.79	4.89	4.99	5.12	6.00	7.86	13.61
800	5.47	5.58	5.71	5.85	6.86	8.98	15.56
900	6.15	6.28	6.42	6.58	7.72	10.11	17.50
1,000	6.84	6.98	7.14	7.31	8.57	11.23	19.45
2,000	13.68	13.96	14.27	14.62	17.15	22.46	38.90
3,000	20.52	20.94	21.41	21.93	25.72	33.68	58.35
4,000	27.35	27.92	28.54	29.24	34.30	44.91	77.80
5,000	34.19	34.90	35.68	36.55	42.87	56.14	97.25
6,000	41.03	41.88	42.81	43.86	51.45	67.37	116.70
7,000	47.87	48.85	49.95	51.16	60.02	78.60	136.14
8,000	54.71	55.83	57.08	58.47	68.59	89.82	155.59
9,000	61.55	62.81	64.22	65.78	77.17	101.05	175.04
10,000	68.39	69.79	71.35	73.09	85.74	112.28	194.49
15,000	102.58	104.69	107.03	109.64	128.61	168.42	291.74
20,000	136.77	139.59	142.71	146.19	171.48	224.56	388.99
25,000	170.97	174.48	178.38	182.73	214.36	280.70	486.23
30,000	205.16	209.38	214.06	219.28	257.23	336.84	583.48
35,000	239.36	244.27	249.74	255.82	300.10	392.98	680.72
40,000	273.55	279.17	285.41	292.37	342.97	449.12	777.97
45,000	307.74	314.07	321.09	328.92	385.84	505.26	875.22
50,000	341.94	348.96	356.77	365.46	428.71	561.40	972.46
55,000	376.13	383.86	392.44	402.01	471.58	617.54	1069.71
60,000	410.32	418.76	428.12	438.56	514.45	673.68	1166.96
65,000	444.52	453.65	463.80	475.10	557.32	729.82	1264.20
70,000	478.71	488.55	499.47	511.65	600.20	785.96	1361.45
75,000	512.91	523.45	535.15	548.20	643.07	842.10	1458.69
80,000	547.10	558.34	570.83	584.74	685.94	898.24	1555.94
85,000	581.29	593.24	606.50	621.29	728.81	954.38	1653.19
90,000	615.49	628.14	642.18	657.84	771.68	1010.52	1750.43
95,000	649.68	663.03	677.86	694.38	814.55	1066.66	1847.68
100,000	683.87	697.93	713.53	730.93	857.42	1122.80	1944.93
110,000	752.26	767.72	784.89	804.02	943.17	1235.08	2139.42
120,000	820.65	837.51	856.24	877.11	1028.91	1347.36	2333.91
130,000	889.04	907.31	927.59	950.21	1114.65	1459.64	2528.40
140,000	957.42	977.10	998.95	1023.30	1200.39	1571.92	2722.90
150,000	1025.81	1046.89	1070.30	1096.39	1286.13	1684.20	2917.39
200,000	1367.75	1395.86	1427.07	1461.86	1714.85	2245.60	3889.85
250,000	1709.69	1744.82	1783.83	1827.32	2143.56	2807.00	4862.32
300,000	2051.62	2093.78	2140.60	2192.78	2572.27	3368.40	5834.78
350,000	2393.56	2442.75	2497.37	2558.25	3000.98	3929.80	6807.24
400,000	2735.50	2791.71	2854.13	2923.71	3429.69	4491.20	7779.70
450,000	3077.44	3140.68	3210.90	3289.18	3858.40	5052.60	8752.17
500,000	3419.37	3489.64	3567.67	3654.64	4287.11	5614.00	9724.63
550,000	3761.31	3838.60	3924.43	4020.11	4715.83	6175.41	10697.09
600,000	4103.25	4187.57	4281.20	4385.57	5144.54	6736.81	11669.56
650,000	4445.19	4536.53	4637.97	4751.03	5573.25	7298.21	12642.02
700,000	4787.12	4885.50	4994.73	5116.50	6001.96	7859.61	13614.48
750,000	5129.06	5234.46	5351.50	5481.96	6430.67	8421.01	14586.95
800,000	5471.00	5583.42	5708.27	5847.43	6859.38	8982.41	15559.41
850,000	5812.94	5932.39	6065.03	6212.89	7288.09	9543.81	16531.87
900,000	6154.87	6281.35	6421.80	6578.35	7716.81	10105.21	17504.34
950,000	6496.81	6630.32	6778.57	6943.82	8145.52	10666.61	18476.80
1,000,000	6838.75	6979.28	7135.34	7309.28	8574.23	11228.01	19449.26

Monthly Payments
Necessary to Amortize a Loan

AMOUNT BORROWED	YEARS REMAINING IN TERM						
	30	29	28	27	26	25	24
100	0.63	0.64	0.65	0.66	0.66	0.68	0.69
200	1.26	1.28	1.29	1.31	1.33	1.35	1.37
300	1.90	1.92	1.94	1.97	1.99	2.03	2.06
400	2.53	2.56	2.59	2.62	2.66	2.70	2.75
500	3.16	3.20	3.24	3.28	3.32	3.38	3.43
600	3.79	3.84	3.88	3.93	3.99	4.05	4.12
700	4.42	4.47	4.53	4.59	4.65	4.73	4.81
800	5.06	5.11	5.18	5.24	5.32	5.40	5.49
900	5.69	5.75	5.82	5.90	5.98	6.08	6.18
1,000	6.32	6.39	6.47	6.56	6.65	6.75	6.87
2,000	12.64	12.78	12.94	13.11	13.30	13.50	13.73
3,000	18.96	19.18	19.41	19.67	19.95	20.26	20.60
4,000	25.28	25.57	25.88	26.22	26.60	27.01	27.46
5,000	31.60	31.96	32.35	32.78	33.25	33.76	34.33
6,000	37.92	38.35	38.82	39.33	39.90	40.51	41.19
7,000	44.24	44.74	45.29	45.89	46.54	47.26	48.06
8,000	50.57	51.14	51.76	52.44	53.19	54.02	54.92
9,000	56.89	57.53	58.23	59.00	59.84	60.77	61.79
10,000	63.21	63.92	64.70	65.56	66.49	67.52	68.65
15,000	94.81	95.88	97.05	98.33	99.74	101.28	102.98
20,000	126.41	127.84	129.40	131.11	132.98	135.04	137.31
25,000	158.02	159.80	161.75	163.89	166.23	168.80	171.64
30,000	189.62	191.76	194.10	196.67	199.48	202.56	205.96
35,000	221.22	223.72	226.46	229.44	232.72	236.32	240.29
40,000	252.83	255.69	258.81	262.22	265.97	270.08	274.62
45,000	284.43	287.65	291.16	295.00	299.21	303.84	308.94
50,000	316.03	319.61	323.51	327.78	332.46	337.60	343.27
55,000	347.64	351.57	355.86	360.56	365.70	371.36	377.60
60,000	379.24	383.53	388.21	393.33	398.95	405.12	411.93
65,000	410.84	415.49	420.56	426.11	432.20	438.88	446.25
70,000	442.45	447.45	452.91	458.89	465.44	472.65	480.58
75,000	474.05	479.41	485.26	491.67	498.69	506.41	514.91
80,000	505.65	511.37	517.61	524.44	531.93	540.17	549.23
85,000	537.26	543.33	549.96	557.22	565.18	573.93	583.56
90,000	568.86	575.29	582.31	590.00	598.43	607.69	617.89
95,000	600.46	607.25	614.67	622.78	631.67	641.45	652.22
100,000	632.07	639.21	647.02	655.55	664.92	675.21	686.54
110,000	695.27	703.13	711.72	721.11	731.41	742.73	755.20
120,000	758.48	767.06	776.42	786.67	797.90	810.25	823.85
130,000	821.69	830.98	841.12	852.22	864.39	877.77	892.51
140,000	884.90	894.90	905.82	917.78	930.88	945.29	961.16
150,000	948.10	958.82	970.52	983.33	997.38	1012.81	1029.81
200,000	1264.14	1278.43	1294.03	1311.11	1329.84	1350.41	1373.09
250,000	1580.17	1598.03	1617.54	1638.89	1662.29	1688.02	1716.36
300,000	1896.20	1917.64	1941.05	1966.66	1994.75	2025.62	2059.63
350,000	2212.24	2237.24	2264.56	2294.44	2327.21	2363.23	2402.90
400,000	2528.27	2556.85	2588.06	2622.22	2659.67	2700.83	2746.17
450,000	2844.31	2876.46	2911.57	2950.00	2992.13	3038.43	3089.44
500,000	3160.34	3196.06	3235.08	3277.77	3324.59	3376.04	3432.71
550,000	3476.37	3515.67	3558.59	3605.55	3657.05	3713.64	3775.98
600,000	3792.41	3835.28	3882.10	3933.33	3989.51	4051.24	4119.26
650,000	4108.44	4154.88	4205.60	4261.11	4321.97	4388.85	4462.53
700,000	4424.48	4474.49	4529.11	4588.88	4654.42	4726.45	4805.80
750,000	4740.51	4794.09	4852.62	4916.66	4986.88	5064.05	5149.07
800,000	5056.54	5113.70	5176.13	5244.44	5319.34	5401.66	5492.34
850,000	5372.58	5433.31	5499.64	5572.22	5651.80	5739.26	5835.61
900,000	5688.61	5752.91	5823.14	5899.99	5984.26	6076.86	6178.88
950,000	6004.65	6072.52	6146.65	6227.77	6316.72	6414.47	6522.16
1,000,000	6320.68	6392.13	6470.16	6555.55	6649.18	6752.07	6865.43

Monthly Payments $6^1/_2$%
Necessary to Amortize a Loan

AMOUNT BORROWED	YEARS REMAINING IN TERM						
	23	22	21	20	15	10	5
100	0.70	0.71	0.73	0.75	0.87	1.14	1.96
200	1.40	1.43	1.46	1.49	1.74	2.27	3.91
300	2.10	2.14	2.19	2.24	2.61	3.41	5.87
400	2.80	2.85	2.91	2.98	3.48	4.54	7.83
500	3.50	3.56	3.64	3.73	4.36	5.68	9.78
600	4.19	4.28	4.37	4.47	5.23	6.81	11.74
700	4.89	4.99	5.10	5.22	6.10	7.95	13.70
800	5.59	5.70	5.83	5.96	6.97	9.08	15.65
900	6.29	6.42	6.56	6.71	7.84	10.22	17.61
1,000	6.99	7.13	7.28	7.46	8.71	11.35	19.57
2,000	13.98	14.26	14.57	14.91	17.42	22.71	39.13
3,000	20.97	21.39	21.85	22.37	26.13	34.06	58.70
4,000	27.96	28.52	29.13	29.82	34.84	45.42	78.26
5,000	34.95	35.65	36.42	37.28	43.56	56.77	97.83
6,000	41.94	42.78	43.70	44.73	52.27	68.13	117.40
7,000	48.93	49.91	50.99	52.19	60.98	79.48	136.96
8,000	55.93	57.04	58.27	59.65	69.69	90.84	156.53
9,000	62.92	64.16	65.55	67.10	78.40	102.19	176.10
10,000	69.91	71.29	72.84	74.56	87.11	113.55	195.66
15,000	104.86	106.94	109.25	111.84	130.67	170.32	293.49
20,000	139.81	142.59	145.67	149.11	174.22	227.10	391.32
25,000	174.77	178.23	182.09	186.39	217.78	283.87	489.15
30,000	209.72	213.88	218.51	223.67	261.33	340.64	586.98
35,000	244.67	249.53	254.93	260.95	304.89	397.42	684.82
40,000	279.63	285.18	291.35	298.23	348.44	454.19	782.65
45,000	314.58	320.82	327.76	335.51	392.00	510.97	880.48
50,000	349.53	356.47	364.18	372.79	435.55	567.74	978.31
55,000	384.49	392.12	400.60	410.07	479.11	624.51	1076.14
60,000	419.44	427.76	437.02	447.34	522.66	681.29	1173.97
65,000	454.39	463.41	473.44	484.62	566.22	738.06	1271.80
70,000	489.35	499.06	509.85	521.90	609.78	794.84	1369.63
75,000	524.30	534.70	546.27	559.18	653.33	851.61	1467.46
80,000	559.25	570.35	582.69	596.46	696.89	908.38	1565.29
85,000	594.20	606.00	619.11	633.74	740.44	965.16	1663.12
90,000	629.16	641.65	655.53	671.02	784.00	1021.93	1760.95
95,000	664.11	677.29	691.94	708.29	827.55	1078.71	1858.78
100,000	699.06	712.94	728.36	745.57	871.11	1135.48	1956.61
110,000	768.97	784.23	801.20	820.13	958.22	1249.03	2152.28
120,000	838.88	855.53	874.04	894.69	1045.33	1362.58	2347.94
130,000	908.78	926.82	946.87	969.25	1132.44	1476.12	2543.60
140,000	978.69	998.11	1019.71	1043.80	1219.55	1589.67	2739.26
150,000	1048.60	1069.41	1092.54	1118.36	1306.66	1703.22	2934.92
200,000	1398.13	1425.88	1456.73	1491.15	1742.21	2270.96	3913.23
250,000	1747.66	1782.35	1820.91	1863.93	2177.77	2838.70	4891.54
300,000	2097.19	2138.82	2185.09	2236.72	2613.32	3406.44	5869.84
350,000	2446.73	2495.29	2549.27	2609.51	3048.88	3974.18	6848.15
400,000	2796.26	2851.76	2913.45	2982.29	3484.43	4541.92	7826.46
450,000	3145.79	3208.23	3277.63	3355.08	3919.98	5109.66	8804.77
500,000	3495.32	3564.69	3641.81	3727.87	4355.54	5677.40	9783.07
550,000	3844.86	3921.16	4006.00	4100.65	4791.09	6245.14	10761.38
600,000	4194.39	4277.63	4370.18	4473.44	5226.64	6812.88	11739.69
650,000	4543.92	4634.10	4734.36	4846.23	5662.20	7380.62	12718.00
700,000	4893.45	4990.57	5098.54	5219.01	6097.75	7948.36	13696.30
750,000	5242.99	5347.04	5462.72	5591.80	6533.31	8516.10	14674.61
800,000	5592.52	5703.51	5826.90	5964.59	6968.86	9083.84	15652.92
850,000	5942.05	6059.98	6191.08	6337.37	7404.41	9651.58	16631.23
900,000	6291.58	6416.45	6555.27	6710.16	7839.97	10219.32	17609.53
950,000	6641.11	6772.92	6919.45	7082.94	8275.52	10787.06	18587.84
1,000,000	6990.65	7129.39	7283.63	7455.73	8711.07	11354.80	19566.15

6³/₄%

Monthly Payments
Necessary to Amortize a Loan

AMOUNT BORROWED	YEARS REMAINING IN TERM						
	30	29	28	27	26	25	24
100	0.65	0.66	0.66	0.67	0.68	0.69	0.70
200	1.30	1.31	1.33	1.34	1.36	1.38	1.40
300	1.95	1.97	1.99	2.01	2.04	2.07	2.11
400	2.59	2.62	2.65	2.69	2.72	2.76	2.81
500	3.24	3.28	3.32	3.36	3.40	3.45	3.51
600	3.89	3.93	3.98	4.03	4.08	4.15	4.21
700	4.54	4.59	4.64	4.70	4.77	4.84	4.91
800	5.19	5.24	5.31	5.37	5.45	5.53	5.62
900	5.84	5.90	5.97	6.04	6.13	6.22	6.32
1,000	6.49	6.56	6.63	6.72	6.81	6.91	7.02
2,000	12.97	13.11	13.26	13.43	13.62	13.82	14.04
3,000	19.46	19.67	19.90	20.15	20.42	20.73	21.06
4,000	25.94	26.22	26.53	26.86	27.23	27.64	28.08
5,000	32.43	32.78	33.16	33.58	34.04	34.55	35.10
6,000	38.92	39.34	39.79	40.30	40.85	41.45	42.12
7,000	45.40	45.89	46.43	47.01	47.66	48.36	49.14
8,000	51.89	52.45	53.06	53.73	54.46	55.27	56.17
9,000	58.37	59.00	59.69	60.44	61.27	62.18	63.19
10,000	64.86	65.56	66.32	67.16	68.08	69.09	70.21
15,000	97.29	98.34	99.48	100.74	102.12	103.64	105.31
20,000	129.72	131.12	132.65	134.32	136.16	138.18	140.41
25,000	162.15	163.90	165.81	167.90	170.20	172.73	175.52
30,000	194.58	196.68	198.97	201.48	204.24	207.27	210.62
35,000	227.01	229.45	232.13	235.06	238.28	241.82	245.72
40,000	259.44	262.23	265.29	268.64	272.32	276.36	280.83
45,000	291.87	295.01	298.45	302.22	306.36	310.91	315.93
50,000	324.30	327.79	331.61	335.80	340.40	345.46	351.04
55,000	356.73	360.57	364.77	369.38	374.44	380.00	386.14
60,000	389.16	393.35	397.94	402.96	408.48	414.55	421.24
65,000	421.59	426.13	431.10	436.54	442.52	449.09	456.35
70,000	454.02	458.91	464.26	470.12	476.56	483.64	491.45
75,000	486.45	491.69	497.42	503.70	510.60	518.18	526.55
80,000	518.88	524.47	530.58	537.28	544.64	552.73	561.66
85,000	551.31	557.25	563.74	570.86	578.68	587.27	596.76
90,000	583.74	590.03	596.90	604.44	612.72	621.82	631.86
95,000	616.17	622.81	630.07	638.02	646.75	656.37	666.97
100,000	648.60	655.58	663.23	671.60	680.79	690.91	702.07
110,000	713.46	721.14	729.55	738.76	748.87	760.00	772.28
120,000	778.32	786.70	795.87	805.92	816.95	829.09	842.49
130,000	843.18	852.26	862.19	873.08	885.03	898.18	912.69
140,000	908.04	917.82	928.52	940.24	953.11	967.28	982.90
150,000	972.90	983.38	994.84	1007.40	1021.19	1036.37	1053.11
200,000	1297.20	1311.17	1326.45	1343.20	1361.59	1381.82	1404.14
250,000	1621.50	1638.96	1658.07	1679.00	1701.99	1727.28	1755.18
300,000	1945.79	1966.75	1989.68	2014.80	2042.38	2072.73	2106.21
350,000	2270.09	2294.55	2321.29	2350.60	2382.78	2418.19	2457.25
400,000	2594.39	2622.34	2652.91	2686.40	2723.18	2763.65	2808.28
450,000	2918.69	2950.13	2984.52	3022.20	3063.58	3109.10	3159.32
500,000	3242.99	3277.92	3316.13	3358.00	3403.97	3454.56	3510.36
550,000	3567.29	3605.72	3647.75	3693.80	3744.37	3800.01	3861.39
600,000	3891.59	3933.51	3979.36	4029.60	4084.77	4145.47	4212.43
650,000	4215.89	4261.30	4310.97	4365.40	4425.16	4490.92	4563.46
700,000	4540.19	4589.09	4642.59	4701.20	4765.56	4836.38	4914.50
750,000	4864.49	4916.89	4974.20	5037.00	5105.96	5181.84	5265.53
800,000	5188.78	5244.68	5305.82	5372.80	5446.36	5527.29	5616.57
850,000	5513.08	5572.47	5637.43	5708.61	5786.75	5872.75	5967.60
900,000	5837.38	5900.26	5969.04	6044.41	6127.15	6218.20	6318.64
950,000	6161.68	6228.06	6300.66	6380.21	6467.55	6563.66	6669.68
1,000,000	6485.98	6555.85	6632.27	6716.01	6807.95	6909.12	7020.71

YEARS REMAINING IN TERM

AMOUNT BORROWED	23	22	21	20	15	10	5
100	0.71	0.73	0.74	0.76	0.88	1.15	1.97
200	1.43	1.46	1.49	1.52	1.77	2.30	3.94
300	2.14	2.18	2.23	2.28	2.65	3.44	5.91
400	2.86	2.91	2.97	3.04	3.54	4.59	7.87
500	3.57	3.64	3.72	3.80	4.42	5.74	9.84
600	4.29	4.37	4.46	4.56	5.31	6.89	11.81
700	5.00	5.10	5.20	5.32	6.19	8.04	13.78
800	5.72	5.82	5.95	6.08	7.08	9.19	15.75
900	6.43	6.55	6.69	6.84	7.96	10.33	17.72
1,000	7.14	7.28	7.43	7.60	8.85	11.48	19.68
2,000	14.29	14.56	14.87	15.21	17.70	22.96	39.37
3,000	21.43	21.84	22.30	22.81	26.55	34.45	59.05
4,000	28.58	29.12	29.73	30.41	35.40	45.93	78.73
5,000	35.72	36.41	37.17	38.02	44.25	57.41	98.42
6,000	42.86	43.69	44.60	45.62	53.09	68.89	118.10
7,000	50.01	50.97	52.03	53.23	61.94	80.38	137.78
8,000	57.15	58.25	59.47	60.83	70.79	91.86	157.47
9,000	64.30	65.53	66.90	68.43	79.64	103.34	177.15
10,000	71.44	72.81	74.33	76.04	88.49	114.82	196.83
15,000	107.16	109.22	111.50	114.05	132.74	172.24	295.25
20,000	142.88	145.62	148.67	152.07	176.98	229.65	393.67
25,000	178.60	182.03	185.84	190.09	221.23	287.06	492.09
30,000	214.32	218.43	223.00	228.11	265.47	344.47	590.50
35,000	250.04	254.84	260.17	266.13	309.72	401.88	688.92
40,000	285.77	291.24	297.34	304.15	353.96	459.30	787.34
45,000	321.49	327.65	334.50	342.16	398.21	516.71	885.76
50,000	357.21	364.05	371.67	380.18	442.45	574.12	984.17
55,000	392.93	400.46	408.84	418.20	486.70	631.53	1082.59
60,000	428.65	436.86	446.01	456.22	530.95	688.94	1181.01
65,000	464.37	473.27	483.17	494.24	575.19	746.36	1279.42
70,000	500.09	509.67	520.34	532.25	619.44	803.77	1377.84
75,000	535.81	546.08	557.51	570.27	663.68	861.18	1476.26
80,000	571.53	582.48	594.67	608.29	707.93	918.59	1574.68
85,000	607.25	618.89	631.84	646.31	752.17	976.00	1673.09
90,000	642.97	655.29	669.01	684.33	796.42	1033.42	1771.51
95,000	678.69	691.70	706.18	722.35	840.66	1090.83	1869.93
100,000	714.41	728.11	743.34	760.36	884.91	1148.24	1968.35
110,000	785.86	800.92	817.68	836.40	973.40	1263.07	2165.18
120,000	857.30	873.73	892.01	912.44	1061.89	1377.89	2362.02
130,000	928.74	946.54	966.35	988.47	1150.38	1492.71	2558.85
140,000	1000.18	1019.35	1040.68	1064.51	1238.87	1607.54	2755.68
150,000	1071.62	1092.16	1115.01	1140.55	1327.36	1722.36	2952.52
200,000	1428.83	1456.21	1486.69	1520.73	1769.82	2296.48	3936.69
250,000	1786.03	1820.26	1858.36	1900.91	2212.27	2870.60	4920.87
300,000	2143.24	2184.32	2230.03	2281.09	2654.73	3444.72	5905.04
350,000	2500.45	2548.37	2601.70	2661.27	3097.18	4018.84	6889.21
400,000	2857.65	2912.42	2973.37	3041.46	3539.64	4592.96	7873.38
450,000	3214.86	3276.47	3345.04	3421.64	3982.09	5167.09	8857.56
500,000	3572.07	3640.53	3716.72	3801.82	4424.55	5741.21	9841.73
550,000	3929.28	4004.58	4088.39	4182.00	4867.00	6315.33	10825.90
600,000	4286.48	4368.63	4460.06	4562.18	5309.46	6889.45	11810.08
650,000	4643.69	4732.68	4831.73	4942.37	5751.91	7463.57	12794.25
700,000	5000.90	5096.74	5203.40	5322.55	6194.37	8037.69	13778.42
750,000	5358.10	5460.79	5575.07	5702.73	6636.82	8611.81	14762.60
800,000	5715.31	5824.84	5946.74	6082.91	7079.28	9185.93	15746.77
850,000	6072.52	6188.89	6318.42	6463.09	7521.73	9760.05	16730.94
900,000	6429.72	6552.95	6690.09	6843.28	7964.19	10334.17	17715.11
950,000	6786.93	6917.00	7061.76	7223.46	8406.64	10908.29	18699.29
1,000,000	7144.14	7281.05	7433.43	7603.64	8849.09	11482.41	19683.46

Monthly Payments
Necessary to Amortize a Loan

AMOUNT BORROWED	YEARS REMAINING IN TERM						
	30	29	28	27	26	25	24
100	0.67	0.67	0.68	0.69	0.70	0.71	0.72
200	1.33	1.34	1.36	1.38	1.39	1.41	1.44
300	2.00	2.02	2.04	2.06	2.09	2.12	2.15
400	2.66	2.69	2.72	2.75	2.79	2.83	2.87
500	3.33	3.36	3.40	3.44	3.48	3.53	3.59
600	3.99	4.03	4.08	4.13	4.18	4.24	4.31
700	4.66	4.70	4.76	4.81	4.88	4.95	5.02
800	5.32	5.38	5.44	5.50	5.57	5.65	5.74
900	5.99	6.05	6.12	6.19	6.27	6.36	6.46
1,000	6.65	6.72	6.80	6.88	6.97	7.07	7.18
2,000	13.31	13.44	13.59	13.76	13.94	14.14	14.36
3,000	19.96	20.16	20.39	20.63	20.91	21.20	21.53
4,000	26.61	26.89	27.18	27.51	27.87	28.27	28.71
5,000	33.27	33.61	33.98	34.39	34.84	35.34	35.89
6,000	39.92	40.33	40.78	41.27	41.81	42.41	43.07
7,000	46.57	47.05	47.57	48.15	48.78	49.47	50.24
8,000	53.22	53.77	54.37	55.03	55.75	56.54	57.42
9,000	59.88	60.49	61.16	61.90	62.72	63.61	64.60
10,000	66.53	67.21	67.96	68.78	69.68	70.68	71.78
15,000	99.80	100.82	101.94	103.17	104.53	106.02	107.66
20,000	133.06	134.43	135.92	137.56	139.37	141.36	143.55
25,000	166.33	168.03	169.90	171.95	174.21	176.69	179.44
30,000	199.59	201.64	203.88	206.34	209.05	212.03	215.33
35,000	232.86	235.25	237.86	240.74	243.89	247.37	251.22
40,000	266.12	268.85	271.84	275.13	278.74	282.71	287.10
45,000	299.39	302.46	305.82	309.52	313.58	318.05	322.99
50,000	332.65	336.07	339.80	343.91	348.42	353.39	358.88
55,000	365.92	369.67	373.78	378.30	383.26	388.73	394.77
60,000	399.18	403.28	407.77	412.69	418.10	424.07	430.66
65,000	432.45	436.88	441.75	447.08	452.94	459.41	466.54
70,000	465.71	470.49	475.73	481.47	487.79	494.75	502.43
75,000	498.98	504.10	509.71	515.86	522.63	530.08	538.32
80,000	532.24	537.70	543.69	550.25	557.47	565.42	574.21
85,000	565.51	571.31	577.67	584.64	592.31	600.76	610.10
90,000	598.77	604.92	611.65	619.03	627.15	636.10	645.98
95,000	632.04	638.52	645.63	653.42	662.00	671.44	681.87
100,000	665.30	672.13	679.61	687.81	696.84	706.78	717.76
110,000	731.83	739.34	747.57	756.60	766.52	777.46	789.54
120,000	798.36	806.56	815.53	825.38	836.21	848.14	861.31
130,000	864.89	873.77	883.49	894.16	905.89	918.81	933.09
140,000	931.42	940.98	951.45	962.94	975.57	989.49	1004.86
150,000	997.95	1008.20	1019.41	1031.72	1045.26	1060.17	1076.64
200,000	1330.60	1344.26	1359.22	1375.63	1393.68	1413.56	1435.52
250,000	1663.26	1680.33	1699.02	1719.54	1742.09	1766.95	1794.40
300,000	1995.91	2016.39	2038.83	2063.44	2090.51	2120.34	2153.28
350,000	2328.56	2352.46	2378.63	2407.35	2438.93	2473.73	2512.16
400,000	2661.21	2688.52	2718.43	2751.26	2787.35	2827.12	2871.04
450,000	2993.86	3024.59	3058.24	3095.17	3135.77	3180.51	3229.92
500,000	3326.51	3360.65	3398.04	3439.07	3484.19	3533.90	3588.80
550,000	3659.16	3696.72	3737.85	3782.98	3832.61	3887.29	3947.68
600,000	3991.81	4032.78	4077.65	4126.89	4181.03	4240.68	4306.56
650,000	4324.47	4368.85	4417.46	4470.80	4529.44	4594.06	4665.44
700,000	4657.12	4704.91	4757.26	4814.70	4877.86	4947.45	5024.32
750,000	4989.77	5040.98	5097.06	5158.61	5226.28	5300.84	5383.20
800,000	5322.42	5377.04	5436.87	5502.52	5574.70	5654.23	5742.08
850,000	5655.07	5713.11	5776.67	5846.43	5923.12	6007.62	6100.96
900,000	5987.72	6049.17	6116.48	6190.33	6271.54	6361.01	6459.84
950,000	6320.37	6385.24	6456.28	6534.24	6619.96	6714.40	6818.72
1,000,000	6653.02	6721.30	6796.09	6878.15	6968.38	7067.79	7177.60

Monthly Payments 7%
Necessary to Amortize a Loan

AMOUNT BORROWED	\multicolumn{7}{c}{YEARS REMAINING IN TERM}
	23	22	21	20	15	10	5
100	0.73	0.74	0.76	0.78	0.90	1.16	1.98
200	1.46	1.49	1.52	1.55	1.80	2.32	3.96
300	2.19	2.23	2.28	2.33	2.70	3.48	5.94
400	2.92	2.97	3.03	3.10	3.60	4.64	7.92
500	3.65	3.72	3.79	3.88	4.49	5.81	9.90
600	4.38	4.46	4.55	4.65	5.39	6.97	11.88
700	5.11	5.20	5.31	5.43	6.29	8.13	13.86
800	5.84	5.95	6.07	6.20	7.19	9.29	15.84
900	6.57	6.69	6.83	6.98	8.09	10.45	17.82
1,000	7.30	7.43	7.58	7.75	8.99	11.61	19.80
2,000	14.60	14.87	15.17	15.51	17.98	23.22	39.60
3,000	21.90	22.30	22.75	23.26	26.96	34.83	59.40
4,000	29.20	29.74	30.34	31.01	35.95	46.44	79.20
5,000	36.50	37.17	37.92	38.76	44.94	58.05	99.01
6,000	43.80	44.61	45.51	46.52	53.93	69.67	118.81
7,000	51.09	52.04	53.09	54.27	62.92	81.28	138.61
8,000	58.39	59.47	60.68	62.02	71.91	92.89	158.41
9,000	65.69	66.91	68.26	69.78	80.89	104.50	178.21
10,000	72.99	74.34	75.85	77.53	89.88	116.11	198.01
15,000	109.49	111.51	113.77	116.29	134.82	174.16	297.02
20,000	145.98	148.68	151.69	155.05	179.77	232.22	396.02
25,000	182.48	185.86	189.62	193.82	224.71	290.27	495.03
30,000	218.98	223.03	227.54	232.59	269.65	348.33	594.04
35,000	255.47	260.20	265.47	271.35	314.59	406.38	693.04
40,000	291.97	297.37	303.39	310.12	359.53	464.43	792.05
45,000	328.46	334.54	341.31	348.88	404.47	522.49	891.05
50,000	364.96	371.71	379.24	387.65	449.41	580.54	990.06
55,000	401.46	408.88	417.16	426.41	494.36	638.60	1089.07
60,000	437.95	446.05	455.08	465.18	539.30	696.65	1188.07
65,000	474.45	483.23	493.01	503.94	584.24	754.71	1287.08
70,000	510.94	520.40	530.93	542.71	629.18	812.76	1386.08
75,000	547.44	557.57	568.85	581.47	674.12	870.81	1485.09
80,000	583.94	594.74	606.78	620.24	719.06	928.87	1584.10
85,000	620.43	631.91	644.70	659.00	764.00	986.92	1683.10
90,000	656.93	669.08	682.62	697.77	808.95	1044.98	1782.11
95,000	693.42	706.25	720.55	736.53	853.89	1103.03	1881.11
100,000	729.92	743.42	758.47	775.30	898.83	1161.08	1980.12
110,000	802.91	817.77	834.32	852.83	988.71	1277.19	2178.13
120,000	875.90	892.11	910.17	930.36	1078.59	1393.30	2376.14
130,000	948.89	966.45	986.01	1007.89	1168.48	1509.41	2574.16
140,000	1021.89	1040.79	1061.86	1085.42	1258.36	1625.52	2772.17
150,000	1094.88	1115.14	1137.71	1162.95	1348.24	1741.63	2970.18
200,000	1459.84	1486.85	1516.94	1550.60	1797.66	2322.17	3960.24
250,000	1824.80	1858.56	1896.18	1938.25	2247.07	2902.71	4950.30
300,000	2189.76	2230.27	2275.42	2325.90	2696.48	3483.25	5940.36
350,000	2554.72	2601.98	2654.65	2713.55	3145.90	4063.80	6930.42
400,000	2919.68	2973.70	3033.89	3101.20	3595.31	4644.34	7920.48
450,000	3284.64	3345.41	3413.12	3488.85	4044.73	5224.88	8910.54
500,000	3649.60	3717.12	3792.36	3876.49	4494.14	5805.42	9900.60
550,000	4014.56	4088.83	4171.59	4264.14	4943.56	6385.97	10890.66
600,000	4379.52	4460.54	4550.83	4651.79	5392.97	6966.51	11880.72
650,000	4744.47	4832.26	4930.07	5039.44	5842.38	7547.05	12870.78
700,000	5109.43	5203.97	5309.30	5427.09	6291.80	8127.59	13860.84
750,000	5474.39	5575.68	5688.54	5814.74	6741.21	8708.14	14850.90
800,000	5839.35	5947.39	6067.77	6202.39	7190.63	9288.68	15840.96
850,000	6204.31	6319.10	6447.01	6590.04	7640.04	9869.22	16831.02
900,000	6569.27	6690.82	6826.25	6977.69	8089.45	10449.76	17821.08
950,000	6934.23	7062.53	7205.48	7365.34	8538.87	11030.31	18811.14
1,000,000	7299.19	7434.24	7584.72	7752.99	8988.28	11610.85	19801.20

7¼%

Monthly Payments
Necessary to Amortize a Loan

AMOUNT BORROWED	YEARS REMAINING IN TERM						
	30	29	28	27	26	25	24
100	0.68	0.69	0.70	0.70	0.71	0.72	0.73
200	1.36	1.38	1.39	1.41	1.43	1.45	1.47
300	2.05	2.07	2.09	2.11	2.14	2.17	2.20
400	2.73	2.76	2.78	2.82	2.85	2.89	2.93
500	3.41	3.44	3.48	3.52	3.57	3.61	3.67
600	4.09	4.13	4.18	4.23	4.28	4.34	4.40
700	4.78	4.82	4.87	4.93	4.99	5.06	5.14
800	5.46	5.51	5.57	5.63	5.70	5.78	5.87
900	6.14	6.20	6.27	6.34	6.42	6.51	6.60
1,000	6.82	6.89	6.96	7.04	7.13	7.23	7.34
2,000	13.64	13.78	13.92	14.08	14.26	14.46	14.67
3,000	20.47	20.67	20.88	21.13	21.39	21.68	22.01
4,000	27.29	27.55	27.85	28.17	28.52	28.91	29.34
5,000	34.11	34.44	34.81	35.21	35.65	36.14	36.68
6,000	40.93	41.33	41.77	42.25	42.78	43.37	44.02
7,000	47.75	48.22	48.73	49.29	49.91	50.60	51.35
8,000	54.57	55.11	55.69	56.34	57.04	57.82	58.69
9,000	61.40	62.00	62.65	63.38	64.17	65.05	66.02
10,000	68.22	68.88	69.62	70.42	71.30	72.28	73.36
15,000	102.33	103.33	104.42	105.63	106.96	108.42	110.04
20,000	136.44	137.77	139.23	140.84	142.61	144.56	146.72
25,000	170.54	172.21	174.04	176.05	178.26	180.70	183.40
30,000	204.65	206.65	208.85	211.26	213.91	216.84	220.08
35,000	238.76	241.10	243.65	246.47	249.57	252.98	256.76
40,000	272.87	275.54	278.46	281.68	285.22	289.12	293.44
45,000	306.98	309.98	313.27	316.89	320.87	325.26	330.12
50,000	341.09	344.42	348.08	352.10	356.52	361.40	366.80
55,000	375.20	378.86	382.89	387.31	392.17	397.54	403.48
60,000	409.31	413.31	417.69	422.52	427.83	433.68	440.16
65,000	443.41	447.75	452.50	457.73	463.48	469.82	476.84
70,000	477.52	482.19	487.31	492.94	499.13	505.96	513.52
75,000	511.63	516.63	522.12	528.15	534.78	542.11	550.20
80,000	545.74	551.07	556.93	563.36	570.43	578.25	586.88
85,000	579.85	585.52	591.73	598.56	606.09	614.39	623.56
90,000	613.96	619.96	626.54	633.77	641.74	650.53	660.24
95,000	648.07	654.40	661.35	668.98	677.39	686.67	696.92
100,000	682.18	688.84	696.16	704.19	713.04	722.81	733.61
110,000	750.39	757.73	765.77	774.61	784.35	795.09	806.97
120,000	818.61	826.61	835.39	845.03	855.65	867.37	880.33
130,000	886.83	895.50	905.00	915.45	926.96	939.65	953.69
140,000	955.05	964.38	974.62	985.87	998.26	1011.93	1027.05
150,000	1023.26	1033.26	1044.24	1056.29	1069.56	1084.21	1100.41
200,000	1364.35	1377.69	1392.31	1408.39	1426.09	1445.61	1467.21
250,000	1705.44	1722.11	1740.39	1760.48	1782.61	1807.02	1834.01
300,000	2046.53	2066.53	2088.47	2112.58	2139.13	2168.42	2200.82
350,000	2387.62	2410.95	2436.55	2464.68	2495.65	2529.82	2567.62
400,000	2728.71	2755.37	2784.63	2816.78	2852.17	2891.23	2934.42
450,000	3069.79	3099.79	3132.71	3168.87	3208.69	3252.63	3301.22
500,000	3410.88	3444.22	3480.78	3520.97	3565.22	3614.03	3668.03
550,000	3751.97	3788.64	3828.86	3873.07	3921.74	3975.44	4034.83
600,000	4093.06	4133.06	4176.94	4225.16	4278.26	4336.84	4401.63
650,000	4434.15	4477.48	4525.02	4577.26	4634.78	4698.24	4768.43
700,000	4775.23	4821.90	4873.10	4929.36	4991.30	5059.65	5135.24
750,000	5116.32	5166.32	5221.18	5281.45	5347.82	5421.05	5502.04
800,000	5457.41	5510.75	5569.26	5633.55	5704.34	5782.45	5868.84
850,000	5798.50	5855.17	5917.33	5985.65	6060.87	6143.86	6235.64
900,000	6139.59	6199.59	6265.41	6337.75	6417.39	6505.26	6602.45
950,000	6480.67	6544.01	6613.49	6689.84	6773.91	6866.67	6969.25
1,000,000	6821.76	6888.43	6961.57	7041.94	7130.43	7228.07	7336.05

Monthly Payments

7¹/₄%

Necessary to Amortize a Loan

AMOUNT BORROWED	YEARS REMAINING IN TERM						
	23	22	21	20	15	10	5
100	0.75	0.76	0.77	0.79	0.91	1.17	1.99
200	1.49	1.52	1.55	1.58	1.83	2.35	3.98
300	2.24	2.28	2.32	2.37	2.74	3.52	5.98
400	2.98	3.04	3.09	3.16	3.65	4.70	7.97
500	3.73	3.79	3.87	3.95	4.56	5.87	9.96
600	4.47	4.55	4.64	4.74	5.48	7.04	11.95
700	5.22	5.31	5.42	5.53	6.39	8.22	13.94
800	5.96	6.07	6.19	6.32	7.30	9.39	15.94
900	6.71	6.83	6.96	7.11	8.22	10.57	17.93
1,000	7.46	7.59	7.74	7.90	9.13	11.74	19.92
2,000	14.91	15.18	15.47	15.81	18.26	23.48	39.84
3,000	22.37	22.77	23.21	23.71	27.39	35.22	59.76
4,000	29.82	30.36	30.95	31.62	36.51	46.96	79.68
5,000	37.28	37.94	38.69	39.52	45.64	58.70	99.60
6,000	44.73	45.53	46.42	47.42	54.77	70.44	119.52
7,000	52.19	53.12	54.16	55.33	63.90	82.18	139.44
8,000	59.65	60.71	61.90	63.23	73.03	93.92	159.35
9,000	67.10	68.30	69.64	71.13	82.16	105.66	179.27
10,000	74.56	75.89	77.37	79.04	91.29	117.40	199.19
15,000	111.84	113.83	116.06	118.56	136.93	176.10	298.79
20,000	149.12	151.78	154.75	158.08	182.57	234.80	398.39
25,000	186.39	189.72	193.44	197.59	228.22	293.50	497.98
30,000	223.67	227.67	232.12	237.11	273.86	352.20	597.58
35,000	260.95	265.61	270.81	276.63	319.50	410.90	697.18
40,000	298.23	303.56	309.50	316.15	365.15	469.60	796.77
45,000	335.51	341.50	348.19	355.67	410.79	528.30	896.37
50,000	372.79	379.45	386.87	395.19	456.43	587.01	995.97
55,000	410.07	417.39	425.56	434.71	502.07	645.71	1095.56
60,000	447.35	455.34	464.25	474.23	547.72	704.41	1195.16
65,000	484.63	493.28	502.94	513.74	593.36	763.11	1294.76
70,000	521.91	531.23	541.62	553.26	639.00	821.81	1394.36
75,000	559.18	569.17	580.31	592.78	684.65	880.51	1493.95
80,000	596.46	607.11	619.00	632.30	730.29	939.21	1593.55
85,000	633.74	645.06	657.68	671.82	775.93	997.91	1693.15
90,000	671.02	683.00	696.37	711.34	821.58	1056.61	1792.74
95,000	708.30	720.95	735.06	750.86	867.22	1115.31	1892.34
100,000	745.58	758.89	773.75	790.38	912.86	1174.01	1991.94
110,000	820.14	834.78	851.12	869.41	1004.15	1291.41	2191.13
120,000	894.69	910.67	928.50	948.45	1095.44	1408.81	2390.32
130,000	969.25	986.56	1005.87	1027.49	1186.72	1526.21	2589.52
140,000	1043.81	1062.45	1083.25	1106.53	1278.01	1643.61	2788.71
150,000	1118.37	1138.34	1160.62	1185.56	1369.29	1761.02	2987.90
200,000	1491.16	1517.79	1547.49	1580.75	1825.73	2348.02	3983.87
250,000	1863.95	1897.23	1934.37	1975.94	2282.16	2935.03	4979.84
300,000	2236.74	2276.68	2321.24	2371.13	2738.59	3522.03	5975.81
350,000	2609.53	2656.13	2708.11	2766.32	3195.02	4109.04	6971.78
400,000	2982.31	3035.57	3094.99	3161.50	3651.45	4696.04	7967.74
450,000	3355.10	3415.02	3481.86	3556.69	4107.88	5283.05	8963.71
500,000	3727.89	3794.47	3868.73	3951.88	4564.31	5870.05	9959.68
550,000	4100.68	4173.91	4255.61	4347.07	5020.75	6457.06	10955.65
600,000	4473.47	4553.36	4642.48	4742.26	5477.18	7044.06	11951.62
650,000	4846.26	4932.81	5029.35	5137.44	5933.61	7631.07	12947.58
700,000	5219.05	5312.25	5416.23	5532.63	6390.04	8218.07	13943.55
750,000	5591.84	5691.70	5803.10	5927.82	6846.47	8805.08	14939.52
800,000	5964.63	6071.15	6189.97	6323.01	7302.90	9392.08	15935.49
850,000	6337.42	6450.59	6576.85	6718.20	7759.33	9979.09	16931.46
900,000	6710.21	6830.04	6963.72	7113.38	8215.77	10566.09	17927.43
950,000	7083.00	7209.49	7350.59	7508.57	8672.20	11153.10	18923.39
1,000,000	7455.79	7588.93	7737.47	7903.76	9128.63	11740.10	19919.36

7½%

Monthly Payments
Necessary to Amortize a Loan

AMOUNT BORROWED	YEARS REMAINING IN TERM						
	30	29	28	27	26	25	24
100	0.70	0.71	0.71	0.72	0.73	0.74	0.75
200	1.40	1.41	1.43	1.44	1.46	1.48	1.50
300	2.10	2.12	2.14	2.16	2.19	2.22	2.25
400	2.80	2.82	2.85	2.88	2.92	2.96	3.00
500	3.50	3.53	3.56	3.60	3.65	3.69	3.75
600	4.20	4.23	4.28	4.32	4.38	4.43	4.50
700	4.89	4.94	4.99	5.05	5.11	5.17	5.25
800	5.59	5.65	5.70	5.77	5.84	5.91	6.00
900	6.29	6.35	6.42	6.49	6.56	6.65	6.75
1,000	6.99	7.06	7.13	7.21	7.29	7.39	7.50
2,000	13.98	14.11	14.26	14.41	14.59	14.78	14.99
3,000	20.98	21.17	21.39	21.62	21.88	22.17	22.49
4,000	27.97	28.23	28.51	28.83	29.18	29.56	29.98
5,000	34.96	35.29	35.64	36.04	36.47	36.95	37.48
6,000	41.95	42.34	42.77	43.24	43.76	44.34	44.98
7,000	48.95	49.40	49.90	50.45	51.06	51.73	52.47
8,000	55.94	56.46	57.03	57.66	58.35	59.12	59.97
9,000	62.93	63.51	64.16	64.87	65.65	66.51	67.46
10,000	69.92	70.57	71.29	72.07	72.94	73.90	74.96
15,000	104.88	105.86	106.93	108.11	109.41	110.85	112.44
20,000	139.84	141.14	142.57	144.15	145.88	147.80	149.92
25,000	174.80	176.43	178.22	180.18	182.35	184.75	187.40
30,000	209.76	211.72	213.86	216.22	218.82	221.70	224.88
35,000	244.73	247.00	249.50	252.26	255.29	258.65	262.36
40,000	279.69	282.29	285.15	288.29	291.76	295.60	299.84
45,000	314.65	317.57	320.79	324.33	328.23	332.55	337.32
50,000	349.61	352.86	356.43	360.37	364.70	369.50	374.80
55,000	384.57	388.15	392.08	396.40	401.17	406.45	412.28
60,000	419.53	423.43	427.72	432.44	437.64	443.39	449.76
65,000	454.49	458.72	463.36	468.48	474.11	480.34	487.24
70,000	489.45	494.00	499.01	504.51	510.59	517.29	524.72
75,000	524.41	529.29	534.65	540.55	547.06	554.24	562.20
80,000	559.37	564.58	570.29	576.59	583.53	591.19	599.68
85,000	594.33	599.86	605.94	612.62	620.00	628.14	637.16
90,000	629.29	635.15	641.58	648.66	656.47	665.09	674.64
95,000	664.25	670.43	677.22	684.70	692.94	702.04	712.12
100,000	699.21	705.72	712.87	720.73	729.41	738.99	749.60
110,000	769.14	776.29	784.15	792.81	802.35	812.89	824.57
120,000	839.06	846.86	855.44	864.88	875.29	886.79	899.53
130,000	908.98	917.44	926.73	936.95	948.23	960.69	974.49
140,000	978.90	988.01	998.01	1009.03	1021.17	1034.59	1049.45
150,000	1048.82	1058.58	1069.30	1081.10	1094.11	1108.49	1124.41
200,000	1398.43	1411.44	1425.74	1441.47	1458.81	1477.98	1499.21
250,000	1748.04	1764.30	1782.17	1801.83	1823.52	1847.48	1874.01
300,000	2097.64	2117.16	2138.60	2162.20	2188.22	2216.97	2248.81
350,000	2447.25	2470.02	2495.04	2522.57	2552.93	2586.47	2623.62
400,000	2796.86	2822.88	2851.47	2882.94	2917.63	2955.96	2998.42
450,000	3146.47	3175.74	3207.90	3243.30	3282.33	3325.46	3373.22
500,000	3496.07	3528.60	3564.34	3603.67	3647.04	3694.96	3748.02
550,000	3845.68	3881.46	3920.77	3964.04	4011.74	4064.45	4122.83
600,000	4195.29	4234.32	4277.21	4324.40	4376.44	4433.95	4497.63
650,000	4544.89	4587.18	4633.64	4684.77	4741.15	4803.44	4872.43
700,000	4894.50	4940.04	4990.07	5045.14	5105.85	5172.94	5247.23
750,000	5244.11	5292.90	5346.51	5405.50	5470.56	5542.43	5622.04
800,000	5593.72	5645.76	5702.94	5765.87	5835.26	5911.93	5996.84
850,000	5943.32	5998.62	6059.37	6126.24	6199.96	6281.43	6371.64
900,000	6292.93	6351.48	6415.81	6486.60	6564.67	6650.92	6746.44
950,000	6642.54	6704.34	6772.24	6846.97	6929.37	7020.42	7121.25
1,000,000	6992.15	7057.20	7128.68	7207.34	7294.07	7389.91	7496.05

Monthly Payments 7½%

Necessary to Amortize a Loan

AMOUNT BORROWED	YEARS REMAINING IN TERM						
	23	22	21	20	15	10	5
100	0.76	0.77	0.79	0.81	0.93	1.19	2.00
200	1.52	1.55	1.58	1.61	1.85	2.37	4.01
300	2.28	2.32	2.37	2.42	2.78	3.56	6.01
400	3.05	3.10	3.16	3.22	3.71	4.75	8.02
500	3.81	3.87	3.95	4.03	4.64	5.94	10.02
600	4.57	4.65	4.73	4.83	5.56	7.12	12.02
700	5.33	5.42	5.52	5.64	6.49	8.31	14.03
800	6.09	6.20	6.31	6.44	7.42	9.50	16.03
900	6.85	6.97	7.10	7.25	8.34	10.68	18.03
1,000	7.61	7.75	7.89	8.06	9.27	11.87	20.04
2,000	15.23	15.49	15.78	16.11	18.54	23.74	40.08
3,000	22.84	23.24	23.67	24.17	27.81	35.61	60.11
4,000	30.46	30.98	31.57	32.22	37.08	47.48	80.15
5,000	38.07	38.73	39.46	40.28	46.35	59.35	100.19
6,000	45.68	46.47	47.35	48.34	55.62	71.22	120.23
7,000	53.30	54.22	55.24	56.39	64.89	83.09	140.27
8,000	60.91	61.96	63.13	64.45	74.16	94.96	160.30
9,000	68.53	69.71	71.02	72.50	83.43	106.83	180.34
10,000	76.14	77.45	78.92	80.56	92.70	118.70	200.38
15,000	114.21	116.18	118.37	120.84	139.05	178.05	300.57
20,000	152.28	154.90	157.83	161.12	185.40	237.40	400.76
25,000	190.35	193.63	197.29	201.40	231.75	296.75	500.95
30,000	228.42	232.35	236.75	241.68	278.10	356.11	601.14
35,000	266.49	271.08	276.21	281.96	324.45	415.46	701.33
40,000	304.56	309.80	315.67	322.24	370.80	474.81	801.52
45,000	342.63	348.53	355.12	362.52	417.16	534.16	901.71
50,000	380.69	387.26	394.58	402.80	463.51	593.51	1001.90
55,000	418.76	425.98	434.04	443.08	509.86	652.86	1102.09
60,000	456.83	464.71	473.50	483.36	556.21	712.21	1202.28
65,000	494.90	503.43	512.96	523.64	602.56	771.56	1302.47
70,000	532.97	542.16	552.42	563.92	648.91	830.91	1402.66
75,000	571.04	580.88	591.87	604.19	695.26	890.26	1502.85
80,000	609.11	619.61	631.33	644.47	741.61	949.61	1603.04
85,000	647.18	658.33	670.79	684.75	787.96	1008.97	1703.23
90,000	685.25	697.06	710.25	725.03	834.31	1068.32	1803.42
95,000	723.32	735.78	749.71	765.31	880.66	1127.67	1903.61
100,000	761.39	774.51	789.17	805.59	927.01	1187.02	2003.79
110,000	837.53	851.96	868.08	886.15	1019.71	1305.72	2204.17
120,000	913.67	929.41	947.00	966.71	1112.41	1424.42	2404.55
130,000	989.81	1006.86	1025.92	1047.27	1205.12	1543.12	2604.93
140,000	1065.94	1084.31	1104.83	1127.83	1297.82	1661.82	2805.31
150,000	1142.08	1161.77	1183.75	1208.39	1390.52	1780.53	3005.69
200,000	1522.78	1549.02	1578.33	1611.19	1854.02	2374.04	4007.59
250,000	1903.47	1936.28	1972.92	2013.98	2317.53	2967.54	5009.49
300,000	2284.17	2323.53	2367.50	2416.78	2781.04	3561.05	6011.38
350,000	2664.86	2710.79	2762.08	2819.58	3244.54	4154.56	7013.28
400,000	3045.56	3098.04	3156.66	3222.37	3708.05	4748.07	8015.18
450,000	3426.25	3485.30	3551.25	3625.17	4171.56	5341.58	9017.08
500,000	3806.95	3872.55	3945.83	4027.97	4635.06	5935.09	10018.97
550,000	4187.64	4259.81	4340.41	4430.76	5098.57	6528.60	11020.87
600,000	4568.34	4647.06	4735.00	4833.56	5562.07	7122.11	12022.77
650,000	4949.03	5034.32	5129.58	5236.36	6025.58	7715.61	13024.67
700,000	5329.72	5421.57	5524.16	5639.15	6489.09	8309.12	14026.56
750,000	5710.42	5808.83	5918.75	6041.95	6952.59	8902.63	15028.46
800,000	6091.11	6196.08	6313.33	6444.75	7416.10	9496.14	16030.36
850,000	6471.81	6583.34	6707.91	6847.54	7879.61	10089.65	17032.26
900,000	6852.50	6970.59	7102.49	7250.34	8343.11	10683.16	18034.15
950,000	7233.20	7357.85	7497.08	7653.14	8806.62	11276.67	19036.05
1,000,000	7613.89	7745.10	7891.66	8055.93	9270.12	11870.18	20037.95

Monthly Payments
Necessary to Amortize a Loan

AMOUNT BORROWED	YEARS REMAINING IN TERM						
	30	29	28	27	26	25	24
100	0.72	0.72	0.73	0.74	0.75	0.76	0.77
200	1.43	1.45	1.46	1.47	1.49	1.51	1.53
300	2.15	2.17	2.19	2.21	2.24	2.27	2.30
400	2.87	2.89	2.92	2.95	2.98	3.02	3.06
500	3.58	3.61	3.65	3.69	3.73	3.78	3.83
600	4.30	4.34	4.38	4.42	4.48	4.53	4.59
700	5.01	5.06	5.11	5.16	5.22	5.29	5.36
800	5.73	5.78	5.84	5.90	5.97	6.04	6.13
900	6.45	6.50	6.57	6.64	6.71	6.80	6.89
1,000	7.16	7.23	7.30	7.37	7.46	7.55	7.66
2,000	14.33	14.46	14.59	14.75	14.92	15.11	15.32
3,000	21.49	21.68	21.89	22.12	22.38	22.66	22.97
4,000	28.66	28.91	29.19	29.50	29.84	30.21	30.63
5,000	35.82	36.14	36.49	36.87	37.30	37.77	38.29
6,000	42.98	43.37	43.78	44.25	44.76	45.32	45.95
7,000	50.15	50.59	51.08	51.62	52.21	52.87	53.60
8,000	57.31	57.82	58.38	58.99	59.67	60.43	61.26
9,000	64.48	65.05	65.68	66.37	67.13	67.98	68.92
10,000	71.64	72.28	72.97	73.74	74.59	75.53	76.58
15,000	107.46	108.41	109.46	110.61	111.89	113.30	114.86
20,000	143.28	144.55	145.95	147.49	149.19	151.07	153.15
25,000	179.10	180.69	182.43	184.36	186.48	188.83	191.44
30,000	214.92	216.83	218.92	221.23	223.78	226.60	229.73
35,000	250.74	252.96	255.41	258.10	261.07	264.37	268.01
40,000	286.56	289.10	291.89	294.97	298.37	302.13	306.30
45,000	322.39	325.24	328.38	331.84	335.67	339.90	344.59
50,000	358.21	361.38	364.87	368.72	372.96	377.66	382.88
55,000	394.03	397.52	401.35	405.59	410.26	415.43	421.17
60,000	429.85	433.65	437.84	442.46	447.56	453.20	459.45
65,000	465.67	469.79	474.33	479.33	484.85	490.96	497.74
70,000	501.49	505.93	510.82	516.20	522.15	528.73	536.03
75,000	537.31	542.07	547.30	553.07	559.45	566.50	574.32
80,000	573.13	578.20	583.79	589.94	596.74	604.26	612.60
85,000	608.95	614.34	620.28	626.82	634.04	642.03	650.89
90,000	644.77	650.48	656.76	663.69	671.33	679.80	689.18
95,000	680.59	686.62	693.25	700.56	708.63	717.56	727.47
100,000	716.41	722.76	729.74	737.43	745.93	755.33	765.76
110,000	788.05	795.03	802.71	811.17	820.52	830.86	842.33
120,000	859.69	867.31	875.68	884.92	895.11	906.39	918.91
130,000	931.34	939.58	948.66	958.66	969.71	981.93	995.48
140,000	1002.98	1011.86	1021.63	1032.40	1044.30	1057.46	1072.06
150,000	1074.62	1084.13	1094.60	1106.15	1118.89	1132.99	1148.63
200,000	1432.82	1445.51	1459.47	1474.86	1491.85	1510.66	1531.51
250,000	1791.03	1806.89	1824.34	1843.58	1864.82	1888.32	1914.39
300,000	2149.24	2168.27	2189.21	2212.29	2237.78	2265.99	2297.27
350,000	2507.44	2529.65	2554.08	2581.01	2610.74	2643.65	2680.14
400,000	2865.65	2891.02	2918.95	2949.72	2983.71	3021.32	3063.02
450,000	3223.86	3252.40	3283.81	3318.44	3356.67	3398.98	3445.90
500,000	3582.06	3613.78	3648.68	3687.15	3729.64	3776.64	3828.78
550,000	3940.27	3975.16	4013.55	4055.87	4102.60	4154.31	4211.66
600,000	4298.47	4336.53	4378.42	4424.58	4475.56	4531.97	4594.53
650,000	4656.68	4697.91	4743.29	4793.30	4848.53	4909.64	4977.41
700,000	5014.89	5059.29	5108.15	5162.01	5221.49	5287.30	5360.29
750,000	5373.09	5420.67	5473.02	5530.73	5594.45	5664.97	5743.17
800,000	5731.30	5782.05	5837.89	5899.44	5967.42	6042.63	6126.04
850,000	6089.50	6143.42	6202.76	6268.16	6340.38	6420.29	6508.92
900,000	6447.71	6504.80	6567.63	6636.87	6713.34	6797.96	6891.80
950,000	6805.92	6866.18	6932.49	7005.59	7086.31	7175.62	7274.68
1,000,000	7164.12	7227.56	7297.36	7374.30	7459.27	7553.29	7657.56

Monthly Payments

Necessary to Amortize a Loan

7³/₄%

AMOUNT BORROWED	23	22	21	20	15	10	5
			YEARS REMAINING IN TERM				
100	0.78	0.79	0.80	0.82	0.94	1.20	2.02
200	1.55	1.58	1.61	1.64	1.88	2.40	4.03
300	2.33	2.37	2.41	2.46	2.82	3.60	6.05
400	3.11	3.16	3.22	3.28	3.77	4.80	8.06
500	3.89	3.95	4.02	4.10	4.71	6.00	10.08
600	4.66	4.74	4.83	4.93	5.65	7.20	12.09
700	5.44	5.53	5.63	5.75	6.59	8.40	14.11
800	6.22	6.32	6.44	6.57	7.53	9.60	16.13
900	7.00	7.11	7.24	7.39	8.47	10.80	18.14
1,000	7.77	7.90	8.05	8.21	9.41	12.00	20.16
2,000	15.55	15.81	16.09	16.42	18.83	24.00	40.31
3,000	23.32	23.71	24.14	24.63	28.24	36.00	60.47
4,000	31.09	31.61	32.19	32.84	37.65	48.00	80.63
5,000	38.87	39.51	40.24	41.05	47.06	60.01	100.78
6,000	46.64	47.42	48.28	49.26	56.48	72.01	120.94
7,000	54.41	55.32	56.33	57.47	65.89	84.01	141.10
8,000	62.19	63.22	64.38	65.68	75.30	96.01	161.26
9,000	69.96	71.12	72.43	73.89	84.71	108.01	181.41
10,000	77.73	79.03	80.47	82.09	94.13	120.01	201.57
15,000	116.60	118.54	120.71	123.14	141.19	180.02	302.35
20,000	155.47	158.05	160.95	164.19	188.26	240.02	403.14
25,000	194.34	197.57	201.18	205.24	235.32	300.03	503.92
30,000	233.20	237.08	241.42	246.28	282.38	360.03	604.71
35,000	272.07	276.60	281.65	287.33	329.45	420.04	705.49
40,000	310.94	316.11	321.89	328.38	376.51	480.04	806.28
45,000	349.81	355.62	362.13	369.43	423.57	540.05	907.06
50,000	388.67	395.14	402.36	410.47	470.64	600.05	1007.85
55,000	427.54	434.65	442.60	451.52	517.70	660.06	1108.63
60,000	466.41	474.16	482.84	492.57	564.77	720.06	1209.42
65,000	505.28	513.68	523.07	533.62	611.83	780.07	1310.20
70,000	544.14	553.19	563.31	574.66	658.89	840.07	1410.99
75,000	583.01	592.70	603.55	615.71	705.96	900.08	1511.77
80,000	621.88	632.22	643.78	656.76	753.02	960.09	1612.56
85,000	660.75	671.73	684.02	697.81	800.08	1020.09	1713.34
90,000	699.61	711.25	724.25	738.85	847.15	1080.10	1814.13
95,000	738.48	750.76	764.49	779.90	894.21	1140.10	1914.91
100,000	777.35	790.27	804.73	820.95	941.28	1200.11	2015.70
110,000	855.08	869.30	885.20	903.04	1035.40	1320.12	2217.27
120,000	932.82	948.33	965.67	985.14	1129.53	1440.13	2418.84
130,000	1010.55	1027.35	1046.15	1067.23	1223.66	1560.14	2620.40
140,000	1088.29	1106.38	1126.62	1149.33	1317.79	1680.15	2821.97
150,000	1166.02	1185.41	1207.09	1231.42	1411.91	1800.16	3023.54
200,000	1554.70	1580.55	1609.45	1641.90	1882.55	2400.21	4031.39
250,000	1943.37	1975.68	2011.82	2052.37	2353.19	3000.27	5039.24
300,000	2332.04	2370.82	2414.18	2462.85	2823.83	3600.32	6047.09
350,000	2720.72	2765.95	2816.55	2873.32	3294.47	4200.37	7054.94
400,000	3109.39	3161.09	3218.91	3283.79	3765.10	4800.43	8062.78
450,000	3498.07	3556.23	3621.27	3694.27	4235.74	5400.48	9070.63
500,000	3886.74	3951.36	4023.64	4104.74	4706.38	6000.53	10078.48
550,000	4275.41	4346.50	4426.00	4515.22	5177.02	6600.58	11086.33
600,000	4664.09	4741.64	4828.36	4925.69	5647.65	7200.64	12094.18
650,000	5052.76	5136.77	5230.73	5336.17	6118.29	7800.69	13102.02
700,000	5441.44	5531.91	5633.09	5746.64	6588.93	8400.74	14109.87
750,000	5830.11	5927.05	6035.45	6157.11	7059.57	9000.80	15117.72
800,000	6218.79	6322.18	6437.82	6567.59	7530.21	9600.85	16125.57
850,000	6607.46	6717.32	6840.18	6978.06	8000.84	10200.90	17133.42
900,000	6996.13	7112.45	7242.54	7388.54	8471.48	10800.96	18141.26
950,000	7384.81	7507.59	7644.91	7799.01	8942.12	11401.01	19149.11
1,000,000	7773.48	7902.73	8047.27	8209.49	9412.76	12001.06	20156.96

Monthly Payments
Necessary to Amortize a Loan

AMOUNT BORROWED	YEARS REMAINING IN TERM						
	30	29	28	27	26	25	24
100	0.73	0.74	0.75	0.75	0.76	0.77	0.78
200	1.47	1.48	1.49	1.51	1.53	1.54	1.56
300	2.20	2.22	2.24	2.26	2.29	2.32	2.35
400	2.94	2.96	2.99	3.02	3.05	3.09	3.13
500	3.67	3.70	3.73	3.77	3.81	3.86	3.91
600	4.40	4.44	4.48	4.53	4.58	4.63	4.69
700	5.14	5.18	5.23	5.28	5.34	5.40	5.47
800	5.87	5.92	5.97	6.03	6.10	6.17	6.26
900	6.60	6.66	6.72	6.79	6.86	6.95	7.04
1,000	7.34	7.40	7.47	7.54	7.63	7.72	7.82
2,000	14.68	14.80	14.94	15.09	15.25	15.44	15.64
3,000	22.01	22.20	22.40	22.63	22.88	23.15	23.46
4,000	29.35	29.60	29.87	30.17	30.50	30.87	31.28
5,000	36.69	37.00	37.34	37.71	38.13	38.59	39.10
6,000	44.03	44.40	44.81	45.26	45.76	46.31	46.92
7,000	51.36	51.80	52.27	52.80	53.38	54.03	54.74
8,000	58.70	59.20	59.74	60.34	61.01	61.75	62.56
9,000	66.04	66.60	67.21	67.89	68.63	69.46	70.38
10,000	73.38	73.99	74.68	75.43	76.26	77.18	78.21
15,000	110.06	110.99	112.01	113.14	114.39	115.77	117.31
20,000	146.75	147.99	149.35	150.86	152.52	154.36	156.41
25,000	183.44	184.99	186.69	188.57	190.65	192.95	195.51
30,000	220.13	221.98	224.03	226.28	228.78	231.54	234.62
35,000	256.82	258.98	261.37	264.00	266.91	270.14	273.72
40,000	293.51	295.98	298.70	301.71	305.04	308.73	312.82
45,000	330.19	332.98	336.04	339.43	343.17	347.32	351.92
50,000	366.88	369.97	373.38	377.14	381.30	385.91	391.03
55,000	403.57	406.97	410.72	414.85	419.43	424.50	430.13
60,000	440.26	443.97	448.06	452.57	457.56	463.09	469.23
65,000	476.95	480.96	485.39	490.28	495.69	501.68	508.34
70,000	513.64	517.96	522.73	528.00	533.82	540.27	547.44
75,000	550.32	554.96	560.07	565.71	571.95	578.86	586.54
80,000	587.01	591.96	597.41	603.42	610.08	617.45	625.64
85,000	623.70	628.95	634.74	641.14	648.21	656.04	664.75
90,000	660.39	665.95	672.08	678.85	686.34	694.63	703.85
95,000	697.08	702.95	709.42	716.57	724.47	733.23	742.95
100,000	733.76	739.95	746.76	754.28	762.60	771.82	782.05
110,000	807.14	813.94	821.43	829.71	838.86	849.00	860.26
120,000	880.52	887.93	896.11	905.14	915.12	926.18	938.46
130,000	953.89	961.93	970.79	980.56	991.38	1003.36	1016.67
140,000	1027.27	1035.92	1045.46	1055.99	1067.64	1080.54	1094.88
150,000	1100.65	1109.92	1120.14	1131.42	1143.90	1157.72	1173.08
200,000	1467.53	1479.89	1493.52	1508.56	1525.20	1543.63	1564.11
250,000	1834.41	1849.86	1866.90	1885.70	1906.50	1929.54	1955.14
300,000	2201.29	2219.84	2240.28	2262.84	2287.79	2315.45	2346.16
350,000	2568.18	2589.81	2613.66	2639.98	2669.09	2701.36	2737.19
400,000	2935.06	2959.78	2987.03	3017.12	3050.39	3087.26	3128.22
450,000	3301.94	3329.76	3360.41	3394.26	3431.69	3473.17	3519.24
500,000	3668.82	3699.73	3733.79	3771.40	3812.99	3859.08	3910.27
550,000	4035.71	4069.70	4107.17	4148.54	4194.29	4244.99	4301.30
600,000	4402.59	4439.67	4480.55	4525.68	4575.59	4630.90	4692.32
650,000	4769.47	4809.65	4853.93	4902.82	4956.89	5016.81	5083.35
700,000	5136.35	5179.62	5227.31	5279.96	5338.19	5402.71	5474.38
750,000	5503.23	5549.59	5600.69	5657.10	5719.49	5788.62	5865.41
800,000	5870.12	5919.57	5974.07	6034.24	6100.78	6174.53	6256.43
850,000	6237.00	6289.54	6347.45	6411.38	6482.08	6560.44	6647.46
900,000	6603.88	6659.51	6720.83	6788.52	6863.38	6946.35	7038.49
950,000	6970.76	7029.49	7094.21	7165.66	7244.68	7332.25	7429.51
1,000,000	7337.65	7399.46	7467.59	7542.80	7625.98	7718.16	7820.54

Monthly Payments   8%
Necessary to Amortize a Loan

AMOUNT BORROWED	YEARS REMAINING IN TERM						
	23	22	21	20	15	10	5
100	0.79	0.81	0.82	0.84	0.96	1.21	2.03
200	1.59	1.61	1.64	1.67	1.91	2.43	4.06
300	2.38	2.42	2.46	2.51	2.87	3.64	6.08
400	3.17	3.22	3.28	3.35	3.82	4.85	8.11
500	3.97	4.03	4.10	4.18	4.78	6.07	10.14
600	4.76	4.84	4.92	5.02	5.73	7.28	12.17
700	5.55	5.64	5.74	5.86	6.69	8.49	14.19
800	6.35	6.45	6.56	6.69	7.65	9.71	16.22
900	7.14	7.26	7.38	7.53	8.60	10.92	18.25
1,000	7.93	8.06	8.20	8.36	9.56	12.13	20.28
2,000	15.87	16.12	16.41	16.73	19.11	24.27	40.55
3,000	23.80	24.19	24.61	25.09	28.67	36.40	60.83
4,000	31.74	32.25	32.82	33.46	38.23	48.53	81.11
5,000	39.67	40.31	41.02	41.82	47.78	60.66	101.38
6,000	47.61	48.37	49.23	50.19	57.34	72.80	121.66
7,000	55.54	56.43	57.43	58.55	66.90	84.93	141.93
8,000	63.48	64.49	65.63	66.92	76.45	97.06	162.21
9,000	71.41	72.56	73.84	75.28	86.01	109.19	182.49
10,000	79.35	80.62	82.04	83.64	95.57	121.33	202.76
15,000	119.02	120.93	123.06	125.47	143.35	181.99	304.15
20,000	158.69	161.24	164.09	167.29	191.13	242.66	405.53
25,000	198.36	201.54	205.11	209.11	238.91	303.32	506.91
30,000	238.04	241.85	246.13	250.93	286.70	363.98	608.29
35,000	277.71	282.16	287.15	292.75	334.48	424.65	709.67
40,000	317.38	322.47	328.17	334.58	382.26	485.31	811.06
45,000	357.05	362.78	369.19	376.40	430.04	545.97	912.44
50,000	396.73	403.09	410.21	418.22	477.83	606.64	1013.82
55,000	436.40	443.40	451.24	460.04	525.61	667.30	1115.20
60,000	476.07	483.71	492.26	501.86	573.39	727.97	1216.58
65,000	515.74	524.02	533.28	543.69	621.17	788.63	1317.97
70,000	555.42	564.32	574.30	585.51	668.96	849.29	1419.35
75,000	595.09	604.63	615.32	627.33	716.74	909.96	1520.73
80,000	634.76	644.94	656.34	669.15	764.52	970.62	1622.11
85,000	674.43	685.25	697.36	710.97	812.30	1031.28	1723.49
90,000	714.11	725.56	738.39	752.80	860.09	1091.95	1824.88
95,000	753.78	765.87	779.41	794.62	907.87	1152.61	1926.26
100,000	793.45	806.18	820.43	836.44	955.65	1213.28	2027.64
110,000	872.80	886.80	902.47	920.08	1051.22	1334.60	2230.40
120,000	952.14	967.41	984.51	1003.73	1146.78	1455.93	2433.17
130,000	1031.49	1048.03	1066.56	1087.37	1242.35	1577.26	2635.93
140,000	1110.83	1128.65	1148.60	1171.02	1337.91	1698.59	2838.70
150,000	1190.18	1209.27	1230.64	1254.66	1433.48	1819.91	3041.46
200,000	1586.91	1612.36	1640.86	1672.88	1911.30	2426.55	4055.28
250,000	1983.63	2015.42	2051.07	2091.10	2389.13	3033.19	5069.10
300,000	2380.36	2418.53	2461.28	2509.32	2866.96	3639.83	6082.92
350,000	2777.08	2821.62	2871.50	2927.54	3344.78	4246.47	7096.74
400,000	3173.81	3224.71	3281.71	3345.76	3822.61	4853.10	8110.56
450,000	3570.54	3627.80	3691.93	3763.98	4300.43	5459.74	9124.38
500,000	3967.26	4030.89	4102.14	4182.20	4778.26	6066.38	10138.20
550,000	4363.99	4433.98	4512.35	4600.42	5256.09	6673.02	11152.02
600,000	4760.72	4837.07	4922.57	5018.64	5733.91	7279.66	12165.84
650,000	5157.44	5240.16	5332.78	5436.86	6211.74	7886.29	13179.66
700,000	5554.17	5643.25	5743.00	5855.08	6689.56	8492.93	14193.48
750,000	5950.89	6046.33	6153.21	6273.30	7167.39	9099.57	15207.30
800,000	6347.62	6449.42	6563.42	6691.52	7645.22	9706.21	16221.12
850,000	6744.35	6852.51	6973.64	7109.74	8123.04	10312.85	17234.94
900,000	7141.07	7255.60	7383.85	7527.96	8600.87	10919.48	18248.75
950,000	7537.80	7658.69	7794.07	7946.18	9078.69	11526.12	19262.57
1,000,000	7934.53	8061.78	8204.28	8364.40	9556.52	12132.76	20276.39

Monthly Payments
Necessary to Amortize a Loan

AMOUNT BORROWED	YEARS REMAINING IN TERM						
	30	29	28	27	26	25	24
100	0.75	0.76	0.76	0.77	0.78	0.79	0.80
200	1.50	1.51	1.53	1.54	1.56	1.58	1.60
300	2.25	2.27	2.29	2.31	2.34	2.37	2.40
400	3.01	3.03	3.06	3.09	3.12	3.15	3.19
500	3.76	3.79	3.82	3.86	3.90	3.94	3.99
600	4.51	4.54	4.58	4.63	4.68	4.73	4.79
700	5.26	5.30	5.35	5.40	5.46	5.52	5.59
800	6.01	6.06	6.11	6.17	6.24	6.31	6.39
900	6.76	6.82	6.88	6.94	7.01	7.10	7.19
1,000	7.51	7.57	7.64	7.71	7.79	7.88	7.98
2,000	15.03	15.15	15.28	15.43	15.59	15.77	15.97
3,000	22.54	22.72	22.92	23.14	23.38	23.65	23.95
4,000	30.05	30.29	30.56	30.85	31.18	31.54	31.94
5,000	37.56	37.86	38.20	38.56	38.97	39.42	39.92
6,000	45.08	45.44	45.84	46.28	46.77	47.31	47.91
7,000	52.59	53.01	53.48	53.99	54.56	55.19	55.89
8,000	60.10	60.58	61.11	61.70	62.35	63.08	63.88
9,000	67.61	68.16	68.75	69.42	70.15	70.96	71.86
10,000	75.13	75.73	76.39	77.13	77.94	78.85	79.85
15,000	112.69	113.59	114.59	115.69	116.91	118.27	119.77
20,000	150.25	151.46	152.79	154.26	155.88	157.69	159.70
25,000	187.82	189.32	190.98	192.82	194.85	197.11	199.62
30,000	225.38	227.19	229.18	231.38	233.83	236.54	239.55
35,000	262.94	265.05	267.38	269.95	272.80	275.96	279.47
40,000	300.51	302.91	305.57	308.51	311.77	315.38	319.40
45,000	338.07	340.78	343.77	347.07	350.74	354.80	359.32
50,000	375.63	378.64	381.97	385.64	389.71	394.23	399.25
55,000	413.20	416.51	420.16	424.20	428.68	433.65	439.17
60,000	450.76	454.37	458.36	462.77	467.65	473.07	479.10
65,000	488.32	492.24	496.55	501.33	506.62	512.49	519.02
70,000	525.89	530.10	534.75	539.89	545.59	551.92	558.95
75,000	563.45	567.96	572.95	578.46	584.56	591.34	598.87
80,000	601.01	605.83	611.14	617.02	623.53	630.76	638.80
85,000	638.58	643.69	649.34	655.59	662.50	670.18	678.72
90,000	676.14	681.56	687.54	694.15	701.48	709.61	718.65
95,000	713.70	719.42	725.73	732.71	740.45	749.03	758.57
100,000	751.27	757.29	763.93	771.28	779.42	788.45	798.50
110,000	826.39	833.01	840.32	848.41	857.36	867.30	878.35
120,000	901.52	908.74	916.72	925.53	935.30	946.14	958.20
130,000	976.65	984.47	993.11	1002.66	1013.24	1024.99	1038.05
140,000	1051.77	1060.20	1069.50	1079.79	1091.18	1103.83	1117.90
150,000	1126.90	1135.93	1145.90	1156.92	1169.13	1182.68	1197.75
200,000	1502.53	1514.57	1527.86	1542.56	1558.83	1576.90	1596.99
250,000	1878.17	1893.21	1909.83	1928.20	1948.54	1971.13	1996.24
300,000	2253.80	2271.86	2291.79	2313.83	2338.25	2365.35	2395.49
350,000	2629.43	2650.50	2673.76	2699.47	2727.96	2759.58	2794.74
400,000	3005.07	3029.14	3055.72	3085.11	3117.67	3153.80	3193.99
450,000	3380.70	3407.79	3437.69	3470.75	3507.38	3548.03	3593.24
500,000	3756.33	3786.43	3819.65	3856.39	3897.09	3942.25	3992.49
550,000	4131.97	4165.07	4201.62	4242.03	4286.79	4336.48	4391.74
600,000	4507.60	4543.71	4583.58	4627.67	4676.50	4730.70	4790.98
650,000	4883.23	4922.36	4965.55	5013.31	5066.21	5124.93	5190.23
700,000	5258.87	5301.00	5347.51	5398.95	5455.92	5519.15	5589.48
750,000	5634.50	5679.64	5729.48	5784.59	5845.63	5913.38	5988.73
800,000	6010.13	6058.28	6111.44	6170.22	6235.34	6307.60	6387.98
850,000	6385.77	6436.93	6493.41	6555.86	6625.04	6701.83	6787.23
900,000	6761.40	6815.57	6875.37	6941.50	7014.75	7096.05	7186.48
950,000	7137.03	7194.21	7257.34	7327.14	7404.46	7490.28	7585.73
1,000,000	7512.67	7572.86	7639.30	7712.78	7794.17	7884.50	7984.97

Monthly Payments 8¼%
Necessary to Amortize a Loan

YEARS REMAINING IN TERM

AMOUNT BORROWED	23	22	21	20	15	10	5
100	0.81	0.82	0.84	0.85	0.97	1.23	2.04
200	1.62	1.64	1.67	1.70	1.94	2.45	4.08
300	2.43	2.47	2.51	2.56	2.91	3.68	6.12
400	3.24	3.29	3.35	3.41	3.88	4.91	8.16
500	4.05	4.11	4.18	4.26	4.85	6.13	10.20
600	4.86	4.93	5.02	5.11	5.82	7.36	12.24
700	5.67	5.76	5.85	5.96	6.79	8.59	14.28
800	6.48	6.58	6.69	6.82	7.76	9.81	16.32
900	7.29	7.40	7.53	7.67	8.73	11.04	18.36
1,000	8.10	8.22	8.36	8.52	9.70	12.27	20.40
2,000	16.19	16.44	16.73	17.04	19.40	24.53	40.79
3,000	24.29	24.67	25.09	25.56	29.10	36.80	61.19
4,000	32.39	32.89	33.45	34.08	38.81	49.06	81.59
5,000	40.48	41.11	41.81	42.60	48.51	61.33	101.98
6,000	48.58	49.33	50.18	51.12	58.21	73.59	122.38
7,000	56.68	57.56	58.54	59.64	67.91	85.86	142.77
8,000	64.78	65.78	66.90	68.17	77.61	98.12	163.17
9,000	72.87	74.00	75.26	76.69	87.31	110.39	183.57
10,000	80.97	82.22	83.63	85.21	97.01	122.65	203.96
15,000	121.45	123.33	125.44	127.81	145.52	183.98	305.94
20,000	161.94	164.44	167.25	170.41	194.03	245.31	407.93
25,000	202.42	205.56	209.07	213.02	242.54	306.63	509.91
30,000	242.90	246.67	250.88	255.62	291.04	367.96	611.89
35,000	283.39	287.78	292.69	298.22	339.55	429.28	713.87
40,000	323.88	328.89	334.51	340.83	388.06	490.61	815.85
45,000	364.36	370.00	376.32	383.43	436.56	551.94	917.83
50,000	404.85	411.11	418.13	426.03	485.07	613.26	1019.81
55,000	445.33	452.22	459.95	468.64	533.58	674.59	1121.79
60,000	485.82	493.33	501.76	511.24	582.08	735.92	1223.78
65,000	526.30	534.45	543.57	553.84	630.59	797.24	1325.76
70,000	566.79	575.56	585.39	596.45	679.10	858.57	1427.74
75,000	607.27	616.67	627.20	639.05	727.61	919.89	1529.72
80,000	647.76	657.78	669.01	681.65	776.11	981.22	1631.70
85,000	688.24	698.89	710.83	724.26	824.62	1042.55	1733.68
90,000	728.73	740.00	752.64	766.86	873.13	1103.87	1835.66
95,000	769.21	781.11	794.45	809.46	921.63	1165.20	1937.64
100,000	809.70	822.22	836.27	852.07	970.14	1226.53	2039.63
110,000	890.67	904.45	919.89	937.27	1067.15	1349.18	2243.59
120,000	971.64	986.67	1003.52	1022.48	1164.17	1471.83	2447.55
130,000	1052.61	1068.89	1087.15	1107.69	1261.18	1594.48	2651.51
140,000	1133.58	1151.11	1170.77	1192.89	1358.20	1717.14	2855.48
150,000	1214.55	1233.33	1254.40	1278.10	1455.21	1839.79	3059.44
200,000	1619.40	1644.45	1672.53	1704.13	1940.28	2453.05	4079.25
250,000	2024.25	2055.56	2090.67	2130.16	2425.35	3066.32	5099.06
300,000	2429.10	2466.67	2508.80	2556.20	2910.42	3679.58	6118.88
350,000	2833.95	2877.78	2926.93	2982.23	3395.49	4292.84	7138.69
400,000	3238.80	3288.89	3345.06	3408.26	3880.56	4906.11	8158.50
450,000	3643.65	3700.00	3763.20	3834.30	4365.63	5519.37	9178.31
500,000	4048.50	4111.12	4181.33	4260.33	4850.70	6132.63	10198.13
550,000	4453.35	4522.23	4599.46	4686.36	5335.77	6745.89	11217.94
600,000	4858.20	4933.34	5017.60	5112.39	5820.84	7359.16	12237.75
650,000	5263.05	5344.45	5435.73	5538.43	6305.91	7972.42	13257.56
700,000	5667.90	5755.56	5853.86	5964.46	6790.98	8585.68	14277.38
750,000	6072.75	6166.67	6272.00	6390.49	7276.05	9198.95	15297.19
800,000	6477.60	6577.79	6690.13	6816.53	7761.12	9812.21	16317.00
850,000	6882.45	6988.90	7108.26	7242.56	8246.19	10425.47	17336.81
900,000	7287.30	7400.01	7526.39	7668.59	8731.26	11038.74	18356.63
950,000	7692.15	7811.12	7944.53	8094.62	9216.33	11652.00	19376.44
1,000,000	8097.00	8222.23	8362.66	8520.66	9701.40	12265.26	20396.25

8½% Monthly Payments
Necessary to Amortize a Loan

AMOUNT BORROWED	YEARS REMAINING IN TERM						
	30	29	28	27	26	25	24
100	0.77	0.77	0.78	0.79	0.80	0.81	0.82
200	1.54	1.55	1.56	1.58	1.59	1.61	1.63
300	2.31	2.32	2.34	2.37	2.39	2.42	2.45
400	3.08	3.10	3.12	3.15	3.19	3.22	3.26
500	3.84	3.87	3.91	3.94	3.98	4.03	4.08
600	4.61	4.65	4.69	4.73	4.78	4.83	4.89
700	5.38	5.42	5.47	5.52	5.57	5.64	5.71
800	6.15	6.20	6.25	6.31	6.37	6.44	6.52
900	6.92	6.97	7.03	7.10	7.17	7.25	7.34
1,000	7.69	7.75	7.81	7.88	7.96	8.05	8.15
2,000	15.38	15.50	15.62	15.77	15.93	16.10	16.30
3,000	23.07	23.24	23.44	23.65	23.89	24.16	24.45
4,000	30.76	30.99	31.25	31.54	31.86	32.21	32.60
5,000	38.45	38.74	39.06	39.42	39.82	40.26	40.75
6,000	46.13	46.49	46.87	47.31	47.78	48.31	48.90
7,000	53.82	54.23	54.69	55.19	55.75	56.37	57.06
8,000	61.51	61.98	62.50	63.07	63.71	64.42	65.21
9,000	69.20	69.73	70.31	70.96	71.67	72.47	73.36
10,000	76.89	77.48	78.12	78.84	79.64	80.52	81.51
15,000	115.34	116.22	117.19	118.26	119.46	120.78	122.26
20,000	153.78	154.95	156.25	157.68	159.28	161.05	163.02
25,000	192.23	193.69	195.31	197.11	199.09	201.31	203.77
30,000	230.67	232.43	234.37	236.53	238.91	241.57	244.52
35,000	269.12	271.17	273.44	275.95	278.73	281.83	285.28
40,000	307.57	309.91	312.50	315.37	318.55	322.09	326.03
45,000	346.01	348.65	351.56	354.79	358.37	362.35	366.79
50,000	384.46	387.39	390.62	394.21	398.19	402.61	407.54
55,000	422.90	426.12	429.69	433.63	438.01	442.87	448.30
60,000	461.35	464.86	468.75	473.05	477.83	483.14	489.05
65,000	499.79	503.60	507.81	512.47	517.65	523.40	529.80
70,000	538.24	542.34	546.87	551.89	557.47	563.66	570.56
75,000	576.69	581.08	585.94	591.32	597.28	603.92	611.31
80,000	615.13	619.82	625.00	630.74	637.10	644.18	652.07
85,000	653.58	658.55	664.06	670.16	676.92	684.44	692.82
90,000	692.02	697.29	703.12	709.58	716.74	724.70	733.57
95,000	730.47	736.03	742.19	749.00	756.56	764.97	774.33
100,000	768.91	774.77	781.25	788.42	796.38	805.23	815.08
110,000	845.80	852.25	859.37	867.26	876.02	885.75	896.59
120,000	922.70	929.72	937.50	946.11	955.66	966.27	978.10
130,000	999.59	1007.20	1015.62	1024.95	1035.29	1046.80	1059.61
140,000	1076.48	1084.68	1093.75	1103.79	1114.93	1127.32	1141.12
150,000	1153.37	1162.16	1171.87	1182.63	1194.57	1207.84	1222.62
200,000	1537.83	1549.54	1562.49	1576.84	1592.76	1610.45	1630.16
250,000	1922.28	1936.93	1953.12	1971.05	1990.95	2013.07	2037.71
300,000	2306.74	2324.31	2343.74	2365.26	2389.14	2415.68	2445.25
350,000	2691.20	2711.70	2734.37	2759.47	2787.33	2818.29	2852.79
400,000	3075.65	3099.08	3124.99	3153.68	3185.52	3220.91	3260.33
450,000	3460.11	3486.47	3515.61	3547.89	3583.71	3623.52	3667.87
500,000	3844.57	3873.85	3906.24	3942.11	3981.90	4026.14	4075.41
550,000	4229.02	4261.24	4296.86	4336.32	4380.09	4428.75	4482.95
600,000	4613.48	4648.62	4687.48	4730.53	4778.28	4831.36	4890.49
650,000	4997.94	5036.01	5078.11	5124.74	5176.47	5233.98	5298.04
700,000	5382.39	5423.39	5468.73	5518.95	5574.66	5636.59	5705.58
750,000	5766.85	5810.78	5859.36	5913.16	5972.85	6039.20	6113.12
800,000	6151.31	6198.16	6249.98	6307.37	6371.04	6441.82	6520.66
850,000	6535.76	6585.55	6640.60	6701.58	6769.23	6844.43	6928.20
900,000	6920.22	6972.93	7031.23	7095.79	7167.42	7247.04	7335.74
950,000	7304.68	7360.32	7421.85	7490.00	7565.61	7649.66	7743.28
1,000,000	7689.13	7747.70	7812.47	7884.21	7963.80	8052.27	8150.82

Monthly Payments 8½%
Necessary to Amortize a Loan

AMOUNT BORROWED	YEARS REMAINING IN TERM						
	23	22	21	20	15	10	5
100	0.83	0.84	0.85	0.87	0.98	1.24	2.05
200	1.65	1.68	1.70	1.74	1.97	2.48	4.10
300	2.48	2.52	2.56	2.60	2.95	3.72	6.15
400	3.30	3.35	3.41	3.47	3.94	4.96	8.21
500	4.13	4.19	4.26	4.34	4.92	6.20	10.26
600	4.96	5.03	5.11	5.21	5.91	7.44	12.31
700	5.78	5.87	5.97	6.07	6.89	8.68	14.36
800	6.61	6.71	6.82	6.94	7.88	9.92	16.41
900	7.43	7.55	7.67	7.81	8.86	11.16	18.46
1,000	8.26	8.38	8.52	8.68	9.85	12.40	20.52
2,000	16.52	16.77	17.04	17.36	19.69	24.80	41.03
3,000	24.78	25.15	25.57	26.03	29.54	37.20	61.55
4,000	33.04	33.54	34.09	34.71	39.39	49.59	82.07
5,000	41.30	41.92	42.61	43.39	49.24	61.99	102.58
6,000	49.57	50.30	51.13	52.07	59.08	74.39	123.10
7,000	57.83	58.69	59.66	60.75	68.93	86.79	143.62
8,000	66.09	67.07	68.18	69.43	78.78	99.19	164.13
9,000	74.35	75.46	76.70	78.10	88.63	111.59	184.65
10,000	82.61	83.84	85.22	86.78	98.47	123.99	205.17
15,000	123.91	125.76	127.84	130.17	147.71	185.98	307.75
20,000	165.22	167.68	170.45	173.56	196.95	247.97	410.33
25,000	206.52	209.60	213.06	216.96	246.18	309.96	512.91
30,000	247.83	251.52	255.67	260.35	295.42	371.96	615.50
35,000	289.13	293.44	298.28	303.74	344.66	433.95	718.08
40,000	330.43	335.36	340.90	347.13	393.90	495.94	820.66
45,000	371.74	377.28	383.51	390.52	443.13	557.94	923.24
50,000	413.04	419.20	426.12	433.91	492.37	619.93	1025.83
55,000	454.35	461.12	468.73	477.30	541.61	681.92	1128.41
60,000	495.65	503.04	511.34	520.69	590.84	743.91	1230.99
65,000	536.96	544.96	553.96	564.09	640.08	805.91	1333.57
70,000	578.26	586.88	596.57	607.48	689.32	867.90	1436.16
75,000	619.56	628.80	639.18	650.87	738.55	929.89	1538.74
80,000	660.87	670.72	681.79	694.26	787.79	991.89	1641.32
85,000	702.17	712.65	724.40	737.65	837.03	1053.88	1743.91
90,000	743.48	754.57	767.02	781.04	886.27	1115.87	1846.49
95,000	784.78	796.49	809.63	824.43	935.50	1177.86	1949.07
100,000	826.09	838.41	852.24	867.82	984.74	1239.86	2051.65
110,000	908.70	922.25	937.46	954.61	1083.21	1363.84	2256.82
120,000	991.30	1006.09	1022.69	1041.39	1181.69	1487.83	2461.98
130,000	1073.91	1089.93	1107.91	1128.17	1280.16	1611.81	2667.15
140,000	1156.52	1173.77	1193.13	1214.95	1378.64	1735.80	2872.31
150,000	1239.13	1257.61	1278.36	1301.73	1477.11	1859.79	3077.48
200,000	1652.17	1676.81	1704.48	1735.65	1969.48	2479.71	4103.31
250,000	2065.22	2096.02	2130.60	2169.56	2461.85	3099.64	5129.13
300,000	2478.26	2515.22	2556.72	2603.47	2954.22	3719.57	6154.96
350,000	2891.30	2934.42	2982.84	3037.38	3446.59	4339.50	7180.79
400,000	3304.35	3353.62	3408.96	3471.29	3938.96	4959.43	8206.61
450,000	3717.39	3772.83	3835.08	3905.20	4431.33	5579.36	9232.44
500,000	4130.43	4192.03	4261.20	4339.12	4923.70	6199.28	10258.27
550,000	4543.48	4611.23	4687.32	4773.03	5416.07	6819.21	11284.09
600,000	4956.52	5030.44	5113.44	5206.94	5908.44	7439.14	12309.92
650,000	5369.56	5449.64	5539.55	5640.85	6400.81	8059.07	13335.75
700,000	5782.61	5868.84	5965.67	6074.76	6893.18	8679.00	14361.57
750,000	6195.65	6288.05	6391.79	6508.67	7385.55	9298.93	15387.40
800,000	6608.69	6707.25	6817.91	6942.59	7877.92	9918.86	16413.23
850,000	7021.74	7126.45	7244.03	7376.50	8370.29	10538.78	17439.05
900,000	7434.78	7545.66	7670.15	7810.41	8862.66	11158.71	18464.88
950,000	7847.82	7964.86	8096.27	8244.32	9355.03	11778.64	19490.70
1,000,000	8260.87	8384.06	8522.39	8678.23	9847.40	12398.57	20516.53

Monthly Payments
Necessary to Amortize a Loan

YEARS REMAINING IN TERM

AMOUNT BORROWED	30	29	28	27	26	25	24
100	0.79	0.79	0.80	0.81	0.81	0.82	0.83
200	1.57	1.58	1.60	1.61	1.63	1.64	1.66
300	2.36	2.38	2.40	2.42	2.44	2.47	2.50
400	3.15	3.17	3.19	3.22	3.25	3.29	3.33
500	3.93	3.96	3.99	4.03	4.07	4.11	4.16
600	4.72	4.75	4.79	4.83	4.88	4.93	4.99
700	5.51	5.55	5.59	5.64	5.69	5.76	5.82
800	6.29	6.34	6.39	6.45	6.51	6.58	6.65
900	7.08	7.13	7.19	7.25	7.32	7.40	7.49
1,000	7.87	7.92	7.99	8.06	8.13	8.22	8.32
2,000	15.73	15.85	15.97	16.11	16.27	16.44	16.64
3,000	23.60	23.77	23.96	24.17	24.40	24.66	24.95
4,000	31.47	31.70	31.95	32.23	32.54	32.89	33.27
5,000	39.34	39.62	39.94	40.29	40.67	41.11	41.59
6,000	47.20	47.54	47.92	48.34	48.81	49.33	49.91
7,000	55.07	55.47	55.91	56.40	56.94	57.55	58.23
8,000	62.94	63.39	63.90	64.46	65.08	65.77	66.54
9,000	70.80	71.32	71.88	72.51	73.21	73.99	74.86
10,000	78.67	79.24	79.87	80.57	81.35	82.21	83.18
15,000	118.01	118.86	119.81	120.86	122.02	123.32	124.77
20,000	157.34	158.48	159.74	161.14	162.70	164.43	166.36
25,000	196.68	198.10	199.68	201.43	203.37	205.54	207.95
30,000	236.01	237.72	239.61	241.71	244.05	246.64	249.54
35,000	275.35	277.34	279.55	282.00	284.72	287.75	291.13
40,000	314.68	316.96	319.48	322.28	325.39	328.86	332.72
45,000	354.02	356.58	359.42	362.57	366.07	369.96	374.31
50,000	393.35	396.20	399.35	402.85	406.74	411.07	415.90
55,000	432.69	435.82	439.29	443.14	447.42	452.18	457.49
60,000	472.02	475.44	479.22	483.42	488.09	493.29	499.08
65,000	511.36	515.06	519.16	523.71	528.76	534.39	540.67
70,000	550.69	554.68	559.09	563.99	569.44	575.50	582.26
75,000	590.03	594.30	599.03	604.28	610.11	616.61	623.85
80,000	629.36	633.92	638.96	644.56	650.79	657.71	665.44
85,000	668.70	673.54	678.90	684.85	691.46	698.82	707.03
90,000	708.03	713.16	718.83	725.13	732.14	739.93	748.63
95,000	747.37	752.78	758.77	765.42	772.81	781.04	790.22
100,000	786.70	792.40	798.71	805.70	813.49	822.14	831.81
110,000	865.37	871.64	878.58	886.28	894.83	904.36	914.99
120,000	944.04	950.88	958.45	966.85	976.17	986.57	998.17
130,000	1022.71	1030.11	1038.32	1047.42	1057.53	1068.79	1081.35
140,000	1101.38	1109.35	1118.19	1127.99	1138.88	1151.00	1164.53
150,000	1180.05	1188.59	1198.06	1208.56	1220.23	1233.22	1247.71
200,000	1573.40	1584.79	1597.41	1611.41	1626.97	1644.29	1663.61
250,000	1966.75	1980.99	1996.76	2014.26	2033.71	2055.36	2079.51
300,000	2360.10	2377.19	2396.12	2417.11	2440.45	2466.43	2495.42
350,000	2753.45	2773.39	2795.47	2819.97	2847.19	2877.50	2911.32
400,000	3146.80	3169.58	3194.82	3222.82	3253.93	3288.57	3327.22
450,000	3540.15	3565.78	3594.17	3625.67	3660.68	3699.65	3743.13
500,000	3933.50	3961.98	3993.53	4028.52	4067.42	4110.72	4159.03
550,000	4326.85	4358.18	4392.88	4431.38	4474.16	4521.79	4574.93
600,000	4720.20	4754.38	4792.23	4834.23	4880.90	4932.86	4990.83
650,000	5113.55	5150.57	5191.58	5237.08	5287.64	5343.93	5406.74
700,000	5506.90	5546.77	5590.94	5639.93	5694.38	5755.01	5822.64
750,000	5900.25	5942.97	5990.29	6042.79	6101.13	6166.08	6238.54
800,000	6293.60	6339.17	6389.64	6445.64	6507.87	6577.15	6654.45
850,000	6686.95	6735.37	6788.99	6848.49	6914.61	6988.22	7070.35
900,000	7080.30	7131.56	7188.35	7251.34	7321.35	7399.29	7486.25
950,000	7473.65	7527.76	7587.70	7654.20	7728.09	7810.36	7902.15
1,000,000	7867.00	7923.96	7987.05	8057.05	8134.83	8221.44	8318.06

Monthly Payments 8¾%
Necessary to Amortize a Loan

AMOUNT BORROWED	YEARS REMAINING IN TERM						
	23	22	21	20	15	10	5
100	0.84	0.85	0.87	0.88	1.00	1.25	2.06
200	1.69	1.71	1.74	1.77	2.00	2.51	4.13
300	2.53	2.56	2.61	2.65	3.00	3.76	6.19
400	3.37	3.42	3.47	3.53	4.00	5.01	8.25
500	4.21	4.27	4.34	4.42	5.00	6.27	10.32
600	5.06	5.13	5.21	5.30	6.00	7.52	12.38
700	5.90	5.98	6.08	6.19	7.00	8.77	14.45
800	6.74	6.84	6.95	7.07	8.00	10.03	16.51
900	7.58	7.69	7.82	7.95	9.00	11.28	18.57
1,000	8.43	8.55	8.68	8.84	9.99	12.53	20.64
2,000	16.85	17.09	17.37	17.67	19.99	25.07	41.27
3,000	25.28	25.64	26.05	26.51	29.98	37.60	61.91
4,000	33.70	34.19	34.73	35.35	39.98	50.13	82.55
5,000	42.13	42.74	43.42	44.19	49.97	62.66	103.19
6,000	50.56	51.28	52.10	53.02	59.97	75.20	123.82
7,000	58.98	59.83	60.78	61.86	69.96	87.73	144.46
8,000	67.41	68.38	69.47	70.70	79.96	100.26	165.10
9,000	75.83	76.93	78.15	79.53	89.95	112.79	185.74
10,000	84.26	85.47	86.83	88.37	99.94	125.33	206.37
15,000	126.39	128.21	130.25	132.56	149.92	187.99	309.56
20,000	168.52	170.94	173.67	176.74	199.89	250.65	412.74
25,000	210.65	213.68	217.09	220.93	249.86	313.32	515.93
30,000	252.78	256.42	260.50	265.11	299.83	375.98	619.12
35,000	294.91	299.15	303.92	309.30	349.81	438.64	722.30
40,000	337.04	341.89	347.34	353.48	399.78	501.31	825.49
45,000	379.17	384.63	390.76	397.67	449.75	563.97	928.68
50,000	421.31	427.36	434.17	441.86	499.72	626.63	1031.86
55,000	463.44	470.10	477.59	486.04	549.70	689.30	1135.05
60,000	505.57	512.83	521.01	530.23	599.67	751.96	1238.23
65,000	547.70	555.57	564.42	574.41	649.64	814.62	1341.42
70,000	589.83	598.31	607.84	618.60	699.61	877.29	1444.61
75,000	631.96	641.04	651.26	662.78	749.59	939.95	1547.79
80,000	674.09	683.78	694.68	706.97	799.56	1002.61	1650.98
85,000	716.22	726.52	738.09	751.15	849.53	1065.28	1754.16
90,000	758.35	769.25	781.51	795.34	899.50	1127.94	1857.35
95,000	800.48	811.99	824.93	839.53	949.48	1190.60	1960.54
100,000	842.61	854.72	868.34	883.71	999.45	1253.27	2063.72
110,000	926.87	940.20	955.18	972.08	1099.39	1378.59	2270.10
120,000	1011.13	1025.67	1042.01	1060.45	1199.34	1503.92	2476.47
130,000	1095.39	1111.14	1128.85	1148.82	1299.28	1629.25	2682.84
140,000	1179.65	1196.61	1215.68	1237.19	1399.23	1754.57	2889.21
150,000	1263.92	1282.09	1302.52	1325.57	1499.17	1879.90	3095.58
200,000	1685.22	1709.45	1736.69	1767.42	1998.90	2506.54	4127.45
250,000	2106.53	2136.81	2170.86	2209.28	2498.62	3133.17	5159.31
300,000	2527.83	2564.17	2605.03	2651.13	2998.35	3759.80	6191.17
350,000	2949.14	2991.53	3039.21	3092.99	3498.07	4386.44	7223.03
400,000	3370.44	3418.90	3473.38	3534.84	3997.79	5013.07	8254.89
450,000	3791.75	3846.26	3907.55	3976.70	4497.52	5639.70	9286.75
500,000	4213.05	4273.62	4341.72	4418.55	4997.24	6266.34	10318.62
550,000	4634.36	4700.98	4775.90	4860.41	5496.97	6892.97	11350.48
600,000	5055.66	5128.34	5210.07	5302.26	5996.69	7519.61	12382.34
650,000	5476.97	5555.71	5644.24	5744.12	6496.42	8146.24	13414.20
700,000	5898.27	5983.07	6078.41	6185.97	6996.14	8772.87	14446.06
750,000	6319.58	6410.43	6512.59	6627.83	7495.86	9399.51	15477.92
800,000	6740.88	6837.79	6946.76	7069.69	7995.59	10026.14	16509.79
850,000	7162.19	7265.15	7380.93	7511.54	8495.31	10652.77	17541.65
900,000	7583.49	7692.52	7815.10	7953.40	8995.04	11279.41	18573.51
950,000	8004.80	8119.88	8249.28	8395.25	9494.76	11906.04	19605.37
1,000,000	8426.10	8547.24	8683.45	8837.11	9994.49	12532.68	20637.23

Monthly Payments
Necessary to Amortize a Loan

AMOUNT BORROWED	YEARS REMAINING IN TERM						
	30	29	28	27	26	25	24
100	0.80	0.81	0.82	0.82	0.83	0.84	0.85
200	1.61	1.62	1.63	1.65	1.66	1.68	1.70
300	2.41	2.43	2.45	2.47	2.49	2.52	2.55
400	3.22	3.24	3.27	3.29	3.32	3.36	3.39
500	4.02	4.05	4.08	4.12	4.15	4.20	4.24
600	4.83	4.86	4.90	4.94	4.98	5.04	5.09
700	5.63	5.67	5.71	5.76	5.82	5.87	5.94
800	6.44	6.48	6.53	6.59	6.65	6.71	6.79
900	7.24	7.29	7.35	7.41	7.48	7.55	7.64
1,000	8.05	8.10	8.16	8.23	8.31	8.39	8.49
2,000	16.09	16.20	16.33	16.46	16.61	16.78	16.97
3,000	24.14	24.30	24.49	24.69	24.92	25.18	25.46
4,000	32.18	32.41	32.65	32.93	33.23	33.57	33.95
5,000	40.23	40.51	40.81	41.16	41.54	41.96	42.43
6,000	48.28	48.61	48.98	49.39	49.84	50.35	50.92
7,000	56.32	56.71	57.14	57.62	58.15	58.74	59.41
8,000	64.37	64.81	65.30	65.85	66.46	67.14	67.89
9,000	72.42	72.91	73.47	74.08	74.77	75.53	76.38
10,000	80.46	81.02	81.63	82.31	83.07	83.92	84.87
15,000	120.69	121.52	122.44	123.47	124.61	125.88	127.30
20,000	160.92	162.03	163.26	164.63	166.14	167.84	169.73
25,000	201.16	202.54	204.07	205.78	207.68	209.80	212.17
30,000	241.39	243.05	244.89	246.94	249.22	251.76	254.60
35,000	281.62	283.56	285.70	288.09	290.75	293.72	297.03
40,000	321.85	324.06	326.52	329.25	332.29	335.68	339.47
45,000	362.08	364.57	367.33	370.41	373.83	377.64	381.90
50,000	402.31	405.08	408.15	411.56	415.36	419.60	424.33
55,000	442.54	445.59	448.96	452.72	456.90	461.56	466.77
60,000	482.77	486.09	489.78	493.88	498.43	503.52	509.20
65,000	523.00	526.60	530.59	535.03	539.97	545.48	551.63
70,000	563.24	567.11	571.41	576.19	581.51	587.44	594.07
75,000	603.47	607.62	612.22	617.34	623.04	629.40	636.50
80,000	643.70	648.13	653.04	658.50	664.58	671.36	678.93
85,000	683.93	688.63	693.85	699.66	706.11	713.32	721.36
90,000	724.16	729.14	734.67	740.81	747.65	755.28	763.80
95,000	764.39	769.65	775.48	781.97	789.19	797.24	806.23
100,000	804.62	810.16	816.30	823.13	830.72	839.20	848.66
110,000	885.08	891.17	897.93	905.44	913.80	923.12	933.53
120,000	965.55	972.19	979.56	987.75	996.87	1007.04	1018.40
130,000	1046.01	1053.20	1061.19	1070.06	1079.94	1090.96	1103.26
140,000	1126.47	1134.22	1142.82	1152.38	1163.01	1174.87	1188.13
150,000	1206.93	1215.24	1224.45	1234.69	1246.09	1258.79	1273.00
200,000	1609.25	1620.32	1632.60	1646.25	1661.45	1678.39	1697.33
250,000	2011.56	2025.39	2040.75	2057.81	2076.81	2097.99	2121.66
300,000	2413.87	2430.47	2448.90	2469.38	2492.17	2517.59	2545.99
350,000	2816.18	2835.55	2857.05	2880.94	2907.53	2937.19	2970.33
400,000	3218.49	3240.63	3265.20	3292.50	3322.89	3356.79	3394.66
450,000	3620.80	3645.71	3673.35	3704.06	3738.26	3776.38	3818.99
500,000	4023.11	4050.79	4081.50	4115.63	4153.62	4195.98	4243.32
550,000	4425.42	4455.87	4489.65	4527.19	4568.98	4615.58	4667.65
600,000	4827.74	4860.95	4897.80	4938.75	4984.34	5035.18	5091.99
650,000	5230.05	5266.02	5305.95	5350.32	5399.70	5454.78	5516.32
700,000	5632.36	5671.10	5714.10	5761.88	5815.06	5874.37	5940.65
750,000	6034.67	6076.18	6122.25	6173.44	6230.43	6293.97	6364.98
800,000	6436.98	6481.26	6530.40	6585.00	6645.79	6713.57	6789.31
850,000	6839.30	6886.34	6938.55	6996.57	7061.15	7133.17	7213.65
900,000	7241.60	7291.42	7346.70	7408.13	7476.51	7552.77	7637.98
950,000	7643.91	7696.50	7754.85	7819.69	7891.87	7972.37	8062.31
1,000,000	8046.23	8101.58	8163.00	8231.25	8307.23	8391.96	8486.64

Monthly Payments 9%
Necessary to Amortize a Loan

AMOUNT BORROWED	YEARS REMAINING IN TERM						
	23	22	21	20	15	10	5
100	0.86	0.87	0.88	0.90	1.01	1.27	2.08
200	1.72	1.74	1.77	1.80	2.03	2.53	4.15
300	2.58	2.61	2.65	2.70	3.04	3.80	6.23
400	3.44	3.48	3.54	3.60	4.06	5.07	8.30
500	4.30	4.36	4.42	4.50	5.07	6.33	10.38
600	5.16	5.23	5.31	5.40	6.09	7.60	12.46
700	6.01	6.10	6.19	6.30	7.10	8.87	14.53
800	6.87	6.97	7.08	7.20	8.11	10.13	16.61
900	7.73	7.84	7.96	8.10	9.13	11.40	18.68
1,000	8.59	8.71	8.85	9.00	10.14	12.67	20.76
2,000	17.19	17.42	17.69	17.99	20.29	25.34	41.52
3,000	25.78	26.14	26.54	26.99	30.43	38.00	62.28
4,000	34.37	34.85	35.38	35.99	40.57	50.67	83.03
5,000	42.96	43.56	44.23	44.99	50.71	63.34	103.79
6,000	51.56	52.27	53.07	53.98	60.86	76.01	124.55
7,000	60.15	60.98	61.92	62.98	71.00	88.67	145.31
8,000	68.74	69.69	70.77	71.98	81.14	101.34	166.07
9,000	77.33	78.41	79.61	80.98	91.28	114.01	186.83
10,000	85.93	87.12	88.46	89.97	101.43	126.68	207.58
15,000	128.89	130.68	132.69	134.96	152.14	190.01	311.38
20,000	171.85	174.23	176.92	179.95	202.85	253.35	415.17
25,000	214.82	217.79	221.15	224.93	253.57	316.69	518.96
30,000	257.78	261.35	265.37	269.92	304.28	380.03	622.75
35,000	300.74	304.91	309.60	314.90	354.99	443.37	726.54
40,000	343.71	348.47	353.83	359.89	405.71	506.70	830.33
45,000	386.67	392.03	398.06	404.88	456.42	570.04	934.13
50,000	429.63	435.59	442.29	449.86	507.13	633.38	1037.92
55,000	472.60	479.15	486.52	494.85	557.85	696.72	1141.71
60,000	515.56	522.70	530.75	539.84	608.56	760.05	1245.50
65,000	558.52	566.26	574.98	584.82	659.27	823.39	1349.29
70,000	601.49	609.82	619.21	629.81	709.99	886.73	1453.08
75,000	644.45	653.38	663.44	674.79	760.70	950.07	1556.88
80,000	687.41	696.94	707.66	719.78	811.41	1013.41	1660.67
85,000	730.38	740.50	751.89	764.77	862.13	1076.74	1764.46
90,000	773.34	784.06	796.12	809.75	912.84	1140.08	1868.25
95,000	816.30	827.62	840.35	854.74	963.55	1203.42	1972.04
100,000	859.27	871.17	884.58	899.73	1014.27	1266.76	2075.84
110,000	945.19	958.29	973.04	989.70	1115.69	1393.43	2283.42
120,000	1031.12	1045.41	1061.50	1079.67	1217.12	1520.11	2491.00
130,000	1117.05	1132.53	1149.96	1169.64	1318.55	1646.79	2698.59
140,000	1202.98	1219.64	1238.41	1259.62	1419.97	1773.46	2906.17
150,000	1288.90	1306.76	1326.87	1349.59	1521.40	1900.14	3113.75
200,000	1718.54	1742.35	1769.16	1799.45	2028.53	2533.52	4151.67
250,000	2148.17	2177.94	2211.45	2249.31	2535.67	3166.89	5189.59
300,000	2577.80	2613.52	2653.74	2699.18	3042.80	3800.27	6227.51
350,000	3007.44	3049.11	3096.03	3149.04	3549.93	4433.65	7265.42
400,000	3437.07	3484.70	3538.32	3598.90	4057.07	5067.03	8303.34
450,000	3866.71	3920.28	3980.61	4048.77	4564.20	5700.41	9341.26
500,000	4296.34	4355.87	4422.91	4498.63	5071.33	6333.79	10379.18
550,000	4725.97	4791.46	4865.20	4948.49	5578.47	6967.17	11417.10
600,000	5155.61	5227.05	5307.49	5398.36	6085.60	7600.55	12455.01
650,000	5585.24	5662.63	5749.78	5848.22	6592.73	8233.93	13492.93
700,000	6014.88	6098.22	6192.07	6298.08	7099.87	8867.30	14530.85
750,000	6444.51	6533.81	6634.36	6747.94	7607.00	9500.68	15568.77
800,000	6874.15	6969.39	7076.65	7197.81	8114.13	10134.06	16606.68
850,000	7303.78	7404.98	7518.94	7647.67	8621.27	10767.44	17644.60
900,000	7733.41	7840.57	7961.23	8097.53	9128.40	11400.82	18682.52
950,000	8163.05	8276.16	8403.52	8547.40	9635.53	12034.20	19720.44
1,000,000	8592.68	8711.74	8845.81	8997.26	10142.67	12667.58	20758.36

9¼%

Monthly Payments
Necessary to Amortize a Loan

AMOUNT BORROWED	YEARS REMAINING IN TERM						
	30	29	28	27	26	25	24
100	0.82	0.83	0.83	0.84	0.85	0.86	0.87
200	1.65	1.66	1.67	1.68	1.70	1.71	1.73
300	2.47	2.48	2.50	2.52	2.54	2.57	2.60
400	3.29	3.31	3.34	3.36	3.39	3.43	3.46
500	4.11	4.14	4.17	4.20	4.24	4.28	4.33
600	4.94	4.97	5.00	5.04	5.09	5.14	5.19
700	5.76	5.80	5.84	5.88	5.94	5.99	6.06
800	6.58	6.62	6.67	6.73	6.78	6.85	6.93
900	7.40	7.45	7.51	7.57	7.63	7.71	7.79
1,000	8.23	8.28	8.34	8.41	8.48	8.56	8.66
2,000	16.45	16.56	16.68	16.81	16.96	17.13	17.31
3,000	24.68	24.84	25.02	25.22	25.44	25.69	25.97
4,000	32.91	33.12	33.36	33.63	33.92	34.26	34.63
5,000	41.13	41.40	41.70	42.03	42.40	42.82	43.28
6,000	49.36	49.68	50.04	50.44	50.89	51.38	51.94
7,000	57.59	57.96	58.38	58.85	59.37	59.95	60.60
8,000	65.81	66.24	66.72	67.25	67.85	68.51	69.25
9,000	74.04	74.52	75.06	75.66	76.33	77.07	77.91
10,000	82.27	82.81	83.40	84.07	84.81	85.64	86.57
15,000	123.40	124.21	125.10	126.10	127.21	128.46	129.85
20,000	164.54	165.61	166.81	168.14	169.62	171.28	173.13
25,000	205.67	207.01	208.51	210.17	212.02	214.10	216.41
30,000	246.80	248.42	250.21	252.20	254.43	256.91	259.70
35,000	287.94	289.82	291.91	294.24	296.83	299.73	302.98
40,000	329.07	331.22	333.61	336.27	339.24	342.55	346.26
45,000	370.20	372.62	375.31	378.31	381.64	385.37	389.54
50,000	411.34	414.03	417.01	420.34	424.05	428.19	432.83
55,000	452.47	455.43	458.71	462.37	466.45	471.01	476.11
60,000	493.61	496.83	500.42	504.41	508.86	513.83	519.39
65,000	534.74	538.23	542.12	546.44	551.26	556.65	562.68
70,000	575.87	579.64	583.82	588.48	593.67	599.47	605.96
75,000	617.01	621.04	625.52	630.51	636.07	642.29	649.24
80,000	658.14	662.44	667.22	672.54	678.48	685.11	692.52
85,000	699.27	703.84	708.92	714.58	720.88	727.92	735.81
90,000	740.41	745.25	750.62	756.61	763.29	770.74	779.09
95,000	781.54	786.65	792.33	798.64	805.69	813.56	822.37
100,000	822.68	828.05	834.03	840.68	848.10	856.38	865.66
110,000	904.94	910.86	917.43	924.75	932.91	942.02	952.22
120,000	987.21	993.66	1008.84	1008.81	1017.72	1027.66	1038.79
130,000	1069.48	1076.47	1084.23	1092.88	1102.53	1113.30	1125.35
140,000	1151.75	1159.27	1167.64	1176.95	1187.33	1198.93	1211.92
150,000	1234.01	1242.08	1251.04	1261.02	1272.14	1284.57	1298.48
200,000	1645.35	1656.10	1668.05	1681.36	1696.19	1712.76	1731.31
250,000	2056.69	2070.13	2085.07	2101.70	2120.24	2140.95	2164.14
300,000	2468.03	2484.15	2502.08	2522.04	2544.29	2569.15	2596.97
350,000	2879.36	2898.18	2919.09	2942.38	2968.34	2997.34	3029.79
400,000	3290.70	3312.20	3336.11	3362.72	3392.39	3425.53	3462.62
450,000	3702.04	3726.23	3753.12	3783.05	3816.43	3853.72	3895.45
500,000	4113.38	4140.25	4170.13	4203.39	4240.48	4281.91	4328.28
550,000	4524.71	4554.28	4587.15	4623.73	4664.53	4710.10	4761.10
600,000	4936.05	4968.31	5004.16	5044.07	5088.58	5138.29	5193.93
650,000	5347.39	5382.33	5421.17	5464.41	5512.63	5566.48	5626.76
700,000	5758.73	5796.36	5838.19	5884.75	5936.67	5994.67	6059.59
750,000	6170.07	6210.38	6255.20	6305.09	6360.72	6422.86	6492.41
800,000	6581.40	6624.41	6672.21	6725.43	6784.77	6851.05	6925.24
850,000	6992.74	7038.43	7089.23	7145.77	7208.82	7279.25	7358.07
900,000	7404.08	7452.46	7506.24	7566.11	7632.87	7707.44	7790.90
950,000	7815.42	7866.48	7923.25	7986.45	8056.92	8135.63	8223.72
1,000,000	8226.75	8280.51	8340.27	8406.79	8480.96	8563.82	8656.55

AMOUNT BORROWED	YEARS REMAINING IN TERM						
	23	22	21	20	15	10	5
100	0.88	0.89	0.90	0.92	1.03	1.28	2.09
200	1.75	1.78	1.80	1.83	2.06	2.56	4.18
300	2.63	2.66	2.70	2.75	3.09	3.84	6.26
400	3.50	3.55	3.60	3.66	4.12	5.12	8.35
500	4.38	4.44	4.50	4.58	5.15	6.40	10.44
600	5.26	5.33	5.41	5.50	6.18	7.68	12.53
700	6.13	6.21	6.31	6.41	7.20	8.96	14.62
800	7.01	7.10	7.21	7.33	8.23	10.24	16.70
900	7.88	7.99	8.11	8.24	9.26	11.52	18.79
1,000	8.76	8.88	9.01	9.16	10.29	12.80	20.88
2,000	17.52	17.76	18.02	18.32	20.58	25.61	41.76
3,000	26.28	26.63	27.03	27.48	30.88	38.41	62.64
4,000	35.04	35.51	36.04	36.63	41.17	51.21	83.52
5,000	43.80	44.39	45.05	45.79	51.46	64.02	104.40
6,000	52.56	53.27	54.06	54.95	61.75	76.82	125.28
7,000	61.32	62.14	63.07	64.11	72.04	89.62	146.16
8,000	70.08	71.02	72.08	73.27	82.34	102.43	167.04
9,000	78.85	79.90	81.09	82.43	92.63	115.23	187.92
10,000	87.61	88.78	90.09	91.59	102.92	128.03	208.80
15,000	131.41	133.16	135.14	137.38	154.38	192.05	313.20
20,000	175.21	177.55	180.19	183.17	205.84	256.07	417.60
25,000	219.01	221.94	225.24	228.97	257.30	320.08	522.00
30,000	262.82	266.33	270.28	274.76	308.76	384.10	626.40
35,000	306.62	310.71	315.33	320.55	360.22	448.11	730.80
40,000	350.42	355.10	360.38	366.35	411.68	512.13	835.20
45,000	394.23	399.49	405.43	412.14	463.14	576.15	939.60
50,000	438.03	443.88	450.47	457.93	514.60	640.16	1043.99
55,000	481.83	488.26	495.52	503.73	566.06	704.18	1148.39
60,000	525.63	532.65	540.57	549.52	617.52	768.20	1252.79
65,000	569.44	577.04	585.61	595.31	668.97	832.21	1357.19
70,000	613.24	621.43	630.66	641.11	720.43	896.23	1461.59
75,000	657.04	665.82	675.71	686.90	771.89	960.25	1565.99
80,000	700.85	710.20	720.76	732.69	823.35	1024.26	1670.39
85,000	744.65	754.59	765.80	778.49	874.81	1088.28	1774.79
90,000	788.45	798.98	810.85	824.28	926.27	1152.29	1879.19
95,000	832.25	843.37	855.90	870.07	977.73	1216.31	1983.59
100,000	876.06	887.75	900.94	915.87	1029.19	1280.33	2087.99
110,000	963.66	976.53	991.04	1007.45	1132.11	1408.36	2296.79
120,000	1051.27	1065.31	1081.13	1099.04	1235.03	1536.39	2505.59
130,000	1138.87	1154.08	1171.23	1190.63	1337.95	1664.43	2714.39
140,000	1226.48	1242.86	1261.32	1282.21	1440.87	1792.46	2923.19
150,000	1314.09	1331.63	1351.42	1373.80	1543.79	1920.49	3131.98
200,000	1752.11	1775.51	1801.89	1831.73	2058.38	2560.65	4175.98
250,000	2190.14	2219.39	2252.36	2289.67	2572.98	3200.82	5219.97
300,000	2628.17	2663.26	2702.83	2747.60	3087.58	3840.98	6263.97
350,000	3066.20	3107.14	3153.31	3205.53	3602.17	4481.15	7307.96
400,000	3504.23	3551.02	3603.78	3663.47	4116.77	5121.31	8351.96
450,000	3942.26	3994.89	4054.25	4121.40	4631.37	5761.47	9395.95
500,000	4380.29	4438.77	4504.72	4579.33	5145.96	6401.64	10439.95
550,000	4818.31	4882.65	4955.20	5037.27	5660.56	7041.80	11483.94
600,000	5256.34	5326.53	5405.67	5495.20	6175.15	7681.96	12527.94
650,000	5694.37	5770.40	5856.14	5953.13	6689.75	8322.13	13571.93
700,000	6132.40	6214.28	6306.61	6411.07	7204.35	8962.29	14615.93
750,000	6570.43	6658.16	6757.09	6869.00	7718.94	9602.45	15659.92
800,000	7008.46	7102.03	7207.56	7326.93	8233.54	10242.62	16703.92
850,000	7446.49	7545.91	7658.03	7784.87	8748.13	10882.78	17747.91
900,000	7884.51	7989.79	8108.50	8242.80	9262.73	11522.94	18791.91
950,000	8322.54	8433.67	8558.98	8700.73	9777.33	12163.11	19835.90
1,000,000	8760.57	8877.54	9009.45	9158.67	10291.92	12803.27	20879.90

9½%

Monthly Payments
Necessary to Amortize a Loan

YEARS REMAINING IN TERM

AMOUNT BORROWED	30	29	28	27	26	25	24
100	0.84	0.85	0.85	0.86	0.87	0.87	0.88
200	1.68	1.69	1.70	1.72	1.73	1.75	1.77
300	2.52	2.54	2.56	2.58	2.60	2.62	2.65
400	3.36	3.38	3.41	3.43	3.46	3.49	3.53
500	4.20	4.23	4.26	4.29	4.33	4.37	4.41
600	5.05	5.08	5.11	5.15	5.19	5.24	5.30
700	5.89	5.92	5.96	6.01	6.06	6.12	6.18
800	6.73	6.77	6.82	6.87	6.92	6.99	7.06
900	7.57	7.61	7.67	7.73	7.79	7.86	7.94
1,000	8.41	8.46	8.52	8.58	8.66	8.74	8.83
2,000	16.82	16.92	17.04	17.17	17.31	17.47	17.66
3,000	25.23	25.38	25.56	25.75	25.97	26.21	26.48
4,000	33.63	33.84	34.08	34.33	34.62	34.95	35.31
5,000	42.04	42.30	42.59	42.92	43.28	43.68	44.14
6,000	50.45	50.76	51.11	51.50	51.94	52.42	52.97
7,000	58.86	59.23	59.63	60.09	60.59	61.16	61.79
8,000	67.27	67.69	68.15	68.67	69.25	69.90	70.62
9,000	75.68	76.15	76.67	77.25	77.90	78.63	79.45
10,000	84.09	84.61	85.19	85.84	86.56	87.37	88.28
15,000	126.13	126.91	127.78	128.75	129.84	131.05	132.42
20,000	168.17	169.21	170.38	171.67	173.12	174.74	176.55
25,000	210.21	211.52	212.97	214.59	216.40	218.42	220.69
30,000	252.26	253.82	255.56	257.51	259.68	262.11	264.83
35,000	294.30	296.13	298.16	300.43	302.96	305.79	308.97
40,000	336.34	338.43	340.75	343.34	346.24	349.48	353.11
45,000	378.38	380.73	383.35	386.26	389.52	393.16	397.25
50,000	420.43	423.04	425.94	429.18	432.80	436.85	441.39
55,000	462.47	465.34	468.53	472.10	476.08	480.53	485.53
60,000	504.51	507.64	511.13	515.02	519.36	524.22	529.66
65,000	546.56	549.95	553.72	557.93	562.64	567.90	573.80
70,000	588.60	592.25	596.32	600.85	605.92	611.59	617.94
75,000	630.64	634.55	638.91	643.77	649.20	655.27	662.08
80,000	672.68	676.86	681.51	686.69	692.48	698.96	706.22
85,000	714.73	719.16	724.10	729.61	735.76	742.64	750.36
90,000	756.77	761.46	766.69	772.53	779.04	786.33	794.50
95,000	798.81	803.77	809.29	815.44	822.32	830.01	838.64
100,000	840.85	846.07	851.88	858.36	865.60	873.70	882.77
110,000	924.94	930.68	937.07	944.20	952.16	961.07	971.05
120,000	1009.03	1015.29	1022.26	1030.03	1038.72	1048.44	1059.33
130,000	1093.11	1099.89	1107.45	1115.87	1125.28	1135.81	1147.61
140,000	1177.20	1184.50	1192.63	1201.71	1211.84	1223.18	1235.88
150,000	1261.28	1269.11	1277.82	1287.54	1298.40	1310.54	1324.16
200,000	1681.71	1692.14	1703.76	1716.72	1731.20	1747.39	1765.55
250,000	2102.14	2115.18	2129.70	2145.90	2164.00	2184.24	2206.94
300,000	2522.56	2538.21	2555.65	2575.08	2596.80	2621.09	2648.32
350,000	2942.99	2961.25	2981.59	3004.26	3029.60	3057.94	3089.71
400,000	3363.42	3384.29	3407.53	3433.45	3462.40	3494.79	3531.10
450,000	3783.84	3807.32	3833.47	3862.63	3895.19	3931.63	3972.49
500,000	4204.27	4230.36	4259.41	4291.81	4327.99	4368.48	4413.87
550,000	4624.70	4653.39	4685.35	4720.99	4760.79	4805.33	4855.26
600,000	5045.13	5076.43	5111.29	5150.17	5193.59	5242.18	5296.65
650,000	5465.55	5499.46	5537.23	5579.35	5626.39	5679.03	5738.04
700,000	5885.98	5922.50	5963.17	6008.53	6059.19	6115.88	6179.42
750,000	6306.41	6345.54	6389.11	6437.71	6491.99	6552.72	6620.81
800,000	6726.83	6768.57	6815.05	6866.89	6924.79	6989.57	7062.20
850,000	7147.26	7191.61	7240.99	7296.07	7357.59	7426.42	7503.59
900,000	7567.69	7614.64	7666.94	7725.25	7790.39	7863.27	7944.97
950,000	7988.11	8037.68	8092.88	8154.43	8223.19	8300.12	8386.36
1,000,000	8408.54	8460.71	8518.82	8583.61	8655.99	8736.97	8827.75

Monthly Payments 9¹/₂%
Necessary to Amortize a Loan

YEARS REMAINING IN TERM

AMOUNT BORROWED	23	22	21	20	15	10	5
100	0.89	0.90	0.92	0.93	1.04	1.29	2.10
200	1.79	1.81	1.83	1.86	2.09	2.59	4.20
300	2.68	2.71	2.75	2.80	3.13	3.88	6.30
400	3.57	3.62	3.67	3.73	4.18	5.18	8.40
500	4.46	4.52	4.59	4.66	5.22	6.47	10.50
600	5.36	5.43	5.50	5.59	6.27	7.76	12.60
700	6.25	6.33	6.42	6.52	7.31	9.06	14.70
800	7.14	7.24	7.34	7.46	8.35	10.35	16.80
900	8.04	8.14	8.26	8.39	9.40	11.65	18.90
1,000	8.93	9.04	9.17	9.32	10.44	12.94	21.00
2,000	17.86	18.09	18.35	18.64	20.88	25.88	42.00
3,000	26.79	27.13	27.52	27.96	31.33	38.82	63.01
4,000	35.72	36.18	36.70	37.29	41.77	51.76	84.01
5,000	44.65	45.22	45.87	46.61	52.21	64.70	105.01
6,000	53.58	54.27	55.05	55.93	62.65	77.64	126.01
7,000	62.51	63.31	64.22	65.25	73.10	90.58	147.01
8,000	71.44	72.36	73.39	74.57	83.54	103.52	168.01
9,000	80.37	81.40	82.57	83.89	93.98	116.46	189.02
10,000	89.30	90.45	91.74	93.21	104.42	129.40	210.02
15,000	133.95	135.67	137.62	139.82	156.63	194.10	315.03
20,000	178.59	180.89	183.49	186.43	208.84	258.80	420.04
25,000	223.24	226.12	229.36	233.03	261.06	323.49	525.05
30,000	267.89	271.34	275.23	279.64	313.27	388.19	630.06
35,000	312.54	316.56	321.10	326.25	365.48	452.89	735.07
40,000	357.19	361.78	366.97	372.85	417.69	517.59	840.07
45,000	401.84	407.01	412.85	419.46	469.90	582.29	945.08
50,000	446.49	452.23	458.72	466.07	522.11	646.99	1050.09
55,000	491.14	497.45	504.59	512.67	574.32	711.69	1155.10
60,000	535.78	542.68	550.46	559.28	626.53	776.39	1260.11
65,000	580.43	587.90	596.33	605.89	678.75	841.08	1365.12
70,000	625.08	633.12	642.20	652.49	730.96	905.78	1470.13
75,000	669.73	678.35	688.08	699.10	783.17	970.48	1575.14
80,000	714.38	723.57	733.95	745.70	835.38	1035.18	1680.15
85,000	759.03	768.79	779.82	792.31	887.59	1099.88	1785.16
90,000	803.68	814.02	825.69	838.92	939.80	1164.58	1890.17
95,000	848.33	859.24	871.56	885.52	992.01	1229.28	1995.18
100,000	892.97	904.46	917.43	932.13	1044.22	1293.98	2100.19
110,000	982.27	994.91	1009.18	1025.34	1148.65	1423.37	2310.20
120,000	1071.57	1085.35	1100.92	1118.56	1253.07	1552.77	2520.22
130,000	1160.87	1175.80	1192.66	1211.77	1357.49	1682.17	2730.24
140,000	1250.16	1266.25	1284.41	1304.98	1461.91	1811.57	2940.26
150,000	1339.46	1356.69	1376.15	1398.20	1566.34	1940.96	3150.28
200,000	1785.95	1808.92	1834.87	1864.26	2088.45	2587.95	4200.37
250,000	2232.44	2261.15	2293.59	2330.33	2610.56	3234.94	5250.47
300,000	2678.92	2713.38	2752.30	2796.39	3132.67	3881.93	6300.56
350,000	3125.41	3165.61	3211.02	3262.46	3654.79	4528.91	7350.65
400,000	3571.90	3617.85	3669.74	3728.52	4176.90	5175.90	8400.74
450,000	4018.38	4070.08	4128.45	4194.59	4699.01	5822.89	9450.84
500,000	4464.87	4522.31	4587.17	4660.66	5221.12	6469.88	10500.93
550,000	4911.36	4974.54	5045.89	5126.72	5743.24	7116.87	11551.02
600,000	5357.85	5426.77	5504.61	5592.79	6265.35	7763.85	12601.02
650,000	5804.33	5879.00	5963.32	6058.85	6787.46	8410.84	13651.21
700,000	6250.82	6331.23	6422.04	6524.92	7309.57	9057.83	14701.30
750,000	6697.31	6783.46	6880.76	6990.98	7831.69	9704.82	15751.40
800,000	7143.79	7235.69	7339.47	7457.05	8353.80	10351.80	16801.49
850,000	7590.28	7687.92	7798.19	7923.12	8875.91	10998.79	17851.58
900,000	8036.77	8140.15	8256.91	8389.18	9398.02	11645.78	18901.68
950,000	8483.26	8592.38	8715.63	8855.25	9920.13	12292.77	19951.77
1,000,000	8929.74	9044.61	9174.34	9321.31	10442.25	12939.76	21001.86

9³/₄%

Monthly Payments
Necessary to Amortize a Loan

AMOUNT BORROWED	YEARS REMAINING IN TERM						
	30	29	28	27	26	25	24
100	0.86	0.86	0.87	0.88	0.88	0.89	0.90
200	1.72	1.73	1.74	1.75	1.77	1.78	1.80
300	2.58	2.59	2.61	2.63	2.65	2.67	2.70
400	3.44	3.46	3.48	3.50	3.53	3.56	3.60
500	4.30	4.32	4.35	4.38	4.42	4.46	4.50
600	5.15	5.19	5.22	5.26	5.30	5.35	5.40
700	6.01	6.05	6.09	6.13	6.18	6.24	6.30
800	6.87	6.91	6.96	7.01	7.07	7.13	7.20
900	7.73	7.78	7.83	7.89	7.95	8.02	8.10
1,000	8.59	8.64	8.70	8.76	8.83	8.91	9.00
2,000	17.18	17.28	17.40	17.52	17.66	17.82	18.00
3,000	25.77	25.93	26.10	26.29	26.50	26.73	27.00
4,000	34.37	34.57	34.79	35.05	35.33	35.65	36.00
5,000	42.96	43.21	43.49	43.81	44.16	44.56	45.00
6,000	51.55	51.85	52.19	52.57	52.99	53.47	54.00
7,000	60.14	60.50	60.89	61.33	61.83	62.38	63.00
8,000	68.73	69.14	69.59	70.09	70.66	71.29	72.00
9,000	77.32	77.78	78.29	78.86	79.49	80.20	81.00
10,000	85.92	86.42	86.99	87.62	88.32	89.11	90.00
15,000	128.87	129.63	130.48	131.43	132.48	133.67	135.00
20,000	171.83	172.84	173.97	175.23	176.65	178.23	180.00
25,000	214.79	216.05	217.47	219.04	220.81	222.78	225.00
30,000	257.75	259.26	260.96	262.85	264.97	267.34	270.00
35,000	300.70	302.48	304.45	306.66	309.13	311.90	315.00
40,000	343.66	345.69	347.94	350.47	353.29	356.45	360.00
45,000	386.62	388.90	391.44	394.28	397.45	401.01	405.01
50,000	429.58	432.11	434.93	438.08	441.61	445.57	450.01
55,000	472.53	475.32	478.42	481.89	485.77	490.13	495.01
60,000	515.49	518.53	521.92	525.70	529.94	534.68	540.01
65,000	558.45	561.74	565.41	569.51	574.10	579.24	585.01
70,000	601.41	604.95	608.90	613.32	618.26	623.80	630.01
75,000	644.37	648.16	652.40	657.13	662.42	668.35	675.02
80,000	687.32	691.37	695.89	700.94	706.58	712.91	720.02
85,000	730.28	734.58	739.38	744.74	750.74	757.47	765.02
90,000	773.24	777.79	782.87	788.55	794.90	802.02	810.02
95,000	816.20	821.00	826.37	832.36	839.07	846.58	855.02
100,000	859.15	864.21	869.86	876.17	883.23	891.14	900.02
110,000	945.07	950.64	956.85	963.79	971.55	980.25	990.02
120,000	1030.99	1037.06	1043.83	1051.40	1059.87	1069.36	1080.02
130,000	1116.90	1123.48	1130.82	1139.02	1148.19	1158.48	1170.03
140,000	1202.82	1209.90	1217.81	1226.64	1236.52	1247.59	1260.03
150,000	1288.73	1296.32	1304.79	1314.25	1324.84	1336.71	1350.03
200,000	1718.31	1728.43	1739.72	1752.34	1766.45	1782.27	1800.04
250,000	2147.89	2160.54	2174.65	2190.42	2208.07	2227.84	2250.05
300,000	2577.46	2592.64	2609.58	2628.51	2649.68	2673.41	2700.06
350,000	3007.04	3024.75	3044.51	3066.59	3091.29	3118.98	3150.07
400,000	3436.62	3456.86	3479.44	3504.68	3532.91	3564.55	3600.08
450,000	3866.19	3888.97	3914.37	3942.76	3974.52	4010.12	4050.09
500,000	4295.77	4321.07	4349.30	4380.84	4416.13	4455.69	4500.10
550,000	4725.35	4753.18	4784.24	4818.93	4857.75	4901.26	4950.11
600,000	5154.93	5185.29	5219.17	5257.01	5299.36	5346.82	5400.12
650,000	5584.50	5617.40	5654.10	5695.10	5740.97	5792.39	5850.13
700,000	6014.08	6049.50	6089.03	6133.18	6182.59	6237.96	6300.14
750,000	6443.66	6481.61	6523.96	6571.27	6624.20	6683.53	6750.15
800,000	6873.24	6913.72	6958.89	7009.35	7065.81	7129.10	7200.16
850,000	7302.81	7345.83	7393.82	7447.44	7507.43	7574.67	7650.17
900,000	7732.39	7777.93	7828.75	7885.52	7949.04	8020.24	8100.18
950,000	8161.97	8210.04	8263.68	8323.60	8390.65	8465.81	8550.19
1,000,000	8591.54	8642.15	8698.61	8761.69	8832.27	8911.37	9000.20

Monthly Payments
Necessary to Amortize a Loan

9³/₄%

AMOUNT BORROWED	YEARS REMAINING IN TERM						
	23	22	21	20	15	10	5
100	0.91	0.92	0.93	0.95	1.06	1.31	2.11
200	1.82	1.84	1.87	1.90	2.12	2.62	4.22
300	2.73	2.76	2.80	2.85	3.18	3.92	6.34
400	3.64	3.69	3.74	3.79	4.24	5.23	8.45
500	4.55	4.61	4.67	4.74	5.30	6.54	10.56
600	5.46	5.53	5.60	5.69	6.36	7.85	12.67
700	6.37	6.45	6.54	6.64	7.42	9.15	14.79
800	7.28	7.37	7.47	7.59	8.47	10.46	16.90
900	8.19	8.29	8.41	8.54	9.53	11.77	19.01
1,000	9.10	9.21	9.34	9.49	10.59	13.08	21.12
2,000	18.20	18.43	18.68	18.97	21.19	26.15	42.25
3,000	27.30	27.64	28.02	28.46	31.78	39.23	63.37
4,000	36.40	36.85	37.36	37.94	42.37	52.31	84.50
5,000	45.50	46.06	46.70	47.43	52.97	65.39	105.62
6,000	54.60	55.28	56.04	56.91	63.56	78.46	126.75
7,000	63.70	64.49	65.38	66.40	74.16	91.54	147.87
8,000	72.80	73.70	74.72	75.88	84.75	104.62	168.99
9,000	81.90	82.92	84.06	85.37	95.34	117.69	190.12
10,000	91.00	92.13	93.40	94.85	105.94	130.77	211.24
15,000	136.50	138.19	140.11	142.28	158.90	196.16	316.86
20,000	182.00	184.26	186.81	189.70	211.87	261.54	422.48
25,000	227.50	230.32	233.51	237.13	264.84	326.93	528.11
30,000	273.01	276.39	280.21	284.56	317.81	392.31	633.73
35,000	318.51	322.45	326.92	331.98	370.78	457.70	739.35
40,000	364.01	368.52	373.62	379.41	423.75	523.08	844.97
45,000	409.51	414.58	420.32	426.83	476.71	588.47	950.59
50,000	455.01	460.65	467.02	474.26	529.68	653.85	1056.21
55,000	500.51	506.71	513.73	521.68	582.65	719.24	1161.83
60,000	546.01	552.78	560.43	569.11	635.62	784.62	1267.45
65,000	591.51	598.84	607.13	616.54	688.59	850.01	1373.08
70,000	637.01	644.90	653.83	663.96	741.55	915.39	1478.70
75,000	682.51	690.97	700.54	711.39	794.52	980.78	1584.32
80,000	728.01	737.03	747.24	758.81	847.49	1046.16	1689.94
85,000	773.51	783.10	793.94	806.24	900.46	1111.55	1795.56
90,000	819.02	829.16	840.64	853.67	953.43	1176.93	1901.18
95,000	864.52	875.23	887.34	901.09	1006.39	1242.32	2006.80
100,000	910.02	921.29	934.05	948.52	1059.36	1307.70	2112.42
110,000	1001.02	1013.42	1027.45	1043.37	1165.30	1438.47	2323.67
120,000	1092.02	1105.55	1120.86	1138.22	1271.24	1569.24	2534.91
130,000	1183.02	1197.68	1214.26	1233.07	1377.17	1700.01	2746.15
140,000	1274.02	1289.81	1307.67	1327.92	1483.11	1830.78	2957.39
150,000	1365.03	1381.94	1401.07	1422.78	1589.04	1961.55	3168.64
200,000	1820.03	1842.59	1868.09	1897.03	2118.73	2615.40	4224.85
250,000	2275.04	2303.23	2335.12	2371.29	2648.41	3269.26	5281.06
300,000	2730.05	2763.88	2802.14	2845.55	3178.09	3923.11	6337.27
350,000	3185.06	3224.52	3269.16	3319.81	3707.77	4576.96	7393.49
400,000	3640.07	3685.17	3736.19	3794.07	4237.45	5230.81	8449.70
450,000	4095.08	4145.82	4203.21	4268.33	4767.13	5884.66	9505.91
500,000	4550.08	4606.46	4670.23	4742.58	5296.81	6538.51	10562.12
550,000	5005.09	5067.11	5137.26	5216.84	5826.49	7192.36	11618.33
600,000	5460.10	5527.76	5604.28	5691.10	6356.17	7846.21	12674.55
650,000	5915.11	5988.40	6071.30	6165.36	6885.86	8500.07	13730.76
700,000	6370.12	6449.05	6538.33	6639.62	7415.54	9153.92	14786.97
750,000	6825.13	6909.70	7005.35	7113.88	7945.22	9807.77	15843.18
800,000	7280.13	7370.34	7472.37	7588.13	8474.90	10461.62	16899.39
850,000	7735.14	7830.99	7939.40	8062.39	9004.58	11115.47	17955.61
900,000	8190.15	8291.64	8406.42	8536.65	9534.26	11769.32	19011.82
950,000	8645.16	8752.28	8873.45	9010.91	10063.95	12423.17	20068.03
1,000,000	9100.17	9212.93	9340.47	9485.17	10593.63	13077.02	21124.24

10%

Monthly Payments
Necessary to Amortize a Loan

AMOUNT BORROWED	YEARS REMAINING IN TERM						
	30	29	28	27	26	25	24
100	0.88	0.88	0.89	0.89	0.90	0.91	0.92
200	1.76	1.76	1.78	1.79	1.80	1.82	1.83
300	2.63	2.65	2.66	2.68	2.70	2.73	2.75
400	3.51	3.53	3.55	3.58	3.60	3.63	3.67
500	4.39	4.41	4.44	4.47	4.50	4.54	4.59
600	5.27	5.29	5.33	5.36	5.41	5.45	5.50
700	6.14	6.18	6.22	6.26	6.31	6.36	6.42
800	7.02	7.06	7.10	7.15	7.21	7.27	7.34
900	7.90	7.94	7.99	8.05	8.11	8.18	8.26
1,000	8.78	8.82	8.88	8.94	9.01	9.09	9.17
2,000	17.55	17.65	17.76	17.88	18.02	18.17	18.35
3,000	26.33	26.47	26.64	26.82	27.03	27.26	27.52
4,000	35.10	35.30	35.52	35.76	36.04	36.35	36.70
5,000	43.88	44.12	44.40	44.70	45.05	45.44	45.87
6,000	52.65	52.95	53.28	53.65	54.06	54.52	55.04
7,000	61.43	61.77	62.16	62.59	63.07	63.61	64.22
8,000	70.21	70.60	71.04	71.53	72.08	72.70	73.39
9,000	78.98	79.42	79.92	80.47	81.09	81.78	82.56
10,000	87.76	88.25	88.80	89.41	90.10	90.87	91.74
15,000	131.64	132.37	133.19	134.11	135.15	136.31	137.61
20,000	175.51	176.50	177.59	178.82	180.20	181.74	183.48
25,000	219.39	220.62	221.99	223.52	225.24	227.18	229.35
30,000	263.27	264.74	266.39	268.23	270.29	272.61	275.22
35,000	307.15	308.87	310.79	312.93	315.34	318.05	321.09
40,000	351.03	352.99	355.18	357.64	360.39	363.48	366.96
45,000	394.91	397.11	399.58	402.34	405.44	408.92	412.82
50,000	438.79	441.24	443.98	447.05	450.49	454.35	458.69
55,000	482.66	485.36	488.38	491.75	495.54	499.79	504.56
60,000	526.54	529.49	532.78	536.46	540.59	545.22	550.43
65,000	570.42	573.61	577.17	581.16	585.64	590.66	596.30
70,000	614.30	617.73	621.57	625.87	630.68	636.09	642.17
75,000	658.18	661.86	665.97	670.57	675.73	681.53	688.04
80,000	702.06	705.98	710.37	715.28	720.78	726.96	733.91
85,000	745.94	750.11	754.77	759.98	765.83	772.40	779.78
90,000	789.81	794.23	799.16	804.69	810.88	817.83	825.65
95,000	833.69	838.35	843.56	849.39	855.93	863.27	871.52
100,000	877.57	882.48	887.96	894.10	900.98	908.70	917.39
110,000	965.33	970.72	976.76	983.51	991.07	999.57	1009.13
120,000	1053.09	1058.97	1065.55	1072.92	1081.17	1090.44	1100.87
130,000	1140.84	1147.22	1154.35	1162.33	1171.27	1181.31	1192.61
140,000	1228.60	1235.47	1243.14	1251.74	1261.37	1272.18	1284.34
150,000	1316.36	1323.72	1331.94	1341.15	1351.47	1363.05	1376.08
200,000	1755.14	1764.95	1775.92	1788.20	1801.95	1817.40	1834.78
250,000	2193.93	2206.19	2219.90	2235.24	2252.44	2271.75	2293.47
300,000	2632.71	2647.43	2663.88	2682.29	2702.93	2726.10	2752.17
350,000	3071.50	3088.67	3107.86	3129.34	3153.42	3180.45	3210.86
400,000	3510.29	3529.91	3551.84	3576.39	3603.91	3634.80	3669.55
450,000	3949.07	3971.15	3995.82	4023.44	4054.40	4089.15	4128.25
500,000	4387.86	4412.39	4439.80	4470.49	4504.88	4543.50	4586.94
550,000	4826.64	4853.62	4883.78	4917.54	4955.37	4997.85	5045.64
600,000	5265.43	5294.86	5327.76	5364.59	5405.86	5452.20	5504.33
650,000	5704.22	5736.10	5771.74	5811.64	5856.35	5906.55	5963.03
700,000	6143.00	6177.34	6215.72	6258.68	6306.84	6360.91	6421.72
750,000	6581.79	6618.58	6659.70	6705.73	6757.33	6815.26	6880.42
800,000	7020.57	7059.82	7103.68	7152.78	7207.82	7269.61	7339.11
850,000	7459.36	7501.06	7547.66	7599.83	7658.30	7723.96	7797.80
900,000	7898.14	7942.29	7991.64	8046.88	8108.79	8178.31	8256.50
950,000	8336.93	8383.53	8435.62	8493.93	8559.28	8632.66	8715.19
1,000,000	8775.72	8824.77	8879.60	8940.98	9009.77	9087.01	9173.89

Monthly Payments

10%

Necessary to Amortize a Loan

YEARS REMAINING IN TERM

AMOUNT BORROWED	23	22	21	20	15	10	5
100	0.93	0.94	0.95	0.97	1.07	1.32	2.12
200	1.85	1.88	1.90	1.93	2.15	2.64	4.25
300	2.78	2.81	2.85	2.90	3.22	3.96	6.37
400	3.71	3.75	3.80	3.86	4.30	5.29	8.50
500	4.64	4.69	4.75	4.83	5.37	6.61	10.62
600	5.56	5.63	5.70	5.79	6.45	7.93	12.75
700	6.49	6.57	6.66	6.76	7.52	9.25	14.87
800	7.42	7.51	7.61	7.72	8.60	10.57	17.00
900	8.34	8.44	8.56	8.69	9.67	11.89	19.12
1,000	9.27	9.38	9.51	9.65	10.75	13.22	21.25
2,000	18.54	18.76	19.02	19.30	21.49	26.43	42.49
3,000	27.82	28.15	28.52	28.95	32.24	39.65	63.74
4,000	37.09	37.53	38.03	38.60	42.98	52.86	84.99
5,000	46.36	46.91	47.54	48.25	53.73	66.08	106.24
6,000	55.63	56.29	57.05	57.90	64.48	79.29	127.48
7,000	64.90	65.68	66.55	67.55	75.22	92.51	148.73
8,000	74.17	75.06	76.06	77.20	85.97	105.72	169.98
9,000	83.45	84.44	85.57	86.85	96.71	118.94	191.22
10,000	92.72	93.82	95.08	96.50	107.46	132.15	212.47
15,000	139.08	140.74	142.62	144.75	161.19	198.23	318.71
20,000	185.44	187.65	190.16	193.00	214.92	264.30	424.94
25,000	231.80	234.56	237.70	241.26	268.65	330.38	531.18
30,000	278.15	281.47	285.23	289.51	322.38	396.45	637.41
35,000	324.51	328.39	332.77	337.76	376.11	462.53	743.65
40,000	370.87	375.30	380.31	386.01	429.84	528.60	849.88
45,000	417.23	422.21	427.85	434.26	483.57	594.68	956.12
50,000	463.59	469.12	475.39	482.51	537.30	660.75	1062.35
55,000	509.95	516.04	522.93	530.76	591.03	726.83	1168.59
60,000	556.31	562.95	570.47	579.01	644.76	792.90	1274.82
65,000	602.67	609.86	618.01	627.26	698.49	858.98	1381.06
70,000	649.03	656.77	665.55	675.52	752.22	925.06	1487.29
75,000	695.39	703.68	713.09	723.77	805.95	991.13	1593.53
80,000	741.75	750.60	760.62	772.02	859.68	1057.21	1699.76
85,000	788.10	797.51	808.16	820.27	913.41	1123.28	1806.00
90,000	834.46	844.42	855.70	868.52	967.14	1189.36	1912.23
95,000	880.82	891.33	903.24	916.77	1020.87	1255.43	2018.47
100,000	927.18	938.25	950.78	965.02	1074.61	1321.51	2124.70
110,000	1019.90	1032.07	1045.86	1061.52	1182.07	1453.66	2337.17
120,000	1112.62	1125.90	1140.94	1158.03	1289.53	1585.81	2549.65
130,000	1205.34	1219.72	1236.01	1254.53	1396.99	1717.96	2762.12
140,000	1298.05	1313.54	1331.09	1351.03	1504.45	1850.11	2974.59
150,000	1390.77	1407.37	1426.17	1447.53	1611.91	1982.26	3187.06
200,000	1854.36	1876.49	1901.56	1930.04	2149.21	2643.01	4249.41
250,000	2317.95	2345.61	2376.95	2412.55	2686.51	3303.77	5311.76
300,000	2781.54	2814.74	2852.34	2895.06	3223.82	3964.52	6374.11
350,000	3245.14	3283.86	3327.73	3377.58	3761.12	4625.28	7436.47
400,000	3708.73	3752.98	3803.12	3860.09	4298.42	5286.03	8498.82
450,000	4172.32	4222.11	4278.51	4342.60	4835.72	5946.78	9561.17
500,000	4635.91	4691.23	4753.90	4825.11	5373.03	6607.54	10623.52
550,000	5099.50	5160.35	5229.29	5307.62	5910.33	7268.29	11685.87
600,000	5563.09	5629.48	5704.68	5790.13	6447.63	7929.04	12748.23
650,000	6026.68	6098.60	6180.07	6272.64	6984.93	8589.80	13810.58
700,000	6490.27	6567.72	6655.46	6755.15	7522.24	9250.55	14872.93
750,000	6953.86	7036.84	7130.85	7237.66	8059.54	9911.31	15935.28
800,000	7417.45	7505.97	7606.24	7720.17	8596.84	10572.06	16997.64
850,000	7881.04	7975.09	8081.63	8202.68	9134.14	11232.81	18059.99
900,000	8344.63	8444.21	8557.02	8685.19	9671.45	11893.57	19122.34
950,000	8808.23	8913.34	9032.41	9167.71	10208.75	12554.32	20184.69
1,000,000	9271.82	9382.46	9507.80	9650.22	10746.05	13215.07	21247.04

10¼% **Monthly Payments**
Necessary to Amortize a Loan

AMOUNT BORROWED	YEARS REMAINING IN TERM						
	30	**29**	**28**	**27**	**26**	**25**	**24**
100	0.90	0.90	0.91	0.91	0.92	0.93	0.93
200	1.79	1.80	1.81	1.82	1.84	1.85	1.87
300	2.69	2.70	2.72	2.74	2.76	2.78	2.80
400	3.58	3.60	3.62	3.65	3.68	3.71	3.74
500	4.48	4.50	4.53	4.56	4.59	4.63	4.67
600	5.38	5.41	5.44	5.47	5.51	5.56	5.61
700	6.27	6.31	6.34	6.39	6.43	6.48	6.54
800	7.17	7.21	7.25	7.30	7.35	7.41	7.48
900	8.06	8.11	8.16	8.21	8.27	8.34	8.41
1,000	8.96	9.01	9.06	9.12	9.19	9.26	9.35
2,000	17.92	18.02	18.12	18.24	18.38	18.53	18.70
3,000	26.88	27.03	27.19	27.36	27.57	27.79	28.05
4,000	35.84	36.03	36.25	36.49	36.75	37.06	37.40
5,000	44.81	45.04	45.31	45.61	45.94	46.32	46.74
6,000	53.77	54.05	54.37	54.73	55.13	55.58	56.09
7,000	62.73	63.06	63.43	63.85	64.32	64.85	65.44
8,000	71.69	72.07	72.49	72.97	73.51	74.11	74.79
9,000	80.65	81.08	81.56	82.09	82.70	83.37	84.14
10,000	89.61	90.09	90.62	91.21	91.88	92.64	93.49
15,000	134.42	135.13	135.93	136.82	137.83	138.96	140.23
20,000	179.22	180.17	181.24	182.43	183.77	185.28	186.98
25,000	224.03	225.21	226.54	228.04	229.71	231.60	233.72
30,000	268.83	270.26	271.85	273.64	275.65	277.91	280.46
35,000	313.64	315.30	317.16	319.25	321.60	324.23	327.21
40,000	358.44	360.34	362.47	364.86	367.54	370.55	373.95
45,000	403.25	405.38	407.78	410.46	413.48	416.87	420.69
50,000	448.05	450.43	453.09	456.07	459.42	463.19	467.44
55,000	492.86	495.47	498.40	501.68	505.37	509.51	514.18
60,000	537.66	540.51	543.71	547.29	551.31	555.83	560.93
65,000	582.47	585.55	589.01	592.89	597.25	602.15	607.67
70,000	627.27	630.60	634.32	638.50	643.19	648.47	654.41
75,000	672.08	675.64	679.63	684.11	689.13	694.79	701.16
80,000	716.88	720.68	724.94	729.72	735.08	741.11	747.90
85,000	761.69	765.73	770.25	775.32	781.02	787.43	794.65
90,000	806.49	810.77	815.56	820.93	826.96	833.74	841.39
95,000	851.30	855.81	860.87	866.54	872.90	880.06	888.13
100,000	896.10	900.85	906.18	912.14	918.85	926.38	934.88
110,000	985.71	990.94	996.79	1003.36	1010.73	1019.02	1028.36
120,000	1075.32	1081.02	1087.41	1094.57	1102.61	1111.66	1121.85
130,000	1164.93	1171.11	1178.03	1185.79	1194.50	1204.30	1215.34
140,000	1254.54	1261.20	1268.65	1277.00	1286.38	1296.94	1308.83
150,000	1344.15	1351.28	1359.26	1368.22	1378.27	1389.57	1402.31
200,000	1792.20	1801.71	1812.35	1824.29	1837.69	1852.77	1869.75
250,000	2240.25	2252.13	2265.44	2280.36	2297.11	2315.96	2337.19
300,000	2688.30	2702.56	2718.53	2736.43	2756.54	2779.15	2804.63
350,000	3136.35	3152.99	3171.62	3192.50	3215.96	3242.34	3272.07
400,000	3584.41	3603.41	3624.70	3648.58	3675.38	3705.53	3739.51
450,000	4032.46	4053.84	4077.79	4104.65	4134.81	4168.72	4206.94
500,000	4480.51	4504.27	4530.88	4560.72	4594.23	4631.92	4674.38
550,000	4928.56	4954.70	4983.97	5016.79	5053.65	5095.11	5141.82
600,000	5376.61	5405.12	5437.06	5472.86	5513.07	5558.30	5609.26
650,000	5824.66	5855.55	5890.14	5928.94	5972.50	6021.49	6076.70
700,000	6272.71	6305.98	6343.23	6385.01	6431.92	6484.68	6544.14
750,000	6720.76	6756.40	6796.32	6841.08	6891.34	6947.87	7011.57
800,000	7168.81	7206.83	7249.41	7297.15	7350.76	7411.07	7479.01
850,000	7616.86	7657.26	7702.50	7753.22	7810.19	7874.26	7946.45
900,000	8064.91	8107.68	8155.58	8209.30	8269.61	8337.45	8413.89
950,000	8512.96	8558.11	8608.67	8665.37	8729.03	8800.64	8881.33
1,000,000	8961.01	9008.54	9061.76	9121.44	9188.46	9263.83	9348.77

Monthly Payments 10¼%
Necessary to Amortize a Loan

AMOUNT BORROWED	YEARS REMAINING IN TERM						
	23	22	21	20	15	10	5
100	0.94	0.96	0.97	0.98	1.09	1.34	2.14
200	1.89	1.91	1.94	1.96	2.18	2.67	4.27
300	2.83	2.87	2.90	2.94	3.27	4.01	6.41
400	3.78	3.82	3.87	3.93	4.36	5.34	8.55
500	4.72	4.78	4.84	4.91	5.45	6.68	10.69
600	5.67	5.73	5.81	5.89	6.54	8.01	12.82
700	6.61	6.69	6.77	6.87	7.63	9.35	14.96
800	7.56	7.64	7.74	7.85	8.72	10.68	17.10
900	8.50	8.60	8.71	8.83	9.81	12.02	19.23
1,000	9.44	9.55	9.68	9.82	10.90	13.35	21.37
2,000	18.89	19.11	19.35	19.63	21.80	26.71	42.74
3,000	28.33	28.66	29.03	29.45	32.70	40.06	64.11
4,000	37.78	38.21	38.71	39.27	43.60	53.42	85.48
5,000	47.22	47.77	48.38	49.08	54.50	66.77	106.85
6,000	56.67	57.32	58.06	58.90	65.40	80.12	128.22
7,000	66.11	66.87	67.73	68.72	76.30	93.48	149.59
8,000	75.56	76.43	77.41	78.53	87.20	106.83	170.96
9,000	85.00	85.98	87.09	88.35	98.10	120.19	192.33
10,000	94.45	95.53	96.76	98.16	109.00	133.54	213.70
15,000	141.67	143.30	145.14	147.25	163.49	200.31	320.55
20,000	188.89	191.06	193.53	196.33	217.99	267.08	427.41
25,000	236.12	238.83	241.91	245.41	272.49	333.85	534.26
30,000	283.34	286.60	290.29	294.49	326.99	400.62	641.11
35,000	330.56	334.36	338.67	343.58	381.48	467.39	747.96
40,000	377.79	382.13	387.05	392.66	435.98	534.16	854.81
45,000	425.01	429.89	435.43	441.74	490.48	600.93	961.66
50,000	472.23	477.66	483.82	490.82	544.98	667.70	1068.51
55,000	519.46	525.43	532.20	539.90	599.47	734.46	1175.36
60,000	566.68	573.19	580.58	588.99	653.97	801.23	1282.22
65,000	613.90	620.96	628.96	638.07	708.47	868.00	1389.07
70,000	661.13	668.72	677.34	687.15	762.97	934.77	1495.92
75,000	708.35	716.49	725.72	736.23	817.46	1001.54	1602.77
80,000	755.57	764.25	774.11	785.31	871.96	1068.31	1709.62
85,000	802.80	812.02	822.49	834.40	926.46	1135.08	1816.47
90,000	850.02	859.79	870.87	883.48	980.96	1201.85	1923.32
95,000	897.24	907.55	919.25	932.56	1035.45	1268.62	2030.18
100,000	944.47	955.32	967.63	981.64	1089.95	1335.39	2137.03
110,000	1038.91	1050.85	1064.39	1079.81	1198.95	1468.93	2350.73
120,000	1133.36	1146.38	1161.16	1177.97	1307.94	1602.47	2564.43
130,000	1227.81	1241.91	1257.92	1276.14	1416.94	1736.01	2778.13
140,000	1322.25	1337.45	1354.68	1374.30	1525.93	1869.55	2991.84
150,000	1416.70	1432.98	1451.45	1472.47	1634.93	2003.09	3205.54
200,000	1888.93	1910.64	1935.26	1963.29	2179.90	2670.78	4274.05
250,000	2361.17	2388.30	2419.08	2454.11	2724.88	3338.48	5342.57
300,000	2833.40	2865.95	2902.89	2944.93	3269.85	4006.17	6411.08
350,000	3305.63	3343.61	3386.71	3435.75	3814.83	4673.87	7479.59
400,000	3777.86	3821.27	3870.53	3926.57	4359.80	5341.56	8548.11
450,000	4250.10	4298.93	4354.34	4417.40	4904.78	6009.26	9616.62
500,000	4722.33	4776.59	4838.16	4908.22	5449.75	6676.95	10685.13
550,000	5194.56	5254.25	5321.97	5399.04	5994.73	7344.65	11753.65
600,000	5666.80	5731.91	5805.79	5889.86	6539.71	8012.34	12822.16
650,000	6139.03	6209.57	6289.60	6380.68	7084.68	8680.04	13890.67
700,000	6611.26	6687.23	6773.42	6871.50	7629.66	9347.73	14959.18
750,000	7083.50	7164.89	7257.24	7362.33	8174.63	10015.43	16027.70
800,000	7555.73	7642.55	7741.05	7853.15	8719.61	10683.12	17096.21
850,000	8027.96	8120.21	8224.87	8343.97	9264.58	11350.82	18164.72
900,000	8500.20	8597.86	8708.68	8834.79	9809.56	12018.51	19233.24
950,000	8972.43	9075.52	9192.50	9325.61	10354.53	12686.21	20301.75
1,000,000	9444.66	9553.18	9676.31	9816.43	10899.51	13353.90	21370.26

10½%

Monthly Payments
Necessary to Amortize a Loan

YEARS REMAINING IN TERM

AMOUNT BORROWED	30	29	28	27	26	25	24
100	0.91	0.92	0.92	0.93	0.94	0.94	0.95
200	1.83	1.84	1.85	1.86	1.87	1.89	1.90
300	2.74	2.76	2.77	2.79	2.81	2.83	2.86
400	3.66	3.68	3.70	3.72	3.75	3.78	3.81
500	4.57	4.60	4.62	4.65	4.68	4.72	4.76
600	5.49	5.52	5.55	5.58	5.62	5.67	5.71
700	6.40	6.44	6.47	6.51	6.56	6.61	6.67
800	7.32	7.35	7.40	7.44	7.49	7.55	7.62
900	8.23	8.27	8.32	8.37	8.43	8.50	8.57
1,000	9.15	9.19	9.25	9.30	9.37	9.44	9.52
2,000	18.29	18.39	18.49	18.61	18.74	18.88	19.05
3,000	27.44	27.58	27.74	27.91	28.10	28.33	28.57
4,000	36.59	36.77	36.98	37.21	37.47	37.77	38.10
5,000	45.74	45.97	46.23	46.52	46.84	47.21	47.62
6,000	54.88	55.16	55.47	55.82	56.21	56.65	57.15
7,000	64.03	64.35	64.72	65.12	65.58	66.09	66.67
8,000	73.18	73.55	73.96	74.42	74.95	75.53	76.20
9,000	82.33	82.74	83.21	83.73	84.31	84.98	85.72
10,000	91.47	91.93	92.45	93.03	93.68	94.42	95.25
15,000	137.21	137.90	138.68	139.55	140.52	141.63	142.87
20,000	182.95	183.87	184.90	186.06	187.37	188.84	190.50
25,000	228.68	229.84	231.13	232.58	234.21	236.05	238.12
30,000	274.42	275.80	277.35	279.09	281.05	283.25	285.74
35,000	320.16	321.77	323.58	325.61	327.89	330.46	333.37
40,000	365.90	367.74	369.80	372.12	374.73	377.67	380.99
45,000	411.63	413.70	416.03	418.64	421.57	424.88	428.62
50,000	457.37	459.67	462.25	465.15	468.41	472.09	476.24
55,000	503.11	505.64	508.48	511.67	515.26	519.30	523.86
60,000	548.84	551.60	554.70	558.18	562.10	566.51	571.49
65,000	594.58	597.57	600.93	604.70	608.94	613.72	619.11
70,000	640.32	643.54	647.15	651.21	655.78	660.93	666.74
75,000	686.05	689.51	693.38	697.73	702.62	708.14	714.36
80,000	731.79	735.47	739.60	744.24	749.46	755.35	761.98
85,000	777.53	781.44	785.83	790.76	796.30	802.55	809.61
90,000	823.27	827.41	832.05	837.27	843.15	849.76	857.23
95,000	869.00	873.37	878.28	883.79	889.99	896.97	904.86
100,000	914.74	919.34	924.50	930.30	936.83	944.18	952.48
110,000	1006.21	1011.27	1016.95	1023.33	1030.51	1038.60	1047.73
120,000	1097.69	1103.21	1109.40	1116.36	1124.20	1133.02	1142.98
130,000	1189.16	1195.14	1201.85	1209.40	1217.88	1227.44	1238.23
140,000	1280.64	1287.08	1294.31	1302.43	1311.56	1321.85	1333.47
150,000	1372.11	1379.01	1386.76	1395.46	1405.24	1416.27	1428.72
200,000	1829.48	1838.68	1849.01	1860.61	1873.66	1888.36	1904.96
250,000	2286.85	2298.35	2311.26	2325.76	2342.07	2360.45	2381.20
300,000	2744.22	2758.02	2773.51	2790.91	2810.49	2832.55	2857.44
350,000	3201.59	3217.69	3235.76	3256.06	3278.90	3304.64	3333.68
400,000	3658.96	3677.36	3698.01	3721.22	3747.32	3776.73	3809.92
450,000	4116.33	4137.03	4160.27	4186.37	4215.73	4248.82	4286.16
500,000	4573.70	4596.70	4622.52	4651.52	4684.15	4720.91	4762.40
550,000	5031.07	5056.37	5084.77	5116.67	5152.56	5193.00	5238.64
600,000	5488.44	5516.04	5547.02	5581.82	5620.98	5665.09	5714.89
650,000	5945.81	5975.71	6009.27	6046.98	6089.39	6137.18	6191.13
700,000	6403.18	6435.38	6471.53	6512.13	6557.80	6609.27	6667.37
750,000	6860.54	6895.05	6933.78	6977.28	7026.22	7081.36	7143.61
800,000	7317.91	7354.73	7396.03	7442.43	7494.63	7553.45	7619.85
850,000	7775.28	7814.40	7858.28	7907.58	7963.05	8025.54	8096.09
900,000	8232.65	8274.07	8320.53	8372.73	8431.46	8497.64	8572.33
950,000	8690.02	8733.74	8782.78	8837.89	8899.88	8969.73	9048.57
1,000,000	9147.39	9193.41	9245.04	9303.04	9368.29	9441.82	9524.81

Monthly Payments 10½%
Necessary to Amortize a Loan

AMOUNT BORROWED	YEARS REMAINING IN TERM						
	23	22	21	20	15	10	5
100	0.96	0.97	0.98	1.00	1.11	1.35	2.15
200	1.92	1.95	1.97	2.00	2.21	2.70	4.30
300	2.89	2.92	2.95	3.00	3.32	4.05	6.45
400	3.85	3.89	3.94	3.99	4.42	5.40	8.60
500	4.81	4.86	4.92	4.99	5.53	6.75	10.75
600	5.77	5.84	5.91	5.99	6.63	8.10	12.90
700	6.73	6.81	6.89	6.99	7.74	9.45	15.05
800	7.69	7.78	7.88	7.99	8.84	10.79	17.20
900	8.66	8.75	8.86	8.99	9.95	12.14	19.34
1,000	9.62	9.73	9.85	9.98	11.05	13.49	21.49
2,000	19.24	19.45	19.69	19.97	22.11	26.99	42.99
3,000	28.86	29.18	29.54	29.95	33.16	40.48	64.48
4,000	38.47	38.90	39.38	39.94	44.22	53.97	85.98
5,000	48.09	48.63	49.23	49.92	55.27	67.47	107.47
6,000	57.71	58.35	59.08	59.90	66.32	80.96	128.96
7,000	67.33	68.08	68.92	69.89	77.38	94.45	150.46
8,000	76.95	77.80	78.77	79.87	88.43	107.95	171.95
9,000	86.57	87.53	88.61	89.85	99.49	121.44	193.45
10,000	96.19	97.25	98.46	99.84	110.54	134.93	214.94
15,000	144.28	145.88	147.69	149.76	165.81	202.40	322.41
20,000	192.37	194.50	196.92	199.68	221.08	269.87	429.88
25,000	240.47	243.13	246.15	249.59	276.35	337.34	537.35
30,000	288.56	291.75	295.38	299.51	331.62	404.80	644.82
35,000	336.65	340.38	344.61	349.43	386.89	472.27	752.29
40,000	384.75	389.00	393.84	399.35	442.16	539.74	859.76
45,000	432.84	437.63	443.07	449.27	497.43	607.21	967.23
50,000	480.93	486.25	492.30	499.19	552.70	674.67	1074.70
55,000	529.03	534.88	541.53	549.11	607.97	742.14	1182.16
60,000	577.12	583.50	590.76	599.03	663.24	809.61	1289.63
65,000	625.21	632.13	639.99	648.95	718.51	877.08	1397.10
70,000	673.31	680.75	689.22	698.87	773.78	944.54	1504.57
75,000	721.40	729.38	738.45	748.78	829.05	1012.01	1612.04
80,000	769.49	778.01	787.68	798.70	884.32	1079.48	1719.51
85,000	817.59	826.63	836.91	848.62	939.59	1146.95	1826.98
90,000	865.68	875.26	886.14	898.54	994.86	1214.41	1934.45
95,000	913.77	923.88	935.37	948.46	1050.13	1281.88	2041.92
100,000	961.87	972.51	984.60	998.38	1105.40	1349.35	2149.39
110,000	1058.05	1069.76	1083.06	1098.22	1215.94	1484.28	2364.33
120,000	1154.24	1167.01	1181.52	1198.06	1326.48	1619.22	2579.27
130,000	1250.43	1264.26	1279.98	1297.89	1437.02	1754.15	2794.21
140,000	1346.61	1361.51	1378.44	1397.73	1547.56	1889.09	3009.15
150,000	1442.80	1458.76	1476.90	1497.57	1658.10	2024.02	3224.09
200,000	1923.73	1945.01	1969.20	1996.76	2210.80	2698.70	4298.78
250,000	2404.67	2431.27	2461.50	2495.95	2763.50	3373.37	5373.48
300,000	2885.60	2917.52	2953.80	2995.14	3316.20	4048.05	6448.17
350,000	3366.54	3403.77	3446.10	3494.33	3868.90	4722.72	7522.87
400,000	3847.47	3890.03	3938.39	3993.52	4421.60	5397.40	8597.56
450,000	4328.40	4376.28	4430.69	4492.71	4974.30	6072.07	9672.26
500,000	4809.34	4862.54	4922.99	4991.90	5526.99	6746.75	10746.95
550,000	5290.27	5348.79	5415.29	5491.09	6079.69	7421.42	11821.65
600,000	5771.20	5835.04	5907.59	5990.28	6632.39	8096.10	12896.34
650,000	6252.14	6321.30	6399.89	6489.47	7185.09	8770.77	13971.04
700,000	6733.07	6807.55	6892.19	6988.66	7737.79	9445.45	15045.73
750,000	7214.00	7293.80	7384.49	7487.85	8290.49	10120.12	16120.43
800,000	7694.94	7780.06	7876.79	7987.04	8843.19	10794.80	17195.12
850,000	8175.87	8266.31	8369.09	8486.23	9395.89	11469.47	18269.82
900,000	8656.81	8752.56	8861.39	8985.42	9948.59	12144.15	19344.51
950,000	9137.74	9238.82	9353.69	9484.61	10501.29	12818.82	20419.21
1,000,000	9618.67	9725.07	9845.99	9983.80	11053.99	13493.50	21493.90

10³/₄% Monthly Payments
Necessary to Amortize a Loan

YEARS REMAINING IN TERM

AMOUNT BORROWED	30	29	28	27	26	25	24
100	0.93	0.94	0.94	0.95	0.95	0.96	0.97
200	1.87	1.88	1.89	1.90	1.91	1.92	1.94
300	2.80	2.81	2.83	2.85	2.86	2.89	2.91
400	3.73	3.75	3.77	3.79	3.82	3.85	3.88
500	4.67	4.69	4.71	4.74	4.77	4.81	4.85
600	5.60	5.63	5.66	5.69	5.73	5.77	5.82
700	6.53	6.57	6.60	6.64	6.68	6.73	6.79
800	7.47	7.50	7.54	7.59	7.64	7.70	7.76
900	8.40	8.44	8.49	8.54	8.59	8.66	8.73
1,000	9.33	9.38	9.43	9.49	9.55	9.62	9.70
2,000	18.67	18.76	18.86	18.97	19.10	19.24	19.40
3,000	28.00	28.14	28.29	28.46	28.65	28.86	29.11
4,000	37.34	37.52	37.72	37.94	38.20	38.48	38.81
5,000	46.67	46.90	47.15	47.43	47.75	48.10	48.51
6,000	56.01	56.28	56.58	56.91	57.30	57.73	58.21
7,000	65.34	65.66	66.01	66.40	66.84	67.35	67.91
8,000	74.68	75.03	75.44	75.89	76.39	76.97	77.62
9,000	84.01	84.41	84.86	85.37	85.94	86.59	87.32
10,000	93.35	93.79	94.29	94.86	95.49	96.21	97.02
15,000	140.02	140.69	141.44	142.29	143.24	144.31	145.53
20,000	186.70	187.59	188.59	189.71	190.98	192.42	194.04
25,000	233.37	234.48	235.73	237.14	238.73	240.52	242.55
30,000	280.04	281.38	282.88	284.57	286.48	288.63	291.06
35,000	326.72	328.28	330.03	332.00	334.22	336.73	339.57
40,000	373.39	375.17	377.18	379.43	381.97	384.84	388.08
45,000	420.07	422.07	424.32	426.86	429.72	432.94	436.59
50,000	466.74	468.97	471.47	474.29	477.46	481.05	485.10
55,000	513.41	515.86	518.62	521.72	525.21	529.15	533.61
60,000	560.09	562.76	565.76	569.14	572.95	577.26	582.12
65,000	606.76	609.66	612.91	616.57	620.70	625.36	630.63
70,000	653.44	656.55	660.06	664.00	668.45	673.46	679.14
75,000	700.11	703.45	707.20	711.43	716.19	721.57	727.65
80,000	746.79	750.35	754.35	758.86	763.94	769.67	776.16
85,000	793.46	797.24	801.50	806.29	811.69	817.78	824.67
90,000	840.13	844.14	848.65	853.72	859.43	865.88	873.18
95,000	886.81	891.04	895.79	901.15	907.18	913.99	921.69
100,000	933.48	937.93	942.94	948.57	954.92	962.09	970.20
110,000	1026.83	1031.73	1037.23	1043.43	1050.42	1058.30	1067.22
120,000	1120.18	1125.52	1131.53	1138.29	1145.91	1154.51	1164.24
130,000	1213.53	1219.31	1225.82	1233.15	1241.40	1250.72	1261.26
140,000	1306.87	1313.11	1320.12	1328.00	1336.89	1346.93	1358.28
150,000	1400.22	1406.90	1414.41	1422.86	1432.39	1443.14	1455.30
200,000	1866.96	1875.87	1885.88	1897.15	1909.85	1924.19	1940.40
250,000	2333.70	2344.83	2357.35	2371.43	2387.31	2405.23	2425.50
300,000	2800.44	2813.80	2828.82	2845.72	2864.77	2886.28	2910.60
350,000	3267.18	3282.77	3300.29	3320.01	3342.23	3367.32	3395.69
400,000	3733.93	3751.74	3771.76	3794.30	3819.70	3848.37	3880.79
450,000	4200.67	4220.70	4243.23	4268.58	4297.16	4329.42	4365.89
500,000	4667.41	4689.67	4714.70	4742.87	4774.62	4810.46	4850.99
550,000	5134.15	5158.64	5186.17	5217.16	5252.08	5291.51	5336.09
600,000	5600.89	5627.60	5657.64	5691.44	5729.55	5772.56	5821.19
650,000	6067.63	6096.57	6129.11	6165.73	6207.01	6253.60	6306.29
700,000	6534.37	6565.54	6600.58	6640.02	6684.47	6734.65	6791.39
750,000	7001.11	7034.50	7072.05	7114.30	7161.93	7215.70	7276.49
800,000	7467.85	7503.47	7543.52	7588.59	7639.39	7696.74	7761.59
850,000	7934.59	7972.44	8014.99	8062.88	8116.86	8177.79	8246.69
900,000	8401.33	8441.40	8486.46	8537.16	8594.32	8658.83	8731.79
950,000	8868.07	8910.37	8957.93	9011.45	9071.78	9139.88	9216.89
1,000,000	9334.81	9379.34	9429.40	9485.74	9549.24	9620.93	9701.99

Monthly Payments
Necessary to Amortize a Loan

10¾%

AMOUNT BORROWED	YEARS REMAINING IN TERM						
	23	**22**	**21**	**20**	**15**	**10**	**5**
100	0.98	0.99	1.00	1.02	1.12	1.36	2.16
200	1.96	1.98	2.00	2.03	2.24	2.73	4.32
300	2.94	2.97	2.97	3.05	3.36	4.09	6.49
400	3.92	3.96	4.01	4.06	4.48	5.45	8.65
500	4.90	4.95	5.01	5.08	5.60	6.82	10.81
600	5.88	5.94	6.01	6.09	6.73	8.18	12.97
700	6.86	6.93	7.01	7.11	7.85	9.54	15.13
800	7.84	7.92	8.01	8.12	8.97	10.91	17.29
900	8.81	8.91	9.02	9.14	10.09	12.27	19.46
1,000	9.79	9.90	10.02	10.15	11.21	13.63	21.62
2,000	19.59	19.80	20.03	20.30	22.42	27.27	43.24
3,000	29.38	29.69	30.05	30.46	33.63	40.90	64.85
4,000	39.18	39.59	40.07	40.61	44.84	54.54	86.47
5,000	48.97	49.49	50.08	50.76	56.05	68.17	108.09
6,000	58.76	59.39	60.10	60.91	67.26	81.80	129.71
7,000	68.56	69.29	70.12	71.07	78.47	95.44	151.33
8,000	78.35	79.18	80.13	81.22	89.68	109.07	172.94
9,000	88.14	89.08	90.15	91.37	100.89	122.70	194.56
10,000	97.94	98.98	100.17	101.52	112.09	136.34	216.18
15,000	146.91	148.47	150.25	152.28	168.14	204.51	324.27
20,000	195.88	197.96	200.34	203.05	224.19	272.68	432.36
25,000	244.85	247.45	250.42	253.81	280.24	340.85	540.45
30,000	293.81	296.94	300.50	304.57	336.28	409.02	648.54
35,000	342.78	346.43	350.59	355.33	392.33	477.19	756.63
40,000	391.75	395.92	400.67	406.09	448.38	545.35	864.72
45,000	440.72	445.41	450.76	456.85	504.43	613.52	972.81
50,000	489.69	494.90	500.84	507.61	560.47	681.69	1080.90
55,000	538.66	544.40	550.92	558.38	616.52	749.86	1188.99
60,000	587.63	593.89	601.01	609.14	672.57	818.03	1297.08
65,000	636.60	643.38	651.09	659.90	728.62	886.20	1405.17
70,000	685.57	692.87	701.18	710.66	784.66	954.37	1513.26
75,000	734.54	742.36	751.26	761.42	840.71	1022.54	1621.35
80,000	783.51	791.85	801.34	812.18	896.76	1090.71	1729.44
85,000	832.47	841.34	851.43	862.94	952.81	1158.88	1837.53
90,000	881.44	890.83	901.51	913.71	1008.85	1227.05	1945.62
95,000	930.41	940.32	951.60	964.47	1064.90	1295.22	2053.71
100,000	979.38	989.81	1001.68	1015.23	1120.95	1363.39	2161.80
110,000	1077.32	1088.79	1101.85	1116.75	1233.04	1499.73	2377.97
120,000	1175.20	1187.77	1202.02	1218.27	1345.14	1636.06	2594.15
130,000	1273.20	1286.75	1302.18	1319.80	1457.23	1772.40	2810.33
140,000	1371.13	1385.73	1402.35	1421.32	1569.33	1908.74	3026.51
150,000	1469.07	1484.71	1502.52	1522.84	1681.42	2045.08	3242.69
200,000	1958.76	1979.62	2003.36	2030.46	2241.90	2726.77	4323.59
250,000	2448.46	2474.52	2504.20	2538.07	2802.37	3408.47	5404.49
300,000	2938.15	2969.43	3005.04	3045.69	3362.84	4090.16	6485.39
350,000	3427.84	3464.33	3505.88	3553.30	3923.32	4771.85	7566.28
400,000	3917.53	3959.24	4006.72	4060.92	4483.79	5453.55	8647.18
450,000	4407.22	4454.14	4507.56	4568.53	5044.27	6135.24	9728.08
500,000	4896.91	4949.05	5008.40	5076.14	5604.74	6816.93	10808.98
550,000	5386.60	5443.95	5509.24	5583.76	6165.21	7498.63	11889.87
600,000	5876.29	5938.86	6010.08	6091.37	6725.69	8180.32	12970.77
650,000	6365.98	6433.76	6510.92	6598.99	7286.16	8862.01	14051.67
700,000	6855.67	6928.67	7011.76	7106.60	7846.64	9543.71	15132.57
750,000	7345.37	7423.57	7512.59	7614.22	8407.11	10225.40	16213.47
800,000	7835.06	7918.48	8013.43	8121.83	8967.58	10907.09	17294.36
850,000	8324.75	8413.38	8514.27	8629.45	9528.06	11588.79	18375.26
900,000	8814.44	8908.29	9015.11	9137.06	10088.53	12270.48	19456.16
950,000	9304.13	9403.19	9515.95	9644.68	10649.01	12952.17	20537.06
1,000,000	9793.82	9896.10	10016.79	10152.29	11209.48	13633.87	21617.95

11%

Monthly Payments
Necessary to Amortize a Loan

AMOUNT BORROWED	YEARS REMAINING IN TERM						
	30	29	28	27	26	25	24
100	0.95	0.96	0.96	0.97	0.97	0.98	0.99
200	1.90	1.91	1.92	1.93	1.95	1.96	1.98
300	2.86	2.87	2.88	2.90	2.92	2.94	2.96
400	3.81	3.83	3.85	3.87	3.89	3.92	3.95
500	4.76	4.78	4.81	4.83	4.87	4.90	4.94
600	5.71	5.74	5.77	5.80	5.84	5.88	5.93
700	6.67	6.70	6.73	6.77	6.81	6.86	6.92
800	7.62	7.65	7.69	7.74	7.79	7.84	7.90
900	8.57	8.61	8.65	8.70	8.76	8.82	8.89
1,000	9.52	9.57	9.61	9.67	9.73	9.80	9.88
2,000	19.05	19.13	19.23	19.34	19.46	19.60	19.76
3,000	28.57	28.70	28.84	29.01	29.19	29.40	29.64
4,000	38.09	38.27	38.46	38.68	38.93	39.20	39.52
5,000	47.62	47.83	48.07	48.35	48.66	49.01	49.40
6,000	57.14	57.40	57.69	58.02	58.39	58.81	59.28
7,000	66.66	66.96	67.30	67.69	68.12	68.61	69.16
8,000	76.19	76.53	76.92	77.36	77.85	78.41	79.04
9,000	85.71	86.10	86.53	87.03	87.58	88.21	88.92
10,000	95.23	95.66	96.15	96.70	97.31	98.01	98.80
15,000	142.85	143.49	144.22	145.04	145.97	147.02	148.20
20,000	190.46	191.33	192.30	193.39	194.63	196.02	197.61
25,000	238.08	239.16	240.37	241.74	243.28	245.03	247.01
30,000	285.70	286.99	288.44	290.09	291.94	294.03	296.41
35,000	333.31	334.82	336.52	338.43	340.59	343.04	345.81
40,000	380.93	382.65	384.59	386.78	389.25	392.05	395.21
45,000	428.55	430.48	432.67	435.13	437.91	441.05	444.61
50,000	476.16	478.31	480.74	483.48	486.56	490.06	494.01
55,000	523.78	526.15	528.81	531.82	535.22	539.06	543.41
60,000	571.39	573.98	576.89	580.17	583.88	588.07	592.82
65,000	619.01	621.81	624.96	628.52	632.53	637.07	642.22
70,000	666.63	669.64	673.04	676.87	681.19	686.08	691.62
75,000	714.24	717.47	721.11	725.21	729.85	735.08	741.02
80,000	761.86	765.30	769.18	773.56	778.50	784.09	790.42
85,000	809.47	813.14	817.26	821.91	827.16	833.10	839.82
90,000	857.09	860.97	865.33	870.26	875.81	882.10	889.22
95,000	904.71	908.80	913.41	918.60	924.47	931.11	938.63
100,000	952.32	956.63	961.48	966.95	973.13	980.11	988.03
110,000	1047.56	1052.29	1057.63	1063.65	1070.44	1078.12	1086.83
120,000	1142.79	1147.96	1153.78	1160.34	1167.75	1176.14	1185.63
130,000	1238.02	1243.62	1249.92	1257.04	1265.07	1274.15	1284.43
140,000	1333.25	1339.28	1346.07	1353.73	1362.38	1372.16	1383.24
150,000	1428.49	1434.94	1442.22	1450.43	1459.69	1470.17	1482.04
200,000	1904.65	1913.26	1922.96	1933.90	1946.25	1960.23	1976.05
250,000	2380.81	2391.57	2403.70	2417.38	2432.82	2450.28	2470.07
300,000	2856.97	2869.89	2884.44	2900.85	2919.38	2940.34	2964.08
350,000	3333.13	3348.20	3365.18	3384.33	3405.95	3430.40	3458.09
400,000	3809.29	3826.52	3845.92	3867.80	3892.51	3920.45	3952.11
450,000	4285.46	4304.83	4326.66	4351.28	4379.07	4410.51	4446.12
500,000	4761.62	4783.15	4807.40	4834.75	4865.64	4900.57	4940.13
550,000	5237.78	5261.46	5288.14	5318.23	5352.20	5390.62	5434.15
600,000	5713.94	5739.78	5768.88	5801.70	5838.76	5880.68	5928.16
650,000	6190.10	6218.09	6249.62	6285.18	6325.33	6370.73	6422.17
700,000	6666.26	6696.41	6730.36	6768.65	6811.89	6860.79	6916.19
750,000	7142.43	7174.72	7211.10	7252.13	7298.45	7350.85	7410.20
800,000	7618.59	7653.04	7691.84	7735.60	7785.02	7840.90	7904.21
850,000	8094.75	8131.35	8172.58	8219.08	8271.58	8330.96	8398.23
900,000	8570.91	8609.66	8653.32	8702.55	8758.15	8821.02	8892.24
950,000	9047.07	9087.98	9134.06	9186.03	9244.71	9311.07	9386.25
1,000,000	9523.23	9566.29	9614.80	9669.50	9731.27	9801.13	9880.27

Monthly Payments 11%
Necessary to Amortize a Loan

AMOUNT BORROWED	YEARS REMAINING IN TERM						
	23	22	21	20	15	10	5
100	1.00	1.01	1.02	1.03	1.14	1.38	2.17
200	1.99	2.01	2.04	2.06	2.27	2.76	4.35
300	2.99	3.02	3.06	3.10	3.41	4.13	6.52
400	3.99	4.03	4.08	4.13	4.55	5.51	8.70
500	4.99	5.04	5.09	5.16	5.68	6.89	10.87
600	5.98	6.04	6.11	6.19	6.82	8.27	13.05
700	6.98	7.05	7.13	7.23	7.96	9.64	15.22
800	7.98	8.06	8.15	8.26	9.09	11.02	17.39
900	8.97	9.07	9.17	9.29	10.23	12.40	19.57
1,000	9.97	10.07	10.19	10.32	11.37	13.78	21.74
2,000	19.94	20.14	20.38	20.64	22.73	27.55	43.48
3,000	29.91	30.22	30.57	30.97	34.10	41.33	65.23
4,000	39.88	40.29	40.75	41.29	45.46	55.10	86.97
5,000	49.85	50.36	50.94	51.61	56.83	68.88	108.71
6,000	59.82	60.43	61.13	61.93	68.20	82.65	130.45
7,000	69.79	70.51	71.32	72.25	79.56	96.43	152.20
8,000	79.76	80.58	81.51	82.58	90.93	110.20	173.94
9,000	89.73	90.65	91.70	92.90	102.29	123.98	195.68
10,000	99.70	100.72	101.89	103.22	113.66	137.75	217.42
15,000	149.55	151.08	152.83	154.83	170.49	206.63	326.14
20,000	199.40	201.44	203.77	206.44	227.32	275.50	434.85
25,000	249.25	251.81	254.72	258.05	284.15	344.38	543.56
30,000	299.10	302.17	305.66	309.66	340.98	413.25	652.27
35,000	348.95	352.53	356.60	361.27	397.81	482.13	760.98
40,000	398.80	402.89	407.55	412.88	454.64	551.00	869.70
45,000	448.65	453.25	458.49	464.48	511.47	619.88	978.41
50,000	498.50	503.61	509.44	516.09	568.30	688.75	1087.12
55,000	548.35	553.97	560.38	567.70	625.13	757.63	1195.83
60,000	598.20	604.33	611.32	619.31	681.96	826.50	1304.55
65,000	648.06	654.70	662.27	670.92	738.79	895.38	1413.26
70,000	697.91	705.06	713.21	722.53	795.62	964.25	1521.97
75,000	747.76	755.42	764.15	774.14	852.45	1033.13	1630.68
80,000	797.61	805.78	815.10	825.75	909.28	1102.00	1739.39
85,000	847.46	856.14	866.04	877.36	966.11	1170.88	1848.11
90,000	897.31	906.50	916.98	928.97	1022.94	1239.75	1956.82
95,000	947.16	956.86	967.93	980.58	1079.77	1308.63	2065.53
100,000	997.01	1007.22	1018.87	1032.19	1136.60	1377.50	2174.24
110,000	1096.71	1107.95	1120.76	1135.41	1250.26	1515.25	2391.67
120,000	1196.41	1208.67	1222.65	1238.63	1363.92	1653.00	2609.09
130,000	1296.11	1309.39	1324.53	1341.84	1477.58	1790.75	2826.51
140,000	1395.81	1410.11	1426.42	1445.06	1591.24	1928.50	3043.94
150,000	1495.51	1510.84	1528.31	1548.28	1704.90	2066.25	3261.36
200,000	1994.02	2014.45	2037.74	2064.38	2273.19	2755.00	4348.48
250,000	2492.52	2518.06	2547.18	2580.47	2841.49	3443.75	5435.61
300,000	2991.02	3021.67	3056.61	3096.57	3409.79	4132.50	6522.73
350,000	3489.53	3525.28	3566.05	3612.66	3978.09	4821.25	7609.85
400,000	3988.03	4028.89	4075.48	4128.75	4546.39	5510.00	8696.97
450,000	4486.54	4532.51	4584.92	4644.85	5114.69	6198.75	9784.09
500,000	4985.04	5036.12	5094.35	5160.94	5682.98	6887.50	10871.21
550,000	5483.54	5539.73	5603.79	5677.04	6251.28	7576.25	11958.33
600,000	5982.05	6043.34	6113.23	6193.13	6819.58	8265.00	13045.45
650,000	6480.55	6546.95	6622.66	6709.22	7387.88	8953.75	14132.57
700,000	6979.06	7050.56	7132.10	7225.32	7956.18	9642.50	15219.70
750,000	7477.56	7554.18	7641.53	7741.41	8524.48	10331.25	16306.82
800,000	7976.06	8057.79	8150.97	8257.51	9092.78	11020.00	17393.94
850,000	8474.57	8561.40	8660.40	8773.60	9661.07	11708.75	18481.06
900,000	8973.07	9065.01	9169.84	9289.70	10229.37	12397.50	19568.18
950,000	9471.58	9568.62	9679.27	9805.79	10797.67	13086.25	20655.30
1,000,000	9970.08	10072.23	10188.71	10321.88	11365.97	13775.00	21742.42

11¼%

Monthly Payments
Necessary to Amortize a Loan

AMOUNT BORROWED	YEARS REMAINING IN TERM						
	30	29	28	27	26	25	24
100	0.97	0.98	0.98	0.99	0.99	1.00	1.01
200	1.94	1.95	1.96	1.97	1.98	2.00	2.01
300	2.91	2.93	2.94	2.96	2.97	2.99	3.02
400	3.89	3.90	3.92	3.94	3.97	3.99	4.02
500	4.86	4.88	4.90	4.93	4.96	4.99	5.03
600	5.83	5.85	5.88	5.91	5.95	5.99	6.04
700	6.80	6.83	6.86	6.90	6.94	6.99	7.04
800	7.77	7.80	7.84	7.88	7.93	7.99	8.05
900	8.74	8.78	8.82	8.87	8.92	8.98	9.05
1,000	9.71	9.75	9.80	9.85	9.91	9.98	10.06
2,000	19.43	19.51	19.60	19.71	19.83	19.96	20.12
3,000	29.14	29.26	29.40	29.56	29.74	29.95	30.18
4,000	38.85	39.02	39.20	39.42	39.66	39.93	40.24
5,000	48.56	48.77	49.01	49.27	49.57	49.91	50.30
6,000	58.28	58.53	58.81	59.13	59.49	59.89	60.36
7,000	67.99	68.28	68.61	68.98	69.40	69.88	70.42
8,000	77.70	78.03	78.41	78.83	79.31	79.86	80.48
9,000	87.41	87.79	88.21	88.69	89.23	89.84	90.54
10,000	97.13	97.54	98.01	98.54	99.14	99.82	100.60
15,000	145.69	146.31	147.02	147.81	148.72	149.74	150.89
20,000	194.25	195.08	196.02	197.09	198.29	199.65	201.19
25,000	242.82	243.86	245.03	246.36	247.86	249.56	251.49
30,000	291.38	292.63	294.04	295.63	297.43	299.47	301.79
35,000	339.94	341.40	343.04	344.90	347.00	349.38	352.09
40,000	388.50	390.17	392.05	394.17	396.57	399.30	402.38
45,000	437.07	438.94	441.05	443.44	446.15	449.21	452.68
50,000	485.63	487.71	490.06	492.71	495.72	499.12	502.98
55,000	534.19	536.48	539.07	541.99	545.29	549.03	553.28
60,000	582.76	585.25	588.07	591.26	594.86	598.94	603.58
65,000	631.32	634.03	637.08	640.53	644.43	648.86	653.88
70,000	679.88	682.80	686.08	689.80	694.00	698.77	704.17
75,000	728.45	731.57	735.09	739.07	743.58	748.68	754.47
80,000	777.01	780.34	784.10	788.34	793.15	798.59	804.77
85,000	825.57	829.11	833.10	837.61	842.72	848.50	855.07
90,000	874.14	877.88	882.11	886.89	892.29	898.42	905.37
95,000	922.70	926.65	931.12	936.16	941.86	948.33	955.66
100,000	971.26	975.42	980.12	985.43	991.43	998.24	1005.96
110,000	1068.39	1072.97	1078.13	1083.97	1090.58	1098.06	1106.56
120,000	1165.51	1170.51	1176.15	1182.52	1189.72	1197.89	1207.15
130,000	1262.64	1268.05	1274.16	1281.06	1288.87	1297.71	1307.75
140,000	1359.77	1365.59	1372.17	1379.60	1388.01	1397.54	1408.35
150,000	1456.89	1463.14	1470.18	1478.14	1487.15	1497.36	1508.94
200,000	1942.52	1950.85	1960.24	1970.86	1982.87	1996.48	2011.92
250,000	2428.15	2438.56	2450.30	2463.57	2478.59	2495.60	2514.90
300,000	2913.78	2926.27	2940.36	2956.29	2974.30	2994.72	3017.89
350,000	3399.41	3413.98	3430.42	3449.00	3470.02	3493.84	3520.87
400,000	3885.05	3901.69	3920.48	3941.72	3965.74	3992.96	4023.85
450,000	4370.68	4389.41	4410.55	4434.43	4461.46	4492.08	4526.83
500,000	4856.31	4877.12	4900.61	4927.15	4957.17	4991.20	5029.81
550,000	5341.94	5364.83	5390.67	5419.86	5452.89	5490.32	5532.79
600,000	5827.57	5852.54	5880.73	5912.58	5948.61	5989.44	6035.77
650,000	6313.20	6340.25	6370.79	6405.29	6444.33	6488.56	6538.75
700,000	6798.83	6827.96	6860.85	6898.01	6940.04	6987.68	7041.73
750,000	7284.46	7315.68	7350.91	7390.72	7435.76	7486.80	7544.71
800,000	7770.09	7803.39	7840.97	7883.43	7931.48	7985.92	8047.70
850,000	8255.72	8291.10	8331.03	8376.15	8427.20	8485.04	8550.68
900,000	8741.35	8778.81	8821.09	8868.86	8922.91	8984.16	9053.66
950,000	9226.98	9266.52	9311.15	9361.58	9418.63	9483.28	9556.64
1,000,000	9712.61	9754.23	9801.21	9854.29	9914.35	9982.40	10059.62

Monthly Payments 11¼%
Necessary to Amortize a Loan

AMOUNT BORROWED	YEARS REMAINING IN TERM						
	23	22	21	20	15	10	5
100	1.01	1.02	1.04	1.05	1.15	1.39	2.19
200	2.03	2.05	2.07	2.10	2.30	2.78	4.37
300	3.04	3.07	3.11	3.15	3.46	4.18	6.56
400	4.06	4.10	4.14	4.20	4.61	5.57	8.75
500	5.07	5.12	5.18	5.25	5.76	6.96	10.93
600	6.09	6.15	6.22	6.30	6.91	8.35	13.12
700	7.10	7.17	7.25	7.34	8.07	9.74	15.31
800	8.12	8.20	8.29	8.39	9.22	11.13	17.49
900	9.13	9.22	9.33	9.44	10.37	12.53	19.68
1,000	10.15	10.25	10.36	10.49	11.52	13.92	21.87
2,000	20.29	20.49	20.72	20.99	23.05	27.83	43.73
3,000	30.44	30.74	31.09	31.48	34.57	41.75	65.60
4,000	40.59	40.99	41.45	41.97	46.09	55.67	87.47
5,000	50.74	51.24	51.81	52.46	57.62	69.58	109.34
6,000	60.88	61.48	62.17	62.96	69.14	83.50	131.20
7,000	71.03	71.73	72.53	73.45	80.66	97.42	153.07
8,000	81.18	81.98	82.89	83.94	92.19	111.34	174.94
9,000	91.33	92.23	93.26	94.43	103.71	125.25	196.81
10,000	101.47	102.47	103.62	104.93	115.23	139.17	218.67
15,000	152.21	153.71	155.43	157.39	172.85	208.75	328.01
20,000	202.95	204.95	207.23	209.85	230.47	278.34	437.35
25,000	253.69	256.19	259.04	262.31	288.09	347.92	546.68
30,000	304.42	307.42	310.85	314.78	345.70	417.51	656.02
35,000	355.16	358.66	362.66	367.24	403.32	487.09	765.36
40,000	405.90	409.90	414.47	419.70	460.94	556.68	874.69
45,000	456.63	461.14	466.28	472.17	518.56	626.26	984.03
50,000	507.37	512.37	518.09	524.63	576.17	695.84	1093.37
55,000	558.11	563.61	569.89	577.09	633.79	765.43	1202.70
60,000	608.85	614.85	621.70	629.55	691.41	835.01	1312.04
65,000	659.58	666.08	673.51	682.02	749.02	904.60	1421.38
70,000	710.32	717.32	725.32	734.48	806.64	974.18	1530.71
75,000	761.06	768.56	777.13	786.94	864.26	1043.77	1640.05
80,000	811.79	819.80	828.94	839.40	921.88	1113.35	1749.38
85,000	862.53	871.03	880.75	891.87	979.49	1182.94	1858.72
90,000	913.27	922.27	932.55	944.33	1037.11	1252.52	1968.06
95,000	964.00	973.51	984.36	996.79	1094.73	1322.10	2077.39
100,000	1014.74	1024.75	1036.17	1049.26	1152.34	1391.69	2186.73
110,000	1116.22	1127.22	1139.79	1154.18	1267.58	1530.86	2405.40
120,000	1217.69	1229.69	1243.41	1259.11	1382.81	1670.03	2624.08
130,000	1319.16	1332.17	1347.02	1364.03	1498.05	1809.20	2842.75
140,000	1420.64	1434.64	1450.64	1468.96	1613.28	1948.37	3061.42
150,000	1522.11	1537.12	1554.26	1573.88	1728.52	2087.53	3280.10
200,000	2029.48	2049.49	2072.34	2098.51	2304.69	2783.38	4373.46
250,000	2536.85	2561.86	2590.43	2623.14	2880.86	3479.22	5466.83
300,000	3044.23	3074.24	3108.51	3147.77	3457.03	4175.07	6560.19
350,000	3551.60	3586.61	3626.60	3672.40	4033.21	4870.91	7653.56
400,000	4058.97	4098.98	4144.68	4197.02	4609.38	5566.76	8746.92
450,000	4566.34	4611.36	4662.77	4721.65	5185.55	6262.60	9840.29
500,000	5073.71	5123.73	5180.86	5246.28	5761.72	6958.45	10933.65
550,000	5581.08	5636.10	5698.94	5770.91	6337.90	7654.29	12027.02
600,000	6088.45	6148.47	6217.03	6295.54	6914.07	8350.14	13120.38
650,000	6595.82	6660.85	6735.11	6820.16	7490.24	9045.98	14213.75
700,000	7103.19	7173.22	7253.20	7344.79	8066.41	9741.83	15307.12
750,000	7610.56	7685.59	7771.28	7869.42	8642.58	10437.67	16400.48
800,000	8117.94	8197.97	8289.37	8394.05	9218.76	11133.52	17493.85
850,000	8625.31	8710.34	8807.46	8918.68	9794.93	11829.36	18587.21
900,000	9132.68	9222.71	9325.54	9443.30	10371.10	12525.21	19680.58
950,000	9640.05	9735.09	9843.63	9967.93	10947.27	13221.05	20773.94
1,000,000	10147.42	10247.46	10361.71	10492.56	11523.45	13916.89	21867.31

11½%

Monthly Payments
Necessary to Amortize a Loan

AMOUNT BORROWED	YEARS REMAINING IN TERM						
	30	29	28	27	26	25	24
100	0.99	0.99	1.00	1.00	1.01	1.02	1.02
200	1.98	1.99	2.00	2.01	2.02	2.03	2.05
300	2.97	2.98	3.00	3.01	3.03	3.05	3.07
400	3.96	3.98	4.00	4.02	4.04	4.07	4.10
500	4.95	4.97	4.99	5.02	5.05	5.08	5.12
600	5.94	5.97	5.99	6.02	6.06	6.10	6.14
700	6.93	6.96	6.99	7.03	7.07	7.12	7.17
800	7.92	7.95	7.99	8.03	8.08	8.13	8.19
900	8.91	8.95	8.99	9.04	9.09	9.15	9.22
1,000	9.90	9.94	9.99	10.04	10.10	10.16	10.24
2,000	19.81	19.89	19.98	20.08	20.20	20.33	20.48
3,000	29.71	29.83	29.97	30.12	30.30	30.49	30.72
4,000	39.61	39.77	39.95	40.16	40.39	40.66	40.96
5,000	49.51	49.72	49.94	50.20	50.49	50.82	51.20
6,000	59.42	59.66	59.93	60.24	60.59	60.99	61.44
7,000	69.32	69.60	69.92	70.28	70.69	71.15	71.68
8,000	79.22	79.54	79.91	80.32	80.79	81.32	81.92
9,000	89.13	89.49	89.90	90.36	90.89	91.48	92.16
10,000	99.03	99.43	99.89	100.40	100.98	101.65	102.40
15,000	148.54	149.15	149.83	150.60	151.48	152.47	153.60
20,000	198.06	198.86	199.77	200.80	201.97	203.29	204.80
25,000	247.57	248.58	249.71	251.00	252.46	254.12	256.00
30,000	297.09	298.29	299.66	301.20	302.95	304.94	307.20
35,000	346.60	348.01	349.60	351.40	353.45	355.76	358.40
40,000	396.12	397.72	399.54	401.60	403.94	406.59	409.60
45,000	445.63	447.44	449.49	451.80	454.43	457.41	460.80
50,000	495.15	497.16	499.43	502.00	504.92	508.23	512.00
55,000	544.66	546.87	549.37	552.20	555.41	559.06	563.20
60,000	594.17	596.59	599.32	602.40	605.91	609.88	614.40
65,000	643.69	646.30	649.26	652.61	656.40	660.70	665.60
70,000	693.20	696.02	699.20	702.81	706.89	711.53	716.80
75,000	742.72	745.73	749.14	753.01	757.38	762.35	768.00
80,000	792.23	795.45	799.09	803.21	807.88	813.18	819.20
85,000	841.75	845.17	849.03	853.41	858.37	864.00	870.40
90,000	891.26	894.88	898.97	903.61	908.86	914.82	921.60
95,000	940.78	944.60	948.92	953.81	959.35	965.65	972.80
100,000	990.29	994.31	998.86	1004.01	1009.84	1016.47	1024.00
110,000	1089.32	1093.74	1098.75	1104.41	1110.83	1118.12	1126.40
120,000	1188.35	1193.17	1198.63	1204.81	1211.81	1219.76	1228.80
130,000	1287.38	1292.61	1298.52	1305.21	1312.80	1321.41	1331.20
140,000	1386.41	1392.04	1398.40	1405.61	1413.78	1423.06	1433.60
150,000	1485.44	1491.47	1498.29	1506.01	1514.77	1524.70	1536.00
200,000	1980.58	1988.62	1997.72	2008.02	2019.69	2032.94	2048.00
250,000	2475.73	2485.78	2497.15	2510.02	2524.61	2541.17	2560.00
300,000	2970.87	2982.94	2996.58	3012.02	3029.53	3049.41	3072.00
350,000	3466.02	3480.09	3496.01	3514.03	3534.45	3557.64	3584.01
400,000	3961.17	3977.25	3995.44	4016.03	4039.38	4065.88	4096.01
450,000	4456.31	4474.40	4494.87	4518.03	4544.30	4574.11	4608.01
500,000	4951.46	4971.56	4994.30	5020.04	5049.22	5082.34	5120.01
550,000	5446.60	5468.72	5493.73	5522.04	5554.14	5590.58	5632.01
600,000	5941.75	5965.87	5993.16	6024.05	6059.06	6098.81	6144.01
650,000	6436.89	6463.03	6492.59	6526.05	6563.99	6607.05	6656.01
700,000	6932.04	6960.18	6992.02	7028.05	7068.91	7115.28	7168.01
750,000	7427.19	7457.34	7491.45	7530.06	7573.83	7623.52	7680.01
800,000	7922.33	7954.50	7990.88	8032.06	8078.75	8131.75	8192.01
850,000	8417.48	8451.65	8490.30	8534.07	8583.67	8639.99	8704.01
900,000	8912.62	8948.81	8989.73	9036.07	9088.60	9148.22	9216.01
950,000	9407.77	9445.97	9489.16	9538.07	9593.52	9656.46	9728.01
1,000,000	9902.91	9943.12	9988.59	10040.08	10098.44	10164.69	10240.02

Monthly Payments 11¾%
Necessary to Amortize a Loan

YEARS REMAINING IN TERM

AMOUNT BORROWED	23	22	21	20	15	10	5
100	1.05	1.06	1.07	1.08	1.18	1.42	2.21
200	2.10	2.12	2.14	2.17	2.37	2.84	4.42
300	3.15	3.18	3.21	3.25	3.55	4.26	6.64
400	4.20	4.24	4.28	4.33	4.74	5.68	8.85
500	5.25	5.30	5.36	5.42	5.92	7.10	11.06
600	6.30	6.36	6.43	6.50	7.10	8.52	13.27
700	7.35	7.42	7.50	7.59	8.29	9.94	15.48
800	8.40	8.48	8.57	8.67	9.47	11.36	17.69
900	9.45	9.54	9.64	9.75	10.66	12.78	19.91
1,000	10.51	10.60	10.71	10.84	11.84	14.20	22.12
2,000	21.01	21.20	21.42	21.67	23.68	28.41	44.24
3,000	31.52	31.80	32.13	32.51	35.52	42.61	66.35
4,000	42.02	42.40	42.84	43.35	47.37	56.81	88.47
5,000	52.53	53.01	53.55	54.19	59.21	71.01	110.59
6,000	63.03	63.61	64.27	65.02	71.05	85.22	132.71
7,000	73.54	74.21	74.98	75.86	82.89	99.42	154.83
8,000	84.04	84.81	85.69	86.70	94.73	113.62	176.95
9,000	94.55	95.41	96.40	97.53	106.57	127.83	199.06
10,000	105.05	106.01	107.11	108.37	118.41	142.03	221.18
15,000	157.58	159.02	160.66	162.56	177.62	213.04	331.77
20,000	210.10	212.02	214.22	216.74	236.83	284.06	442.37
25,000	262.63	265.03	267.77	270.93	296.03	355.07	552.96
30,000	315.16	318.03	321.33	325.11	355.24	426.09	663.55
35,000	367.68	371.04	374.88	379.30	414.45	497.10	774.14
40,000	420.21	424.04	428.44	433.48	473.65	568.12	884.73
45,000	472.74	477.05	481.99	487.67	532.86	639.13	995.32
50,000	525.26	530.05	535.54	541.85	592.07	710.15	1105.92
55,000	577.79	583.06	589.10	596.04	651.27	781.16	1216.51
60,000	630.31	636.06	642.65	650.22	710.48	852.18	1327.10
65,000	682.84	689.07	696.21	704.41	769.69	923.19	1437.69
70,000	735.37	742.07	749.76	758.59	828.89	994.21	1548.28
75,000	787.89	795.08	803.32	812.78	888.10	1065.22	1658.87
80,000	840.42	848.08	856.87	866.97	947.31	1136.24	1769.47
85,000	892.94	901.09	910.42	921.15	1006.51	1207.25	1880.06
90,000	945.47	954.10	963.98	975.34	1065.72	1278.27	1990.65
95,000	998.00	1007.10	1017.53	1029.52	1124.92	1349.28	2101.24
100,000	1050.52	1060.11	1071.09	1083.71	1184.13	1420.29	2211.83
110,000	1155.58	1166.12	1178.20	1192.08	1302.54	1562.32	2433.02
120,000	1260.63	1272.13	1285.31	1300.45	1420.96	1704.35	2654.20
130,000	1365.68	1378.14	1392.41	1408.82	1539.37	1846.38	2875.38
140,000	1470.73	1484.15	1499.52	1517.19	1657.78	1988.41	3096.56
150,000	1575.78	1590.16	1606.63	1625.56	1776.20	2130.44	3317.75
200,000	2101.05	2120.21	2142.18	2167.41	2368.26	2840.59	4423.66
250,000	2626.31	2650.26	2677.72	2709.27	2960.33	3550.74	5529.58
300,000	3151.57	3180.32	3213.26	3251.12	3552.39	4260.88	6635.50
350,000	3676.83	3710.37	3748.81	3792.97	4144.46	4971.03	7741.41
400,000	4202.09	4240.42	4284.35	4334.83	4736.53	5681.18	8847.33
450,000	4727.35	4770.48	4819.90	4876.68	5328.59	6391.33	9953.24
500,000	5252.62	5300.53	5355.44	5418.54	5920.66	7101.47	11059.16
550,000	5777.88	5830.58	5890.98	5960.39	6512.72	7811.62	12165.08
600,000	6303.14	6360.63	6426.53	6502.24	7104.79	8521.77	13270.99
650,000	6828.40	6890.69	6962.07	7044.10	7696.85	9231.91	14376.91
700,000	7353.66	7420.74	7497.62	7585.95	8288.92	9942.06	15482.82
750,000	7878.92	7950.79	8033.16	8127.80	8880.99	10652.21	16588.74
800,000	8404.19	8480.85	8568.70	8669.66	9473.05	11362.36	17694.66
850,000	8929.45	9010.90	9104.25	9211.51	10065.12	12072.50	18800.57
900,000	9454.71	9540.95	9639.79	9753.36	10657.18	12782.65	19906.49
950,000	9979.97	10071.01	10175.34	10295.22	11249.25	13492.80	21012.40
1,000,000	10505.23	10601.06	10710.88	10837.07	11841.31	14202.95	22118.32

Monthly Payments
Necessary to Amortize a Loan

YEARS REMAINING IN TERM

AMOUNT BORROWED	30	29	28	27	26	25	24
100	1.03	1.03	1.04	1.04	1.05	1.05	1.06
200	2.06	2.06	2.07	2.08	2.09	2.11	2.12
300	3.09	3.10	3.11	3.12	3.14	3.16	3.18
400	4.11	4.13	4.15	4.17	4.19	4.21	4.24
500	5.14	5.16	5.18	5.21	5.23	5.27	5.30
600	6.17	6.19	6.22	6.25	6.28	6.32	6.36
700	7.20	7.23	7.26	7.29	7.33	7.37	7.42
800	8.23	8.26	8.29	8.33	8.38	8.43	8.48
900	9.26	9.29	9.33	9.37	9.42	9.48	9.54
1,000	10.29	10.32	10.37	10.41	10.47	10.53	10.60
2,000	20.57	20.65	20.73	20.83	20.94	21.06	21.21
3,000	30.86	30.97	31.10	31.24	31.41	31.60	31.81
4,000	41.14	41.29	41.46	41.66	41.88	42.13	42.42
5,000	51.43	51.62	51.83	52.07	52.35	52.66	53.02
6,000	61.72	61.94	62.20	62.49	62.82	63.19	63.62
7,000	72.00	72.27	72.56	72.90	73.29	73.73	74.23
8,000	82.29	82.59	82.93	83.32	83.76	84.26	84.83
9,000	92.58	92.91	93.30	93.73	94.23	94.79	95.43
10,000	102.86	103.24	103.66	104.14	104.70	105.32	106.04
15,000	154.29	154.85	155.49	156.22	157.04	157.98	159.06
20,000	205.72	206.47	207.32	208.29	209.39	210.64	212.08
25,000	257.15	258.09	259.15	260.36	261.74	263.31	265.10
30,000	308.58	309.71	310.98	312.43	314.09	315.97	318.11
35,000	360.01	361.33	362.81	364.51	366.43	368.63	371.13
40,000	411.45	412.94	414.65	416.58	418.78	421.29	424.15
45,000	462.88	464.56	466.48	468.65	471.13	473.95	477.17
50,000	514.31	516.18	518.31	520.72	523.48	526.61	530.19
55,000	565.74	567.80	570.14	572.80	575.82	579.27	583.21
60,000	617.17	619.42	621.97	624.87	628.17	631.93	636.23
65,000	668.60	671.03	673.80	676.94	680.52	684.60	689.25
70,000	720.03	722.65	725.63	729.01	732.87	737.26	742.27
75,000	771.46	774.27	777.46	781.09	785.21	789.92	795.29
80,000	822.89	825.89	829.29	833.16	837.56	842.58	848.31
85,000	874.32	877.50	881.12	885.23	889.91	895.24	901.32
90,000	925.75	929.12	932.95	937.30	942.26	947.90	954.34
95,000	977.18	980.74	984.78	989.38	994.60	1000.56	1007.36
100,000	1028.61	1032.36	1036.61	1041.45	1046.95	1053.22	1060.38
110,000	1131.47	1135.59	1140.27	1145.59	1151.65	1158.55	1166.42
120,000	1234.34	1238.83	1243.94	1249.74	1256.34	1263.87	1272.46
130,000	1337.20	1342.07	1347.60	1353.88	1361.04	1369.19	1378.50
140,000	1440.06	1445.30	1451.26	1458.03	1465.73	1474.51	1484.53
150,000	1542.92	1548.54	1554.92	1562.17	1570.43	1579.84	1590.57
200,000	2057.23	2064.72	2073.23	2082.90	2093.90	2106.45	2120.76
250,000	2571.53	2580.90	2591.53	2603.62	2617.38	2633.06	2650.95
300,000	3085.84	3097.08	3109.84	3124.35	3140.86	3159.67	3181.15
350,000	3600.14	3613.26	3628.15	3645.07	3664.33	3686.28	3711.34
400,000	4114.45	4129.44	4146.45	4165.80	4187.81	4212.90	4241.53
450,000	4628.76	4645.61	4664.76	4686.52	4711.29	4739.51	4771.72
500,000	5143.06	5161.79	5183.06	5207.24	5234.76	5266.12	5301.91
550,000	5657.37	5677.97	5701.37	5727.97	5758.24	5792.73	5832.10
600,000	6171.68	6194.15	6219.68	6248.69	6281.71	6319.34	6362.29
650,000	6685.98	6710.33	6737.98	6769.42	6805.19	6845.96	6892.48
700,000	7200.29	7226.51	7256.29	7290.14	7328.67	7372.57	7422.67
750,000	7714.59	7742.69	7774.60	7810.87	7852.14	7899.18	7952.86
800,000	8228.90	8258.87	8292.90	8331.59	8375.62	8425.79	8483.06
850,000	8743.21	8775.05	8811.21	8852.32	8899.10	8952.41	9013.25
900,000	9257.51	9291.23	9329.52	9373.04	9422.57	9479.02	9543.44
950,000	9771.82	9807.41	9847.82	9893.76	9946.05	10005.63	10073.63
1,000,000	10286.13	10323.59	10366.13	10414.49	10469.52	10532.24	10603.82

Monthly Payments 12%
Necessary to Amortize a Loan

AMOUNT BORROWED	YEARS REMAINING IN TERM						
	23	22	21	20	15	10	5
100	1.07	1.08	1.09	1.10	1.20	1.43	2.22
200	2.14	2.16	2.18	2.20	2.40	2.87	4.45
300	3.21	3.23	3.27	3.30	3.60	4.30	6.67
400	4.27	4.31	4.35	4.40	4.80	5.74	8.90
500	5.34	5.39	5.44	5.51	6.00	7.17	11.12
600	6.41	6.47	6.53	6.61	7.20	8.61	13.35
700	7.48	7.55	7.62	7.71	8.40	10.04	15.57
800	8.55	8.62	8.71	8.81	9.60	11.48	17.80
900	9.62	9.70	9.80	9.91	10.80	12.91	20.02
1,000	10.69	10.78	10.89	11.01	12.00	14.35	22.24
2,000	21.37	21.56	21.77	22.02	24.00	28.69	44.49
3,000	32.06	32.34	32.66	33.03	36.01	43.04	66.73
4,000	42.74	43.12	43.55	44.04	48.01	57.39	88.98
5,000	53.43	53.90	54.43	55.05	60.01	71.74	111.22
6,000	64.11	64.68	65.32	66.07	72.01	86.08	133.47
7,000	74.80	75.46	76.21	77.08	84.01	100.43	155.71
8,000	85.49	86.24	87.10	88.09	96.01	114.78	177.96
9,000	96.17	97.01	97.98	99.10	108.02	129.12	200.20
10,000	106.86	107.79	108.87	110.11	120.02	143.47	222.44
15,000	160.28	161.69	163.30	165.16	180.03	215.21	333.67
20,000	213.71	215.59	217.74	220.22	240.03	286.94	444.89
25,000	267.14	269.48	272.17	275.27	300.04	358.68	556.11
30,000	320.57	323.38	326.61	330.33	360.05	430.41	667.33
35,000	374.00	377.28	381.04	385.38	420.06	502.15	778.56
40,000	427.43	431.18	435.48	440.43	480.07	573.88	889.78
45,000	480.85	485.07	489.91	495.49	540.08	645.62	1001.00
50,000	534.28	538.97	544.35	550.54	600.08	717.35	1112.22
55,000	587.71	592.87	598.78	605.60	660.09	789.09	1223.44
60,000	641.14	646.76	653.22	660.65	720.10	860.83	1334.67
65,000	694.57	700.66	707.65	715.71	780.11	932.56	1445.89
70,000	748.00	754.56	762.09	770.76	840.12	1004.30	1557.11
75,000	801.42	808.45	816.52	825.81	900.13	1076.03	1668.33
80,000	854.85	862.35	870.96	880.87	960.13	1147.77	1779.56
85,000	908.28	916.25	925.39	935.92	1020.14	1219.50	1890.78
90,000	961.71	970.14	979.83	990.98	1080.15	1291.24	2002.00
95,000	1015.14	1024.04	1034.26	1046.03	1140.16	1362.97	2113.22
100,000	1068.56	1077.94	1088.70	1101.09	1200.17	1434.71	2224.44
110,000	1175.42	1185.73	1197.57	1211.19	1320.18	1578.18	2446.89
120,000	1282.28	1293.53	1306.44	1321.30	1440.20	1721.65	2669.33
130,000	1389.13	1401.32	1415.31	1431.41	1560.22	1865.12	2891.78
140,000	1495.99	1509.11	1524.18	1541.52	1680.24	2008.59	3114.22
150,000	1602.85	1616.91	1633.05	1651.63	1800.25	2152.06	3336.67
200,000	2137.13	2155.88	2177.40	2202.17	2400.34	2869.42	4448.89
250,000	2671.41	2694.85	2721.75	2752.72	3000.42	3586.77	5561.11
300,000	3205.69	3233.82	3266.10	3303.26	3600.50	4304.13	6673.33
350,000	3739.98	3772.78	3810.45	3853.80	4200.59	5021.48	7785.56
400,000	4274.26	4311.75	4354.80	4404.34	4800.67	5738.84	8897.78
450,000	4808.54	4850.72	4899.15	4954.89	5400.76	6456.19	10010.00
500,000	5342.82	5389.69	5443.50	5505.43	6000.84	7173.55	11122.22
550,000	5877.11	5928.66	5987.85	6055.97	6600.92	7890.90	12234.45
600,000	6411.39	6467.63	6532.20	6606.52	7201.01	8608.26	13346.67
650,000	6945.67	7006.60	7076.55	7157.06	7801.09	9325.61	14458.89
700,000	7479.95	7545.57	7620.90	7707.60	8401.18	10042.97	15571.11
750,000	8014.24	8084.54	8165.25	8258.15	9001.26	10760.32	16683.34
800,000	8548.52	8623.51	8709.60	8808.69	9601.34	11477.68	17795.56
850,000	9082.80	9162.48	9253.95	9359.23	10201.43	12195.03	18907.78
900,000	9617.08	9701.45	9798.30	9909.78	10801.51	12912.39	20020.00
950,000	10151.37	10240.41	10342.65	10460.32	11401.60	13629.74	21132.23
1,000,000	10685.65	10779.38	10887.00	11010.86	12001.68	14347.09	22244.45

12¼%

Monthly Payments
Necessary to Amortize a Loan

AMOUNT BORROWED	YEARS REMAINING IN TERM						
	30	29	28	27	26	25	24
100	1.05	1.05	1.06	1.06	1.07	1.07	1.08
200	2.10	2.10	2.11	2.12	2.13	2.14	2.16
300	3.14	3.15	3.17	3.18	3.20	3.22	3.24
400	4.19	4.21	4.22	4.24	4.26	4.29	4.31
500	5.24	5.26	5.28	5.30	5.33	5.36	5.39
600	6.29	6.31	6.33	6.36	6.39	6.43	6.47
700	7.34	7.36	7.39	7.42	7.46	7.50	7.55
800	8.38	8.41	8.44	8.48	8.53	8.57	8.63
900	9.43	9.46	9.50	9.54	9.59	9.65	9.71
1,000	10.48	10.52	10.56	10.60	10.66	10.72	10.79
2,000	20.96	21.03	21.11	21.21	21.31	21.43	21.57
3,000	31.44	31.55	31.67	31.81	31.97	32.15	32.36
4,000	41.92	42.06	42.22	42.41	42.63	42.87	43.15
5,000	52.39	52.58	52.78	53.02	53.28	53.59	53.94
6,000	62.87	63.09	63.34	63.62	63.94	64.30	64.72
7,000	73.35	73.61	73.89	74.22	74.60	75.02	75.51
8,000	83.83	84.12	84.45	84.82	85.25	85.74	86.30
9,000	94.31	94.64	95.01	95.43	95.91	96.46	97.08
10,000	104.79	105.15	105.56	106.03	106.56	107.17	107.87
15,000	157.18	157.73	158.34	159.05	159.85	160.76	161.81
20,000	209.58	210.30	211.12	212.06	213.13	214.35	215.74
25,000	261.97	262.88	263.91	265.08	266.41	267.94	269.68
30,000	314.37	315.45	316.69	318.09	319.69	321.52	323.62
35,000	366.76	368.03	369.47	371.11	372.98	375.11	377.55
40,000	419.16	420.60	422.25	424.12	426.26	428.70	431.49
45,000	471.55	473.18	475.03	477.14	479.54	482.28	485.42
50,000	523.95	525.75	527.81	530.15	532.82	535.87	539.36
55,000	576.34	578.33	580.59	583.17	586.11	589.46	593.29
60,000	628.74	630.91	633.37	636.18	639.39	643.05	647.23
65,000	681.13	683.48	686.15	689.20	692.67	696.63	701.17
70,000	733.53	736.06	738.93	742.21	745.95	750.22	755.10
75,000	785.92	788.63	791.72	795.23	799.23	803.81	809.04
80,000	838.32	841.21	844.50	848.24	852.52	857.40	862.97
85,000	890.71	893.78	897.28	901.26	905.80	910.98	916.91
90,000	943.11	946.36	950.06	954.27	959.08	964.57	970.85
95,000	995.50	998.93	1002.84	1007.29	1012.36	1018.16	1024.78
100,000	1047.90	1051.51	1055.62	1060.30	1065.65	1071.74	1078.72
110,000	1152.69	1156.66	1161.18	1166.34	1172.21	1178.92	1186.59
120,000	1257.48	1261.81	1266.75	1272.37	1278.77	1286.09	1294.46
130,000	1362.27	1366.96	1372.31	1378.40	1385.34	1393.27	1402.33
140,000	1467.06	1472.11	1477.87	1484.43	1491.90	1500.44	1510.20
150,000	1571.84	1577.26	1583.43	1590.46	1598.47	1607.62	1618.08
200,000	2095.79	2103.02	2111.24	2120.61	2131.29	2143.49	2157.43
250,000	2619.74	2628.77	2639.05	2650.76	2664.11	2679.36	2696.79
300,000	3143.69	3154.53	3166.86	3180.91	3196.94	3215.23	3236.15
350,000	3667.64	3680.28	3694.67	3711.07	3729.76	3751.10	3775.51
400,000	4191.59	4206.04	4222.49	4241.22	4262.58	4286.98	4314.87
450,000	4715.53	4731.79	4750.30	4771.37	4795.41	4822.85	4854.23
500,000	5239.48	5257.55	5278.11	5301.52	5328.23	5358.72	5393.58
550,000	5763.43	5783.30	5805.92	5831.68	5861.05	5894.59	5932.94
600,000	6287.38	6309.06	6333.73	6361.83	6393.87	6430.46	6472.30
650,000	6811.33	6834.81	6861.54	6891.98	6926.70	6966.33	7011.66
700,000	7335.28	7360.57	7389.35	7422.13	7459.52	7502.21	7551.02
750,000	7859.22	7886.32	7917.16	7952.29	7992.34	8038.08	8090.38
800,000	8383.17	8412.08	8444.97	8482.44	8525.17	8573.95	8629.73
850,000	8907.12	8937.83	8972.78	9012.59	9057.99	9109.82	9169.09
900,000	9431.07	9463.59	9500.59	9542.74	9590.81	9645.69	9708.45
950,000	9955.02	9989.34	10028.40	10072.90	10123.63	10181.57	10247.81
1,000,000	10478.96	10515.10	10556.21	10603.05	10656.46	10717.44	10787.17

AMOUNT BORROWED	YEARS REMAINING IN TERM						
	23	22	21	20	15	10	5
100	1.09	1.10	1.11	1.12	1.22	1.45	2.24
200	2.17	2.19	2.21	2.24	2.43	2.90	4.47
300	3.26	3.29	3.32	3.36	3.65	4.35	6.71
400	4.35	4.38	4.43	4.47	4.87	5.80	8.95
500	5.43	5.48	5.53	5.59	6.08	7.25	11.19
600	6.52	6.58	6.64	6.71	7.30	8.70	13.42
700	7.61	7.67	7.74	7.83	8.51	10.14	15.66
800	8.69	8.77	8.85	8.95	9.73	11.59	17.90
900	9.78	9.86	9.96	10.07	10.95	13.04	20.13
1,000	10.87	10.96	11.06	11.19	12.16	14.49	22.37
2,000	21.73	21.92	22.13	22.37	24.33	28.98	44.74
3,000	32.60	32.88	33.19	33.56	36.49	43.48	67.11
4,000	43.47	43.83	44.26	44.74	48.65	57.97	89.48
5,000	54.34	54.79	55.32	55.93	60.81	72.46	111.85
6,000	65.20	65.75	66.38	67.11	72.98	86.95	134.23
7,000	76.07	76.71	77.45	78.30	85.14	101.44	156.60
8,000	86.94	87.67	88.51	89.49	97.30	115.94	178.97
9,000	97.80	98.63	99.58	100.67	109.47	130.43	201.34
10,000	108.67	109.59	110.64	111.86	121.63	144.92	223.71
15,000	163.01	164.38	165.96	167.78	182.44	217.38	335.56
20,000	217.34	219.17	221.28	223.71	243.26	289.84	447.42
25,000	271.68	273.97	276.60	279.64	304.07	362.30	559.27
30,000	326.01	328.76	331.92	335.57	364.89	434.76	671.13
35,000	380.35	383.55	387.24	391.50	425.70	507.22	782.98
40,000	434.68	438.35	442.56	447.43	486.52	579.68	894.84
45,000	489.02	493.14	497.88	503.35	547.33	652.14	1006.69
50,000	543.35	547.93	553.21	559.28	608.15	724.60	1118.55
55,000	597.69	602.73	608.53	615.21	668.96	797.06	1230.40
60,000	652.02	657.52	663.85	671.14	729.78	869.52	1342.26
65,000	706.36	712.31	719.17	727.07	790.59	941.98	1454.11
70,000	760.69	767.11	774.49	783.00	851.41	1014.44	1565.97
75,000	815.03	821.90	829.81	838.92	912.22	1086.90	1677.82
80,000	869.36	876.70	885.13	894.85	973.04	1159.36	1789.68
85,000	923.70	931.49	940.45	950.78	1033.85	1231.82	1901.53
90,000	978.03	986.28	995.77	1006.71	1094.67	1304.28	2013.39
95,000	1032.37	1041.08	1051.09	1062.64	1155.48	1376.74	2125.24
100,000	1086.70	1095.87	1106.41	1118.56	1216.30	1449.20	2237.10
110,000	1195.37	1205.46	1217.05	1230.42	1337.93	1594.12	2460.81
120,000	1304.04	1315.04	1327.69	1342.28	1459.56	1739.04	2684.52
130,000	1412.71	1424.63	1438.33	1454.13	1581.19	1883.96	2908.23
140,000	1521.39	1534.22	1548.97	1565.99	1702.82	2028.88	3131.94
150,000	1630.06	1643.80	1659.62	1677.85	1824.45	2173.80	3355.65
200,000	2173.41	2191.74	2212.82	2237.13	2432.60	2898.40	4474.20
250,000	2716.76	2739.67	2766.03	2796.41	3040.75	3623.00	5592.75
300,000	3260.11	3287.61	3319.23	3355.69	3648.90	4347.60	6711.30
350,000	3803.46	3835.54	3872.44	3914.98	4257.05	5072.20	7829.85
400,000	4346.81	4383.48	4425.64	4474.26	4865.19	5796.79	8948.39
450,000	4890.17	4931.41	4978.85	5033.54	5473.34	6521.39	10066.94
500,000	5433.52	5479.35	5532.05	5592.82	6081.49	7245.99	11185.49
550,000	5976.87	6027.28	6085.26	6152.11	6689.64	7970.59	12304.04
600,000	6520.22	6575.22	6638.46	6711.39	7297.79	8695.19	13422.59
650,000	7063.57	7123.15	7191.67	7270.67	7905.94	9419.79	14541.14
700,000	7606.93	7671.08	7744.87	7829.95	8514.09	10144.39	15659.69
750,000	8150.28	8219.02	8298.08	8389.24	9122.24	10868.99	16778.24
800,000	8693.63	8766.95	8851.28	8948.52	9730.39	11593.59	17896.79
850,000	9236.98	9314.89	9404.49	9507.80	10338.54	12318.19	19015.34
900,000	9780.33	9862.82	9957.69	10067.08	10946.69	13042.79	20133.89
950,000	10323.68	10410.76	10510.90	10626.36	11554.84	13767.39	21252.44
1,000,000	10867.04	10958.69	11064.10	11185.65	12162.99	14491.99	22370.99

12½%

Monthly Payments
Necessary to Amortize a Loan

AMOUNT BORROWED	YEARS REMAINING IN TERM						
	30	29	28	27	26	25	24
100	1.07	1.07	1.07	1.08	1.08	1.09	1.10
200	2.13	2.14	2.15	2.16	2.17	2.18	2.19
300	3.20	3.21	3.22	3.24	3.25	3.27	3.29
400	4.27	4.28	4.30	4.32	4.34	4.36	4.39
500	5.34	5.35	5.37	5.40	5.42	5.45	5.49
600	6.40	6.42	6.45	6.48	6.51	6.54	6.58
700	7.47	7.50	7.52	7.55	7.59	7.63	7.68
800	8.54	8.57	8.60	8.63	8.68	8.72	8.78
900	9.61	9.64	9.67	9.71	9.76	9.81	9.87
1,000	10.67	10.71	10.75	10.79	10.84	10.90	10.97
2,000	21.35	21.41	21.49	21.58	21.69	21.81	21.94
3,000	32.02	32.12	32.24	32.38	32.53	32.71	32.91
4,000	42.69	42.83	42.99	43.17	43.38	43.61	43.89
5,000	53.36	53.54	53.74	53.96	54.22	54.52	54.86
6,000	64.04	64.24	64.48	64.75	65.07	65.42	65.83
7,000	74.71	74.95	75.23	75.55	75.91	76.32	76.80
8,000	85.38	85.66	85.98	86.34	86.75	87.23	87.77
9,000	96.05	96.37	96.72	97.13	97.60	98.13	98.74
10,000	106.73	107.07	107.47	107.92	108.44	109.04	109.71
15,000	160.09	160.61	161.21	161.89	162.66	163.55	164.57
20,000	213.45	214.15	214.94	215.85	216.89	218.07	219.43
25,000	266.81	267.69	268.68	269.81	271.11	272.59	274.29
30,000	320.18	321.22	322.41	323.77	325.33	327.11	329.14
35,000	373.54	374.76	376.15	377.74	379.55	381.62	384.00
40,000	426.90	428.30	429.89	431.70	433.77	436.14	438.86
45,000	480.27	481.83	483.62	485.66	487.99	490.66	493.72
50,000	533.63	535.37	537.36	539.62	542.21	545.18	548.57
55,000	586.99	588.91	591.09	593.59	596.44	599.69	603.43
60,000	640.35	642.44	644.83	647.55	650.66	654.21	658.29
65,000	693.72	695.98	698.56	701.51	704.88	708.73	713.14
70,000	747.08	749.52	752.30	755.47	759.10	763.25	768.00
75,000	800.44	803.06	806.03	809.44	813.32	817.77	822.86
80,000	853.81	856.59	859.77	863.40	867.54	872.28	877.72
85,000	907.17	910.13	913.51	917.36	921.76	926.80	932.57
90,000	960.53	963.67	967.24	971.32	975.98	981.32	987.43
95,000	1013.89	1017.20	1020.98	1025.28	1030.21	1035.84	1042.29
100,000	1067.26	1070.74	1074.71	1079.25	1084.43	1090.35	1097.14
110,000	1173.98	1177.82	1182.18	1187.17	1192.87	1199.39	1206.86
120,000	1280.71	1284.89	1289.66	1295.10	1301.31	1308.42	1316.57
130,000	1387.44	1391.96	1397.13	1403.02	1409.76	1417.46	1426.29
140,000	1494.16	1499.04	1504.60	1510.95	1518.20	1526.50	1536.00
150,000	1600.89	1606.11	1612.07	1618.87	1626.64	1635.53	1645.72
200,000	2134.52	2141.48	2149.43	2158.49	2168.85	2180.71	2194.29
250,000	2668.14	2676.85	2686.78	2698.12	2711.07	2725.89	2742.86
300,000	3201.77	3212.22	3224.14	3237.74	3253.28	3271.06	3291.43
350,000	3735.40	3747.59	3761.50	3777.36	3795.50	3816.24	3840.01
400,000	4269.03	4282.96	4298.85	4316.99	4337.71	4361.42	4388.58
450,000	4802.66	4818.33	4836.21	4856.61	4879.92	4906.59	4937.15
500,000	5336.29	5353.71	5373.57	5396.23	5422.14	5451.77	5485.72
550,000	5869.92	5889.08	5910.92	5935.86	5964.35	5996.95	6034.29
600,000	6403.55	6424.45	6448.28	6475.48	6506.56	6542.12	6582.87
650,000	6937.18	6959.82	6985.63	7015.10	7048.78	7087.30	7131.44
700,000	7470.80	7495.19	7522.99	7554.73	7590.99	7632.48	7680.01
750,000	8004.43	8030.56	8060.35	8094.35	8133.20	8177.66	8228.58
800,000	8538.06	8565.93	8597.70	8633.97	8675.42	8722.83	8777.16
850,000	9071.69	9101.30	9135.06	9173.60	9217.63	9268.01	9325.73
900,000	9605.32	9636.67	9672.42	9713.22	9759.85	9813.19	9874.30
950,000	10138.95	10172.04	10209.77	10252.84	10302.06	10358.36	10422.87
1,000,000	10672.58	10707.41	10747.13	10792.47	10844.27	10903.54	10971.44

Monthly Payments 12½%
Necessary to Amortize a Loan

AMOUNT BORROWED	YEARS REMAINING IN TERM						
	23	22	21	20	15	10	5
100	1.10	1.11	1.12	1.14	1.23	1.46	2.25
200	2.21	2.23	2.25	2.27	2.47	2.93	4.50
300	3.31	3.34	3.37	3.41	3.70	4.39	6.75
400	4.42	4.46	4.50	4.54	4.93	5.86	9.00
500	5.52	5.57	5.62	5.68	6.16	7.32	11.25
600	6.63	6.68	6.75	6.82	7.40	8.78	13.50
700	7.73	7.80	7.87	7.95	8.63	10.25	15.75
800	8.84	8.91	8.99	9.09	9.86	11.71	18.00
900	9.94	10.03	10.12	10.23	11.09	13.17	20.25
1,000	11.05	11.14	11.24	11.36	12.33	14.64	22.50
2,000	22.10	22.28	22.48	22.72	24.65	29.28	45.00
3,000	33.15	33.42	33.73	34.08	36.98	43.91	67.49
4,000	44.20	44.56	44.97	45.45	49.30	58.55	89.99
5,000	55.25	55.69	56.21	56.81	61.63	73.19	112.49
6,000	66.30	66.83	67.45	68.17	73.95	87.83	134.99
7,000	77.35	77.97	78.70	79.53	86.28	102.46	157.49
8,000	88.39	89.11	89.94	90.89	98.60	117.10	179.98
9,000	99.44	100.25	101.18	102.25	110.93	131.74	202.48
10,000	110.49	111.39	112.42	113.61	123.25	146.38	224.98
15,000	165.74	167.08	168.63	170.42	184.88	219.56	337.47
20,000	220.99	222.78	224.84	227.23	246.50	292.75	449.96
25,000	276.23	278.47	281.05	284.04	308.13	365.94	562.45
30,000	331.48	334.17	337.27	340.84	369.76	439.13	674.94
35,000	386.73	389.86	393.48	397.65	431.38	512.32	787.43
40,000	441.97	445.56	449.69	454.46	493.01	585.50	899.92
45,000	497.22	501.25	505.90	511.26	554.63	658.69	1012.41
50,000	552.47	556.95	562.11	568.07	616.26	731.88	1124.90
55,000	607.72	612.64	618.32	624.88	677.89	805.07	1237.39
60,000	662.96	668.34	674.53	681.68	739.51	878.26	1349.88
65,000	718.21	724.03	730.74	738.49	801.14	951.45	1462.37
70,000	773.46	779.73	786.95	795.30	862.77	1024.63	1574.86
75,000	828.70	835.42	843.16	852.11	924.39	1097.82	1687.35
80,000	883.95	891.12	899.37	908.91	986.02	1171.01	1799.84
85,000	939.20	946.81	955.59	965.72	1047.64	1244.20	1912.32
90,000	994.44	1002.51	1011.80	1022.53	1109.27	1317.39	2024.81
95,000	1049.69	1058.20	1068.01	1079.33	1170.90	1390.57	2137.30
100,000	1104.94	1113.90	1124.22	1136.14	1232.52	1463.76	2249.79
110,000	1215.43	1225.29	1236.64	1249.75	1355.77	1610.14	2474.77
120,000	1325.92	1336.67	1349.06	1363.37	1479.03	1756.51	2699.75
130,000	1436.42	1448.06	1461.48	1476.98	1602.28	1902.89	2924.73
140,000	1546.91	1559.45	1573.91	1590.60	1725.53	2049.27	3149.71
150,000	1657.41	1670.84	1686.33	1704.21	1848.78	2195.64	3374.69
200,000	2209.87	2227.79	2248.44	2272.28	2465.04	2927.52	4499.59
250,000	2762.34	2784.74	2810.55	2840.35	3081.31	3659.40	5624.48
300,000	3314.81	3341.69	3372.65	3408.42	3697.57	4391.29	6749.38
350,000	3867.28	3898.64	3934.76	3976.49	4313.83	5123.17	7874.28
400,000	4419.75	4455.58	4496.87	4544.56	4930.09	5855.05	8999.18
450,000	4972.22	5012.53	5058.98	5112.63	5546.35	6586.93	10124.07
500,000	5524.68	5569.48	5621.09	5680.70	6162.61	7318.81	11248.97
550,000	6077.15	6126.43	6183.20	6248.77	6778.87	8050.69	12373.87
600,000	6629.62	6683.37	6745.31	6816.84	7395.13	8782.57	13498.76
650,000	7182.09	7240.32	7307.42	7384.91	8011.39	9514.45	14623.66
700,000	7734.56	7797.27	7869.53	7952.98	8627.65	10246.33	15748.56
750,000	8287.03	8354.22	8431.64	8521.05	9243.92	10978.21	16873.45
800,000	8839.49	8911.17	8993.74	9089.12	9860.18	11710.09	17998.35
850,000	9391.96	9468.11	9555.85	9657.19	10476.44	12441.97	19123.25
900,000	9944.43	10025.06	10117.96	10225.26	11092.70	13173.86	20248.14
950,000	10496.90	10582.01	10680.07	10793.34	11708.96	13905.74	21373.04
1,000,000	11049.37	11138.96	11242.18	11361.41	12325.22	14637.62	22497.94

12³/₄%

Monthly Payments
Necessary to Amortize a Loan

AMOUNT BORROWED	YEARS REMAINING IN TERM						
	30	29	28	27	26	25	24
100	1.09	1.09	1.09	1.10	1.10	1.11	1.12
200	2.17	2.18	2.19	2.20	2.21	2.22	2.23
300	3.26	3.27	3.28	3.29	3.31	3.33	3.35
400	4.35	4.36	4.38	4.39	4.41	4.44	4.46
500	5.43	5.45	5.47	5.49	5.52	5.55	5.58
600	6.52	6.54	6.56	6.59	6.62	6.65	6.69
700	7.61	7.63	7.66	7.69	7.72	7.76	7.81
800	8.69	8.72	8.75	8.79	8.83	8.87	8.93
900	9.78	9.81	9.84	9.88	9.93	9.98	10.04
1,000	10.87	10.90	10.94	10.98	11.03	11.09	11.16
2,000	21.73	21.80	21.88	21.97	22.07	22.18	22.31
3,000	32.60	32.70	32.82	32.95	33.10	33.27	33.47
4,000	43.47	43.60	43.76	43.93	44.13	44.36	44.63
5,000	54.33	54.50	54.69	54.91	55.16	55.45	55.78
6,000	65.20	65.40	65.63	65.90	66.20	66.54	66.94
7,000	76.07	76.30	76.57	76.88	77.23	77.63	78.10
8,000	86.94	87.20	87.51	87.86	88.26	88.72	89.25
9,000	97.80	98.10	98.45	98.84	99.30	99.81	100.41
10,000	108.67	109.00	109.39	109.83	110.33	110.91	111.57
15,000	163.00	163.51	164.08	164.74	165.49	166.36	167.35
20,000	217.34	218.01	218.78	219.65	220.66	221.81	223.13
25,000	271.67	272.51	273.47	274.57	275.82	277.26	278.92
30,000	326.01	327.01	328.17	329.48	330.99	332.72	334.70
35,000	380.34	381.52	382.86	384.40	386.15	388.17	390.48
40,000	434.68	436.02	437.55	439.31	441.32	443.62	446.26
45,000	489.01	490.52	492.25	494.22	496.48	499.07	502.05
50,000	543.35	545.02	546.94	549.14	551.65	554.53	557.83
55,000	597.68	599.53	601.64	604.05	606.81	609.98	613.61
60,000	652.02	654.03	656.33	658.96	661.98	665.43	669.40
65,000	706.35	708.53	711.03	713.88	717.14	720.88	725.18
70,000	760.69	763.03	765.72	768.79	772.31	776.34	780.96
75,000	815.02	817.54	820.41	823.70	827.47	831.79	836.75
80,000	869.35	872.04	875.11	878.62	882.64	887.24	892.53
85,000	923.69	926.54	929.80	933.53	937.80	942.69	948.31
90,000	978.02	981.04	984.50	988.44	992.96	998.15	1004.10
95,000	1032.36	1035.55	1039.19	1043.36	1048.13	1053.60	1059.88
100,000	1086.69	1090.05	1093.88	1098.27	1103.29	1109.05	1115.66
110,000	1195.36	1199.05	1203.27	1208.10	1213.62	1219.96	1227.23
120,000	1304.03	1308.06	1312.66	1317.93	1323.95	1330.86	1338.79
130,000	1412.70	1417.06	1422.05	1427.75	1434.28	1441.77	1450.36
140,000	1521.37	1526.07	1531.44	1537.58	1544.61	1552.67	1561.93
150,000	1630.04	1635.07	1640.83	1647.41	1654.94	1663.58	1673.49
200,000	2173.39	2180.10	2187.77	2196.54	2206.59	2218.10	2231.32
250,000	2716.73	2725.12	2734.71	2745.68	2758.24	2772.63	2789.16
300,000	3260.08	3270.15	3281.65	3294.81	3309.88	3327.16	3346.99
350,000	3803.43	3815.17	3828.60	3843.95	3861.53	3881.68	3904.82
400,000	4346.77	4360.20	4375.54	4393.09	4413.18	4436.21	4462.65
450,000	4890.12	4905.22	4922.48	4942.22	4964.82	4990.74	5020.48
500,000	5433.47	5450.25	5469.42	5491.36	5516.47	5545.26	5578.31
550,000	5976.81	5995.27	6016.37	6040.49	6068.12	6099.79	6136.14
600,000	6520.16	6540.30	6563.31	6589.63	6619.77	6654.31	6693.97
650,000	7063.51	7085.32	7110.25	7138.77	7171.41	7208.84	7251.80
700,000	7606.85	7630.35	7657.19	7687.90	7723.06	7763.37	7809.63
750,000	8150.20	8175.37	8204.14	8237.04	8274.71	8317.89	8367.47
800,000	8693.55	8720.40	8751.08	8786.17	8826.35	8872.42	8925.30
850,000	9236.89	9265.42	9298.02	9335.31	9378.00	9426.94	9483.13
900,000	9780.24	9810.45	9844.96	9884.44	9929.65	9981.47	10040.96
950,000	10323.59	10355.47	10391.91	10433.58	10481.30	10536.00	10598.79
1,000,000	10866.93	10900.49	10938.85	10982.72	11032.94	11090.52	11156.62

AMOUNT BORROWED	YEARS REMAINING IN TERM						
	23	22	21	20	15	10	5
100	1.12	1.13	1.14	1.15	1.25	1.48	2.26
200	2.25	2.26	2.28	2.31	2.50	2.96	4.53
300	3.37	3.40	3.43	3.46	3.75	4.44	6.79
400	4.49	4.53	4.57	4.62	5.00	5.91	9.05
500	5.62	5.66	5.71	5.77	6.24	7.39	11.31
600	6.74	6.79	6.85	6.92	7.49	8.87	13.58
700	7.86	7.92	7.99	8.08	8.74	10.35	15.84
800	8.99	9.06	9.14	9.23	9.99	11.83	18.10
900	10.11	10.19	10.28	10.38	11.24	13.31	20.36
1,000	11.23	11.32	11.42	11.54	12.49	14.78	22.63
2,000	22.47	22.64	22.84	23.08	24.98	29.57	45.25
3,000	33.70	33.96	34.26	34.61	37.47	44.35	67.88
4,000	44.93	45.28	45.68	46.15	49.95	59.14	90.50
5,000	56.16	56.60	57.11	57.69	62.44	73.92	113.13
6,000	67.40	67.92	68.53	69.23	74.93	88.70	135.75
7,000	78.63	79.24	79.95	80.77	87.42	103.49	158.38
8,000	89.86	90.56	91.37	92.30	99.91	118.27	181.00
9,000	101.09	101.88	102.79	103.84	112.40	133.06	203.63
10,000	112.33	113.20	114.21	115.38	124.88	147.84	226.25
15,000	168.49	169.80	171.32	173.07	187.33	221.76	339.38
20,000	224.65	226.40	228.42	230.76	249.77	295.68	452.51
25,000	280.82	283.00	285.53	288.45	312.21	369.60	565.63
30,000	336.98	339.60	342.64	346.14	374.65	443.52	678.76
35,000	393.14	396.21	399.74	403.83	437.09	517.44	791.89
40,000	449.30	452.81	456.85	461.52	499.53	591.36	905.01
45,000	505.47	509.41	513.95	519.22	561.98	665.28	1018.14
50,000	561.63	566.01	571.06	576.91	624.42	739.20	1131.27
55,000	617.79	622.61	628.17	634.60	686.86	813.12	1244.39
60,000	673.96	679.21	685.27	692.29	749.30	887.04	1357.52
65,000	730.12	735.81	742.38	749.98	811.74	960.96	1470.64
70,000	786.28	792.41	799.48	807.67	874.19	1034.88	1583.77
75,000	842.45	849.01	856.59	865.36	936.63	1108.80	1696.90
80,000	898.61	905.61	913.70	923.05	999.07	1182.72	1810.02
85,000	954.77	962.21	970.80	980.74	1061.51	1256.64	1923.15
90,000	1010.94	1018.81	1027.91	1038.43	1123.95	1330.56	2036.28
95,000	1067.10	1075.41	1085.01	1096.12	1186.40	1404.48	2149.40
100,000	1123.26	1132.02	1142.12	1153.81	1248.84	1478.40	2262.53
110,000	1235.59	1245.22	1256.33	1269.19	1373.72	1626.24	2488.78
120,000	1347.91	1358.42	1370.54	1384.57	1498.60	1774.08	2715.04
130,000	1460.24	1471.62	1484.76	1499.96	1623.49	1921.92	2941.29
140,000	1572.57	1584.82	1598.97	1615.34	1748.37	2069.76	3167.54
150,000	1684.89	1698.02	1713.18	1730.72	1873.26	2217.60	3393.80
200,000	2246.52	2264.03	2284.24	2307.62	2497.67	2956.80	4525.06
250,000	2808.15	2830.04	2855.30	2884.53	3122.09	3696.00	5656.33
300,000	3369.79	3396.05	3426.36	3461.43	3746.51	4435.19	6787.59
350,000	3931.42	3962.05	3997.42	4038.34	4370.93	5174.39	7918.86
400,000	4493.05	4528.06	4568.48	4615.25	4995.35	5913.59	9050.12
450,000	5054.68	5094.07	5139.54	5192.15	5619.77	6652.79	10181.39
500,000	5616.31	5660.08	5710.60	5769.06	6244.18	7391.99	11312.65
550,000	6177.94	6226.09	6281.66	6345.96	6868.60	8131.19	12443.92
600,000	6739.57	6792.09	6852.72	6922.87	7493.02	8870.39	13575.18
650,000	7301.20	7358.10	7423.78	7499.78	8117.44	9609.59	14706.45
700,000	7862.83	7924.11	7994.84	8076.68	8741.86	10348.79	15837.71
750,000	8424.46	8490.12	8565.90	8653.59	9366.28	11087.99	16968.98
800,000	8986.09	9056.13	9136.96	9230.49	9990.70	11827.18	18100.24
850,000	9547.73	9622.05	9708.02	9807.40	10615.11	12566.38	19231.51
900,000	10109.36	10188.14	10279.08	10384.30	11239.53	13305.58	20362.77
950,000	10670.99	10754.15	10850.14	10961.21	11863.95	14044.78	21494.04
1,000,000	11232.62	11320.16	11421.20	11538.12	12488.37	14783.98	22625.30

13% Monthly Payments
Necessary to Amortize a Loan

AMOUNT BORROWED	\multicolumn{7}{c}{YEARS REMAINING IN TERM}						
	30	29	28	27	26	25	24
100	1.11	1.11	1.11	1.12	1.12	1.13	1.13
200	2.21	2.22	2.23	2.23	2.24	2.26	2.27
300	3.32	3.33	3.34	3.35	3.37	3.38	3.40
400	4.42	4.44	4.45	4.47	4.49	4.51	4.54
500	5.53	5.55	5.57	5.59	5.61	5.64	5.67
600	6.64	6.66	6.68	6.70	6.73	6.77	6.81
700	7.74	7.77	7.79	7.82	7.86	7.89	7.94
800	8.85	8.88	8.91	8.94	8.98	9.02	9.07
900	9.96	9.98	10.02	10.06	10.10	10.15	10.21
1,000	11.06	11.09	11.13	11.17	11.22	11.28	11.34
2,000	22.12	22.19	22.26	22.35	22.44	22.56	22.69
3,000	33.19	33.28	33.39	33.52	33.67	33.84	34.03
4,000	44.25	44.38	44.53	44.70	44.89	45.11	45.37
5,000	55.31	55.47	55.66	55.87	56.11	56.39	56.71
6,000	66.37	66.57	66.79	67.04	67.33	67.67	68.06
7,000	77.43	77.66	77.92	78.22	78.56	78.95	79.40
8,000	88.50	88.75	89.05	89.39	89.78	90.23	90.74
9,000	99.56	99.85	100.18	100.56	101.00	101.51	102.08
10,000	110.62	110.94	111.31	111.74	112.22	112.78	113.43
15,000	165.93	166.41	166.97	167.61	168.34	169.18	170.14
20,000	221.24	221.89	222.63	223.48	224.45	225.57	226.85
25,000	276.55	277.36	278.28	279.34	280.56	281.96	283.57
30,000	331.86	332.83	333.94	335.21	336.67	338.35	340.28
35,000	387.17	388.30	389.60	391.08	392.79	394.74	396.99
40,000	442.48	443.77	445.25	446.95	448.90	451.13	453.71
45,000	497.79	499.24	500.91	502.82	505.01	507.53	510.42
50,000	553.10	554.72	556.57	558.69	561.12	563.92	567.13
55,000	608.41	610.19	612.22	614.56	617.23	620.31	623.85
60,000	663.72	665.66	667.88	670.43	673.35	676.70	680.56
65,000	719.03	721.13	723.54	726.29	729.46	733.09	737.27
70,000	774.34	776.60	779.19	782.16	785.57	789.48	793.99
75,000	829.65	832.07	834.85	838.03	841.68	845.88	850.70
80,000	884.96	887.55	890.51	893.90	897.80	902.27	907.41
85,000	940.27	943.02	946.16	949.77	953.91	958.66	964.13
90,000	995.58	998.49	1001.82	1005.64	1010.02	1015.05	1020.84
95,000	1050.89	1053.96	1057.48	1061.51	1066.13	1071.44	1077.55
100,000	1106.20	1109.43	1113.13	1117.38	1122.24	1127.84	1134.27
110,000	1216.82	1220.38	1224.45	1229.11	1234.47	1240.62	1247.69
120,000	1327.44	1331.32	1335.76	1340.85	1346.69	1353.40	1361.12
130,000	1438.06	1442.26	1447.07	1452.59	1458.92	1466.19	1474.55
140,000	1548.68	1553.20	1558.39	1564.33	1571.14	1578.97	1587.97
150,000	1659.30	1664.15	1669.70	1676.06	1683.37	1691.75	1701.40
200,000	2212.40	2218.86	2226.27	2234.75	2244.49	2255.67	2268.53
250,000	2765.50	2773.58	2782.83	2793.44	2805.61	2819.59	2835.67
300,000	3318.60	3328.30	3339.40	3352.13	3366.73	3383.51	3402.80
350,000	3871.70	3883.01	3895.97	3910.82	3927.85	3947.42	3969.93
400,000	4424.80	4437.73	4452.53	4469.50	4488.98	4511.34	4537.07
450,000	4977.90	4992.44	5009.10	5028.19	5050.10	5075.26	5104.20
500,000	5531.00	5547.16	5565.67	5586.88	5611.22	5639.18	5671.33
550,000	6084.10	6101.88	6122.23	6145.57	6172.34	6203.09	6238.47
600,000	6637.20	6656.59	6678.80	6704.26	6733.46	6767.01	6805.60
650,000	7190.30	7211.31	7235.37	7262.94	7294.58	7330.93	7372.73
700,000	7743.40	7766.02	7791.93	7821.63	7855.71	7894.85	7939.87
750,000	8296.50	8320.74	8348.50	8380.32	8416.83	8458.76	8507.00
800,000	8849.60	8875.45	8905.07	8939.01	8977.95	9022.68	9074.13
850,000	9402.70	9430.17	9461.63	9497.70	9539.07	9586.60	9641.27
900,000	9955.80	9984.89	10018.20	10056.38	10100.19	10150.52	10208.40
950,000	10508.90	10539.60	10574.77	10615.07	10661.32	10714.44	10775.53
1,000,000	11062.00	11094.32	11131.33	11173.76	11222.44	11278.35	11342.67

Monthly Payments 13%
Necessary to Amortize a Loan

AMOUNT BORROWED	YEARS REMAINING IN TERM						
	23	22	21	20	15	10	5
100	1.14	1.15	1.16	1.17	1.27	1.49	2.28
200	2.28	2.30	2.32	2.34	2.53	2.99	4.55
300	3.43	3.45	3.48	3.51	3.80	4.48	6.83
400	4.57	4.60	4.64	4.69	5.06	5.97	9.10
500	5.71	5.75	5.80	5.86	6.33	7.47	11.38
600	6.85	6.90	6.96	7.03	7.59	8.96	13.65
700	7.99	8.05	8.12	8.20	8.86	10.45	15.93
800	9.13	9.20	9.28	9.37	10.12	11.94	18.20
900	10.28	10.35	10.44	10.54	11.39	13.44	20.48
1,000	11.42	11.50	11.60	11.72	12.65	14.93	22.75
2,000	22.83	23.00	23.20	23.43	25.30	29.86	45.51
3,000	34.25	34.51	34.80	35.15	37.96	44.79	68.26
4,000	45.67	46.01	46.40	46.86	50.61	59.72	91.01
5,000	57.08	57.51	58.01	58.58	63.26	74.66	113.77
6,000	68.50	69.01	69.61	70.29	75.91	89.59	136.52
7,000	79.92	80.52	81.21	82.01	88.57	104.52	159.27
8,000	91.33	92.02	92.81	93.73	101.22	119.45	182.02
9,000	102.75	103.52	104.41	105.44	113.87	134.38	204.78
10,000	114.17	115.02	116.01	117.16	126.52	149.31	227.53
15,000	171.25	172.53	174.02	175.74	189.79	223.97	341.30
20,000	228.34	230.05	232.02	234.32	253.05	298.62	455.06
25,000	285.42	287.56	290.03	292.89	316.31	373.28	568.83
30,000	342.50	345.07	348.03	351.47	379.57	447.93	682.59
35,000	399.59	402.58	406.04	410.05	442.83	522.59	796.36
40,000	456.67	460.09	464.05	468.63	506.10	597.24	910.12
45,000	513.75	517.60	522.05	527.21	569.36	671.90	1023.89
50,000	570.84	575.11	580.06	585.79	632.62	746.55	1137.65
55,000	627.92	632.62	638.06	644.37	695.88	821.21	1251.42
60,000	685.01	690.14	696.07	702.95	759.15	895.86	1365.18
65,000	742.09	747.65	754.07	761.52	822.41	970.52	1478.95
70,000	799.17	805.16	812.08	820.10	885.67	1045.18	1592.72
75,000	856.26	862.67	870.09	878.68	948.93	1119.83	1706.48
80,000	913.34	920.18	928.09	937.26	1012.19	1194.49	1820.25
85,000	970.42	977.69	986.10	995.84	1075.46	1269.14	1934.01
90,000	1027.51	1035.20	1044.10	1054.42	1138.72	1343.80	2047.78
95,000	1084.59	1092.72	1102.11	1113.00	1201.98	1418.45	2161.54
100,000	1141.68	1150.23	1160.11	1171.58	1265.24	1493.11	2275.31
110,000	1255.84	1265.25	1276.13	1288.73	1391.77	1642.42	2502.84
120,000	1370.01	1380.27	1392.14	1405.89	1518.29	1791.73	2730.37
130,000	1484.18	1495.29	1508.15	1523.05	1644.81	1941.04	2957.90
140,000	1598.35	1610.32	1624.16	1640.21	1771.34	2090.35	3185.43
150,000	1712.51	1725.34	1740.17	1757.36	1897.86	2239.66	3412.96
200,000	2283.35	2300.45	2320.23	2343.15	2530.48	2986.21	4550.61
250,000	2854.19	2875.57	2900.29	2928.94	3163.11	3732.77	5688.27
300,000	3425.03	3450.68	3480.34	3514.73	3795.73	4479.32	6825.92
350,000	3995.87	4025.79	4060.40	4100.51	4428.35	5225.88	7963.58
400,000	4566.70	4600.91	4640.46	4686.30	5060.97	5972.43	9101.23
450,000	5137.54	5176.02	5220.51	5272.09	5693.59	6718.98	10238.88
500,000	5708.38	5751.13	5800.57	5857.88	6326.21	7465.54	11376.54
550,000	6279.22	6326.24	6380.63	6443.67	6958.83	8212.09	12514.19
600,000	6850.06	6901.36	6960.69	7029.45	7591.45	8958.64	13651.84
650,000	7420.89	7476.47	7540.74	7615.24	8224.07	9705.20	14789.50
700,000	7991.73	8051.58	8120.80	8201.03	8856.70	10451.75	15927.15
750,000	8562.57	8626.70	8700.86	8786.82	9489.32	11198.31	17064.80
800,000	9133.41	9201.81	9280.91	9372.61	10121.94	11944.86	18202.46
850,000	9704.25	9776.92	9860.97	9958.39	10754.56	12691.41	19340.11
900,000	10275.08	10352.04	10441.03	10544.18	11387.18	13437.97	20477.77
950,000	10845.92	10927.15	11021.08	11129.97	12019.80	14184.52	21615.42
1,000,000	11416.76	11502.26	11601.14	11715.76	12652.42	14931.07	22753.07

13¼%

Monthly Payments
Necessary to Amortize a Loan

YEARS REMAINING IN TERM

AMOUNT BORROWED	30	29	28	27	26	25	24
100	1.13	1.13	1.13	1.14	1.14	1.15	1.15
200	2.25	2.26	2.26	2.27	2.28	2.29	2.31
300	3.38	3.39	3.40	3.41	3.42	3.44	3.46
400	4.50	4.52	4.53	4.55	4.57	4.59	4.61
500	5.63	5.64	5.66	5.68	5.71	5.73	5.76
600	6.75	6.77	6.79	6.82	6.85	6.88	6.92
700	7.88	7.90	7.93	7.96	7.99	8.03	8.07
800	9.01	9.03	9.06	9.09	9.13	9.17	9.22
900	10.13	10.16	10.19	10.23	10.27	10.32	10.38
1,000	11.26	11.29	11.32	11.37	11.41	11.47	11.53
2,000	22.52	22.58	22.65	22.73	22.83	22.93	23.06
3,000	33.77	33.87	33.97	34.10	34.24	34.40	34.59
4,000	45.03	45.16	45.30	45.46	45.65	45.87	46.12
5,000	56.29	56.44	56.62	56.83	57.06	57.34	57.65
6,000	67.55	67.73	67.95	68.19	68.48	68.80	69.18
7,000	78.80	79.02	79.27	79.56	79.89	80.27	80.71
8,000	90.06	90.31	90.60	90.92	91.30	91.74	92.24
9,000	101.32	101.60	101.92	102.29	102.71	103.20	103.77
10,000	112.58	112.89	113.25	113.66	114.13	114.67	115.30
15,000	168.87	169.33	169.87	170.48	171.19	172.01	172.94
20,000	225.15	225.78	226.49	227.31	228.25	229.34	230.59
25,000	281.44	282.22	283.11	284.14	285.32	286.68	288.24
30,000	337.73	338.67	339.74	340.97	342.38	344.01	345.89
35,000	394.02	395.11	396.36	397.80	399.45	401.35	403.53
40,000	450.31	451.55	452.98	454.62	456.51	458.68	461.18
45,000	506.60	508.00	509.61	511.45	513.57	516.02	518.83
50,000	562.89	564.44	566.23	568.28	570.64	573.35	576.48
55,000	619.18	620.89	622.85	625.11	627.70	630.69	634.13
60,000	675.46	677.33	679.47	681.93	684.76	688.02	691.77
65,000	731.75	733.78	736.10	738.76	741.83	745.36	749.42
70,000	788.04	790.22	792.72	795.59	798.89	802.69	807.07
75,000	844.33	846.66	849.34	852.42	855.95	860.03	864.72
80,000	900.62	903.11	905.96	909.25	913.02	917.36	922.36
85,000	956.91	959.55	962.59	966.07	970.08	974.70	980.01
90,000	1013.20	1016.00	1019.21	1022.90	1027.15	1032.03	1037.66
95,000	1069.48	1072.44	1075.83	1079.73	1084.21	1089.37	1095.31
100,000	1125.77	1128.88	1132.46	1136.56	1141.27	1146.70	1152.96
110,000	1238.35	1241.77	1245.70	1250.21	1255.40	1261.37	1268.25
120,000	1350.93	1354.66	1358.95	1363.87	1369.53	1376.04	1383.55
130,000	1463.51	1467.55	1472.19	1477.52	1483.65	1490.71	1498.84
140,000	1576.08	1580.44	1585.44	1591.18	1597.78	1605.38	1614.14
150,000	1688.66	1693.33	1698.68	1704.84	1711.91	1720.05	1729.43
200,000	2251.55	2257.77	2264.91	2273.11	2282.55	2293.40	2305.91
250,000	2814.43	2822.21	2831.14	2841.39	2853.18	2866.75	2882.39
300,000	3377.32	3386.65	3397.37	3409.67	3423.82	3440.10	3458.87
350,000	3940.21	3951.10	3963.60	3977.95	3994.45	4013.45	4035.35
400,000	4503.10	4515.54	4529.82	4546.23	4565.09	4586.80	4611.82
450,000	5065.98	5079.98	5096.05	5114.51	5135.73	5160.15	5188.30
500,000	5628.87	5644.42	5662.28	5682.79	5706.36	5733.50	5764.78
550,000	6191.75	6208.87	6228.51	6251.06	6277.00	6306.85	6341.26
600,000	6754.64	6773.31	6794.73	6819.34	6847.64	6880.20	6917.74
650,000	7317.53	7337.75	7360.96	7387.62	7418.27	7453.55	7494.21
700,000	7880.41	7902.19	7927.19	7955.90	7988.91	8026.90	8070.69
750,000	8443.30	8466.64	8493.42	8524.18	8559.55	8600.25	8647.17
800,000	9006.19	9031.08	9059.65	9092.46	9130.18	9173.60	9223.65
850,000	9569.07	9595.52	9625.87	9660.74	9700.82	9746.95	9800.13
900,000	10131.96	10159.96	10192.10	10229.01	10271.45	10320.30	10376.60
950,000	10694.85	10724.41	10758.33	10797.29	10842.09	10893.65	10953.08
1,000,000	11257.74	11288.85	11324.56	11365.57	11412.73	11467.00	11529.56

Monthly Payments 13¼%
Necessary to Amortize a Loan

AMOUNT BORROWED	YEARS REMAINING IN TERM						
	23	22	21	20	15	10	5
100	1.16	1.17	1.18	1.19	1.28	1.51	2.29
200	2.32	2.34	2.36	2.38	2.56	3.02	4.58
300	3.48	3.51	3.53	3.57	3.85	4.52	6.86
400	4.64	4.67	4.71	4.76	5.13	6.03	9.15
500	5.80	5.84	5.89	5.95	6.41	7.54	11.44
600	6.96	7.01	7.07	7.14	7.69	9.05	13.73
700	8.12	8.18	8.25	8.33	8.97	10.56	16.02
800	9.28	9.35	9.43	9.52	10.25	12.06	18.31
900	10.44	10.52	10.60	10.70	11.54	13.57	20.59
1,000	11.60	11.69	11.78	11.89	12.82	15.08	22.88
2,000	23.20	23.37	23.56	23.79	25.63	30.16	45.76
3,000	34.81	35.06	35.35	35.68	38.45	45.24	68.64
4,000	46.41	46.74	47.13	47.58	51.27	60.32	91.53
5,000	58.01	58.43	58.91	59.47	64.09	75.39	114.41
6,000	69.61	70.11	70.69	71.37	76.90	90.47	137.29
7,000	81.21	81.80	82.47	83.26	89.72	105.55	160.17
8,000	92.81	93.48	94.26	95.15	102.54	120.63	183.05
9,000	104.42	105.17	106.04	107.05	115.36	135.71	205.93
10,000	116.02	116.85	117.82	118.94	128.17	150.79	228.81
15,000	174.03	175.28	176.73	178.41	192.26	226.18	343.22
20,000	232.04	233.71	235.64	237.89	256.35	301.58	457.63
25,000	290.04	292.13	294.55	297.36	320.43	376.97	572.03
30,000	348.05	350.56	353.46	356.83	384.52	452.37	686.44
35,000	406.06	408.98	412.37	416.30	448.61	527.76	800.84
40,000	464.07	467.41	471.28	475.77	512.69	603.16	915.25
45,000	522.08	525.84	530.19	535.24	576.78	678.55	1029.66
50,000	580.09	584.26	589.10	594.72	640.87	753.94	1144.06
55,000	638.10	642.69	648.01	654.19	704.96	829.34	1258.47
60,000	696.11	701.12	706.92	713.66	769.04	904.73	1372.88
65,000	754.11	759.54	765.83	773.13	833.13	980.13	1487.28
70,000	812.12	817.97	824.74	832.60	897.22	1055.52	1601.69
75,000	870.13	876.39	883.65	892.07	961.30	1130.92	1716.09
80,000	928.14	934.82	942.56	951.54	1025.39	1206.31	1830.50
85,000	986.15	993.25	1001.47	1011.02	1089.48	1281.71	1944.91
90,000	1044.16	1051.67	1060.38	1070.49	1153.56	1357.10	2059.31
95,000	1102.17	1110.10	1119.29	1129.96	1217.65	1432.49	2173.72
100,000	1160.18	1168.53	1178.20	1189.43	1281.74	1507.89	2288.13
110,000	1276.19	1285.38	1296.02	1308.37	1409.91	1658.68	2516.94
120,000	1392.21	1402.23	1413.84	1427.32	1538.08	1809.47	2745.75
130,000	1508.23	1519.08	1531.66	1546.26	1666.26	1960.26	2974.56
140,000	1624.25	1635.94	1649.48	1665.20	1794.43	2111.04	3203.38
150,000	1740.26	1752.79	1767.30	1784.15	1922.60	2261.83	3432.19
200,000	2320.35	2337.05	2356.40	2378.86	2563.47	3015.78	4576.25
250,000	2900.44	2921.31	2945.50	2973.58	3204.34	3769.72	5720.31
300,000	3480.53	3505.58	3534.59	3568.29	3845.21	4523.67	6864.38
350,000	4060.62	4089.84	4123.69	4163.01	4486.08	5277.61	8008.44
400,000	4640.71	4674.10	4712.79	4757.72	5126.95	6031.56	9152.50
450,000	5220.79	5258.36	5301.89	5352.44	5767.81	6785.50	10296.56
500,000	5800.88	5842.63	5890.99	5947.15	6408.68	7539.45	11440.63
550,000	6380.97	6426.89	6480.09	6541.87	7049.55	8293.39	12584.69
600,000	6961.06	7011.15	7069.19	7136.58	7690.42	9047.33	13728.75
650,000	7541.15	7595.42	7658.29	7731.30	8331.29	9801.28	14872.82
700,000	8121.24	8179.68	8247.39	8326.02	8972.16	10555.22	16016.88
750,000	8701.32	8763.94	8836.49	8920.73	9613.02	11309.17	17160.94
800,000	9281.41	9348.20	9425.59	9515.45	10253.89	12063.11	18305.00
850,000	9861.50	9932.47	10014.68	10110.16	10894.76	12817.06	19449.07
900,000	10441.59	10516.73	10603.78	10704.88	11535.63	13571.00	20593.13
950,000	11021.68	11100.99	11192.88	11299.59	12176.50	14324.95	21737.19
1,000,000	11601.77	11685.25	11781.98	11894.31	12817.36	15078.89	22881.26

13½%

Monthly Payments
Necessary to Amortize a Loan

YEARS REMAINING IN TERM

AMOUNT BORROWED	30	29	28	27	26	25	24
100	1.15	1.15	1.15	1.16	1.16	1.17	1.17
200	2.29	2.30	2.30	2.31	2.32	2.33	2.34
300	3.44	3.45	3.46	3.47	3.48	3.50	3.52
400	4.58	4.59	4.61	4.62	4.64	4.66	4.69
500	5.73	5.74	5.76	5.78	5.80	5.83	5.86
600	6.87	6.89	6.91	6.93	6.96	6.99	7.03
700	8.02	8.04	8.06	8.09	8.12	8.16	8.20
800	9.16	9.19	9.21	9.25	9.28	9.33	9.37
900	10.31	10.34	10.37	10.40	10.44	10.49	10.55
1,000	11.45	11.48	11.52	11.56	11.60	11.66	11.72
2,000	22.91	22.97	23.04	23.12	23.21	23.31	23.43
3,000	34.36	34.45	34.56	34.67	34.81	34.97	35.15
4,000	45.82	45.94	46.07	46.23	46.42	46.63	46.87
5,000	57.27	57.42	57.59	57.79	58.02	58.28	58.59
6,000	68.72	68.90	69.11	69.35	69.62	69.94	70.30
7,000	80.18	80.39	80.63	80.91	81.23	81.60	82.02
8,000	91.63	91.87	92.15	92.46	92.83	93.25	93.74
9,000	103.09	103.36	103.67	104.02	104.43	104.91	105.46
10,000	114.54	114.84	115.18	115.58	116.04	116.56	117.17
15,000	171.81	172.26	172.78	173.37	174.06	174.85	175.76
20,000	229.08	229.68	230.37	231.16	232.08	233.13	234.35
25,000	286.35	287.10	287.96	288.95	290.09	291.41	292.93
30,000	343.62	344.52	345.55	346.74	348.11	349.69	351.52
35,000	400.89	401.94	403.15	404.53	406.13	407.98	410.10
40,000	458.16	459.36	460.74	462.32	464.15	466.26	468.69
45,000	515.44	516.78	518.33	520.12	522.17	524.54	527.28
50,000	572.71	574.20	575.92	577.91	580.19	582.82	585.86
55,000	629.98	631.62	633.52	635.70	638.21	641.10	644.45
60,000	687.25	689.04	691.11	693.49	696.23	699.39	703.04
65,000	744.52	746.46	748.70	751.28	754.25	757.67	761.62
70,000	801.79	803.88	806.29	809.07	812.26	815.95	820.21
75,000	859.06	861.30	863.89	866.86	870.28	874.23	878.80
80,000	916.33	918.72	921.48	924.65	928.30	932.52	937.38
85,000	973.60	976.15	979.07	982.44	986.32	990.80	995.97
90,000	1030.87	1033.57	1036.66	1040.23	1044.34	1049.08	1054.55
95,000	1088.14	1090.99	1094.26	1098.02	1102.36	1107.36	1113.14
100,000	1145.41	1148.41	1151.85	1155.81	1160.38	1165.64	1171.73
110,000	1259.95	1263.25	1267.03	1271.39	1276.42	1282.21	1288.90
120,000	1374.49	1378.09	1382.22	1386.97	1392.45	1398.77	1406.07
130,000	1489.04	1492.93	1497.40	1502.56	1508.49	1515.34	1523.25
140,000	1603.58	1607.77	1612.59	1618.14	1624.53	1631.90	1640.42
150,000	1718.12	1722.61	1727.77	1733.72	1740.57	1748.47	1757.59
200,000	2290.82	2296.81	2303.70	2311.62	2320.76	2331.29	2343.45
250,000	2863.53	2871.01	2879.62	2889.53	2900.95	2914.11	2929.32
300,000	3436.24	3445.22	3455.55	3467.44	3481.13	3496.93	3515.18
350,000	4008.94	4019.42	4031.47	4045.34	4061.32	4079.76	4101.04
400,000	4581.65	4593.62	4607.40	4623.25	4641.51	4662.58	4686.91
450,000	5154.35	5167.83	5183.32	5201.15	5221.70	5245.40	5272.77
500,000	5727.06	5742.03	5759.24	5779.06	5801.89	5828.22	5858.64
550,000	6299.77	6316.23	6335.17	6356.97	6382.08	6411.05	6444.50
600,000	6872.47	6890.44	6911.09	6934.87	6962.27	6993.87	7030.36
650,000	7445.18	7464.64	7487.02	7512.78	7542.46	7576.69	7616.23
700,000	8017.89	8038.84	8062.94	8090.69	8122.65	8159.51	8202.09
750,000	8590.59	8613.04	8638.87	8668.59	8702.84	8742.34	8787.95
800,000	9163.30	9187.25	9214.79	9246.50	9283.03	9325.16	9373.82
850,000	9736.00	9761.45	9790.72	9824.40	9863.22	9907.98	9959.68
900,000	10308.71	10335.65	10366.64	10402.31	10443.40	10490.80	10545.54
950,000	10881.42	10909.86	10942.57	10980.22	11023.59	11073.63	11131.41
1,000,000	11454.12	11484.06	11518.49	11558.12	11603.78	11656.45	11717.27

Monthly Payments   13½%
Necessary to Amortize a Loan

AMOUNT BORROWED	YEARS REMAINING IN TERM						
	23	22	21	20	15	10	5
100	1.18	1.19	1.20	1.21	1.30	1.52	2.30
200	2.36	2.37	2.39	2.41	2.60	3.05	4.60
300	3.54	3.56	3.59	3.62	3.89	4.57	6.90
400	4.72	4.75	4.79	4.83	5.19	6.09	9.20
500	5.89	5.93	5.98	6.04	6.49	7.61	11.50
600	7.07	7.12	7.18	7.24	7.79	9.14	13.81
700	8.25	8.31	8.37	8.45	9.09	10.66	16.11
800	9.43	9.50	9.57	9.66	10.39	12.18	18.41
900	10.61	10.68	10.77	10.87	11.68	13.70	20.71
1,000	11.79	11.87	11.96	12.07	12.98	15.23	23.01
2,000	23.58	23.74	23.93	24.15	25.97	30.45	46.02
3,000	35.36	35.61	35.89	36.22	38.95	45.68	69.03
4,000	47.15	47.48	47.85	48.29	51.93	60.91	92.04
5,000	58.94	59.35	59.82	60.37	64.92	76.14	115.05
6,000	70.73	71.21	71.78	72.44	77.90	91.36	138.06
7,000	82.51	83.08	83.75	84.52	90.88	106.59	161.07
8,000	94.30	94.95	95.71	96.59	103.87	121.82	184.08
9,000	106.09	106.82	107.67	108.66	116.85	137.05	207.09
10,000	117.88	118.69	119.64	120.74	129.83	152.27	230.10
15,000	176.81	178.04	179.46	181.11	194.75	228.41	345.15
20,000	235.75	237.38	239.27	241.47	259.66	304.55	460.20
25,000	294.69	296.73	299.09	301.84	324.58	380.69	575.25
30,000	353.63	356.07	358.91	362.21	389.50	456.82	690.30
35,000	412.57	415.42	418.73	422.58	454.41	532.96	805.34
40,000	471.50	474.76	478.55	482.95	519.33	609.10	920.39
45,000	530.44	534.11	538.37	543.32	584.24	685.23	1035.44
50,000	589.38	593.46	598.18	603.69	649.16	761.37	1150.49
55,000	648.32	652.80	658.00	664.06	714.08	837.51	1265.54
60,000	707.26	712.15	717.82	724.42	778.99	913.65	1380.59
65,000	766.19	771.49	777.64	784.79	843.91	989.78	1495.64
70,000	825.13	830.84	837.46	845.16	908.82	1065.92	1610.69
75,000	884.07	890.18	897.28	905.53	973.74	1142.06	1725.74
80,000	943.01	949.53	957.10	965.90	1038.65	1218.19	1840.79
85,000	1001.95	1008.87	1016.91	1026.27	1103.57	1294.33	1955.84
90,000	1060.89	1068.22	1076.73	1086.64	1168.49	1370.47	2070.89
95,000	1119.82	1127.57	1136.55	1147.01	1233.40	1446.61	2185.94
100,000	1178.76	1186.91	1196.37	1207.37	1298.32	1522.74	2300.98
110,000	1296.64	1305.60	1316.01	1328.11	1428.15	1675.02	2531.08
120,000	1414.51	1424.29	1435.64	1448.85	1557.98	1827.29	2761.18
130,000	1532.39	1542.98	1555.28	1569.59	1687.81	1979.57	2991.28
140,000	1650.27	1661.67	1674.92	1690.32	1817.65	2131.84	3221.38
150,000	1768.14	1780.37	1794.55	1811.06	1947.48	2284.11	3451.48
200,000	2357.52	2373.82	2392.74	2414.75	2596.64	3045.49	4601.97
250,000	2946.90	2967.28	2990.92	3018.44	3245.80	3806.86	5752.46
300,000	3536.28	3560.73	3589.11	3622.12	3894.96	4568.23	6902.95
350,000	4125.66	4154.19	4187.29	4225.81	4544.11	5329.60	8053.45
400,000	4715.05	4747.64	4785.48	4829.50	5193.27	6090.97	9203.94
450,000	5304.43	5341.10	5383.66	5433.19	5842.43	6852.34	10354.43
500,000	5893.81	5934.55	5981.85	6036.87	6491.59	7613.71	11504.92
550,000	6483.19	6528.01	6580.03	6640.56	7140.75	8375.09	12655.42
600,000	7072.57	7121.46	7178.22	7244.25	7789.91	9136.46	13805.91
650,000	7661.95	7714.92	7776.40	7847.94	8439.07	9897.83	14956.40
700,000	8251.33	8308.37	8374.59	8451.62	9088.23	10659.20	16106.89
750,000	8840.71	8901.83	8972.77	9055.31	9737.39	11420.57	17257.38
800,000	9430.09	9495.28	9570.96	9659.00	10386.55	12181.94	18407.88
850,000	10019.47	10088.74	10169.14	10262.68	11035.71	12943.31	19558.37
900,000	10608.85	10682.20	10767.33	10866.37	11684.87	13704.69	20708.86
950,000	11198.23	11275.65	11365.51	11470.06	12334.03	14466.06	21859.35
1,000,000	11787.61	11869.11	11963.70	12073.75	12983.19	15227.43	23009.85

13¾%

Monthly Payments
Necessary to Amortize a Loan

AMOUNT BORROWED	YEARS REMAINING IN TERM						
	30	29	28	27	26	25	24
100	1.17	1.17	1.17	1.18	1.18	1.18	1.19
200	2.33	2.34	2.34	2.35	2.36	2.37	2.38
300	3.50	3.50	3.51	3.53	3.54	3.55	3.57
400	4.66	4.67	4.69	4.70	4.72	4.74	4.76
500	5.83	5.84	5.86	5.88	5.90	5.92	5.95
600	6.99	7.01	7.03	7.05	7.08	7.11	7.14
700	8.16	8.18	8.20	8.23	8.26	8.29	8.33
800	9.32	9.34	9.37	9.40	9.44	9.48	9.52
900	10.49	10.51	10.54	10.58	10.62	10.66	10.72
1,000	11.65	11.68	11.71	11.75	11.80	11.85	11.91
2,000	23.30	23.36	23.43	23.50	23.59	23.69	23.81
3,000	34.95	35.04	35.14	35.25	35.39	35.54	35.72
4,000	46.60	46.72	46.85	47.01	47.18	47.39	47.62
5,000	58.26	58.40	58.57	58.76	58.98	59.23	59.53
6,000	69.91	70.08	70.28	70.51	70.77	71.08	71.43
7,000	81.56	81.76	81.99	82.26	82.57	82.93	83.34
8,000	93.21	93.44	93.70	94.01	94.36	94.77	95.25
9,000	104.86	105.12	105.42	105.76	106.16	106.62	107.15
10,000	116.51	116.80	117.13	117.51	117.96	118.47	119.06
15,000	174.77	175.20	175.70	176.27	176.93	177.70	178.59
20,000	233.02	233.60	234.26	235.03	235.91	236.93	238.12
25,000	291.28	292.00	292.83	293.78	294.89	296.17	297.64
30,000	349.53	350.40	351.39	352.54	353.87	355.40	357.17
35,000	407.79	408.80	409.96	411.30	412.85	414.63	416.70
40,000	466.05	467.20	468.52	470.06	471.82	473.87	476.23
45,000	524.30	525.60	527.09	528.81	530.80	533.10	535.76
50,000	582.56	584.00	585.66	587.57	589.78	592.33	595.29
55,000	640.81	642.40	644.22	646.33	648.76	651.57	654.82
60,000	699.07	700.79	702.79	705.08	707.73	710.80	714.35
65,000	757.32	759.19	761.35	763.84	766.71	770.03	773.88
70,000	815.58	817.59	819.92	822.60	825.69	829.27	833.40
75,000	873.83	875.99	878.48	881.35	884.67	888.50	892.93
80,000	932.09	934.39	937.05	940.11	943.65	947.73	952.46
85,000	990.35	992.79	995.61	998.87	1002.62	1006.97	1011.99
90,000	1048.60	1051.19	1054.18	1057.62	1061.60	1066.20	1071.52
95,000	1106.86	1109.59	1112.74	1116.38	1120.58	1125.43	1131.05
100,000	1165.11	1167.99	1171.31	1175.14	1179.56	1184.67	1190.58
110,000	1281.62	1284.79	1288.44	1292.65	1297.51	1303.13	1309.64
120,000	1398.14	1401.59	1405.57	1410.17	1415.47	1421.60	1428.69
130,000	1514.65	1518.39	1522.70	1527.68	1533.43	1540.07	1547.75
140,000	1631.16	1635.19	1639.83	1645.19	1651.38	1658.53	1666.81
150,000	1747.67	1751.99	1756.97	1762.71	1769.34	1777.00	1785.87
200,000	2330.23	2335.98	2342.62	2350.28	2359.12	2369.33	2381.15
250,000	2912.78	2919.98	2928.28	2937.85	2948.89	2961.66	2976.44
300,000	3495.34	3503.97	3513.93	3525.41	3538.67	3554.00	3571.73
350,000	4077.89	4087.97	4099.59	4112.98	4128.45	4146.33	4167.02
400,000	4660.45	4671.97	4685.24	4700.55	4718.23	4738.66	4762.31
450,000	5243.01	5255.96	5270.90	5288.12	5308.01	5331.00	5357.60
500,000	5825.56	5839.96	5856.55	5875.69	5897.79	5923.33	5952.89
550,000	6408.12	6423.96	6442.21	6463.26	6487.57	6515.66	6548.18
600,000	6990.68	7007.95	7027.86	7050.83	7077.35	7108.00	7143.46
650,000	7573.23	7591.95	7613.52	7638.40	7667.13	7700.33	7738.75
700,000	8155.79	8175.94	8199.17	8225.97	8256.90	8292.66	8334.04
750,000	8738.34	8759.94	8784.83	8813.54	8846.68	8884.99	8929.33
800,000	9320.90	9343.93	9370.48	9401.10	9436.46	9477.33	9524.62
850,000	9903.46	9927.93	9956.14	9988.67	10026.24	10069.66	10119.91
900,000	10486.01	10511.92	10541.79	10576.24	10616.02	10661.99	10715.20
950,000	11068.57	11095.92	11127.45	11163.81	11205.80	11254.33	11310.48
1,000,000	11651.13	11679.92	11713.10	11751.38	11795.58	11846.66	11905.77

Monthly Payments 13¾%
Necessary to Amortize a Loan

AMOUNT BORROWED	YEARS REMAINING IN TERM						
	23	22	21	20	15	10	5
100	1.20	1.21	1.21	1.23	1.31	1.54	2.31
200	2.39	2.41	2.43	2.45	2.63	3.08	4.63
300	3.59	3.62	3.64	3.68	3.94	4.61	6.94
400	4.79	4.82	4.86	4.90	5.26	6.15	9.26
500	5.99	6.03	6.07	6.13	6.57	7.69	11.57
600	7.18	7.23	7.29	7.35	7.89	9.23	13.88
700	8.38	8.44	8.50	8.58	9.20	10.76	16.20
800	9.58	9.64	9.72	9.80	10.52	12.30	18.51
900	10.78	10.85	10.93	11.03	11.83	13.84	20.82
1,000	11.97	12.05	12.15	12.25	13.15	15.38	23.14
2,000	23.95	24.11	24.29	24.51	26.30	30.75	46.28
3,000	35.92	36.16	36.44	36.76	39.45	46.13	69.42
4,000	47.90	48.22	48.59	49.02	52.60	61.51	92.56
5,000	59.87	60.27	60.73	61.27	65.75	76.88	115.69
6,000	71.85	72.32	72.88	73.52	78.90	92.26	138.83
7,000	83.82	84.38	85.02	85.78	92.05	107.64	161.97
8,000	95.79	96.43	97.17	98.03	105.20	123.01	185.11
9,000	107.77	108.48	109.32	110.29	118.35	138.39	208.25
10,000	119.74	120.54	121.46	122.54	131.50	153.77	231.39
15,000	179.61	180.81	182.19	183.81	197.25	230.65	347.08
20,000	239.49	241.08	242.93	245.08	263.00	307.53	462.78
25,000	299.36	301.34	303.66	306.35	328.75	384.42	578.47
30,000	359.23	361.61	364.39	367.62	394.50	461.30	694.17
35,000	419.10	421.88	425.12	428.89	460.25	538.18	809.86
40,000	478.97	482.15	485.85	490.16	525.99	615.07	925.55
45,000	538.84	542.42	546.58	551.43	591.74	691.95	1041.25
50,000	598.71	602.69	607.31	612.70	657.49	768.83	1156.94
55,000	658.59	662.96	668.04	673.97	723.24	845.72	1272.64
60,000	718.46	723.23	728.78	735.24	788.99	922.60	1388.33
65,000	778.33	783.50	789.51	796.51	854.74	999.48	1504.02
70,000	838.20	843.77	850.24	857.78	920.49	1076.37	1619.72
75,000	898.07	904.03	910.97	919.05	986.24	1153.25	1735.41
80,000	957.94	964.30	971.70	980.32	1051.99	1230.13	1851.11
85,000	1017.81	1024.57	1032.43	1041.59	1117.74	1307.02	1966.80
90,000	1077.68	1084.84	1093.16	1102.86	1183.49	1383.90	2082.50
95,000	1137.56	1145.11	1153.90	1164.14	1249.24	1460.78	2198.19
100,000	1197.43	1205.38	1214.63	1225.41	1314.99	1537.67	2313.88
110,000	1317.17	1325.92	1336.09	1347.95	1446.49	1691.43	2545.27
120,000	1436.91	1446.46	1457.55	1470.49	1577.98	1845.20	2776.66
130,000	1556.66	1566.99	1579.01	1593.03	1709.48	1998.97	3008.05
140,000	1676.40	1687.53	1700.48	1715.57	1840.98	2152.74	3239.44
150,000	1796.14	1808.07	1821.94	1838.11	1972.48	2306.50	3470.83
200,000	2394.86	2410.76	2429.25	2450.81	2629.97	3075.34	4627.77
250,000	2993.57	3013.45	3036.57	3063.51	3287.47	3844.17	5784.71
300,000	3592.28	3616.14	3643.88	3676.22	3944.96	4613.00	6941.65
350,000	4191.00	4218.83	4251.19	4288.92	4602.46	5381.84	8098.60
400,000	4789.71	4821.52	4858.51	4901.62	5259.95	6150.67	9255.54
450,000	5388.42	5424.21	5465.82	5514.32	5917.44	6919.51	10412.48
500,000	5987.14	6026.90	6073.14	6127.03	6574.94	7688.34	11569.42
550,000	6585.85	6629.59	6680.45	6739.73	7232.43	8457.17	12726.36
600,000	7184.57	7232.28	7287.76	7352.43	7889.92	9226.01	13883.31
650,000	7783.28	7834.97	7895.07	7965.13	8547.42	9994.84	15040.25
700,000	8381.99	8437.66	8502.39	8577.84	9204.91	10763.68	16197.19
750,000	8980.71	9040.34	9109.70	9190.54	9862.40	11532.51	17354.13
800,000	9579.42	9643.03	9717.02	9803.24	10519.90	12301.34	18511.08
850,000	10178.14	10245.72	10324.33	10415.95	11177.39	13070.18	19668.02
900,000	10776.85	10848.41	10931.64	11028.65	11834.89	13839.01	20824.96
950,000	11375.56	11451.10	11538.96	11641.35	12492.38	14607.85	21981.90
1,000,000	11974.28	12053.79	12146.27	12254.05	13149.87	15376.68	23138.84

14% Monthly Payments
Necessary to Amortize a Loan

AMOUNT BORROWED	YEARS REMAINING IN TERM						
	30	29	28	27	26	25	24
100	1.18	1.19	1.19	1.19	1.20	1.20	1.21
200	2.37	2.38	2.38	2.39	2.40	2.41	2.42
300	3.55	3.56	3.57	3.58	3.60	3.61	3.63
400	4.74	4.75	4.76	4.78	4.80	4.82	4.84
500	5.92	5.94	5.95	5.97	5.99	6.02	6.05
600	7.11	7.13	7.15	7.17	7.19	7.22	7.26
700	8.29	8.31	8.34	8.36	8.39	8.43	8.47
800	9.48	9.50	9.53	9.56	9.59	9.63	9.68
900	10.66	10.69	10.72	10.75	10.79	10.83	10.89
1,000	11.85	11.88	11.91	11.95	11.99	12.04	12.10
2,000	23.70	23.75	23.82	23.89	23.98	24.08	24.19
3,000	35.55	35.63	35.73	35.84	35.96	36.11	36.29
4,000	47.39	47.51	47.63	47.78	47.95	48.15	48.38
5,000	59.24	59.38	59.54	59.73	59.94	60.19	60.48
6,000	71.09	71.26	71.45	71.67	71.93	72.23	72.57
7,000	82.94	83.13	83.36	83.62	83.92	84.26	84.67
8,000	94.79	95.01	95.27	95.56	95.90	96.30	96.76
9,000	106.64	106.89	107.18	107.51	107.89	108.34	108.86
10,000	118.49	118.76	119.08	119.45	119.88	120.38	120.95
15,000	177.73	178.15	178.63	179.18	179.82	180.56	181.43
20,000	236.97	237.53	238.17	238.91	239.76	240.75	241.90
25,000	296.22	296.91	297.71	298.63	299.70	300.94	302.38
30,000	355.46	356.29	357.25	358.36	359.64	361.13	362.85
35,000	414.71	415.67	416.79	418.09	419.58	421.32	423.33
40,000	473.95	475.06	476.33	477.81	479.52	481.50	483.80
45,000	533.19	534.44	535.88	537.54	539.46	541.69	544.28
50,000	592.44	593.82	595.42	597.27	599.40	601.88	604.75
55,000	651.68	653.20	654.96	656.99	659.34	662.07	665.23
60,000	710.92	712.58	714.50	716.72	719.28	722.26	725.70
65,000	770.17	771.97	774.04	776.45	779.23	782.44	786.18
70,000	829.41	831.35	833.59	836.17	839.17	842.63	846.65
75,000	888.65	890.73	893.13	895.90	899.11	902.82	907.13
80,000	947.90	950.11	952.67	955.63	959.05	963.01	967.60
85,000	1007.14	1009.49	1012.21	1015.35	1018.99	1023.20	1028.08
90,000	1066.38	1068.88	1071.75	1075.08	1078.93	1083.38	1088.55
95,000	1125.63	1128.26	1131.29	1134.81	1138.87	1143.57	1149.03
100,000	1184.87	1187.64	1190.84	1194.53	1198.81	1203.76	1209.50
110,000	1303.36	1306.40	1309.92	1313.99	1318.69	1324.14	1330.45
120,000	1421.85	1425.17	1429.01	1433.44	1438.57	1444.51	1451.41
130,000	1540.33	1543.93	1548.09	1552.89	1558.45	1564.89	1572.36
140,000	1658.82	1662.70	1667.17	1672.35	1678.33	1685.27	1693.31
150,000	1777.31	1781.46	1786.25	1791.80	1798.21	1805.64	1814.26
200,000	2369.74	2375.28	2381.67	2389.06	2397.62	2407.52	2419.01
250,000	2962.18	2969.10	2977.09	2986.33	2997.02	3009.40	3023.76
300,000	3554.62	3562.92	3572.51	3583.60	3596.42	3611.28	3628.51
350,000	4147.05	4156.74	4167.93	4180.86	4195.83	4213.16	4233.26
400,000	4739.49	4750.56	4763.35	4778.13	4795.23	4815.04	4838.02
450,000	5331.92	5344.38	5358.76	5375.39	5394.64	5416.92	5442.77
500,000	5924.36	5938.20	5954.18	5972.66	5994.04	6018.81	6047.52
550,000	6516.79	6532.02	6549.60	6569.93	6593.45	6620.69	6652.27
600,000	7109.23	7125.84	7145.02	7167.19	7192.85	7222.57	7257.03
650,000	7701.67	7719.66	7740.44	7764.46	7792.25	7824.45	7861.78
700,000	8294.10	8313.48	8335.85	8361.73	8391.66	8426.33	8466.53
750,000	8886.54	8907.30	8931.27	8958.99	8991.06	9028.21	9071.28
800,000	9478.97	9501.12	9526.69	9556.26	9590.47	9630.09	9676.03
850,000	10071.41	10094.93	10122.11	10153.52	10189.87	10231.97	10280.79
900,000	10663.85	10688.75	10717.53	10750.79	10789.27	10833.85	10885.54
950,000	11256.28	11282.57	11312.95	11348.06	11388.68	11435.73	11490.29
1,000,000	11848.72	11876.39	11908.36	11945.32	11988.08	12037.61	12095.04

Monthly Payments 14%
Necessary to Amortize a Loan

AMOUNT BORROWED	YEARS REMAINING IN TERM						
	23	22	21	20	15	10	5
100	1.22	1.22	1.23	1.24	1.33	1.55	2.33
200	2.43	2.45	2.47	2.49	2.66	3.11	4.65
300	3.65	3.67	3.70	3.73	4.00	4.66	6.98
400	4.86	4.90	4.93	4.97	5.33	6.21	9.31
500	6.08	6.12	6.16	6.22	6.66	7.76	11.63
600	7.30	7.34	7.40	7.46	7.99	9.32	13.96
700	8.51	8.57	8.63	8.70	9.32	10.87	16.29
800	9.73	9.79	9.86	9.95	10.65	12.42	18.61
900	10.95	11.02	11.10	11.19	11.99	13.97	20.94
1,000	12.16	12.24	12.33	12.44	13.32	15.53	23.27
2,000	24.32	24.48	24.66	24.87	26.63	31.05	46.54
3,000	36.49	36.72	36.99	37.31	39.95	46.58	69.80
4,000	48.65	48.96	49.32	49.74	53.27	62.11	93.07
5,000	60.81	61.20	61.65	62.18	66.59	77.63	116.34
6,000	72.97	73.44	73.98	74.61	79.90	93.16	139.61
7,000	85.13	85.68	86.31	87.05	93.22	108.69	162.88
8,000	97.29	97.91	98.64	99.48	106.54	124.21	186.15
9,000	109.46	110.15	110.97	111.92	119.86	139.74	209.41
10,000	121.62	122.39	123.30	124.35	133.17	155.27	232.68
15,000	182.43	183.59	184.95	186.53	199.76	232.90	349.02
20,000	243.23	244.79	246.59	248.70	266.35	310.53	465.37
25,000	304.04	305.98	308.24	310.88	332.94	388.17	581.71
30,000	364.85	367.18	369.89	373.06	399.52	465.80	698.05
35,000	425.66	428.38	431.54	435.23	466.11	543.43	814.39
40,000	486.47	489.57	493.19	497.41	532.70	621.07	930.73
45,000	547.28	550.77	554.84	559.58	599.28	698.70	1047.07
50,000	608.09	611.96	616.48	621.76	665.87	776.33	1163.41
55,000	668.90	673.16	678.13	683.94	732.46	853.97	1279.75
60,000	729.70	734.36	739.78	746.11	799.04	931.60	1396.10
65,000	790.51	795.55	801.43	808.29	865.63	1009.23	1512.44
70,000	851.32	856.75	863.08	870.46	932.22	1086.87	1628.78
75,000	912.13	917.95	924.73	932.64	998.81	1164.50	1745.12
80,000	972.94	979.14	986.37	994.82	1065.39	1242.13	1861.46
85,000	1033.75	1040.34	1048.02	1056.99	1131.98	1319.76	1977.80
90,000	1094.56	1101.54	1109.67	1119.17	1198.57	1397.40	2094.14
95,000	1155.36	1162.73	1171.32	1181.34	1265.15	1475.03	2210.48
100,000	1216.17	1223.93	1232.97	1243.52	1331.74	1552.66	2326.83
110,000	1337.79	1346.32	1356.26	1367.87	1464.92	1707.93	2559.51
120,000	1459.41	1468.72	1479.56	1492.22	1598.09	1863.20	2792.19
130,000	1581.03	1591.11	1602.86	1616.58	1731.26	2018.46	3024.87
140,000	1702.64	1713.50	1726.15	1740.93	1864.44	2173.73	3257.56
150,000	1824.26	1835.89	1849.45	1865.28	1997.61	2329.00	3490.24
200,000	2432.35	2447.86	2465.93	2487.04	2663.48	3105.33	4653.65
250,000	3040.43	3059.82	3082.42	3108.80	3329.35	3881.66	5817.06
300,000	3648.52	3671.79	3698.90	3730.56	3995.22	4657.99	6980.48
350,000	4256.61	4283.75	4315.38	4352.32	4661.09	5434.33	8143.89
400,000	4864.69	4895.72	4931.87	4974.08	5326.97	6210.66	9307.30
450,000	5472.78	5507.68	5548.35	5595.84	5992.84	6986.99	10470.71
500,000	6080.87	6119.65	6164.84	6217.60	6658.71	7763.32	11634.13
550,000	6688.95	6731.61	6781.32	6839.36	7324.58	8539.65	12797.54
600,000	7297.04	7343.58	7397.80	7461.12	7990.45	9315.99	13960.95
650,000	7905.13	7955.54	8014.29	8082.89	8656.32	10092.32	15124.36
700,000	8513.21	8567.51	8630.77	8704.65	9322.19	10868.65	16287.78
750,000	9121.30	9179.47	9247.25	9326.41	9988.06	11644.98	17451.19
800,000	9729.38	9791.44	9863.74	9948.17	10653.93	12421.31	18614.60
850,000	10337.47	10403.40	10480.22	10569.93	11319.80	13197.65	19778.01
900,000	10945.56	11015.36	11096.70	11191.69	11985.67	13973.98	20941.43
950,000	11553.64	11627.33	11713.19	11813.45	12651.54	14750.31	22104.84
1,000,000	12161.73	12239.29	12329.67	12435.21	13317.41	15526.64	23268.25

14¹/₄%

Monthly Payments
Necessary to Amortize a Loan

YEARS REMAINING IN TERM

AMOUNT BORROWED	30	29	28	27	26	25	24
100	1.20	1.21	1.21	1.21	1.22	1.22	1.23
200	2.41	2.41	2.42	2.43	2.44	2.45	2.46
300	3.61	3.62	3.63	3.64	3.65	3.67	3.69
400	4.82	4.83	4.84	4.86	4.87	4.89	4.91
500	6.02	6.04	6.05	6.07	6.09	6.11	6.14
600	7.23	7.24	7.26	7.28	7.31	7.34	7.37
700	8.43	8.45	8.47	8.50	8.53	8.56	8.60
800	9.64	9.66	9.68	9.71	9.75	9.78	9.83
900	10.84	10.87	10.89	10.93	10.96	11.01	11.06
1,000	12.05	12.07	12.10	12.14	12.18	12.23	12.29
2,000	24.09	24.15	24.21	24.28	24.36	24.46	24.57
3,000	36.14	36.22	36.31	36.42	36.54	36.69	36.86
4,000	48.19	48.29	48.42	48.56	48.73	48.92	49.14
5,000	60.23	60.37	60.52	60.70	60.91	61.15	61.43
6,000	72.28	72.44	72.63	72.84	73.09	73.38	73.71
7,000	84.33	84.51	84.73	84.98	85.27	85.60	86.00
8,000	96.37	96.59	96.83	97.12	97.45	97.83	98.28
9,000	108.42	108.66	108.94	109.26	109.63	110.06	110.57
10,000	120.47	120.73	121.04	121.40	121.81	122.29	122.85
15,000	180.70	181.10	181.56	182.10	182.72	183.44	184.28
20,000	240.94	241.47	242.09	242.80	243.63	244.59	245.70
25,000	301.17	301.84	302.61	303.50	304.53	305.73	307.13
30,000	361.41	362.20	363.13	364.20	365.44	366.88	368.55
35,000	421.64	422.57	423.65	424.90	426.34	428.02	429.98
40,000	481.87	482.94	484.17	485.60	487.25	489.17	491.40
45,000	542.11	543.31	544.69	546.30	548.16	550.32	552.83
50,000	602.34	603.67	605.21	607.00	609.06	611.46	614.25
55,000	662.58	664.04	665.73	667.70	669.97	672.61	675.68
60,000	722.81	724.41	726.26	728.40	730.88	733.76	737.10
65,000	783.05	784.78	786.78	789.09	791.78	794.90	798.53
70,000	843.28	845.14	847.30	849.79	852.69	856.05	859.95
75,000	903.52	905.51	907.82	910.49	913.60	917.20	921.38
80,000	963.75	965.88	968.34	971.19	974.50	978.34	982.80
85,000	1023.98	1026.24	1028.86	1031.89	1035.41	1039.49	1044.23
90,000	1084.22	1086.61	1089.38	1092.59	1096.31	1100.63	1105.65
95,000	1144.45	1146.98	1149.90	1153.29	1157.22	1161.78	1167.08
100,000	1204.69	1207.35	1210.43	1213.99	1218.13	1222.93	1228.51
110,000	1325.16	1328.08	1331.47	1335.39	1339.94	1345.22	1351.36
120,000	1445.62	1448.82	1452.51	1456.79	1461.75	1467.51	1474.21
130,000	1566.09	1569.55	1573.55	1578.19	1583.57	1589.81	1597.06
140,000	1686.56	1690.29	1694.60	1699.59	1705.38	1712.10	1719.91
150,000	1807.03	1811.02	1815.64	1820.99	1827.19	1834.39	1842.76
200,000	2409.37	2414.69	2420.85	2427.98	2436.25	2445.86	2457.01
250,000	3011.72	3018.37	3026.06	3034.98	3045.32	3057.32	3071.26
300,000	3614.06	3622.04	3631.28	3641.98	3654.38	3668.78	3685.52
350,000	4216.40	4225.71	4236.49	4248.97	4263.45	4280.25	4299.77
400,000	4818.75	4829.39	4841.70	4855.97	4872.51	4891.71	4914.02
450,000	5421.09	5433.06	5446.91	5462.96	5481.57	5503.17	5528.27
500,000	6023.44	6036.73	6052.13	6069.96	6090.64	6114.64	6142.53
550,000	6625.78	6640.41	6657.34	6676.95	6699.70	6726.10	6756.78
600,000	7228.12	7244.08	7262.55	7283.95	7308.76	7337.57	7371.03
650,000	7830.47	7847.75	7867.76	7890.95	7917.83	7949.03	7985.28
700,000	8432.81	8451.43	8472.98	8497.94	8526.89	8560.49	8599.54
750,000	9035.15	9055.10	9078.19	9104.94	9135.96	9171.96	9213.79
800,000	9637.50	9658.77	9683.40	9711.93	9745.02	9783.42	9828.04
850,000	10239.84	10262.44	10288.61	10318.93	10354.08	10394.88	10442.29
900,000	10842.18	10866.12	10893.83	10925.93	10963.15	11006.35	11056.55
950,000	11444.53	11469.79	11499.04	11532.92	11572.21	11617.81	11670.80
1,000,000	12046.87	12073.46	12104.25	12139.92	12181.27	12229.28	12285.05

Monthly Payments 14¼%
Necessary to Amortize a Loan

AMOUNT BORROWED	YEARS REMAINING IN TERM						
	23	22	21	20	15	10	5
100	1.23	1.24	1.25	1.26	1.35	1.57	2.34
200	2.47	2.49	2.50	2.52	2.70	3.14	4.68
300	3.70	3.73	3.75	3.79	4.05	4.70	7.02
400	4.94	4.97	5.01	5.05	5.39	6.27	9.36
500	6.17	6.21	6.26	6.31	6.74	7.84	11.70
600	7.41	7.46	7.51	7.57	8.09	9.41	14.04
700	8.64	8.70	8.76	8.83	9.44	10.97	16.38
800	9.88	9.94	10.01	10.09	10.79	12.54	18.72
900	11.11	11.18	11.26	11.36	12.14	14.11	21.06
1,000	12.35	12.43	12.51	12.62	13.49	15.68	23.40
2,000	24.70	24.85	25.03	25.23	26.97	31.35	46.80
3,000	37.05	37.28	37.54	37.85	40.46	47.03	70.19
4,000	49.40	49.70	50.06	50.47	53.94	62.71	93.59
5,000	61.75	62.13	62.57	63.09	67.43	78.39	116.99
6,000	74.10	74.55	75.08	75.70	80.91	94.06	140.39
7,000	86.45	86.98	87.60	88.32	94.40	109.74	163.79
8,000	98.80	99.40	100.11	100.94	107.89	125.42	187.18
9,000	111.15	111.83	112.62	113.55	121.37	141.10	210.58
10,000	123.50	124.26	125.14	126.17	134.86	156.77	233.98
15,000	185.25	186.38	187.71	189.26	202.29	235.16	350.97
20,000	247.00	248.51	250.28	252.34	269.72	313.55	467.96
25,000	308.75	310.64	312.85	315.43	337.14	391.93	584.95
30,000	370.50	372.77	375.42	378.52	404.57	470.32	701.94
35,000	432.25	434.90	437.99	441.60	472.00	548.71	818.93
40,000	494.00	497.02	500.56	504.69	539.43	627.09	935.92
45,000	555.75	559.15	563.12	567.77	606.86	705.48	1052.91
50,000	617.50	621.28	625.69	630.86	674.29	783.87	1169.90
55,000	679.25	683.41	688.26	693.95	741.72	862.25	1286.89
60,000	741.00	745.54	750.83	757.03	809.15	940.64	1403.88
65,000	802.75	807.66	813.40	820.12	876.58	1019.03	1520.87
70,000	864.50	869.79	875.97	883.20	944.01	1097.41	1637.86
75,000	926.25	931.92	938.54	946.29	1011.43	1175.80	1754.85
80,000	988.00	994.05	1001.11	1009.38	1078.86	1254.18	1871.85
85,000	1049.75	1056.17	1063.68	1072.46	1146.29	1332.57	1988.84
90,000	1111.50	1118.30	1126.25	1135.55	1213.72	1410.96	2105.83
95,000	1173.25	1180.43	1188.82	1198.63	1281.15	1489.34	2222.82
100,000	1235.00	1242.56	1251.39	1261.72	1348.58	1567.73	2339.81
110,000	1358.49	1366.81	1376.53	1387.89	1483.44	1724.50	2573.79
120,000	1481.99	1491.07	1501.67	1514.06	1618.30	1881.28	2807.77
130,000	1605.49	1615.33	1626.80	1640.23	1753.15	2038.05	3041.75
140,000	1728.99	1739.58	1751.94	1766.41	1888.01	2194.82	3275.73
150,000	1852.49	1863.84	1877.08	1892.58	2022.87	2351.60	3509.71
200,000	2469.99	2485.12	2502.78	2523.44	2697.16	3135.46	4679.61
250,000	3087.49	3106.40	3128.47	3154.30	3371.45	3919.33	5849.52
300,000	3704.99	3727.68	3754.17	3785.16	4045.74	4703.19	7019.42
350,000	4322.48	4348.95	4379.86	4416.02	4720.03	5487.06	8189.32
400,000	4939.98	4970.23	5005.55	5046.88	5394.32	6270.92	9359.23
450,000	5557.48	5591.51	5631.25	5677.74	6068.61	7054.79	10529.13
500,000	6174.98	6212.79	6256.94	6308.59	6742.90	7838.66	11699.03
550,000	6792.47	6834.07	6882.64	6939.45	7417.19	8622.52	12868.94
600,000	7409.97	7455.35	7508.33	7570.31	8091.48	9406.39	14038.84
650,000	8027.47	8076.63	8134.02	8201.17	8765.77	10190.25	15208.74
700,000	8644.97	8697.91	8759.72	8832.03	9440.06	10974.12	16378.64
750,000	9262.46	9319.19	9385.41	9462.89	10114.35	11757.98	17548.55
800,000	9879.96	9940.47	10011.11	10093.75	10788.64	12541.85	18718.45
850,000	10497.46	10561.75	10636.80	10724.61	11462.93	13325.71	19888.35
900,000	11114.96	11183.03	11262.50	11355.47	12137.22	14109.58	21058.26
950,000	11732.45	11804.31	11888.19	11986.33	12811.51	14893.45	22228.16
1,000,000	12349.95	12425.58	12513.88	12617.19	13485.80	15677.31	23398.06

14¹/₂%

Monthly Payments
Necessary to Amortize a Loan

AMOUNT BORROWED	YEARS REMAINING IN TERM						
	30	29	28	27	26	25	24
100	1.22	1.23	1.23	1.23	1.24	1.24	1.25
200	2.45	2.45	2.46	2.47	2.48	2.48	2.50
300	3.67	3.68	3.69	3.70	3.71	3.73	3.74
400	4.90	4.91	4.92	4.93	4.95	4.97	4.99
500	6.12	6.14	6.15	6.17	6.19	6.21	6.24
600	7.35	7.36	7.38	7.40	7.43	7.45	7.49
700	8.57	8.59	8.61	8.63	8.66	8.70	8.73
800	9.80	9.82	9.84	9.87	9.90	9.94	9.98
900	11.02	11.04	11.07	11.10	11.14	11.18	11.23
1,000	12.25	12.27	12.30	12.34	12.38	12.42	12.48
2,000	24.49	24.54	24.60	24.67	24.75	24.84	24.95
3,000	36.74	36.81	36.90	37.01	37.13	37.26	37.43
4,000	48.98	49.08	49.20	49.34	49.50	49.69	49.90
5,000	61.23	61.36	61.50	61.68	61.88	62.11	62.38
6,000	73.47	73.63	73.80	74.01	74.25	74.53	74.85
7,000	85.72	85.90	86.11	86.35	86.63	86.95	87.33
8,000	97.96	98.17	98.41	98.68	99.00	99.37	99.81
9,000	110.21	110.44	110.71	111.02	111.38	111.79	112.28
10,000	122.46	122.71	123.01	123.35	123.75	124.22	124.76
15,000	183.68	184.07	184.51	185.03	185.63	186.32	187.14
20,000	244.91	245.42	246.01	246.70	247.50	248.43	249.52
25,000	306.14	306.78	307.52	308.38	309.38	310.54	311.89
30,000	367.37	368.13	369.02	370.05	371.25	372.65	374.27
35,000	428.59	429.49	430.53	431.73	433.13	434.76	436.65
40,000	489.82	490.84	492.03	493.41	495.00	496.87	499.03
45,000	551.05	552.20	553.53	555.08	556.88	558.97	561.41
50,000	612.28	613.56	615.04	616.76	618.76	621.08	623.79
55,000	673.51	674.91	676.54	678.43	680.63	683.19	686.17
60,000	734.73	736.27	738.04	740.11	742.51	745.30	748.55
65,000	795.96	797.62	799.55	801.78	804.38	807.41	810.93
70,000	857.19	858.98	861.05	863.46	866.26	869.51	873.30
75,000	918.42	920.33	922.56	925.14	928.13	931.62	935.68
80,000	979.64	981.69	984.06	986.81	990.01	993.73	998.06
85,000	1040.87	1043.04	1045.56	1048.49	1051.89	1055.84	1060.44
90,000	1102.10	1104.40	1107.07	1110.16	1113.76	1117.95	1122.82
95,000	1163.33	1165.75	1168.57	1171.84	1175.64	1180.05	1185.20
100,000	1224.56	1227.11	1230.07	1233.51	1237.51	1242.16	1247.58
110,000	1347.01	1349.82	1353.08	1356.87	1361.26	1366.38	1372.34
120,000	1469.47	1472.53	1476.09	1480.22	1485.01	1490.60	1497.09
130,000	1591.92	1595.24	1599.10	1603.57	1608.77	1614.81	1621.85
140,000	1714.38	1717.95	1722.10	1726.92	1732.52	1739.03	1746.61
150,000	1836.83	1840.67	1845.11	1850.27	1856.27	1863.24	1871.37
200,000	2449.11	2454.22	2460.15	2467.03	2475.02	2484.33	2495.16
250,000	3061.39	3067.78	3075.18	3083.79	3093.78	3105.41	3118.95
300,000	3673.67	3681.33	3690.22	3700.54	3712.54	3726.49	3742.73
350,000	4285.95	4294.89	4305.26	4317.30	4331.29	4347.57	4366.52
400,000	4898.22	4908.44	4920.29	4934.06	4950.05	4968.65	4990.31
450,000	5510.50	5522.00	5535.33	5550.81	5568.81	5589.73	5614.10
500,000	6122.78	6135.55	6150.37	6167.57	6187.56	6210.81	6237.89
550,000	6735.06	6749.11	6765.40	6784.33	6806.32	6831.90	6861.68
600,000	7347.34	7362.66	7380.44	7401.09	7425.07	7452.98	7485.47
650,000	7959.61	7976.22	7995.48	8017.84	8043.83	8074.06	8109.26
700,000	8571.89	8589.77	8610.51	8634.60	8662.59	8695.14	8733.05
750,000	9184.17	9203.33	9225.55	9251.36	9281.34	9316.22	9356.84
800,000	9796.45	9816.88	9840.59	9868.11	9900.10	9937.30	9980.62
850,000	10408.73	10430.44	10455.62	10484.87	10518.86	10558.38	10604.41
900,000	11021.00	11043.99	11070.66	11101.63	11137.61	11179.47	11228.20
950,000	11633.28	11657.55	11685.70	11718.39	11756.37	11800.55	11851.99
1,000,000	12245.56	12271.10	12300.74	12335.14	12375.12	12421.63	12475.78

AMOUNT BORROWED	YEARS REMAINING IN TERM						
	23	22	21	20	15	10	5
100	1.25	1.26	1.27	1.28	1.37	1.58	2.35
200	2.51	2.52	2.54	2.56	2.73	3.17	4.71
300	3.76	3.78	3.81	3.84	4.10	4.75	7.06
400	5.02	5.05	5.08	5.12	5.46	6.33	9.41
500	6.27	6.31	6.35	6.40	6.83	7.91	11.76
600	7.52	7.57	7.62	7.68	8.19	9.50	14.12
700	8.78	8.83	8.89	8.96	9.56	11.08	16.47
800	10.03	10.09	10.16	10.24	10.92	12.66	18.82
900	11.29	11.35	11.43	11.52	12.29	14.25	21.18
1,000	12.54	12.61	12.70	12.80	13.66	15.83	23.53
2,000	25.08	25.23	25.40	25.60	27.31	31.66	47.06
3,000	37.62	37.84	38.10	38.40	40.97	47.49	70.58
4,000	50.16	50.45	50.80	51.20	54.62	63.31	94.11
5,000	62.69	63.06	63.49	64.00	68.28	79.14	117.64
6,000	75.23	75.68	76.19	76.80	81.93	94.97	141.17
7,000	87.77	88.29	88.89	89.60	95.59	110.80	164.70
8,000	100.31	100.90	101.59	102.40	109.24	126.63	188.23
9,000	112.85	113.51	114.29	115.20	122.90	142.46	211.75
10,000	125.39	126.13	126.99	128.00	136.55	158.29	235.28
15,000	188.08	189.19	190.48	192.00	204.83	237.43	352.92
20,000	250.78	252.25	253.98	256.00	273.10	316.57	470.57
25,000	313.47	315.32	317.47	320.00	341.38	395.72	588.21
30,000	376.17	378.38	380.97	384.00	409.65	474.86	705.85
35,000	438.86	441.44	444.46	448.00	477.93	554.00	823.49
40,000	501.56	504.51	507.96	512.00	546.20	633.15	941.13
45,000	564.25	567.57	571.45	576.00	614.48	712.29	1058.77
50,000	626.95	630.63	634.94	640.00	682.75	791.43	1176.41
55,000	689.64	693.70	698.44	704.00	751.03	870.58	1294.06
60,000	752.34	756.76	761.93	768.00	819.30	949.72	1411.70
65,000	815.03	819.82	825.43	832.00	887.58	1028.86	1529.34
70,000	877.72	882.89	888.92	896.00	955.85	1108.01	1646.98
75,000	940.42	945.95	952.42	960.00	1024.13	1187.15	1764.62
80,000	1003.11	1009.01	1015.91	1024.00	1092.40	1266.29	1882.26
85,000	1065.81	1072.07	1079.41	1088.00	1160.68	1345.44	1999.90
90,000	1128.50	1135.14	1142.90	1152.00	1228.95	1424.58	2117.55
95,000	1191.20	1198.20	1206.39	1216.00	1297.23	1503.72	2235.19
100,000	1253.89	1261.26	1269.89	1280.00	1365.50	1582.87	2352.83
110,000	1379.28	1387.39	1396.88	1408.00	1502.05	1741.15	2588.11
120,000	1504.67	1513.52	1523.87	1536.00	1638.60	1899.44	2823.39
130,000	1630.06	1639.64	1650.86	1664.00	1775.15	2057.73	3058.68
140,000	1755.45	1765.77	1777.84	1792.00	1911.70	2216.02	3293.96
150,000	1880.84	1891.90	1904.83	1920.00	2048.25	2374.30	3529.24
200,000	2507.78	2522.53	2539.78	2560.00	2731.00	3165.74	4705.66
250,000	3134.73	3153.16	3174.72	3199.99	3413.75	3957.17	5882.07
300,000	3761.68	3783.79	3809.67	3839.99	4096.50	4748.60	7058.48
350,000	4388.62	4414.43	4444.61	4479.99	4779.25	5540.04	8234.90
400,000	5015.57	5045.06	5079.55	5119.99	5462.00	6331.47	9411.31
450,000	5642.51	5675.69	5714.50	5759.99	6144.75	7122.91	10587.73
500,000	6269.46	6306.32	6349.44	6399.99	6827.50	7914.34	11764.14
550,000	6896.40	6936.95	6984.39	7039.99	7510.25	8705.77	12940.55
600,000	7523.35	7567.59	7619.33	7679.99	8193.01	9497.21	14116.97
650,000	8150.30	8198.22	8254.28	8319.99	8875.76	10288.64	15293.38
700,000	8777.24	8828.85	8889.22	8959.98	9558.51	11080.08	16469.80
750,000	9404.19	9459.48	9524.16	9599.98	10241.26	11871.51	17646.21
800,000	10031.13	10090.11	10159.11	10239.98	10924.01	12662.94	18822.62
850,000	10658.08	10720.75	10794.05	10879.98	11606.76	13454.38	19999.04
900,000	11285.03	11351.38	11429.00	11519.98	12289.51	14245.81	21175.45
950,000	11911.97	11982.01	12063.94	12159.98	12972.26	15037.24	22351.87
1,000,000	12538.92	12612.64	12698.89	12799.98	13655.01	15828.68	23528.28

14³/₄% Monthly Payments
Necessary to Amortize a Loan

YEARS REMAINING IN TERM

AMOUNT BORROWED	30	29	28	27	26	25	24
100	1.24	1.25	1.25	1.25	1.26	1.26	1.27
200	2.49	2.49	2.50	2.51	2.51	2.52	2.53
300	3.73	3.74	3.75	3.76	3.77	3.78	3.80
400	4.98	4.99	5.00	5.01	5.03	5.05	5.07
500	6.22	6.23	6.25	6.27	6.28	6.31	6.33
600	7.47	7.48	7.50	7.52	7.54	7.57	7.60
700	8.71	8.73	8.75	8.77	8.80	8.83	8.87
800	9.96	9.98	10.00	10.02	10.06	10.09	10.13
900	11.20	11.22	11.25	11.28	11.31	11.35	11.40
1,000	12.44	12.47	12.50	12.53	12.57	12.61	12.67
2,000	24.89	24.94	25.00	25.06	25.14	25.23	25.33
3,000	37.33	37.41	37.49	37.59	37.71	37.84	38.00
4,000	49.78	49.88	49.99	50.12	50.28	50.46	50.67
5,000	62.22	62.35	62.49	62.65	62.85	63.07	63.34
6,000	74.67	74.82	74.99	75.19	75.42	75.69	76.00
7,000	87.11	87.28	87.48	87.72	87.99	88.30	88.67
8,000	99.56	99.75	99.98	100.25	100.56	100.92	101.34
9,000	112.00	112.22	112.48	112.78	113.13	113.53	114.00
10,000	124.45	124.69	124.98	125.31	125.70	126.15	126.67
15,000	186.67	187.04	187.47	187.96	188.54	189.22	190.01
20,000	248.90	249.39	249.96	250.62	251.39	252.29	253.34
25,000	311.12	311.73	312.44	313.27	314.24	315.37	316.68
30,000	373.34	374.08	374.93	375.93	377.09	378.44	380.02
35,000	435.57	436.42	437.42	438.58	439.94	441.51	443.35
40,000	497.79	498.77	499.91	501.24	502.78	504.59	506.69
45,000	560.01	561.12	562.40	563.89	565.63	567.66	570.02
50,000	622.24	623.46	624.89	626.55	628.48	630.73	633.36
55,000	684.46	685.81	687.38	689.20	691.33	693.81	696.70
60,000	746.69	748.16	749.87	751.86	754.18	756.88	760.03
65,000	808.91	810.50	812.36	814.51	817.02	819.95	823.37
70,000	871.13	872.85	874.85	877.17	879.87	883.03	886.70
75,000	933.36	935.20	937.33	939.82	942.72	946.10	950.04
80,000	995.58	997.54	999.82	1002.48	1005.57	1009.17	1013.38
85,000	1057.80	1059.89	1062.31	1065.13	1068.42	1072.25	1076.71
90,000	1120.03	1122.24	1124.80	1127.79	1131.26	1135.32	1140.05
95,000	1182.25	1184.58	1187.29	1190.44	1194.11	1198.39	1203.38
100,000	1244.48	1246.93	1249.78	1253.10	1256.96	1261.46	1266.72
110,000	1368.92	1371.62	1374.76	1378.41	1382.66	1387.61	1393.39
120,000	1493.37	1496.31	1499.74	1503.72	1508.35	1513.76	1520.06
130,000	1617.82	1621.01	1624.71	1629.03	1634.05	1639.90	1646.74
140,000	1742.27	1745.70	1749.69	1754.34	1759.75	1766.05	1773.41
150,000	1866.71	1870.39	1874.67	1879.65	1885.44	1892.20	1900.08
200,000	2488.95	2493.86	2499.56	2506.19	2513.92	2522.93	2533.44
250,000	3111.19	3117.32	3124.45	3132.74	3142.40	3153.66	3166.80
300,000	3733.43	3740.78	3749.34	3759.29	3770.88	3784.39	3800.16
350,000	4355.67	4364.25	4374.23	4385.84	4399.36	4415.13	4433.52
400,000	4977.90	4987.71	4999.12	5012.39	5027.84	5045.86	5066.88
450,000	5600.14	5611.18	5624.01	5638.94	5656.32	5676.59	5700.24
500,000	6222.38	6234.64	6248.90	6265.49	6284.80	6307.32	6333.60
550,000	6844.62	6858.10	6873.79	6892.03	6913.29	6938.06	6966.96
600,000	7466.85	7481.57	7498.68	7518.58	7541.77	7568.79	7600.32
650,000	8089.09	8105.03	8123.56	8145.13	8170.25	8199.52	8233.68
700,000	8711.33	8728.49	8748.45	8771.68	8798.73	8830.25	8867.04
750,000	9333.57	9351.96	9373.34	9398.23	9427.21	9460.99	9500.40
800,000	9955.81	9975.42	9998.23	10024.78	10055.69	10091.72	10133.76
850,000	10578.04	10598.89	10623.12	10651.33	10684.17	10722.45	10767.12
900,000	11200.28	11222.35	11248.01	11277.87	11312.65	11353.18	11400.48
950,000	11822.52	11845.81	11872.90	11904.42	11941.13	11983.92	12033.84
1,000,000	12444.76	12469.28	12497.79	12530.97	12569.61	12614.65	12667.20

AMOUNT BORROWED	YEARS REMAINING IN TERM						
	23	22	21	20	15	10	5
100	1.27	1.28	1.29	1.30	1.38	1.60	2.37
200	2.55	2.56	2.58	2.60	2.77	3.20	4.73
300	3.82	3.84	3.87	3.90	4.15	4.79	7.10
400	5.09	5.12	5.15	5.19	5.53	6.39	9.46
500	6.36	6.40	6.44	6.49	6.91	7.99	11.83
600	7.64	7.68	7.73	7.79	8.30	9.59	14.20
700	8.91	8.96	9.02	9.09	9.68	11.19	16.56
800	10.18	10.24	10.31	10.39	11.06	12.78	18.93
900	11.46	11.52	11.60	11.69	12.44	14.38	21.29
1,000	12.73	12.80	12.88	12.98	13.83	15.98	23.66
2,000	25.46	25.60	25.77	25.97	27.65	31.96	47.32
3,000	38.19	38.40	38.65	38.95	41.48	47.94	70.98
4,000	50.91	51.20	51.54	51.93	55.30	63.92	94.64
5,000	63.64	64.00	64.42	64.92	69.13	79.90	118.29
6,000	76.37	76.80	77.31	77.90	82.95	95.88	141.95
7,000	89.10	89.60	90.19	90.88	96.78	111.87	165.61
8,000	101.83	102.40	103.08	103.87	110.60	127.85	189.27
9,000	114.56	115.20	115.96	116.85	124.43	143.83	212.93
10,000	127.29	128.00	128.85	129.84	138.25	159.81	236.59
15,000	190.93	192.01	193.27	194.75	207.38	239.71	354.88
20,000	254.57	256.01	257.69	259.67	276.50	319.61	473.18
25,000	318.22	320.01	322.12	324.59	345.63	399.52	591.47
30,000	381.86	384.01	386.54	389.51	414.75	479.42	709.77
35,000	445.50	448.02	450.96	454.42	483.88	559.33	828.06
40,000	509.14	512.02	515.39	519.34	553.00	639.23	946.36
45,000	572.79	576.02	579.81	584.26	622.13	719.13	1064.65
50,000	636.43	640.02	644.23	649.18	691.25	799.04	1182.95
55,000	700.07	704.02	708.66	714.10	760.38	878.94	1301.24
60,000	763.72	768.03	773.08	779.01	829.50	958.84	1419.53
65,000	827.36	832.03	837.50	843.93	898.63	1038.75	1537.83
70,000	891.00	896.03	901.93	908.85	967.75	1118.65	1656.12
75,000	954.65	960.03	966.35	973.77	1036.88	1198.56	1774.42
80,000	1018.29	1024.04	1030.77	1038.68	1106.00	1278.46	1892.71
85,000	1081.93	1088.04	1095.20	1103.60	1175.13	1358.36	2011.01
90,000	1145.57	1152.04	1159.62	1168.52	1244.25	1438.27	2129.30
95,000	1209.22	1216.04	1224.04	1233.44	1313.38	1518.17	2247.60
100,000	1272.86	1280.04	1288.47	1298.36	1382.50	1598.07	2365.89
110,000	1400.15	1408.05	1417.31	1428.19	1520.75	1757.88	2602.48
120,000	1527.43	1536.05	1546.16	1558.03	1659.00	1917.69	2839.07
130,000	1654.72	1664.06	1675.01	1687.86	1797.25	2077.50	3075.66
140,000	1782.00	1792.06	1803.85	1817.70	1935.51	2237.30	3312.25
150,000	1909.29	1920.07	1932.70	1947.53	2073.76	2397.11	3548.84
200,000	2545.72	2560.09	2576.93	2596.71	2765.01	3196.15	4731.78
250,000	3182.15	3200.11	3221.16	3245.89	3456.26	3995.19	5914.73
300,000	3818.58	3840.13	3865.40	3895.07	4147.51	4794.22	7097.67
350,000	4455.01	4480.16	4509.63	4544.24	4838.76	5593.26	8280.62
400,000	5091.44	5120.18	5153.86	5193.42	5530.02	6392.30	9463.56
450,000	5727.87	5760.20	5798.09	5842.60	6221.27	7191.33	10646.51
500,000	6364.30	6400.22	6442.33	6491.78	6912.52	7990.37	11829.45
550,000	7000.73	7040.25	7086.56	7140.95	7603.77	8789.41	13012.40
600,000	7637.16	7680.27	7730.79	7790.13	8295.02	9588.45	14195.34
650,000	8273.59	8320.29	8375.03	8439.31	8986.27	10387.48	15378.29
700,000	8910.02	8960.31	9019.26	9088.49	9677.53	11186.52	16561.23
750,000	9546.45	9600.34	9663.49	9737.66	10368.78	11985.56	17744.18
800,000	10182.88	10240.36	10307.72	10386.84	11060.03	12784.59	18927.12
850,000	10819.31	10880.38	10951.96	11036.02	11751.28	13583.63	20110.07
900,000	11455.74	11520.40	11596.19	11685.20	12442.53	14382.67	21293.01
950,000	12092.17	12160.42	12240.42	12334.38	13133.79	15181.71	22475.96
1,000,000	12728.60	12800.45	12884.65	12983.55	13825.04	15980.74	23658.90

15% Monthly Payments
Necessary to Amortize a Loan

AMOUNT BORROWED	YEARS REMAINING IN TERM						
	30	29	28	27	26	25	24
100	1.26	1.27	1.27	1.27	1.28	1.28	1.29
200	2.53	2.53	2.54	2.55	2.55	2.56	2.57
300	3.79	3.80	3.81	3.82	3.83	3.84	3.86
400	5.06	5.07	5.08	5.09	5.11	5.12	5.14
500	6.32	6.33	6.35	6.36	6.38	6.40	6.43
600	7.59	7.60	7.62	7.64	7.66	7.68	7.72
700	8.85	8.87	8.89	8.91	8.94	8.97	9.00
800	10.12	10.13	10.16	10.18	10.21	10.25	10.29
900	11.38	11.40	11.43	11.45	11.49	11.53	11.57
1,000	12.64	12.67	12.70	12.73	12.76	12.81	12.86
2,000	25.29	25.34	25.39	25.45	25.53	25.62	25.72
3,000	37.93	38.00	38.09	38.18	38.29	38.42	38.58
4,000	50.58	50.67	50.78	50.91	51.06	51.23	51.44
5,000	63.22	63.34	63.48	63.64	63.82	64.04	64.30
6,000	75.87	76.01	76.17	76.36	76.59	76.85	77.16
7,000	88.51	88.68	88.87	89.09	89.35	89.66	90.02
8,000	101.16	101.34	101.56	101.82	102.12	102.47	102.87
9,000	113.80	114.01	114.26	114.55	114.88	115.27	115.73
10,000	126.44	126.68	126.95	127.27	127.65	128.08	128.59
15,000	189.67	190.02	190.43	190.91	191.47	192.12	192.89
20,000	252.89	253.36	253.91	254.55	255.29	256.17	257.19
25,000	316.11	316.70	317.38	318.18	319.12	320.21	321.48
30,000	379.33	380.04	380.86	381.82	382.94	384.25	385.78
35,000	442.56	443.38	444.34	445.46	446.76	448.29	450.08
40,000	505.78	506.72	507.82	509.10	510.59	512.33	514.37
45,000	569.00	570.06	571.29	572.73	574.41	576.37	578.67
50,000	632.22	633.40	634.77	636.37	638.24	640.42	642.96
55,000	695.44	696.74	698.25	700.01	702.06	704.46	707.26
60,000	758.67	760.08	761.72	763.64	765.88	768.50	771.56
65,000	821.89	823.42	825.20	827.28	829.71	832.54	835.85
70,000	885.11	886.76	888.68	890.92	893.53	896.58	900.15
75,000	948.33	950.10	952.15	954.55	957.35	960.62	964.45
80,000	1011.56	1013.44	1015.63	1018.19	1021.18	1024.66	1028.74
85,000	1074.78	1076.78	1079.11	1081.83	1085.00	1088.71	1093.04
90,000	1138.00	1140.12	1142.59	1145.46	1148.82	1152.75	1157.34
95,000	1201.22	1203.46	1206.06	1209.10	1212.65	1216.79	1221.63
100,000	1264.44	1266.80	1269.54	1272.74	1276.47	1280.83	1285.93
110,000	1390.89	1393.48	1396.49	1400.01	1404.12	1408.91	1414.52
120,000	1517.33	1520.16	1523.45	1527.29	1531.76	1537.00	1543.12
130,000	1643.78	1646.84	1650.40	1654.56	1659.41	1665.08	1671.71
140,000	1770.22	1773.52	1777.36	1781.83	1787.06	1793.16	1800.30
150,000	1896.67	1900.20	1904.31	1909.11	1914.71	1921.25	1928.89
200,000	2528.89	2533.59	2539.08	2545.48	2552.94	2561.66	2571.86
250,000	3161.11	3166.99	3173.85	3181.84	3191.18	3202.08	3214.82
300,000	3793.33	3800.39	3808.62	3818.21	3829.41	3842.49	3857.79
350,000	4425.55	4433.79	4443.39	4454.58	4467.65	4482.91	4500.75
400,000	5057.78	5067.19	5078.16	5090.95	5105.88	5123.32	5143.72
450,000	5690.00	5700.59	5712.93	5727.32	5744.12	5763.74	5786.68
500,000	6322.22	6333.99	6347.70	6363.69	6382.35	6404.15	6429.65
550,000	6954.44	6967.38	6982.47	7000.06	7020.59	7044.57	7072.61
600,000	7586.66	7600.78	7617.24	7636.43	7658.82	7684.98	7715.58
650,000	8218.89	8234.18	8252.01	8272.80	8297.06	8325.40	8358.54
700,000	8851.11	8867.58	8886.78	8909.16	8935.29	8965.81	9001.50
750,000	9483.33	9500.98	9521.55	9545.53	9573.53	9606.23	9644.47
800,000	10115.55	10134.38	10156.32	10181.90	10211.76	10246.64	10287.43
850,000	10747.77	10767.78	10791.09	10818.27	10850.00	10887.06	10930.40
900,000	11380.00	11401.17	11425.86	11454.64	11488.23	11527.48	11573.36
950,000	12012.22	12034.57	12060.63	12091.01	12126.47	12167.89	12216.33
1,000,000	12644.44	12667.97	12695.40	12727.38	12764.70	12808.31	12859.29

Monthly Payments 15%
Necessary to Amortize a Loan

AMOUNT BORROWED	YEARS REMAINING IN TERM						
	23	22	21	20	15	10	5
100	1.29	1.30	1.31	1.32	1.40	1.61	2.38
200	2.58	2.60	2.61	2.63	2.80	3.23	4.76
300	3.88	3.90	3.92	3.95	4.20	4.84	7.14
400	5.17	5.20	5.23	5.27	5.60	6.45	9.52
500	6.46	6.49	6.54	6.58	7.00	8.07	11.89
600	7.75	7.79	7.84	7.90	8.40	9.68	14.27
700	9.04	9.09	9.15	9.22	9.80	11.29	16.65
800	10.34	10.39	10.46	10.53	11.20	12.91	19.03
900	11.63	11.69	11.76	11.85	12.60	14.52	21.41
1,000	12.92	12.99	13.07	13.17	14.00	16.13	23.79
2,000	25.84	25.98	26.14	26.34	27.99	32.27	47.58
3,000	38.76	38.97	39.21	39.50	41.99	48.40	71.37
4,000	51.68	51.96	52.28	52.67	55.98	64.53	95.16
5,000	64.59	64.94	65.36	65.84	69.98	80.67	118.95
6,000	77.51	77.93	78.43	79.01	83.98	96.80	142.74
7,000	90.43	90.92	91.50	92.18	97.97	112.93	166.53
8,000	103.35	103.91	104.57	105.34	111.97	129.07	190.32
9,000	116.27	116.90	117.64	118.51	125.96	145.20	214.11
10,000	129.19	129.89	130.71	131.68	139.96	161.33	237.90
15,000	193.78	194.83	196.07	197.52	209.94	242.00	356.85
20,000	258.38	259.78	261.42	263.36	279.92	322.67	475.80
25,000	322.97	324.72	326.78	329.20	349.90	403.34	594.75
30,000	387.57	389.67	392.14	395.04	419.88	484.00	713.70
35,000	452.16	454.61	457.49	460.88	489.86	564.67	832.65
40,000	516.76	519.56	522.85	526.72	559.83	645.34	951.60
45,000	581.35	584.50	588.20	592.56	629.81	726.01	1070.55
50,000	645.95	649.45	653.56	658.39	699.79	806.67	1189.50
55,000	710.54	714.39	718.91	724.23	769.77	887.34	1308.45
60,000	775.14	779.34	784.27	790.07	839.75	968.01	1427.40
65,000	839.73	844.28	849.63	855.91	909.73	1048.68	1546.35
70,000	904.33	909.23	914.98	921.75	979.71	1129.34	1665.30
75,000	968.92	974.17	980.34	987.59	1049.69	1210.01	1784.24
80,000	1033.52	1039.12	1045.69	1053.43	1119.67	1290.68	1903.19
85,000	1098.11	1104.06	1111.05	1119.27	1189.65	1371.35	2022.14
90,000	1162.71	1169.01	1176.41	1185.11	1259.63	1452.01	2141.09
95,000	1227.30	1233.95	1241.76	1250.95	1329.61	1532.68	2260.04
100,000	1291.90	1298.90	1307.12	1316.79	1399.59	1613.35	2378.99
110,000	1421.09	1428.79	1437.83	1448.47	1539.55	1774.68	2616.89
120,000	1550.28	1558.68	1568.54	1580.15	1679.50	1936.02	2854.79
130,000	1679.47	1688.57	1699.25	1711.83	1819.46	2097.35	3092.69
140,000	1808.66	1818.46	1829.96	1843.51	1959.42	2258.69	3330.59
150,000	1937.85	1948.35	1960.68	1975.18	2099.38	2420.02	3568.49
200,000	2583.80	2597.79	2614.23	2633.58	2799.17	3226.70	4757.99
250,000	3229.75	3247.24	3267.79	3291.97	3498.96	4033.37	5947.48
300,000	3875.70	3896.69	3921.35	3950.37	4198.76	4840.05	7136.98
350,000	4521.65	4546.14	4574.91	4608.76	4898.55	5646.72	8326.48
400,000	5167.59	5195.59	5228.47	5267.16	5598.35	6453.40	9515.97
450,000	5813.54	5845.04	5882.03	5925.55	6298.14	7260.07	10705.47
500,000	6459.49	6494.49	6535.59	6583.95	6997.94	8066.75	11894.97
550,000	7105.44	7143.94	7189.14	7242.34	7697.73	8873.42	13084.46
600,000	7751.39	7793.38	7842.70	7900.74	8397.52	9680.10	14273.96
650,000	8397.34	8442.83	8496.26	8559.13	9097.32	10486.77	15463.45
700,000	9043.29	9092.28	9149.82	9217.53	9797.11	11293.45	16652.95
750,000	9689.24	9741.73	9803.38	9875.92	10496.90	12100.12	17842.45
800,000	10335.19	10391.18	10456.94	10534.32	11196.70	12906.80	19031.94
850,000	10981.14	11040.63	11110.50	11192.71	11896.49	13713.47	20221.44
900,000	11627.09	11690.08	11764.05	11851.11	12596.28	14520.15	21410.94
950,000	12273.04	12339.53	12417.61	12509.50	13296.08	15326.82	22600.43
1,000,000	12918.99	12988.97	13071.17	13167.90	13995.87	16133.50	23789.93

Table 2
Payment Adjustments for ARMs

Table 2 provides an easy way to calculate the change in monthly payments when the interest rate is adjusted. Each pair of facing pages in the table covers a different preadjustment interest rate, ranging from 2 percent to 15 percent in $1/4$ percent increments. The far left-hand column shows postadjustment interest rates in percent, ranging from 3 percentage points below the preadjustment rate to 4 percentage points above. Because adjustable-rate mortgages are typically set at 2 or more percentage points above a base rate, and because base rates have never been negative, the designers of these tables set a floor of interest rate expectations at 2 percent. Because of that floor, pages with old interest rates below 5 percent do not show changes to interest rates below 2 percent, so a full 3-percentage-point drop will not be accommodated. There is space on those table pages to show higher rates than 4 percentage points above the preadjustment rate, so that was provided.

The body of the table indicates the percentage change in the monthly payment for remaining loan terms of 30 to 20 years in one-year increments, plus 15, 10, and 5 years. To calculate the new payment, multiply the old payment by the percentage in the table and add or subtract that amount to or from the old payment.

Example

An adjustable-rate mortgage with a 30-year term was originated at a 6 percent interest rate. The original principal was $100,000. This caused the initial payment to be $599.55. At the end of year 1, interest rates have increased such that this becomes an 8 percent–rate loan with 29 years remaining in term.

1. See page 184, which offers a "6 percent Old Rate" in the table heading and 29 under "Years Remaining in Term."
2. Find the new interest rate, 8 percent, in the "New Rate (%)" column.
3. Find the intersection of the 8 percent row with the 29-year column.
4. The percentage shown at that intersection is 21.90 percent.
5. The previous payment of $599.55 must be increased by 21.90 percent of itself to derive the new payment.
   (a) 21.90% × $599.55 = $131.30
   (b) $599.55 + $131.30 = $730.85

2%
Old Rate

Payment Adjustments
(As % of Old Payment)

NEW RATE (%)	YEARS REMAINING IN TERM						
	30	29	28	27	26	25	24
2.000	0.00	0.00	0.00	0.00	0.00	0.00	0.00
2.125	1.70	1.65	1.60	1.55	1.49	1.44	1.39
2.250	3.42	3.31	3.21	3.11	3.00	2.90	2.79
2.375	5.15	4.99	4.84	4.68	4.52	4.36	4.20
2.500	6.90	6.69	6.48	6.27	6.06	5.84	5.63
2.625	8.67	8.40	8.14	7.87	7.60	7.33	7.06
2.750	10.45	10.13	9.81	9.49	9.16	8.84	8.51
2.875	12.25	11.87	11.50	11.12	10.74	10.35	9.97
3.000	14.06	13.63	13.20	12.76	12.32	11.88	11.44
3.125	15.90	15.41	14.92	14.42	13.92	13.42	12.92
3.250	17.74	17.20	16.65	16.09	15.53	14.97	14.41
3.375	19.61	19.00	18.39	17.78	17.16	16.54	15.91
3.500	21.49	20.82	20.15	19.47	18.80	18.11	17.43
3.625	23.38	22.66	21.92	21.19	20.44	19.70	18.95
3.750	25.30	24.50	23.71	22.91	22.11	21.30	20.49
3.875	27.22	26.37	25.51	24.65	23.78	22.91	22.03
4.000	29.16	28.25	27.33	26.40	25.47	24.53	23.59
4.125	31.12	30.14	29.16	28.16	27.17	26.17	25.16
4.250	33.09	32.05	31.00	29.94	28.88	27.81	26.74
4.375	35.08	33.97	32.85	31.73	30.60	29.47	28.33
4.500	37.08	35.91	34.72	33.53	32.34	31.14	29.93
4.625	39.10	37.86	36.61	35.35	34.09	32.82	31.54
4.750	41.13	39.82	38.50	37.18	35.85	34.51	33.16
4.875	43.18	41.80	40.41	39.02	37.62	36.21	34.80
5.000	45.24	43.79	42.33	40.87	39.40	37.92	36.44
5.125	47.31	45.79	44.27	42.73	41.19	39.65	38.09
5.250	49.40	47.81	46.21	44.61	43.00	41.38	39.76
5.375	51.50	49.84	48.17	46.50	44.82	43.13	41.43
5.500	53.61	51.88	50.15	48.40	46.64	44.88	43.11
5.625	55.74	53.94	52.13	50.31	48.48	46.65	44.81
5.750	57.88	56.01	54.13	52.24	50.33	48.43	46.51
5.875	60.04	58.09	56.14	54.17	52.20	50.21	48.22
6.000	62.21	60.19	58.16	56.12	54.07	52.01	49.94
6.125	64.39	62.29	60.19	58.08	55.95	53.82	51.68
6.250	66.58	64.41	62.23	60.04	57.84	55.64	53.42
6.375	68.79	66.54	64.29	62.02	59.75	57.46	55.17
6.500	71.01	68.69	66.36	64.02	61.66	59.30	56.93
6.625	73.24	70.84	68.44	66.02	63.59	61.15	58.70
6.750	75.48	73.01	70.53	68.03	65.52	63.01	60.48
6.875	77.73	75.19	72.63	70.05	67.47	64.87	62.27
7.000	80.00	77.37	74.74	72.09	69.42	66.75	64.07
7.125	82.27	79.57	76.86	74.13	71.39	68.64	65.87
7.250	84.56	81.78	78.99	76.19	73.36	70.53	67.69
7.375	86.86	84.01	81.14	78.25	75.35	72.44	69.51
7.500	89.17	86.24	83.29	80.32	77.34	74.35	71.35
7.625	91.49	88.48	85.45	82.41	79.35	76.27	73.19
7.750	93.82	90.73	87.63	84.50	81.36	78.20	75.04
7.875	96.17	93.00	89.81	86.60	83.38	80.15	76.90
8.000	98.52	95.27	92.00	88.72	85.41	82.09	78.76
8.125	100.88	97.55	94.21	90.84	87.45	84.05	80.64
8.250	103.25	99.85	96.42	92.97	89.50	86.02	82.52
8.375	105.64	102.15	98.64	95.11	91.56	87.99	84.41
8.500	108.03	104.46	100.87	97.26	93.63	89.98	86.31
8.625	110.43	106.78	103.11	99.42	95.70	91.97	88.22
8.750	112.84	109.11	105.36	101.58	97.78	93.97	90.14
8.875	115.26	111.45	107.62	103.76	99.88	95.98	92.06
9.000	117.69	113.80	109.88	105.94	101.98	97.99	93.99

Payment Adjustments
(As % of Old Payment)

2%
Old Rate

NEW RATE (%)	YEARS REMAINING IN TERM						
	23	22	21	20	15	10	5
2.000	0.00	0.00	0.00	0.00	0.00	0.00	0.00
2.125	1.34	1.28	1.23	1.17	0.90	0.61	0.31
2.250	2.68	2.58	2.47	2.36	1.80	1.22	0.63
2.375	4.04	3.88	3.71	3.55	2.71	1.84	0.94
2.500	5.41	5.19	4.97	4.75	3.62	2.45	1.25
2.625	6.79	6.51	6.24	5.96	4.53	3.07	1.57
2.750	8.18	7.84	7.51	7.17	5.46	3.69	1.88
2.875	9.58	9.19	8.79	8.40	6.38	4.32	2.20
3.000	10.99	10.54	10.08	9.63	7.32	4.94	2.52
3.125	12.41	11.90	11.39	10.87	8.25	5.57	2.83
3.250	13.84	13.27	12.70	12.12	9.19	6.20	3.15
3.375	15.28	14.65	14.02	13.38	10.14	6.83	3.47
3.500	16.74	16.04	15.34	14.64	11.09	7.47	3.79
3.625	18.20	17.44	16.68	15.92	12.05	8.11	4.11
3.750	19.67	18.85	18.03	17.20	13.01	8.75	4.43
3.875	21.15	20.27	19.38	18.49	13.98	9.39	4.75
4.000	22.65	21.70	20.74	19.79	14.95	10.03	5.07
4.125	24.15	23.14	22.12	21.09	15.92	10.68	5.39
4.250	25.66	24.58	23.50	22.41	16.90	11.33	5.72
4.375	27.19	26.04	24.89	23.73	17.89	11.98	6.04
4.500	28.72	27.50	26.28	25.06	18.88	12.63	6.36
4.625	30.26	28.98	27.69	26.40	19.87	13.29	6.69
4.750	31.82	30.46	29.10	27.74	20.87	13.95	7.01
4.875	33.38	31.96	30.53	29.09	21.88	14.61	7.34
5.000	34.95	33.46	31.96	30.46	22.89	15.27	7.66
5.125	36.53	34.97	33.40	31.82	23.90	15.94	7.99
5.250	38.13	36.49	34.85	33.20	24.92	16.60	8.32
5.375	39.73	38.02	36.30	34.59	25.94	17.27	8.65
5.500	41.34	39.56	37.77	35.98	26.97	17.95	8.98
5.625	42.96	41.10	39.24	37.38	28.01	18.62	9.31
5.750	44.59	42.66	40.72	38.78	29.04	19.30	9.64
5.875	46.22	44.22	42.21	40.20	30.09	19.98	9.97
6.000	47.87	45.79	43.71	41.62	31.13	20.66	10.30
6.125	49.53	47.37	45.21	43.05	32.19	21.34	10.63
6.250	51.19	48.96	46.73	44.49	33.24	22.03	10.96
6.375	52.87	50.56	48.25	45.93	34.30	22.71	11.30
6.500	54.55	52.17	49.78	47.38	35.37	23.40	11.63
6.625	56.24	53.78	51.31	48.84	36.44	24.10	11.96
6.750	57.95	55.40	52.86	50.30	37.51	24.79	12.30
6.875	59.66	57.04	54.41	51.78	38.59	25.49	12.63
7.000	61.37	58.67	55.97	53.26	39.68	26.19	12.97
7.125	63.10	60.32	57.53	54.74	40.76	26.89	13.31
7.250	64.84	61.98	59.11	56.24	41.86	27.59	13.64
7.375	66.58	63.64	60.69	57.74	42.95	28.30	13.98
7.500	68.33	65.31	62.28	59.24	44.06	29.00	14.32
7.625	70.09	66.99	63.88	60.76	45.16	29.71	14.66
7.750	71.86	68.67	65.48	62.28	46.27	30.43	15.00
7.875	73.64	70.37	67.09	63.81	47.39	31.14	15.34
8.000	75.42	72.07	68.71	65.34	48.51	31.86	15.68
8.125	77.21	73.78	70.33	66.88	49.63	32.58	16.02
8.250	79.01	75.49	71.96	68.43	50.76	33.30	16.37
8.375	80.82	77.22	73.60	69.99	51.89	34.02	16.71
8.500	82.64	78.95	75.25	71.55	53.03	34.75	17.05
8.625	84.46	80.68	76.90	73.11	54.17	35.47	17.40
8.750	86.29	82.43	78.56	74.69	55.31	36.20	17.74
8.875	88.13	84.18	80.23	76.27	56.46	36.94	18.09
9.000	89.97	85.94	81.90	77.85	57.62	37.67	18.43

2¼%
Old Rate

Payment Adjustments
(As % of Old Payment)

NEW RATE (%)	YEARS REMAINING IN TERM						
	30	29	28	27	26	25	24
2.000	−3.30	−3.21	−3.11	−3.01	−2.91	−2.81	−2.71
2.125	−1.66	−1.61	−1.56	−1.51	−1.46	−1.41	−1.36
2.250	0.00	0.00	0.00	0.00	0.00	0.00	0.00
2.375	1.68	1.63	1.58	1.53	1.48	1.43	1.37
2.500	3.37	3.27	3.17	3.07	2.97	2.86	2.76
2.625	5.08	4.93	4.77	4.62	4.47	4.31	4.16
2.750	6.80	6.60	6.39	6.19	5.98	5.77	5.56
2.875	8.54	8.29	8.03	7.77	7.51	7.25	6.98
3.000	10.30	9.99	9.68	9.36	9.05	8.73	8.41
3.125	12.07	11.71	11.34	10.97	10.60	10.23	9.85
3.250	13.86	13.44	13.02	12.59	12.17	11.74	11.30
3.375	15.66	15.18	14.71	14.23	13.74	13.26	12.77
3.500	17.48	16.95	16.41	15.87	15.33	14.79	14.24
3.625	19.31	18.72	18.13	17.53	16.93	16.33	15.72
3.750	21.16	20.51	19.86	19.21	18.55	17.88	17.22
3.875	23.02	22.32	21.61	20.89	20.17	19.45	18.72
4.000	24.90	24.13	23.37	22.59	21.81	21.03	20.24
4.125	26.79	25.97	25.14	24.30	23.46	22.62	21.76
4.250	28.70	27.81	26.92	26.03	25.12	24.21	23.30
4.375	30.62	29.67	28.72	27.76	26.80	25.82	24.85
4.500	32.55	31.55	30.53	29.51	28.48	27.45	26.40
4.625	34.50	33.43	32.36	31.27	30.18	29.08	27.97
4.750	36.47	35.33	34.19	33.04	31.89	30.72	29.55
4.875	38.45	37.25	36.04	34.83	33.61	32.38	31.14
5.000	40.44	39.18	37.90	36.62	35.34	34.04	32.74
5.125	42.44	41.12	39.78	38.43	37.08	35.72	34.34
5.250	44.46	43.07	41.67	40.25	38.83	37.40	35.96
5.375	46.49	45.03	43.56	42.08	40.60	39.10	37.59
5.500	48.54	47.01	45.48	43.93	42.37	40.80	39.23
5.625	50.60	49.00	47.40	45.78	44.16	42.52	40.88
5.750	52.67	51.01	49.33	47.65	45.95	44.25	42.53
5.875	54.75	53.02	51.28	49.53	47.76	45.98	44.20
6.000	56.85	55.05	53.24	51.41	49.58	47.73	45.87
6.125	58.96	57.09	55.21	53.31	51.41	49.49	47.56
6.250	61.08	59.14	57.19	55.22	53.24	51.25	49.25
6.375	63.21	61.20	59.18	57.14	55.09	53.03	50.96
6.500	65.36	63.28	61.18	59.07	56.95	54.82	52.67
6.625	67.51	65.36	63.20	61.02	58.82	56.61	54.39
6.750	69.68	67.46	65.22	62.97	60.70	58.42	56.12
6.875	71.86	69.57	67.26	64.93	62.59	60.23	57.86
7.000	74.05	71.69	69.30	66.90	64.49	62.06	59.61
7.125	76.25	73.81	71.36	68.88	66.39	63.89	61.37
7.250	78.47	75.95	73.42	70.88	68.31	65.73	63.14
7.375	80.69	78.10	75.50	72.88	70.24	67.58	64.91
7.500	82.92	80.27	77.59	74.89	72.17	69.44	66.69
7.625	85.17	82.44	79.68	76.91	74.12	71.31	68.49
7.750	87.42	84.62	81.79	78.94	76.07	73.19	70.29
7.875	89.69	86.81	83.91	80.98	78.04	75.07	72.09
8.000	91.96	89.01	86.03	83.03	80.01	76.97	73.91
8.125	94.25	91.22	88.16	85.09	81.99	78.87	75.74
8.250	96.54	93.44	90.31	87.15	83.98	80.78	77.57
8.375	98.84	95.67	92.46	89.23	85.98	82.70	79.41
8.500	101.16	97.90	94.62	91.31	87.98	84.63	81.26
8.625	103.48	100.15	96.79	93.41	90.00	86.57	83.11
8.750	105.81	102.41	98.97	95.51	92.02	88.51	84.97
8.875	108.15	104.67	101.16	97.62	94.05	90.46	86.85
9.000	110.50	106.94	103.35	99.74	96.09	92.42	88.72

Payment Adjustments
(As % of Old Payment)

2¹/₄%
Old Rate

NEW RATE (%)	YEARS REMAINING IN TERM						
	23	22	21	20	15	10	5
2.000	-2.61	-2.51	-2.41	-2.30	-1.77	-1.21	-0.62
2.125	-1.31	-1.26	-1.21	-1.16	-0.89	-0.60	-0.31
2.250	0.00	0.00	0.00	0.00	0.00	0.00	0.00
2.375	1.32	1.27	1.22	1.16	0.89	0.61	0.31
2.500	2.65	2.55	2.44	2.34	1.79	1.22	0.62
2.625	4.00	3.84	3.68	3.52	2.69	1.83	0.94
2.750	5.35	5.14	4.92	4.70	3.59	2.44	1.25
2.875	6.71	6.45	6.17	5.90	4.50	3.06	1.56
3.000	8.09	7.76	7.43	7.10	5.42	3.68	1.88
3.125	9.47	9.09	8.70	8.32	6.34	4.30	2.19
3.250	10.87	10.43	9.98	9.54	7.26	4.92	2.51
3.375	12.27	11.77	11.27	10.77	8.19	5.54	2.83
3.500	13.68	13.13	12.57	12.00	9.13	6.17	3.14
3.625	15.11	14.49	13.87	13.25	10.07	6.80	3.46
3.750	16.54	15.87	15.19	14.50	11.01	7.43	3.78
3.875	17.99	17.25	16.51	15.76	11.96	8.07	4.10
4.000	19.44	18.64	17.84	17.03	12.91	8.71	4.42
4.125	20.91	20.04	19.18	18.30	13.87	9.34	4.74
4.250	22.38	21.45	20.52	19.59	14.84	9.99	5.06
4.375	23.86	22.87	21.88	20.88	15.80	10.63	5.38
4.500	25.36	24.30	23.24	22.18	16.78	11.27	5.70
4.625	26.86	25.74	24.62	23.49	17.76	11.92	6.02
4.750	28.37	27.19	26.00	24.80	18.74	12.57	6.35
4.875	29.89	28.64	27.39	26.12	19.72	13.23	6.67
5.000	31.43	30.11	28.78	27.45	20.72	13.88	7.00
5.125	32.97	31.58	30.19	28.79	21.71	14.54	7.32
5.250	34.52	33.06	31.60	30.13	22.71	15.20	7.65
5.375	36.08	34.55	33.02	31.49	23.72	15.86	7.97
5.500	37.64	36.05	34.45	32.85	24.73	16.52	8.30
5.625	39.22	37.56	35.89	34.21	25.74	17.19	8.63
5.750	40.81	39.08	37.34	35.59	26.76	17.86	8.95
5.875	42.40	40.60	38.79	36.97	27.79	18.53	9.28
6.000	44.01	42.13	40.25	38.36	28.82	19.20	9.61
6.125	45.62	43.67	41.72	39.75	29.85	19.88	9.94
6.250	47.24	45.22	43.19	41.16	30.89	20.55	10.27
6.375	48.87	46.78	44.68	42.57	31.93	21.23	10.60
6.500	50.51	48.35	46.17	43.99	32.98	21.91	10.94
6.625	52.16	49.92	47.67	45.41	34.03	22.60	11.27
6.750	53.82	51.50	49.18	46.84	35.08	23.28	11.60
6.875	55.48	53.09	50.69	48.28	36.14	23.97	11.93
7.000	57.16	54.69	52.21	49.73	37.21	24.66	12.27
7.125	58.84	56.30	53.74	51.18	38.28	25.36	12.60
7.250	60.53	57.91	55.28	52.64	39.35	26.05	12.94
7.375	62.23	59.53	56.82	54.10	40.43	26.75	13.27
7.500	63.93	61.16	58.37	55.58	41.51	27.45	13.61
7.625	65.65	62.79	59.93	57.06	42.60	28.15	13.95
7.750	67.37	64.44	61.50	58.54	43.69	28.85	14.29
7.875	69.10	66.09	63.07	60.04	44.78	29.56	14.62
8.000	70.84	67.75	64.65	61.53	45.88	30.27	14.96
8.125	72.58	69.41	66.23	63.04	46.99	30.98	15.30
8.250	74.33	71.09	67.83	64.55	48.09	31.69	15.64
8.375	76.10	72.77	69.42	66.07	49.21	32.40	15.98
8.500	77.86	74.45	71.03	67.60	50.32	33.12	16.32
8.625	79.64	76.15	72.64	69.13	51.44	33.84	16.67
8.750	81.42	77.85	74.26	70.66	52.57	34.56	17.01
8.875	83.21	79.56	75.89	72.21	53.70	35.28	17.35
9.000	85.01	81.27	77.52	73.76	54.83	36.01	17.70

2¹/₂%
Old Rate

Payment Adjustments
(As % of Old Payment)

NEW RATE (%)	YEARS REMAINING IN TERM						
	30	29	28	27	26	25	24
2.000	−6.45	−6.27	−6.09	−5.90	−5.71	−5.52	−5.33
2.125	−4.86	−4.73	−4.59	−4.44	−4.30	−4.16	−4.01
2.250	−3.26	−3.17	−3.07	−2.98	−2.88	−2.78	−2.69
2.375	−1.64	−1.59	−1.54	−1.49	−1.45	−1.40	−1.35
2.500	0.00	0.00	0.00	0.00	0.00	0.00	0.00
2.625	1.65	1.60	1.56	1.51	1.46	1.41	1.36
2.750	3.32	3.22	3.13	3.03	2.93	2.83	2.73
2.875	5.00	4.86	4.71	4.56	4.41	4.26	4.11
3.000	6.70	6.51	6.31	6.11	5.91	5.71	5.50
3.125	8.42	8.17	7.92	7.67	7.42	7.16	6.90
3.250	10.15	9.85	9.55	9.24	8.94	8.63	8.31
3.375	11.89	11.54	11.18	10.83	10.47	10.10	9.74
3.500	13.65	13.24	12.84	12.43	12.01	11.59	11.17
3.625	15.42	14.96	14.50	14.04	13.57	13.09	12.61
3.750	17.21	16.70	16.18	15.66	15.13	14.60	14.07
3.875	19.01	18.44	17.87	17.29	16.71	16.13	15.53
4.000	20.83	20.20	19.58	18.94	18.30	17.66	17.01
4.125	22.66	21.98	21.29	20.60	19.91	19.20	18.49
4.250	24.50	23.77	23.02	22.28	21.52	20.76	19.99
4.375	26.36	25.57	24.77	23.96	23.14	22.32	21.49
4.500	28.24	27.38	26.52	25.66	24.78	23.90	23.01
4.625	30.12	29.21	28.29	27.36	26.43	25.49	24.54
4.750	32.02	31.05	30.07	29.08	28.09	27.08	26.07
4.875	33.94	32.90	31.86	30.82	29.76	28.69	27.62
5.000	35.86	34.77	33.67	32.56	31.44	30.31	29.17
5.125	37.80	36.65	35.49	34.31	33.13	31.94	30.74
5.250	39.76	38.54	37.31	36.08	34.83	33.58	32.31
5.375	41.72	40.44	39.16	37.86	36.55	35.23	33.90
5.500	43.70	42.36	41.01	39.64	38.27	36.88	35.49
5.625	45.69	44.29	42.87	41.44	40.00	38.55	37.09
5.750	47.69	46.23	44.75	43.25	41.75	40.23	38.70
5.875	49.71	48.18	46.63	45.08	43.50	41.92	40.33
6.000	51.74	50.14	48.53	46.91	45.27	43.62	41.96
6.125	53.78	52.12	50.44	48.75	47.05	45.33	43.60
6.250	55.83	54.10	52.36	50.60	48.83	47.05	45.25
6.375	57.89	56.10	54.29	52.47	50.63	48.77	46.90
6.500	59.97	58.11	56.23	54.34	52.43	50.51	48.57
6.625	62.05	60.13	58.18	56.22	54.25	52.25	50.25
6.750	64.15	62.16	60.15	58.12	56.07	54.01	51.93
6.875	66.26	64.20	62.12	60.02	57.91	55.77	53.63
7.000	68.38	66.25	64.10	61.93	59.75	57.55	55.33
7.125	70.51	68.31	66.09	63.86	61.60	59.33	57.04
7.250	72.65	70.38	68.10	65.79	63.46	61.12	58.76
7.375	74.80	72.47	70.11	67.73	65.34	62.92	60.48
7.500	76.96	74.56	72.13	69.68	67.22	64.73	62.22
7.625	79.13	76.66	74.16	71.65	69.10	66.54	63.96
7.750	81.31	78.77	76.21	73.62	71.00	68.37	65.71
7.875	83.51	80.89	78.26	75.59	72.91	70.20	67.47
8.000	85.71	83.02	80.32	77.58	74.82	72.04	69.24
8.125	87.92	85.16	82.39	79.58	76.75	73.89	71.02
8.250	90.14	87.31	84.46	81.58	78.68	75.75	72.80
8.375	92.36	89.47	86.55	83.60	80.62	77.62	74.59
8.500	94.60	91.64	88.64	85.62	82.57	79.49	76.39
8.625	96.85	93.81	90.75	87.65	84.53	81.37	78.19
8.750	99.10	96.00	92.86	89.69	86.49	83.26	80.01
8.875	101.37	98.19	94.98	91.74	88.46	85.16	81.83
9.000	103.64	100.39	97.11	93.79	90.44	87.06	83.66

Payment Adjustments
(As % of Old Payment)

2¹/₂%
Old Rate

NEW RATE (%)	YEARS REMAINING IN TERM						
	23	22	21	20	15	10	5
2.000	−5.13	−4.93	−4.73	−4.53	−3.49	−2.39	−1.24
2.125	−3.86	−3.71	−3.56	−3.41	−2.63	−1.80	−0.93
2.250	−2.59	−2.49	−2.38	−2.28	−1.76	−1.20	−0.62
2.375	−1.30	−1.25	−1.20	−1.15	−0.88	−0.60	−0.31
2.500	0.00	0.00	0.00	0.00	0.00	0.00	0.00
2.625	1.31	1.26	1.21	1.15	0.88	0.60	0.31
2.750	2.63	2.52	2.42	2.31	1.77	1.21	0.62
2.875	3.95	3.80	3.64	3.48	2.67	1.82	0.93
3.000	5.29	5.08	4.87	4.66	3.57	2.43	1.25
3.125	6.64	6.38	6.11	5.85	4.47	3.04	1.56
3.250	8.00	7.68	7.36	7.04	5.38	3.66	1.87
3.375	9.37	8.99	8.62	8.24	6.29	4.28	2.19
3.500	10.74	10.32	9.88	9.45	7.21	4.90	2.50
3.625	12.13	11.65	11.16	10.66	8.14	5.52	2.82
3.750	13.53	12.99	12.44	11.89	9.06	6.14	3.14
3.875	14.94	14.34	13.73	13.12	10.00	6.77	3.45
4.000	16.35	15.69	15.03	14.36	10.93	7.40	3.77
4.125	17.78	17.06	16.33	15.60	11.87	8.03	4.09
4.250	19.22	18.44	17.65	16.86	12.82	8.66	4.41
4.375	20.66	19.82	18.97	18.12	13.77	9.30	4.73
4.500	22.12	21.21	20.30	19.39	14.73	9.94	5.05
4.625	23.58	22.61	21.64	20.67	15.69	10.58	5.37
4.750	25.05	24.03	22.99	21.95	16.65	11.22	5.69
4.875	26.53	25.45	24.35	23.24	17.62	11.87	6.01
5.000	28.03	26.87	25.71	24.54	18.60	12.51	6.33
5.125	29.53	28.31	27.08	25.85	19.58	13.16	6.66
5.250	31.04	29.75	28.46	27.16	20.56	13.81	6.98
5.375	32.56	31.21	29.85	28.49	21.55	14.47	7.30
5.500	34.08	32.67	31.25	29.81	22.54	15.12	7.63
5.625	35.62	34.14	32.65	31.15	23.54	15.78	7.95
5.750	37.17	35.62	34.06	32.49	24.54	16.44	8.28
5.875	38.72	37.10	35.48	33.84	25.54	17.10	8.61
6.000	40.28	38.60	36.90	35.20	26.56	17.77	8.93
6.125	41.86	40.10	38.34	36.56	27.57	18.44	9.26
6.250	43.44	41.61	39.78	37.94	28.59	19.10	9.59
6.375	45.02	43.13	41.23	39.31	29.61	19.78	9.92
6.500	46.62	44.66	42.69	40.70	30.64	20.45	10.25
6.625	48.23	46.19	44.15	42.09	31.67	21.13	10.58
6.750	49.84	47.74	45.62	43.49	32.71	21.80	10.91
6.875	51.46	49.29	47.10	44.90	33.75	22.48	11.24
7.000	53.09	50.84	48.58	46.31	34.80	23.17	11.57
7.125	54.73	52.41	50.08	47.73	35.85	23.85	11.91
7.250	56.38	53.98	51.58	49.15	36.90	24.54	12.24
7.375	58.03	55.56	53.08	50.59	37.96	25.23	12.57
7.500	59.69	57.15	54.60	52.03	39.03	25.92	12.91
7.625	61.36	58.75	56.12	53.47	40.09	26.61	13.24
7.750	63.04	60.35	57.64	54.92	41.17	27.31	13.58
7.875	64.73	61.96	59.18	56.38	42.24	28.00	13.91
8.000	66.42	63.58	60.72	57.85	43.32	28.70	14.25
8.125	68.12	65.20	62.27	59.32	44.41	29.40	14.59
8.250	69.83	66.83	63.82	60.80	45.49	30.11	14.93
8.375	71.54	68.47	65.38	62.28	46.59	30.81	15.26
8.500	73.26	70.12	66.95	63.77	47.68	31.52	15.60
8.625	74.99	71.77	68.53	65.27	48.78	32.23	15.94
8.750	76.73	73.43	70.11	66.77	49.89	32.94	16.28
8.875	78.47	75.09	71.69	68.28	51.00	33.66	16.62
9.000	80.22	76.77	73.29	69.79	52.11	34.38	16.97

2³/₄%
Payment Adjustments

Old Rate   (As % of Old Payment)

NEW RATE (%)	30	29	28	27	26	25	24
			YEARS REMAINING IN TERM				
2.000	−9.46	−9.20	−8.93	−8.67	−8.39	−8.12	−7.84
2.125	−7.92	−7.70	−7.48	−7.25	−7.03	−6.79	−6.56
2.250	−6.37	−6.19	−6.01	−5.83	−5.64	−5.46	−5.27
2.375	−4.80	−4.66	−4.53	−4.39	−4.25	−4.11	−3.97
2.500	−3.21	−3.12	−3.03	−2.94	−2.85	−2.75	−2.66
2.625	−1.61	−1.57	−1.52	−1.48	−1.43	−1.38	−1.33
2.750	0.00	0.00	0.00	0.00	0.00	0.00	0.00
2.875	1.63	1.58	1.54	1.49	1.44	1.39	1.34
3.000	3.27	3.18	3.09	2.99	2.89	2.80	2.70
3.125	4.93	4.79	4.65	4.50	4.36	4.21	4.06
3.250	6.61	6.42	6.22	6.03	5.84	5.64	5.44
3.375	8.29	8.05	7.81	7.57	7.32	7.07	6.82
3.500	9.99	9.71	9.42	9.12	8.82	8.52	8.22
3.625	11.71	11.37	11.03	10.68	10.33	9.98	9.62
3.750	13.44	13.05	12.66	12.26	11.86	11.45	11.04
3.875	15.19	14.74	14.30	13.85	13.39	12.93	12.47
4.000	16.94	16.45	15.95	15.45	14.94	14.42	13.90
4.125	18.72	18.17	17.62	17.06	16.49	15.92	15.35
4.250	20.50	19.90	19.29	18.68	18.06	17.43	16.80
4.375	22.30	21.65	20.98	20.32	19.64	18.96	18.27
4.500	24.11	23.40	22.69	21.96	21.23	20.49	19.74
4.625	25.94	25.17	24.40	23.62	22.83	22.03	21.23
4.750	27.78	26.96	26.13	25.29	24.44	23.59	22.72
4.875	29.63	28.75	27.87	26.97	26.06	25.15	24.23
5.000	31.50	30.56	29.62	28.66	27.70	26.72	25.74
5.125	33.37	32.38	31.38	30.36	29.34	28.31	27.26
5.250	35.26	34.21	33.15	32.08	30.99	29.90	28.80
5.375	37.17	36.06	34.94	33.80	32.66	31.50	30.34
5.500	39.08	37.91	36.73	35.54	34.33	33.12	31.89
5.625	41.01	39.78	38.54	37.29	36.02	34.74	33.45
5.750	42.95	41.66	40.36	39.04	37.71	36.37	35.02
5.875	44.90	43.55	42.19	40.81	39.42	38.02	36.60
6.000	46.86	45.45	44.03	42.59	41.13	39.67	38.19
6.125	48.84	47.37	45.88	44.38	42.86	41.33	39.78
6.250	50.82	49.29	47.74	46.17	44.59	43.00	41.39
6.375	52.82	51.22	49.61	47.98	46.34	44.68	43.00
6.500	54.83	53.17	51.49	49.80	48.09	46.37	44.63
6.625	56.85	55.13	53.39	51.63	49.86	48.06	46.26
6.750	58.88	57.09	55.29	53.47	51.63	49.77	47.90
6.875	60.92	59.07	57.20	55.32	53.41	51.49	49.55
7.000	62.97	61.06	59.13	57.17	55.20	53.21	51.20
7.125	65.03	63.06	61.06	59.04	57.00	54.94	52.87
7.250	67.10	65.06	63.00	60.92	58.81	56.69	54.54
7.375	69.18	67.08	64.95	62.80	60.63	58.44	56.22
7.500	71.27	69.11	66.91	64.70	62.46	60.19	57.91
7.625	73.38	71.14	68.88	66.60	64.29	61.96	59.61
7.750	75.49	73.19	70.86	68.51	66.14	63.74	61.31
7.875	77.61	75.24	72.85	70.43	67.99	65.52	63.03
8.000	79.74	77.31	74.85	72.36	69.85	67.31	64.75
8.125	81.88	79.38	76.85	74.30	71.72	69.11	66.47
8.250	84.03	81.46	78.87	76.25	73.59	70.92	68.21
8.375	86.18	83.55	80.89	78.20	75.48	72.73	69.95
8.500	88.35	85.65	82.92	80.16	77.37	74.55	71.70
8.625	90.52	87.76	84.96	82.13	79.27	76.38	73.46
8.750	92.70	89.88	87.01	84.11	81.18	78.22	75.23
8.875	94.90	92.00	89.07	86.10	83.10	80.06	77.00
9.000	97.09	94.13	91.13	88.09	85.02	81.92	78.78

Payment Adjustments

(As % of Old Payment)

2³/₄%
Old Rate

NEW RATE (%)	23	22	21	20	15	10	5
				YEARS REMAINING IN TERM			
2.000	−7.56	−7.27	−6.98	−6.69	−5.17	−3.56	−1.85
2.125	−6.32	−6.08	−5.84	−5.60	−4.32	−2.97	−1.54
2.250	−5.08	−4.89	−4.69	−4.49	−3.47	−2.38	−1.23
2.375	−3.82	−3.68	−3.53	−3.38	−2.61	−1.79	−0.93
2.500	−2.56	−2.46	−2.36	−2.26	−1.74	−1.20	−0.62
2.625	−1.28	−1.24	−1.19	−1.13	−0.87	−0.60	−0.31
2.750	0.00	0.00	0.00	0.00	0.00	0.00	0.00
2.875	1.29	1.24	1.19	1.14	0.88	0.60	0.31
3.000	2.60	2.50	2.40	2.29	1.76	1.21	0.62
3.125	3.91	3.76	3.61	3.45	2.65	1.81	0.93
3.250	5.24	5.03	4.82	4.62	3.54	2.42	1.24
3.375	6.57	6.31	6.05	5.79	4.44	3.03	1.56
3.500	7.91	7.60	7.29	6.97	5.34	3.64	1.87
3.625	9.26	8.90	8.53	8.16	6.25	4.26	2.18
3.750	10.62	10.21	9.78	9.36	7.16	4.87	2.50
3.875	12.00	11.52	11.04	10.56	8.08	5.49	2.81
4.000	13.38	12.85	12.31	11.77	9.00	6.11	3.13
4.125	14.77	14.18	13.59	12.99	9.92	6.74	3.44
4.250	16.16	15.52	14.87	14.21	10.85	7.36	3.76
4.375	17.57	16.87	16.16	15.45	11.79	7.99	4.08
4.500	18.99	18.23	17.46	16.69	12.73	8.62	4.40
4.625	20.42	19.60	18.77	17.94	13.67	9.26	4.72
4.750	21.85	20.97	20.09	19.19	14.62	9.89	5.03
4.875	23.30	22.36	21.41	20.46	15.57	10.53	5.35
5.000	24.75	23.75	22.74	21.73	16.53	11.17	5.67
5.125	26.21	25.15	24.08	23.00	17.49	11.81	6.00
5.250	27.68	26.56	25.43	24.29	18.46	12.45	6.32
5.375	29.16	27.98	26.78	25.58	19.43	13.10	6.64
5.500	30.65	29.40	28.15	26.88	20.40	13.75	6.96
5.625	32.15	30.84	29.52	28.18	21.38	14.40	7.29
5.750	33.66	32.28	30.89	29.50	22.37	15.05	7.61
5.875	35.17	33.73	32.28	30.82	23.36	15.70	7.93
6.000	36.69	35.19	33.67	32.14	24.35	16.36	8.26
6.125	38.23	36.65	35.07	33.48	25.35	17.02	8.59
6.250	39.77	38.13	36.48	34.82	26.35	17.68	8.91
6.375	41.31	39.61	37.89	36.16	27.35	18.34	9.24
6.500	42.87	41.10	39.31	37.52	28.36	19.01	9.57
6.625	44.43	42.60	40.74	38.88	29.38	19.68	9.89
6.750	46.01	44.10	42.18	40.25	30.40	20.35	10.22
6.875	47.59	45.61	43.62	41.62	31.42	21.02	10.55
7.000	49.18	47.13	45.07	43.00	32.45	21.69	10.88
7.125	50.77	48.66	46.53	44.39	33.48	22.37	11.21
7.250	52.38	50.19	48.00	45.78	34.52	23.05	11.54
7.375	53.99	51.74	49.47	47.18	35.56	23.73	11.88
7.500	55.61	53.28	50.94	48.59	36.60	24.41	12.21
7.625	57.23	54.84	52.43	50.00	37.65	25.10	12.54
7.750	58.87	56.40	53.92	51.42	38.70	25.78	12.87
7.875	60.51	57.97	55.42	52.85	39.76	26.47	13.21
8.000	62.16	59.55	56.92	54.28	40.82	27.16	13.54
8.125	63.82	61.14	58.44	55.72	41.89	27.86	13.88
8.250	65.48	62.73	59.95	57.16	42.96	28.55	14.21
8.375	67.15	64.33	61.48	58.61	44.03	29.25	14.55
8.500	68.83	65.93	63.01	60.07	45.11	29.95	14.89
8.625	70.51	67.54	64.55	61.53	46.19	30.65	15.23
8.750	72.21	69.16	66.09	63.00	47.28	31.35	15.56
8.875	73.91	70.78	67.64	64.47	48.37	32.06	15.90
9.000	75.61	72.42	69.19	65.95	49.46	32.77	16.24

3%
Old Rate

Payment Adjustments
(As % of Old Payment)

NEW RATE (%)	YEARS REMAINING IN TERM						
	30	29	28	27	26	25	24
2.000	−12.33	−12.00	−11.66	−11.32	−10.97	−10.62	−10.26
2.125	−10.84	−10.55	−10.25	−9.95	−9.64	−9.33	−9.02
2.250	−9.34	−9.08	−8.82	−8.56	−8.30	−8.03	−7.76
2.375	−7.82	−7.60	−7.39	−7.17	−6.94	−6.72	−6.49
2.500	−6.28	−6.11	−5.93	−5.76	−5.58	−5.40	−5.21
2.625	−4.73	−4.60	−4.47	−4.34	−4.20	−4.06	−3.93
2.750	−3.17	−3.08	−2.99	−2.90	−2.81	−2.72	−2.63
2.875	−1.59	−1.55	−1.50	−1.46	−1.41	−1.37	−1.32
3.000	0.00	0.00	0.00	0.00	0.00	0.00	0.00
3.125	1.61	1.56	1.52	1.47	1.42	1.38	1.33
3.250	3.23	3.14	3.04	2.95	2.86	2.76	2.67
3.375	4.86	4.72	4.59	4.45	4.30	4.16	4.02
3.500	6.51	6.33	6.14	5.95	5.76	5.57	5.38
3.625	8.17	7.94	7.71	7.47	7.23	6.99	6.74
3.750	9.85	9.57	9.29	9.00	8.71	8.42	8.12
3.875	11.54	11.21	10.88	10.54	10.20	9.86	9.51
4.000	13.24	12.86	12.48	12.09	11.70	11.31	10.91
4.125	14.95	14.53	14.10	13.66	13.22	12.77	12.32
4.250	16.68	16.21	15.72	15.23	14.74	14.24	13.73
4.375	18.43	17.90	17.36	16.82	16.27	15.72	15.16
4.500	20.18	19.60	19.01	18.42	17.82	17.21	16.60
4.625	21.95	21.32	20.68	20.03	19.38	18.71	18.04
4.750	23.73	23.04	22.35	21.65	20.94	20.22	19.50
4.875	25.52	24.78	24.04	23.28	22.52	21.75	20.96
5.000	27.33	26.54	25.74	24.93	24.11	23.28	22.44
5.125	29.15	28.30	27.44	26.58	25.70	24.82	23.92
5.250	30.98	30.08	29.17	28.24	27.31	26.37	25.41
5.375	32.82	31.86	30.90	29.92	28.93	27.93	26.92
5.500	34.67	33.66	32.64	31.60	30.56	29.50	28.43
5.625	36.54	35.47	34.39	33.30	32.19	31.08	29.95
5.750	38.42	37.29	36.16	35.01	33.84	32.66	31.47
5.875	40.31	39.13	37.93	36.72	35.50	34.26	33.01
6.000	42.21	40.97	39.72	38.45	37.17	35.87	34.56
6.125	44.12	42.82	41.51	40.18	38.84	37.48	36.11
6.250	46.04	44.69	43.32	41.93	40.53	39.11	37.67
6.375	47.98	46.56	45.13	43.69	42.22	40.74	39.25
6.500	49.92	48.45	46.96	45.45	43.93	42.39	40.83
6.625	51.87	50.35	48.80	47.23	45.64	44.04	42.41
6.750	53.84	52.25	50.64	49.01	47.36	45.70	44.01
6.875	55.82	54.17	52.50	50.81	49.10	47.37	45.62
7.000	57.80	56.09	54.36	52.61	50.84	49.04	47.23
7.125	59.80	58.03	56.24	54.42	52.59	50.73	48.85
7.250	61.80	59.98	58.12	56.24	54.34	52.42	50.48
7.375	63.82	61.93	60.01	58.07	56.11	54.13	52.12
7.500	65.85	63.89	61.92	59.91	57.89	55.84	53.76
7.625	67.88	65.87	63.83	61.76	59.67	57.55	55.41
7.750	69.93	67.85	65.75	63.62	61.46	59.28	57.07
7.875	71.98	69.84	67.68	65.48	63.26	61.02	58.74
8.000	74.04	71.84	69.61	67.36	65.07	62.76	60.42
8.125	76.11	73.85	71.56	69.24	66.89	64.51	62.10
8.250	78.19	75.87	73.52	71.13	68.71	66.27	63.79
8.375	80.28	77.90	75.48	73.03	70.54	68.03	65.49
8.500	82.38	79.93	77.45	74.93	72.38	69.80	67.19
8.625	84.48	81.97	79.43	76.85	74.23	71.58	68.90
8.750	86.60	84.02	81.41	78.77	76.09	73.37	70.62
8.875	88.72	86.08	83.41	80.70	77.95	75.17	72.35
9.000	90.85	88.15	85.41	82.63	79.82	76.97	74.08

Payment Adjustments
(As % of Old Payment)

3%
Old Rate

NEW RATE (%)	YEARS REMAINING IN TERM						
	23	22	21	20	15	10	5
2.000	−9.90	−9.53	−9.16	−8.78	−6.82	−4.71	−2.45
2.125	−8.70	−8.37	−8.04	−7.71	−5.98	−4.13	−2.15
2.250	−7.48	−7.20	−6.92	−6.63	−5.14	−3.55	−1.84
2.375	−6.26	−6.03	−5.79	−5.55	−4.30	−2.96	−1.54
2.500	−5.03	−4.84	−4.65	−4.45	−3.45	−2.37	−1.23
2.625	−3.78	−3.64	−3.50	−3.35	−2.59	−1.78	−0.92
2.750	−2.53	−2.44	−2.34	−2.24	−1.73	−1.19	−0.62
2.875	−1.27	−1.22	−1.17	−1.12	−0.87	−0.60	−0.31
3.000	0.00	0.00	0.00	0.00	0.00	0.00	0.00
3.125	1.28	1.23	1.18	1.13	0.87	0.60	0.31
3.250	2.57	2.47	2.37	2.27	1.75	1.20	0.62
3.375	3.87	3.72	3.57	3.42	2.63	1.80	0.93
3.500	5.18	4.98	4.78	4.57	3.52	2.41	1.24
3.625	6.50	6.25	5.99	5.73	4.41	3.02	1.55
3.750	7.82	7.52	7.21	6.90	5.31	3.63	1.87
3.875	9.16	8.80	8.44	8.08	6.21	4.24	2.18
4.000	10.50	10.10	9.68	9.26	7.11	4.85	2.49
4.125	11.86	11.40	10.93	10.46	8.02	5.47	2.81
4.250	13.22	12.71	12.18	11.65	8.93	6.09	3.12
4.375	14.60	14.02	13.44	12.86	9.85	6.71	3.44
4.500	15.98	15.35	14.71	14.07	10.78	7.33	3.75
4.625	17.37	16.68	15.99	15.29	11.70	7.95	4.07
4.750	18.77	18.03	17.28	16.52	12.63	8.58	4.39
4.875	20.17	19.38	18.57	17.76	13.57	9.21	4.70
5.000	21.59	20.73	19.87	19.00	14.51	9.84	5.02
5.125	23.02	22.10	21.18	20.25	15.46	10.48	5.34
5.250	24.45	23.48	22.49	21.50	16.41	11.11	5.66
5.375	25.89	24.86	23.82	22.76	17.36	11.75	5.98
5.500	27.34	26.25	25.15	24.03	18.32	12.39	6.30
5.625	28.80	27.65	26.49	25.31	19.28	13.03	6.62
5.750	30.27	29.06	27.83	26.59	20.25	13.68	6.95
5.875	31.75	30.47	29.18	27.88	21.22	14.33	7.27
6.000	33.23	31.89	30.54	29.18	22.20	14.97	7.59
6.125	34.72	33.32	31.91	30.48	23.18	15.63	7.92
6.250	36.23	34.76	33.29	31.79	24.16	16.28	8.24
6.375	37.73	36.21	34.67	33.11	25.15	16.93	8.56
6.500	39.25	37.66	36.06	34.43	26.14	17.59	8.89
6.625	40.78	39.12	37.45	35.77	27.14	18.25	9.22
6.750	42.31	40.59	38.85	37.10	28.14	18.91	9.54
6.875	43.85	42.06	40.26	38.45	29.15	19.58	9.87
7.000	45.40	43.55	41.68	39.79	30.16	20.24	10.20
7.125	46.95	45.04	43.10	41.15	31.17	20.91	10.53
7.250	48.52	46.53	44.53	42.51	32.19	21.58	10.86
7.375	50.09	48.04	45.97	43.88	33.21	22.26	11.19
7.500	51.67	49.55	47.41	45.26	34.24	22.93	11.52
7.625	53.25	51.07	48.86	46.64	35.27	23.61	11.85
7.750	54.85	52.59	50.32	48.03	36.30	24.29	12.18
7.875	56.45	54.13	51.78	49.42	37.34	24.97	12.51
8.000	58.05	55.66	53.25	50.82	38.38	25.65	12.84
8.125	59.67	57.21	54.73	52.23	39.43	26.33	13.18
8.250	61.29	58.76	56.21	53.64	40.48	27.02	13.51
8.375	62.92	60.32	57.70	55.05	41.54	27.71	13.84
8.500	64.55	61.89	59.19	56.48	42.60	28.40	14.18
8.625	66.20	63.46	60.70	57.91	43.66	29.10	14.51
8.750	67.85	65.04	62.20	59.34	44.73	29.79	14.85
8.875	69.50	66.62	63.72	60.78	45.80	30.49	15.19
9.000	71.16	68.21	65.24	62.23	46.87	31.19	15.53

3¼%
Old Rate

Payment Adjustments
(As % of Old Payment)

NEW RATE (%)	30	29	28	27	26	25	24
					YEARS REMAINING IN TERM		
2.000	−15.07	−14.67	−14.27	−13.86	−13.45	−13.02	−12.59
2.125	−13.63	−13.27	−12.90	−12.53	−12.15	−11.77	−11.38
2.250	−12.17	−11.85	−11.52	−11.18	−10.85	−10.50	−10.16
2.375	−10.70	−10.41	−10.12	−9.83	−9.53	−9.23	−8.92
2.500	−9.21	−8.96	−8.71	−8.46	−8.20	−7.94	−7.68
2.625	−7.71	−7.50	−7.29	−7.08	−6.86	−6.64	−6.42
2.750	−6.20	−6.03	−5.86	−5.69	−5.51	−5.34	−5.16
2.875	−4.67	−4.54	−4.41	−4.28	−4.15	−4.02	−3.88
3.000	−3.13	−3.04	−2.95	−2.87	−2.78	−2.69	−2.60
3.125	−1.57	−1.53	−1.48	−1.44	−1.40	−1.35	−1.30
3.250	0.00	0.00	0.00	0.00	0.00	0.00	0.00
3.375	1.58	1.54	1.50	1.45	1.41	1.36	1.31
3.500	3.18	3.09	3.00	2.91	2.82	2.73	2.64
3.625	4.79	4.66	4.52	4.39	4.25	4.11	3.97
3.750	6.41	6.24	6.06	5.87	5.69	5.50	5.31
3.875	8.05	7.83	7.60	7.37	7.14	6.90	6.67
4.000	9.70	9.43	9.16	8.88	8.60	8.32	8.03
4.125	11.36	11.04	10.72	10.40	10.07	9.74	9.40
4.250	13.04	12.67	12.30	11.93	11.55	11.17	10.78
4.375	14.72	14.31	13.89	13.47	13.04	12.61	12.17
4.500	16.42	15.96	15.50	15.02	14.55	14.06	13.57
4.625	18.14	17.63	17.11	16.59	16.06	15.52	14.98
4.750	19.86	19.30	18.74	18.16	17.58	16.99	16.39
4.875	21.60	20.99	20.37	19.75	19.11	18.47	17.82
5.000	23.35	22.69	22.02	21.34	20.66	19.96	19.26
5.125	25.11	24.40	23.68	22.95	22.21	21.46	20.70
5.250	26.88	26.12	25.35	24.57	23.77	22.97	22.16
5.375	28.67	27.85	27.03	26.19	25.35	24.49	23.62
5.500	30.46	29.60	28.72	27.83	26.93	26.01	25.09
5.625	32.27	31.35	30.42	29.48	28.52	27.55	26.57
5.750	34.09	33.12	32.13	31.13	30.12	29.10	28.06
5.875	35.92	34.90	33.86	32.80	31.73	30.65	29.56
6.000	37.76	36.68	35.59	34.48	33.35	32.21	31.06
6.125	39.61	38.48	37.33	36.16	34.98	33.79	32.58
6.250	41.48	40.29	39.08	37.86	36.62	35.37	34.10
6.375	43.35	42.11	40.85	39.57	38.27	36.96	35.63
6.500	45.23	43.94	42.62	41.28	39.93	38.56	37.17
6.625	47.13	45.77	44.40	43.01	41.59	40.16	38.71
6.750	49.03	47.62	46.19	44.74	43.27	41.78	40.27
6.875	50.95	49.48	47.99	46.48	44.95	43.40	41.83
7.000	52.87	51.35	49.80	48.23	46.65	45.04	43.40
7.125	54.80	53.22	51.62	49.99	48.35	46.68	44.98
7.250	56.75	55.11	53.45	51.76	50.06	48.32	46.57
7.375	58.70	57.01	55.29	53.54	51.77	49.98	48.16
7.500	60.66	58.91	57.13	55.33	53.50	51.65	49.77
7.625	62.63	60.82	58.99	57.12	55.23	53.32	51.38
7.750	64.61	62.75	60.85	58.93	56.98	55.00	52.99
7.875	66.60	64.68	62.72	60.74	58.73	56.69	54.62
8.000	68.60	66.62	64.60	62.56	60.48	58.38	56.25
8.125	70.61	68.57	66.49	64.39	62.25	60.08	57.89
8.250	72.62	70.52	68.39	66.22	64.02	61.79	59.54
8.375	74.65	72.49	70.29	68.07	65.80	63.51	61.19
8.500	76.68	74.46	72.21	69.92	67.59	65.24	62.85
8.625	78.72	76.44	74.13	71.77	69.39	66.97	64.52
8.750	80.76	78.43	76.05	73.64	71.19	68.71	66.19
8.875	82.82	80.42	77.99	75.51	73.00	70.45	67.87
9.000	84.88	82.43	79.93	77.40	74.82	72.21	69.56

Payment Adjustments
3¼%
(As % of Old Payment)

Old Rate

NEW RATE (%)	23	22	21	20	15	10	5
			YEARS REMAINING IN TERM				
2.000	−12.16	−11.72	−11.27	−10.81	−8.42	−5.84	−3.05
2.125	−10.98	−10.58	−10.18	−9.76	−7.60	−5.26	−2.75
2.250	−9.80	−9.44	−9.08	−8.71	−6.77	−4.69	−2.45
2.375	−8.61	−8.29	−7.97	−7.64	−5.94	−4.11	−2.14
2.500	−7.41	−7.13	−6.86	−6.57	−5.11	−3.53	−1.84
2.625	−6.20	−5.97	−5.73	−5.50	−4.27	−2.95	−1.53
2.750	−4.97	−4.79	−4.60	−4.41	−3.42	−2.36	−1.23
2.875	−3.74	−3.61	−3.46	−3.32	−2.57	−1.77	−0.92
3.000	−2.51	−2.41	−2.32	−2.22	−1.72	−1.19	−0.62
3.125	−1.26	−1.21	−1.16	−1.11	−0.86	−0.59	−0.31
3.250	0.00	0.00	0.00	0.00	0.00	0.00	0.00
3.375	1.27	1.22	1.17	1.12	0.87	0.60	0.31
3.500	2.54	2.45	2.35	2.25	1.74	1.19	0.62
3.625	3.83	3.68	3.54	3.39	2.61	1.79	0.93
3.750	5.12	4.93	4.73	4.53	3.49	2.40	1.24
3.875	6.42	6.18	5.93	5.68	4.38	3.00	1.55
4.000	7.74	7.44	7.14	6.84	5.27	3.61	1.86
4.125	9.06	8.71	8.36	8.00	6.16	4.22	2.17
4.250	10.39	9.99	9.58	9.17	7.06	4.83	2.49
4.375	11.72	11.27	10.82	10.35	7.96	5.44	2.80
4.500	13.07	12.57	12.06	11.54	8.87	6.06	3.11
4.625	14.43	13.87	13.30	12.73	9.78	6.68	3.43
4.750	15.79	15.18	14.56	13.93	10.70	7.30	3.74
4.875	17.16	16.50	15.82	15.14	11.62	7.92	4.06
5.000	18.54	17.82	17.09	16.35	12.54	8.54	4.38
5.125	19.93	19.16	18.37	17.58	13.47	9.17	4.69
5.250	21.33	20.50	19.66	18.80	14.40	9.80	5.01
5.375	22.74	21.85	20.95	20.04	15.34	10.43	5.33
5.500	24.15	23.21	22.25	21.28	16.28	11.06	5.65
5.625	25.58	24.57	23.55	22.53	17.23	11.69	5.97
5.750	27.01	25.94	24.87	23.78	18.18	12.33	6.29
5.875	28.45	27.32	26.19	25.04	19.13	12.97	6.61
6.000	29.89	28.71	27.52	26.31	20.09	13.61	6.93
6.125	31.35	30.11	28.85	27.59	21.06	14.26	7.25
6.250	32.81	31.51	30.20	28.87	22.02	14.90	7.57
6.375	34.28	32.92	31.55	30.15	23.00	15.55	7.90
6.500	35.76	34.34	32.90	31.45	23.97	16.20	8.22
6.625	37.25	35.77	34.27	32.75	24.95	16.85	8.54
6.750	38.74	37.20	35.64	34.06	25.94	17.50	8.87
6.875	40.24	38.64	37.01	35.37	26.92	18.16	9.19
7.000	41.75	40.08	38.40	36.69	27.92	18.82	9.52
7.125	43.27	41.54	39.79	38.02	28.91	19.48	9.85
7.250	44.80	43.00	41.18	39.35	29.91	20.14	10.17
7.375	46.33	44.47	42.59	40.69	30.92	20.81	10.50
7.500	47.87	45.94	44.00	42.03	31.93	21.47	10.83
7.625	49.41	47.42	45.41	43.38	32.94	22.14	11.16
7.750	50.97	48.91	46.84	44.74	33.96	22.81	11.49
7.875	52.53	50.41	48.27	46.10	34.98	23.48	11.82
8.000	54.09	51.91	49.70	47.47	36.00	24.16	12.15
8.125	55.67	53.42	51.14	48.84	37.03	24.84	12.48
8.250	57.25	54.93	52.59	50.22	38.07	25.52	12.81
8.375	58.84	56.45	54.05	51.61	39.10	26.20	13.14
8.500	60.43	57.98	55.51	53.00	40.14	26.88	13.48
8.625	62.03	59.52	56.97	54.40	41.19	27.56	13.81
8.750	63.64	61.06	58.44	55.80	42.24	28.25	14.14
8.875	65.25	62.60	59.92	57.21	43.29	28.94	14.48
9.000	66.87	64.16	61.41	58.63	44.34	29.63	14.81

3¹/₂% Payment Adjustments
Old Rate (As % of Old Payment)

NEW RATE (%)	YEARS REMAINING IN TERM						
	30	29	28	27	26	25	24
2.000	−17.69	−17.23	−16.77	−16.30	−15.82	−15.33	−14.84
2.125	−16.29	−15.87	−15.44	−15.01	−14.56	−14.11	−13.66
2.250	−14.88	−14.49	−14.10	−13.70	−13.29	−12.88	−12.46
2.375	−13.45	−13.10	−12.74	−12.38	−12.01	−11.64	−11.26
2.500	−12.01	−11.70	−11.38	−11.05	−10.72	−10.39	−10.05
2.625	−10.55	−10.28	−10.00	−9.71	−9.42	−9.13	−8.83
2.750	−9.09	−8.85	−8.61	−8.36	−8.11	−7.85	−7.59
2.875	−7.61	−7.40	−7.20	−6.99	−6.78	−6.57	−6.35
3.000	−6.11	−5.95	−5.78	−5.62	−5.45	−5.28	−5.10
3.125	−4.60	−4.48	−4.36	−4.23	−4.10	−3.97	−3.84
3.250	−3.08	−3.00	−2.92	−2.83	−2.75	−2.66	−2.57
3.375	−1.55	−1.51	−1.46	−1.42	−1.38	−1.33	−1.29
3.500	0.00	0.00	0.00	0.00	0.00	0.00	0.00
3.625	1.56	1.52	1.48	1.43	1.39	1.34	1.30
3.750	3.13	3.05	2.96	2.88	2.79	2.70	2.61
3.875	4.72	4.59	4.46	4.33	4.20	4.06	3.92
4.000	6.32	6.15	5.97	5.80	5.62	5.44	5.25
4.125	7.93	7.71	7.50	7.27	7.05	6.82	6.59
4.250	9.55	9.29	9.03	8.76	8.49	8.21	7.93
4.375	11.19	10.88	10.57	10.26	9.94	9.62	9.29
4.500	12.84	12.49	12.13	11.77	11.40	11.03	10.65
4.625	14.50	14.10	13.70	13.29	12.87	12.45	12.02
4.750	16.17	15.72	15.27	14.82	14.35	13.88	13.40
4.875	17.85	17.36	16.86	16.36	15.84	15.32	14.79
5.000	19.55	19.01	18.46	17.91	17.34	16.77	16.19
5.125	21.25	20.67	20.07	19.47	18.85	18.23	17.60
5.250	22.97	22.34	21.69	21.04	20.37	19.70	19.02
5.375	24.70	24.02	23.32	22.62	21.90	21.18	20.44
5.500	26.44	25.71	24.97	24.21	23.44	22.66	21.88
5.625	28.20	27.41	26.62	25.81	24.99	24.16	23.32
5.750	29.96	29.13	28.28	27.42	26.55	25.66	24.77
5.875	31.73	30.85	29.95	29.04	28.12	27.18	26.23
6.000	33.52	32.58	31.63	30.67	29.69	28.70	27.69
6.125	35.31	34.33	33.33	32.31	31.28	30.23	29.17
6.250	37.12	36.08	35.03	33.96	32.87	31.77	30.65
6.375	38.93	37.84	36.74	35.61	34.47	33.32	32.14
6.500	40.76	39.62	38.46	37.28	36.09	34.87	33.64
6.625	42.59	41.40	40.19	38.96	37.71	36.44	35.15
6.750	44.44	43.19	41.93	40.64	39.34	38.01	36.67
6.875	46.29	45.00	43.68	42.33	40.97	39.59	38.19
7.000	48.16	46.81	45.43	44.04	42.62	41.18	39.72
7.125	50.03	48.63	47.20	45.75	44.27	42.78	41.26
7.250	51.92	50.46	48.97	47.47	45.94	44.38	42.80
7.375	53.81	52.30	50.76	49.19	47.61	45.99	44.36
7.500	55.71	54.14	52.55	50.93	49.28	47.61	45.92
7.625	57.62	56.00	54.35	52.67	50.97	49.24	47.49
7.750	59.54	57.87	56.16	54.43	52.67	50.88	49.06
7.875	61.47	59.74	57.98	56.19	54.37	52.52	50.65
8.000	63.41	61.62	59.80	57.96	56.08	54.17	52.24
8.125	65.35	63.51	61.64	59.73	57.80	55.83	53.83
8.250	67.30	65.41	63.48	61.51	59.52	57.49	55.44
8.375	69.26	67.31	65.33	63.31	61.25	59.17	57.05
8.500	71.23	69.23	67.18	65.10	62.99	60.84	58.66
8.625	73.21	71.15	69.05	66.91	64.74	62.53	60.29
8.750	75.19	73.08	70.92	68.72	66.49	64.22	61.92
8.875	77.19	75.01	72.80	70.54	68.25	65.92	63.56
9.000	79.19	76.96	74.68	72.37	70.02	67.63	65.20

Payment Adjustments

(As % of Old Payment)

3¹/₂%
Old Rate

NEW RATE (%)	YEARS REMAINING IN TERM						
	23	22	21	20	15	10	5
2.000	−14.34	−13.82	−13.30	−12.77	−9.98	−6.95	−3.65
2.125	−13.19	−12.72	−12.24	−11.75	−9.18	−6.38	−3.35
2.250	−12.04	−11.60	−11.16	−10.72	−8.36	−5.81	−3.05
2.375	−10.87	−10.48	−10.08	−9.68	−7.55	−5.24	−2.75
2.500	−9.70	−9.35	−8.99	−8.63	−6.73	−4.67	−2.44
2.625	−8.52	−8.21	−7.90	−7.58	−5.90	−4.09	−2.14
2.750	−7.33	−7.06	−6.79	−6.52	−5.07	−3.51	−1.84
2.875	−6.13	−5.91	−5.68	−5.45	−4.24	−2.93	−1.53
3.000	−4.92	−4.74	−4.56	−4.37	−3.40	−2.35	−1.23
3.125	−3.71	−3.57	−3.43	−3.29	−2.56	−1.77	−0.92
3.250	−2.48	−2.39	−2.30	−2.20	−1.71	−1.18	−0.61
3.375	−1.24	−1.20	−1.15	−1.10	−0.86	−0.59	−0.31
3.500	0.00	0.00	0.00	0.00	0.00	0.00	0.00
3.625	1.25	1.21	1.16	1.11	0.86	0.59	0.31
3.750	2.51	2.42	2.33	2.23	1.73	1.19	0.62
3.875	3.79	3.64	3.50	3.35	2.60	1.79	0.93
4.000	5.06	4.87	4.68	4.49	3.47	2.39	1.24
4.125	6.35	6.11	5.87	5.63	4.35	2.99	1.55
4.250	7.65	7.36	7.07	6.77	5.23	3.59	1.86
4.375	8.95	8.62	8.27	7.93	6.12	4.20	2.17
4.500	10.27	9.88	9.48	9.09	7.01	4.81	2.48
4.625	11.59	11.15	10.70	10.25	7.91	5.42	2.79
4.750	12.92	12.43	11.93	11.43	8.81	6.03	3.11
4.875	14.26	13.71	13.16	12.61	9.71	6.64	3.42
5.000	15.60	15.01	14.41	13.79	10.62	7.26	3.74
5.125	16.96	16.31	15.65	14.99	11.53	7.88	4.05
5.250	18.32	17.62	16.91	16.19	12.45	8.50	4.37
5.375	19.70	18.94	18.17	17.40	13.37	9.12	4.68
5.500	21.07	20.26	19.44	18.61	14.30	9.75	5.00
5.625	22.46	21.60	20.72	19.83	15.23	10.38	5.32
5.750	23.86	22.94	22.00	21.06	16.16	11.01	5.63
5.875	25.26	24.28	23.29	22.29	17.10	11.64	5.95
6.000	26.67	25.64	24.59	23.53	18.04	12.27	6.27
6.125	28.09	27.00	25.90	24.78	18.99	12.91	6.59
6.250	29.52	28.37	27.21	26.03	19.94	13.55	6.91
6.375	30.95	29.75	28.53	27.29	20.89	14.19	7.23
6.500	32.40	31.13	29.85	28.56	21.85	14.83	7.56
6.625	33.85	32.52	31.18	29.83	22.82	15.47	7.88
6.750	35.30	33.92	32.52	31.11	23.78	16.12	8.20
6.875	36.77	35.33	33.87	32.39	24.76	16.77	8.52
7.000	38.24	36.74	35.22	33.68	25.73	17.42	8.85
7.125	39.72	38.16	36.58	34.98	26.71	18.07	9.17
7.250	41.21	39.58	37.94	36.28	27.69	18.72	9.50
7.375	42.70	41.02	39.31	37.59	28.68	19.38	9.82
7.500	44.20	42.46	40.69	38.91	29.67	20.04	10.15
7.625	45.71	43.90	42.08	40.23	30.67	20.70	10.48
7.750	47.22	45.36	43.47	41.55	31.67	21.36	10.80
7.875	48.74	46.82	44.86	42.89	32.67	22.03	11.13
8.000	50.27	48.28	46.27	44.22	33.68	22.69	11.46
8.125	51.81	49.75	47.67	45.57	34.69	23.36	11.79
8.250	53.35	51.23	49.09	46.92	35.71	24.03	12.12
8.375	54.90	52.72	50.51	48.27	36.73	24.71	12.45
8.500	56.45	54.21	51.94	49.64	37.75	25.38	12.78
8.625	58.01	55.71	53.37	51.00	38.78	26.06	13.11
8.750	59.58	57.21	54.81	52.37	39.81	26.74	13.44
8.875	61.16	58.72	56.25	53.75	40.84	27.42	13.78
9.000	62.74	60.24	57.70	55.14	41.88	28.10	14.11

3¾%
Old Rate

Payment Adjustments
(As % of Old Payment)

NEW RATE (%)	YEARS REMAINING IN TERM						
	30	29	28	27	26	25	24
2.000	−20.19	−19.68	−19.17	−18.64	−18.10	−17.56	−17.00
2.125	−18.83	−18.36	−17.87	−17.38	−16.88	−16.37	−15.85
2.250	−17.46	−17.02	−16.57	−16.11	−15.65	−15.17	−14.69
2.375	−16.08	−15.67	−15.25	−14.83	−14.40	−13.96	−13.52
2.500	−14.68	−14.31	−13.93	−13.54	−13.14	−12.74	−12.33
2.625	−13.27	−12.93	−12.59	−12.24	−11.88	−11.51	−11.14
2.750	−11.85	−11.54	−11.24	−10.92	−10.60	−10.27	−9.94
2.875	−10.41	−10.14	−9.87	−9.59	−9.31	−9.02	−8.73
3.000	−8.96	−8.73	−8.50	−8.26	−8.01	−7.76	−7.51
3.125	−7.50	−7.31	−7.11	−6.91	−6.70	−6.50	−6.28
3.250	−6.03	−5.87	−5.71	−5.55	−5.38	−5.22	−5.04
3.375	−4.54	−4.42	−4.30	−4.18	−4.05	−3.93	−3.80
3.500	−3.04	−2.96	−2.88	−2.80	−2.71	−2.63	−2.54
3.625	−1.53	−1.49	−1.44	−1.40	−1.36	−1.32	−1.27
3.750	0.00	0.00	0.00	0.00	0.00	0.00	0.00
3.875	1.54	1.50	1.46	1.41	1.37	1.33	1.28
4.000	3.09	3.01	2.92	2.84	2.75	2.67	2.58
4.125	4.65	4.53	4.40	4.27	4.14	4.01	3.88
4.250	6.22	6.06	5.89	5.72	5.55	5.37	5.19
4.375	7.81	7.60	7.39	7.18	6.96	6.74	6.51
4.500	9.41	9.16	8.90	8.64	8.38	8.11	7.84
4.625	11.02	10.72	10.42	10.12	9.81	9.50	9.18
4.750	12.64	12.30	11.96	11.61	11.25	10.89	10.52
4.875	14.27	13.89	13.50	13.10	12.70	12.29	11.88
5.000	15.92	15.49	15.05	14.61	14.16	13.70	13.24
5.125	17.57	17.10	16.62	16.13	15.63	15.13	14.61
5.250	19.24	18.72	18.19	17.65	17.11	16.56	15.99
5.375	20.91	20.35	19.78	19.19	18.60	17.99	17.38
5.500	22.60	21.99	21.37	20.74	20.09	19.44	18.78
5.625	24.30	23.64	22.97	22.29	21.60	20.90	20.18
5.750	26.01	25.31	24.59	23.86	23.12	22.36	21.60
5.875	27.73	26.98	26.21	25.43	24.64	23.84	23.02
6.000	29.46	28.66	27.85	27.02	26.17	25.32	24.45
6.125	31.20	30.35	29.49	28.61	27.72	26.81	25.89
6.250	32.95	32.05	31.14	30.21	29.27	28.31	27.33
6.375	34.71	33.77	32.80	31.82	30.83	29.81	28.79
6.500	36.48	35.49	34.47	33.44	32.39	31.33	30.25
6.625	38.26	37.22	36.15	35.07	33.97	32.85	31.72
6.750	40.05	38.96	37.84	36.71	35.56	34.38	33.19
6.875	41.85	40.71	39.54	38.36	37.15	35.92	34.68
7.000	43.66	42.46	41.25	40.01	38.75	37.47	36.17
7.125	45.48	44.23	42.96	41.67	40.36	39.03	37.67
7.250	47.30	46.01	44.69	43.34	41.98	40.59	39.18
7.375	49.14	47.79	46.42	45.02	43.60	42.16	40.69
7.500	50.98	49.58	48.16	46.71	45.24	43.74	42.21
7.625	52.83	51.38	49.91	48.41	46.88	45.32	43.74
7.750	54.69	53.19	51.67	50.11	48.53	46.91	45.28
7.875	56.56	55.01	53.43	51.82	50.18	48.51	46.82
8.000	58.44	56.84	55.20	53.54	51.84	50.12	48.37
8.125	60.33	58.67	56.98	55.27	53.52	51.73	49.92
8.250	62.22	60.51	58.77	57.00	55.19	53.36	51.49
8.375	64.12	62.36	60.57	58.74	56.88	54.98	53.06
8.500	66.03	64.22	62.37	60.49	58.57	56.62	54.63
8.625	67.95	66.08	64.18	62.24	60.27	58.26	56.22
8.750	69.87	67.95	66.00	64.01	61.98	59.91	57.81
8.875	71.80	69.83	67.82	65.78	63.69	61.56	59.40
9.000	73.74	71.72	69.66	67.55	65.41	63.23	61.00

Payment Adjustments
(As % of Old Payment)

3³/₄%
Old Rate

NEW RATE (%)	YEARS REMAINING IN TERM						
	23	22	21	20	15	10	5
2.000	−16.44	−15.86	−15.27	−14.67	−11.51	−8.04	−4.24
2.125	−15.32	−14.78	−14.23	−13.67	−10.72	−7.48	−3.94
2.250	−14.20	−13.69	−13.18	−12.66	−9.92	−6.92	−3.64
2.375	−13.06	−12.60	−12.13	−11.65	−9.12	−6.35	−3.34
2.500	−11.92	−11.49	−11.06	−10.62	−8.31	−5.79	−3.04
2.625	−10.77	−10.38	−9.99	−9.59	−7.50	−5.22	−2.74
2.750	−9.60	−9.26	−8.91	−8.56	−6.68	−4.65	−2.44
2.875	−8.43	−8.13	−7.82	−7.51	−5.86	−4.07	−2.13
3.000	−7.26	−6.99	−6.73	−6.46	−5.04	−3.50	−1.83
3.125	−6.07	−5.85	−5.63	−5.40	−4.21	−2.92	−1.53
3.250	−4.87	−4.70	−4.52	−4.33	−3.38	−2.34	−1.22
3.375	−3.67	−3.53	−3.40	−3.26	−2.54	−1.76	−0.92
3.500	−2.45	−2.36	−2.27	−2.18	−1.70	−1.17	−0.61
3.625	−1.23	−1.19	−1.14	−1.09	−0.85	−0.59	−0.31
3.750	0.00	0.00	0.00	0.00	0.00	0.00	0.00
3.875	1.24	1.19	1.15	1.10	0.85	0.59	0.31
4.000	2.49	2.40	2.30	2.21	1.71	1.18	0.62
4.125	3.74	3.61	3.46	3.32	2.58	1.78	0.92
4.250	5.01	4.82	4.63	4.44	3.45	2.37	1.23
4.375	6.28	6.05	5.81	5.57	4.32	2.97	1.54
4.500	7.56	7.28	7.00	6.71	5.19	3.57	1.85
4.625	8.85	8.52	8.19	7.85	6.07	4.18	2.16
4.750	10.15	9.77	9.39	9.00	6.96	4.78	2.47
4.875	11.46	11.03	10.59	10.15	7.85	5.39	2.79
5.000	12.77	12.29	11.80	11.31	8.74	6.00	3.10
5.125	14.09	13.56	13.02	12.48	9.64	6.61	3.41
5.250	15.42	14.84	14.25	13.65	10.54	7.23	3.73
5.375	16.76	16.13	15.49	14.84	11.45	7.84	4.04
5.500	18.10	17.42	16.73	16.02	12.36	8.46	4.36
5.625	19.46	18.72	17.98	17.22	13.27	9.08	4.67
5.750	20.82	20.03	19.23	18.42	14.19	9.70	4.99
5.875	22.19	21.35	20.49	19.62	15.11	10.33	5.30
6.000	23.57	22.67	21.76	20.84	16.04	10.95	5.62
6.125	24.95	24.00	23.04	22.06	16.97	11.58	5.94
6.250	26.34	25.34	24.32	23.28	17.90	12.21	6.26
6.375	27.74	26.68	25.61	24.51	18.84	12.84	6.58
6.500	29.15	28.03	26.90	25.75	19.79	13.48	6.90
6.625	30.56	29.39	28.20	27.00	20.73	14.12	7.22
6.750	31.98	30.76	29.51	28.25	21.68	14.75	7.54
6.875	33.41	32.13	30.83	29.50	22.64	15.39	7.86
7.000	34.85	33.51	32.15	30.77	23.60	16.04	8.18
7.125	36.29	34.89	33.47	32.03	24.56	16.68	8.50
7.250	37.74	36.29	34.81	33.31	25.53	17.33	8.83
7.375	39.20	37.68	36.15	34.59	26.50	17.98	9.15
7.500	40.66	39.09	37.49	35.88	27.47	18.63	9.47
7.625	42.13	40.50	38.85	37.17	28.45	19.28	9.80
7.750	43.61	41.92	40.21	38.47	29.43	19.94	10.12
7.875	45.10	43.35	41.57	39.77	30.42	20.59	10.45
8.000	46.59	44.78	42.94	41.08	31.41	21.25	10.78
8.125	48.08	46.21	44.32	42.39	32.41	21.91	11.10
8.250	49.59	47.66	45.70	43.71	33.40	22.58	11.43
8.375	51.10	49.11	47.09	45.04	34.41	23.24	11.76
8.500	52.61	50.56	48.48	46.37	35.41	23.91	12.09
8.625	54.14	52.03	49.88	47.71	36.42	24.58	12.42
8.750	55.67	53.50	51.29	49.05	37.43	25.25	12.75
8.875	57.20	54.97	52.70	50.40	38.45	25.92	13.08
9.000	58.75	56.45	54.12	51.75	39.47	26.60	13.41

4%
Old Rate

Payment Adjustments
(As % of Old Payment)

NEW RATE (%)	YEARS REMAINING IN TERM						
	30	29	28	27	26	25	24
2.000	−22.58	−22.03	−21.46	−20.89	−20.30	−19.70	−19.09
2.125	−21.26	−20.74	−20.21	−19.66	−19.11	−18.54	−17.96
2.250	−19.93	−19.44	−18.94	−18.43	−17.91	−17.37	−16.83
2.375	−18.59	−18.13	−17.66	−17.18	−16.69	−16.20	−15.69
2.500	−17.24	−16.81	−16.37	−15.93	−15.47	−15.01	−14.54
2.625	−15.87	−15.47	−15.07	−14.66	−14.24	−13.81	−13.37
2.750	−14.49	−14.13	−13.76	−13.38	−13.00	−12.60	−12.20
2.875	−13.10	−12.77	−12.43	−12.09	−11.74	−11.39	−11.02
3.000	−11.69	−11.40	−11.10	−10.79	−10.48	−10.16	−9.84
3.125	−10.27	−10.01	−9.75	−9.48	−9.20	−8.92	−8.64
3.250	−8.84	−8.62	−8.39	−8.16	−7.92	−7.68	−7.43
3.375	−7.40	−7.21	−7.02	−6.82	−6.62	−6.42	−6.21
3.500	−5.94	−5.79	−5.64	−5.48	−5.32	−5.16	−4.99
3.625	−4.47	−4.36	−4.24	−4.13	−4.00	−3.88	−3.76
3.750	−3.00	−2.92	−2.84	−2.76	−2.68	−2.60	−2.51
3.875	−1.50	−1.46	−1.43	−1.39	−1.34	−1.30	−1.26
4.000	0.00	0.00	0.00	0.00	0.00	0.00	0.00
4.125	1.52	1.48	1.44	1.40	1.35	1.31	1.27
4.250	3.04	2.96	2.88	2.80	2.72	2.63	2.55
4.375	4.58	4.46	4.34	4.22	4.09	3.96	3.83
4.500	6.13	5.97	5.81	5.64	5.48	5.30	5.13
4.625	7.69	7.49	7.29	7.08	6.87	6.65	6.43
4.750	9.26	9.02	8.78	8.53	8.27	8.01	7.75
4.875	10.85	10.56	10.28	9.98	9.68	9.38	9.07
5.000	12.44	12.12	11.79	11.45	11.10	10.75	10.40
5.125	14.05	13.68	13.30	12.92	12.53	12.14	11.73
5.250	15.67	15.25	14.83	14.41	13.97	13.53	13.08
5.375	17.29	16.84	16.37	15.90	15.42	14.93	14.43
5.500	18.93	18.43	17.92	17.40	16.88	16.34	15.79
5.625	20.58	20.03	19.48	18.92	18.34	17.76	17.16
5.750	22.24	21.65	21.05	20.44	19.82	19.19	18.54
5.875	23.90	23.27	22.63	21.97	21.30	20.62	19.93
6.000	25.58	24.90	24.21	23.51	22.79	22.06	21.32
6.125	27.27	26.55	25.81	25.06	24.29	23.52	22.72
6.250	28.97	28.20	27.42	26.62	25.80	24.98	24.13
6.375	30.68	29.86	29.03	28.18	27.32	26.44	25.55
6.500	32.39	31.53	30.65	29.76	28.85	27.92	26.98
6.625	34.12	33.21	32.29	31.34	30.38	29.40	28.41
6.750	35.86	34.90	33.93	32.94	31.92	30.89	29.85
6.875	37.60	36.60	35.58	34.54	33.47	32.39	31.29
7.000	39.36	38.31	37.24	36.14	35.03	33.90	32.75
7.125	41.12	40.02	38.90	37.76	36.60	35.42	34.21
7.250	42.89	41.75	40.58	39.39	38.17	36.94	35.68
7.375	44.67	43.48	42.26	41.02	39.76	38.47	37.16
7.500	46.46	45.22	43.95	42.66	41.34	40.00	38.64
7.625	48.26	46.97	45.65	44.31	42.94	41.55	40.13
7.750	50.06	48.72	47.36	45.97	44.55	43.10	41.63
7.875	51.87	50.49	49.07	47.63	46.16	44.66	43.13
8.000	53.70	52.26	50.80	49.30	47.78	46.22	44.64
8.125	55.52	54.04	52.53	50.98	49.40	47.79	46.16
8.250	57.36	55.83	54.26	52.67	51.04	49.37	47.68
8.375	59.21	57.62	56.01	54.36	52.68	50.96	49.21
8.500	61.06	59.43	57.76	56.06	54.32	52.55	50.75
8.625	62.92	61.24	59.52	57.77	55.98	54.15	52.29
8.750	64.78	63.05	61.29	59.48	57.64	55.76	53.84
8.875	66.66	64.88	63.06	61.20	59.30	57.37	55.40
9.000	68.54	66.71	64.84	62.93	60.98	58.99	56.96

Payment Adjustments

(As % of Old Payment)

4%
Old Rate

NEW RATE (%)	YEARS REMAINING IN TERM						
	23	22	21	20	15	10	5
2.000	−18.47	−17.83	−17.18	−16.52	−13.00	−9.12	−4.83
2.125	−17.38	−16.78	−16.16	−15.54	−12.22	−8.56	−4.53
2.250	−16.28	−15.71	−15.14	−14.55	−11.44	−8.01	−4.23
2.375	−15.17	−14.64	−14.10	−13.56	−10.65	−7.45	−3.93
2.500	−14.05	−13.56	−13.06	−12.55	−9.86	−6.89	−3.63
2.625	−12.93	−12.48	−12.02	−11.55	−9.06	−6.33	−3.33
2.750	−11.80	−11.38	−10.96	−10.53	−8.26	−5.76	−3.03
2.875	−10.66	−10.28	−9.90	−9.51	−7.45	−5.20	−2.73
3.000	−9.51	−9.17	−8.83	−8.48	−6.64	−4.63	−2.43
3.125	−8.35	−8.05	−7.75	−7.44	−5.82	−4.06	−2.13
3.250	−7.18	−6.92	−6.66	−6.40	−5.00	−3.48	−1.83
3.375	−6.00	−5.79	−5.57	−5.35	−4.18	−2.91	−1.52
3.500	−4.82	−4.65	−4.47	−4.29	−3.35	−2.33	−1.22
3.625	−3.63	−3.50	−3.37	−3.23	−2.52	−1.75	−0.92
3.750	−2.43	−2.34	−2.25	−2.16	−1.69	−1.17	−0.61
3.875	−1.22	−1.17	−1.13	−1.08	−0.84	−0.59	−0.31
4.000	0.00	0.00	0.00	0.00	0.00	0.00	0.00
4.125	1.23	1.18	1.14	1.09	0.85	0.59	0.31
4.250	2.46	2.37	2.28	2.19	1.70	1.18	0.61
4.375	3.70	3.57	3.43	3.29	2.56	1.77	0.92
4.500	4.95	4.77	4.59	4.40	3.42	2.36	1.23
4.625	6.21	5.98	5.75	5.52	4.29	2.96	1.54
4.750	7.48	7.20	6.92	6.64	5.16	3.56	1.85
4.875	8.75	8.43	8.10	7.77	6.03	4.16	2.16
5.000	10.03	9.66	9.29	8.91	6.91	4.76	2.47
5.125	11.32	10.91	10.48	10.05	7.79	5.37	2.78
5.250	12.62	12.15	11.68	11.20	8.68	5.97	3.09
5.375	13.93	13.41	12.89	12.35	9.57	6.58	3.40
5.500	15.24	14.67	14.10	13.52	10.46	7.19	3.72
5.625	16.56	15.94	15.32	14.68	11.36	7.80	4.03
5.750	17.89	17.22	16.55	15.86	12.26	8.42	4.35
5.875	19.22	18.51	17.78	17.04	13.17	9.04	4.66
6.000	20.57	19.80	19.02	18.23	14.08	9.66	4.98
6.125	21.92	21.10	20.27	19.42	15.00	10.28	5.29
6.250	23.28	22.40	21.52	20.62	15.92	10.90	5.61
6.375	24.64	23.72	22.78	21.82	16.84	11.52	5.92
6.500	26.01	25.04	24.04	23.04	17.77	12.15	6.24
6.625	27.39	26.36	25.32	24.25	18.70	12.78	6.56
6.750	28.78	27.70	26.60	25.48	19.63	13.41	6.88
6.875	30.18	29.04	27.88	26.71	20.57	14.05	7.20
7.000	31.58	30.38	29.17	27.94	21.51	14.68	7.52
7.125	32.98	31.74	30.47	29.18	22.46	15.32	7.84
7.250	34.40	33.10	31.77	30.43	23.41	15.96	8.16
7.375	35.82	34.46	33.08	31.68	24.37	16.60	8.48
7.500	37.25	35.84	34.40	32.94	25.32	17.24	8.80
7.625	38.68	37.21	35.72	34.20	26.29	17.89	9.13
7.750	40.13	38.60	37.05	35.47	27.25	18.53	9.45
7.875	41.57	39.99	38.38	36.75	28.22	19.18	9.77
8.000	43.03	41.39	39.72	38.03	29.20	19.84	10.10
8.125	44.49	42.79	41.07	39.32	30.17	20.49	10.42
8.250	45.96	44.20	42.42	40.61	31.16	21.14	10.75
8.375	47.43	45.62	43.78	41.91	32.14	21.80	11.08
8.500	48.91	47.04	45.14	43.21	33.13	22.46	11.40
8.625	50.40	48.47	46.51	44.52	34.12	23.12	11.73
8.750	51.89	49.90	47.88	45.83	35.12	23.79	12.06
8.875	53.39	51.34	49.26	47.15	36.12	24.45	12.39
9.000	54.89	52.79	50.65	48.47	37.12	25.12	12.72

4¼%
Old Rate

Payment Adjustments
(As % of Old Payment)

NEW RATE (%)	YEARS REMAINING IN TERM						
	30	29	28	27	26	25	24
2.000	−24.86	−24.27	−23.66	−23.04	−22.41	−21.76	−21.10
2.125	−23.59	−23.02	−22.44	−21.85	−21.25	−20.63	−20.00
2.250	−22.30	−21.76	−21.21	−20.65	−20.08	−19.49	−18.90
2.375	−21.00	−20.49	−19.97	−19.44	−18.90	−18.35	−17.78
2.500	−19.68	−19.20	−18.72	−18.22	−17.71	−17.19	−16.66
2.625	−18.35	−17.91	−17.45	−16.98	−16.51	−16.02	−15.53
2.750	−17.01	−16.60	−16.17	−15.74	−15.30	−14.85	−14.39
2.875	−15.66	−15.28	−14.89	−14.49	−14.08	−13.66	−13.23
3.000	−14.30	−13.95	−13.59	−13.22	−12.85	−12.46	−12.08
3.125	−12.92	−12.60	−12.28	−11.94	−11.61	−11.26	−10.91
3.250	−11.53	−11.25	−10.96	−10.66	−10.36	−10.05	−9.73
3.375	−10.13	−9.88	−9.62	−9.36	−9.09	−8.82	−8.54
3.500	−8.72	−8.50	−8.28	−8.06	−7.82	−7.59	−7.35
3.625	−7.30	−7.11	−6.93	−6.74	−6.54	−6.35	−6.15
3.750	−5.86	−5.71	−5.56	−5.41	−5.25	−5.10	−4.93
3.875	−4.41	−4.30	−4.19	−4.07	−3.96	−3.84	−3.71
4.000	−2.95	−2.88	−2.80	−2.73	−2.65	−2.57	−2.48
4.125	−1.48	−1.44	−1.41	−1.37	−1.33	−1.29	−1.25
4.250	0.00	0.00	0.00	0.00	0.00	0.00	0.00
4.375	1.49	1.46	1.42	1.38	1.34	1.30	1.25
4.500	3.00	2.92	2.84	2.76	2.68	2.60	2.52
4.625	4.51	4.40	4.28	4.16	4.04	3.92	3.79
4.750	6.04	5.89	5.73	5.57	5.40	5.24	5.07
4.875	7.58	7.38	7.19	6.98	6.78	6.57	6.36
5.000	9.12	8.89	8.65	8.41	8.16	7.91	7.65
5.125	10.68	10.41	10.13	9.84	9.55	9.26	8.96
5.250	12.25	11.94	11.62	11.29	10.96	10.62	10.27
5.375	13.83	13.47	13.11	12.74	12.37	11.98	11.59
5.500	15.42	15.02	14.62	14.20	13.78	13.36	12.92
5.625	17.02	16.58	16.13	15.68	15.21	14.74	14.25
5.750	18.63	18.15	17.66	17.16	16.65	16.13	15.60
5.875	20.25	19.72	19.19	18.65	18.09	17.53	16.95
6.000	21.87	21.31	20.73	20.14	19.54	18.93	18.31
6.125	23.51	22.91	22.28	21.65	21.01	20.35	19.68
6.250	25.16	24.51	23.85	23.17	22.47	21.77	21.05
6.375	26.82	26.12	25.41	24.69	23.95	23.20	22.43
6.500	28.48	27.75	26.99	26.22	25.44	24.64	23.82
6.625	30.16	29.38	28.58	27.76	26.93	26.08	25.22
6.750	31.84	31.02	30.17	29.31	28.43	27.54	26.62
6.875	33.54	32.67	31.78	30.87	29.94	29.00	28.03
7.000	35.24	34.33	33.39	32.43	31.46	30.47	29.45
7.125	36.95	35.99	35.01	34.01	32.98	31.94	30.88
7.250	38.67	37.67	36.64	35.59	34.52	33.42	32.31
7.375	40.40	39.35	38.27	37.18	36.06	34.91	33.75
7.500	42.13	41.04	39.92	38.77	37.60	36.41	35.19
7.625	43.88	42.74	41.57	40.38	39.16	37.92	36.65
7.750	45.63	44.44	43.23	41.99	40.72	39.43	38.11
7.875	47.39	46.16	44.90	43.61	42.29	40.95	39.57
8.000	49.16	47.88	46.57	45.23	43.87	42.47	41.05
8.125	50.93	49.61	48.25	46.86	45.45	44.00	42.53
8.250	52.72	51.34	49.94	48.50	47.04	45.54	44.01
8.375	54.51	53.09	51.64	50.15	48.64	47.09	45.50
8.500	56.30	54.84	53.34	51.81	50.24	48.64	47.00
8.625	58.11	56.60	55.05	53.47	51.85	50.20	48.51
8.750	59.92	58.36	56.77	55.13	53.47	51.76	50.02
8.875	61.74	60.13	58.49	56.81	55.09	53.33	51.54
9.000	63.56	61.91	60.22	58.49	56.72	54.91	53.06

Payment Adjustments
(As % of Old Payment)

$4^1/4\%$ Old Rate

NEW RATE (%)	YEARS REMAINING IN TERM						
	23	22	21	20	15	10	5
2.000	−20.42	−19.73	−19.03	−18.31	−14.46	−10.18	−5.41
2.125	−19.36	−18.70	−18.03	−17.35	−13.69	−9.63	−5.11
2.250	−18.29	−17.66	−17.03	−16.38	−12.92	−9.08	−4.82
2.375	−17.21	−16.62	−16.02	−15.41	−12.14	−8.53	−4.52
2.500	−16.12	−15.57	−15.00	−14.43	−11.36	−7.97	−4.22
2.625	−15.02	−14.50	−13.98	−13.44	−10.58	−7.42	−3.92
2.750	−13.92	−13.44	−12.95	−12.45	−9.79	−6.86	−3.63
2.875	−12.80	−12.36	−11.91	−11.45	−9.00	−6.30	−3.33
3.000	−11.68	−11.27	−10.86	−10.44	−8.20	−5.74	−3.03
3.125	−10.55	−10.18	−9.81	−9.42	−7.40	−5.17	−2.73
3.250	−9.41	−9.08	−8.75	−8.40	−6.59	−4.61	−2.43
3.375	−8.26	−7.97	−7.68	−7.38	−5.78	−4.04	−2.12
3.500	−7.11	−6.86	−6.60	−6.34	−4.97	−3.47	−1.82
3.625	−5.94	−5.73	−5.52	−5.30	−4.15	−2.89	−1.52
3.750	−4.77	−4.60	−4.43	−4.25	−3.33	−2.32	−1.22
3.875	−3.59	−3.46	−3.33	−3.20	−2.50	−1.74	−0.91
4.000	−2.40	−2.32	−2.23	−2.14	−1.67	−1.16	−0.61
4.125	−1.20	−1.16	−1.12	−1.07	−0.84	−0.58	−0.31
4.250	0.00	0.00	0.00	0.00	0.00	0.00	0.00
4.375	1.21	1.17	1.12	1.08	0.84	0.59	0.31
4.500	2.43	2.35	2.26	2.17	1.69	1.17	0.61
4.625	3.66	3.53	3.40	3.26	2.54	1.76	0.92
4.750	4.90	4.72	4.54	4.36	3.40	2.35	1.23
4.875	6.14	5.92	5.69	5.46	4.26	2.95	1.54
5.000	7.39	7.12	6.85	6.58	5.12	3.54	1.84
5.125	8.65	8.34	8.02	7.69	5.99	4.14	2.15
5.250	9.92	9.56	9.19	8.82	6.86	4.74	2.46
5.375	11.19	10.78	10.37	9.95	7.73	5.34	2.77
5.500	12.47	12.02	11.56	11.09	8.61	5.94	3.08
5.625	13.76	13.26	12.75	12.23	9.50	6.55	3.40
5.750	15.06	14.51	13.95	13.38	10.39	7.16	3.71
5.875	16.36	15.76	15.15	14.53	11.28	7.77	4.02
6.000	17.67	17.03	16.37	15.70	12.17	8.38	4.33
6.125	18.99	18.29	17.59	16.86	13.07	8.99	4.65
6.250	20.32	19.57	18.81	18.04	13.97	9.61	4.96
6.375	21.65	20.85	20.04	19.22	14.88	10.23	5.28
6.500	22.99	22.14	21.28	20.40	15.80	10.85	5.59
6.625	24.34	23.44	22.52	21.59	16.71	11.47	5.91
6.750	25.69	24.74	23.77	22.79	17.63	12.09	6.23
6.875	27.05	26.05	25.03	23.99	18.55	12.72	6.54
7.000	28.42	27.36	26.29	25.20	19.48	13.35	6.86
7.125	29.79	28.69	27.56	26.42	20.41	13.98	7.18
7.250	31.17	30.02	28.84	27.64	21.35	14.61	7.50
7.375	32.56	31.35	30.12	28.86	22.28	15.24	7.82
7.500	33.95	32.69	31.40	30.10	23.23	15.88	8.14
7.625	35.35	34.04	32.70	31.33	24.17	16.52	8.46
7.750	36.76	35.39	34.00	32.57	25.12	17.15	8.78
7.875	38.18	36.75	35.30	33.82	26.08	17.80	9.10
8.000	39.60	38.12	36.61	35.08	27.03	18.44	9.43
8.125	41.02	39.49	37.93	36.34	28.00	19.09	9.75
8.250	42.45	40.86	39.25	37.60	28.96	19.73	10.07
8.375	43.89	42.25	40.57	38.87	29.93	20.38	10.40
8.500	45.34	43.64	41.91	40.14	30.90	21.04	10.72
8.625	46.79	45.03	43.24	41.42	31.88	21.69	11.05
8.750	48.24	46.43	44.59	42.71	32.86	22.34	11.37
8.875	49.71	47.84	45.94	44.00	33.84	23.00	11.70
9.000	51.17	49.25	47.29	45.30	34.83	23.66	12.03

4¹/₂%
Old Rate

Payment Adjustments
(As % of Old Payment)

NEW RATE (%)	YEARS REMAINING IN TERM						
	30	29	28	27	26	25	24
2.000	−27.05	−26.42	−25.77	−25.11	−24.44	−23.74	−23.04
2.125	−25.81	−25.21	−24.59	−23.95	−23.31	−22.64	−21.97
2.250	−24.56	−23.98	−23.39	−22.79	−22.17	−21.54	−20.89
2.375	−23.30	−22.74	−22.18	−21.61	−21.02	−20.42	−19.80
2.500	−22.02	−21.50	−20.96	−20.42	−19.86	−19.29	−18.71
2.625	−20.73	−20.24	−19.73	−19.22	−18.69	−18.15	−17.60
2.750	−19.43	−18.97	−18.49	−18.01	−17.51	−17.01	−16.49
2.875	−18.12	−17.68	−17.24	−16.79	−16.32	−15.85	−15.37
3.000	−16.79	−16.39	−15.98	−15.55	−15.12	−14.68	−14.23
3.125	−15.46	−15.08	−14.70	−14.31	−13.92	−13.51	−13.10
3.250	−14.11	−13.77	−13.42	−13.06	−12.70	−12.33	−11.95
3.375	−12.75	−12.44	−12.12	−11.80	−11.47	−11.13	−10.79
3.500	−11.38	−11.10	−10.82	−10.53	−10.23	−9.93	−9.63
3.625	−9.99	−9.75	−9.50	−9.25	−8.99	−8.72	−8.45
3.750	−8.60	−8.39	−8.17	−7.96	−7.73	−7.50	−7.27
3.875	−7.19	−7.02	−6.84	−6.65	−6.47	−6.27	−6.08
4.000	−5.78	−5.63	−5.49	−5.34	−5.19	−5.04	−4.88
4.125	−4.35	−4.24	−4.13	−4.02	−3.91	−3.79	−3.67
4.250	−2.91	−2.84	−2.77	−2.69	−2.61	−2.54	−2.46
4.375	−1.46	−1.42	−1.39	−1.35	−1.31	−1.27	−1.23
4.500	0.00	0.00	0.00	0.00	0.00	0.00	0.00
4.625	1.47	1.43	1.40	1.36	1.32	1.28	1.24
4.750	2.95	2.88	2.80	2.73	2.65	2.57	2.49
4.875	4.45	4.33	4.22	4.11	3.99	3.87	3.74
5.000	5.95	5.80	5.65	5.49	5.34	5.17	5.01
5.125	7.46	7.27	7.08	6.89	6.69	6.49	6.28
5.250	8.98	8.76	8.53	8.29	8.06	7.81	7.56
5.375	10.52	10.25	9.98	9.71	9.43	9.14	8.85
5.500	12.06	11.76	11.45	11.13	10.81	10.48	10.14
5.625	13.61	13.27	12.92	12.56	12.20	11.83	11.45
5.750	15.17	14.79	14.40	14.01	13.60	13.18	12.76
5.875	16.75	16.33	15.89	15.45	15.00	14.55	14.08
6.000	18.33	17.87	17.39	16.91	16.42	15.92	15.40
6.125	19.92	19.42	18.90	18.38	17.84	17.30	16.74
6.250	21.52	20.98	20.42	19.85	19.27	18.68	18.08
6.375	23.13	22.54	21.95	21.34	20.71	20.08	19.42
6.500	24.75	24.12	23.48	22.83	22.16	21.48	20.78
6.625	26.37	25.71	25.02	24.33	23.61	22.89	22.14
6.750	28.01	27.30	26.57	25.83	25.08	24.30	23.51
6.875	29.65	28.90	28.13	27.35	26.55	25.73	24.89
7.000	31.30	30.51	29.70	28.87	28.02	27.16	26.27
7.125	32.97	32.13	31.28	30.40	29.51	28.60	27.66
7.250	34.64	33.76	32.86	31.94	31.00	30.04	29.06
7.375	36.31	35.39	34.45	33.49	32.50	31.49	30.46
7.500	38.00	37.03	36.05	35.04	34.01	32.95	31.87
7.625	39.69	38.68	37.65	36.60	35.52	34.42	33.29
7.750	41.39	40.34	39.27	38.17	37.04	35.89	34.72
7.875	43.10	42.01	40.89	39.74	38.57	37.37	36.15
8.000	44.82	43.68	42.52	41.32	40.11	38.86	37.58
8.125	46.54	45.36	44.15	42.91	41.65	40.35	39.03
8.250	48.27	47.05	45.79	44.51	43.20	41.85	40.48
8.375	50.01	48.74	47.44	46.11	44.75	43.36	41.93
8.500	51.75	50.44	49.10	47.72	46.31	44.87	43.39
8.625	53.51	52.15	50.76	49.34	47.88	46.39	44.86
8.750	55.26	53.87	52.43	50.96	49.45	47.91	46.34
8.875	57.03	55.59	54.11	52.59	51.03	49.44	47.82
9.000	58.80	57.31	55.79	54.22	52.62	50.98	49.30

Payment Adjustments $4^1/_2\%$
(As % of Old Payment)
Old Rate

NEW RATE (%)	YEARS REMAINING IN TERM						
	23	22	21	20	15	10	5
2.000	−22.31	−21.57	−20.81	−20.04	−15.88	−11.22	−5.98
2.125	−21.27	−20.57	−19.84	−19.10	−15.13	−10.68	−5.69
2.250	−20.23	−19.55	−18.86	−18.15	−14.37	−10.13	−5.39
2.375	−19.17	−18.53	−17.87	−17.20	−13.60	−9.59	−5.10
2.500	−18.11	−17.50	−16.88	−16.24	−12.84	−9.04	−4.80
2.625	−17.04	−16.46	−15.88	−15.27	−12.07	−8.49	−4.51
2.750	−15.96	−15.42	−14.87	−14.30	−11.29	−7.94	−4.21
2.875	−14.87	−14.37	−13.85	−13.32	−10.51	−7.38	−3.91
3.000	−13.78	−13.31	−12.83	−12.34	−9.73	−6.83	−3.62
3.125	−12.67	−12.24	−11.80	−11.34	−8.94	−6.27	−3.32
3.250	−11.56	−11.16	−10.76	−10.35	−8.15	−5.71	−3.02
3.375	−10.44	−10.08	−9.71	−9.34	−7.35	−5.15	−2.72
3.500	−9.31	−8.99	−8.66	−8.33	−6.55	−4.59	−2.42
3.625	−8.17	−7.89	−7.60	−7.31	−5.75	−4.02	−2.12
3.750	−7.03	−6.79	−6.54	−6.28	−4.94	−3.45	−1.82
3.875	−5.88	−5.67	−5.47	−5.25	−4.12	−2.88	−1.52
4.000	−4.72	−4.55	−4.39	−4.22	−3.31	−2.31	−1.21
4.125	−3.55	−3.43	−3.30	−3.17	−2.49	−1.74	−0.91
4.250	−2.37	−2.29	−2.21	−2.12	−1.66	−1.16	−0.61
4.375	−1.19	−1.15	−1.11	−1.06	−0.83	−0.58	−0.30
4.500	0.00	0.00	0.00	0.00	0.00	0.00	0.00
4.625	1.20	1.16	1.11	1.07	0.84	0.58	0.31
4.750	2.41	2.32	2.23	2.15	1.68	1.17	0.61
4.875	3.62	3.49	3.36	3.23	2.52	1.75	0.92
5.000	4.84	4.67	4.49	4.32	3.37	2.34	1.22
5.125	6.07	5.85	5.63	5.41	4.23	2.93	1.53
5.250	7.31	7.05	6.78	6.51	5.08	3.53	1.84
5.375	8.55	8.25	7.94	7.62	5.94	4.12	2.15
5.500	9.80	9.45	9.09	8.73	6.81	4.72	2.46
5.625	11.06	10.66	10.26	9.85	7.68	5.31	2.77
5.750	12.33	11.88	11.43	10.98	8.55	5.92	3.08
5.875	13.60	13.11	12.61	12.11	9.43	6.52	3.39
6.000	14.88	14.34	13.80	13.24	10.31	7.12	3.70
6.125	16.17	15.58	14.99	14.39	11.19	7.73	4.01
6.250	17.46	16.83	16.19	15.53	12.08	8.34	4.32
6.375	18.76	18.08	17.39	16.69	12.97	8.95	4.64
6.500	20.07	19.34	18.60	17.85	13.87	9.56	4.95
6.625	21.38	20.61	19.82	19.02	14.77	10.18	5.27
6.750	22.70	21.88	21.04	20.19	15.68	10.79	5.58
6.875	24.03	23.16	22.27	21.36	16.58	11.41	5.90
7.000	25.37	24.45	23.51	22.55	17.49	12.03	6.21
7.125	26.71	25.74	24.75	23.74	18.41	12.65	6.53
7.250	28.06	27.04	25.99	24.93	19.33	13.28	6.85
7.375	29.41	28.34	27.25	26.13	20.25	13.91	7.16
7.500	30.77	29.65	28.50	27.34	21.18	14.53	7.48
7.625	32.14	30.97	29.77	28.55	22.11	15.17	7.80
7.750	33.51	32.29	31.04	29.76	23.04	15.80	8.12
7.875	34.89	33.62	32.31	30.99	23.98	16.43	8.44
8.000	36.28	34.95	33.59	32.21	24.92	17.07	8.76
8.125	37.67	36.29	34.88	33.44	25.87	17.71	9.08
8.250	39.07	37.64	36.17	34.68	26.82	18.35	9.40
8.375	40.48	38.99	37.47	35.92	27.77	18.99	9.73
8.500	41.89	40.35	38.77	37.17	28.73	19.63	10.05
8.625	43.30	41.71	40.08	38.43	29.68	20.28	10.37
8.750	44.72	43.08	41.40	39.68	30.65	20.93	10.70
8.875	46.15	44.45	42.72	40.95	31.61	21.58	11.02
9.000	47.58	45.83	44.04	42.22	32.59	22.23	11.35

4³/₄%
Old Rate

Payment Adjustments
(As % of Old Payment)

NEW RATE (%)	YEARS REMAINING IN TERM						
	30	29	28	27	26	25	24
2.000	−29.14	−28.48	−27.80	−27.10	−26.39	−25.65	−24.91
2.125	−27.94	−27.30	−26.64	−25.97	−25.29	−24.58	−23.86
2.250	−26.72	−26.11	−25.48	−24.84	−24.18	−23.50	−22.81
2.375	−25.50	−24.91	−24.31	−23.69	−23.06	−22.41	−21.75
2.500	−24.26	−23.69	−23.12	−22.53	−21.93	−21.31	−20.68
2.625	−23.00	−22.47	−21.92	−21.36	−20.79	−20.20	−19.60
2.750	−21.74	−21.23	−20.72	−20.18	−19.64	−19.08	−18.52
2.875	−20.46	−19.99	−19.50	−19.00	−18.48	−17.96	−17.42
3.000	−19.18	−18.73	−18.27	−17.80	−17.32	−16.82	−16.32
3.125	−17.88	−17.46	−17.03	−16.59	−16.14	−15.68	−15.21
3.250	−16.57	−16.18	−15.78	−15.37	−14.95	−14.52	−14.09
3.375	−15.25	−14.89	−14.52	−14.14	−13.76	−13.36	−12.96
3.500	−13.92	−13.59	−13.25	−12.90	−12.55	−12.19	−11.82
3.625	−12.57	−12.28	−11.97	−11.66	−11.34	−11.01	−10.67
3.750	−11.22	−10.95	−10.68	−10.40	−10.11	−9.82	−9.52
3.875	−9.86	−9.62	−9.38	−9.13	−8.88	−8.62	−8.36
4.000	−8.48	−8.28	−8.07	−7.86	−7.64	−7.42	−7.19
4.125	−7.09	−6.92	−6.75	−6.57	−6.39	−6.20	−6.01
4.250	−5.69	−5.56	−5.42	−5.27	−5.13	−4.98	−4.82
4.375	−4.29	−4.18	−4.08	−3.97	−3.86	−3.75	−3.63
4.500	−2.87	−2.80	−2.73	−2.66	−2.58	−2.51	−2.43
4.625	−1.44	−1.40	−1.37	−1.33	−1.30	−1.26	−1.22
4.750	0.00	0.00	0.00	0.00	0.00	0.00	0.00
4.875	1.45	1.41	1.38	1.34	1.30	1.27	1.23
5.000	2.91	2.84	2.77	2.69	2.62	2.54	2.46
5.125	4.38	4.27	4.16	4.05	3.94	3.82	3.70
5.250	5.86	5.71	5.57	5.42	5.27	5.11	4.95
5.375	7.35	7.17	6.98	6.80	6.60	6.41	6.21
5.500	8.85	8.63	8.41	8.18	7.95	7.71	7.47
5.625	10.35	10.10	9.84	9.58	9.30	9.03	8.74
5.750	11.87	11.58	11.28	10.98	10.67	10.35	10.02
5.875	13.40	13.07	12.73	12.39	12.04	11.68	11.31
6.000	14.93	14.57	14.19	13.81	13.41	13.01	12.60
6.125	16.48	16.07	15.66	15.24	14.80	14.36	13.90
6.250	18.03	17.59	17.14	16.67	16.19	15.71	15.21
6.375	19.60	19.11	18.62	18.11	17.60	17.07	16.52
6.500	21.17	20.65	20.11	19.57	19.01	18.43	17.85
6.625	22.75	22.19	21.61	21.02	20.42	19.81	19.18
6.750	24.34	23.74	23.12	22.49	21.85	21.19	20.51
6.875	25.93	25.29	24.64	23.97	23.28	22.58	21.86
7.000	27.54	26.86	26.16	25.45	24.72	23.97	23.21
7.125	29.15	28.43	27.70	26.94	26.17	25.37	24.56
7.250	30.77	30.01	29.24	28.44	27.62	26.78	25.93
7.375	32.40	31.60	30.78	29.94	29.08	28.20	27.30
7.500	34.04	33.20	32.34	31.45	30.55	29.62	28.67
7.625	35.68	34.80	33.90	32.97	32.02	31.05	30.06
7.750	37.34	36.41	35.47	34.50	33.50	32.49	31.44
7.875	39.00	38.03	37.05	36.03	34.99	33.93	32.84
8.000	40.66	39.66	38.63	37.57	36.49	35.38	34.24
8.125	42.34	41.29	40.22	39.12	37.99	36.83	35.65
8.250	44.02	42.93	41.82	40.67	39.50	38.30	37.06
8.375	45.71	44.58	43.42	42.23	41.01	39.76	38.49
8.500	47.40	46.23	45.03	43.80	42.53	41.24	39.91
8.625	49.10	47.89	46.65	45.37	44.06	42.72	41.34
8.750	50.81	49.56	48.27	46.95	45.60	44.21	42.78
8.875	52.53	51.23	49.90	48.54	47.14	45.70	44.23
9.000	54.25	52.91	51.54	50.13	48.68	47.20	45.68

Payment Adjustments 4³/₄%

(As % of Old Payment)   Old Rate

NEW RATE (%)	23	22	21	20	15	10	5
				YEARS REMAINING IN TERM			
2.000	−24.14	−23.35	−22.54	−21.72	−17.27	−12.24	−6.55
2.125	−23.12	−22.37	−21.59	−20.80	−16.53	−11.71	−6.26
2.250	−22.10	−21.38	−20.63	−19.87	−15.78	−11.17	−5.97
2.375	−21.07	−20.38	−19.67	−18.94	−15.03	−10.63	−5.68
2.500	−20.03	−19.37	−18.69	−18.00	−14.28	−10.09	−5.38
2.625	−18.99	−18.36	−17.71	−17.05	−13.52	−9.55	−5.09
2.750	−17.93	−17.34	−16.73	−16.10	−12.75	−9.00	−4.79
2.875	−16.87	−16.31	−15.73	−15.14	−11.99	−8.45	−4.50
3.000	−15.80	−15.27	−14.73	−14.18	−11.22	−7.90	−4.20
3.125	−14.72	−14.23	−13.72	−13.21	−10.44	−7.35	−3.91
3.250	−13.64	−13.18	−12.71	−12.23	−9.66	−6.80	−3.61
3.375	−12.54	−12.12	−11.69	−11.24	−8.88	−6.24	−3.31
3.500	−11.44	−11.05	−10.66	−10.25	−8.09	−5.69	−3.01
3.625	−10.33	−9.98	−9.62	−9.26	−7.30	−5.13	−2.71
3.750	−9.21	−8.90	−8.58	−8.25	−6.51	−4.57	−2.42
3.875	−8.09	−7.81	−7.53	−7.24	−5.71	−4.00	−2.12
4.000	−6.96	−6.72	−6.48	−6.23	−4.90	−3.44	−1.81
4.125	−5.82	−5.62	−5.41	−5.21	−4.10	−2.87	−1.51
4.250	−4.67	−4.51	−4.34	−4.18	−3.29	−2.30	−1.21
4.375	−3.51	−3.39	−3.27	−3.14	−2.47	−1.73	−0.91
4.500	−2.35	−2.27	−2.19	−2.10	−1.65	−1.15	−0.61
4.625	−1.18	−1.14	−1.10	−1.05	−0.83	−0.58	−0.30
4.750	0.00	0.00	0.00	0.00	0.00	0.00	0.00
4.875	1.19	1.14	1.10	1.06	0.83	0.58	0.30
5.000	2.38	2.30	2.21	2.12	1.67	1.16	0.61
5.125	3.58	3.45	3.33	3.20	2.51	1.75	0.92
5.250	4.79	4.62	4.45	4.27	3.35	2.33	1.22
5.375	6.00	5.79	5.58	5.36	4.20	2.92	1.53
5.500	7.22	6.97	6.71	6.45	5.05	3.51	1.84
5.625	8.45	8.15	7.85	7.54	5.90	4.10	2.14
5.750	9.69	9.35	9.00	8.64	6.76	4.69	2.45
5.875	10.93	10.55	10.15	9.75	7.62	5.29	2.76
6.000	12.18	11.75	11.31	10.86	8.49	5.89	3.07
6.125	13.44	12.96	12.48	11.98	9.36	6.49	3.38
6.250	14.70	14.18	13.65	13.11	10.23	7.09	3.69
6.375	15.97	15.41	14.83	14.24	11.11	7.69	4.00
6.500	17.25	16.64	16.01	15.37	11.99	8.30	4.31
6.625	18.53	17.87	17.20	16.52	12.88	8.91	4.63
6.750	19.82	19.12	18.40	17.66	13.77	9.52	4.94
6.875	21.12	20.37	19.60	18.82	14.66	10.13	5.25
7.000	22.42	21.62	20.81	19.97	15.56	10.74	5.57
7.125	23.73	22.89	22.02	21.14	16.46	11.36	5.88
7.250	25.05	24.15	23.24	22.31	17.36	11.97	6.20
7.375	26.37	25.43	24.47	23.48	18.27	12.59	6.51
7.500	27.70	26.71	25.70	24.66	19.18	13.21	6.83
7.625	29.04	28.00	26.93	25.85	20.09	13.84	7.15
7.750	30.38	29.29	28.17	27.04	21.01	14.46	7.46
7.875	31.73	30.59	29.42	28.23	21.94	15.09	7.78
8.000	33.08	31.89	30.68	29.44	22.86	15.72	8.10
8.125	34.44	33.20	31.93	30.64	23.79	16.35	8.42
8.250	35.80	34.52	33.20	31.85	24.72	16.98	8.74
8.375	37.18	35.84	34.47	33.07	25.66	17.62	9.06
8.500	38.55	37.16	35.74	34.29	26.60	18.25	9.38
8.625	39.94	38.50	37.02	35.52	27.54	18.89	9.70
8.750	41.32	39.83	38.31	36.75	28.49	19.53	10.02
8.875	42.72	41.18	39.60	37.99	29.44	20.17	10.35
9.000	44.12	42.52	40.89	39.23	30.40	20.82	10.67

5%
Old Rate

Payment Adjustments
(As % of Old Payment)

NEW RATE (%)	YEARS REMAINING IN TERM						
	30	29	28	27	26	25	24
2.000	-31.15	-30.45	-29.74	-29.01	-28.26	-27.49	-26.71
2.125	-29.98	-29.31	-28.62	-27.91	-27.19	-26.45	-25.69
2.250	-28.79	-28.15	-27.49	-26.81	-26.11	-25.39	-24.66
2.375	-27.60	-26.98	-26.34	-25.69	-25.02	-24.33	-23.63
2.500	-26.39	-25.80	-25.19	-24.56	-23.92	-23.26	-22.58
2.625	-25.18	-24.61	-24.02	-23.42	-22.81	-22.18	-21.53
2.750	-23.95	-23.41	-22.85	-22.28	-21.69	-21.09	-20.47
2.875	-22.71	-22.19	-21.66	-21.12	-20.56	-19.99	-19.40
3.000	-21.46	-20.97	-20.47	-19.95	-19.42	-18.88	-18.33
3.125	-20.20	-19.74	-19.26	-18.77	-18.27	-17.76	-17.24
3.250	-18.93	-18.49	-18.05	-17.59	-17.12	-16.64	-16.15
3.375	-17.64	-17.24	-16.82	-16.39	-15.95	-15.50	-15.04
3.500	-16.35	-15.97	-15.58	-15.19	-14.78	-14.36	-13.94
3.625	-15.05	-14.70	-14.34	-13.97	-13.60	-13.21	-12.82
3.750	-13.73	-13.41	-13.08	-12.75	-12.40	-12.05	-11.69
3.875	-12.40	-12.11	-11.82	-11.51	-11.20	-10.88	-10.56
4.000	-11.07	-10.81	-10.54	-10.27	-9.99	-9.71	-9.42
4.125	-9.72	-9.49	-9.26	-9.02	-8.77	-8.52	-8.27
4.250	-8.36	-8.16	-7.96	-7.76	-7.55	-7.33	-7.11
4.375	-6.99	-6.83	-6.66	-6.48	-6.31	-6.13	-5.94
4.500	-5.61	-5.48	-5.35	-5.21	-5.06	-4.92	-4.77
4.625	-4.22	-4.12	-4.02	-3.92	-3.81	-3.70	-3.59
4.750	-2.83	-2.76	-2.69	-2.62	-2.55	-2.47	-2.40
4.875	-1.42	-1.38	-1.35	-1.31	-1.28	-1.24	-1.20
5.000	0.00	0.00	0.00	0.00	0.00	0.00	0.00
5.125	1.43	1.40	1.36	1.32	1.29	1.25	1.21
5.250	2.87	2.80	2.73	2.66	2.58	2.51	2.43
5.375	4.31	4.21	4.11	4.00	3.89	3.77	3.66
5.500	5.77	5.63	5.49	5.35	5.20	5.05	4.89
5.625	7.23	7.06	6.89	6.70	6.52	6.33	6.13
5.750	8.71	8.50	8.29	8.07	7.85	7.62	7.38
5.875	10.19	9.95	9.70	9.44	9.18	8.91	8.64
6.000	11.69	11.41	11.12	10.83	10.52	10.22	9.90
6.125	13.19	12.87	12.55	12.22	11.88	11.53	11.17
6.250	14.70	14.35	13.98	13.61	13.23	12.84	12.44
6.375	16.22	15.83	15.43	15.02	14.60	14.17	13.73
6.500	17.74	17.32	16.88	16.43	15.97	15.50	15.02
6.625	19.28	18.82	18.34	17.85	17.35	16.84	16.32
6.750	20.82	20.32	19.81	19.28	18.74	18.19	17.62
6.875	22.37	21.84	21.28	20.72	20.14	19.54	18.93
7.000	23.93	23.36	22.77	22.16	21.54	20.90	20.25
7.125	25.50	24.89	24.26	23.61	22.95	22.27	21.57
7.250	27.08	26.43	25.76	25.07	24.37	23.64	22.90
7.375	28.66	27.97	27.26	26.54	25.79	25.03	24.24
7.500	30.25	29.52	28.78	28.01	27.22	26.41	25.58
7.625	31.85	31.08	30.30	29.49	28.66	27.81	26.93
7.750	33.46	32.65	31.82	30.97	30.10	29.21	28.29
7.875	35.07	34.23	33.36	32.47	31.55	30.62	29.65
8.000	36.69	35.81	34.90	33.97	33.01	32.03	31.02
8.125	38.31	37.39	36.45	35.47	34.47	33.45	32.40
8.250	39.95	38.99	38.00	36.99	35.94	34.87	33.78
8.375	41.59	40.59	39.56	38.51	37.42	36.31	35.16
8.500	43.24	42.20	41.13	40.03	38.90	37.74	36.55
8.625	44.89	43.81	42.70	41.56	40.39	39.19	37.95
8.750	46.55	45.43	44.28	43.10	41.89	40.64	39.36
8.875	48.22	47.06	45.87	44.64	43.39	42.09	40.77
9.000	49.89	48.69	47.46	46.19	44.89	43.55	42.18

Payment Adjustments
(As % of Old Payment)

5%
Old Rate

NEW RATE (%)	YEARS REMAINING IN TERM						
	23	22	21	20	15	10	5
2.000	−25.90	−25.07	−24.22	−23.34	−18.62	−13.25	−7.12
2.125	−24.91	−24.11	−23.29	−22.44	−17.89	−12.72	−6.83
2.250	−23.91	−23.14	−22.35	−21.54	−17.16	−12.19	−6.54
2.375	−22.90	−22.16	−21.40	−20.62	−16.42	−11.65	−6.24
2.500	−21.89	−21.18	−20.45	−19.70	−15.68	−11.12	−5.95
2.625	−20.87	−20.19	−19.49	−18.78	−14.93	−10.58	−5.66
2.750	−19.84	−19.19	−18.53	−17.85	−14.18	−10.04	−5.37
2.875	−18.80	−18.19	−17.56	−16.91	−13.43	−9.50	−5.08
3.000	−17.76	−17.17	−16.58	−15.96	−12.67	−8.96	−4.78
3.125	−16.70	−16.15	−15.59	−15.01	−11.91	−8.41	−4.48
3.250	−15.64	−15.13	−14.60	−14.05	−11.14	−7.87	−4.19
3.375	−14.57	−14.09	−13.60	−13.09	−10.37	−7.32	−3.89
3.500	−13.50	−13.05	−12.59	−12.12	−9.60	−6.77	−3.60
3.625	−12.41	−12.00	−11.58	−11.14	−8.82	−6.21	−3.30
3.750	−11.32	−10.94	−10.56	−10.16	−8.04	−5.66	−3.00
3.875	−10.22	−9.88	−9.53	−9.17	−7.25	−5.10	−2.70
4.000	−9.12	−8.81	−8.50	−8.18	−6.46	−4.54	−2.41
4.125	−8.00	−7.73	−7.46	−7.18	−5.67	−3.98	−2.11
4.250	−6.88	−6.65	−6.41	−6.17	−4.87	−3.42	−1.81
4.375	−5.75	−5.56	−5.36	−5.15	−4.07	−2.85	−1.51
4.500	−4.62	−4.46	−4.30	−4.14	−3.26	−2.29	−1.21
4.625	−3.47	−3.35	−3.23	−3.11	−2.45	−1.72	−0.90
4.750	−2.32	−2.24	−2.16	−2.08	−1.64	−1.15	−0.60
4.875	−1.16	−1.12	−1.08	−1.04	−0.82	−0.57	−0.30
5.000	0.00	0.00	0.00	0.00	0.00	0.00	0.00
5.125	1.17	1.13	1.09	1.05	0.83	0.58	0.31
5.250	2.35	2.27	2.19	2.11	1.66	1.16	0.61
5.375	3.54	3.42	3.29	3.17	2.49	1.74	0.92
5.500	4.73	4.57	4.40	4.23	3.33	2.32	1.22
5.625	5.93	5.73	5.52	5.31	4.17	2.91	1.53
5.750	7.14	6.90	6.64	6.39	5.01	3.49	1.83
5.875	8.35	8.07	7.77	7.47	5.86	4.08	2.14
6.000	9.58	9.24	8.91	8.56	6.71	4.67	2.45
6.125	10.80	10.43	10.05	9.65	7.57	5.27	2.76
6.250	12.04	11.62	11.19	10.75	8.43	5.86	3.06
6.375	13.28	12.82	12.35	11.86	9.29	6.46	3.37
6.500	14.53	14.02	13.50	12.97	10.16	7.06	3.68
6.625	15.78	15.23	14.67	14.09	11.03	7.66	3.99
6.750	17.04	16.45	15.84	15.22	11.90	8.26	4.31
6.875	18.31	17.67	17.01	16.34	12.78	8.86	4.62
7.000	19.58	18.90	18.19	17.48	13.66	9.47	4.93
7.125	20.86	20.13	19.38	18.62	14.55	10.08	5.24
7.250	22.15	21.37	20.58	19.76	15.44	10.69	5.56
7.375	23.44	22.62	21.77	20.91	16.33	11.30	5.87
7.500	24.74	23.87	22.98	22.07	17.23	11.91	6.18
7.625	26.04	25.12	24.19	23.23	18.13	12.53	6.50
7.750	27.35	26.39	25.40	24.40	19.03	13.15	6.82
7.875	28.67	27.66	26.62	25.57	19.94	13.77	7.13
8.000	29.99	28.93	27.85	26.74	20.85	14.39	7.45
8.125	31.32	30.21	29.08	27.92	21.76	15.01	7.77
8.250	32.65	31.50	30.32	29.11	22.68	15.64	8.08
8.375	33.99	32.79	31.56	30.30	23.60	16.27	8.40
8.500	35.34	34.09	32.81	31.50	24.53	16.90	8.72
8.625	36.69	35.39	34.06	32.70	25.46	17.53	9.04
8.750	38.04	36.70	35.32	33.91	26.39	18.16	9.36
8.875	39.40	38.01	36.58	35.12	27.32	18.80	9.68
9.000	40.77	39.33	37.85	36.33	28.26	19.43	10.00

5¼%
Old Rate

Payment Adjustments
(As % of Old Payment)

NEW RATE (%)	YEARS REMAINING IN TERM						
	30	29	28	27	26	25	24
2.250	-30.78	-30.10	-29.41	-28.70	-27.97	-27.22	-26.45
2.375	-29.62	-28.97	-28.30	-27.61	-26.91	-26.18	-25.44
2.500	-28.45	-27.82	-27.17	-26.51	-25.83	-25.14	-24.42
2.625	-27.26	-26.66	-26.04	-25.40	-24.75	-24.08	-23.39
2.750	-26.07	-25.49	-24.90	-24.29	-23.66	-23.02	-22.36
2.875	-24.87	-24.31	-23.74	-23.16	-22.56	-21.95	-21.32
3.000	-23.65	-23.12	-22.58	-22.02	-21.45	-20.87	-20.26
3.125	-22.42	-21.92	-21.41	-20.88	-20.33	-19.78	-19.20
3.250	-21.19	-20.71	-20.22	-19.72	-19.21	-18.68	-18.14
3.375	-19.94	-19.49	-19.03	-18.56	-18.07	-17.57	-17.06
3.500	-18.68	-18.26	-17.83	-17.38	-16.93	-16.46	-15.98
3.625	-17.41	-17.02	-16.61	-16.20	-15.77	-15.34	-14.89
3.750	-16.13	-15.77	-15.39	-15.01	-14.61	-14.20	-13.79
3.875	-14.84	-14.51	-14.16	-13.80	-13.44	-13.06	-12.68
4.000	-13.54	-13.23	-12.92	-12.59	-12.26	-11.92	-11.57
4.125	-12.23	-11.95	-11.67	-11.37	-11.07	-10.76	-10.44
4.250	-10.91	-10.66	-10.41	-10.14	-9.87	-9.60	-9.31
4.375	-9.58	-9.36	-9.14	-8.91	-8.67	-8.42	-8.17
4.500	-8.24	-8.05	-7.86	-7.66	-7.46	-7.25	-7.03
4.625	-6.89	-6.73	-6.57	-6.40	-6.23	-6.06	-5.88
4.750	-5.53	-5.41	-5.28	-5.14	-5.00	-4.86	-4.72
4.875	-4.16	-4.07	-3.97	-3.87	-3.76	-3.66	-3.55
5.000	-2.79	-2.72	-2.66	-2.59	-2.52	-2.45	-2.37
5.125	-1.40	-1.37	-1.33	-1.30	-1.26	-1.23	-1.19
5.250	0.00	0.00	0.00	0.00	0.00	0.00	0.00
5.375	1.41	1.37	1.34	1.31	1.27	1.23	1.20
5.500	2.82	2.76	2.69	2.62	2.55	2.48	2.40
5.625	4.25	4.15	4.05	3.94	3.83	3.72	3.61
5.750	5.68	5.55	5.41	5.27	5.13	4.98	4.83
5.875	7.12	6.96	6.79	6.61	6.43	6.25	6.06
6.000	8.57	8.37	8.17	7.96	7.74	7.52	7.29
6.125	10.03	9.80	9.56	9.31	9.06	8.80	8.53
6.250	11.50	11.23	10.96	10.67	10.38	10.08	9.78
6.375	12.98	12.67	12.36	12.04	11.71	11.38	11.03
6.500	14.46	14.12	13.78	13.42	13.05	12.68	12.29
6.625	15.96	15.58	15.20	14.80	14.40	13.98	13.56
6.750	17.46	17.05	16.63	16.19	15.75	15.30	14.83
6.875	18.96	18.52	18.06	17.59	17.11	16.62	16.11
7.000	20.48	20.00	19.51	19.00	18.48	17.94	17.39
7.125	22.00	21.49	20.96	20.41	19.85	19.28	18.69
7.250	23.54	22.99	22.42	21.83	21.23	20.62	19.99
7.375	25.08	24.49	23.88	23.26	22.62	21.97	21.29
7.500	26.62	26.00	25.36	24.70	24.02	23.32	22.60
7.625	28.18	27.52	26.84	26.14	25.42	24.68	23.92
7.750	29.74	29.04	28.32	27.58	26.83	26.05	25.24
7.875	31.30	30.57	29.82	29.04	28.24	27.42	26.57
8.000	32.88	32.11	31.32	30.50	29.66	28.80	27.91
8.125	34.46	33.65	32.82	31.97	31.09	30.18	29.25
8.250	36.05	35.20	34.34	33.44	32.52	31.57	30.60
8.375	37.64	36.76	35.85	34.92	33.96	32.97	31.95
8.500	39.24	38.33	37.38	36.41	35.40	34.37	33.31
8.625	40.85	39.90	38.91	37.90	36.85	35.78	34.68
8.750	42.46	41.47	40.45	39.40	38.31	37.20	36.05
8.875	44.08	43.06	41.99	40.90	39.77	38.61	37.42
9.000	45.71	44.64	43.54	42.41	41.24	40.04	38.80
9.125	47.34	46.24	45.10	43.93	42.72	41.47	40.19
9.250	48.98	47.84	46.66	45.45	44.20	42.91	41.58

Payment Adjustments
(As % of Old Payment)

5¼%
Old Rate

NEW RATE (%)	YEARS REMAINING IN TERM						
	23	22	21	20	15	10	5
2.250	−25.66	−24.85	−24.01	−23.16	−18.51	−13.19	−7.10
2.375	−24.68	−23.89	−23.09	−22.26	−17.78	−12.67	−6.81
2.500	−23.68	−22.93	−22.16	−21.36	−17.05	−12.14	−6.52
2.625	−22.69	−21.96	−21.22	−20.45	−16.32	−11.61	−6.23
2.750	−21.68	−20.99	−20.27	−19.54	−15.58	−11.07	−5.94
2.875	−20.67	−20.00	−19.32	−18.62	−14.84	−10.54	−5.65
3.000	−19.65	−19.01	−18.36	−17.70	−14.09	−10.00	−5.36
3.125	−18.62	−18.02	−17.40	−16.76	−13.34	−9.46	−5.06
3.250	−17.58	−17.01	−16.43	−15.83	−12.59	−8.92	−4.77
3.375	−16.54	−16.00	−15.45	−14.88	−11.83	−8.38	−4.48
3.500	−15.49	−14.98	−14.46	−13.93	−11.07	−7.84	−4.18
3.625	−14.43	−13.96	−13.47	−12.98	−10.31	−7.29	−3.89
3.750	−13.36	−12.92	−12.47	−12.01	−9.54	−6.74	−3.59
3.875	−12.29	−11.88	−11.47	−11.05	−8.76	−6.19	−3.30
4.000	−11.21	−10.84	−10.46	−10.07	−7.99	−5.64	−3.00
4.125	−10.12	−9.78	−9.44	−9.09	−7.20	−5.08	−2.70
4.250	−9.02	−8.72	−8.42	−8.11	−6.42	−4.53	−2.41
4.375	−7.92	−7.66	−7.39	−7.11	−5.63	−3.96	−2.10
4.500	−6.81	−6.58	−6.35	−6.11	−4.84	−3.41	−1.81
4.625	−5.69	−5.50	−5.31	−5.11	−4.04	−2.84	−1.51
4.750	−4.57	−4.42	−4.26	−4.10	−3.24	−2.28	−1.21
4.875	−3.44	−3.32	−3.20	−3.08	−2.44	−1.71	−0.91
5.000	−2.30	−2.22	−2.14	−2.06	−1.63	−1.15	−0.61
5.125	−1.15	−1.11	−1.07	−1.03	−0.82	−0.57	−0.30
5.250	0.00	0.00	0.00	0.00	0.00	0.00	0.00
5.375	1.16	1.12	1.08	1.04	0.82	0.57	0.30
5.500	2.32	2.25	2.17	2.08	1.64	1.15	0.61
5.625	3.50	3.38	3.26	3.13	2.47	1.73	0.91
5.750	4.68	4.52	4.36	4.19	3.30	2.31	1.22
5.875	5.86	5.66	5.46	5.25	4.13	2.89	1.52
6.000	7.06	6.82	6.57	6.32	4.97	3.47	1.83
6.125	8.26	7.97	7.69	7.39	5.81	4.06	2.13
6.250	9.46	9.14	8.81	8.47	6.66	4.65	2.44
6.375	10.67	10.31	9.94	9.56	7.51	5.24	2.75
6.500	11.89	11.49	11.07	10.64	8.36	5.83	3.06
6.625	13.12	12.67	12.21	11.74	9.22	6.42	3.36
6.750	14.35	13.86	13.35	12.84	10.08	7.02	3.67
6.875	15.59	15.05	14.51	13.94	10.94	7.62	3.98
7.000	16.83	16.25	15.66	15.06	11.81	8.22	4.29
7.125	18.08	17.46	16.82	16.17	12.68	8.82	4.60
7.250	19.34	18.67	17.99	17.29	13.56	9.42	4.92
7.375	20.60	19.89	19.16	18.42	14.43	10.03	5.23
7.500	21.87	21.11	20.34	19.55	15.32	10.63	5.54
7.625	23.14	22.34	21.53	20.69	16.20	11.24	5.85
7.750	24.42	23.58	22.72	21.83	17.09	11.85	6.17
7.875	25.71	24.82	23.91	22.98	17.98	12.47	6.48
8.000	27.00	26.07	25.11	24.13	18.88	13.08	6.80
8.125	28.30	27.32	26.31	25.29	19.78	13.70	7.11
8.250	29.60	28.58	27.52	26.45	20.68	14.32	7.43
8.375	30.91	29.84	28.74	27.61	21.59	14.94	7.74
8.500	32.22	31.11	29.96	28.79	22.50	15.56	8.06
8.625	33.54	32.38	31.19	29.96	23.41	16.18	8.38
8.750	34.87	33.66	32.42	31.14	24.33	16.81	8.70
8.875	36.20	34.94	33.65	32.33	25.25	17.44	9.01
9.000	37.53	36.23	34.89	33.52	26.17	18.06	9.33
9.125	38.88	37.52	36.14	34.72	27.10	18.70	9.65
9.250	40.22	38.82	37.39	35.92	28.03	19.33	9.97

5½%
Old Rate

Payment Adjustments
(As % of Old Payment)

NEW RATE (%)	YEARS REMAINING IN TERM						
	30	29	28	27	26	25	24
2.500	−30.41	−29.75	−29.08	−28.39	−27.68	−26.94	−26.19
2.625	−29.26	−28.63	−27.98	−27.31	−26.62	−25.92	−25.19
2.750	−28.10	−27.49	−26.86	−26.22	−25.56	−24.88	−24.18
2.875	−26.93	−26.34	−25.74	−25.12	−24.49	−23.83	−23.16
3.000	−25.75	−25.19	−24.61	−24.01	−23.40	−22.78	−22.13
3.125	−24.55	−24.02	−23.46	−22.90	−22.31	−21.71	−21.10
3.250	−23.35	−22.84	−22.31	−21.77	−21.22	−20.64	−20.06
3.375	−22.14	−21.65	−21.15	−20.64	−20.11	−19.56	−19.01
3.500	−20.91	−20.45	−19.98	−19.49	−18.99	−18.48	−17.95
3.625	−19.68	−19.24	−18.80	−18.34	−17.87	−17.38	−16.88
3.750	−18.43	−18.03	−17.61	−17.18	−16.73	−16.28	−15.81
3.875	−17.18	−16.80	−16.41	−16.00	−15.59	−15.16	−14.73
4.000	−15.92	−15.56	−15.20	−14.82	−14.44	−14.05	−13.64
4.125	−14.64	−14.32	−13.98	−13.64	−13.28	−12.92	−12.54
4.250	−13.36	−13.06	−12.75	−12.44	−12.11	−11.78	−11.44
4.375	−12.06	−11.79	−11.52	−11.23	−10.94	−10.64	−10.33
4.500	−10.76	−10.52	−10.27	−10.02	−9.76	−9.49	−9.21
4.625	−9.45	−9.24	−9.02	−8.79	−8.56	−8.33	−8.08
4.750	−8.13	−7.94	−7.76	−7.56	−7.36	−7.16	−6.95
4.875	−6.79	−6.64	−6.48	−6.32	−6.16	−5.99	−5.81
5.000	−5.45	−5.33	−5.21	−5.08	−4.94	−4.80	−4.66
5.125	−4.10	−4.01	−3.92	−3.82	−3.72	−3.61	−3.51
5.250	−2.74	−2.68	−2.62	−2.55	−2.49	−2.42	−2.34
5.375	−1.38	−1.35	−1.31	−1.28	−1.25	−1.21	−1.18
5.500	0.00	0.00	0.00	0.00	0.00	0.00	0.00
5.625	1.39	1.35	1.32	1.29	1.25	1.22	1.18
5.750	2.78	2.72	2.65	2.59	2.52	2.45	2.37
5.875	4.18	4.09	3.99	3.89	3.79	3.68	3.57
6.000	5.59	5.47	5.34	5.20	5.06	4.92	4.77
6.125	7.01	6.85	6.69	6.52	6.35	6.17	5.98
6.250	8.44	8.25	8.05	7.85	7.64	7.42	7.20
6.375	9.88	9.65	9.42	9.18	8.94	8.68	8.43
6.500	11.32	11.06	10.80	10.52	10.24	9.95	9.66
6.625	12.77	12.48	12.18	11.87	11.55	11.23	10.89
6.750	14.23	13.91	13.57	13.23	12.87	12.51	12.14
6.875	15.70	15.34	14.97	14.59	14.20	13.80	13.39
7.000	17.17	16.78	16.38	15.96	15.53	15.09	14.64
7.125	18.66	18.23	17.79	17.34	16.87	16.40	15.90
7.250	20.15	19.69	19.21	18.72	18.22	17.70	17.17
7.375	21.64	21.15	20.64	20.11	19.57	19.02	18.45
7.500	23.15	22.62	22.07	21.51	20.93	20.34	19.73
7.625	24.66	24.09	23.51	22.92	22.30	21.67	21.01
7.750	26.18	25.58	24.96	24.33	23.67	23.00	22.31
7.875	27.70	27.07	26.42	25.74	25.05	24.34	23.61
8.000	29.23	28.56	27.88	27.17	26.44	25.69	24.91
8.125	30.77	30.07	29.34	28.60	27.83	27.04	26.22
8.250	32.31	31.58	30.82	30.03	29.23	28.39	27.54
8.375	33.87	33.09	32.30	31.48	30.63	29.76	28.86
8.500	35.42	34.62	33.78	32.92	32.04	31.13	30.19
8.625	36.99	36.14	35.27	34.38	33.45	32.50	31.52
8.750	38.56	37.68	36.77	35.84	34.87	33.88	32.86
8.875	40.13	39.22	38.28	37.30	36.30	35.27	34.20
9.000	41.71	40.76	39.79	38.77	37.73	36.66	35.55
9.125	43.30	42.32	41.30	40.25	39.17	38.05	36.90
9.250	44.89	43.87	42.82	41.73	40.61	39.46	38.26
9.375	46.49	45.44	44.35	43.22	42.06	40.86	39.63
9.500	48.09	47.00	45.88	44.72	43.51	42.28	41.00

Payment Adjustments
(As % of Old Payment)

5½% Old Rate

NEW RATE (%)	YEARS REMAINING IN TERM						
	23	22	21	20	15	10	5
2.500	-25.42	-24.62	-23.81	-22.96	-18.39	-13.13	-7.08
2.625	-24.44	-23.68	-22.89	-22.08	-17.67	-12.61	-6.80
2.750	-23.46	-22.72	-21.96	-21.18	-16.95	-12.08	-6.51
2.875	-22.47	-21.76	-21.03	-20.28	-16.22	-11.56	-6.22
3.000	-21.47	-20.79	-20.09	-19.38	-15.48	-11.03	-5.93
3.125	-20.47	-19.82	-19.15	-18.46	-14.74	-10.49	-5.64
3.250	-19.45	-18.84	-18.20	-17.55	-14.00	-9.96	-5.35
3.375	-18.43	-17.85	-17.24	-16.62	-13.26	-9.42	-5.05
3.500	-17.41	-16.85	-16.28	-15.69	-12.51	-8.88	-4.76
3.625	-16.37	-15.85	-15.31	-14.75	-11.76	-8.34	-4.47
3.750	-15.33	-14.84	-14.33	-13.81	-11.00	-7.80	-4.17
3.875	-14.28	-13.82	-13.35	-12.86	-10.24	-7.25	-3.88
4.000	-13.22	-12.80	-12.36	-11.91	-9.47	-6.71	-3.58
4.125	-12.16	-11.77	-11.36	-10.95	-8.70	-6.16	-3.29
4.250	-11.09	-10.73	-10.36	-9.98	-7.93	-5.61	-2.99
4.375	-10.01	-9.68	-9.35	-9.01	-7.15	-5.06	-2.69
4.500	-8.93	-8.64	-8.34	-8.03	-6.37	-4.50	-2.40
4.625	-7.83	-7.58	-7.32	-7.05	-5.59	-3.95	-2.10
4.750	-6.74	-6.52	-6.29	-6.06	-4.80	-3.39	-1.80
4.875	-5.63	-5.45	-5.26	-5.06	-4.01	-2.83	-1.50
5.000	-4.52	-4.37	-4.22	-4.06	-3.22	-2.27	-1.21
5.125	-3.40	-3.29	-3.17	-3.05	-2.42	-1.70	-0.90
5.250	-2.27	-2.20	-2.12	-2.04	-1.62	-1.14	-0.60
5.375	-1.14	-1.10	-1.06	-1.02	-0.81	-0.57	-0.30
5.500	0.00	0.00	0.00	0.00	0.00	0.00	0.00
5.625	1.15	1.11	1.07	1.03	0.81	0.57	0.30
5.750	2.30	2.22	2.15	2.06	1.63	1.15	0.61
5.875	3.46	3.34	3.23	3.10	2.45	1.72	0.91
6.000	4.62	4.47	4.31	4.15	3.28	2.30	1.21
6.125	5.80	5.60	5.40	5.20	4.11	2.88	1.52
6.250	6.97	6.74	6.50	6.26	4.94	3.46	1.82
6.375	8.16	7.89	7.61	7.32	5.77	4.04	2.13
6.500	9.35	9.04	8.72	8.39	6.61	4.63	2.44
6.625	10.55	10.19	9.83	9.46	7.45	5.21	2.74
6.750	11.75	11.36	10.95	10.54	8.30	5.80	3.05
6.875	12.96	12.53	12.08	11.62	9.15	6.39	3.36
7.000	14.18	13.70	13.21	12.71	10.00	6.99	3.66
7.125	15.40	14.88	14.35	13.80	10.86	7.58	3.97
7.250	16.63	16.07	15.49	14.90	11.72	8.18	4.28
7.375	17.86	17.26	16.64	16.00	12.59	8.78	4.59
7.500	19.10	18.45	17.79	17.11	13.45	9.38	4.90
7.625	20.34	19.66	18.95	18.22	14.32	9.98	5.22
7.750	21.60	20.87	20.11	19.34	15.20	10.58	5.53
7.875	22.85	22.08	21.28	20.47	16.08	11.19	5.84
8.000	24.12	23.30	22.46	21.60	16.96	11.80	6.15
8.125	25.38	24.52	23.64	22.73	17.84	12.41	6.47
8.250	26.66	25.75	24.82	23.87	18.73	13.02	6.78
8.375	27.94	26.99	26.01	25.01	19.62	13.63	7.10
8.500	29.22	28.23	27.21	26.16	20.52	14.25	7.41
8.625	30.51	29.47	28.41	27.31	21.42	14.86	7.73
8.750	31.80	30.72	29.61	28.47	22.32	15.48	8.04
8.875	33.10	31.98	30.82	29.63	23.22	16.10	8.36
9.000	34.41	33.24	32.03	30.80	24.13	16.72	8.68
9.125	35.72	34.50	33.25	31.97	25.04	17.35	8.99
9.250	37.04	35.77	34.48	33.14	25.96	17.97	9.31
9.375	38.36	37.05	35.70	34.32	26.88	18.60	9.63
9.500	39.68	38.33	36.94	35.51	27.80	19.23	9.95

5¾%
Old Rate

Payment Adjustments
(As % of Old Payment)

NEW RATE (%)	YEARS REMAINING IN TERM						
	30	29	28	27	26	25	24
2.750	−30.04	−29.41	−28.75	−28.08	−27.39	−26.67	−25.94
2.875	−28.91	−28.29	−27.66	−27.01	−26.34	−25.65	−24.94
3.000	−27.76	−27.16	−26.56	−25.93	−25.29	−24.62	−23.94
3.125	−26.59	−26.03	−25.44	−24.84	−24.22	−23.58	−22.93
3.250	−25.42	−24.88	−24.32	−23.74	−23.15	−22.54	−21.91
3.375	−24.24	−23.72	−23.19	−22.64	−22.07	−21.49	−20.88
3.500	−23.05	−22.56	−22.05	−21.52	−20.98	−20.42	−19.85
3.625	−21.85	−21.38	−20.90	−20.40	−19.35	−19.35	−18.81
3.750	−20.64	−20.19	−19.74	−19.26	−18.78	−18.28	−17.76
3.875	−19.42	−19.00	−18.57	−18.12	−17.66	−17.19	−16.71
4.000	−18.19	−17.80	−17.39	−16.97	−16.54	−16.10	−15.64
4.125	−16.95	−16.58	−16.20	−15.81	−15.41	−15.00	−14.57
4.250	−15.70	−15.36	−15.01	−14.65	−14.27	−13.89	−13.49
4.375	−14.44	−14.13	−13.80	−13.47	−13.12	−12.77	−12.41
4.500	−13.18	−12.89	−12.59	−12.29	−11.97	−11.65	−11.32
4.625	−11.90	−11.64	−11.37	−11.09	−10.81	−10.52	−10.22
4.750	−10.61	−10.38	−10.14	−9.89	−9.64	−9.38	−9.11
4.875	−9.32	−9.11	−8.90	−8.68	−8.46	−8.23	−7.99
5.000	−8.01	−7.84	−7.65	−7.47	−7.28	−7.08	−6.87
5.125	−6.70	−6.55	−6.40	−6.24	−6.08	−5.92	−5.75
5.250	−5.38	−5.26	−5.13	−5.01	−4.88	−4.75	−4.61
5.375	−4.04	−3.96	−3.86	−3.77	−3.67	−3.57	−3.47
5.500	−2.71	−2.65	−2.58	−2.52	−2.46	−2.39	−2.32
5.625	−1.36	−1.33	−1.30	−1.26	−1.23	−1.20	−1.16
5.750	0.00	0.00	0.00	0.00	0.00	0.00	0.00
5.875	1.36	1.33	1.30	1.27	1.24	1.20	1.17
6.000	2.74	2.68	2.61	2.55	2.48	2.41	2.34
6.125	4.12	4.03	3.93	3.84	3.74	3.63	3.53
6.250	5.51	5.38	5.26	5.13	4.99	4.86	4.71
6.375	6.90	6.75	6.59	6.43	6.26	6.09	5.91
6.500	8.31	8.12	7.93	7.74	7.54	7.33	7.11
6.625	9.72	9.51	9.28	9.05	8.82	8.57	8.32
6.750	11.14	10.89	10.64	10.37	10.10	9.82	9.54
6.875	12.57	12.29	12.00	11.70	11.40	11.08	10.76
7.000	14.00	13.69	13.37	13.04	12.70	12.35	11.98
7.125	15.45	15.10	14.75	14.38	14.00	13.62	13.22
7.250	16.90	16.52	16.13	15.73	15.32	14.89	14.46
7.375	18.35	17.94	17.52	17.09	16.64	16.18	15.70
7.500	19.82	19.37	18.92	18.45	17.96	17.47	16.95
7.625	21.29	20.81	20.32	19.82	19.30	18.76	18.21
7.750	22.76	22.26	21.73	21.19	20.64	20.06	19.47
7.875	24.25	23.71	23.15	22.58	21.98	21.37	20.74
8.000	25.74	25.16	24.57	23.96	23.33	22.68	22.01
8.125	27.23	26.63	26.00	25.36	24.69	24.00	23.29
8.250	28.73	28.10	27.44	26.76	26.05	25.33	24.58
8.375	30.24	29.57	28.88	28.16	27.42	26.66	25.87
8.500	31.76	31.05	30.33	29.57	28.80	27.99	27.17
8.625	33.28	32.54	31.78	30.99	30.18	29.34	28.47
8.750	34.81	34.04	33.24	32.41	31.56	30.68	29.78
8.875	36.34	35.54	34.70	33.84	32.95	32.04	31.09
9.000	37.88	37.04	36.17	35.28	34.35	33.39	32.41
9.125	39.42	38.55	37.65	36.72	35.75	34.76	33.73
9.250	40.97	40.07	39.13	38.16	37.16	36.13	35.06
9.375	42.53	41.59	40.62	39.61	38.57	37.50	36.39
9.500	44.09	43.12	42.11	41.07	39.99	38.88	37.73
9.625	45.65	44.65	43.61	42.53	41.41	40.26	39.07
9.750	47.22	46.18	45.11	43.99	42.84	41.65	40.42

Payment Adjustments 5¾%
(As % of Old Payment)
Old Rate

NEW RATE (%)	YEARS REMAINING IN TERM						
	23	22	21	20	15	10	5
2.750	−25.18	−24.40	−23.60	−22.78	−18.28	−13.08	−7.07
2.875	−24.21	−23.46	−22.69	−21.90	−17.56	−12.56	−6.79
3.000	−23.24	−22.52	−21.77	−21.01	−16.84	−12.03	−6.50
3.125	−22.25	−21.56	−20.85	−20.11	−16.11	−11.51	−6.21
3.250	−21.27	−20.60	−19.92	−19.21	−15.38	−10.98	−5.92
3.375	−20.27	−19.63	−18.98	−18.31	−14.65	−10.45	−5.63
3.500	−19.26	−18.66	−18.04	−17.40	−13.91	−9.92	−5.34
3.625	−18.25	−17.68	−17.09	−16.48	−13.17	−9.38	−5.04
3.750	−17.23	−16.69	−16.13	−15.55	−12.43	−8.84	−4.75
3.875	−16.21	−15.69	−15.17	−14.62	−11.68	−8.31	−4.46
4.000	−15.17	−14.69	−14.20	−13.69	−10.93	−7.77	−4.17
4.125	−14.13	−13.69	−13.22	−12.75	−10.17	−7.22	−3.87
4.250	−13.09	−12.67	−12.24	−11.80	−9.41	−6.68	−3.58
4.375	−12.03	−11.65	−11.25	−10.85	−8.64	−6.13	−3.28
4.500	−10.97	−10.62	−10.26	−9.89	−7.88	−5.59	−2.99
4.625	−9.91	−9.59	−9.26	−8.93	−7.11	−5.04	−2.69
4.750	−8.83	−8.55	−8.26	−7.96	−6.33	−4.48	−2.39
4.875	−7.75	−7.50	−7.25	−6.98	−5.55	−3.93	−2.10
5.000	−6.67	−6.45	−6.23	−6.00	−4.77	−3.38	−1.80
5.125	−5.57	−5.39	−5.20	−5.01	−3.99	−2.82	−1.50
5.250	−4.47	−4.32	−4.18	−4.02	−3.20	−2.26	−1.20
5.375	−3.36	−3.25	−3.14	−3.03	−2.40	−1.70	−0.90
5.500	−2.25	−2.18	−2.10	−2.02	−1.61	−1.13	−0.60
5.625	−1.13	−1.09	−1.05	−1.02	−0.81	−0.57	−0.30
5.750	0.00	0.00	0.00	0.00	0.00	0.00	0.00
5.875	1.13	1.10	1.06	1.02	0.81	0.57	0.30
6.000	2.27	2.20	2.12	2.04	1.62	1.14	0.60
6.125	3.42	3.31	3.19	3.07	2.43	1.71	0.90
6.250	4.57	4.42	4.27	4.11	3.25	2.29	1.21
6.375	5.73	5.54	5.35	5.15	4.07	2.86	1.51
6.500	6.89	6.67	6.43	6.19	4.90	3.44	1.82
6.625	8.06	7.80	7.52	7.24	5.73	4.02	2.12
6.750	9.24	8.93	8.62	8.30	6.56	4.60	2.43
6.875	10.42	10.08	9.72	9.36	7.40	5.19	2.73
7.000	11.61	11.23	10.83	10.43	8.24	5.77	3.04
7.125	12.80	12.38	11.95	11.50	9.08	6.36	3.35
7.250	14.00	13.54	13.06	12.57	9.93	6.95	3.65
7.375	15.21	14.71	14.19	13.66	10.78	7.54	3.96
7.500	16.42	15.88	15.32	14.74	11.63	8.14	4.27
7.625	17.64	17.05	16.45	15.83	12.49	8.73	4.58
7.750	18.86	18.24	17.59	16.93	13.35	9.33	4.89
7.875	20.09	19.42	18.74	18.03	14.21	9.93	5.20
8.000	21.32	20.62	19.89	19.14	15.08	10.53	5.51
8.125	22.56	21.81	21.04	20.25	15.95	11.13	5.82
8.250	23.81	23.02	22.20	21.36	16.83	11.74	6.14
8.375	25.06	24.22	23.37	22.48	17.70	12.34	6.45
8.500	26.32	25.44	24.53	23.61	18.58	12.95	6.76
8.625	27.58	26.66	25.71	24.73	19.47	13.56	7.08
8.750	28.84	27.88	26.89	25.87	20.35	14.17	7.39
8.875	30.11	29.11	28.07	27.01	21.24	14.78	7.70
9.000	31.39	30.34	29.26	28.15	22.14	15.40	8.02
9.125	32.67	31.58	30.45	29.30	23.04	16.02	8.34
9.250	33.96	32.82	31.65	30.45	23.94	16.64	8.65
9.375	35.25	34.07	32.85	31.60	24.84	17.26	8.97
9.500	36.54	35.32	34.06	32.76	25.75	17.88	9.29
9.625	37.84	36.58	35.27	33.93	26.66	18.50	9.60
9.750	39.15	37.84	36.49	35.10	27.57	19.13	9.92

6%
Old Rate

Payment Adjustments
(As % of Old Payment)

NEW RATE (%)	YEARS REMAINING IN TERM						
	30	29	28	27	26	25	24
3.000	-29.68	-29.06	-28.43	-27.77	-27.10	-26.40	-25.68
3.125	-28.55	-27.95	-27.34	-26.71	-26.06	-25.39	-24.69
3.250	-27.41	-26.84	-26.25	-25.64	-25.01	-24.37	-23.70
3.375	-26.26	-25.71	-25.14	-24.56	-23.96	-23.34	-22.70
3.500	-25.10	-24.58	-24.03	-23.47	-22.89	-22.30	-21.69
3.625	-23.93	-23.43	-22.91	-22.38	-21.82	-21.26	-20.67
3.750	-22.76	-22.28	-21.78	-21.27	-20.74	-20.20	-19.65
3.875	-21.57	-21.11	-20.64	-20.16	-19.66	-19.14	-18.61
4.000	-20.37	-19.94	-19.49	-19.03	-18.56	-18.08	-17.57
4.125	-19.16	-18.76	-18.34	-17.91	-17.46	-17.00	-16.53
4.250	-17.95	-17.57	-17.17	-16.77	-16.35	-15.92	-15.48
4.375	-16.72	-16.37	-16.00	-15.62	-15.23	-14.83	-14.41
4.500	-15.49	-15.16	-14.82	-14.47	-14.10	-13.73	-13.35
4.625	-14.25	-13.94	-13.63	-13.30	-12.97	-12.63	-12.27
4.750	-12.99	-12.71	-12.43	-12.13	-11.83	-11.51	-11.19
4.875	-11.73	-11.48	-11.22	-10.95	-10.68	-10.39	-10.10
5.000	-10.46	-10.24	-10.01	-9.77	-9.52	-9.27	-9.01
5.125	-9.18	-8.99	-8.78	-8.57	-8.36	-8.13	-7.90
5.250	-7.90	-7.73	-7.55	-7.37	-7.18	-6.99	-6.79
5.375	-6.60	-6.46	-6.31	-6.16	-6.00	-5.84	-5.68
5.500	-5.30	-5.18	-5.07	-4.94	-4.82	-4.69	-4.56
5.625	-3.99	-3.90	-3.81	-3.72	-3.62	-3.53	-3.43
5.750	-2.66	-2.61	-2.55	-2.49	-2.42	-2.36	-2.29
5.875	-1.34	-1.31	-1.28	-1.25	-1.21	-1.18	-1.15
6.000	0.00	0.00	0.00	0.00	0.00	0.00	0.00
6.125	1.34	1.32	1.29	1.25	1.22	1.19	1.16
6.250	2.70	2.64	2.58	2.52	2.45	2.38	2.32
6.375	4.06	3.97	3.88	3.78	3.69	3.59	3.49
6.500	5.42	5.31	5.18	5.06	4.93	4.80	4.66
6.625	6.80	6.65	6.50	6.34	6.18	6.01	5.84
6.750	8.18	8.00	7.82	7.63	7.44	7.23	7.03
6.875	9.57	9.36	9.15	8.93	8.70	8.46	8.22
7.000	10.97	10.73	10.48	10.23	9.97	9.70	9.42
7.125	12.37	12.10	11.83	11.54	11.24	10.94	10.62
7.250	13.78	13.48	13.17	12.85	12.52	12.18	11.83
7.375	15.20	14.87	14.53	14.18	13.81	13.44	13.05
7.500	16.62	16.26	15.89	15.50	15.11	14.70	14.27
7.625	18.05	17.66	17.26	16.84	16.41	15.96	15.50
7.750	19.49	19.07	18.63	18.18	17.71	17.23	16.74
7.875	20.94	20.48	20.01	19.53	19.03	18.51	17.97
8.000	22.39	21.90	21.40	20.88	20.34	19.79	19.22
8.125	23.84	23.33	22.79	22.24	21.67	21.08	20.47
8.250	25.30	24.76	24.19	23.61	23.00	22.37	21.73
8.375	26.77	26.20	25.60	24.98	24.34	23.67	22.99
8.500	28.25	27.64	27.01	26.35	25.68	24.98	24.25
8.625	29.73	29.09	28.42	27.73	27.02	26.29	25.53
8.750	31.22	30.54	29.84	29.12	28.38	27.60	26.80
8.875	32.71	32.00	31.27	30.52	29.73	28.92	28.09
9.000	34.20	33.47	32.70	31.91	31.10	30.25	29.37
9.125	35.71	34.94	34.14	33.32	32.46	31.58	30.67
9.250	37.22	36.42	35.59	34.73	33.84	32.92	31.96
9.375	38.73	37.90	37.04	36.14	35.22	34.26	33.27
9.500	40.25	39.38	38.49	37.56	36.60	35.60	34.57
9.625	41.77	40.88	39.95	38.99	37.99	36.95	35.89
9.750	43.30	42.37	41.41	40.42	39.38	38.31	37.20
9.875	44.83	43.88	42.88	41.85	40.78	39.67	38.52
10.000	46.37	45.38	44.35	43.29	42.18	41.04	39.85

Payment Adjustments
(As % of Old Payment)

6% Old Rate

NEW RATE (%)	YEARS REMAINING IN TERM						
	23	22	21	20	15	10	5
3.000	-24.94	-24.18	-23.40	-22.59	-18.16	-13.03	-7.06
3.125	-23.98	-23.25	-22.49	-21.71	-17.45	-12.50	-6.77
3.250	-23.01	-22.31	-21.58	-20.83	-16.73	-11.98	-6.48
3.375	-22.04	-21.36	-20.66	-19.94	-16.01	-11.46	-6.19
3.500	-21.06	-20.41	-19.74	-19.05	-15.28	-10.93	-5.90
3.625	-20.07	-19.45	-18.81	-18.15	-14.55	-10.40	-5.61
3.750	-19.07	-18.48	-17.87	-17.24	-13.82	-9.87	-5.32
3.875	-18.07	-17.51	-16.93	-16.33	-13.08	-9.34	-5.03
4.000	-17.06	-16.53	-15.98	-15.42	-12.34	-8.80	-4.74
4.125	-16.04	-15.54	-15.03	-14.49	-11.60	-8.27	-4.45
4.250	-15.02	-14.55	-14.07	-13.57	-10.85	-7.73	-4.16
4.375	-13.99	-13.55	-13.10	-12.63	-10.10	-7.19	-3.86
4.500	-12.95	-12.54	-12.13	-11.69	-9.35	-6.65	-3.57
4.625	-11.91	-11.53	-11.15	-10.75	-8.59	-6.10	-3.27
4.750	-10.86	-10.51	-10.16	-9.80	-7.82	-5.56	-2.98
4.875	-9.80	-9.49	-9.17	-8.84	-7.06	-5.01	-2.68
5.000	-8.74	-8.46	-8.18	-7.88	-6.29	-4.46	-2.39
5.125	-7.67	-7.42	-7.17	-6.92	-5.51	-3.91	-2.09
5.250	-6.59	-6.38	-6.17	-5.94	-4.74	-3.36	-1.79
5.375	-5.51	-5.33	-5.15	-4.97	-3.96	-2.80	-1.50
5.500	-4.42	-4.28	-4.13	-3.98	-3.17	-2.25	-1.20
5.625	-3.32	-3.22	-3.11	-3.00	-2.39	-1.69	-0.90
5.750	-2.22	-2.15	-2.08	-2.00	-1.59	-1.13	-0.60
5.875	-1.11	-1.08	-1.04	-1.00	-0.80	-0.56	-0.30
6.000	0.00	0.00	0.00	0.00	0.00	0.00	0.00
6.125	1.12	1.08	1.05	1.01	0.80	0.57	0.30
6.250	2.25	2.17	2.10	2.02	1.61	1.13	0.60
6.375	3.38	3.27	3.16	3.04	2.42	1.71	0.91
6.500	4.52	4.37	4.22	4.07	3.23	2.28	1.21
6.625	5.66	5.48	5.29	5.10	4.05	2.85	1.51
6.750	6.81	6.59	6.37	6.13	4.87	3.43	1.81
6.875	7.97	7.71	7.45	7.17	5.69	4.00	2.12
7.000	9.13	8.83	8.53	8.22	6.51	4.58	2.42
7.125	10.30	9.96	9.62	9.27	7.34	5.16	2.73
7.250	11.47	11.10	10.72	10.32	8.18	5.75	3.03
7.375	12.65	12.24	11.82	11.38	9.01	6.33	3.34
7.500	13.84	13.39	12.92	12.45	9.85	6.92	3.65
7.625	15.03	14.54	14.03	13.51	10.70	7.51	3.95
7.750	16.22	15.69	15.15	14.59	11.55	8.10	4.26
7.875	17.42	16.86	16.27	15.67	12.40	8.69	4.57
8.000	18.63	18.02	17.40	16.75	13.25	9.28	4.88
8.125	19.84	19.19	18.53	17.84	14.11	9.88	5.19
8.250	21.06	20.37	19.66	18.93	14.97	10.48	5.50
8.375	22.28	21.55	20.80	20.03	15.83	11.08	5.81
8.500	23.51	22.74	21.95	21.13	16.70	11.68	6.12
8.625	24.74	23.93	23.10	22.24	17.57	12.28	6.44
8.750	25.98	25.13	24.25	23.35	18.44	12.89	6.75
8.875	27.22	26.33	25.41	24.46	19.31	13.49	7.06
9.000	28.47	27.54	26.58	25.58	20.19	14.10	7.37
9.125	29.72	28.75	27.74	26.71	21.08	14.71	7.69
9.250	30.98	29.96	28.92	27.84	21.96	15.32	8.00
9.375	32.24	31.19	30.09	28.97	22.85	15.94	8.32
9.500	33.51	32.41	31.28	30.11	23.74	16.55	8.63
9.625	34.78	33.64	32.46	31.25	24.64	17.17	8.95
9.750	36.06	34.87	33.65	32.39	25.54	17.79	9.27
9.875	37.34	36.11	34.85	33.54	26.44	18.41	9.58
10.000	38.62	37.36	36.05	34.70	27.34	19.03	9.90

6¼% Old Rate — Payment Adjustments
(As % of Old Payment)

NEW RATE (%)	YEARS REMAINING IN TERM						
	30	29	28	27	26	25	24
3.250	-29.32	-28.72	-28.10	-27.46	-26.81	-26.13	-25.43
3.375	-28.20	-27.62	-27.02	-26.41	-25.78	-25.12	-24.45
3.500	-27.07	-26.51	-25.94	-25.35	-24.74	-24.11	-23.46
3.625	-25.93	-25.40	-24.85	-24.28	-23.69	-23.09	-22.47
3.750	-24.78	-24.27	-23.75	-23.20	-22.64	-22.06	-21.46
3.875	-23.63	-23.14	-22.63	-22.12	-21.58	-21.03	-20.46
4.000	-22.46	-22.00	-21.52	-21.02	-20.51	-19.98	-19.44
4.125	-21.29	-20.85	-20.39	-19.92	-19.43	-18.93	-18.42
4.250	-20.10	-19.69	-19.25	-18.81	-18.35	-17.88	-17.39
4.375	-18.91	-18.52	-18.11	-17.69	-17.26	-16.81	-16.35
4.500	-17.71	-17.34	-16.96	-16.56	-16.16	-15.74	-15.31
4.625	-16.50	-16.15	-15.80	-15.43	-15.05	-14.66	-14.26
4.750	-15.28	-14.96	-14.63	-14.29	-13.94	-13.57	-13.20
4.875	-14.05	-13.76	-13.45	-13.14	-12.82	-12.48	-12.14
5.000	-12.81	-12.55	-12.27	-11.98	-11.69	-11.38	-11.07
5.125	-11.57	-11.33	-11.07	-10.82	-10.55	-10.27	-9.99
5.250	-10.31	-10.10	-9.87	-9.64	-9.40	-9.16	-8.90
5.375	-9.05	-8.86	-8.67	-8.46	-8.25	-8.04	-7.81
5.500	-7.78	-7.62	-7.45	-7.28	-7.10	-6.91	-6.72
5.625	-6.51	-6.37	-6.23	-6.08	-5.93	-5.77	-5.61
5.750	-5.22	-5.11	-5.00	-4.88	-4.76	-4.63	-4.50
5.875	-3.93	-3.84	-3.76	-3.67	-3.58	-3.48	-3.39
6.000	-2.63	-2.57	-2.51	-2.45	-2.39	-2.33	-2.26
6.125	-1.32	-1.29	-1.26	-1.23	-1.20	-1.17	-1.13
6.250	0.00	0.00	0.00	0.00	0.00	0.00	0.00
6.375	1.32	1.30	1.27	1.24	1.21	1.18	1.14
6.500	2.66	2.60	2.54	2.48	2.42	2.36	2.29
6.625	3.99	3.91	3.82	3.73	3.64	3.54	3.44
6.750	5.34	5.23	5.11	4.99	4.87	4.74	4.60
6.875	6.69	6.55	6.41	6.25	6.10	5.94	5.77
7.000	8.05	7.88	7.71	7.52	7.34	7.14	6.94
7.125	9.42	9.22	9.02	8.80	8.58	8.35	8.12
7.250	10.79	10.57	10.33	10.09	9.83	9.57	9.30
7.375	12.17	11.92	11.65	11.38	11.09	10.80	10.49
7.500	13.56	13.27	12.98	12.67	12.35	12.02	11.69
7.625	14.95	14.64	14.31	13.97	13.62	13.26	12.89
7.750	16.35	16.01	15.65	15.28	14.90	14.50	14.09
7.875	17.76	17.39	17.00	16.60	16.18	15.75	15.30
8.000	19.17	18.77	18.35	17.92	17.47	17.00	16.52
8.125	20.59	20.16	19.71	19.24	18.76	18.26	17.74
8.250	22.02	21.55	21.07	20.57	20.06	19.52	18.97
8.375	23.45	22.95	22.44	21.91	21.36	20.79	20.20
8.500	24.88	24.36	23.82	23.25	22.67	22.07	21.44
8.625	26.32	25.77	25.20	24.60	23.98	23.35	22.68
8.750	27.77	27.19	26.58	25.95	25.30	24.63	23.93
8.875	29.22	28.61	27.97	27.31	26.63	25.92	25.19
9.000	30.68	30.04	29.37	28.68	27.96	27.21	26.44
9.125	32.14	31.47	30.77	30.05	29.30	28.52	27.71
9.250	33.61	32.91	32.18	31.42	30.64	29.82	28.98
9.375	35.09	34.35	33.59	32.80	31.98	31.13	30.25
9.500	36.57	35.80	35.01	34.19	33.33	32.45	31.53
9.625	38.05	37.26	36.43	35.58	34.69	33.76	32.81
9.750	39.54	38.72	37.86	36.97	36.05	35.09	34.10
9.875	41.03	40.18	39.29	38.37	37.41	36.42	35.39
10.000	42.53	41.65	40.73	39.77	38.78	37.75	36.68
10.125	44.03	43.12	42.17	41.18	40.15	39.09	37.98
10.250	45.54	44.60	43.61	42.59	41.53	40.43	39.29

Payment Adjustments
(As % of Old Payment)

6¼%
Old Rate

NEW RATE (%)	YEARS REMAINING IN TERM						
	23	22	21	20	15	10	5
3.250	-24.71	-23.96	-23.19	-22.40	-18.05	-12.97	-7.04
3.375	-23.75	-23.03	-22.29	-21.53	-17.34	-12.45	-6.75
3.500	-22.79	-22.10	-21.39	-20.65	-16.62	-11.93	-6.46
3.625	-21.82	-21.16	-20.48	-19.77	-15.91	-11.41	-6.18
3.750	-20.85	-20.21	-19.56	-18.88	-15.18	-10.88	-5.89
3.875	-19.87	-19.26	-18.64	-17.99	-14.46	-10.35	-5.60
4.000	-18.88	-18.30	-17.71	-17.09	-13.73	-9.83	-5.31
4.125	-17.89	-17.34	-16.77	-16.19	-13.00	-9.30	-5.02
4.250	-16.89	-16.37	-15.83	-15.28	-12.26	-8.77	-4.73
4.375	-15.88	-15.39	-14.88	-14.36	-11.52	-8.23	-4.43
4.500	-14.86	-14.41	-13.93	-13.45	-10.78	-7.70	-4.14
4.625	-13.84	-13.41	-12.97	-12.52	-10.03	-7.16	-3.85
4.750	-12.82	-12.42	-12.01	-11.59	-9.28	-6.62	-3.56
4.875	-11.78	-11.42	-11.04	-10.65	-8.53	-6.08	-3.27
5.000	-10.74	-10.41	-10.07	-9.71	-7.77	-5.54	-2.97
5.125	-9.70	-9.39	-9.08	-8.76	-7.01	-4.99	-2.68
5.250	-8.64	-8.37	-8.10	-7.81	-6.24	-4.44	-2.38
5.375	-7.58	-7.35	-7.10	-6.85	-5.48	-3.89	-2.08
5.500	-6.52	-6.32	-6.10	-5.89	-4.70	-3.34	-1.79
5.625	-5.45	-5.28	-5.10	-4.92	-3.93	-2.79	-1.49
5.750	-4.37	-4.23	-4.09	-3.94	-3.15	-2.23	-1.19
5.875	-3.29	-3.18	-3.08	-2.97	-2.37	-1.68	-0.90
6.000	-2.20	-2.13	-2.06	-1.98	-1.58	-1.12	-0.60
6.125	-1.10	-1.07	-1.03	-0.99	-0.79	-0.56	-0.30
6.250	0.00	0.00	0.00	0.00	0.00	0.00	0.00
6.375	1.11	1.07	1.04	1.00	0.80	0.57	0.30
6.500	2.22	2.15	2.08	2.00	1.60	1.13	0.60
6.625	3.34	3.24	3.13	3.01	2.40	1.70	0.90
6.750	4.47	4.32	4.18	4.03	3.21	2.27	1.21
6.875	5.60	5.42	5.24	5.05	4.02	2.84	1.51
7.000	6.73	6.52	6.30	6.07	4.83	3.41	1.81
7.125	7.88	7.63	7.37	7.10	5.65	3.99	2.11
7.250	9.02	8.74	8.44	8.13	6.47	4.56	2.42
7.375	10.18	9.85	9.52	9.17	7.29	5.14	2.72
7.500	11.33	10.97	10.60	10.22	8.12	5.72	3.03
7.625	12.50	12.10	11.69	11.26	8.95	6.30	3.33
7.750	13.67	13.23	12.78	12.32	9.78	6.89	3.64
7.875	14.84	14.37	13.88	13.37	10.62	7.47	3.95
8.000	16.02	15.51	14.98	14.44	11.46	8.06	4.25
8.125	17.21	16.66	16.09	15.50	12.30	8.65	4.56
8.250	18.40	17.81	17.20	16.57	13.15	9.24	4.87
8.375	19.60	18.97	18.32	17.65	14.00	9.83	5.18
8.500	20.80	20.13	19.44	18.73	14.85	10.43	5.49
8.625	22.00	21.30	20.57	19.81	15.71	11.02	5.80
8.750	23.21	22.47	21.70	20.90	16.57	11.62	6.11
8.875	24.43	23.64	22.83	22.00	17.43	12.22	6.42
9.000	25.65	24.82	23.97	23.09	18.29	12.82	6.73
9.125	26.87	26.01	25.12	24.20	19.16	13.43	7.04
9.250	28.10	27.20	26.27	25.30	20.03	14.03	7.36
9.375	29.34	28.39	27.42	26.41	20.91	14.64	7.67
9.500	30.58	29.59	28.58	27.53	21.79	15.25	7.98
9.625	31.82	30.80	29.74	28.65	22.67	15.86	8.30
9.750	33.07	32.00	30.91	29.77	23.55	16.47	8.61
9.875	34.32	33.22	32.08	30.90	24.44	17.08	8.93
10.000	35.58	34.43	33.25	32.03	25.33	17.70	9.24
10.125	36.84	35.65	34.43	33.16	26.22	18.32	9.56
10.250	38.11	36.88	35.61	34.30	27.12	18.93	9.88

6½%
Old Rate

Payment Adjustments
(As % of Old Payment)

NEW RATE (%)	YEARS REMAINING IN TERM						
	30	29	28	27	26	25	24
3.500	-28.96	-28.38	-27.78	-27.16	-26.52	-25.86	-25.17
3.625	-27.85	-27.29	-26.71	-26.11	-25.50	-24.86	-24.20
3.750	-26.73	-26.19	-25.64	-25.06	-24.47	-23.86	-23.22
3.875	-25.60	-25.09	-24.55	-24.00	-23.43	-22.84	-22.24
4.000	-24.47	-23.97	-23.46	-22.93	-22.39	-21.83	-21.24
4.125	-23.32	-22.85	-22.36	-21.86	-21.34	-20.80	-20.25
4.250	-22.17	-21.72	-21.26	-20.78	-20.28	-19.77	-19.24
4.375	-21.01	-20.58	-20.14	-19.68	-19.21	-18.73	-18.22
4.500	-19.84	-19.43	-19.02	-18.59	-18.14	-17.68	-17.20
4.625	-18.66	-18.28	-17.88	-17.48	-17.06	-16.63	-16.18
4.750	-17.47	-17.11	-16.74	-16.36	-15.97	-15.56	-15.14
4.875	-16.27	-15.94	-15.60	-15.24	-14.88	-14.50	-14.10
5.000	-15.07	-14.76	-14.44	-14.11	-13.77	-13.42	-13.06
5.125	-13.86	-13.57	-13.28	-12.98	-12.66	-12.34	-12.00
5.250	-12.64	-12.38	-12.11	-11.83	-11.55	-11.25	-10.94
5.375	-11.41	-11.17	-10.93	-10.68	-10.42	-10.15	-9.88
5.500	-10.17	-9.96	-9.75	-9.52	-9.29	-9.05	-8.81
5.625	-8.93	-8.74	-8.55	-8.36	-8.15	-7.94	-7.73
5.750	-7.67	-7.51	-7.35	-7.18	-7.01	-6.83	-6.64
5.875	-6.41	-6.28	-6.14	-6.00	-5.86	-5.71	-5.55
6.000	-5.14	-5.04	-4.93	-4.82	-4.70	-4.58	-4.45
6.125	-3.87	-3.79	-3.71	-3.62	-3.53	-3.44	-3.35
6.250	-2.59	-2.53	-2.48	-2.42	-2.36	-2.30	-2.24
6.375	-1.30	-1.27	-1.24	-1.21	-1.18	-1.15	-1.12
6.500	0.00	0.00	0.00	0.00	0.00	0.00	0.00
6.625	1.30	1.28	1.25	1.22	1.19	1.16	1.13
6.750	2.62	2.56	2.51	2.45	2.39	2.33	2.26
6.875	3.93	3.85	3.77	3.68	3.59	3.50	3.40
7.000	5.26	5.15	5.04	4.92	4.80	4.68	4.55
7.125	6.59	6.45	6.31	6.17	6.02	5.86	5.70
7.250	7.93	7.76	7.59	7.42	7.24	7.05	6.85
7.375	9.27	9.08	8.88	8.68	8.47	8.24	8.02
7.500	10.62	10.40	10.18	9.94	9.70	9.45	9.18
7.625	11.98	11.73	11.48	11.21	10.94	10.65	10.36
7.750	13.34	13.07	12.78	12.49	12.18	11.87	11.54
7.875	14.71	14.41	14.10	13.77	13.43	13.08	12.72
8.000	16.09	15.76	15.42	15.06	14.69	14.31	13.91
8.125	17.47	17.11	16.74	16.35	15.95	15.54	15.11
8.250	18.86	18.47	18.07	17.65	17.22	16.77	16.31
8.375	20.25	19.84	19.41	18.96	18.49	18.01	17.51
8.500	21.65	21.21	20.75	20.27	19.77	19.26	18.72
8.625	23.05	22.58	22.09	21.58	21.05	20.51	19.94
8.750	24.46	23.96	23.44	22.90	22.34	21.76	21.16
8.875	25.88	25.35	24.80	24.23	23.64	23.02	22.38
9.000	27.30	26.74	26.16	25.56	24.94	24.29	23.61
9.125	28.73	28.14	27.53	26.90	26.24	25.56	24.85
9.250	30.16	29.54	28.90	28.24	27.55	26.83	26.09
9.375	31.59	30.95	30.28	29.59	28.86	28.11	27.33
9.500	33.03	32.36	31.66	30.94	30.18	29.40	28.58
9.625	34.48	33.78	33.05	32.29	31.50	30.69	29.84
9.750	35.93	35.20	34.44	33.65	32.83	31.98	31.09
9.875	37.38	36.63	35.84	35.02	34.16	33.28	32.36
10.000	38.84	38.06	37.24	36.39	35.50	34.58	33.62
10.125	40.30	39.49	38.64	37.76	36.84	35.89	34.90
10.250	41.77	40.93	40.05	39.14	38.19	37.20	36.17
10.375	43.24	42.38	41.47	40.52	39.54	38.52	37.45
10.500	44.72	43.82	42.89	41.91	40.89	39.84	38.74

Payment Adjustments
(As % of Old Payment)

6½%
Old Rate

NEW RATE (%)	YEARS REMAINING IN TERM						
	23	22	21	20	15	10	5
3.500	-24.47	-23.74	-22.99	-22.21	-17.93	-12.91	-7.02
3.625	-23.52	-22.82	-22.10	-21.35	-17.23	-12.40	-6.74
3.750	-22.57	-21.89	-21.20	-20.48	-16.52	-11.88	-6.45
3.875	-21.61	-20.96	-20.29	-19.60	-15.80	-11.36	-6.16
4.000	-20.64	-20.02	-19.38	-18.72	-15.09	-10.83	-5.88
4.125	-19.67	-19.08	-18.47	-17.84	-14.37	-10.31	-5.59
4.250	-18.69	-18.13	-17.55	-16.95	-13.64	-9.79	-5.30
4.375	-17.71	-17.17	-16.62	-16.05	-12.91	-9.26	-5.01
4.500	-16.71	-16.21	-15.69	-15.15	-12.18	-8.73	-4.72
4.625	-15.72	-15.24	-14.75	-14.24	-11.45	-8.20	-4.43
4.750	-14.71	-14.26	-13.80	-13.33	-10.71	-7.66	-4.14
4.875	-13.70	-13.28	-12.85	-12.41	-9.97	-7.13	-3.84
5.000	-12.68	-12.30	-11.90	-11.48	-9.22	-6.59	-3.55
5.125	-11.66	-11.30	-10.93	-10.55	-8.47	-6.05	-3.26
5.250	-10.63	-10.30	-9.97	-9.62	-7.72	-5.51	-2.96
5.375	-9.59	-9.30	-8.99	-8.68	-6.96	-4.97	-2.67
5.500	-8.55	-8.29	-8.02	-7.74	-6.20	-4.42	-2.38
5.625	-7.50	-7.27	-7.03	-6.79	-5.44	-3.88	-2.08
5.750	-6.45	-6.25	-6.04	-5.83	-4.67	-3.33	-1.78
5.875	-5.39	-5.22	-5.05	-4.87	-3.90	-2.78	-1.49
6.000	-4.32	-4.19	-4.05	-3.91	-3.13	-2.23	-1.19
6.125	-3.25	-3.15	-3.05	-2.94	-2.35	-1.67	-0.90
6.250	-2.17	-2.11	-2.04	-1.97	-1.57	-1.12	-0.60
6.375	-1.09	-1.06	-1.02	-0.98	-0.79	-0.56	-0.30
6.500	0.00	0.00	0.00	0.00	0.00	0.00	0.00
6.625	1.09	1.06	1.03	0.99	0.79	0.56	0.30
6.750	2.20	2.13	2.06	1.98	1.58	1.12	0.60
6.875	3.30	3.20	3.09	2.98	2.38	1.69	0.90
7.000	4.41	4.28	4.13	3.99	3.18	2.25	1.20
7.125	5.53	5.36	5.18	5.00	3.99	2.82	1.50
7.250	6.65	6.45	6.23	6.01	4.79	3.39	1.81
7.375	7.78	7.54	7.29	7.03	5.60	3.96	2.11
7.500	8.91	8.64	8.35	8.05	6.42	4.54	2.41
7.625	10.05	9.74	9.41	9.08	7.23	5.11	2.71
7.750	11.20	10.85	10.48	10.11	8.06	5.69	3.02
7.875	12.35	11.96	11.56	11.15	8.88	6.27	3.32
8.000	13.50	13.08	12.64	12.19	9.70	6.85	3.63
8.125	14.66	14.20	13.72	13.23	10.54	7.43	3.94
8.250	15.83	15.33	14.81	14.28	11.37	8.02	4.24
8.375	17.00	16.46	15.91	15.34	12.21	8.60	4.55
8.500	18.17	17.60	17.01	16.40	13.04	9.19	4.86
8.625	19.35	18.74	18.11	17.46	13.89	9.78	5.17
8.750	20.53	19.89	19.22	18.53	14.73	10.37	5.47
8.875	21.72	21.04	20.33	19.60	15.58	10.97	5.78
9.000	22.92	22.19	21.45	20.67	16.43	11.56	6.09
9.125	24.12	23.36	22.57	21.76	17.29	12.16	6.40
9.250	25.32	24.52	23.69	22.84	18.15	12.76	6.71
9.375	26.53	25.69	24.82	23.93	19.01	13.36	7.03
9.500	27.74	26.86	25.96	25.02	19.87	13.96	7.34
9.625	28.95	28.04	27.10	26.12	20.74	14.56	7.65
9.750	30.18	29.22	28.24	27.22	21.61	15.17	7.96
9.875	31.40	30.41	29.39	28.32	22.48	15.77	8.28
10.000	32.63	31.60	30.54	29.43	23.36	16.38	8.59
10.125	33.87	32.80	31.69	30.55	24.24	16.99	8.90
10.250	35.10	34.00	32.85	31.66	25.12	17.60	9.22
10.375	36.35	35.20	34.01	32.78	26.01	18.22	9.54
10.500	37.59	36.41	35.18	33.91	26.90	18.83	9.85

6¾%
Old Rate

Payment Adjustments
(As % of Old Payment)

NEW RATE (%)	YEARS REMAINING IN TERM						
	30	29	28	27	26	25	24
3.750	-28.60	-28.03	-27.45	-26.85	-26.23	-25.59	-24.92
3.875	-27.50	-26.96	-26.40	-25.82	-25.22	-24.60	-23.96
4.000	-26.39	-25.87	-25.33	-24.78	-24.20	-23.60	-22.99
4.125	-25.28	-24.78	-24.26	-23.73	-23.17	-22.60	-22.01
4.250	-24.15	-23.68	-23.18	-22.67	-22.14	-21.59	-21.02
4.375	-23.02	-22.56	-22.09	-21.60	-21.10	-20.57	-20.03
4.500	-21.88	-21.45	-21.00	-20.53	-20.05	-19.55	-19.04
4.625	-20.73	-20.32	-19.89	-19.45	-18.99	-18.52	-18.03
4.750	-19.57	-19.18	-18.78	-18.36	-17.93	-17.48	-17.02
4.875	-18.41	-18.04	-17.66	-17.27	-16.86	-16.44	-16.00
5.000	-17.23	-16.89	-16.53	-16.17	-15.78	-15.39	-14.98
5.125	-16.05	-15.73	-15.40	-15.05	-14.70	-14.33	-13.95
5.250	-14.86	-14.56	-14.26	-13.94	-13.61	-13.27	-12.91
5.375	-13.66	-13.39	-13.11	-12.81	-12.51	-12.20	-11.87
5.500	-12.46	-12.21	-11.95	-11.68	-11.41	-11.12	-10.82
5.625	-11.25	-11.02	-10.79	-10.55	-10.30	-10.04	-9.77
5.750	-10.02	-9.82	-9.62	-9.40	-9.18	-8.94	-8.71
5.875	-8.80	-8.62	-8.44	-8.25	-8.05	-7.85	-7.64
6.000	-7.56	-7.41	-7.25	-7.09	-6.92	-6.75	-6.57
6.125	-6.32	-6.19	-6.06	-5.92	-5.78	-5.64	-5.49
6.250	-5.07	-4.97	-4.86	-4.75	-4.64	-4.52	-4.40
6.375	-3.81	-3.74	-3.66	-3.57	-3.49	-3.40	-3.31
6.500	-2.55	-2.50	-2.44	-2.39	-2.33	-2.27	-2.21
6.625	-1.28	-1.25	-1.23	-1.20	-1.17	-1.14	-1.11
6.750	0.00	0.00	0.00	0.00	0.00	0.00	0.00
6.875	1.28	1.26	1.23	1.20	1.18	1.15	1.11
7.000	2.58	2.52	2.47	2.41	2.36	2.30	2.23
7.125	3.87	3.80	3.71	3.63	3.54	3.45	3.36
7.250	5.18	5.07	4.97	4.85	4.74	4.62	4.49
7.375	6.49	6.36	6.22	6.08	5.94	5.78	5.63
7.500	7.80	7.65	7.48	7.32	7.14	6.96	6.77
7.625	9.13	8.94	8.75	8.56	8.35	8.14	7.92
7.750	10.46	10.25	10.03	9.80	9.57	9.32	9.07
7.875	11.79	11.55	11.31	11.05	10.79	10.51	10.23
8.000	13.13	12.87	12.59	12.31	12.02	11.71	11.39
8.125	14.48	14.19	13.89	13.57	13.25	12.91	12.56
8.250	15.83	15.51	15.18	14.84	14.49	14.12	13.73
8.375	17.19	16.84	16.49	16.12	15.73	15.33	14.91
8.500	18.55	18.18	17.80	17.39	16.98	16.55	16.10
8.625	19.92	19.52	19.11	18.68	18.23	17.77	17.29
8.750	21.29	20.87	20.43	19.97	19.49	18.99	18.48
8.875	22.67	22.22	21.75	21.26	20.75	20.23	19.68
9.000	24.06	23.58	23.08	22.56	22.02	21.46	20.88
9.125	25.44	24.94	24.41	23.87	23.30	22.70	22.09
9.250	26.84	26.31	25.75	25.18	24.57	23.95	23.30
9.375	28.24	27.68	27.10	26.49	25.86	25.20	24.52
9.500	29.64	29.06	28.44	27.81	27.15	26.46	25.74
9.625	31.05	30.44	29.80	29.13	28.44	27.72	26.96
9.750	32.46	31.82	31.16	30.46	29.73	28.98	28.20
9.875	33.88	33.21	32.52	31.79	31.04	30.25	29.43
10.000	35.30	34.61	33.88	33.13	32.34	31.52	30.67
10.125	36.73	36.01	35.26	34.47	33.65	32.80	31.91
10.250	38.16	37.41	36.63	35.82	34.97	34.08	33.16
10.375	39.59	38.82	38.01	37.17	36.29	35.37	34.41
10.500	41.03	40.23	39.39	38.52	37.61	36.66	35.67
10.625	42.48	41.65	40.78	39.88	38.94	37.95	36.93
10.750	43.92	43.07	42.17	41.24	40.27	39.25	38.19

Payment Adjustments
(As % of Old Payment)

6¾%
Old Rate

NEW RATE (%)	YEARS REMAINING IN TERM						
	23	**22**	**21**	**20**	**15**	**10**	**5**
3.750	-24.23	-23.52	-22.79	-22.03	-17.82	-12.86	-7.01
3.875	-23.29	-22.61	-21.90	-21.17	-17.12	-12.34	-6.72
4.000	-22.35	-21.69	-21.01	-20.30	-16.41	-11.83	-6.44
4.125	-21.40	-20.76	-20.11	-19.44	-15.70	-11.31	-6.15
4.250	-20.44	-19.83	-19.21	-18.56	-14.99	-10.79	-5.86
4.375	-19.47	-18.90	-18.30	-17.68	-14.27	-10.26	-5.57
4.500	-18.50	-17.95	-17.38	-16.80	-13.55	-9.74	-5.29
4.625	-17.53	-17.00	-16.46	-15.91	-12.83	-9.21	-5.00
4.750	-16.54	-16.05	-15.54	-15.01	-12.10	-8.69	-4.71
4.875	-15.55	-15.09	-14.61	-14.11	-11.37	-8.16	-4.42
5.000	-14.56	-14.12	-13.67	-13.21	-10.64	-7.63	-4.13
5.125	-13.56	-13.15	-12.73	-12.29	-9.90	-7.09	-3.83
5.250	-12.55	-12.17	-11.78	-11.38	-9.16	-6.56	-3.54
5.375	-11.54	-11.19	-10.83	-10.46	-8.41	-6.02	-3.25
5.500	-10.52	-10.20	-9.87	-9.53	-7.66	-5.48	-2.96
5.625	-9.49	-9.20	-8.91	-8.60	-6.91	-4.95	-2.67
5.750	-8.46	-8.20	-7.94	-7.66	-6.16	-4.40	-2.37
5.875	-7.42	-7.20	-6.96	-6.72	-5.40	-3.86	-2.08
6.000	-6.38	-6.18	-5.98	-5.78	-4.64	-3.31	-1.78
6.125	-5.33	-5.17	-5.00	-4.83	-3.87	-2.77	-1.49
6.250	-4.28	-4.15	-4.01	-3.87	-3.11	-2.22	-1.19
6.375	-3.21	-3.12	-3.01	-2.91	-2.33	-1.66	-0.89
6.500	-2.15	-2.08	-2.01	-1.94	-1.56	-1.11	-0.60
6.625	-1.08	-1.04	-1.01	-0.97	-0.78	-0.56	-0.30
6.750	0.00	0.00	0.00	0.00	0.00	0.00	0.00
6.875	1.08	1.05	1.01	0.98	0.78	0.56	0.30
7.000	2.17	2.10	2.04	1.96	1.57	1.12	0.60
7.125	3.26	3.16	3.06	2.95	2.36	1.68	0.90
7.250	4.36	4.23	4.09	3.95	3.16	2.24	1.20
7.375	5.47	5.30	5.12	4.95	3.96	2.81	1.50
7.500	6.58	6.37	6.16	5.95	4.76	3.38	1.80
7.625	7.69	7.45	7.21	6.96	5.56	3.95	2.10
7.750	8.81	8.54	8.26	7.97	6.37	4.52	2.41
7.875	9.93	9.63	9.31	8.98	7.18	5.09	2.71
8.000	11.06	10.72	10.37	10.01	7.99	5.66	3.01
8.125	12.20	11.82	11.43	11.03	8.81	6.24	3.32
8.250	13.34	12.93	12.50	12.06	9.63	6.82	3.62
8.375	14.48	14.04	13.57	13.09	10.46	7.40	3.93
8.500	15.63	15.15	14.65	14.13	11.28	7.98	4.23
8.625	16.79	16.27	15.73	15.18	12.11	8.56	4.54
8.750	17.94	17.39	16.82	16.22	12.94	9.15	4.85
8.875	19.11	18.52	17.91	17.27	13.78	9.73	5.15
9.000	20.28	19.65	19.00	18.33	14.62	10.32	5.46
9.125	21.45	20.79	20.10	19.39	15.46	10.91	5.77
9.250	22.63	21.93	21.20	20.45	16.31	11.50	6.08
9.375	23.81	23.07	22.31	21.52	17.15	12.10	6.39
9.500	24.99	24.22	23.42	22.59	18.00	12.69	6.70
9.625	26.18	25.37	24.54	23.67	18.86	13.29	7.01
9.750	27.38	26.53	25.65	24.75	19.71	13.89	7.32
9.875	28.58	27.70	26.78	25.83	20.57	14.49	7.63
10.000	29.78	28.86	27.91	26.92	21.44	15.09	7.94
10.125	30.99	30.03	29.04	28.01	22.30	15.69	8.26
10.250	32.20	31.21	30.17	29.10	23.17	16.30	8.57
10.375	33.42	32.38	31.31	30.20	24.04	16.91	8.88
10.500	34.64	33.57	32.46	31.30	24.92	17.51	9.20
10.625	35.86	34.75	33.60	32.41	25.79	18.12	9.51
10.750	37.09	35.94	34.75	33.52	26.67	18.74	9.83

7%
Old Rate

Payment Adjustments
(As % of Old Payment)

NEW RATE (%)	YEARS REMAINING IN TERM						
	30	29	28	27	26	25	24
4.000	-28.24	-27.70	-27.13	-26.55	-25.94	-25.32	-24.67
4.125	-27.15	-26.63	-26.09	-25.52	-24.94	-24.34	-23.71
4.250	-26.06	-25.55	-25.03	-24.49	-23.93	-23.35	-22.75
4.375	-24.95	-24.47	-23.97	-23.45	-22.91	-22.36	-21.78
4.500	-23.84	-23.38	-22.90	-22.40	-21.89	-21.36	-20.81
4.625	-22.72	-22.28	-21.82	-21.35	-20.86	-20.35	-19.82
4.750	-21.59	-21.17	-20.74	-20.29	-19.82	-19.34	-18.83
4.875	-20.46	-20.06	-19.64	-19.22	-18.77	-18.32	-17.84
5.000	-19.31	-18.94	-18.55	-18.14	-17.72	-17.29	-16.84
5.125	-18.16	-17.80	-17.44	-17.06	-16.66	-16.25	-15.83
5.250	-17.00	-16.67	-16.32	-15.97	-15.60	-15.21	-14.82
5.375	-15.83	-15.52	-15.20	-14.87	-14.52	-14.17	-13.80
5.500	-14.66	-14.37	-14.07	-13.76	-13.45	-13.11	-12.77
5.625	-13.47	-13.21	-12.94	-12.65	-12.36	-12.06	-11.74
5.750	-12.28	-12.04	-11.79	-11.54	-11.27	-10.99	-10.70
5.875	-11.09	-10.87	-10.64	-10.41	-10.17	-9.92	-9.66
6.000	-9.88	-9.69	-9.49	-9.28	-9.06	-8.84	-8.61
6.125	-8.67	-8.50	-8.33	-8.14	-7.95	-7.76	-7.55
6.250	-7.45	-7.31	-7.16	-7.00	-6.84	-6.67	-6.49
6.375	-6.23	-6.11	-5.98	-5.85	-5.71	-5.57	-5.42
6.500	-5.00	-4.90	-4.80	-4.69	-4.58	-4.47	-4.35
6.625	-3.76	-3.68	-3.61	-3.53	-3.44	-3.36	-3.27
6.750	-2.51	-2.46	-2.41	-2.36	-2.30	-2.24	-2.19
6.875	-1.26	-1.23	-1.21	-1.18	-1.15	-1.13	-1.10
7.000	0.00	0.00	0.00	0.00	0.00	0.00	0.00
7.125	1.27	1.24	1.21	1.19	1.16	1.13	1.10
7.250	2.54	2.49	2.44	2.38	2.33	2.27	2.21
7.375	3.81	3.74	3.66	3.58	3.50	3.41	3.32
7.500	5.10	5.00	4.89	4.79	4.67	4.56	4.44
7.625	6.39	6.26	6.13	6.00	5.86	5.71	5.56
7.750	7.68	7.53	7.38	7.21	7.04	6.87	6.69
7.875	8.98	8.81	8.63	8.44	8.24	8.03	7.82
8.000	10.29	10.09	9.88	9.66	9.44	9.20	8.96
8.125	11.60	11.38	11.14	10.90	10.64	10.38	10.10
8.250	12.92	12.67	12.41	12.13	11.85	11.56	11.25
8.375	14.25	13.97	13.68	13.38	13.07	12.74	12.40
8.500	15.57	15.27	14.96	14.63	14.29	13.93	13.56
8.625	16.91	16.58	16.24	15.88	15.51	15.12	14.72
8.750	18.25	17.89	17.52	17.14	16.74	16.32	15.89
8.875	19.59	19.21	18.82	18.42	17.97	17.53	17.06
9.000	20.94	20.54	20.11	19.67	19.21	18.74	18.24
9.125	22.30	21.86	21.42	20.95	20.46	19.95	19.42
9.250	23.65	23.20	22.72	22.22	21.71	21.17	20.61
9.375	25.02	24.54	24.03	23.51	22.96	22.39	21.80
9.500	26.39	25.88	25.35	24.80	24.22	23.62	22.99
9.625	27.76	27.23	26.67	26.09	25.48	24.85	24.19
9.750	29.14	28.58	27.99	27.38	26.75	26.08	25.39
9.875	30.52	29.94	29.32	28.69	28.02	27.32	26.60
10.000	31.91	31.30	30.66	29.99	29.30	28.57	27.81
10.125	33.30	32.66	32.00	31.30	30.58	29.82	29.03
10.250	34.69	34.03	33.34	32.61	31.86	31.07	30.25
10.375	36.09	35.40	34.68	33.93	33.15	32.33	31.47
10.500	37.49	36.78	36.03	35.26	34.44	33.59	32.70
10.625	38.90	38.16	37.39	36.58	35.74	34.85	33.93
10.750	40.31	39.55	38.75	37.91	37.04	36.12	35.17
10.875	41.72	40.94	40.11	39.25	38.34	37.40	36.41
11.000	43.14	42.33	41.48	40.58	39.65	38.67	37.65

Payment Adjustments
(As % of Old Payment)

7%
Old Rate

NEW RATE (%)	YEARS REMAINING IN TERM						
	23	22	21	20	15	10	5
4.000	-24.00	-23.30	-22.58	-21.84	-17.70	-12.80	-6.99
4.125	-23.07	-22.40	-21.70	-20.99	-17.01	-12.29	-6.71
4.250	-22.13	-21.49	-20.82	-20.13	-16.30	-11.77	-6.42
4.375	-21.18	-20.57	-19.93	-19.27	-15.60	-11.26	-6.13
4.500	-20.23	-19.64	-19.03	-18.40	-14.89	-10.74	-5.85
4.625	-19.28	-18.71	-18.13	-17.53	-14.18	-10.22	-5.56
4.750	-18.32	-17.78	-17.22	-16.65	-13.46	-9.70	-5.27
4.875	-17.35	-16.84	-16.31	-15.77	-12.74	-9.17	-4.99
5.000	-16.37	-15.89	-15.39	-14.88	-12.02	-8.65	-4.70
5.125	-15.39	-14.94	-14.47	-13.98	-11.29	-8.12	-4.41
5.250	-14.41	-13.98	-13.54	-13.09	-10.56	-7.59	-4.12
5.375	-13.41	-13.02	-12.61	-12.18	-9.83	-7.06	-3.83
5.500	-12.42	-12.05	-11.67	-11.27	-9.09	-6.53	-3.54
5.625	-11.41	-11.07	-10.72	-10.36	-8.36	-6.00	-3.24
5.750	-10.40	-10.09	-9.77	-9.44	-7.61	-5.46	-2.95
5.875	-9.39	-9.11	-8.82	-8.52	-6.86	-4.92	-2.66
6.000	-8.37	-8.12	-7.86	-7.59	-6.12	-4.38	-2.37
6.125	-7.34	-7.12	-6.89	-6.66	-5.36	-3.84	-2.07
6.250	-6.31	-6.12	-5.93	-5.72	-4.61	-3.30	-1.78
6.375	-5.27	-5.11	-4.95	-4.78	-3.85	-2.75	-1.48
6.500	-4.23	-4.10	-3.97	-3.83	-3.08	-2.20	-1.19
6.625	-3.18	-3.08	-2.98	-2.88	-2.32	-1.66	-0.89
6.750	-2.12	-2.06	-1.99	-1.93	-1.55	-1.11	-0.59
6.875	-1.06	-1.03	-1.00	-0.97	-0.78	-0.55	-0.30
7.000	0.00	0.00	0.00	0.00	0.00	0.00	0.00
7.125	1.07	1.04	1.00	0.97	0.78	0.56	0.30
7.250	2.15	2.08	2.01	1.95	1.56	1.11	0.60
7.375	3.23	3.13	3.03	2.92	2.35	1.67	0.90
7.500	4.31	4.18	4.05	3.91	3.14	2.23	1.20
7.625	5.40	5.24	5.07	4.90	3.93	2.80	1.50
7.750	6.50	6.30	6.10	5.89	4.72	3.36	1.80
7.875	7.60	7.37	7.13	6.89	5.52	3.93	2.10
8.000	8.70	8.44	8.17	7.89	6.32	4.50	2.40
8.125	9.81	9.52	9.21	8.89	7.13	5.07	2.70
8.250	10.93	10.60	10.26	9.90	7.93	5.64	3.01
8.375	12.05	11.69	11.31	10.92	8.75	6.21	3.31
8.500	13.18	12.78	12.36	11.93	9.56	6.78	3.61
8.625	14.30	13.87	13.42	12.96	10.38	7.36	3.92
8.750	15.44	14.97	14.49	13.98	11.19	7.94	4.22
8.875	16.58	16.08	15.55	15.01	12.02	8.52	4.53
9.000	17.72	17.18	16.63	16.05	12.84	9.10	4.83
9.125	18.87	18.30	17.70	17.09	13.67	9.69	5.14
9.250	20.02	19.41	18.78	18.13	14.50	10.27	5.45
9.375	21.18	20.54	19.87	19.18	15.34	10.86	5.76
9.500	22.34	21.66	20.96	20.23	16.18	11.45	6.06
9.625	23.50	22.79	22.05	21.28	17.02	12.04	6.37
9.750	24.67	23.93	23.15	22.34	17.86	12.63	6.68
9.875	25.85	25.06	24.25	23.40	18.71	13.22	6.99
10.000	27.03	26.21	25.36	24.47	19.56	13.82	7.30
10.125	28.21	27.35	26.46	25.54	20.41	14.41	7.61
10.250	29.39	28.50	27.58	26.61	21.26	15.01	7.92
10.375	30.58	29.66	28.69	27.69	22.12	15.61	8.24
10.500	31.78	30.81	29.81	28.77	22.98	16.22	8.55
10.625	32.98	31.98	30.94	29.86	23.85	16.82	8.86
10.750	34.18	33.14	32.07	30.95	24.71	17.42	9.18
10.875	35.38	34.31	33.20	32.04	25.58	18.03	9.49
11.000	36.59	35.48	34.33	33.13	26.45	18.64	9.80

7¼%
Old Rate

Payment Adjustments
(As % of Old Payment)

NEW RATE (%)	YEARS REMAINING IN TERM						
	30	29	28	27	26	25	24
4.250	-27.89	-27.36	-26.81	-26.25	-25.66	-25.05	-24.42
4.375	-26.81	-26.30	-25.78	-25.23	-24.67	-24.08	-23.47
4.500	-25.73	-25.24	-24.73	-24.21	-23.66	-23.10	-22.52
4.625	-24.63	-24.16	-23.68	-23.18	-22.66	-22.12	-21.55
4.750	-23.53	-23.09	-22.62	-22.14	-21.64	-21.12	-20.59
4.875	-22.42	-22.00	-21.56	-21.10	-20.62	-20.13	-19.61
5.000	-21.31	-20.90	-20.48	-20.05	-19.59	-19.12	-18.64
5.125	-20.18	-19.80	-19.40	-18.99	-18.56	-18.11	-17.65
5.250	-19.05	-18.69	-18.31	-17.92	-17.52	-17.09	-16.66
5.375	-17.91	-17.57	-17.22	-16.85	-16.47	-16.07	-15.66
5.500	-16.77	-16.45	-16.12	-15.77	-15.41	-15.04	-14.66
5.625	-15.62	-15.32	-15.01	-14.69	-14.35	-14.01	-13.65
5.750	-14.45	-14.18	-13.89	-13.59	-13.28	-12.96	-12.63
5.875	-13.29	-13.03	-12.77	-12.49	-12.21	-11.92	-11.61
6.000	-12.11	-11.88	-11.64	-11.39	-11.13	-10.86	-10.58
6.125	-10.93	-10.72	-10.50	-10.28	-10.04	-9.80	-9.55
6.250	-9.74	-9.56	-9.36	-9.16	-8.95	-8.74	-8.51
6.375	-8.55	-8.38	-8.21	-8.04	-7.85	-7.66	-7.47
6.500	-7.35	-7.20	-7.06	-6.91	-6.75	-6.59	-6.42
6.625	-6.14	-6.02	-5.90	-5.77	-5.64	-5.50	-5.36
6.750	-4.92	-4.83	-4.73	-4.63	-4.52	-4.41	-4.30
6.875	-3.70	-3.63	-3.56	-3.48	-3.40	-3.32	-3.23
7.000	-2.47	-2.43	-2.38	-2.33	-2.27	-2.22	-2.16
7.125	-1.24	-1.22	-1.19	-1.17	-1.14	-1.11	-1.08
7.250	0.00	0.00	0.00	0.00	0.00	0.00	0.00
7.375	1.25	1.22	1.20	1.17	1.14	1.12	1.09
7.500	2.50	2.45	2.40	2.35	2.29	2.24	2.18
7.625	3.75	3.68	3.61	3.53	3.45	3.37	3.28
7.750	5.02	4.92	4.82	4.72	4.61	4.50	4.38
7.875	6.29	6.17	6.04	5.91	5.78	5.64	5.49
8.000	7.56	7.42	7.27	7.11	6.95	6.78	6.60
8.125	8.84	8.67	8.50	8.32	8.13	7.93	7.72
8.250	10.13	9.94	9.74	9.53	9.31	9.08	8.85
8.375	11.42	11.20	10.98	10.74	10.50	10.24	9.97
8.500	12.71	12.47	12.22	11.96	11.69	11.40	11.11
8.625	14.02	13.75	13.47	13.19	12.88	12.57	12.24
8.750	15.32	15.03	14.73	14.41	14.09	13.74	13.39
8.875	16.63	16.32	15.99	15.65	15.29	14.92	14.53
9.000	17.95	17.61	17.26	16.89	16.50	16.10	15.68
9.125	19.27	18.91	18.53	18.13	17.72	17.29	16.84
9.250	20.60	20.21	19.80	19.38	18.94	18.48	18.00
9.375	21.93	21.51	21.08	20.63	20.17	19.68	19.16
9.500	23.26	22.82	22.37	21.89	21.39	20.88	20.33
9.625	24.60	24.14	23.66	23.15	22.63	22.08	21.51
9.750	25.94	25.46	24.95	24.42	23.87	23.29	22.68
9.875	27.29	26.78	26.25	25.69	25.11	24.50	23.87
10.000	28.64	28.11	27.55	26.97	26.36	25.72	25.05
10.125	30.00	29.44	28.86	28.25	27.61	26.94	26.24
10.250	31.36	30.78	30.17	29.53	28.86	28.16	27.44
10.375	32.72	32.12	31.48	30.82	30.12	29.39	28.63
10.500	34.09	33.46	32.80	32.11	31.38	30.63	29.84
10.625	35.46	34.81	34.12	33.40	32.65	31.86	31.04
10.750	36.84	36.16	35.45	34.70	33.92	33.10	32.25
10.875	38.22	37.52	36.78	36.01	35.20	34.35	33.46
11.000	39.60	38.87	38.11	37.31	36.47	35.60	34.68
11.125	40.99	40.24	39.45	38.62	37.76	36.85	35.90
11.250	42.38	41.60	40.79	39.94	39.04	38.11	37.13

Payment Adjustments
(As % of Old Payment)

7¼%
Old Rate

NEW RATE (%)	YEARS REMAINING IN TERM						
	23	22	21	20	15	10	5
4.250	-23.76	-23.09	-22.38	-21.65	-17.59	-12.75	-6.98
4.375	-22.84	-22.19	-21.51	-20.81	-16.90	-12.23	-6.69
4.500	-21.91	-21.28	-20.63	-19.96	-16.20	-11.72	-6.41
4.625	-20.97	-20.37	-19.75	-19.10	-15.50	-11.21	-6.12
4.750	-20.03	-19.46	-18.86	-18.24	-14.79	-10.69	-5.84
4.875	-19.08	-18.53	-17.96	-17.37	-14.08	-10.18	-5.55
5.000	-18.13	-17.61	-17.06	-16.50	-13.37	-9.66	-5.26
5.125	-17.17	-16.67	-16.16	-15.62	-12.66	-9.13	-4.97
5.250	-16.20	-15.73	-15.25	-14.74	-11.94	-8.61	-4.69
5.375	-15.23	-14.79	-14.33	-13.86	-11.22	-8.09	-4.40
5.500	-14.26	-13.84	-13.41	-12.97	-10.49	-7.56	-4.11
5.625	-13.27	-12.89	-12.49	-12.07	-9.76	-7.03	-3.82
5.750	-12.28	-11.93	-11.56	-11.17	-9.03	-6.50	-3.53
5.875	-11.29	-10.96	-10.62	-10.27	-8.30	-5.97	-3.24
6.000	-10.29	-9.99	-9.68	-9.36	-7.56	-5.44	-2.95
6.125	-9.29	-9.01	-8.73	-8.44	-6.82	-4.90	-2.65
6.250	-8.28	-8.03	-7.78	-7.52	-6.07	-4.36	-2.36
6.375	-7.26	-7.05	-6.83	-6.60	-5.33	-3.82	-2.07
6.500	-6.24	-6.06	-5.87	-5.67	-4.57	-3.28	-1.77
6.625	-5.21	-5.06	-4.90	-4.74	-3.82	-2.74	-1.48
6.750	-4.18	-4.06	-3.93	-3.80	-3.06	-2.20	-1.18
6.875	-3.14	-3.05	-2.95	-2.86	-2.30	-1.65	-0.89
7.000	-2.10	-2.04	-1.97	-1.91	-1.54	-1.10	-0.59
7.125	-1.05	-1.02	-0.99	-0.96	-0.77	-0.55	-0.30
7.250	0.00	0.00	0.00	0.00	0.00	0.00	0.00
7.375	1.06	1.03	0.99	0.96	0.77	0.55	0.30
7.500	2.12	2.06	1.99	1.92	1.55	1.11	0.59
7.625	3.19	3.09	3.00	2.89	2.33	1.66	0.89
7.750	4.26	4.13	4.00	3.87	3.11	2.22	1.19
7.875	5.34	5.18	5.02	4.85	3.90	2.78	1.49
8.000	6.42	6.23	6.03	5.83	4.69	3.34	1.79
8.125	7.51	7.29	7.05	6.81	5.48	3.91	2.09
8.250	8.60	8.34	8.08	7.80	6.27	4.47	2.39
8.375	9.70	9.41	9.11	8.80	7.07	5.04	2.70
8.500	10.80	10.48	10.14	9.80	7.87	5.61	3.00
8.625	11.90	11.55	11.18	10.80	8.68	6.18	3.30
8.750	13.01	12.63	12.23	11.81	9.48	6.75	3.60
8.875	14.13	13.71	13.27	12.82	10.29	7.32	3.91
9.000	15.25	14.79	14.32	13.83	11.11	7.90	4.21
9.125	16.37	15.89	15.38	14.85	11.92	8.48	4.52
9.250	17.50	16.98	16.44	15.88	12.74	9.06	4.82
9.375	18.63	18.08	17.50	16.90	13.56	9.64	5.13
9.500	19.77	19.18	18.57	17.93	14.39	10.22	5.43
9.625	20.91	20.29	19.64	18.97	15.22	10.80	5.74
9.750	22.05	21.40	20.72	20.01	16.05	11.39	6.05
9.875	23.20	22.51	21.80	21.05	16.88	11.97	6.36
10.000	24.36	23.63	22.88	22.10	17.72	12.56	6.67
10.125	25.51	24.76	23.97	23.15	18.56	13.15	6.97
10.250	26.68	25.88	25.06	24.20	19.40	13.75	7.28
10.375	27.84	27.01	26.15	25.26	20.24	14.34	7.59
10.500	29.01	28.15	27.25	26.32	21.09	14.93	7.90
10.625	30.18	29.29	28.35	27.38	21.94	15.53	8.22
10.750	31.36	30.43	29.46	28.45	22.79	16.13	8.53
10.875	32.54	31.57	30.57	29.52	23.65	16.73	8.84
11.000	33.72	32.72	31.68	30.59	24.51	17.33	9.15
11.125	34.91	33.88	32.80	31.67	25.37	17.94	9.47
11.250	36.10	35.03	33.92	32.75	26.23	18.54	9.78

7½%
Old Rate

Payment Adjustments
(As % of Old Payment)

NEW RATE (%)	YEARS REMAINING IN TERM						
	30	29	28	27	26	25	24
4.500	-27.53	-27.03	-26.50	-25.95	-25.38	-24.78	-24.17
4.625	-26.47	-25.98	-25.47	-24.94	-24.39	-23.82	-23.23
4.750	-25.39	-24.92	-24.44	-23.93	-23.40	-22.85	-22.28
4.875	-24.31	-23.86	-23.39	-22.91	-22.40	-21.88	-21.33
5.000	-23.23	-22.79	-22.35	-21.88	-21.40	-20.89	-20.37
5.125	-22.13	-21.72	-21.29	-20.85	-20.38	-19.90	-19.41
5.250	-21.02	-20.63	-20.23	-19.80	-19.37	-18.91	-18.44
5.375	-19.91	-19.54	-19.16	-18.76	-18.34	-17.91	-17.46
5.500	-18.80	-18.45	-18.08	-17.70	-17.31	-16.90	-16.48
5.625	-17.67	-17.34	-17.00	-16.64	-16.27	-15.89	-15.49
5.750	-16.54	-16.23	-15.91	-15.58	-15.23	-14.87	-14.49
5.875	-15.40	-15.11	-14.81	-14.50	-14.18	-13.84	-13.49
6.000	-14.25	-13.99	-13.71	-13.42	-13.12	-12.81	-12.49
6.125	-13.10	-12.86	-12.60	-12.34	-12.06	-11.78	-11.48
6.250	-11.94	-11.72	-11.49	-11.25	-10.99	-10.73	-10.46
6.375	-10.78	-10.57	-10.36	-10.15	-9.92	-9.68	-9.44
6.500	-9.60	-9.42	-9.24	-9.04	-8.84	-8.63	-8.41
6.625	-8.42	-8.27	-8.10	-7.93	-7.76	-7.57	-7.38
6.750	-7.24	-7.10	-6.96	-6.82	-6.66	-6.51	-6.34
6.875	-6.05	-5.93	-5.82	-5.70	-5.57	-5.44	-5.30
7.000	-4.85	-4.76	-4.67	-4.57	-4.47	-4.36	-4.25
7.125	-3.65	-3.58	-3.51	-3.43	-3.36	-3.28	-3.19
7.250	-2.44	-2.39	-2.34	-2.29	-2.24	-2.19	-2.13
7.375	-1.22	-1.20	-1.17	-1.15	-1.12	-1.10	-1.07
7.500	0.00	0.00	0.00	0.00	0.00	0.00	0.00
7.625	1.23	1.20	1.18	1.16	1.13	1.10	1.07
7.750	2.46	2.41	2.37	2.32	2.27	2.21	2.16
7.875	3.70	3.63	3.56	3.48	3.41	3.32	3.24
8.000	4.94	4.85	4.75	4.65	4.55	4.44	4.33
8.125	6.19	6.08	5.96	5.83	5.70	5.57	5.42
8.250	7.44	7.31	7.16	7.01	6.86	6.69	6.52
8.375	8.70	8.54	8.38	8.20	8.02	7.83	7.63
8.500	9.97	9.78	9.59	9.39	9.18	8.96	8.74
8.625	11.24	11.03	10.81	10.59	10.35	10.11	9.85
8.750	12.51	12.28	12.04	11.79	11.53	11.25	10.97
8.875	13.79	13.54	13.27	13.00	12.71	12.40	12.09
9.000	15.08	14.80	14.51	14.21	13.89	13.56	13.21
9.125	16.36	16.06	15.75	15.42	15.08	14.72	14.35
9.250	17.66	17.33	17.00	16.64	16.27	15.89	15.48
9.375	18.96	18.61	18.25	17.87	17.47	17.05	16.62
9.500	20.26	19.89	19.50	19.10	18.67	18.23	17.77
9.625	21.56	21.17	20.76	20.33	19.88	19.41	18.91
9.750	22.87	22.46	22.02	21.57	21.09	20.59	20.07
9.875	24.19	23.75	23.29	22.81	22.30	21.78	21.22
10.000	25.51	25.05	24.56	24.05	23.52	22.97	22.38
10.125	26.83	26.35	25.84	25.30	24.74	24.16	23.55
10.250	28.16	27.65	27.12	26.56	25.97	25.36	24.72
10.375	29.49	28.96	28.40	27.82	27.20	26.56	25.89
10.500	30.82	30.27	29.69	29.08	28.44	27.77	27.06
10.625	32.16	31.59	30.98	30.34	29.68	28.98	28.24
10.750	33.50	32.90	32.27	31.61	30.92	30.19	29.43
10.875	34.85	34.23	33.57	32.89	32.16	31.41	30.62
11.000	36.20	35.55	34.88	34.16	33.41	32.63	31.81
11.125	37.55	36.88	36.18	35.44	34.67	33.85	33.00
11.250	38.91	38.22	37.49	36.73	35.92	35.08	34.20
11.375	40.27	39.55	38.80	38.01	37.18	36.31	35.40
11.500	41.63	40.89	40.12	39.30	38.45	37.55	36.61

Payment Adjustments
(As % of Old Payment)

7½%
Old Rate

NEW RATE (%)	YEARS REMAINING IN TERM						
	23	22	21	20	15	10	5
4.500	-23.53	-22.87	-22.18	-21.47	-17.48	-12.69	-6.96
4.625	-22.61	-21.98	-21.31	-20.63	-16.79	-12.18	-6.68
4.750	-21.69	-21.08	-20.44	-19.78	-16.09	-11.67	-6.39
4.875	-20.76	-20.18	-19.57	-18.93	-15.39	-11.16	-6.11
5.000	-19.83	-19.27	-18.68	-18.08	-14.70	-10.65	-5.82
5.125	-18.89	-18.35	-17.80	-17.22	-13.99	-10.13	-5.54
5.250	-17.94	-17.43	-16.90	-16.35	-13.28	-9.61	-5.25
5.375	-16.99	-16.51	-16.01	-15.48	-12.57	-9.09	-4.96
5.500	-16.04	-15.58	-15.10	-14.61	-11.86	-8.57	-4.67
5.625	-15.07	-14.64	-14.20	-13.73	-11.14	-8.05	-4.39
5.750	-14.11	-13.70	-13.28	-12.85	-10.42	-7.52	-4.10
5.875	-13.13	-12.76	-12.37	-11.96	-9.70	-7.00	-3.81
6.000	-12.15	-11.81	-11.44	-11.07	-8.97	-6.47	-3.52
6.125	-11.17	-10.85	-10.52	-10.17	-8.24	-5.94	-3.23
6.250	-10.18	-9.89	-9.58	-9.27	-7.51	-5.41	-2.94
6.375	-9.19	-8.92	-8.65	-8.36	-6.77	-4.88	-2.65
6.500	-8.19	-7.95	-7.70	-7.45	-6.03	-4.34	-2.35
6.625	-7.18	-6.97	-6.76	-6.53	-5.29	-3.80	-2.06
6.750	-6.17	-5.99	-5.81	-5.61	-4.54	-3.27	-1.77
6.875	-5.15	-5.00	-4.85	-4.69	-3.79	-2.73	-1.48
7.000	-4.13	-4.01	-3.89	-3.76	-3.04	-2.18	-1.18
7.125	-3.11	-3.02	-2.92	-2.83	-2.28	-1.64	-0.89
7.250	-2.08	-2.02	-1.95	-1.89	-1.53	-1.09	-0.59
7.375	-1.04	-1.01	-0.98	-0.95	-0.76	-0.55	-0.30
7.500	0.00	0.00	0.00	0.00	0.00	0.00	0.00
7.625	1.05	1.02	0.98	0.95	0.77	0.55	0.30
7.750	2.10	2.04	1.97	1.91	1.54	1.10	0.60
7.875	3.15	3.06	2.97	2.87	2.31	1.66	0.89
8.000	4.21	4.09	3.96	3.83	3.09	2.21	1.19
8.125	5.28	5.12	4.96	4.80	3.87	2.77	1.49
8.250	6.35	6.16	5.97	5.77	4.65	3.33	1.79
8.375	7.42	7.20	6.98	6.75	5.44	3.89	2.09
8.500	8.50	8.25	7.99	7.73	6.23	4.45	2.39
8.625	9.58	9.30	9.01	8.71	7.02	5.02	2.69
8.750	10.67	10.36	10.03	9.70	7.81	5.58	2.99
8.875	11.76	11.42	11.06	10.69	8.61	6.15	3.29
9.000	12.86	12.48	12.09	11.68	9.41	6.72	3.59
9.125	13.96	13.55	13.13	12.69	10.22	7.29	3.90
9.250	15.06	14.62	14.16	13.69	11.02	7.86	4.20
9.375	16.17	15.70	15.21	14.70	11.83	8.44	4.51
9.500	17.28	16.78	16.25	15.71	12.64	9.01	4.81
9.625	18.40	17.86	17.30	16.72	13.46	9.59	5.12
9.750	19.52	18.95	18.36	17.74	14.28	10.17	5.42
9.875	20.65	20.04	19.42	18.76	15.10	10.75	5.73
10.000	21.78	21.14	20.48	19.79	15.92	11.33	6.03
10.125	22.91	22.24	21.55	20.82	16.75	11.91	6.34
10.250	24.05	23.35	22.61	21.85	17.58	12.50	6.65
10.375	25.19	24.45	23.69	22.89	18.41	13.09	6.96
10.500	26.33	25.56	24.76	23.93	19.24	13.68	7.27
10.625	27.48	26.68	25.85	24.98	20.08	14.27	7.58
10.750	28.63	27.80	26.93	26.02	20.92	14.86	7.89
10.875	29.79	28.92	28.02	27.07	21.76	15.45	8.20
11.000	30.95	30.05	29.11	28.13	22.61	16.05	8.51
11.125	32.11	31.18	30.20	29.19	23.46	16.64	8.82
11.250	33.28	32.31	31.30	30.25	24.31	17.24	9.13
11.375	34.45	33.45	32.40	31.31	25.16	17.84	9.44
11.500	35.62	34.59	33.51	32.38	26.02	18.44	9.76

7¾%
Old Rate

Payment Adjustments
(As % of Old Payment)

NEW RATE (%)	YEARS REMAINING IN TERM						
	30	29	28	27	26	25	24
4.750	-27.19	-26.69	-26.18	-25.65	-25.10	-24.52	-23.92
4.875	-26.13	-25.66	-25.16	-24.65	-24.12	-23.57	-22.99
5.000	-25.07	-24.61	-24.14	-23.65	-23.14	-22.61	-22.05
5.125	-24.00	-23.56	-23.11	-22.64	-22.15	-21.64	-21.11
5.250	-22.92	-22.50	-22.07	-21.62	-21.15	-20.66	-20.16
5.375	-21.84	-21.44	-21.03	-20.60	-20.15	-19.68	-19.20
5.500	-20.75	-20.37	-19.98	-19.57	-19.14	-18.70	-18.24
5.625	-19.65	-19.29	-18.92	-18.53	-18.13	-17.71	-17.27
5.750	-18.54	-18.20	-17.85	-17.49	-17.11	-16.71	-16.30
5.875	-17.43	-17.11	-16.78	-16.44	-16.08	-15.71	-15.32
6.000	-16.31	-16.02	-15.71	-15.38	-15.05	-14.70	-14.34
6.125	-15.19	-14.91	-14.62	-14.32	-14.01	-13.68	-13.35
6.250	-14.06	-13.80	-13.53	-13.26	-12.97	-12.67	-12.35
6.375	-12.92	-12.68	-12.44	-12.18	-11.92	-11.64	-11.35
6.500	-11.77	-11.56	-11.34	-11.10	-10.86	-10.61	-10.34
6.625	-10.62	-10.43	-10.23	-10.02	-9.80	-9.57	-9.33
6.750	-9.47	-9.29	-9.11	-8.93	-8.73	-8.53	-8.32
6.875	-8.30	-8.15	-7.99	-7.83	-7.66	-7.48	-7.30
7.000	-7.13	-7.00	-6.87	-6.73	-6.58	-6.43	-6.27
7.125	-5.96	-5.85	-5.74	-5.62	-5.50	-5.37	-5.24
7.250	-4.78	-4.69	-4.60	-4.51	-4.41	-4.31	-4.20
7.375	-3.59	-3.53	-3.46	-3.39	-3.31	-3.24	-3.16
7.500	-2.40	-2.36	-2.31	-2.26	-2.22	-2.16	-2.11
7.625	-1.20	-1.18	-1.16	-1.14	-1.11	-1.08	-1.06
7.750	0.00	0.00	0.00	0.00	0.00	0.00	0.00
7.875	1.21	1.19	1.16	1.14	1.12	1.09	1.06
8.000	2.42	2.38	2.33	2.28	2.23	2.18	2.13
8.125	3.64	3.58	3.51	3.43	3.36	3.28	3.20
8.250	4.86	4.78	4.69	4.59	4.49	4.38	4.28
8.375	6.09	5.98	5.87	5.75	5.62	5.49	5.36
8.500	7.33	7.20	7.06	6.91	6.76	6.61	6.44
8.625	8.57	8.41	8.25	8.08	7.91	7.72	7.53
8.750	9.81	9.64	9.45	9.26	9.06	8.85	8.63
8.875	11.06	10.86	10.65	10.44	10.21	9.97	9.72
9.000	12.31	12.09	11.86	11.62	11.37	11.10	10.83
9.125	13.57	13.33	13.07	12.81	12.53	12.24	11.93
9.250	14.83	14.57	14.29	14.00	13.70	13.38	13.05
9.375	16.10	15.81	15.51	15.20	14.87	14.52	14.16
9.500	17.37	17.06	16.74	16.40	16.04	15.67	15.28
9.625	18.64	18.31	17.97	17.60	17.22	16.82	16.41
9.750	19.92	19.57	19.20	18.81	18.41	17.98	17.53
9.875	21.21	20.83	20.44	20.03	19.59	19.14	18.67
10.000	22.50	22.10	21.68	21.24	20.79	20.31	19.80
10.125	23.79	23.37	22.93	22.47	21.98	21.47	20.94
10.250	25.08	24.64	24.18	23.69	23.18	22.65	22.09
10.375	26.38	25.92	25.43	24.92	24.38	23.82	23.23
10.500	27.68	27.20	26.69	26.15	25.59	25.00	24.38
10.625	28.99	28.48	27.95	27.39	26.80	26.19	25.54
10.750	30.30	29.77	29.22	28.63	28.02	27.37	26.70
10.875	31.61	31.06	30.48	29.88	29.24	28.56	27.86
11.000	32.93	32.36	31.76	31.12	30.46	29.76	29.03
11.125	34.25	33.66	33.03	32.38	31.68	30.96	30.20
11.250	35.57	34.96	34.31	33.63	32.91	32.16	31.37
11.375	36.90	36.26	35.59	34.89	34.15	33.36	32.54
11.500	38.23	37.57	36.88	36.15	35.38	34.57	33.72
11.625	39.56	38.88	38.17	37.41	36.62	35.78	34.91
11.750	40.90	40.20	39.46	38.68	37.86	37.00	36.09

Payment Adjustments
(As % of Old Payment)

7¾%
Old Rate

NEW RATE (%)	YEARS REMAINING IN TERM						
	23	22	21	20	15	10	5
4.750	-23.30	-22.65	-21.98	-21.28	-17.36	-12.63	-6.95
4.875	-22.39	-21.77	-21.12	-20.45	-16.68	-12.13	-6.66
5.000	-21.48	-20.88	-20.26	-19.61	-15.99	-11.62	-6.38
5.125	-20.56	-19.98	-19.39	-18.77	-15.29	-11.11	-6.09
5.250	-19.63	-19.08	-18.51	-17.92	-14.60	-10.60	-5.81
5.375	-18.70	-18.17	-17.63	-17.07	-13.90	-10.08	-5.52
5.500	-17.76	-17.26	-16.75	-16.21	-13.19	-9.57	-5.24
5.625	-16.82	-16.35	-15.86	-15.35	-12.49	-9.05	-4.95
5.750	-15.87	-15.42	-14.96	-14.48	-11.78	-8.53	-4.66
5.875	-14.92	-14.50	-14.06	-13.61	-11.07	-8.01	-4.38
6.000	-13.96	-13.57	-13.16	-12.73	-10.35	-7.49	-4.09
6.125	-12.99	-12.63	-12.25	-11.85	-9.63	-6.97	-3.80
6.250	-12.03	-11.69	-11.33	-10.97	-8.91	-6.44	-3.51
6.375	-11.05	-10.74	-10.41	-10.08	-8.18	-5.91	-3.22
6.500	-10.07	-9.79	-9.49	-9.18	-7.45	-5.39	-2.93
6.625	-9.09	-8.83	-8.56	-8.28	-6.72	-4.85	-2.64
6.750	-8.10	-7.87	-7.63	-7.38	-5.99	-4.32	-2.35
6.875	-7.10	-6.90	-6.69	-6.47	-5.25	-3.79	-2.06
7.000	-6.10	-5.93	-5.75	-5.56	-4.51	-3.25	-1.77
7.125	-5.10	-4.95	-4.80	-4.64	-3.77	-2.71	-1.47
7.250	-4.09	-3.97	-3.85	-3.72	-3.02	-2.17	-1.18
7.375	-3.07	-2.99	-2.89	-2.80	-2.27	-1.63	-0.89
7.500	-2.05	-2.00	-1.93	-1.87	-1.52	-1.09	-0.59
7.625	-1.03	-1.00	-0.97	-0.94	-0.76	-0.55	-0.30
7.750	0.00	0.00	0.00	0.00	0.00	0.00	0.00
7.875	1.03	1.00	0.97	0.94	0.76	0.55	0.30
8.000	2.07	2.01	1.95	1.89	1.53	1.10	0.59
8.125	3.11	3.03	2.93	2.84	2.30	1.65	0.89
8.250	4.16	4.04	3.92	3.79	3.07	2.20	1.19
8.375	5.21	5.06	4.91	4.75	3.84	2.76	1.49
8.500	6.27	6.09	5.90	5.71	4.62	3.31	1.78
8.625	7.33	7.12	6.90	6.68	5.40	3.87	2.08
8.750	8.40	8.16	7.91	7.64	6.18	4.43	2.38
8.875	9.46	9.19	8.91	8.62	6.97	4.99	2.68
9.000	10.54	10.24	9.92	9.60	7.75	5.55	2.98
9.125	11.62	11.28	10.94	10.58	8.55	6.12	3.28
9.250	12.70	12.34	11.96	11.56	9.34	6.68	3.59
9.375	13.78	13.39	12.98	12.55	10.14	7.25	3.89
9.500	14.87	14.45	14.01	13.54	10.94	7.82	4.19
9.625	15.97	15.51	15.04	14.54	11.74	8.39	4.49
9.750	17.07	16.58	16.07	15.54	12.55	8.97	4.80
9.875	18.17	17.65	17.11	16.54	13.35	9.54	5.10
10.000	19.27	18.72	18.15	17.55	14.16	10.12	5.41
10.125	20.38	19.80	19.19	18.56	14.98	10.69	5.71
10.250	21.50	20.88	20.24	19.57	15.79	11.27	6.02
10.375	22.62	21.97	21.30	20.59	16.61	11.85	6.32
10.500	23.74	23.06	22.35	21.61	17.44	12.44	6.63
10.625	24.86	24.15	23.41	22.64	18.26	13.02	6.94
10.750	25.99	25.25	24.47	23.66	19.09	13.60	7.25
10.875	27.12	26.35	25.54	24.70	19.92	14.19	7.56
11.000	28.26	27.45	26.61	25.73	20.75	14.78	7.86
11.125	29.40	28.56	27.68	26.77	21.59	15.37	8.17
11.250	30.54	29.67	28.76	27.81	22.42	15.96	8.48
11.375	31.68	30.78	29.84	28.85	23.26	16.56	8.79
11.500	32.83	31.90	30.92	29.90	24.11	17.15	9.11
11.625	33.99	33.02	32.01	30.95	24.95	17.75	9.42
11.750	35.14	34.14	33.10	32.01	25.80	18.35	9.73

8%
Old Rate

Payment Adjustments
(As % of Old Payment)

NEW RATE (%)	YEARS REMAINING IN TERM						
	30	29	28	27	26	25	24
5.000	-26.84	-26.37	-25.87	-25.35	-24.82	-24.26	-23.68
5.125	-25.80	-25.34	-24.86	-24.37	-23.85	-23.31	-22.75
5.250	-24.74	-24.30	-23.85	-23.37	-22.88	-22.36	-21.82
5.375	-23.68	-23.26	-22.83	-22.37	-21.90	-21.40	-20.88
5.500	-22.62	-22.22	-21.80	-21.36	-20.91	-20.44	-19.94
5.625	-21.55	-21.17	-20.77	-20.35	-19.92	-19.47	-19.00
5.750	-20.47	-20.10	-19.73	-19.33	-18.92	-18.49	-18.04
5.875	-19.38	-19.04	-18.68	-18.31	-17.91	-17.51	-17.08
6.000	-18.29	-17.97	-17.63	-17.27	-16.91	-16.52	-16.12
6.125	-17.19	-16.89	-16.57	-16.24	-15.89	-15.53	-15.15
6.250	-16.09	-15.80	-15.50	-15.19	-14.87	-14.53	-14.18
6.375	-14.98	-14.71	-14.43	-14.14	-13.84	-13.53	-13.20
6.500	-13.86	-13.61	-13.36	-13.09	-12.81	-12.52	-12.21
6.625	-12.74	-12.51	-12.27	-12.03	-11.77	-11.50	-11.22
6.750	-11.61	-11.40	-11.19	-10.96	-10.73	-10.48	-10.23
6.875	-10.47	-10.29	-10.09	-9.89	-9.68	-9.46	-9.23
7.000	-9.33	-9.17	-8.99	-8.81	-8.62	-8.43	-8.22
7.125	-8.18	-8.04	-7.89	-7.73	-7.56	-7.39	-7.21
7.250	-7.03	-6.91	-6.78	-6.64	-6.50	-6.35	-6.19
7.375	-5.87	-5.77	-5.66	-5.55	-5.43	-5.30	-5.17
7.500	-4.71	-4.63	-4.54	-4.45	-4.35	-4.25	-4.15
7.625	-3.54	-3.48	-3.41	-3.34	-3.27	-3.20	-3.12
7.750	-2.36	-2.32	-2.28	-2.23	-2.19	-2.14	-2.08
7.875	-1.18	-1.16	-1.14	-1.12	-1.10	-1.07	-1.04
8.000	0.00	0.00	0.00	0.00	0.00	0.00	0.00
8.125	1.19	1.17	1.15	1.12	1.10	1.08	1.05
8.250	2.39	2.34	2.30	2.25	2.21	2.16	2.10
8.375	3.59	3.52	3.46	3.39	3.32	3.24	3.16
8.500	4.79	4.71	4.62	4.53	4.43	4.33	4.22
8.625	6.00	5.90	5.79	5.67	5.55	5.42	5.29
8.750	7.21	7.09	6.96	6.82	6.67	6.52	6.36
8.875	8.43	8.29	8.13	7.97	7.80	7.62	7.44
9.000	9.66	9.49	9.31	9.13	8.93	8.73	8.52
9.125	10.88	10.70	10.50	10.29	10.07	9.84	9.60
9.250	12.12	11.91	11.69	11.45	11.21	10.96	10.69
9.375	13.35	13.12	12.88	12.62	12.36	12.08	11.78
9.500	14.59	14.34	14.08	13.80	13.51	13.20	12.88
9.625	15.84	15.57	15.28	14.98	14.66	14.33	13.98
9.750	17.09	16.79	16.49	16.16	15.82	15.46	15.08
9.875	18.34	18.03	17.69	17.35	16.98	16.60	16.19
10.000	19.60	19.26	18.91	18.54	18.15	17.74	17.31
10.125	20.86	20.50	20.13	19.73	19.32	18.88	18.42
10.250	22.12	21.75	21.35	20.93	20.49	20.03	19.54
10.375	23.39	22.99	22.57	22.13	21.67	21.18	20.66
10.500	24.66	24.24	23.80	23.34	22.85	22.33	21.79
10.625	25.94	25.50	25.03	24.55	24.03	23.49	22.92
10.750	27.22	26.76	26.27	25.76	25.22	24.65	24.06
10.875	28.50	28.02	27.51	26.98	26.41	25.82	25.20
11.000	29.79	29.28	28.75	28.20	27.61	26.99	26.34
11.125	31.07	30.55	30.00	29.42	28.81	28.16	27.48
11.250	32.37	31.82	31.25	30.65	30.01	29.34	28.63
11.375	33.66	33.10	32.50	31.87	31.21	30.52	29.78
11.500	34.96	34.38	33.76	33.11	32.42	31.70	30.94
11.625	36.26	35.66	35.02	34.34	33.63	32.88	32.10
11.750	37.57	36.94	36.28	35.58	34.85	34.07	33.26
11.875	38.87	38.23	37.55	36.83	36.07	35.27	34.42
12.000	40.18	39.52	38.82	38.07	37.29	36.46	35.59

Payment Adjustments
(As % of Old Payment)

8% Old Rate

NEW RATE (%)	23	22	21	20	15	10	5
			YEARS REMAINING IN TERM				
5.000	-23.07	-22.44	-21.78	-21.10	-17.25	-12.58	-6.93
5.125	-22.17	-21.56	-20.93	-20.27	-16.57	-12.07	-6.65
5.250	-21.26	-20.68	-20.07	-19.44	-15.88	-11.57	-6.36
5.375	-20.35	-19.79	-19.21	-18.60	-15.19	-11.06	-6.08
5.500	-19.43	-18.90	-18.34	-17.76	-14.50	-10.55	-5.80
5.625	-18.51	-18.00	-17.47	-16.91	-13.80	-10.04	-5.51
5.750	-17.58	-17.09	-16.59	-16.06	-13.10	-9.53	-5.22
5.875	-16.64	-16.18	-15.70	-15.21	-12.40	-9.01	-4.94
6.000	-15.70	-15.27	-14.82	-14.35	-11.70	-8.50	-4.65
6.125	-14.76	-14.35	-13.93	-13.48	-10.99	-7.98	-4.37
6.250	-13.81	-13.43	-13.03	-12.61	-10.28	-7.46	-4.08
6.375	-12.86	-12.50	-12.13	-11.74	-9.56	-6.93	-3.79
6.500	-11.90	-11.57	-11.22	-10.86	-8.85	-6.41	-3.50
6.625	-10.93	-10.63	-10.31	-9.98	-8.13	-5.89	-3.21
6.750	-9.96	-9.68	-9.40	-9.10	-7.40	-5.36	-2.92
6.875	-8.99	-8.74	-8.48	-8.20	-6.68	-4.83	-2.63
7.000	-8.01	-7.78	-7.55	-7.31	-5.95	-4.30	-2.34
7.125	-7.02	-6.83	-6.62	-6.41	-5.21	-3.77	-2.05
7.250	-6.03	-5.87	-5.69	-5.51	-4.48	-3.24	-1.76
7.375	-5.04	-4.90	-4.75	-4.60	-3.74	-2.70	-1.47
7.500	-4.04	-3.93	-3.81	-3.69	-3.00	-2.16	-1.18
7.625	-3.04	-2.95	-2.86	-2.77	-2.25	-1.63	-0.88
7.750	-2.03	-1.97	-1.91	-1.85	-1.50	-1.08	-0.59
7.875	-1.02	-0.99	-0.96	-0.93	-0.75	-0.54	-0.29
8.000	0.00	0.00	0.00	0.00	0.00	0.00	0.00
8.125	1.02	0.99	0.96	0.93	0.76	0.55	0.30
8.250	2.05	1.99	1.93	1.87	1.52	1.09	0.59
8.375	3.08	2.99	2.90	2.81	2.28	1.64	0.89
8.500	4.11	4.00	3.98	3.75	3.04	2.19	1.18
8.625	5.15	5.01	4.86	4.70	3.81	2.74	1.48
8.750	6.20	6.02	5.84	5.65	4.58	3.30	1.78
8.875	7.24	7.04	6.83	6.61	5.36	3.85	2.08
9.000	8.29	8.06	7.82	7.57	6.13	4.41	2.38
9.125	9.35	9.09	8.82	8.53	6.91	4.97	2.68
9.250	10.41	10.12	9.81	9.50	7.70	5.53	2.98
9.375	11.47	11.15	10.82	10.47	8.48	6.09	3.28
9.500	12.54	12.19	11.82	11.44	9.27	6.65	3.58
9.625	13.61	13.23	12.83	12.42	10.06	7.22	3.88
9.750	14.69	14.28	13.85	13.40	10.85	7.78	4.18
9.875	15.77	15.33	14.87	14.38	11.65	8.35	4.48
10.000	16.85	16.38	15.89	15.37	12.45	8.92	4.79
10.125	17.94	17.44	16.91	16.36	13.25	9.49	5.09
10.250	19.03	18.50	17.94	17.36	14.05	10.06	5.39
10.375	20.13	19.56	18.97	18.36	14.86	10.64	5.70
10.500	21.23	20.63	20.01	19.36	15.67	11.22	6.00
10.625	22.33	21.70	21.05	20.37	16.48	11.79	6.31
10.750	23.43	22.78	22.09	21.38	17.30	12.37	6.62
10.875	24.54	23.86	23.14	22.39	18.11	12.95	6.92
11.000	25.65	24.94	24.19	23.40	18.93	13.54	7.23
11.125	26.77	26.02	25.24	24.42	19.76	14.12	7.54
11.250	27.89	27.11	26.30	25.44	20.58	14.71	7.85
11.375	29.01	28.20	27.36	26.47	21.41	15.29	8.15
11.500	30.14	29.30	28.42	27.50	22.24	15.88	8.46
11.625	31.27	30.40	29.48	28.53	23.07	16.47	8.77
11.750	32.40	31.50	30.55	29.56	23.91	17.06	9.08
11.875	33.53	32.60	31.62	30.60	24.75	17.66	9.40
12.000	34.67	33.71	32.70	31.64	25.59	18.25	9.71

8¼%
Old Rate

Payment Adjustments
(As % of Old Payment)

NEW RATE (%)	YEARS REMAINING IN TERM						
	30	29	28	27	26	25	24
5.250	-26.50	-26.04	-25.56	-25.06	-24.54	-24.00	-23.43
5.375	-25.46	-25.02	-24.56	-24.08	-23.58	-23.06	-22.51
5.500	-24.42	-24.00	-23.56	-23.10	-22.62	-22.11	-21.59
5.625	-23.38	-22.97	-22.55	-22.11	-21.65	-21.17	-20.66
5.750	-22.32	-21.93	-21.53	-21.11	-20.67	-20.21	-19.73
5.875	-21.26	-20.89	-20.51	-20.11	-19.69	-19.25	-18.79
6.000	-20.19	-19.84	-19.48	-19.10	-18.70	-18.28	-17.85
6.125	-19.12	-18.79	-18.44	-18.08	-17.70	-17.31	-16.90
6.250	-18.04	-17.73	-17.40	-17.06	-16.71	-16.33	-15.95
6.375	-16.96	-16.66	-16.36	-16.04	-15.70	-15.35	-14.99
6.500	-15.87	-15.59	-15.30	-15.00	-14.69	-14.36	-14.02
6.625	-14.77	-14.51	-14.25	-13.97	-13.67	-13.37	-13.05
6.750	-13.67	-13.43	-13.18	-12.92	-12.65	-12.37	-12.08
6.875	-12.56	-12.34	-12.11	-11.88	-11.63	-11.37	-11.10
7.000	-11.44	-11.24	-11.04	-10.82	-10.60	-10.36	-10.11
7.125	-10.32	-10.14	-9.96	-9.76	-9.56	-9.34	-9.12
7.250	-9.20	-9.04	-8.87	-8.70	-8.52	-8.33	-8.13
7.375	-8.07	-7.93	-7.78	-7.63	-7.47	-7.30	-7.13
7.500	-6.93	-6.81	-6.68	-6.55	-6.42	-6.27	-6.12
7.625	-5.79	-5.69	-5.58	-5.47	-5.36	-5.24	-5.11
7.750	-4.64	-4.56	-4.48	-4.39	-4.30	-4.20	-4.10
7.875	-3.49	-3.43	-3.36	-3.30	-3.23	-3.16	-3.08
8.000	-2.33	-2.29	-2.25	-2.20	-2.16	-2.11	-2.06
8.125	-1.17	-1.15	-1.13	-1.10	-1.08	-1.06	-1.03
8.250	0.00	0.00	0.00	0.00	0.00	0.00	0.00
8.375	1.17	1.15	1.13	1.11	1.09	1.06	1.04
8.500	2.35	2.31	2.27	2.22	2.18	2.13	2.08
8.625	3.53	3.47	3.41	3.34	3.27	3.20	3.12
8.750	4.72	4.64	4.55	4.46	4.37	4.27	4.17
8.875	5.91	5.81	5.70	5.59	5.47	5.35	5.22
9.000	7.10	6.98	6.86	6.72	6.58	6.44	6.28
9.125	8.30	8.16	8.01	7.86	7.70	7.52	7.34
9.250	9.51	9.34	9.18	9.00	8.81	8.62	8.41
9.375	10.71	10.53	10.34	10.14	9.93	9.71	9.48
9.500	11.92	11.72	11.51	11.29	11.06	10.81	10.55
9.625	13.14	12.92	12.69	12.44	12.19	11.92	11.63
9.750	14.36	14.12	13.87	13.60	13.32	13.02	12.71
9.875	15.58	15.32	15.05	14.76	14.46	14.14	13.80
10.000	16.81	16.53	16.24	15.92	15.60	15.25	14.89
10.125	18.04	17.74	17.43	17.09	16.74	16.37	15.98
10.250	19.28	18.96	18.62	18.26	17.89	17.49	17.08
10.375	20.52	20.18	19.82	19.44	19.04	18.62	18.18
10.500	21.76	21.40	21.02	20.62	20.20	19.75	19.28
10.625	23.01	22.63	22.22	21.80	21.36	20.89	20.39
10.750	24.25	23.85	23.43	22.99	22.52	22.02	21.50
10.875	25.51	25.09	24.64	24.18	23.68	23.16	22.62
11.000	26.76	26.32	25.86	25.37	24.85	24.31	23.74
11.125	28.02	27.56	27.08	26.57	26.03	25.46	24.86
11.250	29.28	28.81	28.30	27.77	27.20	26.61	25.98
11.375	30.55	30.05	29.52	28.97	28.38	27.76	27.11
11.500	31.82	31.30	30.75	30.17	29.56	28.92	28.24
11.625	33.09	32.55	31.98	31.38	30.75	30.08	29.38
11.750	34.36	33.81	33.22	32.60	31.94	31.24	30.51
11.875	35.64	35.06	34.45	33.81	33.13	32.41	31.65
12.000	36.92	36.32	35.69	35.03	34.33	33.58	32.80
12.125	38.20	37.59	36.94	36.25	35.52	34.75	33.94
12.250	39.48	38.85	38.18	37.47	36.72	35.93	35.09

Payment Adjustments
(As % of Old Payment)

8¼%
Old Rate

NEW RATE (%)	YEARS REMAINING IN TERM						
	23	22	21	20	15	10	5
5.250	-22.84	-22.22	-21.58	-20.92	-17.14	-12.52	-6.91
5.375	-21.95	-21.35	-20.74	-20.09	-16.46	-12.02	-6.63
5.500	-21.05	-20.48	-19.89	-19.27	-15.78	-11.52	-6.35
5.625	-20.14	-19.60	-19.03	-18.44	-15.09	-11.01	-6.07
5.750	-19.23	-18.71	-18.17	-17.60	-14.40	-10.50	-5.78
5.875	-18.32	-17.82	-17.30	-16.76	-13.71	-9.99	-5.50
6.000	-17.40	-16.92	-16.43	-15.92	-13.02	-9.48	-5.21
6.125	-16.47	-16.02	-15.56	-15.07	-12.32	-8.97	-4.93
6.250	-15.54	-15.12	-14.68	-14.22	-11.62	-8.46	-4.64
6.375	-14.60	-14.21	-13.79	-13.36	-10.91	-7.94	-4.36
6.500	-13.66	-13.29	-12.90	-12.50	-10.21	-7.42	-4.07
6.625	-12.72	-12.37	-12.01	-11.63	-9.50	-6.90	-3.78
6.750	-11.77	-11.45	-11.11	-10.76	-8.79	-6.38	-3.49
6.875	-10.81	-10.52	-10.21	-9.89	-8.07	-5.86	-3.21
7.000	-9.85	-9.58	-9.30	-9.01	-7.35	-5.34	-2.92
7.125	-8.89	-8.65	-8.39	-8.13	-6.63	-4.81	-2.63
7.250	-7.92	-7.70	-7.48	-7.24	-5.90	-4.28	-2.34
7.375	-6.95	-6.75	-6.56	-6.35	-5.18	-3.75	-2.05
7.500	-5.97	-5.80	-5.63	-5.45	-4.45	-3.22	-1.76
7.625	-4.98	-4.85	-4.70	-4.56	-3.71	-2.69	-1.47
7.750	-4.00	-3.89	-3.77	-3.65	-2.97	-2.15	-1.17
7.875	-3.00	-2.92	-2.83	-2.74	-2.24	-1.62	-0.88
8.000	-2.01	-1.95	-1.89	-1.83	-1.49	-1.08	-0.59
8.125	-1.01	-0.98	-0.95	-0.92	-0.75	-0.54	-0.29
8.250	0.00	0.00	0.00	0.00	0.00	0.00	0.00
8.375	1.01	0.98	0.95	0.92	0.75	0.54	0.30
8.500	2.02	1.97	1.91	1.85	1.51	1.09	0.59
8.625	3.04	2.96	2.87	2.78	2.26	1.63	0.89
8.750	4.06	3.95	3.84	3.71	3.02	2.18	1.18
8.875	5.09	4.95	4.80	4.65	3.78	2.73	1.48
9.000	6.12	5.95	5.78	5.59	4.55	3.28	1.77
9.125	7.16	6.96	6.75	6.54	5.32	3.83	2.07
9.250	8.20	7.97	7.73	7.49	6.09	4.39	2.37
9.375	9.24	8.98	8.72	8.44	6.86	4.94	2.67
9.500	10.28	10.00	9.71	9.40	7.64	5.50	2.97
9.625	11.33	11.02	10.70	10.36	8.42	6.06	3.27
9.750	12.39	12.05	11.69	11.32	9.20	6.62	3.57
9.875	13.45	13.08	12.69	12.29	9.98	7.18	3.87
10.000	14.51	14.11	13.69	13.26	10.77	7.74	4.17
10.125	15.57	15.15	14.70	14.23	11.56	8.31	4.47
10.250	16.64	16.19	15.71	15.21	12.35	8.88	4.78
10.375	17.72	17.23	16.72	16.19	13.14	9.44	5.08
10.500	18.79	18.28	17.74	17.17	13.94	10.01	5.38
10.625	19.87	19.33	18.76	18.16	14.74	10.59	5.69
10.750	20.96	20.38	19.78	19.15	15.55	11.16	5.99
10.875	22.04	21.44	20.81	20.14	16.35	11.73	6.29
11.000	23.13	22.50	21.84	21.14	17.16	12.31	6.60
11.125	24.23	23.56	22.87	22.14	17.97	12.89	6.91
11.250	25.32	24.63	23.90	23.14	18.78	13.47	7.21
11.375	26.42	25.70	24.94	24.15	19.60	14.05	7.52
11.500	27.53	26.78	25.99	25.16	20.41	14.63	7.83
11.625	28.63	27.85	27.03	26.17	21.23	15.21	8.13
11.750	29.74	28.93	28.08	27.19	22.06	15.80	8.44
11.875	30.86	30.01	29.13	28.20	22.88	16.39	8.75
12.000	31.97	31.10	30.19	29.23	23.71	16.97	9.06
12.125	33.09	32.19	31.24	30.25	24.54	17.56	9.37
12.250	34.21	33.28	32.30	31.28	25.37	18.15	9.68

8½%
Old Rate

Payment Adjustments
(As % of Old Payment)

NEW RATE (%)	30	29	28	27	26	25	24
	YEARS REMAINING IN TERM						
5.500	-26.16	-25.71	-25.25	-24.77	-24.26	-23.74	-23.19
5.625	-25.13	-24.71	-24.26	-23.80	-23.31	-22.81	-22.28
5.750	-24.10	-23.70	-23.27	-22.82	-22.36	-21.87	-21.36
5.875	-23.07	-22.68	-22.27	-21.84	-21.40	-20.93	-20.44
6.000	-22.03	-21.65	-21.26	-20.86	-20.43	-19.99	-19.52
6.125	-20.98	-20.62	-20.25	-19.86	-19.46	-19.03	-18.59
6.250	-19.92	-19.59	-19.23	-18.87	-18.48	-18.08	-17.66
6.375	-18.86	-18.54	-18.21	-17.86	-17.50	-17.11	-16.72
6.500	-17.80	-17.50	-17.18	-16.85	-16.51	-16.15	-15.77
6.625	-16.73	-16.44	-16.15	-15.84	-15.51	-15.17	-14.82
6.750	-15.65	-15.38	-15.11	-14.82	-14.51	-14.20	-13.87
6.875	-14.56	-14.32	-14.06	-13.79	-13.51	-13.21	-12.91
7.000	-13.48	-13.25	-13.01	-12.76	-12.50	-12.23	-11.94
7.125	-12.38	-12.17	-11.95	-11.72	-11.48	-11.23	-10.97
7.250	-11.28	-11.09	-10.89	-10.68	-10.46	-10.24	-10.00
7.375	-10.18	-10.00	-9.82	-9.64	-9.44	-9.23	-9.02
7.500	-9.06	-8.91	-8.75	-8.59	-8.41	-8.23	-8.03
7.625	-7.95	-7.82	-7.68	-7.53	-7.38	-7.21	-7.05
7.750	-6.83	-6.71	-6.59	-6.47	-6.34	-6.20	-6.05
7.875	-5.70	-5.61	-5.51	-5.40	-5.29	-5.18	-5.05
8.000	-4.57	-4.49	-4.41	-4.33	-4.24	-4.15	-4.05
8.125	-3.44	-3.38	-3.32	-3.25	-3.19	-3.12	-3.05
8.250	-2.30	-2.26	-2.22	-2.17	-2.13	-2.08	-2.03
8.375	-1.15	-1.13	-1.11	-1.09	-1.07	-1.04	-1.02
8.500	0.00	0.00	0.00	0.00	0.00	0.00	0.00
8.625	1.15	1.14	1.12	1.09	1.07	1.05	1.02
8.750	2.31	2.27	2.23	2.19	2.15	2.10	2.05
8.875	3.48	3.42	3.36	3.29	3.23	3.16	3.08
9.000	4.64	4.57	4.49	4.40	4.31	4.22	4.12
9.125	5.82	5.72	5.62	5.51	5.40	5.28	5.16
9.250	6.99	6.88	6.76	6.63	6.49	6.35	6.20
9.375	8.17	8.04	7.90	7.75	7.59	7.43	7.25
9.500	9.36	9.20	9.04	8.87	8.69	8.50	8.30
9.625	10.54	10.37	10.19	10.00	9.80	9.58	9.36
9.750	11.74	11.54	11.34	11.13	10.91	10.67	10.42
9.875	12.93	12.72	12.50	12.26	12.02	11.76	11.48
10.000	14.13	13.90	13.66	13.40	13.13	12.85	12.55
10.125	15.33	15.09	14.82	14.55	14.25	13.95	13.62
10.250	16.54	16.27	15.99	15.69	15.38	15.05	14.70
10.375	17.75	17.46	17.16	16.84	16.50	16.15	15.77
10.500	18.97	18.66	18.34	18.00	17.64	17.26	16.86
10.625	20.18	19.86	19.51	19.15	18.77	18.37	17.94
10.750	21.40	21.06	20.70	20.31	19.91	19.48	19.03
10.875	22.63	22.26	21.88	21.48	21.05	20.60	20.12
11.000	23.85	23.47	23.07	22.64	22.19	21.72	21.22
11.125	25.08	24.68	24.26	23.81	23.34	22.84	22.32
11.250	26.32	25.90	25.46	24.99	24.49	23.97	23.42
11.375	27.55	27.12	26.65	26.16	25.65	25.10	24.52
11.500	28.79	28.34	27.85	27.34	26.80	26.23	25.63
11.625	30.03	29.56	29.06	28.53	27.96	27.37	26.74
11.750	31.28	30.79	30.26	29.71	29.13	28.51	27.86
11.875	32.52	32.02	31.47	30.90	30.29	29.65	28.97
12.000	33.77	33.25	32.69	32.09	31.46	30.80	30.09
12.125	35.03	34.48	33.90	33.29	32.64	31.95	31.22
12.250	36.28	35.72	35.12	34.48	33.81	33.10	32.34
12.375	37.54	36.96	36.34	35.68	34.99	34.25	33.47
12.500	38.80	38.20	37.56	36.89	36.17	35.41	34.61

Payment Adjustments
(As % of Old Payment)

8½%
Old Rate

NEW RATE (%)	YEARS REMAINING IN TERM						
	23	22	21	20	15	10	5
5.500	-22.61	-22.01	-21.39	-20.73	-17.03	-12.47	-6.90
5.625	-21.73	-21.15	-20.55	-19.92	-16.35	-11.97	-6.62
5.750	-20.83	-20.28	-19.70	-19.10	-15.67	-11.47	-6.33
5.875	-19.94	-19.41	-18.85	-18.27	-14.99	-10.96	-6.05
6.000	-19.03	-18.53	-18.00	-17.45	-14.31	-10.46	-5.77
6.125	-18.13	-17.64	-17.14	-16.61	-13.62	-9.95	-5.49
6.250	-17.22	-16.76	-16.28	-15.78	-12.93	-9.44	-5.20
6.375	-16.30	-15.86	-15.41	-14.93	-12.24	-8.93	-4.92
6.500	-15.38	-14.96	-14.54	-14.09	-11.54	-8.42	-4.63
6.625	-14.45	-14.06	-13.66	-13.24	-10.84	-7.90	-4.35
6.750	-13.52	-13.16	-12.78	-12.38	-10.14	-7.39	-4.06
6.875	-12.58	-12.25	-11.89	-11.52	-9.43	-6.87	-3.77
7.000	-11.64	-11.33	-11.00	-10.66	-8.72	-6.35	-3.49
7.125	-10.70	-10.41	-10.11	-9.80	-8.01	-5.83	-3.20
7.250	-9.75	-9.48	-9.21	-8.92	-7.30	-5.31	-2.91
7.375	-8.79	-8.55	-8.31	-8.05	-6.58	-4.79	-2.62
7.500	-7.83	-7.62	-7.40	-7.17	-5.86	-4.26	-2.33
7.625	-6.87	-6.68	-6.49	-6.29	-5.14	-3.74	-2.04
7.750	-5.90	-5.74	-5.57	-5.40	-4.41	-3.21	-1.75
7.875	-4.93	-4.79	-4.66	-4.51	-3.68	-2.68	-1.46
8.000	-3.95	-3.84	-3.73	-3.62	-2.95	-2.14	-1.17
8.125	-2.97	-2.89	-2.81	-2.72	-2.22	-1.61	-0.88
8.250	-1.98	-1.93	-1.87	-1.82	-1.48	-1.08	-0.59
8.375	-0.99	-0.97	-0.94	-0.91	-0.74	-0.54	-0.29
8.500	0.00	0.00	0.00	0.00	0.00	0.00	0.00
8.625	1.00	0.97	0.94	0.91	0.75	0.54	0.29
8.750	2.00	1.95	1.89	1.83	1.49	1.08	0.59
8.875	3.01	2.93	2.84	2.75	2.24	1.62	0.88
9.000	4.02	3.91	3.79	3.68	3.00	2.17	1.18
9.125	5.03	4.90	4.75	4.60	3.75	2.72	1.47
9.250	6.05	5.89	5.72	5.54	4.51	3.26	1.77
9.375	7.07	6.88	6.68	6.47	5.28	3.81	2.07
9.500	8.10	7.88	7.65	7.41	6.04	4.36	2.36
9.625	9.13	8.88	8.62	8.35	6.81	4.92	2.66
9.750	10.16	9.89	9.60	9.30	7.58	5.47	2.96
9.875	11.20	10.90	10.58	10.25	8.35	6.03	3.26
10.000	12.24	11.91	11.56	11.20	9.13	6.59	3.56
10.125	13.28	12.92	12.55	12.16	9.90	7.14	3.86
10.250	14.33	13.94	13.54	13.12	10.68	7.70	4.16
10.375	15.38	14.97	14.53	14.08	11.47	8.27	4.46
10.500	16.44	15.99	15.53	15.04	12.25	8.83	4.76
10.625	17.49	17.02	16.53	16.01	13.04	9.40	5.07
10.750	18.56	18.06	17.53	16.99	13.83	9.96	5.37
10.875	19.62	19.10	18.54	17.96	14.62	10.53	5.67
11.000	20.69	20.14	19.55	18.94	15.42	11.10	5.97
11.125	21.76	21.18	20.57	19.92	16.22	11.67	6.28
11.250	22.84	22.23	21.58	20.91	17.02	12.25	6.58
11.375	23.92	23.27	22.60	21.89	17.82	12.82	6.89
11.500	25.00	24.33	23.62	22.89	18.63	13.40	7.19
11.625	26.08	25.38	24.65	23.88	19.44	13.97	7.50
11.750	27.17	26.44	25.68	24.88	20.25	14.55	7.81
11.875	28.26	27.50	26.71	25.88	21.06	15.13	8.11
12.000	29.35	28.57	27.75	26.88	21.88	15.72	8.42
12.125	30.45	29.64	28.78	27.88	22.69	16.30	8.73
12.250	31.55	30.71	29.82	28.89	23.51	16.88	9.04
12.375	32.65	31.78	30.87	29.90	24.34	17.47	9.35
12.500	33.76	32.86	31.91	30.92	25.16	18.06	9.66

8¾%
Old Rate

Payment Adjustments
(As % of Old Payment)

NEW RATE (%)	YEARS REMAINING IN TERM						
	30	29	28	27	26	25	24
5.750	-25.82	-25.39	-24.95	-24.48	-23.99	-23.48	-22.94
5.875	-24.81	-24.40	-23.97	-23.52	-23.05	-22.56	-22.04
6.000	-23.79	-23.40	-22.98	-22.55	-22.10	-21.63	-21.14
6.125	-22.76	-22.39	-22.00	-21.58	-21.15	-20.70	-20.23
6.250	-21.73	-21.38	-21.00	-20.61	-20.19	-19.76	-19.31
6.375	-20.70	-20.36	-20.00	-19.62	-19.23	-18.82	-18.39
6.500	-19.66	-19.33	-18.99	-18.64	-18.26	-17.87	-17.46
6.625	-18.61	-18.30	-17.98	-17.64	-17.29	-16.92	-16.53
6.750	-17.55	-17.27	-16.96	-16.64	-16.31	-15.96	-15.60
6.875	-16.50	-16.22	-15.94	-15.64	-15.33	-15.00	-14.66
7.000	-15.43	-15.18	-14.91	-14.63	-14.34	-14.03	-13.71
7.125	-14.36	-14.13	-13.88	-13.62	-13.35	-13.06	-12.76
7.250	-13.29	-13.07	-12.84	-12.60	-12.35	-12.08	-11.81
7.375	-12.21	-12.01	-11.80	-11.58	-11.34	-11.10	-10.85
7.500	-11.12	-10.94	-10.75	-10.55	-10.34	-10.11	-9.88
7.625	-10.03	-9.87	-9.69	-9.51	-9.32	-9.12	-8.91
7.750	-8.93	-8.79	-8.63	-8.47	-8.30	-8.13	-7.94
7.875	-7.83	-7.71	-7.57	-7.43	-7.28	-7.13	-6.96
8.000	-6.73	-6.62	-6.50	-6.38	-6.26	-6.12	-5.98
8.125	-5.62	-5.53	-5.43	-5.33	-5.22	-5.11	-4.99
8.250	-4.50	-4.43	-4.35	-4.27	-4.19	-4.10	-4.00
8.375	-3.38	-3.33	-3.27	-3.21	-3.15	-3.08	-3.01
8.500	-2.26	-2.22	-2.19	-2.14	-2.10	-2.06	-2.01
8.625	-1.13	-1.11	-1.09	-1.07	-1.05	-1.03	-1.01
8.750	0.00	0.00	0.00	0.00	0.00	0.00	0.00
8.875	1.14	1.12	1.10	1.08	1.06	1.03	1.01
9.000	2.28	2.24	2.20	2.16	2.12	2.07	2.03
9.125	3.42	3.37	3.31	3.25	3.19	3.12	3.05
9.250	4.57	4.50	4.42	4.34	4.26	4.16	4.07
9.375	5.73	5.63	5.54	5.44	5.33	5.22	5.10
9.500	6.88	6.77	6.66	6.54	6.41	6.27	6.13
9.625	8.04	7.92	7.78	7.64	7.49	7.33	7.16
9.750	9.21	9.06	8.91	8.75	8.57	8.39	8.20
9.875	10.38	10.21	10.04	9.86	9.66	9.46	9.24
10.000	11.55	11.37	11.18	10.97	10.76	10.53	10.29
10.125	12.73	12.53	12.31	12.09	11.85	11.60	11.34
10.250	13.91	13.69	13.46	13.21	12.95	12.68	12.39
10.375	15.09	14.85	14.60	14.34	14.06	13.76	13.45
10.500	16.28	16.02	15.75	15.46	15.16	14.84	14.51
10.625	17.46	17.19	16.90	16.60	16.27	15.93	15.57
10.750	18.66	18.37	18.06	17.73	17.39	17.02	16.64
10.875	19.85	19.54	19.22	18.87	18.50	18.12	17.71
11.000	21.05	20.73	20.38	20.01	19.62	19.21	18.78
11.125	22.26	21.91	21.55	21.16	20.75	20.32	19.86
11.250	23.46	23.10	22.71	22.31	21.88	21.42	20.94
11.375	24.67	24.29	23.89	23.46	23.01	22.53	22.02
11.500	25.88	25.48	25.06	24.61	24.14	23.64	23.11
11.625	27.09	26.68	26.24	25.77	25.27	24.75	24.19
11.750	28.31	27.88	27.42	26.93	26.41	25.87	25.29
11.875	29.53	29.08	28.60	28.09	27.56	26.99	26.38
12.000	30.75	30.28	29.79	29.26	28.70	28.11	27.48
12.125	31.97	31.49	30.98	30.43	29.85	29.23	28.58
12.250	33.20	32.70	32.17	31.60	31.00	30.36	29.68
12.375	34.43	33.91	33.36	32.77	32.15	31.49	30.79
12.500	35.66	35.13	34.56	33.95	33.31	32.62	31.90
12.625	36.90	36.34	35.76	35.13	34.47	33.76	33.01
12.750	38.13	37.56	36.96	36.31	35.63	34.90	34.13

Payment Adjustments
(As % of Old Payment)

8¾%
Old Rate

NEW RATE (%)	YEARS REMAINING IN TERM						
	23	22	21	20	15	10	5
5.750	-22.39	-21.80	-21.19	-20.55	-16.91	-12.41	-6.88
5.875	-21.51	-20.94	-20.36	-19.74	-16.24	-11.91	-6.60
6.000	-20.62	-20.08	-19.52	-18.93	-15.57	-11.42	-6.32
6.125	-19.73	-19.22	-18.68	-18.11	-14.89	-10.91	-6.04
6.250	-18.84	-18.35	-17.83	-17.29	-14.21	-10.41	-5.76
6.375	-17.94	-17.47	-16.98	-16.46	-13.53	-9.90	-5.47
6.500	-17.04	-16.59	-16.12	-15.63	-12.84	-9.40	-5.19
6.625	-16.13	-15.70	-15.26	-14.80	-12.15	-8.89	-4.91
6.750	-15.21	-14.81	-14.40	-13.96	-11.46	-8.38	-4.62
6.875	-14.30	-13.92	-13.53	-13.11	-10.77	-7.87	-4.34
7.000	-13.37	-13.02	-12.65	-12.27	-10.07	-7.36	-4.05
7.125	-12.45	-12.12	-11.78	-11.42	-9.37	-6.84	-3.76
7.250	-11.52	-11.21	-10.89	-10.56	-8.66	-6.32	-3.48
7.375	-10.58	-10.30	-10.01	-9.70	-7.96	-5.81	-3.19
7.500	-9.64	-9.38	-9.12	-8.84	-7.25	-5.29	-2.90
7.625	-8.69	-8.46	-8.22	-7.97	-6.54	-4.77	-2.62
7.750	-7.74	-7.54	-7.33	-7.10	-5.82	-4.24	-2.33
7.875	-6.79	-6.61	-6.42	-6.23	-5.10	-3.72	-2.04
8.000	-5.83	-5.68	-5.52	-5.35	-4.38	-3.19	-1.75
8.125	-4.87	-4.74	-4.61	-4.47	-3.66	-2.66	-1.46
8.250	-3.91	-3.80	-3.69	-3.58	-2.93	-2.13	-1.17
8.375	-2.94	-2.86	-2.78	-2.69	-2.20	-1.60	-0.88
8.500	-1.96	-1.91	-1.85	-1.80	-1.47	-1.07	-0.58
8.625	-0.98	-0.96	-0.93	-0.90	-0.74	-0.54	-0.29
8.750	0.00	0.00	0.00	0.00	0.00	0.00	0.00
8.875	0.99	0.96	0.93	0.90	0.74	0.54	0.29
9.000	1.98	1.92	1.87	1.81	1.48	1.08	0.59
9.125	2.97	2.89	2.81	2.72	2.23	1.62	0.88
9.250	3.97	3.86	3.75	3.64	2.98	2.16	1.18
9.375	4.97	4.84	4.70	4.56	3.73	2.70	1.47
9.500	5.98	5.82	5.65	5.48	4.48	3.25	1.77
9.625	6.99	6.80	6.61	6.40	5.24	3.79	2.06
9.750	8.00	7.79	7.57	7.33	5.99	4.34	2.36
9.875	9.02	8.78	8.53	8.27	6.76	4.89	2.66
10.000	10.04	9.77	9.49	9.20	7.52	5.45	2.96
10.125	11.06	10.77	10.46	10.14	8.29	6.00	3.25
10.250	12.09	11.77	11.43	11.08	9.06	6.55	3.55
10.375	13.12	12.77	12.41	12.03	9.83	7.11	3.85
10.500	14.15	13.78	13.39	12.98	10.60	7.67	4.15
10.625	15.19	14.79	14.37	13.93	11.38	8.23	4.45
10.750	16.23	15.80	15.36	14.88	12.16	8.79	4.75
10.875	17.28	16.82	16.34	15.84	12.94	9.35	5.05
11.000	18.32	17.84	17.33	16.80	13.72	9.91	5.36
11.125	19.37	18.87	18.33	17.77	14.51	10.48	5.66
11.250	20.43	19.89	19.33	18.73	15.30	11.05	5.96
11.375	21.49	20.92	20.33	19.70	16.09	11.61	6.26
11.500	22.55	21.95	21.33	20.68	16.88	12.18	6.57
11.625	23.61	22.99	22.34	21.65	17.68	12.75	6.87
11.750	24.68	24.03	23.35	22.63	18.48	13.33	7.18
11.875	25.74	25.07	24.36	23.61	19.28	13.90	7.48
12.000	26.82	26.12	25.38	24.60	20.08	14.48	7.79
12.125	27.89	27.16	26.39	25.59	20.89	15.06	8.09
12.250	28.97	28.21	27.42	26.58	21.70	15.63	8.40
12.375	30.05	29.27	28.44	27.57	22.51	16.21	8.71
12.500	31.13	30.32	29.47	28.56	23.32	16.80	9.02
12.625	32.22	31.38	30.50	29.56	24.14	17.38	9.33
12.750	33.31	32.44	31.53	30.56	24.95	17.96	9.63

9%
Old Rate

Payment Adjustments
(As % of Old Payment)

NEW RATE (%)	YEARS REMAINING IN TERM						
	30	29	28	27	26	25	24
6.000	-25.49	-25.08	-24.64	-24.19	-23.72	-23.22	-22.70
6.125	-24.48	-24.09	-23.68	-23.24	-22.79	-22.31	-21.81
6.250	-23.48	-23.10	-22.70	-22.29	-21.85	-21.39	-20.91
6.375	-22.46	-22.10	-21.72	-21.32	-20.91	-20.47	-20.01
6.500	-21.45	-21.10	-20.74	-20.36	-19.96	-19.54	-19.10
6.625	-20.42	-20.09	-19.75	-19.39	-19.01	-18.61	-18.19
6.750	-19.39	-19.08	-18.75	-18.41	-18.05	-17.67	-17.27
6.875	-18.36	-18.06	-17.75	-17.43	-17.08	-16.73	-16.35
7.000	-17.31	-17.04	-16.75	-16.44	-16.12	-15.78	-15.42
7.125	-16.27	-16.01	-15.73	-15.45	-15.14	-14.83	-14.49
7.250	-15.22	-14.97	-14.72	-14.45	-14.17	-13.87	-13.56
7.375	-14.16	-13.93	-13.70	-13.45	-13.18	-12.91	-12.62
7.500	-13.10	-12.89	-12.67	-12.44	-12.20	-11.94	-11.67
7.625	-12.03	-11.84	-11.64	-11.43	-11.20	-10.97	-10.72
7.750	-10.96	-10.79	-10.60	-10.41	-10.21	-9.99	-9.77
7.875	-9.89	-9.73	-9.56	-9.39	-9.21	-9.01	-8.81
8.000	-8.81	-8.67	-8.52	-8.36	-8.20	-8.03	-7.85
8.125	-7.72	-7.60	-7.47	-7.33	-7.19	-7.04	-6.88
8.250	-6.63	-6.53	-6.42	-6.30	-6.18	-6.05	-5.91
8.375	-5.54	-5.45	-5.36	-5.26	-5.16	-5.05	-4.94
8.500	-4.44	-4.37	-4.29	-4.22	-4.13	-4.05	-3.96
8.625	-3.33	-3.28	-3.23	-3.17	-3.11	-3.04	-2.97
8.750	-2.23	-2.19	-2.16	-2.12	-2.08	-2.03	-1.99
8.875	-1.12	-1.10	-1.08	-1.06	-1.04	-1.02	-1.00
9.000	0.00	0.00	0.00	0.00	0.00	0.00	0.00
9.125	1.12	1.10	1.08	1.06	1.04	1.02	1.00
9.250	2.24	2.21	2.17	2.13	2.09	2.05	2.00
9.375	3.37	3.32	3.26	3.20	3.14	3.08	3.01
9.500	4.50	4.43	4.36	4.28	4.20	4.11	4.02
9.625	5.64	5.55	5.46	5.36	5.26	5.15	5.03
9.750	6.78	6.67	6.56	6.44	6.32	6.19	6.05
9.875	7.92	7.80	7.67	7.53	7.39	7.23	7.07
10.000	9.07	8.93	8.78	8.62	8.46	8.28	8.10
10.125	10.22	10.06	9.89	9.72	9.53	9.33	9.13
10.250	11.37	11.20	11.01	10.81	10.61	10.39	10.16
10.375	12.53	12.33	12.13	11.92	11.69	11.45	11.19
10.500	13.69	13.48	13.26	13.02	12.77	12.51	12.23
10.625	14.85	14.62	14.38	14.13	13.86	13.58	13.28
10.750	16.02	15.77	15.51	15.24	14.95	14.64	14.32
10.875	17.18	16.92	16.65	16.36	16.05	15.72	15.37
11.000	18.36	18.08	17.79	17.47	17.14	16.79	16.42
11.125	19.53	19.24	18.93	18.59	18.24	17.87	17.48
11.250	20.71	20.40	20.07	19.72	19.35	18.95	18.54
11.375	21.89	21.56	21.22	20.85	20.45	20.04	19.60
11.500	23.08	22.73	22.36	21.98	21.56	21.12	20.66
11.625	24.26	23.90	23.52	23.11	22.67	22.21	21.73
11.750	25.45	25.07	24.67	24.24	23.79	23.31	22.80
11.875	26.64	26.25	25.83	25.38	24.91	24.41	23.87
12.000	27.84	27.43	26.99	26.52	26.03	25.50	24.95
12.125	29.04	28.61	28.15	27.67	27.15	26.61	26.03
12.250	30.23	29.79	29.32	28.81	28.28	27.71	27.11
12.375	31.44	30.98	30.49	29.96	29.41	28.82	28.19
12.500	32.64	32.16	31.66	31.12	30.54	29.93	29.28
12.625	33.85	33.36	32.83	32.27	31.67	31.04	30.37
12.750	35.06	34.55	34.01	33.43	32.81	32.16	31.46
12.875	36.27	35.74	35.18	34.59	33.95	33.27	32.56
13.000	37.48	36.94	36.36	35.75	35.09	34.39	33.65

Payment Adjustments
(As % of Old Payment)

9% Old Rate

NEW RATE (%)	YEARS REMAINING IN TERM						
	23	22	21	20	15	10	5
6.000	-22.16	-21.59	-21.00	-20.37	-16.80	-12.36	-6.87
6.125	-21.29	-20.74	-20.17	-19.57	-16.13	-11.86	-6.59
6.250	-20.41	-19.89	-19.34	-18.76	-15.46	-11.36	-6.31
6.375	-19.53	-19.03	-18.50	-17.95	-14.79	-10.86	-6.02
6.500	-18.64	-18.16	-17.66	-17.13	-14.11	-10.36	-5.74
6.625	-17.75	-17.29	-16.82	-16.31	-13.44	-9.86	-5.46
6.750	-16.86	-16.42	-15.97	-15.49	-12.75	-9.36	-5.18
6.875	-15.96	-15.55	-15.12	-14.66	-12.07	-8.85	-4.89
7.000	-15.05	-14.66	-14.26	-13.83	-11.38	-8.34	-4.61
7.125	-14.14	-13.78	-13.39	-12.99	-10.69	-7.83	-4.33
7.250	-13.23	-12.89	-12.53	-12.15	-10.00	-7.32	-4.04
7.375	-12.31	-11.99	-11.66	-11.31	-9.30	-6.81	-3.76
7.500	-11.39	-11.10	-10.79	-10.46	-8.60	-6.29	-3.47
7.625	-10.46	-10.19	-9.91	-9.61	-7.90	-5.78	-3.18
7.750	-9.53	-9.29	-9.03	-8.76	-7.20	-5.26	-2.90
7.875	-8.60	-8.38	-8.14	-7.90	-6.49	-4.74	-2.61
8.000	-7.66	-7.46	-7.25	-7.03	-5.78	-4.22	-2.32
8.125	-6.72	-6.54	-6.36	-6.17	-5.07	-3.70	-2.03
8.250	-5.77	-5.62	-5.46	-5.30	-4.35	-3.18	-1.74
8.375	-4.82	-4.69	-4.56	-4.42	-3.63	-2.65	-1.45
8.500	-3.86	-3.76	-3.66	-3.55	-2.91	-2.12	-1.16
8.625	-2.90	-2.83	-2.75	-2.66	-2.19	-1.59	-0.87
8.750	-1.94	-1.89	-1.84	-1.78	-1.46	-1.06	-0.58
8.875	-0.97	-0.95	-0.92	-0.89	-0.73	-0.53	-0.29
9.000	0.00	0.00	0.00	0.00	0.00	0.00	0.00
9.125	0.98	0.95	0.92	0.90	0.74	0.54	0.29
9.250	1.95	1.90	1.85	1.79	1.47	1.07	0.59
9.375	2.94	2.86	2.78	2.70	2.21	1.61	0.88
9.500	3.92	3.82	3.71	3.60	2.95	2.15	1.17
9.625	4.91	4.79	4.65	4.51	3.70	2.69	1.47
9.750	5.91	5.75	5.59	5.42	4.45	3.23	1.76
9.875	6.90	6.72	6.54	6.34	5.20	3.78	2.06
10.000	7.90	7.70	7.48	7.26	5.95	4.32	2.36
10.125	8.91	8.68	8.43	8.18	6.70	4.87	2.65
10.250	9.92	9.66	9.39	9.11	7.46	5.42	2.95
10.375	10.93	10.64	10.35	10.03	8.22	5.97	3.25
10.500	11.94	11.63	11.31	10.97	8.99	6.52	3.54
10.625	12.96	12.62	12.27	11.90	9.75	7.07	3.84
10.750	13.98	13.62	13.24	12.84	10.52	7.63	4.14
10.875	15.00	14.62	14.21	13.78	11.29	8.18	4.44
11.000	16.03	15.62	15.18	14.72	12.06	8.74	4.74
11.125	17.06	16.62	16.16	15.67	12.84	9.30	5.04
11.250	18.09	17.63	17.14	16.62	13.61	9.86	5.34
11.375	19.13	18.64	18.12	17.57	14.39	10.43	5.64
11.500	20.17	19.65	19.11	18.53	15.18	10.99	5.95
11.625	21.21	20.67	20.09	19.49	15.96	11.55	6.25
11.750	22.26	21.69	21.08	20.45	16.75	12.12	6.55
11.875	23.31	22.71	22.08	21.41	17.54	12.69	6.86
12.000	24.36	23.73	23.08	22.38	18.33	13.26	7.16
12.125	25.41	24.76	24.08	23.35	19.12	13.83	7.46
12.250	26.47	25.79	25.08	24.32	19.92	14.40	7.77
12.375	27.53	26.83	26.08	25.30	20.72	14.98	8.07
12.500	28.59	27.86	27.09	26.28	21.52	15.55	8.38
12.625	29.66	28.90	28.10	27.26	22.32	16.13	8.69
12.750	30.72	29.94	29.11	28.24	23.13	16.71	8.99
12.875	31.79	30.99	30.13	29.23	23.94	17.29	9.30
13.000	32.87	32.03	31.15	30.22	24.75	17.87	9.61

9¼%
Old Rate

Payment Adjustments
(As % of Old Payment)

NEW RATE (%)	YEARS REMAINING IN TERM						
	30	29	28	27	26	25	24
6.250	-25.16	-24.76	-24.35	-23.91	-23.45	-22.97	-22.47
6.375	-24.17	-23.79	-23.39	-22.97	-22.53	-22.07	-21.58
6.500	-23.17	-22.81	-22.42	-22.02	-21.60	-21.16	-20.69
6.625	-22.17	-21.82	-21.45	-21.07	-20.67	-20.24	-19.80
6.750	-21.16	-20.83	-20.48	-20.11	-19.73	-19.32	-18.90
6.875	-20.15	-19.83	-19.50	-19.15	-18.78	-18.40	-17.99
7.000	-19.13	-18.83	-18.51	-18.18	-17.84	-17.47	-17.09
7.125	-18.11	-17.82	-17.53	-17.21	-16.88	-16.54	-16.17
7.250	-17.08	-16.81	-16.53	-16.24	-15.92	-15.60	-15.25
7.375	-16.05	-15.79	-15.53	-15.25	-14.96	-14.66	-14.33
7.500	-15.01	-14.77	-14.53	-14.27	-14.00	-13.71	-13.41
7.625	-13.96	-13.75	-13.52	-13.28	-13.02	-12.76	-12.48
7.750	-12.92	-12.72	-12.50	-12.28	-12.05	-11.80	-11.54
7.875	-11.86	-11.68	-11.49	-11.28	-11.07	-10.84	-10.60
8.000	-10.81	-10.64	-10.46	-10.28	-10.08	-9.87	-9.66
8.125	-9.75	-9.60	-9.44	-9.27	-9.09	-8.91	-8.71
8.250	-8.68	-8.55	-8.40	-8.26	-8.10	-7.93	-7.76
8.375	-7.61	-7.49	-7.37	-7.24	-7.10	-6.95	-6.80
8.500	-6.54	-6.43	-6.33	-6.22	-6.10	-5.97	-5.84
8.625	-5.46	-5.37	-5.28	-5.19	-5.09	-4.99	-4.88
8.750	-4.37	-4.31	-4.24	-4.16	-4.08	-4.00	-3.91
8.875	-3.29	-3.24	-3.18	-3.13	-3.07	-3.00	-2.94
9.000	-2.19	-2.16	-2.13	-2.09	-2.05	-2.01	-1.96
9.125	-1.10	-1.08	-1.06	-1.05	-1.03	-1.01	-0.98
9.250	0.00	0.00	0.00	0.00	0.00	0.00	0.00
9.375	1.10	1.09	1.07	1.05	1.03	1.01	0.99
9.500	2.21	2.18	2.14	2.10	2.06	2.02	1.98
9.625	3.32	3.27	3.22	3.16	3.10	3.04	2.97
9.750	4.43	4.37	4.30	4.22	4.14	4.06	3.97
9.875	5.55	5.47	5.38	5.29	5.19	5.08	4.97
10.000	6.67	6.57	6.47	6.35	6.24	6.11	5.98
10.125	7.80	7.68	7.56	7.43	7.29	7.14	6.98
10.250	8.93	8.79	8.65	8.50	8.34	8.17	8.00
10.375	10.06	9.91	9.75	9.58	9.40	9.21	9.01
10.500	11.19	11.02	10.85	10.66	10.46	10.25	10.03
10.625	12.33	12.15	11.95	11.75	11.53	11.30	11.05
10.750	13.47	13.27	13.06	12.83	12.60	12.34	12.08
10.875	14.61	14.40	14.17	13.93	13.67	13.39	13.10
11.000	15.76	15.53	15.28	15.02	14.74	14.45	14.14
11.125	16.91	16.66	16.40	16.12	15.82	15.50	15.17
11.250	18.06	17.80	17.52	17.22	16.90	16.56	16.21
11.375	19.22	18.94	18.64	18.32	17.98	17.63	17.25
11.500	20.37	20.08	19.76	19.43	19.07	18.69	18.29
11.625	21.53	21.22	20.89	20.54	20.16	19.76	19.34
11.750	22.70	22.37	22.02	21.65	21.25	20.83	20.39
11.875	23.86	23.52	23.15	22.76	22.35	21.91	21.44
12.000	25.03	24.67	24.29	23.88	23.45	22.99	22.49
12.125	26.20	25.83	25.43	25.00	24.55	24.07	23.55
12.250	27.38	26.99	26.57	26.12	25.65	25.15	24.61
12.375	28.55	28.15	27.71	27.25	26.76	26.23	25.68
12.500	29.73	29.31	28.86	28.38	27.87	27.32	26.74
12.625	30.91	30.47	30.01	29.51	28.98	28.41	27.81
12.750	32.09	31.64	31.16	30.64	30.09	29.50	28.88
12.875	33.28	32.81	32.31	31.78	31.21	30.60	29.95
13.000	34.46	33.98	33.46	32.91	32.32	31.70	31.03
13.125	35.65	35.15	34.62	34.05	33.45	32.80	32.11
13.250	36.84	36.33	35.78	35.19	34.57	33.90	33.19

Payment Adjustments
(As % of Old Payment)

9¼%
Old Rate

NEW RATE (%)	23	22	21	20	15	10	5
6.250	-21.94	-21.38	-20.80	-20.19	-16.69	-12.30	-6.85
6.375	-21.07	-20.54	-19.98	-19.40	-16.03	-11.81	-6.57
6.500	-20.20	-19.69	-19.16	-18.59	-15.36	-11.31	-6.29
6.625	-19.33	-18.84	-18.33	-17.79	-14.69	-10.82	-6.01
6.750	-18.45	-17.98	-17.49	-16.98	-14.02	-10.32	-5.73
6.875	-17.57	-17.12	-16.66	-16.17	-13.34	-9.82	-5.45
7.000	-16.68	-16.26	-15.81	-15.35	-12.67	-9.31	-5.17
7.125	-15.79	-15.39	-14.97	-14.53	-11.99	-8.81	-4.88
7.250	-14.89	-14.52	-14.12	-13.70	-11.30	-8.30	-4.60
7.375	-13.99	-13.64	-13.26	-12.87	-10.62	-7.80	-4.32
7.500	-13.09	-12.76	-12.41	-12.04	-9.93	-7.29	-4.03
7.625	-12.18	-11.87	-11.55	-11.20	-9.24	-6.78	-3.75
7.750	-11.27	-10.98	-10.68	-10.36	-8.54	-6.27	-3.46
7.875	-10.35	-10.09	-9.81	-9.52	-7.85	-5.75	-3.18
8.000	-9.43	-9.19	-8.94	-8.67	-7.15	-5.24	-2.89
8.125	-8.50	-8.29	-8.06	-7.82	-6.44	-4.72	-2.60
8.250	-7.57	-7.38	-7.18	-6.97	-5.74	-4.20	-2.32
8.375	-6.64	-6.47	-6.29	-6.11	-5.03	-3.68	-2.03
8.500	-5.70	-5.56	-5.41	-5.25	-4.32	-3.16	-1.74
8.625	-4.76	-4.64	-4.51	-4.38	-3.61	-2.64	-1.45
8.750	-3.82	-3.72	-3.62	-3.51	-2.89	-2.11	-1.16
8.875	-2.87	-2.80	-2.72	-2.64	-2.17	-1.59	-0.87
9.000	-1.92	-1.87	-1.82	-1.76	-1.45	-1.06	-0.58
9.125	-0.96	-0.94	-0.91	-0.88	-0.73	-0.53	-0.29
9.250	0.00	0.00	0.00	0.00	0.00	0.00	0.00
9.375	0.96	0.94	0.91	0.89	0.73	0.53	0.29
9.500	1.93	1.88	1.83	1.78	1.46	1.07	0.58
9.625	2.90	2.83	2.75	2.67	2.19	1.60	0.88
9.750	3.88	3.78	3.67	3.56	2.93	2.14	1.17
9.875	4.85	4.73	4.60	4.46	3.67	2.68	1.46
10.000	5.84	5.69	5.53	5.37	4.41	3.22	1.76
10.125	6.82	6.65	6.46	6.27	5.16	3.76	2.05
10.250	7.81	7.61	7.40	7.18	5.90	4.30	2.35
10.375	8.80	8.58	8.34	8.09	6.65	4.84	2.64
10.500	9.79	9.55	9.28	9.01	7.40	5.39	2.94
10.625	10.79	10.52	10.23	9.93	8.16	5.94	3.24
10.750	11.79	11.50	11.18	10.85	8.92	6.49	3.53
10.875	12.80	12.47	12.13	11.77	9.67	7.04	3.83
11.000	13.81	13.46	13.09	12.70	10.44	7.59	4.13
11.125	14.82	14.44	14.05	13.63	11.20	8.14	4.43
11.250	15.83	15.43	15.01	14.56	11.97	8.70	4.73
11.375	16.85	16.42	15.97	15.50	12.73	9.25	5.03
11.500	17.87	17.42	16.94	16.44	13.51	9.81	5.33
11.625	18.89	18.41	17.91	17.38	14.28	10.37	5.63
11.750	19.91	19.41	18.88	18.33	15.05	10.93	5.93
11.875	20.94	20.42	19.86	19.27	15.83	11.49	6.23
12.000	21.97	21.42	20.84	20.22	16.61	12.06	6.53
12.125	23.01	22.43	21.82	21.18	17.39	12.62	6.84
12.250	24.04	23.44	22.81	22.13	18.18	13.19	7.14
12.375	25.08	24.46	23.79	23.09	18.97	13.76	7.44
12.500	26.13	25.47	24.78	24.05	19.76	14.33	7.75
12.625	27.17	26.49	25.77	25.01	20.55	14.90	8.05
12.750	28.22	27.51	26.77	25.98	21.34	15.47	8.36
12.875	29.27	28.54	27.77	26.95	22.14	16.04	8.66
13.000	30.32	29.57	28.77	27.92	22.93	16.62	8.97
13.125	31.37	30.60	29.77	28.89	23.74	17.20	9.28
13.250	32.43	31.63	30.77	29.87	24.54	17.77	9.58

9½%
Old Rate

Payment Adjustments
(As % of Old Payment)

NEW RATE (%)	YEARS REMAINING IN TERM						
	30	29	28	27	26	25	24
6.500	-24.83	-24.45	-24.05	-23.63	-23.18	-22.72	-22.23
6.625	-23.85	-23.48	-23.10	-22.69	-22.27	-21.82	-21.35
6.750	-22.86	-22.51	-22.15	-21.76	-21.35	-20.92	-20.47
6.875	-21.87	-21.54	-21.19	-20.82	-20.43	-20.02	-19.58
7.000	-20.88	-20.56	-20.22	-19.87	-19.50	-19.10	-18.69
7.125	-19.88	-19.57	-19.25	-18.92	-18.56	-18.19	-17.80
7.250	-18.87	-18.58	-18.28	-17.96	-17.62	-17.27	-16.90
7.375	-17.86	-17.59	-17.30	-17.00	-16.68	-16.35	-15.99
7.500	-16.84	-16.59	-16.32	-16.03	-15.73	-15.42	-15.09
7.625	-15.82	-15.58	-15.33	-15.06	-14.78	-14.49	-14.17
7.750	-14.80	-14.57	-14.34	-14.09	-13.82	-13.55	-13.26
7.875	-13.77	-13.56	-13.34	-13.11	-12.86	-12.61	-12.33
8.000	-12.74	-12.54	-12.34	-12.13	-11.90	-11.66	-11.41
8.125	-11.70	-11.52	-11.33	-11.14	-10.93	-10.71	-10.48
8.250	-10.65	-10.49	-10.32	-10.15	-9.96	-9.76	-9.55
8.375	-9.61	-9.46	-9.31	-9.15	-8.98	-8.80	-8.61
8.500	-8.56	-8.43	-8.29	-8.15	-8.00	-7.84	-7.67
8.625	-7.50	-7.39	-7.27	-7.14	-7.01	-6.87	-6.72
8.750	-6.44	-6.34	-6.24	-6.13	-6.02	-5.90	-5.77
8.875	-5.38	-5.30	-5.21	-5.12	-5.03	-4.93	-4.82
9.000	-4.31	-4.24	-4.18	-4.11	-4.03	-3.95	-3.86
9.125	-3.24	-3.19	-3.14	-3.08	-3.03	-2.97	-2.90
9.250	-2.16	-2.13	-2.10	-2.06	-2.02	-1.98	-1.94
9.375	-1.08	-1.07	-1.05	-1.03	-1.01	-0.99	-0.97
9.500	0.00	0.00	0.00	0.00	0.00	0.00	0.00
9.625	1.09	1.07	1.05	1.04	1.02	1.00	0.97
9.750	2.18	2.14	2.11	2.07	2.04	2.00	1.95
9.875	3.27	3.22	3.17	3.12	3.06	3.00	2.94
10.000	4.37	4.30	4.24	4.16	4.09	4.01	3.92
10.125	5.47	5.39	5.30	5.21	5.12	5.02	4.91
10.250	6.57	6.47	6.37	6.27	6.15	6.03	5.90
10.375	7.68	7.57	7.45	7.32	7.19	7.05	6.90
10.500	8.79	8.66	8.53	8.38	8.23	8.07	7.90
10.625	9.90	9.76	9.61	9.44	9.27	9.09	8.90
10.750	11.02	10.86	10.69	10.51	10.32	10.12	9.90
10.875	12.13	11.96	11.78	11.58	11.37	11.15	10.91
11.000	13.26	13.07	12.87	12.65	12.42	12.18	11.92
11.125	14.38	14.18	13.96	13.73	13.48	13.22	12.94
11.250	15.51	15.29	15.05	14.80	14.54	14.25	13.95
11.375	16.64	16.40	16.15	15.88	15.60	15.30	14.97
11.500	17.77	17.52	17.25	16.97	16.66	16.34	16.00
11.625	18.91	18.64	18.36	18.05	17.73	17.39	17.02
11.750	20.05	19.76	19.46	19.14	18.80	18.44	18.05
11.875	21.19	20.89	20.57	20.24	19.88	19.49	19.09
12.000	22.33	22.02	21.69	21.33	20.95	20.55	20.12
12.125	23.48	23.15	22.80	22.43	22.03	21.61	21.16
12.250	24.62	24.28	23.92	23.53	23.11	22.67	22.20
12.375	25.77	25.42	25.04	24.63	24.19	23.73	23.24
12.500	26.93	26.55	26.16	25.73	25.28	24.80	24.28
12.625	28.08	27.69	27.28	26.84	26.37	25.87	25.33
12.750	29.24	28.84	28.41	27.95	27.46	26.94	26.38
12.875	30.40	29.98	29.54	29.06	28.55	28.01	27.43
13.000	31.56	31.13	30.67	30.18	29.65	29.09	28.49
13.125	32.72	32.28	31.80	31.29	30.75	30.17	29.55
13.250	33.88	33.43	32.94	32.41	31.85	31.25	30.61
13.375	35.05	34.58	34.07	33.53	32.95	32.33	31.67
13.500	36.22	35.73	35.21	34.65	34.06	33.42	32.73

Payment Adjustments
(As % of Old Payment)

9½%
Old Rate

NEW RATE (%)	YEARS REMAINING IN TERM						
	23	22	21	20	15	10	5
6.500	-21.71	-21.17	-20.61	-20.01	-16.58	-12.25	-6.84
6.625	-20.86	-20.34	-19.79	-19.22	-15.92	-11.76	-6.56
6.750	-20.00	-19.50	-18.98	-18.43	-15.26	-11.26	-6.28
6.875	-19.13	-18.65	-18.15	-17.63	-14.59	-10.77	-6.00
7.000	-18.26	-17.80	-17.33	-16.83	-13.92	-10.27	-5.72
7.125	-17.38	-16.95	-16.50	-16.02	-13.25	-9.77	-5.44
7.250	-16.51	-16.09	-15.66	-15.21	-12.58	-9.27	-5.15
7.375	-15.62	-15.23	-14.82	-14.39	-11.90	-8.77	-4.87
7.500	-14.74	-14.37	-13.98	-13.58	-11.22	-8.27	-4.59
7.625	-13.84	-13.50	-13.14	-12.75	-10.54	-7.76	-4.31
7.750	-12.95	-12.62	-12.28	-11.93	-9.86	-7.25	-4.02
7.875	-12.05	-11.75	-11.43	-11.10	-9.17	-6.75	-3.74
8.000	-11.14	-10.87	-10.57	-10.27	-8.48	-6.24	-3.45
8.125	-10.24	-9.98	-9.71	-9.43	-7.79	-5.72	-3.17
8.250	-9.33	-9.09	-8.85	-8.59	-7.09	-5.21	-2.88
8.375	-8.41	-8.20	-7.98	-7.75	-6.40	-4.70	-2.60
8.500	-7.49	-7.30	-7.11	-6.90	-5.70	-4.18	-2.31
8.625	-6.57	-6.40	-6.23	-6.05	-4.99	-3.66	-2.02
8.750	-5.64	-5.50	-5.35	-5.19	-4.29	-3.15	-1.74
8.875	-4.71	-4.59	-4.47	-4.34	-3.58	-2.63	-1.45
9.000	-3.77	-3.68	-3.58	-3.48	-2.87	-2.10	-1.16
9.125	-2.84	-2.77	-2.69	-2.61	-2.16	-1.58	-0.87
9.250	-1.89	-1.85	-1.80	-1.74	-1.44	-1.05	-0.58
9.375	-0.95	-0.93	-0.90	-0.87	-0.72	-0.53	-0.29
9.500	0.00	0.00	0.00	0.00	0.00	0.00	0.00
9.625	0.95	0.93	0.90	0.88	0.72	0.53	0.29
9.750	1.91	1.86	1.81	1.76	1.45	1.06	0.58
9.875	2.87	2.80	2.72	2.64	2.18	1.59	0.88
10.000	3.83	3.74	3.63	3.53	2.91	2.13	1.17
10.125	4.80	4.68	4.55	4.42	3.64	2.66	1.46
10.250	5.77	5.62	5.47	5.31	4.38	3.20	1.75
10.375	6.74	6.57	6.39	6.21	5.12	3.74	2.05
10.500	7.72	7.52	7.32	7.11	5.86	4.28	2.34
10.625	8.69	8.48	8.25	8.01	6.60	4.82	2.64
10.750	9.68	9.44	9.18	8.92	7.35	5.36	2.93
10.875	10.66	10.40	10.12	9.82	8.10	5.91	3.23
11.000	11.65	11.36	11.06	10.73	8.85	6.45	3.53
11.125	12.64	12.33	12.00	11.65	9.60	7.00	3.82
11.250	13.64	13.30	12.94	12.57	10.35	7.55	4.12
11.375	14.63	14.27	13.89	13.49	11.11	8.10	4.42
11.500	15.63	15.25	14.84	14.41	11.87	8.65	4.72
11.625	16.64	16.23	15.79	15.33	12.63	9.21	5.02
11.750	17.64	17.21	16.75	16.26	13.40	9.76	5.32
11.875	18.65	18.19	17.71	17.19	14.17	10.32	5.62
12.000	19.66	19.18	18.67	18.13	14.93	10.88	5.92
12.125	20.68	20.17	19.63	19.06	15.71	11.44	6.22
12.250	21.70	21.16	20.60	20.00	16.48	12.00	6.52
12.375	22.71	22.16	21.57	20.94	17.25	12.56	6.82
12.500	23.74	23.16	22.54	21.89	18.03	13.12	7.12
12.625	24.76	24.16	23.51	22.83	18.91	13.69	7.43
12.750	25.79	25.16	24.49	23.78	19.59	14.25	7.73
12.875	26.82	26.16	25.47	24.73	20.38	14.82	8.03
13.000	27.85	27.17	26.45	25.69	21.17	15.39	8.34
13.125	28.89	28.18	27.44	26.64	21.95	15.96	8.64
13.250	29.92	29.20	28.42	27.60	22.75	16.53	8.95
13.375	30.96	30.21	29.41	28.56	23.54	17.11	9.26
13.500	32.00	31.23	30.40	29.53	24.33	17.68	9.56

9¾%
Old Rate

Payment Adjustments
(As % of Old Payment)

NEW RATE (%)	YEARS REMAINING IN TERM						
	30	29	28	27	26	25	24
6.750	-24.51	-24.14	-23.75	-23.35	-22.92	-22.47	-21.99
6.875	-23.54	-23.19	-22.82	-22.43	-22.01	-21.58	-21.12
7.000	-22.56	-22.23	-21.87	-21.50	-21.10	-20.69	-20.25
7.125	-21.58	-21.26	-20.92	-20.57	-20.19	-19.79	-19.37
7.250	-20.60	-20.29	-19.97	-19.63	-19.27	-18.89	-18.49
7.375	-19.61	-19.32	-19.01	-18.69	-18.34	-17.98	-17.60
7.500	-18.62	-18.34	-18.05	-17.74	-17.42	-17.07	-16.71
7.625	-17.62	-17.36	-17.08	-16.79	-16.48	-16.16	-15.82
7.750	-16.61	-16.37	-16.11	-15.83	-15.55	-15.24	-14.92
7.875	-15.61	-15.38	-15.13	-14.88	-14.60	-14.32	-14.01
8.000	-14.59	-14.38	-14.15	-13.91	-13.66	-13.39	-13.11
8.125	-13.58	-13.38	-13.17	-12.94	-12.71	-12.46	-12.20
8.250	-12.56	-12.37	-12.18	-11.97	-11.75	-11.52	-11.28
8.375	-11.53	-11.36	-11.18	-11.00	-10.79	-10.58	-10.36
8.500	-10.50	-10.35	-10.19	-10.01	-9.83	-9.64	-9 44
8.625	-9.47	-9.33	-9.19	-9.03	-8.87	-8.69	-8.51
8.750	-8.43	-8.31	-8.18	-8.04	-7.90	-7.74	-7.58
8.875	-7.39	-7.28	-7.17	-7.05	-6.92	-6.79	-6.64
9.000	-6.35	-6.26	-6.16	-6.05	-5.94	-5.83	-5.71
9.125	-5.30	-5.22	-5.14	-5.05	-4.96	-4.87	-4.76
9.250	-4.25	-4.18	-4.12	-4.05	-3.98	-3.90	-3.82
9.375	-3.19	-3.14	-3.10	-3.04	-2.99	-2.93	-2.87
9.500	-2.13	-2.10	-2.07	-2.03	-2.00	-1.96	-1.92
9.625	-1.07	-1.05	-1.04	-1.02	-1.00	-0.98	-0.96
9.750	0.00	0.00	0.00	0.00	0.00	0.00	0.00
9.875	1.07	1.05	1.04	1.02	1.00	0.98	0.96
10.000	2.14	2.11	2.08	2.05	2.01	1.97	1.93
10.125	3.22	3.17	3.13	3.07	3.02	2.96	2.90
10.250	4.30	4.24	4.17	4.11	4 03	3.95	3.87
10.375	5.38	5.31	5.23	5.14	5.05	4.95	4.85
10.500	6.47	6.38	6.28	6.18	6.07	5.95	5.83
10.625	7.56	7.45	7.34	7.22	7.09	6.96	6.81
10.750	8.65	8.53	8.40	8.26	8.12	7.96	7.80
10.875	9.75	9.61	9.47	9.31	9.15	8.97	8.79
11.000	10.84	10.69	10.53	10.36	10.18	9.98	9.78
11.125	11.94	11.78	11.60	11.41	11.21	11.00	10.77
11.250	13.05	12.87	12.68	12.47	12.25	12.02	11.77
11.375	14.15	13.96	13.75	13.53	13.29	13.04	12.77
11.500	15.26	15.05	14.83	14.59	14.34	14.06	13.78
11.625	16.37	16.15	15.91	15.65	15.38	15.09	14.78
11.750	17.49	17.25	16.99	16.72	16.43	16.12	15.79
11.875	18.61	18.35	18.08	17.79	17.48	17.15	16.80
12.000	19.72	19.46	19.17	18.86	18.54	18.19	17.82
12.125	20.84	20.56	20.26	19.94	19.59	19.23	18.83
12.250	21.97	21.67	21.36	21.02	20.65	20.27	19.85
12.375	23.09	22.78	22.45	22.10	21.72	21.31	20.88
12.500	24.22	23.90	23.55	23.18	22.78	22.36	21.90
12.625	25.35	25.01	24.65	24.26	23.85	23.40	22.93
12.750	26.48	26.13	25.75	25.35	24.92	24.45	23.96
12.875	27.62	27.25	26.86	26.44	25.99	25.51	24.99
13.000	28.75	28.37	27.97	27.53	27.06	26.56	26.03
13.125	29.89	29.50	29.08	28.62	28.14	27.62	27.06
13.250	31.03	30.63	30.19	29.72	29.22	28.68	28.10
13.375	32.17	31.75	31.30	30.82	30.30	29.74	29.14
13.500	33.32	32.88	32.42	31.92	31.38	30.80	30.19
13.625	34.46	34.02	33.54	33.02	32.46	31.87	31.23
13.750	35.61	35.15	34.65	34.12	33.55	32.94	32.28

Payment Adjustments
(As % of Old Payment)

9¾%
Old Rate

NEW RATE (%)	YEARS REMAINING IN TERM						
	23	22	21	20	15	10	5
6.750	-21.49	-20.97	-20.42	-19.84	-16.47	-12.19	-6.82
6.875	-20.64	-20.14	-19.61	-19.05	-15.81	-11.70	-6.54
7.000	-19.79	-19.31	-18.80	-18.26	-15.15	-11.21	-6.26
7.125	-18.93	-18.47	-17.98	-17.47	-14.49	-10.72	-5.98
7.250	-18.07	-17.63	-17.16	-16.67	-13.83	-10.22	-5.70
7.375	-17.20	-16.78	-16.34	-15.87	-13.16	-9.73	-5.42
7.500	-16.33	-15.93	-15.51	-15.07	-12.49	-9.23	-5.14
7.625	-15.46	-15.08	-14.68	-14.26	-11.82	-8.73	-4.86
7.750	-14.58	-14.22	-13.84	-13.45	-11.15	-8.23	-4.58
7.875	-13.70	-13.36	-13.01	-12.63	-10.47	-7.72	-4.30
8.000	-12.81	-12.50	-12.16	-11.82	-9.79	-7.22	-4.01
8.125	-11.92	-11.63	-11.32	-10.99	-9.11	-6.72	-3.73
8.250	-11.02	-10.75	-10.47	-10.17	-8.42	-6.21	-3.45
8.375	-10.12	-9.88	-9.61	-9.34	-7.73	-5.70	-3.16
8.500	-9.22	-9.00	-8.76	-8.51	-7.04	-5.19	-2.88
8.625	-8.32	-8.11	-7.90	-7.67	-6.35	-4.68	-2.59
8.750	-7.41	-7.23	-7.03	-6.83	-5.66	-4.16	-2.31
8.875	-6.49	-6.33	-6.17	-5.99	-4.96	-3.65	-2.02
9.000	-5.58	-5.44	-5.30	-5.14	-4.26	-3.13	-1.73
9.125	-4.66	-4.54	-4.42	-4.29	-3.55	-2.61	-1.44
9.250	-3.73	-3.64	-3.54	-3.44	-2.85	-2.09	-1.16
9.375	-2.80	-2.74	-2.66	-2.59	-2.14	-1.57	-0.87
9.500	-1.87	-1.83	-1.78	-1.73	-1.43	-1.05	-0.58
9.625	-0.94	-0.92	-0.89	-0.87	-0.72	-0.53	-0.29
9.750	0.00	0.00	0.00	0.00	0.00	0.00	0.00
9.875	0.94	0.92	0.89	0.87	0.72	0.53	0.29
10.000	1.89	1.84	1.79	1.74	1.44	1.06	0.58
10.125	2.83	2.76	2.69	2.61	2.16	1.59	0.87
10.250	3.79	3.69	3.60	3.49	2.89	2.12	1.16
10.375	4.74	4.62	4.50	4.37	3.61	2.65	1.46
10.500	5.70	5.56	5.41	5.26	4.35	3.18	1.75
10.625	6.66	6.50	6.32	6.14	5.08	3.72	2.04
10.750	7.62	7.44	7.24	7.03	5.81	4.26	2.34
10.875	8.59	8.38	8.16	7.93	6.55	4.80	2.63
11.000	9.56	9.33	9.08	8.82	7.29	5.34	2.93
11.125	10.53	10.28	10.01	9.72	8.03	5.88	3.22
11.250	11.51	11.23	10.93	10.62	8.78	6.42	3.52
11.375	12.49	12.18	11.86	11.52	9.52	6.97	3.81
11.500	13.47	13.14	12.80	12.43	10.27	7.51	4.11
11.625	14.45	14.10	13.73	13.34	11.02	8.06	4.41
11.750	15.44	15.07	14.67	14.25	11.78	8.61	4.71
11.875	16.43	16.03	15.61	15.17	12.53	9.16	5.00
12.000	17.42	17.00	16.56	16.08	13.29	9.71	5.30
12.125	18.42	17.97	17.50	17.00	14.05	10.27	5.60
12.250	19.42	18.95	18.45	17.93	14.81	10.82	5.90
12.375	20.42	19.93	19.41	18.85	15.58	11.38	6.20
12.500	21.42	20.91	20.36	19.78	16.35	11.93	6.50
12.625	22.42	21.89	21.32	20.71	17.11	12.49	6.80
12.750	23.43	22.87	22.28	21.64	17.89	13.05	7.11
12.875	24.44	23.86	23.24	22.58	18.66	13.61	7.41
13.000	25.46	24.85	24.20	23.52	19.43	14.18	7.71
13.125	26.47	25.84	25.17	24.46	20.21	14.74	8.01
13.250	27.49	26.84	26.14	25.40	20.99	15.31	8.32
13.375	28.51	27.83	27.11	26.34	21.77	15.88	8.62
13.500	29.53	28.83	28.08	27.29	22.56	16.44	8.93
13.625	30.56	29.83	29.06	28.24	23.34	17.01	9.23
13.750	31.58	30.84	30.04	29.19	24.13	17.59	9.54

10% Old Rate

Payment Adjustments
(As % of Old Payment)

NEW RATE (%)	YEARS REMAINING IN TERM						
	30	29	28	27	26	25	24
7.000	-24.19	-23.84	-23.46	-23.07	-22.66	-22.22	-21.76
7.125	-23.23	-22.89	-22.53	-22.16	-21.76	-21.34	-20.90
7.250	-22.27	-21.94	-21.60	-21.24	-20.86	-20.46	-20.03
7.375	-21.30	-20.99	-20.66	-20.32	-19.95	-19.57	-19.16
7.500	-20.32	-20.03	-19.72	-19.39	-19.04	-18.68	-18.29
7.625	-19.35	-19.07	-18.77	-18.46	-18.13	-17.78	-17.41
7.750	-18.36	-18.10	-17.82	-17.52	-17.21	-16.88	-16.53
7.875	-17.38	-17.13	-16.86	-16.58	-16.29	-15.97	-15.64
8.000	-16.39	-16.15	-15.90	-15.64	-15.36	-15.06	-14.75
8.125	-15.39	-15.17	-14.94	-14.69	-14.43	-14.15	-13.86
8.250	-14.39	-14.19	-13.97	-13.74	-13.49	-13.23	-12.96
8.375	-13.39	-13.20	-12.99	-12.78	-12.55	-12.31	-12.06
8.500	-12.38	-12.20	-12.02	-11.82	-11.61	-11.39	-11.15
8.625	-11.37	-11.21	-11.04	-10.85	-10.66	-10.46	-10.24
8.750	-10.35	-10.21	-10.05	-9.89	-9.71	-9.53	-9.33
8.875	-9.34	-9.20	-9.06	-8.91	-8.76	-8.59	-8.41
9.000	-8.31	-8.20	-8.07	-7.94	-7.80	-7.65	-7.49
9.125	-7.29	-7.18	-7.07	-6.96	-6.84	-6.70	-6.57
9.250	-6.26	-6.17	-6.07	-5.97	-5.87	-5.76	-5.64
9.375	-5.22	-5.15	-5.07	-4.99	-4.90	-4.81	-4.71
9.500	-4.18	-4.13	-4.06	-4.00	-3.93	-3.85	-3.77
9.625	-3.14	-3.10	-3.05	-3.00	-2.95	-2.89	-2.84
9.750	-2.10	-2.07	-2.04	-2.01	-1.97	-1.93	-1.89
9.875	-1.05	-1.04	-1.02	-1.00	-0.99	-0.97	-0.95
10.000	0.00	0.00	0.00	0.00	0.00	0.00	0.00
10.125	1.05	1.04	1.02	1.01	0.99	0.97	0.95
10.250	2.11	2.08	2.05	2.02	1.98	1.95	1.91
10.375	3.17	3.13	3.08	3.03	2.98	2.92	2.86
10.500	4.24	4.18	4.12	4.05	3.98	3.90	3.83
10.625	5.30	5.23	5.15	5.07	4.98	4.89	4.79
10.750	6.37	6.28	6.19	6.09	5.99	5.88	5.76
10.875	7.44	7.34	7.23	7.12	7.00	6.87	6.73
11.000	8.52	8.40	8.28	8.15	8.01	7.86	7.70
11.125	9.60	9.47	9.33	9.18	9.02	8.85	8.68
11.250	10.68	10.53	10.38	10.21	10.04	9.85	9.65
11.375	11.76	11.60	11.43	11.25	11.06	10.85	10.64
11.500	12.84	12.67	12.49	12.29	12.08	11.86	11.62
11.625	13.93	13.75	13.55	13.34	13.11	12.87	12.61
11.750	15.02	14.82	14.61	14.38	14.14	13.88	13.60
11.875	16.12	15.90	15.67	15.43	15.17	14.89	14.59
12.000	17.21	16.98	16.74	16.48	16.20	15.90	15.59
12.125	18.31	18.07	17.81	17.53	17.24	16.92	16.58
12.250	19.41	19.15	18.88	18.59	18.28	17.94	17.59
12.375	20.51	20.24	19.96	19.65	19.32	18.97	18.59
12.500	21.61	21.33	21.03	20.71	20.36	19.99	19.59
12.625	22.72	22.43	22.11	21.77	21.41	21.02	20.60
12.750	23.83	23.52	23.19	22.84	22.46	22.05	21.61
12.875	24.94	24.62	24.27	23.90	23.51	23.08	22.63
13.000	26.05	25.72	25.36	24.97	24.56	24.11	23.64
13.125	27.17	26.82	26.45	26.04	25.61	25.15	24.66
13.250	28.28	27.92	27.53	27.12	26.67	26.19	25.68
13.375	29.40	29.03	28.63	28.19	27.73	27.23	26.70
13.500	30.52	30.13	29.72	29.27	28.79	28.28	27.72
13.625	31.64	31.24	30.81	30.35	29.85	29.32	28.75
13.750	32.77	32.35	31.91	31.43	30.92	30.37	29.78
13.875	33.89	33.47	33.01	32.52	31.99	31.42	30.81
14.000	35.02	34.58	34.11	33.60	33.06	32.47	31.84

Payment Adjustments
(As % of Old Payment)

10%
Old Rate

NEW RATE (%)	YEARS REMAINING IN TERM						
	23	22	21	20	15	10	5
7.000	-21.28	-20.76	-20.23	-19.66	-16.36	-12.14	-6.81
7.125	-20.43	-19.94	-19.42	-18.88	-15.71	-11.65	-6.53
7.250	-19.59	-19.12	-18.62	-18.10	-15.05	-11.16	-6.25
7.375	-18.74	-18.29	-17.81	-17.31	-14.39	-10.67	-5.97
7.500	-17.88	-17.45	-17.00	-16.52	-13.74	-10.18	-5.69
7.625	-17.02	-16.61	-16.18	-15.73	-13.07	-9.68	-5.41
7.750	-16.16	-15.77	-15.36	-14.93	-12.41	-9.19	-5.13
7.875	-15.29	-14.93	-14.54	-14.13	-11.74	-8.69	-4.85
8.000	-14.42	-14.08	-13.71	-13.32	-11.07	-8.19	-4.57
8.125	-13.55	-13.22	-12.88	-12.52	-10.40	-7.69	-4.29
8.250	-12.67	-12.37	-12.04	-11.71	-9.72	-7.19	-4.00
8.375	-11.79	-11.51	-11.21	-10.89	-9.04	-6.68	-3.72
8.500	-10.90	-10.64	-10.36	-10.07	-8.36	-6.18	-3.44
8.625	-10.01	-9.77	-9.52	-9.25	-7.68	-5.67	-3.15
8.750	-9.12	-8.90	-8.67	-8.43	-6.99	-5.16	-2.87
8.875	-8.23	-8.03	-7.82	-7.60	-6.31	-4.65	-2.59
9.000	-7.33	-7.15	-6.96	-6.77	-5.62	-4.14	-2.30
9.125	-6.42	-6.27	-6.10	-5.93	-4.92	-3.63	-2.01
9.250	-5.51	-5.38	-5.24	-5.09	-4.23	-3.12	-1.73
9.375	-4.60	-4.49	-4.38	-4.25	-3.53	-2.60	-1.44
9.500	-3.69	-3.60	-3.51	-3.41	-2.83	-2.08	-1.15
9.625	-2.77	-2.71	-2.64	-2.56	-2.12	-1.57	-0.87
9.750	-1.85	-1.81	-1.76	-1.71	-1.42	-1.04	-0.58
9.875	-0.93	-0.91	-0.88	-0.86	-0.71	-0.52	-0.29
10.000	0.00	0.00	0.00	0.00	0.00	0.00	0.00
10.125	0.93	0.91	0.88	0.86	0.71	0.52	0.29
10.250	1.86	1.82	1.77	1.72	1.43	1.05	0.58
10.375	2.80	2.73	2.66	2.59	2.15	1.58	0.87
10.500	3.74	3.65	3.56	3.46	2.87	2.11	1.16
10.625	4.68	4.57	4.45	4.33	3.59	2.64	1.45
10.750	5.63	5.50	5.35	5.20	4.31	3.17	1.75
10.875	6.58	6.42	6.26	6.08	5.04	3.70	2.04
11.000	7.53	7.35	7.16	6.96	5.77	4.24	2.33
11.125	8.49	8.28	8.07	7.84	6.50	4.77	2.63
11.250	9.44	9.22	8.98	8.73	7.23	5.31	2.92
11.375	10.40	10.16	9.89	9.62	7.97	5.85	3.21
11.500	11.37	11.10	10.81	10.51	8.71	6.39	3.51
11.625	12.33	12.04	11.73	11.40	9.45	6.93	3.80
11.750	13.30	12.99	12.65	12.30	10.19	7.48	4.10
11.875	14.27	13.94	13.58	13.20	10.94	8.02	4.40
12.000	15.25	14.89	14.51	14.10	11.68	8.57	4.69
12.125	16.23	15.84	15.44	15.00	12.43	9.11	4.99
12.250	17.20	16.80	16.37	15.91	13.19	9.66	5.29
12.375	18.19	17.76	17.30	16.82	13.94	10.21	5.59
12.500	19.17	18.72	18.24	17.73	14.70	10.76	5.89
12.625	20.16	19.69	19.18	18.65	15.45	11.32	6.19
12.750	21.15	20.65	20.12	19.56	16.21	11.87	6.49
12.875	22.14	21.62	21.07	20.48	16.98	12.43	6.79
13.000	23.13	22.59	22.02	21.40	17.74	12.98	7.09
13.125	24.13	23.57	22.97	22.33	18.51	13.54	7.39
13.250	25.13	24.54	23.92	23.25	19.27	14.10	7.69
13.375	26.13	25.52	24.87	24.18	20.05	14.66	7.99
13.500	27.13	26.50	25.83	25.11	20.82	15.23	8.30
13.625	28.14	27.49	26.79	26.05	21.59	15.79	8.60
13.750	29.15	28.47	27.75	26.98	22.37	16.36	8.90
13.875	30.16	29.46	28.71	27.92	23.15	16.92	9.21
14.000	31.17	30.45	29.68	28.86	23.93	17.49	9.51

10¼% Old Rate — Payment Adjustments (As % of Old Payment)

NEW RATE (%)	30	29	28	27	26	25	24
			YEARS REMAINING IN TERM				
7.250	-23.87	-23.53	-23.18	-22.80	-22.40	-21.98	-21.53
7.375	-22.92	-22.60	-22.26	-21.89	-21.51	-21.10	-20.68
7.500	-21.97	-21.66	-21.33	-20.98	-20.62	-20.23	-19.82
7.625	-21.01	-20.72	-20.40	-20.07	-19.72	-19.35	-18.96
7.750	-20.05	-19.77	-19.47	-19.15	-18.82	-18.46	-18.09
7.875	-19.09	-18.82	-18.53	-18.23	-17.91	-17.58	-17.22
8.000	-18.12	-17.86	-17.59	-17.31	-17.00	-16.68	-16.35
8.125	-17.14	-16.90	-16.65	-16.38	-16.09	-15.79	-15.47
8.250	-16.16	-15.94	-15.70	-15.44	-15.17	-14.89	-14.59
8.375	-15.18	-14.97	-14.74	-14.51	-14.25	-13.99	-13.70
8.500	-14.19	-14.00	-13.79	-13.56	-13.33	-13.08	-12.81
8.625	-13.20	-13.02	-12.82	-12.62	-12.40	-12.17	-11.92
8.750	-12.21	-12.04	-11.86	-11.67	-11.47	-11.25	-11.03
8.875	-11.21	-11.06	-10.89	-10.72	-10.53	-10.33	-10.13
9.000	-10.21	-10.07	-9.92	-9.76	-9.59	-9.41	-9.22
9.125	-9.20	-9.08	-8.94	-8.80	-8.65	-8.49	-8.31
9.250	-8.19	-8.08	-7.96	-7.83	-7.70	-7.56	-7.40
9.375	-7.18	-7.08	-6.98	-6.87	-6.75	-6.62	-6.49
9.500	-6.17	-6.08	-5.99	-5.90	-5.80	-5.69	-5.57
9.625	-5.15	-5.08	-5.00	-4.92	-4.84	-4.75	-4.65
9.750	-4.12	-4.07	-4.01	-3.94	-3.88	-3.80	-3.73
9.875	-3.10	-3.06	-3.01	-2.96	-2.91	-2.86	-2.80
10.000	-2.07	-2.04	-2.01	-1.98	-1.94	-1.91	-1.87
10.125	-1.04	-1.02	-1.01	-0.99	-0.97	-0.96	-0.94
10.250	0.00	0.00	0.00	0.00	0.00	0.00	0.00
10.375	1.04	1.02	1.01	0.99	0.98	0.96	0.94
10.500	2.08	2.05	2.02	1.99	1.96	1.92	1.88
10.625	3.12	3.08	3.04	2.99	2.94	2.89	2.83
10.750	4.17	4.12	4.06	3.99	3.93	3.85	3.78
10.875	5.22	5.15	5.08	5.00	4.92	4.83	4.73
11.000	6.27	6.19	6.10	6.01	5.91	5.80	5.69
11.125	7.33	7.23	7.13	7.02	6.90	6.78	6.64
11.250	8.39	8.28	8.16	8.03	7.90	7.76	7.60
11.375	9.45	9.32	9.19	9.05	8.90	8.74	8.57
11.500	10.51	10.37	10.23	10.07	9.90	9.72	9.53
11.625	11.58	11.43	11.27	11.09	10.91	10.71	10.50
11.750	12.64	12.48	12.31	12.12	11.92	11.70	11.47
11.875	13.72	13.54	13.35	13.15	12.93	12.70	12.45
12.000	14.79	14.60	14.39	14.18	13.94	13.69	13.42
12.125	15.86	15.66	15.44	15.21	14.96	14.69	14.40
12.250	16.94	16.72	16.49	16.24	15.98	15.69	15.39
12.375	18.02	17.79	17.54	17.28	17.00	16.69	16.37
12.500	19.10	18.86	18.60	18.32	18.02	17.70	17.36
12.625	20.18	19.93	19.66	19.36	19.05	18.71	18.35
12.750	21.27	21.00	20.71	20.41	20.07	19.72	19.34
12.875	22.36	22.08	21.78	21.45	21.10	20.73	20.33
13.000	23.45	23.15	22.84	22.50	22.14	21.75	21.33
13.125	24.54	24.23	23.90	23.55	23.17	22.76	22.33
13.250	25.63	25.31	24.97	24.60	24.21	23.78	23.33
13.375	26.73	26.40	26.04	25.66	25.25	24.80	24.33
13.500	27.82	27.48	27.11	26.71	26.29	25.83	25.33
13.625	28.92	28.57	28.18	27.77	27.33	26.85	26.34
13.750	30.02	29.65	29.26	28.83	28.37	27.88	27.35
13.875	31.12	30.74	30.34	29.89	29.42	28.91	28.36
14.000	32.23	31.83	31.41	30.96	30.47	29.94	29.38
14.125	33.33	32.93	32.49	32.02	31.52	30.98	30.39
14.250	34.44	34.02	33.58	33.09	32.57	32.01	31.41

Payment Adjustments 10¼%
(As % of Old Payment)
Old Rate

NEW RATE (%)	YEARS REMAINING IN TERM						
	23	22	21	20	15	10	5
7.250	-21.06	-20.56	-20.04	-19.48	-16.25	-12.08	-6.79
7.375	-20.22	-19.75	-19.24	-18.71	-15.60	-11.60	-6.51
7.500	-19.38	-18.93	-18.44	-17.93	-14.95	-11.11	-6.23
7.625	-18.54	-18.10	-17.64	-17.15	-14.30	-10.62	-5.96
7.750	-17.69	-17.28	-16.84	-16.37	-13.64	-10.13	-5.68
7.875	-16.84	-16.45	-16.03	-15.58	-12.98	-9.64	-5.40
8.000	-15.99	-15.61	-15.21	-14.79	-12.32	-9.14	-5.12
8.125	-15.13	-14.77	-14.40	-14.00	-11.66	-8.65	-4.84
8.250	-14.27	-13.93	-13.58	-13.20	-10.99	-8.15	-4.56
8.375	-13.40	-13.09	-12.75	-12.40	-10.32	-7.65	-4.28
8.500	-12.53	-12.24	-11.92	-11.59	-9.65	-7.15	-3.99
8.625	-11.66	-11.39	-11.09	-10.79	-8.98	-6.65	-3.71
8.750	-10.78	-10.53	-10.26	-9.98	-8.30	-6.15	-3.43
8.875	-9.90	-9.67	-9.42	-9.16	-7.62	-5.65	-3.15
9.000	-9.02	-8.81	-8.58	-8.35	-6.94	-5.14	-2.86
9.125	-8.13	-7.94	-7.74	-7.52	-6.26	-4.63	-2.58
9.250	-7.24	-7.07	-6.89	-6.70	-5.57	-4.12	-2.29
9.375	-6.35	-6.20	-6.04	-5.87	-4.89	-3.61	-2.01
9.500	-5.45	-5.32	-5.19	-5.04	-4.20	-3.10	-1.72
9.625	-4.55	-4.44	-4.33	-4.21	-3.50	-2.59	-1.44
9.750	-3.65	-3.56	-3.47	-3.37	-2.81	-2.07	-1.15
9.875	-2.74	-2.68	-2.61	-2.54	-2.11	-1.56	-0.86
10.000	-1.83	-1.79	-1.74	-1.69	-1.41	-1.04	-0.58
10.125	-0.92	-0.90	-0.87	-0.85	-0.71	-0.52	-0.29
10.250	0.00	0.00	0.00	0.00	0.00	0.00	0.00
10.375	0.92	0.90	0.88	0.85	0.71	0.52	0.29
10.500	1.84	1.80	1.75	1.71	1.42	1.05	0.58
10.625	2.77	2.70	2.63	2.56	2.13	1.57	0.87
10.750	3.70	3.61	3.52	3.42	2.84	2.10	1.16
10.875	4.63	4.52	4.41	4.28	3.56	2.62	1.45
11.000	5.56	5.43	5.30	5.15	4.28	3.15	1.74
11.125	6.50	6.35	6.19	6.02	5.00	3.68	2.03
11.250	7.44	7.27	7.08	6.89	5.72	4.22	2.33
11.375	8.38	8.19	7.98	7.76	6.45	4.75	2.62
11.500	9.33	9.11	8.88	8.64	7.18	5.28	2.91
11.625	10.28	10.04	9.79	9.52	7.91	5.82	3.21
11.750	11.23	10.97	10.69	10.40	8.64	6.36	3.50
11.875	12.18	11.90	11.60	11.28	9.38	6.90	3.80
12.000	13.14	12.84	12.51	12.17	10.11	7.44	4.09
12.125	14.10	13.77	13.43	13.06	10.85	7.98	4.39
12.250	15.06	14.71	14.34	13.95	11.59	8.52	4.68
12.375	16.02	15.65	15.26	14.84	12.34	9.07	4.98
12.500	16.99	16.60	16.18	15.74	13.08	9.61	5.28
12.625	17.96	17.55	17.11	16.64	13.83	10.16	5.58
12.750	18.93	18.50	18.03	17.54	14.58	10.71	5.87
12.875	19.90	19.45	18.96	18.44	15.33	11.26	6.17
13.000	20.88	20.40	19.89	19.35	16.08	11.81	6.47
13.125	21.86	21.36	20.83	20.26	16.84	12.36	6.77
13.250	22.84	22.32	21.76	21.17	17.60	12.92	7.07
13.375	23.82	23.28	22.70	22.08	18.36	13.47	7.37
13.500	24.81	24.24	23.64	23.00	19.12	14.03	7.67
13.625	25.79	25.21	24.58	23.91	19.88	14.59	7.97
13.750	26.78	26.18	25.53	24.83	20.65	15.15	8.28
13.875	27.78	27.15	26.47	25.75	21.41	15.71	8.58
14.000	28.77	28.12	27.42	26.68	22.18	16.27	8.88
14.125	29.76	29.09	28.37	27.60	22.96	16.83	9.19
14.250	30.76	30.07	29.32	28.53	23.73	17.40	9.49

10½%
Old Rate

Payment Adjustments
(As % of Old Payment)

NEW RATE (%)	YEARS REMAINING IN TERM						
	30	29	28	27	26	25	24
7.500	-23.56	-23.24	-22.89	-22.53	-22.14	-21.73	-21.30
7.625	-22.62	-22.31	-21.98	-21.63	-21.26	-20.87	-20.45
7.750	-21.68	-21.38	-21.07	-20.73	-20.38	-20.00	-19.60
7.875	-20.73	-20.45	-20.15	-19.83	-19.49	-19.13	-18.75
8.000	-19.78	-19.51	-19.23	-18.92	-18.60	-18.26	-17.89
8.125	-18.83	-18.57	-18.30	-18.01	-17.70	-17.38	-17.03
8.250	-17.87	-17.63	-17.37	-17.09	-16.80	-16.49	-16.17
8.375	-16.91	-16.68	-16.43	-16.17	-15.90	-15.61	-15.30
8.500	-15.94	-15.73	-15.50	-15.25	-14.99	-14.72	-14.43
8.625	-14.97	-14.77	-14.55	-14.32	-14.08	-13.82	-13.55
8.750	-14.00	-13.81	-13.61	-13.39	-13.17	-12.93	-12.67
8.875	-13.02	-12.84	-12.66	-12.46	-12.25	-12.02	-11.79
9.000	-12.04	-11.88	-11.70	-11.52	-11.33	-11.12	-10.90
9.125	-11.05	-10.90	-10.75	-10.58	-10.40	-10.21	-10.01
9.250	-10.06	-9.93	-9.79	-9.63	-9.47	-9.30	-9.12
9.375	-9.07	-8.95	-8.82	-8.69	-8.54	-8.38	-8.22
9.500	-8.08	-7.97	-7.86	-7.73	-7.60	-7.47	-7.32
9.625	-7.08	-6.98	-6.88	-6.78	-6.66	-6.54	-6.41
9.750	-6.08	-6.00	-5.91	-5.82	-5.72	-5.62	-5.51
9.875	-5.07	-5.00	-4.93	-4.86	-4.78	-4.69	-4.60
10.000	-4.06	-4.01	-3.95	-3.89	-3.83	-3.76	-3.68
10.125	-3.05	-3.01	-2.97	-2.92	-2.87	-2.82	-2.77
10.250	-2.04	-2.01	-1.98	-1.95	-1.92	-1.89	-1.85
10.375	-1.02	-1.01	-0.99	-0.98	-0.96	-0.94	-0.93
10.500	0.00	0.00	0.00	0.00	0.00	0.00	0.00
10.625	1.02	1.01	1.00	0.98	0.96	.0.95	0.93
10.750	2.05	2.02	1.99	1.96	1.93	1.90	1.86
10.875	3.08	3.04	3.00	2.95	2.90	2.85	2.79
11.000	4.11	4.06	4.00	3.94	3.87	3.81	3.73
11.125	5.14	5.08	5.01	4.93	4.85	4.76	4.67
11.250	6.18	6.10	6.02	5.93	5.83	5.73	5.61
11.375	7.22	7.13	7.03	6.92	6.81	6.69	6.56
11.500	8.26	8.15	8.04	7.92	7.79	7.66	7.51
11.625	9.30	9.19	9.06	8.92	8.78	8.63	8.46
11.750	10.35	10.22	10.08	9.93	9.77	9.60	9.41
11.875	11.40	11.26	11.10	10.94	10.76	10.57	10.37
12.000	12.45	12.29	12.13	11.95	11.75	11.55	11.33
12.125	13.50	13.33	13.15	12.96	12.75	12.53	12.29
12.250	14.56	14.38	14.18	13.97	13.75	13.51	13.25
12.375	15.61	15.42	15.21	14.99	14.75	14.49	14.22
12.500	16.67	16.47	16.25	16.01	15.76	15.48	15.19
12.625	17.73	17.52	17.28	17.03	16.76	16.47	16.16
12.750	18.80	18.57	18.32	18.06	17.77	17.46	17.13
12.875	19.86	19.62	19.36	19.08	18.78	18.46	18.11
13.000	20.93	20.68	20.40	20.11	19.79	19.45	19.09
13.125	22.00	21.73	21.45	21.14	20.81	20.45	20.07
13.250	23.07	22.79	22.49	22.17	21.82	21.45	21.05
13.375	24.14	23.85	23.54	23.20	22.84	22.45	22.03
13.500	25.22	24.92	24.59	24.24	23.86	23.46	23.02
13.625	26.29	25.98	25.64	25.28	24.88	24.46	24.01
13.750	27.37	27.05	26.70	26.32	25.91	25.47	25.00
13.875	28.45	28.11	27.75	27.36	26.94	26.48	25.99
14.000	29.53	29.18	28.81	28.40	27.96	27.49	26.98
14.125	30.61	30.25	29.87	29.45	28.99	28.51	27.98
14.250	31.70	31.33	30.93	30.49	30.03	29.52	28.98
14.375	32.78	32.40	31.99	31.54	31.06	30.54	29.98
14.500	33.87	33.48	33.05	32.59	32.10	31.56	30.98

Payment Adjustments 10½%
(As % of Old Payment)
Old Rate

NEW RATE (%)	YEARS REMAINING IN TERM						
	23	22	21	20	15	10	5
7.500	-20.84	-20.36	-19.85	-19.31	-16.14	-12.03	-6.77
7.625	-20.02	-19.55	-19.06	-18.54	-15.49	-11.55	-6.50
7.750	-19.18	-18.74	-18.27	-17.77	-14.85	-11.06	-6.22
7.875	-18.35	-17.92	-17.47	-17.00	-14.20	-10.57	-5.94
8.000	-17.51	-17.10	-16.67	-16.22	-13.55	-10.08	-5.66
8.125	-16.67	-16.28	-15.87	-15.44	-12.89	-9.59	-5.39
8.250	-15.82	-15.45	-15.07	-14.66	-12.24	-9.10	-5.11
8.375	-14.97	-14.62	-14.26	-13.87	-11.58	-8.61	-4.83
8.500	-14.12	-13.79	-13.44	-13.08	-10.92	-8.11	-4.55
8.625	-13.26	-12.95	-12.63	-12.28	-10.25	-7.62	-4.27
8.750	-12.40	-12.11	-11.81	-11.49	-9.58	-7.12	-3.99
8.875	-11.53	-11.27	-10.98	-10.69	-8.92	-6.62	-3.70
9.000	-10.67	-10.42	-10.16	-9.88	-8.24	-6.12	-3.42
9.125	-9.80	-9.57	-9.33	-9.07	-7.57	-5.62	-3.14
9.250	-8.92	-8.71	-8.50	-8.26	-6.89	-5.12	-2.86
9.375	-8.04	-7.86	-7.66	-7.45	-6.22	-4.61	-2.57
9.500	-7.16	-7.00	-6.82	-6.64	-5.53	-4.10	-2.29
9.625	-6.28	-6.13	-5.98	-5.82	-4.85	-3.60	-2.01
9.750	-5.39	-5.27	-5.13	-4.99	-4.16	-3.09	-1.72
9.875	-4.50	-4.40	-4.29	-4.17	-3.48	-2.58	-1.43
10.000	-3.61	-3.52	-3.43	-3.34	-2.79	-2.06	-1.15
10.125	-2.71	-2.65	-2.58	-2.51	-2.09	-1.55	-0.86
10.250	-1.81	-1.77	-1.72	-1.68	-1.40	-1.03	-0.58
10.375	-0.91	-0.89	-0.86	-0.84	-0.70	-0.52	-0.29
10.500	0.00	0.00	0.00	0.00	0.00	0.00	0.00
10.625	0.91	0.89	0.87	0.84	0.70	0.52	0.29
10.750	1.82	1.78	1.73	1.69	1.41	1.04	0.58
10.875	2.74	2.67	2.61	2.54	2.11	1.56	0.87
11.000	3.65	3.57	3.48	3.39	2.82	2.09	1.16
11.125	4.57	4.47	4.36	4.24	3.53	2.61	1.45
11.250	5.50	5.37	5.24	5.10	4.25	3.14	1.74
11.375	6.42	6.28	6.12	5.95	4.96	3.67	2.03
11.500	7.35	7.18	7.01	6.82	5.68	4.19	2.32
11.625	8.28	8.09	7.89	7.68	6.40	4.73	2.61
11.750	9.22	9.01	8.78	8.55	7.12	5.26	2.91
11.875	10.15	9.92	9.68	9.42	7.85	5.79	3.20
12.000	11.09	10.84	10.57	10.29	8.57	6.33	3.49
12.125	12.03	11.76	11.47	11.16	9.30	6.86	3.79
12.250	12.98	12.68	12.37	12.04	10.03	7.40	4.08
12.375	13.92	13.61	13.27	12.92	10.76	7.94	4.38
12.500	14.87	14.54	14.18	13.80	11.50	8.48	4.67
12.625	15.83	15.47	15.09	14.68	12.24	9.02	4.97
12.750	16.78	16.40	16.00	15.57	12.98	9.56	5.26
12.875	17.74	17.34	16.91	16.46	13.72	10.11	5.56
13.000	18.69	18.27	17.83	17.35	14.46	10.65	5.86
13.125	19.65	19.21	18.74	18.24	15.21	11.20	6.16
13.250	20.62	20.16	19.66	19.14	15.95	11.75	6.45
13.375	21.58	21.10	20.58	20.03	16.70	12.30	6.75
13.500	22.55	22.05	21.51	20.93	17.45	12.85	7.05
13.625	23.52	22.99	22.43	21.84	18.21	13.40	7.35
13.750	24.49	23.95	23.36	22.74	18.96	13.96	7.65
13.875	25.46	24.90	24.29	23.65	19.72	14.51	7.95
14.000	26.44	25.85	25.23	24.55	20.48	15.07	8.25
14.125	27.42	26.81	26.16	25.46	21.24	15.62	8.56
14.250	28.40	27.77	27.10	26.38	22.00	16.18	8.86
14.375	29.38	28.73	28.03	27.29	22.76	16.74	9.16
14.500	30.36	29.69	28.98	28.21	23.53	17.31	9.46

10¾%
Old Rate

Payment Adjustments
(As % of Old Payment)

NEW RATE (%)	YEARS REMAINING IN TERM						
	30	29	28	27	26	25	24
7.750	-23.25	-22.94	-22.61	-22.26	-21.89	-21.49	-21.07
7.875	-22.33	-22.03	-21.71	-21.37	-21.02	-20.64	-20.23
8.000	-21.39	-21.11	-20.81	-20.48	-20.14	-19.78	-19.39
8.125	-20.46	-20.19	-19.90	-19.59	-19.26	-18.91	-18.55
8.250	-19.52	-19.26	-18.98	-18.69	-18.38	-18.05	-17.70
8.375	-18.58	-18.33	-18.07	-17.79	-17.49	-17.18	-16.84
8.500	-17.63	-17.40	-17.15	-16.88	-16.60	-16.30	-15.99
8.625	-16.68	-16.46	-16.22	-15.97	-15.71	-15.43	-15.13
8.750	-15.72	-15.52	-15.30	-15.06	-14.81	-14.55	-14.26
8.875	-14.77	-14.57	-14.37	-14.15	-13.91	-13.66	-13.40
9.000	-13.80	-13.62	-13.43	-13.23	-13.01	-12.77	-12.53
9.125	-12.84	-12.67·	-12.49	-12.30	-12.10	-11.88	-11.65
9.250	-11.87	-11.72	-11.55	-11.37	-11.19	-10.99	-10.78
9.375	-10.90	-10.76	-10.61	-10.44	-10.27	-10.09	-9.89
9.500	-9.92	-9.79	-9.66	-9.51	-9.35	-9.19	-9.01
9.625	-8.94	-8.83	-8.71	-8.57	-8.43	-8.28	-8.12
9.750	-7.96	-7.86	-7.75	-7.63	-7.51	-7.38	-7.23
9.875	-6.98	-6.89	-6.79	-6.69	-6.58	-6.46	-6.34
10.000	-5.99	-5.91	-5.83	-5.74	-5.65	-5.55	-5.44
10.125	-5.00	-4.93	-4.87	-4.79	-4.72	-4.63	-4.54
10.250	-4.00	-3.95	-3.90	-3.84	-3.78	-3.71	-3.64
10.375	-3.01	-2.97	-2.93	-2.88	-2.84	-2.79	-2.74
10.500	-2.01	-1.98	-1.96	-1.93	-1.89	-1.86	-1.83
10.625	-1.01	-0.99	-0.98	-0.96	-0.95	-0.93	-0.91
10.750	0.00	0.00	0.00	0.00	0.00	0.00	0.00
10.875	1.01	1.00	0.98	0.97	0.95	0.94	0.92
11.000	2.02	1.99	1.97	1.94	1.91	1.87	1.84
11.125	3.03	2.99	2.95	2.91	2.86	2.81	2.76
11.250	4.05	4.00	3.94	3.89	3.82	3.76	3.69
11.375	5.07	5.00	4.94	4.86	4.79	4.70	4.61
11.500	6.09	6.01	5.93	5.84	5.75	5.65	5.55
11.625	7.11	7.02	6.93	6.83	6.72	6.60	6.48
11.750	8.13	8.03	7.93	7.81	7.69	7.56	7.42
11.875	9.16	9.05	8.93	8.80	8.66	8.51	8.35
12.000	10.19	10.07	9.93	9.79	9.64	9.47	9.30
12.125	11.22	11.09	10.94	10.78	10.61	10.43	10.24
12.250	12.26	12.11	11.95	11.78	11.59	11.40	11.19
12.375	13.29	13.13	12.96	12.78	12.58	12.36	12.13
12.500	14.33	14.16	13.97	13.78	13.56	13.33	13.08
12.625	15.37	15.19	14.99	14.78	14.55	14.30	14.04
12.750	16.41	16.22	16.01	15.78	15.54	15.27	14.99
12.875	17.46	17.25	17.03	16.79	16.53	16.25	15.95
13.000	18.50	18.28	18.05	17.80	17.52	17.23	16.91
13.125	19.55	19.32	19.07	18.81	18.52	18.21	17.87
13.250	20.60	20.36	20.10	19.82	19.51	19.19	18.84
13.375	21.65	21.40	21.13	20.83	20.51	20.17	19.80
13.500	22.70	22.44	22.16	21.85	21.52	21.16	20.77
13.625	23.76	23.48	23.19	22.87	22.52	22.14	21.74
13.750	24.81	24.53	24.22	23.88	23.52	23.13	22.71
13.875	25.87	25.57	25.25	24.91	24.53	24.13	23.69
14.000	26.93	26.62	26.29	25.93	25.54	25.12	24.67
14.125	27.99	27.67	27.33	26.95	26.55	26.11	25.64
14.250	29.05	28.72	28.37	27.98	27.56	27.11	26.62
14.375	30.12	29.78	29.41	29.01	28.58	28.11	27.61
14.500	31.18	30.83	30.45	30.04	29.59	29.11	28.59
14.625	32.25	31.89	31.50	31.07	30.61	30.11	29.58
14.750	33.32	32.94	32.54	32.10	31.63	31.12	30.56

Payment Adjustments 10¾%
(As % of Old Payment)
Old Rate

NEW RATE (%)	YEARS REMAINING IN TERM						
	23	22	21	20	15	10	5
7.750	-20.63	-20.16	-19.66	-19.14	-16.03	-11.98	-6.76
7.875	-19.81	-19.36	-18.88	-18.38	-15.39	-11.49	-6.48
8.000	-18.98	-18.55	-18.09	-17.61	-14.75	-11.01	-6.21
8.125	-18.16	-17.74	-17.31	-16.84	-14.10	-10.52	-5.93
8.250	-17.33	-16.93	-16.51	-16.07	-13.45	-10.04	-5.65
8.375	-16.49	-16.12	-15.72	-15.30	-12.80	-9.55	-5.37
8.500	-15.65	-15.30	-14.92	-14.52	-12.15	-9.06	-5.09
8.625	-14.81	-14.47	-14.12	-13.74	-11.50	-8.57	-4.82
8.750	-13.97	-13.65	-13.31	-12.95	-10.84	-8.08	-4.54
8.875	-13.12	-12.82	-12.50	-12.17	-10.18	-7.58	-4.26
9.000	-12.26	-11.99	-11.69	-11.38	-9.52	-7.09	-3.98
9.125	-11.41	-11.15	-10.87	-10.58	-8.85	-6.59	-3.70
9.250	-10.55	-10.31	-10.06	-9.79	-8.19	-6.09	-3.41
9.375	-9.69	-9.47	-9.24	-8.99	-7.52	-5.59	-3.13
9.500	-8.82	-8.62	-8.41	-8.19	-6.84	-5.09	-2.85
9.625	-7.95	-7.77	-7.58	-7.38	-6.17	-4.59	-2.57
9.750	-7.08	-6.92	-6.75	-6.57	-5.49	-4.08	-2.28
9.875	-6.21	-6.07	-5.92	-5.76	-4.82	-3.58	-2.00
10.000	-5.33	-5.21	-5.08	-4.95	-4.13	-3.07	-1.72
10.125	-4.45	-4.35	-4.24	-4.13	-3.45	-2.56	-1.43
10.250	-3.57	-3.48	-3.40	-3.31	-2.77	-2.05	-1.15
10.375	-2.68	-2.62	-2.55	-2.49	-2.08	-1.54	-0.86
10.500	-1.79	-1.75	-1.71	-1.66	-1.39	-1.03	-0.57
10.625	-0.90	-0.88	-0.85	-0.83	-0.69	-0.52	-0.29
10.750	0.00	0.00	0.00	0.00	0.00	0.00	0.00
10.875	0.90	0.88	0.86	0.83	0.70	0.52	0.29
11.000	1.80	1.76	1.72	1.67	1.40	1.03	0.58
11.125	2.70	2.64	2.58	2.51	2.10	1.55	0.86
11.250	3.61	3.53	3.44	3.35	2.80	2.08	1.15
11.375	4.52	4.42	4.31	4.20	3.51	2.60	1.44
11.500	5.43	5.31	5.18	5.04	4.21	3.12	1.73
11.625	6.35	6.20	6.05	5.89	4.92	3.65	2.02
11.750	7.26	7.10	6.93	6.75	5.64	4.17	2.32
11.875	8.18	8.00	7.81	7.60	6.35	4.70	2.61
12.000	9.11	8.90	8.69	8.46	7.07	5.23	2.90
12.125	10.03	9.81	9.57	9.32	7.79	5.76	3.19
12.250	10.96	10.72	10.46	10.18	8.51	6.29	3.48
12.375	11.89	11.62	11.34	11.04	9.23	6.83	3.78
12.500	12.82	12.54	12.23	11.91	9.95	7.36	4.07
12.625	13.75	13.45	13.13	12.78	10.68	7.90	4.37
12.750	14.69	14.37	14.02	13.65	11.41	8.44	4.66
12.875	15.63	15.29	14.92	14.52	12.14	8.97	4.95
13.000	16.57	16.21	15.82	15.40	12.87	9.51	5.25
13.125	17.51	17.13	16.72	16.28	13.61	10.06	5.55
13.250	18.46	18.06	17.62	17.16	14.34	10.60	5.84
13.375	19.41	18.98	18.53	18.04	15.08	11.14	6.14
13.500	20.36	19.91	19.44	18.93	15.82	11.69	6.44
13.625	21.31	20.84	20.35	19.81	16.57	12.23	6.74
13.750	22.26	21.78	21.26	20.70	17.31	12.78	7.04
13.875	23.22	22.71	22.17	21.59	18.06	13.33	7.33
14.000	24.18	23.65	23.09	22.49	18.80	13.88	7.63
14.125	25.14	24.59	24.01	23.38	19.56	14.43	7.93
14.250	26.10	25.53	24.93	24.28	20.31	14.99	8.23
14.375	27.06	26.48	25.85	25.18	21.06	15.54	8.53
14.500	28.03	27.42	26.78	26.08	21.82	16.10	8.84
14.625	29.00	28.37	27.70	26.98	22.57	16.66	9.14
14.750	29.97	29.32	28.63	27.89	23.33	17.21	9.44

11%
Old Rate

Payment Adjustments
(As % of Old Payment)

NEW RATE (%)	YEARS REMAINING IN TERM						
	30	29	28	27	26	25	24
8.000	-22.95	-22.65	-22.33	-21.99	-21.63	-21.25	-20.85
8.125	-22.03	-21.75	-21.44	-21.12	-20.77	-20.41	-20.02
8.250	-21.11	-20.84	-20.55	-20.24	-19.91	-19.56	-19.18
8.375	-20.19	-19.93	-19.65	-19.35	-19.04	-18.70	-18.34
8.500	-19.26	-19.01	-18.75	-18.46	-18.16	-17.84	-17.50
8.625	-18.33	-18.09	-17.84	-17.57	-17.29	-16.98	-16.66
8.750	-17.39	-17.17	-16.93	-16.68	-16.41	-16.12	-15.81
8.875	-16.45	-16.24	-16.02	-15.78	-15.52	-15.25	-14.96
9.000	-15.51	-15.31	-15.10	-14.87	-14.63	-14.38	-14.11
9.125	-14.56	-14.38	-14.18	-13.97	-13.74	-13.50	-13.25
9.250	-13.61	-13.44	-13.26	-13.06	-12.85	-12.62	-12.39
9.375	-12.66	-12.50	-12.33	-12.15	-11.95	-11.74	-11.52
9.500	-11.71	-11.56	-11.40	-11.23	-11.05	-10.86	-10.65
9.625	-10.75	-10.61	-10.47	-10.31	-10.15	-9.97	-9.78
9.750	-9.78	-9.66	-9.53	-9.39	-9.24	-9.08	-8.91
9.875	-8.82	-8.71	-8.59	-8.46	-8.33	-8.18	-8.03
10.000	-7.85	-7.75	-7.65	-7.53	-7.41	-7.29	-7.15
10.125	-6.88	-6.79	-6.70	-6.60	-6.50	-6.39	-6.27
10.250	-5.90	-5.83	-5.75	-5.67	-5.58	-5.48	-5.38
10.375	-4.93	-4.87	-4.80	-4.73	-4.66	-4.58	-4.49
10.500	-3.95	-3.90	-3.85	-3.79	-3.73	-3.67	-3.60
10.625	-2.96	-2.93	-2.89	-2.85	-2.80	-2.75	-2.70
10.750	-1.98	-1.95	-1.93	-1.90	-1.87	-1.84	-1.80
10.875	-0.99	-0.98	-0.97	-0.95	-0.94	-0.92	-0.90
11.000	0.00	0.00	0.00	0.00	0.00	0.00	0.00
11.125	0.99	0.98	0.97	0.95	0.94	0.92	0.91
11.250	1.99	1.96	1.94	1.91	1.88	1.85	1.82
11.375	2.99	2.95	2.91	2.87	2.83	2.78	2.73
11.500	3.99	3.94	3.89	3.83	3.77	3.71	3.64
11.625	4.99	4.93	4.87	4.80	4.72	4.64	4.56
11.750	5.99	5.92	5.85	5.76	5.68	5.58	5.48
11.875	7.00	6.92	6.83	6.73	6.63	6.52	6.40
12.000	8.01	7.92	7.81	7.70	7.59	7.46	7.32
12.125	9.02	8.92	8.80	8.68	8.55	8.40	8.25
12.250	10.04	9.92	9.79	9.65	9.51	9.35	9.18
12.375	11.05	10.92	10.78	10.63	10.47	10.30	10.11
12.500	12.07	11.93	11.78	11.61	11.44	11.25	11.04
12.625	13.09	12.94	12.77	12.60	12.41	12.20	11.98
12.750	14.11	13.95	13.77	13.58	13.38	13.16	12.92
12.875	15.13	14.96	14.77	14.57	14.35	14.11	13.86
13.000	16.16	15.97	15.77	15.56	15.32	15.07	14.80
13.125	17.18	16.99	16.78	16.55	16.30	16.03	15.75
13.250	18.21	18.01	17.78	17.54	17.28	17.00	16.69
13.375	19.24	19.03	18.79	18.54	18.26	17.96	17.64
13.500	20.28	20.05	19.80	19.53	19.24	18.93	18.59
13.625	21.31	21.07	20.81	20.53	20.23	19.90	19.55
13.750	22.34	22.09	21.82	21.53	21.21	20.87	20.50
13.875	23.38	23.12	22.84	22.53	22.20	21.84	21.46
14.000	24.42	24.15	23.85	23.54	23.19	22.82	22.42
14.125	25.46	25.18	24.87	24.54	24.18	23.80	23.38
14.250	26.50	26.21	25.89	25.55	25.18	24.77	24.34
14.375	27.54	27.24	26.91	26.56	26.17	25.75	25.30
14.500	28.59	28.27	27.94	27.57	27.17	26.74	26.27
14.625	29.63	29.31	28.96	28.58	28.17	27.72	27.24
14.750	30.68	30.35	29.99	29.59	29.17	28.71	28.21
14.875	31.73	31.38	31.01	30.61	30.17	29.69	29.18
15.000	32.77	32.42	32.04	31.62	31.17	30.68	30.15

Payment Adjustments
(As % of Old Payment)

11% Old Rate

NEW RATE (%)	YEARS REMAINING IN TERM						
	23	22	21	20	15	10	5
8.000	-20.42	-19.96	-19.48	-18.96	-15.92	-11.92	-6.74
8.125	-19.60	-19.17	-18.70	-18.21	-15.28	-11.44	-6.47
8.250	-18.79	-18.37	-17.92	-17.45	-14.65	-10.96	-6.19
8.375	-17.97	-17.57	-17.14	-16.69	-14.00	-10.48	-5.91
8.500	-17.14	-16.76	-16.35	-15.92	-13.36	-9.99	-5.64
8.625	-16.32	-15.95	-15.57	-15.16	-12.71	-9.51	-5.36
8.750	-15.49	-15.14	-14.77	-14.38	-12.07	-9.02	-5.08
8.875	-14.65	-14.33	-13.98	-13.61	-11.42	-8.53	-4.80
9.000	-13.82	-13.51	-13.18	-12.83	-10.76	-8.04	-4.53
9.125	-12.97	-12.69	-12.38	-12.05	-10.11	-7.55	-4.25
9.250	-12.13	-11.86	-11.57	-11.27	-9.45	-7.05	-3.97
9.375	-11.28	-11.03	-10.77	-10.48	-8.79	-6.56	-3.69
9.500	-10.43	-10.20	-9.96	-9.69	-8.13	-6.06	-3.41
9.625	-9.58	-9.37	-9.14	-8.90	-7.46	-5.57	-3.13
9.750	-8.73	-8.53	-8.33	-8.11	-6.79	-5.07	-2.84
9.875	-7.87	-7.69	-7.51	-7.31	-6.13	-4.57	-2.56
10.000	-7.00	-6.85	-6.68	-6.51	-5.45	-4.06	-2.28
10.125	-6.14	-6.00	-5.86	-5.70	-4.78	-3.56	-2.00
10.250	-5.27	-5.15	-5.03	-4.90	-4.10	-3.06	-1.71
10.375	-4.40	-4.30	-4.20	-4.09	-3.43	-2.55	-1.43
10.500	-3.52	-3.45	-3.36	-3.28	-2.74	-2.04	-1.14
10.625	-2.65	-2.59	-2.53	-2.46	-2.06	-1.53	-0.86
10.750	-1.77	-1.73	-1.69	-1.64	-1.38	-1.02	-0.57
10.875	-0.89	-0.87	-0.84	-0.82	-0.69	-0.51	-0.29
11.000	0.00	0.00	0.00	0.00	0.00	0.00	0.00
11.125	0.89	0.87	0.85	0.83	0.69	0.51	0.29
11.250	1.78	1.74	1.70	1.65	1.39	1.03	0.58
11.375	2.67	2.61	2.55	2.48	2.08	1.55	0.86
11.500	3.57	3.49	3.41	3.32	2.78	2.07	1.15
11.625	4.47	4.37	4.26	4.15	3.48	2.59	1.44
11.750	5.37	5.25	5.13	4.99	4.18	3.11	1.73
11.875	6.27	6.13	5.99	5.83	4.89	3.63	2.02
12.000	7.18	7.02	6.85	6.68	5.59	4.15	2.31
12.125	8.09	7.91	7.72	7.52	6.30	4.68	2.60
12.250	9.00	8.80	8.59	8.37	7.01	5.21	2.89
12.375	9.91	9.69	9.46	9.22	7.73	5.73	3.18
12.500	10.83	10.59	10.34	10.07	8.44	6.26	3.48
12.625	11.74	11.49	11.22	10.93	9.16	6.79	3.77
12.750	12.66	12.39	12.10	11.78	9.88	7.32	4.06
12.875	13.59	13.29	12.98	12.64	10.60	7.86	4.35
13.000	14.51	14.20	13.86	13.50	11.32	8.39	4.65
13.125	15.44	15.11	14.75	14.37	12.04	8.93	4.94
13.250	16.37	16.01	15.64	15.23	12.77	9.47	5.24
13.375	17.30	16.93	16.53	16.10	13.50	10.00	5.53
13.500	18.23	17.84	17.42	16.97	14.23	10.54	5.83
13.625	19.17	18.76	18.32	17.84	14.96	11.09	6.13
13.750	20.10	19.67	19.21	18.72	15.70	11.63	6.42
13.875	21.04	20.59	20.11	19.60	16.43	12.17	6.72
14.000	21.98	21.52	21.01	20.47	17.17	12.72	7.02
14.125	22.93	22.44	21.92	21.35	17.91	13.26	7.32
14.250	23.87	23.36	22.82	22.24	18.65	13.81	7.61
14.375	24.82	24.29	23.73	23.12	19.39	14.36	7.91
14.500	25.77	25.22	24.64	24.01	20.14	14.91	8.21
14.625	26.72	26.15	25.55	24.90	20.89	15.46	8.51
14.750	27.67	27.09	26.46	25.79	21.64	16.01	8.81
14.875	28.62	28.02	27.37	26.68	22.39	16.57	9.12
15.000	29.58	28.96	28.29	27.57	23.14	17.12	9.42

11¼%
Old Rate

Payment Adjustments
(As % of Old Payment)

NEW RATE (%)	YEARS REMAINING IN TERM						
	30	29	28	27	26	25	24
8.250	-22.65	-22.36	-22.06	-21.73	-21.39	-21.02	-20.62
8.375	-21.74	-21.47	-21.18	-20.86	-20.53	-20.18	-19.80
8.500	-20.83	-20.57	-20.29	-19.99	-19.67	-19.34	-18.97
8.625	-19.92	-19.67	-19.40	-19.12	-18.81	-18.49	-18.15
8.750	-19.00	-18.76	-18.51	-18.24	-17.95	-17.64	-17.31
8.875	-18.08	-17.86	-17.61	-17.36	-17.08	-16.79	-16.48
9.000	-17.16	-16.94	-16.71	-16.47	-16.21	-15.93	-15.64
9.125	-16.23	-16.03	-15.81	-15.58	-15.34	-15.07	-14.79
9.250	-15.30	-15.11	-14.91	-14.69	-14.46	-14.21	-13.95
9.375	-14.36	-14.19	-14.00	-13.79	-13.58	-13.35	-13.10
9.500	-13.43	-13.26	-13.08	-12.89	-12.69	-12.48	-12.25
9.625	-12.49	-12.33	-12.17	-11.99	-11.81	-11.60	-11.39
9.750	-11.54	-11.40	-11.25	-11.09	-10.91	-10.73	-10.53
9.875	-10.60	-10.47	-10.33	-10.18	-10.02	-9.85	-9.67
10.000	-9.65	-9.53	-9.40	-9.27	-9.12	-8.97	-8.80
10.125	-8.69	-8.59	-8.48	-8.35	-8.22	-8.09	-7.94
10.250	-7.74	-7.64	-7.54	-7.44	-7.32	-7.20	-7.07
10.375	-6.78	-6.70	-6.61	-6.52	-6.42	-6.31	-6.19
10.500	-5.82	-5.75	-5.67	-5.59	-5.51	-5.42	-5.32
10.625	-4.86	-4.80	-4.74	-4.67	-4.60	-4.52	-4.44
10.750	-3.89	-3.84	-3.79	-3.74	-3.68	-3.62	-3.56
10.875	-2.92	-2.89	-2.85	-2.81	-2.77	-2.72	-2.67
11.000	-1.95	-1.93	-1.90	-1.88	-1.85	-1.82	-1.78
11.125	-0.98	-0.96	-0.95	-0.94	-0.92	-0.91	-0.89
11.250	0.00	0.00	0.00	0.00	0.00	0.00	0.00
11.375	0.98	0.97	0.95	0.94	0.93	0.91	0.90
11.500	1.96	1.94	1.91	1.89	1.86	1.83	1.79
11.625	2.94	2.91	2.87	2.83	2.79	2.74	2.69
11.750	3.93	3.88	3.83	3.78	3.72	3.66	3.60
11.875	4.92	4.86	4.80	4.73	4.66	4.58	4.50
12.000	5.90	5.84	5.76	5.68	5.60	5.51	5.41
12.125	6.90	6.82	6.73	6.64	6.54	6.43	6.32
12.250	7.89	7.80	7.70	7.60	7.49	7.36	7.23
12.375	8.89	8.78	8.68	8.56	8.43	8.29	8.15
12.500	9.88	9.77	9.65	9.52	9.38	9.23	9.06
12.625	10.88	10.76	10.63	10.48	10.33	10.16	9.98
12.750	11.88	11.75	11.61	11.45	11.28	11.10	10.90
12.875	12.89	12.74	12.59	12.42	12.24	12.04	11.83
13.000	13.89	13.74	13.57	13.39	13.19	12.98	12.75
13.125	14.90	14.73	14.56	14.36	14.15	13.93	13.68
13.250	15.91	15.73	15.54	15.34	15.11	14.87	14.61
13.375	16.92	16.73	16.53	16.31	16.08	15.82	15.54
13.500	17.93	17.73	17.52	17.29	17.04	16.77	16.48
13.625	18.94	18.74	18.51	18.27	18.01	17.72	17.41
13.750	19.96	19.74	19.51	19.25	18.97	18.68	18.35
13.875	20.98	20.75	20.50	20.23	19.94	19.63	19.29
14.000	21.99	21.76	21.50	21.22	20.92	20.59	20.23
14.125	23.01	22.77	22.50	22.21	21.89	21.55	21.18
14.250	24.03	23.78	23.50	23.19	22.86	22.51	22.12
14.375	25.06	24.79	24.50	24.18	23.84	23.47	23.07
14.500	26.08	25.80	25.50	25.18	24.82	24.44	24.02
14.625	27.10	26.82	26.51	26.17	25.80	25.40	24.97
14.750	28.13	27.83	27.51	27.16	26.78	26.37	25.92
14.875	29.16	28.85	28.52	28.16	27.77	27.34	26.88
15.000	30.19	29.87	29.53	29.16	28.75	28.31	27.83
15.125	31.22	30.89	30.54	30.15	29.74	29.28	28.79
15.250	32.25	31.91	31.55	31.15	30.72	30.26	29.75

Payment Adjustments 11¼%
(As % of Old Payment)   Old Rate

NEW RATE (%)	YEARS REMAINING IN TERM						
	23	22	21	20	15	10	5
8.250	-20.21	-19.76	-19.29	-18.79	-15.81	-11.87	-6.73
8.375	-19.40	-18.98	-18.52	-18.04	-15.18	-11.39	-6.45
8.500	-18.59	-18.18	-17.75	-17.29	-14.54	-10.91	-6.18
8.625	-17.78	-17.39	-16.98	-16.54	-13.91	-10.43	-5.90
8.750	-16.96	-16.59	-16.20	-15.78	-13.27	-9.95	-5.63
8.875	-16.14	-15.79	-15.42	-15.02	-12.63	-9.46	-5.35
9.000	-15.32	-14.99	-14.63	-14.25	-11.98	-8.98	-5.07
9.125	-14.50	-14.18	-13.84	-13.48	-11.34	-8.49	-4.79
9.250	-13.67	-13.37	-13.05	-12.71	-10.69	-8.00	-4.52
9.375	-12.84	-12.55	-12.26	-11.94	-10.04	-7.51	-4.24
9.500	-12.00	-11.74	-11.46	-11.16	-9.38	-7.02	-3.96
9.625	-11.16	-10.92	-10.66	-10.38	-8.73	-6.53	-3.68
9.750	-10.32	-10.10	-9.86	-9.60	-8.07	-6.03	-3.40
9.875	-9.48	-9.27	-9.05	-8.82	-7.41	-5.54	-3.12
10.000	-8.63	-8.44	-8.24	-8.03	-6.75	-5.04	-2.84
10.125	-7.78	-7.61	-7.43	-7.24	-6.08	-4.55	-2.56
10.250	-6.93	-6.78	-6.61	-6.44	-5.41	-4.05	-2.27
10.375	-6.07	-5.94	-5.80	-5.65	-4.75	-3.55	-1.99
10.500	-5.21	-5.10	-4.98	-4.85	-4.07	-3.04	-1.71
10.625	-4.35	-4.25	-4.15	-4.05	-3.40	-2.54	-1.42
10.750	-3.48	-3.41	-3.33	-3.24	-2.72	-2.03	-1.14
10.875	-2.62	-2.56	-2.50	-2.44	-2.05	-1.53	-0.86
11.000	-1.75	-1.71	-1.67	-1.63	-1.37	-1.02	-0.57
11.125	-0.88	-0.86	-0.84	-0.81	-0.68	-0.51	-0.29
11.250	0.00	0.00	0.00	0.00	0.00	0.00	0.00
11.375	0.88	0.86	0.84	0.82	0.69	0.51	0.29
11.500	1.76	1.72	1.68	1.64	1.37	1.02	0.57
11.625	2.64	2.58	2.52	2.46	2.07	1.54	0.86
11.750	3.53	3.45	3.37	3.28	2.76	2.06	1.15
11.875	4.41	4.32	4.22	4.11	3.45	2.57	1.44
12.000	5.30	5.19	5.07	4.94	4.15	3.09	1.72
12.125	6.20	6.06	5.92	5.77	4.85	3.61	2.01
12.250	7.09	6.94	6.78	6.61	5.55	4.13	2.30
12.375	7.99	7.82	7.64	7.44	6.25	4.65	2.59
12.500	8.89	8.70	8.50	8.28	6.96	5.18	2.88
12.625	9.79	9.58	9.36	9.12	7.66	5.70	3.17
12.750	10.69	10.47	10.22	9.96	8.37	6.23	3.47
12.875	11.60	11.36	11.09	10.81	9.08	6.76	3.76
13.000	12.51	12.24	11.96	11.66	9.80	7.29	4.05
13.125	13.42	13.14	12.83	12.51	10.51	7.82	4.34
13.250	14.33	14.03	13.71	13.36	11.23	8.35	4.64
13.375	15.25	14.93	14.58	14.21	11.95	8.88	4.93
13.500	16.16	15.82	15.46	15.07	12.67	9.42	5.22
13.625	17.08	16.72	16.34	15.93	13.39	9.95	5.52
13.750	18.00	17.63	17.22	16.79	14.11	10.49	5.81
13.875	18.93	18.53	18.11	17.65	14.84	11.03	6.11
14.000	19.85	19.44	18.99	18.51	15.57	11.57	6.41
14.125	20.78	20.35	19.88	19.38	16.30	12.11	6.70
14.250	21.71	21.26	20.77	20.25	17.03	12.65	7.00
14.375	22.64	22.17	21.66	21.12	17.76	13.19	7.30
14.500	23.57	23.08	22.56	21.99	18.50	13.74	7.60
14.625	24.50	24.00	23.45	22.86	19.23	14.28	7.89
14.750	25.44	24.91	24.35	23.74	19.97	14.83	8.19
14.875	26.37	25.83	25.25	24.62	20.71	15.38	8.49
15.000	27.31	26.75	26.15	25.50	21.46	15.93	8.79
15.125	28.25	27.68	27.05	26.38	22.20	16.48	9.09
15.250	29.20	28.60	27.96	27.26	22.94	17.03	9.39

11½%
Old Rate

Payment Adjustments
(As % of Old Payment)

NEW RATE (%)	YEARS REMAINING IN TERM						
	30	29	28	27	26	25	24
8.500	-22.35	-22.08	-21.79	-21.47	-21.14	-20.78	-20.40
8.625	-21.46	-21.20	-20.91	-20.61	-20.29	-19.95	-19.59
8.750	-20.56	-20.31	-20.04	-19.75	-19.44	-19.12	-18.77
8.875	-19.66	-19.42	-19.16	-18.89	-18.59	-18.28	-17.95
9.000	-18.75	-18.52	-18.28	-18.02	-17.74	-17.44	-17.12
9.125	-17.84	-17.62	-17.39	-17.14	-16.88	-16.60	-16.29
9.250	-16.93	-16.72	-16.50	-16.27	-16.02	-15.75	-15.46
9.375	-16.01	-15.82	-15.61	-15.39	-15.15	-14.90	-14.63
9.500	-15.09	-14.91	-14.71	-14.51	-14.28	-14.05	-13.79
9.625	-14.17	-14.00	-13.82	-13.62	-13.41	-13.19	-12.95
9.750	-13.24	-13.08	-12.91	-12.73	-12.54	-12.33	-12.11
9.875	-12.31	-12.17	-12.01	-11.84	-11.66	-11.47	-11.26
10.000	-11.38	-11.25	-11.10	-10.95	-10.78	-10.60	-10.41
10.125	-10.45	-10.32	-10.19	-10.05	-9.90	-9.73	-9.56
10.250	-9.51	-9.40	-9.28	-9.15	-9.01	-8.86	-8.70
10.375	-8.57	-8.47	-8.36	-8.25	-8.12	-7.99	-7.85
10.500	-7.63	-7.54	-7.44	-7.34	-7.23	-7.11	-6.98
10.625	-6.68	-6.61	-6.52	-6.43	-6.34	-6.23	-6.12
10.750	-5.74	-5.67	-5.60	-5.52	-5.44	-5.35	-5.25
10.875	-4.79	-4.73	-4.67	-4.61	-4.54	-4.46	-4.39
11.000	-3.83	-3.79	-3.74	-3.69	-3.64	-3.58	-3.51
11.125	-2.88	-2.85	-2.81	-2.77	-2.73	-2.69	-2.64
11.250	-1.92	-1.90	-1.88	-1.85	-1.82	-1.79	-1.76
11.375	-0.96	-0.95	-0.94	-0.93	-0.91	-0.90	-0.88
11.500	0.00	0.00	0.00	0.00	0.00	0.00	0.00
11.625	0.96	0.95	0.94	0.93	0.92	0.90	0.88
11.750	1.93	1.91	1.89	1.86	1.83	1.80	1.77
11.875	2.90	2.87	2.83	2.79	2.75	2.71	2.66
12.000	3.87	3.83	3.78	3.73	3.67	3.62	3.55
12.125	4.84	4.79	4.73	4.67	4.60	4.53	4.45
12.250	5.82	5.75	5.68	5.61	5.53	5.44	5.34
12.375	6.79	6.72	6.64	6.55	6.45	6.35	6.24
12.500	7.77	7.69	7.59	7.49	7.39	7.27	7.14
12.625	8.75	8.66	8.55	8.44	8.32	8.19	8.05
12.750	9.73	9.63	9.51	9.39	9.25	9.11	8.95
12.875	10.72	10.60	10.48	10.34	10.19	10.03	9.86
13.000	11.70	11.58	11.44	11.29	11.13	10.96	10.77
13.125	12.69	12.56	12.41	12.25	12.07	11.88	11.68
13.250	13.68	13.53	13.37	13.20	13.01	12.81	12.59
13.375	14.67	14.52	14.34	14.16	13.96	13.74	13.51
13.500	15.66	15.50	15.32	15.12	14.91	14.68	14.43
13.625	16.66	16.48	16.29	16.08	15.86	15.61	15.35
13.750	17.65	17.47	17.26	17.04	16.81	16.55	16.27
13.875	18.65	18.45	18.24	18.01	17.76	17.49	17.19
14.000	19.65	19.44	19.22	18.98	18.71	18.43	18.12
14.125	20.65	20.43	20.20	19.94	19.67	19.37	19.04
14.250	21.65	21.43	21.18	20.91	20.63	20.31	19.97
14.375	22.65	22.42	22.16	21.89	21.58	21.26	20.90
14.500	23.66	23.41	23.15	22.86	22.54	22.20	21.83
14.625	24.66	24.41	24.13	23.83	23.51	23.15	22.77
14.750	25.67	25.41	25.12	24.81	24.47	24.10	23.70
14.875	26.68	26.40	26.11	25.79	25.44	25.05	24.64
15.000	27.68	27.40	27.10	26.77	26.40	26.01	25.58
15.125	28.69	28.41	28.09	27.75	27.37	26.96	26.52
15.250	29.71	29.41	29.08	28.73	28.34	27.92	27.46
15.375	30.72	30.41	30.08	29.71	29.31	28.88	28.40
15.500	31.73	31.42	31.07	30.69	30.28	29.84	29.35

Payment Adjustments
(As % of Old Payment)

11½% Old Rate

NEW RATE (%)	23	22	21	20	15	10	5
	YEARS REMAINING IN TERM						
8.500	-20.00	-19.57	-19.11	-18.62	-15.70	-11.81	-6.71
8.625	-19.20	-18.79	-18.35	-17.88	-15.08	-11.34	-6.44
8.750	-18.40	-18.00	-17.58	-17.13	-14.44	-10.86	-6.16
8.875	-17.59	-17.21	-16.81	-16.38	-13.81	-10.38	-5.89
9.000	-16.78	-16.42	-16.04	-15.63	-13.18	-9.90	-5.61
9.125	-15.97	-15.63	-15.27	-14.88	-12.54	-9.42	-5.34
9.250	-15.16	-14.83	-14.49	-14.12	-11.90	-8.94	-5.06
9.375	-14.34	-14.03	-13.71	-13.36	-11.26	-8.45	-4.78
9.500	-13.52	-13.23	-12.92	-12.59	-10.61	-7.96	-4.51
9.625	-12.70	-12.42	-12.14	-11.83	-9.97	-7.48	-4.23
9.750	-11.87	-11.62	-11.35	-11.06	-9.32	-6.99	-3.95
9.875	-11.04	-10.80	-10.55	-10.28	-8.66	-6.50	-3.67
10.000	-10.21	-9.99	-9.76	-9.51	-8.01	-6.01	-3.39
10.125	-9.37	-9.17	-8.96	-8.73	-7.36	-5.51	-3.11
10.250	-8.53	-8.35	-8.16	-7.95	-6.70	-5.02	-2.83
10.375	-7.69	-7.53	-7.35	-7.17	-6.04	-4.52	-2.55
10.500	-6.85	-6.70	-6.55	-6.38	-5.37	-4.03	-2.27
10.625	-6.00	-5.87	-5.74	-5.59	-4.71	-3.53	-1.99
10.750	-5.15	-5.04	-4.93	-4.80	-4.04	-3.03	-1.70
10.875	-4.30	-4.21	-4.11	-4.01	-3.38	-2.53	-1.42
11.000	-3.45	-3.37	-3.29	-3.21	-2.70	-2.02	-1.14
11.125	-2.59	-2.53	-2.47	-2.41	-2.03	-1.52	-0.85
11.250	-1.73	-1.69	-1.65	-1.61	-1.36	-1.01	-0.57
11.375	-0.87	-0.85	-0.83	-0.81	-0.68	-0.51	-0.29
11.500	0.00	0.00	0.00	0.00	0.00	0.00	0.00
11.625	0.87	0.85	0.83	0.81	0.68	0.51	0.29
11.750	1.74	1.70	1.66	1.62	1.36	1.02	0.57
11.875	2.61	2.56	2.50	2.43	2.05	1.53	0.86
12.000	3.48	3.41	3.33	3.25	2.74	2.05	1.15
12.125	4.36	4.27	4.17	4.07	3.43	2.56	1.43
12.250	5.24	5.13	5.01	4.89	4.12	3.08	1.72
12.375	6.12	6.00	5.86	5.71	4.81	3.59	2.01
12.500	7.01	6.86	6.70	6.54	5.51	4.11	2.30
12.625	7.89	7.73	7.55	7.36	6.20	4.63	2.59
12.750	8.78	8.60	8.40	8.19	6.90	5.15	2.88
12.875	9.67	9.47	9.26	9.03	7.60	5.67	3.17
13.000	10.57	10.35	10.11	9.86	8.31	6.20	3.46
13.125	11.46	11.22	10.97	10.70	9.01	6.72	3.75
13.250	12.36	12.10	11.83	11.53	9.72	7.25	4.04
13.375	13.26	12.98	12.69	12.37	10.43	7.78	4.33
13.500	14.16	13.87	13.55	13.22	11.14	8.31	4.62
13.625	15.06	14.75	14.42	14.06	11.85	8.84	4.92
13.750	15.96	15.64	15.29	14.91	12.57	9.37	5.21
13.875	16.87	16.53	16.16	15.76	13.28	9.90	5.51
14.000	17.78	17.42	17.03	16.61	14.00	10.43	5.80
14.125	18.69	18.31	17.90	17.46	14.72	10.97	6.10
14.250	19.60	19.20	18.78	18.31	15.44	11.51	6.39
14.375	20.52	20.10	19.65	19.17	16.17	12.04	6.69
14.500	21.43	21.00	20.53	20.03	16.89	12.58	6.98
14.625	22.35	21.90	21.41	20.89	17.62	13.12	7.28
14.750	23.27	22.80	22.29	21.75	18.35	13.66	7.58
14.875	24.19	23.70	23.18	22.61	19.08	14.21	7.87
15.000	25.11	24.61	24.06	23.48	19.81	14.75	8.17
15.125	26.04	25.52	24.95	24.34	20.54	15.30	8.47
15.250	26.96	26.42	25.84	25.21	21.28	15.84	8.77
15.375	27.89	27.34	26.73	26.08	22.01	16.39	9.07
15.500	28.82	28.25	27.63	26.95	22.75	16.94	9.37

11¾%
Old Rate

Payment Adjustments
(As % of Old Payment)

NEW RATE (%)	YEARS REMAINING IN TERM						
	30	29	28	27	26	25	24
8.750	-22.06	-21.80	-21.52	-21.22	-20.89	-20.55	-20.18
8.875	-21.18	-20.93	-20.66	-20.37	-20.06	-19.73	-19.38
9.000	-20.29	-20.05	-19.79	-19.51	-19.22	-18.90	-18.57
9.125	-19.40	-19.17	-18.92	-18.66	-18.37	-18.07	-17.75
9.250	-18.50	-18.28	-18.05	-17.80	-17.53	-17.24	-16.94
9.375	-17.60	-17.39	-17.17	-16.93	-16.68	-16.41	-16.12
9.500	-16.70	-16.50	-16.29	-16.07	-15.83	-15.57	-15.29
9.625	-15.79	-15.61	-15.41	-15.20	-14.97	-14.73	-14.47
9.750	-14.89	-14.71	-14.53	-14.33	-14.11	-13.88	-13.64
9.875	-13.97	-13.81	-13.64	-13.45	-13.25	-13.04	-12.81
10.000	-13.06	-12.91	-12.75	-12.57	-12.39	-12.19	-11.97
10.125	-12.14	-12.00	-11.85	-11.69	-11.52	-11.33	-11.13
10.250	-11.23	-11.10	-10.96	-10.81	-10.65	-10.48	-10.29
10.375	-10.30	-10.19	-10.06	-9.92	-9.78	-9.62	-9.45
10.500	-9.38	-9.27	-9.16	-9.03	-8.90	-8.76	-8.60
10.625	-8.45	-8.36	-8.25	-8.14	-8.02	-7.89	-7.76
10.750	-7.52	-7.44	-7.35	-7.25	-7.14	-7.03	-6.90
10.875	-6.59	-6.52	-6.44	-6.35	-6.26	-6.16	-6.05
11.000	-5.66	-5.59	-5.52	-5.45	-5.37	-5.28	-5.19
11.125	-4.72	-4.67	-4.61	-4.55	-4.48	-4.41	-4.33
11.250	-3.78	-3.74	-3.69	-3.64	-3.59	-3.53	-3.47
11.375	-2.84	-2.81	-2.77	-2.74	-2.70	-2.65	-2.61
11.500	-1.89	-1.87	-1.85	-1.83	-1.80	-1.77	-1.74
11.625	-0.95	-0.94	-0.93	-0.91	-0.90	-0.89	-0.87
11.750	0.00	0.00	0.00	0.00	0.00	0.00	0.00
11.875	0.95	0.94	0.93	0.92	0.90	0.89	0.87
12.000	1.90	1.88	1.86	1.83	1.81	1.78	1.75
12.125	2.86	2.83	2.79	2.76	2.72	2.67	2.63
12.250	3.81	3.77	3.73	3.68	3.63	3.57	3.51
12.375	4.77	4.72	4.66	4.60	4.54	4.47	4.39
12.500	5.73	5.67	5.60	5.53	5.45	5.37	5.28
12.625	6.69	6.62	6.54	6.46	6.37	6.27	6.17
12.750	7.66	7.57	7.49	7.39	7.29	7.18	7.05
12.875	8.62	8.53	8.43	8.32	8.21	8.08	7.95
13.000	9.59	9.49	9.38	9.26	9.13	8.99	8.84
13.125	10.56	10.45	10.33	10.20	10.05	9.90	9.74
13.250	11.53	11.41	11.28	11.13	10.98	10.81	10.63
13.375	12.50	12.37	12.23	12.08	11.91	11.73	11.53
13.500	13.47	13.33	13.18	13.02	12.84	12.64	12.43
13.625	14.45	14.30	14.14	13.96	13.77	13.56	13.34
13.750	15.43	15.27	15.09	14.91	14.70	14.48	14.24
13.875	16.40	16.24	16.05	15.85	15.64	15.40	15.15
14.000	17.38	17.21	17.01	16.80	16.58	16.33	16.06
14.125	18.36	18.18	17.98	17.75	17.51	17.25	16.97
14.250	19.35	19.15	18.94	18.71	18.45	18.18	17.88
14.375	20.33	20.13	19.90	19.66	19.40	19.11	18.80
14.500	21.31	21.10	20.87	20.62	20.34	20.04	19.71
14.625	22.30	22.08	21.84	21.57	21.28	20.97	20.63
14.750	23.29	23.06	22.81	22.53	22.23	21.90	21.55
14.875	24.28	24.04	23.78	23.49	23.18	22.84	22.47
15.000	25.27	25.02	24.75	24.45	24.13	23.78	23.39
15.125	26.26	26.00	25.72	25.41	25.08	24.71	24.32
15.250	27.25	26.98	26.69	26.38	26.03	25.65	25.24
15.375	28.24	27.97	27.67	27.34	26.98	26.59	26.17
15.500	29.24	28.95	28.65	28.31	27.94	27.54	27.10
15.625	30.23	29.94	29.62	29.28	28.90	28.48	28.03
15.750	31.23	30.93	30.60	30.24	29.85	29.43	28.96

Payment Adjustments 11¾%
(As % of Old Payment) Old Rate

NEW RATE (%)	YEARS REMAINING IN TERM						
	23	22	21	20	15	10	5
8.750	-19.79	-19.37	-18.93	-18.46	-15.60	-11.76	-6.70
8.875	-19.00	-18.60	-18.17	-17.72	-14.97	-11.29	-6.42
9.000	-18.21	-17.82	-17.41	-16.98	-14.35	-10.81	-6.15
9.125	-17.41	-17.04	-16.65	-16.23	-13.72	-10.33	-5.87
9.250	-16.61	-16.26	-15.89	-15.49	-13.08	-9.85	-5.60
9.375	-15.80	-15.47	-15.12	-14.74	-12.45	-9.38	-5.32
9.500	-15.00	-14.68	-14.35	-13.99	-11.82	-8.89	-5.05
9.625	-14.19	-13.89	-13.57	-13.23	-11.18	-8.41	-4.77
9.750	-13.37	-13.09	-12.79	-12.47	-10.54	-7.93	-4.49
9.875	-12.56	-12.30	-12.01	-11.71	-9.89	-7.44	-4.22
10.000	-11.74	-11.50	-11.23	-10.95	-9.25	-6.96	-3.94
10.125	-10.92	-10.69	-10.45	-10.19	-8.60	-6.47	-3.66
10.250	-10.10	-9.88	-9.66	-9.42	-7.95	-5.98	-3.38
10.375	-9.27	-9.08	-8.87	-8.65	-7.30	-5.49	-3.10
10.500	-8.44	-8.26	-8.07	-7.87	-6.65	-5.00	-2.82
10.625	-7.61	-7.45	-7.28	-7.10	-5.99	-4.50	-2.54
10.750	-6.77	-6.63	-6.48	-6.32	-5.34	-4.01	-2.26
10.875	-5.93	-5.81	-5.68	-5.54	-4.68	-3.51	-1.98
11.000	-5.09	-4.99	-4.88	-4.75	-4.01	-3.01	-1.70
11.125	-4.25	-4.16	-4.07	-3.97	-3.35	-2.51	-1.42
11.250	-3.41	-3.34	-3.26	-3.18	-2.68	-2.01	-1.14
11.375	-2.56	-2.51	-2.45	-2.39	-2.02	-1.51	-0.85
11.500	-1.71	-1.67	-1.64	-1.59	-1.35	-1.01	-0.57
11.625	-0.86	-0.84	-0.82	-0.80	-0.67	-0.51	-0.29
11.750	0.00	0.00	0.00	0.00	0.00	0.00	0.00
11.875	0.86	0.84	0.82	0.80	0.68	0.51	0.28
12.000	1.72	1.68	1.64	1.60	1.35	1.01	0.57
12.125	2.58	2.53	2.47	2.41	2.03	1.52	0.86
12.250	3.44	3.37	3.30	3.22	2.72	2.03	1.14
12.375	4.31	4.22	4.13	4.03	3.40	2.55	1.43
12.500	5.18	5.07	4.96	4.84	4.09	3.06	1.72
12.625	6.05	5.93	5.79	5.65	4.77	3.57	2.00
12.750	6.92	6.78	6.63	6.47	5.46	4.09	2.29
12.875	7.80	7.64	7.47	7.29	6.16	4.61	2.58
13.000	8.68	8.50	8.31	8.11	6.85	5.13	2.87
13.125	9.56	9.36	9.15	8.93	7.55	5.65	3.16
13.250	10.44	10.23	10.00	9.76	8.24	6.17	3.45
13.375	11.32	11.09	10.85	10.58	8.94	6.69	3.74
13.500	12.21	11.96	11.70	11.41	9.64	7.21	4.03
13.625	13.09	12.83	12.55	12.24	10.35	7.74	4.32
13.750	13.98	13.70	13.40	13.08	11.05	8.26	4.61
13.875	14.88	14.58	14.26	13.91	11.76	8.79	4.91
14.000	15.77	15.45	15.11	14.75	12.47	9.32	5.20
14.125	16.66	16.33	15.97	15.59	13.18	9.85	5.49
14.250	17.56	17.21	16.83	16.43	13.89	10.38	5.78
14.375	18.46	18.09	17.70	17.27	14.60	10.91	6.08
14.500	19.36	18.98	18.56	18.11	15.32	11.45	6.37
14.625	20.26	19.86	19.43	18.96	16.03	11.98	6.67
14.750	21.16	20.75	20.29	19.81	16.75	12.52	6.96
14.875	22.07	21.63	21.16	20.66	17.47	13.05	7.26
15.000	22.98	22.52	22.04	21.51	18.19	13.59	7.56
15.125	23.89	23.42	22.91	22.36	18.92	14.13	7.85
15.250	24.80	24.31	23.78	23.22	19.64	14.67	8.15
15.375	25.71	25.20	24.66	24.07	20.37	15.21	8.45
15.500	26.62	26.10	25.54	24.93	21.10	15.76	8.75
15.625	27.53	27.00	26.42	25.79	21.83	16.30	9.05
15.750	28.45	27.90	27.30	26.65	22.56	16.85	9.35

12%
Old Rate

Payment Adjustments
(As % of Old Payment)

NEW RATE (%)	YEARS REMAINING IN TERM						
	30	**29**	**28**	**27**	**26**	**25**	**24**
9.000	-21.78	-21.52	-21.25	-20.96	-20.65	-20.32	-19.97
9.125	-20.90	-20.66	-20.40	-20.12	-19.82	-19.51	-19.17
9.250	-20.02	-19.79	-19.54	-19.28	-18.99	-18.69	-18.36
9.375	-19.14	-18.92	-18.68	-18.43	-18.16	-17.87	-17.56
9.500	-18.25	-18.04	-17.82	-17.58	-17.32	-17.05	-16.75
9.625	-17.37	-17.17	-16.96	-16.73	-16.48	-16.22	-15.94
9.750	-16.47	-16.29	-16.09	-15.87	-15.64	-15.39	-15.12
9.875	-15.58	-15.40	-15.21	-15.01	-14.79	-14.56	-14.31
10.000	-14.68	-14.52	-14.34	-14.15	-13.94	-13.72	-13.48
10.125	-13.78	-13.63	-13.46	-13.28	-13.09	-12.88	-12.66
10.250	-12.88	-12.74	-12.58	-12.42	-12.24	-12.04	-11.84
10.375	-11.98	-11.84	-11.70	-11.55	-11.38	-11.20	-11.01
10.500	-11.07	-10.95	-10.81	-10.67	-10.52	-10.35	-10.18
10.625	-10.16	-10.05	-9.93	-9.80	-9.66	-9.50	-9.34
10.750	-9.25	-9.15	-9.04	-8.92	-8.79	-8.65	-8.50
10.875	-8.33	-8.24	-8.14	-8.04	-7.92	-7.80	-7.67
11.000	-7.42	-7.34	-7.25	-7.15	-7.05	-6.94	-6.82
11.125	-6.50	-6.43	-6.35	-6.27	-6.18	-6.08	-5.98
11.250	-5.58	-5.52	-5.45	-5.38	-5.30	-5.22	-5.13
11.375	-4.65	-4.60	-4.55	-4.49	-4.42	-4.36	-4.28
11.500	-3.73	-3.69	-3.64	-3.60	-3.54	-3.49	-3.43
11.625	-2.80	-2.77	-2.73	-2.70	-2.66	-2.62	-2.58
11.750	-1.87	-1.85	-1.83	-1.80	-1.78	-1.75	-1.72
11.875	-0.93	-0.92	-0.91	-0.90	-0.89	-0.88	-0.86
12.000	0.00	0.00	0.00	0.00	0.00	0.00	0.00
12.125	0.94	0.93	0.92	0.90	0.89	0.88	0.86
12.250	1.87	1.86	1.83	1.81	1.79	1.76	1.73
12.375	2.81	2.79	2.75	2.72	2.68	2.64	2.60
12.500	3.76	3.72	3.68	3.63	3.58	3.53	3.47
12.625	4.70	4.65	4.60	4.54	4.48	4.41	4.34
12.750	5.65	5.59	5.52	5.46	5.38	5.30	5.21
12.875	6.59	6.53	6.45	6.37	6.29	6.19	6.09
13.000	7.54	7.47	7.38	7.29	7.19	7.08	6.97
13.125	8.49	8.41	8.31	8.21	8.10	7.98	7.85
13.250	9.45	9.35	9.25	9.13	9.01	8.88	8.73
13.375	10.40	10.29	10.18	10.06	9.92	9.77	9.61
13.500	11.36	11.24	11.12	10.98	10.83	10.67	10.50
13.625	12.31	12.19	12.05	11.91	11.75	11.58	11.39
13.750	13.27	13.14	12.99	12.84	12.67	12.48	12.28
13.875	14.23	14.09	13.94	13.77	13.58	13.39	13.17
14.000	15.19	15.04	14.88	14.70	14.50	14.29	14.06
14.125	16.15	16.00	15.82	15.63	15.43	15.20	14.96
14.250	17.12	16.95	16.77	16.57	16.35	16.11	15.85
14.375	18.08	17.91	17.71	17.50	17.27	17.03	16.75
14.500	19.05	18.86	18.66	18.44	18.20	17.94	17.65
14.625	20.02	19.82	19.61	19.38	19.13	18.85	18.56
14.750	20.99	20.78	20.56	20.32	20.06	19.77	19.46
14.875	21.96	21.75	21.52	21.26	20.99	20.69	20.36
15.000	22.93	22.71	22.47	22.21	21.92	21.61	21.27
15.125	23.90	23.67	23.43	23.15	22.86	22.53	22.18
15.250	24.87	24.64	24.38	24.10	23.79	23.46	23.09
15.375	25.85	25.60	25.34	25.05	24.73	24.38	24.00
15.500	26.82	26.57	26.30	26.00	25.67	25.31	24.91
15.625	27.80	27.54	27.26	26.95	26.61	26.23	25.83
15.750	28.78	28.51	28.22	27.90	27.55	27.16	26.74
15.875	29.76	29.48	29.18	28.85	28.49	28.09	27.66
16.000	30.74	30.45	30.14	29.80	29.43	29.02	28.58

Payment Adjustments
(As % of Old Payment)

12%
Old Rate

NEW RATE (%)	YEARS REMAINING IN TERM						
	23	22	21	20	15	10	5
9.000	-19.59	-19.18	-18.75	-18.29	-15.49	-11.71	-6.68
9.125	-18.80	-18.41	-18.00	-17.56	-14.87	-11.23	-6.41
9.250	-18.02	-17.64	-17.25	-16.82	-14.25	-10.76	-6.13
9.375	-17.23	-16.87	-16.49	-16.08	-13.62	-10.29	-5.86
9.500	-16.43	-16.09	-15.73	-15.34	-12.99	-9.81	-5.59
9.625	-15.64	-15.31	-14.97	-14.60	-12.36	-9.33	-5.31
9.750	-14.84	-14.53	-14.21	-13.86	-11.73	-8.85	-5.04
9.875	-14.04	-13.75	-13.44	-13.11	-11.10	-8.37	-4.76
10.000	-13.23	-12.96	-12.67	-12.36	-10.46	-7.89	-4.48
10.125	-12.42	-12.17	-11.90	-11.60	-9.82	-7.41	-4.21
10.250	-11.61	-11.38	-11.12	-10.85	-9.18	-6.92	-3.93
10.375	-10.80	-10.58	-10.34	-10.09	-8.54	-6.44	-3.65
10.500	-9.99	-9.78	-9.56	-9.33	-7.90	-5.95	-3.37
10.625	-9.17	-8.98	-8.78	-8.56	-7.25	-5.46	-3.10
10.750	-8.35	-8.18	-7.99	-7.80	-6.60	-4.97	-2.82
10.875	-7.52	-7.37	-7.20	-7.03	-5.95	-4.48	-2.54
11.000	-6.70	-6.56	-6.41	-6.26	-5.30	-3.99	-2.26
11.125	-5.87	-5.75	-5.62	-5.48	-4.64	-3.49	-1.98
11.250	-5.04	-4.93	-4.82	-4.71	-3.98	-3.00	-1.70
11.375	-4.20	-4.12	-4.03	-3.93	-3.33	-2.50	-1.41
11.500	-3.37	-3.30	-3.23	-3.15	-2.66	-2.00	-1.13
11.625	-2.53	-2.48	-2.42	-2.36	-2.00	-1.51	-0.85
11.750	-1.69	-1.65	-1.62	-1.58	-1.34	-1.00	-0.57
11.875	-0.85	-0.83	-0.81	-0.79	-0.67	-0.50	-0.28
12.000	0.00	0.00	0.00	0.00	0.00	0.00	0.00
12.125	0.85	0.83	0.81	0.79	0.67	0.50	0.28
12.250	1.70	1.66	1.63	1.59	1.34	1.01	0.57
12.375	2.55	2.50	2.44	2.38	2.02	1.52	0.85
12.500	3.40	3.34	3.26	3.18	2.70	2.03	1.14
12.625	4.26	4.18	4.08	3.99	3.37	2.53	1.43
12.750	5.12	5.02	4.91	4.79	4.06	3.05	1.71
12.875	5.98	5.86	5.73	5.59	4.74	3.56	2.00
13.000	6.84	6.71	6.56	6.40	5.42	4.07	2.29
13.125	7.71	7.55	7.39	7.21	6.11	4.58	2.57
13.250	8.57	8.40	8.22	8.02	6.80	5.10	2.86
13.375	9.44	9.26	9.05	8.84	7.49	5.62	3.15
13.500	10.31	10.11	9.89	9.65	8.18	6.14	3.44
13.625	11.19	10.97	10.73	10.47	8.87	6.66	3.73
13.750	12.06	11.82	11.57	11.29	9.57	7.18	4.02
13.875	12.94	12.68	12.41	12.11	10.26	7.70	4.31
14.000	13.81	13.54	13.25	12.94	10.96	8.22	4.60
14.125	14.69	14.41	14.10	13.76	11.66	8.75	4.89
14.250	15.58	15.27	14.94	14.59	12.37	9.27	5.19
14.375	16.46	16.14	15.79	15.42	13.07	9.80	5.48
14.500	17.34	17.01	16.64	16.25	13.78	10.33	5.77
14.625	18.23	17.88	17.49	17.08	14.48	10.86	6.06
14.750	19.12	18.75	18.35	17.92	15.19	11.39	6.36
14.875	20.01	19.62	19.20	18.75	15.90	11.92	6.65
15.000	20.90	20.50	20.06	19.59	16.62	12.45	6.95
15.125	21.79	21.38	20.92	20.43	17.33	12.99	7.24
15.250	22.69	22.25	21.78	21.27	18.05	13.52	7.54
15.375	23.58	23.13	22.64	22.11	18.76	14.06	7.83
15.500	24.48	24.02	23.51	22.96	19.48	14.59	8.13
15.625	25.38	24.90	24.37	23.80	20.20	15.13	8.43
15.750	26.28	25.78	25.24	24.65	20.93	15.67	8.73
15.875	27.18	26.67	26.11	25.50	21.65	16.22	9.02
16.000	28.09	27.56	26.98	26.35	22.37	16.76	9.32

NEW RATE (%)	YEARS REMAINING IN TERM						
	30	29	28	27	26	25	24
9.250	-21.49	-21.25	-20.99	-20.71	-20.41	-20.09	-19.75
9.375	-20.63	-20.40	-20.15	-19.88	-19.60	-19.29	-18.96
9.500	-19.76	-19.54	-19.30	-19.05	-18.77	-18.48	-18.16
9.625	-18.89	-18.68	-18.45	-18.21	-17.95	-17.67	-17.37
9.750	-18.01	-17.81	-17.60	-17.37	-17.12	-16.85	-16.57
9.875	-17.13	-16.94	-16.74	-16.52	-16.29	-16.03	-15.76
10.000	-16.25	-16.08	-15.88	-15.68	-15.45	-15.21	-14.96
10.125	-15.37	-15.20	-15.02	-14.83	-14.62	-14.39	-14.15
10.250	-14.49	-14.33	-14.16	-13.97	-13.78	-13.56	-13.33
10.375	-13.60	-13.45	-13.29	-13.12	-12.93	-12.73	-12.52
10.500	-12.71	-12.57	-12.42	-12.26	-12.09	-11.90	-11.70
10.625	-11.81	-11.69	-11.55	-11.40	-11.24	-11.07	-10.88
10.750	-10.92	-10.80	-10.67	-10.54	-10.39	-10.23	-10.06
10.875	-10.02	-9.91	-9.80	-9.67	-9.54	-9.39	-9.23
11.000	-9.12	-9.02	-8.92	-8.80	-8.68	-8.55	-8.41
11.125	-8.22	-8.13	-8.04	-7.93	-7.82	-7.71	-7.58
11.250	-7.31	-7.24	-7.15	-7.06	-6.96	-6.86	-6.74
11.375	-6.41	-6.34	-6.27	-6.19	-6.10	-6.01	-5.91
11.500	-5.50	-5.44	-5.38	-5.31	-5.24	-5.16	-5.07
11.625	-4.59	-4.54	-4.49	-4.43	-4.37	-4.30	-4.23
11.750	-3.67	-3.63	-3.59	-3.55	-3.50	-3.45	-3.39
11.875	-2.76	-2.73	-2.70	-2.66	-2.63	-2.59	-2.55
12.000	-1.84	-1.82	-1.80	-1.78	-1.75	-1.73	-1.70
12.125	-0.92	-0.91	-0.90	-0.89	-0.88	-0.87	-0.85
12.250	0.00	0.00	0.00	0.00	0.00	0.00	0.00
12.375	0.92	0.91	0.90	0.89	0.88	0.87	0.85
12.500	1.85	1.83	1.81	1.79	1.76	1.74	1.71
12.625	2.77	2.75	2.72	2.68	2.65	2.61	2.57
12.750	3.70	3.67	3.62	3.58	3.53	3.48	3.42
12.875	4.63	4.59	4.54	4.48	4.42	4.36	4.29
13.000	5.56	5.51	5.45	5.38	5.31	5.23	5.15
13.125	6.50	6.43	6.36	6.29	6.20	6.11	6.01
13.250	7.43	7.36	7.28	7.19	7.10	6.99	6.88
13.375	8.37	8.29	8.20	8.10	7.99	7.88	7.75
13.500	9.31	9.21	9.12	9.01	8.89	8.76	8.62
13.625	10.25	10.15	10.04	9.92	9.79	9.65	9.50
13.750	11.19	11.08	10.96	10.83	10.69	10.54	10.37
13.875	12.13	12.01	11.88	11.74	11.59	11.43	11.25
14.000	13.07	12.95	12.81	12.66	12.50	12.32	12.12
14.125	14.02	13.88	13.74	13.58	13.40	13.21	13.00
14.250	14.96	14.82	14.66	14.49	14.31	14.11	13.89
14.375	15.91	15.76	15.59	15.41	15.22	15.00	14.77
14.500	16.86	16.70	16.53	16.34	16.13	15.90	15.65
14.625	17.81	17.64	17.46	17.26	17.04	16.80	16.54
14.750	18.76	18.58	18.39	18.18	17.95	17.70	17.43
14.875	19.71	19.53	19.33	19.11	18.87	18.60	18.32
15.000	20.66	20.47	20.26	20.04	19.78	19.51	19.21
15.125	21.62	21.42	21.20	20.96	20.70	20.41	20.10
15.250	22.57	22.37	22.14	21.89	21.62	21.32	21.00
15.375	23.53	23.32	23.08	22.82	22.54	22.23	21.89
15.500	24.49	24.27	24.02	23.76	23.46	23.14	22.79
15.625	25.45	25.22	24.97	24.69	24.38	24.05	23.69
15.750	26.41	26.17	25.91	25.62	25.31	24.96	24.59
15.875	27.37	27.12	26.85	26.56	26.23	25.88	25.49
16.000	28.33	28.08	27.80	27.49	27.16	26.79	26.39
16.125	29.29	29.03	28.75	28.43	28.09	27.71	27.29
16.250	30.25	29.99	29.69	29.37	29.02	28.63	28.20

Payment Adjustments 12¼%
(As % of Old Payment) Old Rate

NEW RATE (%)	23	22	21	20	15	10	5
			YEARS REMAINING IN TERM				
9.250	-19.38	-18.99	-18.57	-18.12	-15.38	-11.65	-6.66
9.375	-18.61	-18.23	-17.83	-17.40	-14.77	-11.18	-6.39
9.500	-17.83	-17.47	-17.08	-16.67	-14.15	-10.71	-6.12
9.625	-17.04	-16.70	-16.33	-15.94	-13.53	-10.24	-5.85
9.750	-16.26	-15.93	-15.58	-15.20	-12.90	-9.76	-5.57
9.875	-15.47	-15.16	-14.82	-14.47	-12.28	-9.29	-5.30
10.000	-14.68	-14.38	-14.07	-13.73	-11.65	-8.81	-5.02
10.125	-13.89	-13.61	-13.31	-12.99	-11.02	-8.33	-4.75
10.250	-13.09	-12.83	-12.54	-12.24	-10.39	-7.85	-4.47
10.375	-12.29	-12.04	-11.78	-11.49	-9.75	-7.37	-4.20
10.500	-11.49	-11.26	-11.01	-10.74	-9.12	-6.89	-3.92
10.625	-10.68	-10.47	-10.24	-9.99	-8.48	-6.41	-3.64
10.750	-9.88	-9.68	-9.47	-9.24	-7.84	-5.92	-3.37
10.875	-9.07	-8.88	-8.69	-8.48	-7.20	-5.44	-3.09
11.000	-8.25	-8.09	-7.91	-7.72	-6.55	-4.95	-2.81
11.125	-7.44	-7.29	-7.13	-6.96	-5.91	-4.46	-2.53
11.250	-6.62	-6.49	-6.35	-6.20	-5.26	-3.97	-2.25
11.375	-5.80	-5.69	-5.56	-5.43	-4.61	-3.48	-1.97
11.500	-4.98	-4.88	-4.78	-4.66	-3.96	-2.98	-1.69
11.625	-4.16	-4.07	-3.99	-3.89	-3.30	-2.49	-1.41
11.750	-3.33	-3.26	-3.19	-3.12	-2.64	-1.99	-1.13
11.875	-2.50	-2.45	-2.40	-2.34	-1.99	-1.50	-0.85
12.000	-1.67	-1.64	-1.60	-1.56	-1.33	-1.00	-0.57
12.125	-0.84	-0.82	-0.80	-0.78	-0.66	-0.50	-0.28
12.250	0.00	0.00	0.00	0.00	0.00	0.00	0.00
12.375	0.84	0.82	0.80	0.78	0.67	0.50	0.28
12.500	1.68	1.65	1.61	1.57	1.33	1.01	0.57
12.625	2.52	2.47	2.42	2.36	2.00	1.51	0.85
12.750	3.36	3.30	3.23	3.15	2.68	2.01	1.14
12.875	4.21	4.13	4.04	3.94	3.35	2.52	1.42
13.000	5.06	4.96	4.85	4.74	4.02	3.03	1.71
13.125	5.91	5.79	5.67	5.54	4.70	3.54	1.99
13.250	6.76	6.63	6.49	6.34	5.38	4.05	2.28
13.375	7.62	7.47	7.31	7.14	6.06	4.56	2.57
13.500	8.47	8.31	8.13	7.94	6.74	5.07	2.86
13.625	9.33	9.15	8.95	8.74	7.43	5.59	3.14
13.750	10.19	9.99	9.78	9.55	8.11	6.11	3.43
13.875	11.05	10.84	10.61	10.36	8.80	6.62	3.72
14.000	11.91	11.69	11.44	11.17	9.49	7.14	4.01
14.125	12.78	12.53	12.27	11.98	10.18	7.66	4.30
14.250	13.65	13.39	13.10	12.80	10.88	8.18	4.59
14.375	14.51	14.24	13.94	13.61	11.57	8.70	4.88
14.500	15.38	15.09	14.78	14.43	12.27	9.22	5.17
14.625	16.26	15.95	15.61	15.25	12.97	9.75	5.46
14.750	17.13	16.81	16.45	16.07	13.66	10.27	5.76
14.875	18.01	17.67	17.30	16.90	14.37	10.80	6.05
15.000	18.88	18.53	18.14	17.72	15.07	11.33	6.34
15.125	19.76	19.39	18.99	18.55	15.77	11.86	6.64
15.250	20.64	20.25	19.83	19.38	16.48	12.39	6.93
15.375	21.52	21.12	20.68	20.21	17.19	12.92	7.22
15.500	22.40	21.99	21.53	21.04	17.90	13.45	7.52
15.625	23.29	22.86	22.38	21.87	18.61	13.98	7.81
15.750	24.17	23.73	23.24	22.71	19.32	14.52	8.11
15.875	25.06	24.60	24.09	23.54	20.04	15.05	8.41
16.000	25.95	25.47	24.95	24.38	20.75	15.59	8.70
16.125	26.84	26.34	25.81	25.22	21.47	16.13	9.00
16.250	27.73	27.22	26.66	26.06	22.19	16.67	9.30

12½%
Old Rate

Payment Adjustments
(As % of Old Payment)

NEW RATE (%)	YEARS REMAINING IN TERM						
	30	29	28	27	26	25	24
9.500	-21.21	-20.98	-20.73	-20.47	-20.18	-19.87	-19.54
9.625	-20.36	-20.14	-19.90	-19.64	-19.37	-19.07	-18.75
9.750	-19.50	-19.29	-19.06	-18.82	-18.55	-18.27	-17.97
9.875	-18.64	-18.44	-18.22	-17.99	-17.74	-17.47	-17.18
10.000	-17.77	-17.58	-17.38	-17.16	-16.92	-16.66	-16.38
10.125	-16.91	-16.73	-16.53	-16.32	-16.09	-15.85	-15.59
10.250	-16.04	-15.87	-15.68	-15.48	-15.27	-15.04	-14.79
10.375	-15.17	-15.00	-14.83	-14.64	-14.44	-14.22	-13.99
10.500	-14.29	-14.14	-13.98	-13.80	-13.61	-13.41	-13.19
10.625	-13.41	-13.27	-13.12	-12.96	-12.78	-12.59	-12.38
10.750	-12.53	-12.40	-12.26	-12.11	-11.94	-11.76	-11.57
10.875	-11.65	-11.53	-11.40	-11.26	-11.10	-10.94	-10.76
11.000	-10.77	-10.66	-10.54	-10.41	-10.26	-10.11	-9.95
11.125	-9.88	-9.78	-9.67	-9.55	-9.42	-9.28	-9.13
11.250	-8.99	-8.90	-8.80	-8.69	-8.58	-8.45	-8.31
11.375	-8.10	-8.02	-7.93	-7.83	-7.73	-7.61	-7.49
11.500	-7.21	-7.14	-7.06	-6.97	-6.88	-6.78	-6.67
11.625	-6.32	-6.25	-6.18	-6.11	-6.03	-5.94	-5.84
11.750	-5.42	-5.37	-5.31	-5.24	-5.17	-5.10	-5.01
11.875	-4.52	-4.48	-4.43	-4.37	-4.31	-4.25	-4.18
12.000	-3.62	-3.58	-3.55	-3.50	-3.46	-3.41	-3.35
12.125	-2.72	-2.69	-2.66	-2.63	-2.59	-2.56	-2.52
12.250	-1.81	-1.80	-1.78	-1.76	-1.73	-1.71	-1.68
12.375	-0.91	-0.90	-0.89	-0.88	-0.87	-0.85	-0.84
12.500	0.00	0.00	0.00	0.00	0.00	0.00	0.00
12.625	0.91	0.90	0.89	0.88	0.87	0.86	0.84
12.750	1.82	1.80	1.78	1.76	1.74	1.71	1.69
12.875	2.73	2.71	2.68	2.65	2.61	2.58	2.53
13.000	3.65	3.61	3.57	3.53	3.49	3.44	3.38
13.125	4.56	4.52	4.47	4.42	4.36	4.30	4.23
13.250	5.48	5.43	5.37	5.31	5.24	5.17	5.09
13.375	6.40	6.34	6.27	6.20	6.12	6.04	5.94
13.500	7.32	7.25	7.18	7.09	7.00	6.91	6.80
13.625	8.25	8.17	8.08	7.99	7.89	7.78	7.66
13.750	9.17	9.08	8.99	8.89	8.77	8.65	8.52
13.875	10.09	10.00	9.90	9.78	9.66	9.52	9.38
14.000	11.02	10.92	10.81	10.68	10.55	10.40	10.24
14.125	11.95	11.84	11.72	11.58	11.44	11.28	11.11
14.250	12.88	12.76	12.63	12.48	12.33	12.16	11.97
14.375	13.81	13.68	13.54	13.39	13.22	13.04	12.84
14.500	14.74	14.60	14.46	14.29	14.12	13.92	13.71
14.625	15.67	15.53	15.37	15.20	15.01	14.81	14.58
14.750	16.60	16.45	16.29	16.11	15.91	15.69	15.46
14.875	17.54	17.38	17.21	17.02	16.81	16.58	16.33
15.000	18.48	18.31	18.13	17.93	17.71	17.47	17.21
15.125	19.41	19.24	19.05	18.84	18.61	18.36	18.08
15.250	20.35	20.17	19.97	19.75	19.51	19.25	18.96
15.375	21.29	21.10	20.90	20.67	20.42	20.14	19.84
15.500	22.23	22.04	21.82	21.58	21.32	21.04	20.73
15.625	23.17	22.97	22.75	22.50	22.23	21.93	21.61
15.750	24.11	23.90	23.67	23.42	23.14	22.83	22.49
15.875	25.06	24.84	24.60	24.34	24.05	23.73	23.38
16.000	26.00	25.78	25.53	25.26	24.96	24.63	24.27
16.125	26.95	26.71	26.46	26.18	25.87	25.53	25.16
16.250	27.89	27.65	27.39	27.10	26.78	26.43	26.05
16.375	28.84	28.59	28.32	28.02	27.70	27.33	26.94
16.500	29.79	29.53	29.26	28.95	28.61	28.24	27.83

Payment Adjustments 12½%
(As % of Old Payment) — Old Rate

NEW RATE (%)	YEARS REMAINING IN TERM						
	23	22	21	20	15	10	5
9.500	-19.18	-18.80	-18.39	-17.96	-15.28	-11.60	-6.65
9.625	-18.41	-18.05	-17.66	-17.24	-14.66	-11.13	-6.38
9.750	-17.64	-17.29	-16.92	-16.51	-14.05	-10.66	-6.11
9.875	-16.87	-16.53	-16.17	-15.79	-13.43	-10.19	-5.83
10.000	-16.09	-15.77	-15.43	-15.06	-12.81	-9.72	-5.56
10.125	-15.31	-15.00	-14.68	-14.33	-12.19	-9.25	-5.29
10.250	-14.52	-14.24	-13.93	-13.60	-11.57	-8.77	-5.01
10.375	-13.74	-13.47	-13.18	-12.86	-10.94	-8.29	-4.74
10.500	-12.95	-12.69	-12.42	-12.13	-10.31	-7.82	-4.46
10.625	-12.16	-11.92	-11.66	-11.39	-9.68	-7.34	-4.19
10.750	-11.36	-11.14	-10.90	-10.64	-9.05	-6.86	-3.91
10.875	-10.57	-10.36	-10.14	-9.90	-8.42	-6.38	-3.64
11.000	-9.77	-9.58	-9.37	-9.15	-7.78	-5.89	-3.36
11.125	-8.97	-8.79	-8.60	-8.40	-7.15	-5.41	-3.08
11.250	-8.16	-8.00	-7.83	-7.65	-6.51	-4.92	-2.80
11.375	-7.36	-7.21	-7.06	-6.89	-5.86	-4.44	-2.53
11.500	-6.55	-6.42	-6.28	-6.14	-5.22	-3.95	-2.25
11.625	-5.74	-5.63	-5.51	-5.38	-4.57	-3.46	-1.97
11.750	-4.92	-4.83	-4.73	-4.61	-3.93	-2.97	-1.69
11.875	-4.11	-4.03	-3.94	-3.85	-3.28	-2.48	-1.41
12.000	-3.29	-3.23	-3.16	-3.09	-2.63	-1.99	-1.13
12.125	-2.47	-2.42	-2.37	-2.32	-1.97	-1.49	-0.85
12.250	-1.65	-1.62	-1.58	-1.55	-1.32	-1.00	-0.56
12.375	-0.83	-0.81	-0.79	-0.77	-0.66	-0.50	-0.28
12.500	0.00	0.00	0.00	0.00	0.00	0.00	0.00
12.625	0.83	0.81	0.80	0.78	0.66	0.50	0.28
12.750	1.66	1.63	1.59	1.56	1.32	1.00	0.57
12.875	2.49	2.44	2.39	2.34	1.99	1.50	0.85
13.000	3.32	3.26	3.19	3.12	2.65	2.00	1.13
13.125	4.16	4.08	4.00	3.90	3.32	2.51	1.42
13.250	5.00	4.90	4.80	4.69	3.99	3.01	1.70
13.375	5.84	5.73	5.61	5.48	4.66	3.52	1.99
13.500	6.68	6.55	6.42	6.27	5.34	4.03	2.27
13.625	7.52	7.38	7.23	7.06	6.01	4.54	2.56
13.750	8.37	8.21	8.04	7.86	6.69	5.05	2.85
13.875	9.22	9.04	8.86	8.65	7.37	5.56	3.14
14.000	10.07	9.88	9.67	9.45	8.05	6.07	3.42
14.125	10.92	10.71	10.49	10.25	8.73	6.59	3.71
14.250	11.77	11.55	11.31	11.05	9.42	7.10	4.00
14.375	12.62	12.39	12.13	11.86	10.10	7.62	4.29
14.500	13.48	13.23	12.96	12.66	10.79	8.14	4.58
14.625	14.34	14.07	13.78	13.47	11.48	8.66	4.87
14.750	15.20	14.92	14.61	14.28	12.17	9.18	5.16
14.875	16.06	15.76	15.44	15.09	12.86	9.70	5.45
15.000	16.92	16.61	16.27	15.90	13.55	10.22	5.74
15.125	17.78	17.46	17.10	16.71	14.25	10.74	6.03
15.250	18.65	18.31	17.93	17.53	14.95	11.27	6.33
15.375	19.52	19.16	18.77	18.35	15.65	11.79	6.62
15.500	20.38	20.01	19.61	19.16	16.35	12.32	6.91
15.625	21.25	20.87	20.44	19.98	17.05	12.85	7.21
15.750	22.13	21.72	21.28	20.81	17.75	13.38	7.50
15.875	23.00	22.58	22.13	21.63	18.46	13.91	7.80
16.000	23.87	23.44	22.97	22.45	19.16	14.44	8.09
16.125	24.75	24.30	23.81	23.28	19.87	14.97	8.39
16.250	25.62	25.16	24.66	24.11	20.58	15.51	8.68
16.375	26.50	26.02	25.50	24.94	21.29	16.04	8.98
16.500	27.38	26.89	26.35	25.77	22.00	16.58	9.27

12¾%
Old Rate

Payment Adjustments
(As % of Old Payment)

NEW RATE (%)	YEARS REMAINING IN TERM						
	30	29	28	27	26	25	24
9.750	-20.94	-20.72	-20.48	-20.22	-19.95	-19.65	-19.33
9.875	-20.09	-19.88	-19.65	-19.41	-19.14	-18.86	-18.55
10.000	-19.24	-19.04	-18.83	-18.59	-18.34	-18.07	-17.77
10.125	-18.39	-18.20	-17.99	-17.77	-17.53	-17.27	-16.99
10.250	-17.54	-17.36	-17.16	-16.95	-16.72	-16.47	-16.20
10.375	-16.68	-16.51	-16.32	-16.12	-15.90	-15.67	-15.42
10.500	-15.82	-15.66	-15.48	-15.29	-15.09	-14.87	-14.63
10.625	-14.96	-14.81	-14.64	-14.46	-14.27	-14.06	-13.83
10.750	-14.10	-13.95	-13.80	-13.63	-13.45	-13.25	-13.04
10.875	-13.23	-13.10	-12.95	-12.79	-12.62	-12.44	-12.24
11.000	-12.37	-12.24	-12.10	-11.96	-11.80	-11.63	-11.44
11.125	-11.49	-11.38	-11.25	-11.12	-10.97	-10.81	-10.64
11.250	-10.62	-10.52	-10.40	-10.27	-10.14	-9.99	-9.83
11.375	-9.75	-9.65	-9.54	-9.43	-9.31	-9.17	-9.03
11.500	-8.87	-8.78	-8.69	-8.58	-8.47	-8.35	-8.22
11.625	-7.99	-7.91	-7.83	-7.73	-7.63	-7.52	-7.40
11.750	-7.11	-7.04	-6.97	-6.88	-6.79	-6.70	-6.59
11.875	-6.23	-6.17	-6.10	-6.03	-5.95	-5.87	-5.77
12.000	-5.34	-5.29	-5.24	-5.17	-5.11	-5.03	-4.95
12.125	-4.46	-4.41	-4.37	-4.32	-4.26	-4.20	-4.13
12.250	-3.57	-3.54	-3.50	-3.46	-3.41	-3.36	-3.31
12.375	-2.68	-2.65	-2.63	-2.60	-2.56	-2.53	-2.49
12.500	-1.79	-1.77	-1.75	-1.73	-1.71	-1.69	-1.66
12.625	-0.90	-0.89	-0.88	-0.87	-0.86	-0.84	-0.83
12.750	0.00	0.00	0.00	0.00	0.00	0.00	0.00
12.875	0.90	0.89	0.88	0.87	0.86	0.85	0.83
13.000	1.79	1.78	1.76	1.74	1.72	1.69	1.67
13.125	2.69	2.67	2.64	2.61	2.58	2.54	2.50
13.250	3.60	3.56	3.53	3.49	3.44	3.39	3.34
13.375	4.50	4.46	4.41	4.36	4.31	4.25	4.18
13.500	5.40	5.35	5.30	5.24	5.17	5.10	5.03
13.625	6.31	6.25	6.19	6.12	6.04	5.96	5.87
13.750	7.22	7.15	7.08	7.00	6.91	6.82	6.71
13.875	8.12	8.05	7.97	7.88	7.78	7.68	7.56
14.000	9.03	8.95	8.86	8.76	8.66	8.54	8.41
14.125	9.95	9.86	9.76	9.65	9.53	9.40	9.26
14.250	10.86	10.76	10.65	10.54	10.41	10.27	10.11
14.375	11.77	11.67	11.55	11.42	11.29	11.13	10.97
14.500	12.69	12.57	12.45	12.31	12.17	12.00	11.82
14.625	13.60	13.48	13.35	13.20	13.05	12.87	12.68
14.750	14.52	14.39	14.25	14.10	13.93	13.74	13.54
14.875	15.44	15.30	15.15	14.99	14.81	14.61	14.40
15.000	16.36	16.21	16.06	15.89	15.70	15.49	15.26
15.125	17.28	17.13	16.96	16.78	16.58	16.36	16.12
15.250	18.20	18.04	17.87	17.68	17.47	17.24	16.99
15.375	19.12	18.96	18.78	18.58	18.36	18.12	17.85
15.500	20.04	19.87	19.68	19.48	19.25	19.00	18.72
15.625	20.97	20.79	20.59	20.38	20.14	19.88	19.59
15.750	21.89	21.71	21.51	21.28	21.03	20.76	20.46
15.875	22.82	22.63	22.42	22.18	21.93	21.64	21.33
16.000	23.75	23.55	23.33	23.09	22.82	22.53	22.20
16.125	24.68	24.47	24.24	23.99	23.72	23.41	23.08
16.250	25.60	25.39	25.16	24.90	24.61	24.30	23.95
16.375	26.53	26.32	26.07	25.81	25.51	25.19	24.83
16.500	27.46	27.24	26.99	26.71	26.41	26.08	25.71
16.625	28.40	28.16	27.91	27.62	27.31	26.97	26.59
16.750	29.33	29.09	28.83	28.53	28.21	27.86	27.47

Payment Adjustments 12¾%
(As % of Old Payment) Old Rate

NEW RATE (%)	23	22	21	20	15	10	5
			YEARS REMAINING IN TERM				
9.750	-18.98	-18.61	-18.22	-17.79	-15.17	-11.55	-6.63
9.875	-18.22	-17.87	-17.49	-17.08	-14.56	-11.08	-6.36
10.000	-17.46	-17.12	-16.75	-16.36	-13.95	-10.61	-6.09
10.125	-16.69	-16.36	-16.02	-15.64	-13.34	-10.14	-5.82
10.250	-15.92	-15.61	-15.28	-14.92	-12.72	-9.67	-5.55
10.375	-15.14	-14.85	-14.54	-14.20	-12.11	-9.20	-5.27
10.500	-14.37	-14.09	-13.79	-13.47	-11.49	-8.73	-5.00
10.625	-13.59	-13.33	-13.05	-12.74	-10.86	-8.25	-4.73
10.750	-12.81	-12.56	-12.30	-12.01	-10.24	-7.78	-4.45
10.875	-12.03	-11.79	-11.55	-11.28	-9.62	-7.30	-4.18
11.000	-11.24	-11.02	-10.79	-10.54	-8.99	-6.83	-3.90
11.125	-10.45	-10.25	-10.03	-9.80	-8.36	-6.35	-3.63
11.250	-9.66	-9.48	-9.28	-9.06	-7.73	-5.86	-3.35
11.375	-8.87	-8.70	-8.52	-8.32	-7.09	-5.38	-3.07
11.500	-8.07	-7.92	-7.75	-7.57	-6.46	-4.90	-2.80
11.625	-7.28	-7.14	-6.99	-6.83	-5.82	-4.42	-2.52
11.750	-6.48	-6.35	-6.22	-6.08	-5.18	-3.93	-2.24
11.875	-5.67	-5.57	-5.45	-5.32	-4.54	-3.44	-1.96
12.000	-4.87	-4.78	-4.68	-4.57	-3.90	-2.96	-1.68
12.125	-4.06	-3.99	-3.90	-3.81	-3.25	-2.47	-1.40
12.250	-3.25	-3.19	-3.13	-3.05	-2.61	-1.98	-1.12
12.375	-2.44	-2.40	-2.35	-2.29	-1.96	-1.48	-0.84
12.500	-1.63	-1.60	-1.57	-1.53	-1.31	-0.99	-0.56
12.625	-0.82	-0.80	-0.78	-0.77	-0.65	-0.50	-0.28
12.750	0.00	0.00	0.00	0.00	0.00	0.00	0.00
12.875	0.82	0.80	0.79	0.77	0.66	0.50	0.28
13.000	1.64	1.61	1.58	1.54	1.31	0.99	0.56
13.125	2.46	2.42	2.37	2.31	1.97	1.49	0.85
13.250	3.29	3.23	3.16	3.09	2.63	1.99	1.13
13.375	4.11	4.04	3.95	3.86	3.30	2.50	1.42
13.500	4.94	4.85	4.75	4.64	3.96	3.00	1.70
13.625	5.77	5.66	5.55	5.42	4.63	3.50	1.98
13.750	6.60	6.48	6.35	6.21	5.30	4.01	2.27
13.875	7.44	7.30	7.15	6.99	5.97	4.52	2.56
14.000	8.27	8.12	7.95	7.78	6.64	5.02	2.84
14.125	9.11	8.94	8.76	8.56	7.31	5.53	3.13
14.250	9.95	9.77	9.57	9.35	7.99	6.04	3.42
14.375	10.79	10.59	10.38	10.14	8.66	6.55	3.70
14.500	11.63	11.42	11.19	10.94	9.34	7.07	3.99
14.625	12.47	12.25	12.00	11.73	10.02	7.58	4.28
14.750	13.32	13.08	12.81	12.53	10.70	8.10	4.57
14.875	14.16	13.91	13.63	13.33	11.39	8.61	4.86
15.000	15.01	14.74	14.45	14.13	12.07	9.13	5.15
15.125	15.86	15.58	15.27	14.93	12.76	9.65	5.44
15.250	16.71	16.41	16.09	15.73	13.45	10.17	5.73
15.375	17.57	17.25	16.91	16.53	14.14	10.69	6.02
15.500	18.42	18.09	17.73	17.34	14.83	11.21	6.31
15.625	19.28	18.93	18.56	18.15	15.52	11.73	6.60
15.750	20.13	19.77	19.38	18.96	16.21	12.26	6.90
15.875	20.99	20.62	20.21	19.77	16.91	12.78	7.19
16.000	21.85	21.46	21.04	20.58	17.61	13.31	7.48
16.125	22.71	22.31	21.87	21.39	18.30	13.83	7.78
16.250	23.57	23.16	22.70	22.21	19.00	14.36	8.07
16.375	24.44	24.01	23.54	23.02	19.71	14.89	8.36
16.500	25.30	24.86	24.37	23.84	20.41	15.42	8.66
16.625	26.17	25.71	25.21	24.66	21.11	15.96	8.96
16.750	27.04	26.56	26.05	25.48	21.82	16.49	9.25

13%
Old Rate

Payment Adjustments
(As % of Old Payment)

NEW RATE (%)	YEARS REMAINING IN TERM						
	30	29	28	27	26	25	24
10.000	-20.67	-20.46	-20.23	-19.98	-19.72	-19.43	-19.12
10.125	-19.83	-19.63	-19.41	-19.18	-18.92	-18.65	-18.35
10.250	-18.99	-18.80	-18.59	-18.37	-18.12	-17.86	-17.58
10.375	-18.15	-17.97	-17.77	-17.77	-17.56	-17.32	-17.07	-16.80
10.500	-17.31	-17.13	-16.95	-16.74	-16.52	-16.28	-16.03
10.625	-16.46	-16.30	-16.12	-15.93	-15.72	-15.49	-15.25
10.750	-15.61	-15.46	-15.29	-15.11	-14.91	-14.70	-14.46
10.875	-14.76	-14.62	-14.46	-14.29	-14.10	-13.90	-13.68
11.000	-13.91	-13.77	-13.62	-13.46	-13.29	-13.10	-12.89
11.125	-13.06	-12.93	-12.79	-12.64	-12.47	-12.30	-12.10
11.250	-12.20	-12.08	-11.95	-11.81	-11.66	-11.49	-11.31
11.375	-11.34	-11.23	-11.11	-10.98	-10.84	-10.68	-10.52
11.500	-10.48	-10.38	-10.27	-10.15	-10.02	-9.87	-9.72
11.625	-9.61	-9.52	-9.42	-9.31	-9.19	-9.06	-8.92
11.750	-8.75	-8.67	-8.57	-8.47	-8.37	-8.25	-8.12
11.875	-7.88	-7.81	-7.73	-7.64	-7.54	-7.43	-7.32
12.000	-7.01	-6.95	-6.87	-6.80	-6.71	-6.62	-6.51
12.125	-6.14	-6.08	-6.02	-5.95	-5.88	-5.80	-5.71
12.250	-5.27	-5.22	-5.17	-5.11	-5.04	-4.97	-4.90
12.375	-4.40	-4.36	-4.31	-4.26	-4.21	-4.15	-4.09
12.500	-3.52	-3.49	-3.45	-3.41	-3.37	-3.32	-3.27
12.625	-2.64	-2.62	-2.59	-2.56	-2.53	-2.50	-2.46
12.750	-1.76	-1.75	-1.73	-1.71	-1.69	-1.67	-1.64
12.875	-0.88	-0.87	-0.87	-0.86	-0.85	-0 83	-0.82
13.000	0.00	0.00	0.00	0.00	0.00	0.00	0.00
13.125	0.88	0.88	0.87	0.86	0.85	0.84	0.82
13.250	1.77	1.75	1.74	1.72	1.70	1.67	1.65
13.375	2.66	2.63	2.61	2.58	2.55	2.51	2.47
13.500	3.54	3.51	3.48	3.44	3.40	3.35	3.30
13.625	4.43	4.39	4.35	4.30	4.25	4.19	4.13
13.750	5.33	5.28	5.23	5.17	5.11	5.04	4.96
13.875	6.22	6.16	6.10	6.04	5.96	5.88	5.80
14.000	7.11	7.05	6.98	6.91	6.82	6.73	6.63
14.125	8.01	7.94	7.86	7.78	7.68	7.58	7.47
14.250	8.90	8.83	8.74	8.65	8.54	8.43	8.31
14.375	9.80	9.72	9.62	9.52	9.41	9.28	9.15
14.500	10.70	10.61	10.51	10.39	10.27	10.14	9.99
14.625	11.60	11.50	11.39	11.27	11.14	10.99	10.83
14.750	12.50	12.39	12.28	12.15	12.00	11.85	11.68
14.875	13.40	13.29	13.16	13.02	12.87	12.71	12.52
15.000	14.31	14.18	14.05	13.90	13.74	13.57	13.37
15.125	15.21	15.08	14.94	14.78	14.61	14.43	14.22
15.250	16.11	15.98	15.83	15.67	15.49	15.29	15.07
15.375	17.02	16.88	16.72	16.55	16.36	16.15	15.92
15.500	17.93	17.78	17.62	17.43	17.24	17.02	16.77
15.625	18.84	18.68	18.51	18.32	18.11	17.88	17.63
15.750	19.74	19.58	19.40	19.21	18.99	18.75	18.49
15.875	20.65	20.49	20.30	20.09	19.87	19.62	19.34
16.000	21.57	21.39	21.20	20.98	20.75	20.49	20.20
16.125	22.48	22.30	22.09	21.87	21.63	21.36	21.06
16.250	23.39	23.20	22.99	22.76	22.51	22.23	21.92
16.375	24.30	24.11	23.89	23.66	23.39	23.10	22.78
16.500	25.22	25.02	24.79	24.55	24.28	23.98	23.65
16.625	26.13	25.92	25.70	25.44	25.16	24.85	24.51
16.750	27.05	26.83	26.60	26.34	26.05	25.73	25.37
16.875	27.96	27.74	27.50	27.23	26.93	26.60	26.24
17.000	28.88	28.66	28.41	28.13	27.82	27.48	27.11

Payment Adjustments
(As % of Old Payment)

13% Old Rate

NEW RATE (%)	YEARS REMAINING IN TERM						
	23	22	21	20	15	10	5
10.000	-18.79	-18.43	-18.04	-17.63	-15.07	-11.49	-6.62
10.125	-18.03	-17.69	-17.32	-16.92	-14.46	-11.03	-6.35
10.250	-17.27	-16.95	-16.59	-16.21	-13.85	-10.56	-6.08
10.375	-16.51	-16.20	-15.86	-15.50	-13.25	-10.10	-5.81
10.500	-15.75	-15.45	-15.13	-14.78	-12.63	-9.63	-5.53
10.625	-14.98	-14.70	-14.39	-14.07	-12.02	-9.16	-5.26
10.750	-14.22	-13.95	-13.66	-13.34	-11.40	-8.69	-4.99
10.875	-13.44	-13.19	-12.92	-12.62	-10.79	-8.22	-4.72
11.000	-12.67	-12.43	-12.17	-11.90	-10.17	-7.74	-4.44
11.125	-11.90	-11.67	-11.43	-11.17	-9.55	-7.27	-4.17
11.250	-11.12	-10.91	-10.68	-10.44	-8.92	-6.79	-3.89
11.375	-10.34	-10.14	-9.93	-9.71	-8.30	-6.32	-3.62
11.500	-9.56	-9.38	-9.18	-8.97	-7.67	-5.84	-3.34
11.625	-8.77	-8.61	-8.43	-8.24	-7.04	-5.36	-3.07
11.750	-7.98	-7.83	-7.67	-7.50	-6.41	-4.88	-2.79
11.875	-7.19	-7.06	-6.92	-6.76	-5.78	-4.39	-2.51
12.000	-6.40	-6.28	-6.16	-6.02	-5.14	-3.91	-2.24
12.125	-5.61	-5.51	-5.39	-5.27	-4.51	-3.43	-1.96
12.250	-4.82	-4.73	-4.63	-4.52	-3.87	-2.94	-1.68
12.375	-4.02	-3.94	-3.86	-3.78	-3.23	-2.45	-1.40
12.500	-3.22	-3.16	-3.09	-3.02	-2.59	-1.97	-1.12
12.625	-2.42	-2.37	-2.32	-2.27	-1.94	-1.48	-0.84
12.750	-1.61	-1.58	-1.55	-1.52	-1.30	-0.98	-0.56
12.875	-0.81	-0.79	-0.78	-0.76	-0.65	-0.49	-0.28
13.000	0.00	0.00	0.00	0.00	0.00	0.00	0.00
13.125	0.81	0.79	0.78	0.76	0.65	0.49	0.28
13.250	1.62	1.59	1.56	1.52	1.30	0.99	0.56
13.375	2.43	2.39	2.34	2.29	1.96	1.49	0.85
13.500	3.25	3.19	3.13	3.06	2.61	1.98	1.13
13.625	4.06	3.99	3.91	3.82	3.27	2.48	1.41
13.750	4.88	4.80	4.70	4.59	3.93	2.98	1.70
13.875	5.70	5.60	5.49	5.37	4.59	3.49	1.98
14.000	6.53	6.41	6.28	6.14	5.26	3.99	2.26
14.125	7.35	7.22	7.07	6.92	5.92	4.49	2.55
14.250	8.17	8.03	7.87	7.69	6.59	5.00	2.83
14.375	9.00	8.84	8.66	8.47	7.25	5.50	3.12
14.500	9.83	9.65	9.46	9.25	7.92	6.01	3.41
14.625	10.66	10.47	10.26	10.04	8.60	6.52	3.69
14.750	11.49	11.29	11.06	10.82	9.27	7.03	3.98
14.875	12.32	12.11	11.87	11.61	9.94	7.54	4.27
15.000	13.16	12.93	12.67	12.39	10.62	8.05	4.56
15.125	13.99	13.75	13.48	13.18	11.30	8.57	4.85
15.250	14.83	14.57	14.29	13.97	11.97	9.08	5.13
15.375	15.67	15.40	15.09	14.77	12.66	9.60	5.42
15.500	16.51	16.22	15.91	15.56	13.34	10.11	5.71
15.625	17.35	17.05	16.72	16.36	14.02	10.63	6.00
15.750	18.20	17.88	17.53	17.15	14.71	11.15	6.30
15.875	19.04	18.71	18.35	17.95	15.39	11.67	6.59
16.000	19.89	19.54	19.16	18.75	16.08	12.19	6.88
16.125	20.73	20.37	19.98	19.55	16.77	12.71	7.17
16.250	21.58	21.21	20.80	20.35	17.46	13.24	7.46
16.375	22.43	22.04	21.62	21.16	18.15	13.76	7.76
16.500	23.28	22.88	22.44	21.96	18.85	14.29	8.05
16.625	24.13	23.72	23.27	22.77	19.54	14.81	8.34
16.750	24.99	24.56	24.09	23.58	20.24	15.34	8.64
16.875	25.84	25.40	24.92	24.39	20.94	15.87	8.93
17.000	26.70	26.24	25.74	25.20	21.64	16.40	9.23

13¼%
Old Rate

Payment Adjustments
(As % of Old Payment)

NEW RATE (%)	YEARS REMAINING IN TERM						
	30	29	28	27	26	25	24
10.250	-20.40	-20.20	-19.98	-19.75	-19.49	-19.21	-18.91
10.375	-19.57	-19.38	-19.17	-18.95	-18.70	-18.44	-18.15
10.500	-18.75	-18.56	-18.36	-18.15	-17.91	-17.66	-17.39
10.625	-17.91	-17.74	-17.55	-17.34	-17.12	-16.88	-16.62
10.750	-17.08	-16.92	-16.73	-16.54	-16.33	-16.10	-15.85
10.875	-16.25	-16.09	-15.92	-15.73	-15.53	-15.31	-15.08
11.000	-15.41	-15.26	-15.10	-14.92	-14.73	-14.53	-14.31
11.125	-14.57	-14.43	-14.28	-14.11	-13.93	-13.74	-13.53
11.250	-13.72	-13.59	-13.45	-13.30	-13.13	-12.95	-12.75
11.375	-12.88	-12.76	-12.63	-12.48	-12.32	-12.15	-11.97
11.500	-12.03	-11.92	-11.80	-11.66	-11.52	-11.36	-11.18
11.625	-11.19	-11.08	-10.97	-10.84	-10.71	-10.56	-10.40
11.750	-10.34	-10.24	-10.13	-10.02	-9.89	-9.76	-9.61
11.875	-9.48	-9.40	-9.30	-9.19	-9.08	-8.96	-8.82
12.000	-8.63	-8.55	-8.46	-8.37	-8.26	-8.15	-8.03
12.125	-7.77	-7.70	-7.62	-7.54	-7.45	-7.35	-7.24
12.250	-6.92	-6.85	-6.78	-6.71	-6.63	-6.54	-6.44
12.375	-6.06	-6.00	-5.94	-5.88	-5.80	-5.73	-5.64
12.500	-5.20	-5.15	-5.10	-5.04	-4.98	-4.91	-4.84
12.625	-4.34	-4.30	-4.25	-4.21	-4.16	-4.10	-4.04
12.750	-3.47	-3.44	-3.41	-3.37	-3.33	-3.28	-3.23
12.875	-2.61	-2.58	-2.56	-2.53	-2.50	-2.47	-2.43
13.000	-1.74	-1.72	-1.71	-1.69	-1.67	-1.65	-1.62
13.125	-0.87	-0.86	-0.85	-0.84	-0.83	-0.82	-0.81
13.250	0.00	0.00	0.00	0.00	0.00	0.00	0.00
13.375	0.87	0.86	0.86	0.85	0.84	0.83	0.81
13.500	1.74	1.73	1.71	1.69	1.67	1.65	1.63
13.625	2.62	2.60	2.57	2.54	2.51	2.48	2.44
13.750	3.49	3.46	3.43	3.39	3.35	3.31	3.26
13.875	4.37	4.33	4.29	4.25	4.20	4.14	4.08
14.000	5.25	5.20	5.16	5.10	5.04	4.98	4.90
14.125	6.13	6.08	6.02	5.96	5.89	5.81	5.73
14.250	7.01	6.95	6.88	6.81	6.73	6.65	6.55
14.375	7.89	7.83	7.75	7.67	7.58	7.49	7.38
14.500	8.77	8.70	8.62	8.53	8.43	8.32	8.21
14.625	9.66	9.58	9.49	9.39	9.28	9.17	9.04
14.750	10.54	10.46	10.36	10.25	10.14	10.01	9.87
14.875	11.43	11.34	11.23	11.12	10.99	10.85	10.70
15.000	12.32	12.22	12.10	11.98	11.85	11.70	11.53
15.125	13.21	13.10	12.98	12.85	12.70	12.54	12.37
15.250	14.10	13.98	13.85	13.71	13.56	13.39	13.20
15.375	14.99	14.86	14.73	14.58	14.42	14.24	14.04
15.500	15.88	15.75	15.61	15.45	15.28	15.09	14.88
15.625	16.77	16.64	16.49	16.32	16.14	15.94	15.72
15.750	17.66	17.52	17.37	17.19	17.00	16.80	16.56
15.875	18.56	18.41	18.25	18.07	17.87	17.65	17.41
16.000	19.45	19.30	19.13	18.94	18.73	18.50	18.25
16.125	20.35	20.19	20.01	19.82	19.60	19.36	19.10
16.250	21.24	21.08	20.90	20.69	20.47	20.22	19.94
16.375	22.14	21.97	21.78	21.57	21.33	21.08	20.79
16.500	23.04	22.86	22.66	22.45	22.20	21.94	21.64
16.625	23.94	23.75	23.55	23.32	23.07	22.80	22.49
16.750	24.84	24.65	24.44	24.20	23.95	23.66	23.34
16.875	25.74	25.54	25.33	25.08	24.82	24.52	24.19
17.000	26.64	26.44	26.21	25.97	25.69	25.39	25.05
17.125	27.54	27.33	27.10	26.85	26.56	26.25	25.90
17.250	28.44	28.23	27.99	27.73	27.44	27.12	26.76

Payment Adjustments 13¼%
(As % of Old Payment)   Old Rate

NEW RATE (%)	YEARS REMAINING IN TERM						
	23	22	21	20	15	10	5
10.250	-18.59	-18.25	-17.87	-17.47	-14.96	-11.44	-6.60
10.375	-17.84	-17.51	-17.15	-16.77	-14.36	-10.98	-6.33
10.500	-17.09	-16.77	-16.43	-16.06	-13.76	-10.51	-6.06
10.625	-16.34	-16.04	-15.71	-15.36	-13.15	-10.05	-5.79
10.750	-15.58	-15.29	-14.98	-14.65	-12.54	-9.58	-5.52
10.875	-14.83	-14.55	-14.25	-13.93	-11.94	-9.12	-5.25
11.000	-14.06	-13.80	-13.52	-13.22	-11.32	-8.65	-4.98
11.125	-13.30	-13.06	-12.79	-12.50	-10.71	-8.18	-4.70
11.250	-12.54	-12.30	-12.05	-11.78	-10.09	-7.71	-4.43
11.375	-11.77	-11.55	-11.32	-11.06	-9.48	-7.23	-4.16
11.500	-11.00	-10.80	-10.58	-10.34	-8.86	-6.76	-3.88
11.625	-10.23	-10.04	-9.84	-9.62	-8.24	-6.29	-3.61
11.750	-9.45	-9.28	-9.09	-8.89	-7.61	-5.81	-3.33
11.875	-8.67	-8.52	-8.34	-8.16	-6.99	-5.33	-3.06
12.000	-7.90	-7.75	-7.60	-7.43	-6.36	-4.85	-2.78
12.125	-7.12	-6.99	-6.85	-6.69	-5.74	-4.37	-2.51
12.250	-6.33	-6.22	-6.09	-5.96	-5.11	-3.89	-2.23
12.375	-5.55	-5.45	-5.34	-5.22	-4.47	-3.41	-1.95
12.500	-4.76	-4.68	-4.58	-4.48	-3.84	-2.93	-1.67
12.625	-3.97	-3.90	-3.82	-3.74	-3.20	-2.44	-1.40
12.750	-3.18	-3.12	-3.06	-2.99	-2.57	-1.96	-1.12
12.875	-2.39	-2.35	-2.30	-2.25	-1.93	-1.47	-0.84
13.000	-1.59	-1.57	-1.53	-1.50	-1.29	-0.98	-0.56
13.125	-0.80	-0.78	-0.77	-0.75	-0.64	-0.49	-0.28
13.250	0.00	0.00	0.00	0.00	0.00	0.00	0.00
13.375	0.80	0.79	0.77	0.75	0.65	0.49	0.28
13.500	1.60	1.57	1.54	1.51	1.29	0.98	0.56
13.625	2.41	2.36	2.32	2.27	1.94	1.48	0.84
13.750	3.21	3.15	3.09	3.02	2.59	1.98	1.13
13.875	4.02	3.95	3.87	3.79	3.25	2.47	1.41
14.000	4.83	4.74	4.65	4.55	3.90	2.97	1.69
14.125	5.64	5.54	5.43	5.31	4.56	3.47	1.97
14.250	6.45	6.34	6.21	6.08	5.21	3.97	2.26
14.375	7.26	7.14	7.00	6.84	5.87	4.47	2.54
14.500	8.08	7.94	7.78	7.61	6.54	4.97	2.83
14.625	8.89	8.74	8.57	8.39	7.20	5.48	3.11
14.750	9.71	9.54	9.36	9.16	7.86	5.98	3.40
14.875	10.53	10.35	10.15	9.93	8.53	6.49	3.68
15.000	11.35	11.16	10.94	10.71	9.19	6.99	3.97
15.125	12.18	11.97	11.74	11.48	9.86	7.50	4.26
15.250	13.00	12.78	12.53	12.26	10.53	8.01	4.55
15.375	13.83	13.59	13.33	13.04	11.21	8.52	4.83
15.500	14.65	14.40	14.13	13.83	11.88	9.03	5.12
15.625	15.48	15.22	14.93	14.61	12.55	9.55	5.41
15.750	16.31	16.03	15.73	15.39	13.23	10.06	5.70
15.875	17.14	16.85	16.53	16.18	13.91	10.58	5.99
16.000	17.97	17.67	17.33	16.97	14.59	11.09	6.28
16.125	18.81	18.49	18.14	17.76	15.27	11.61	6.57
16.250	19.64	19.31	18.95	18.55	15.95	12.13	6.86
16.375	20.48	20.13	19.75	19.34	16.63	12.65	7.15
16.500	21.32	20.96	20.56	20.13	17.32	13.17	7.44
16.625	22.15	21.78	21.37	20.93	18.00	13.69	7.74
16.750	22.99	22.61	22.19	21.72	18.69	14.21	8.03
16.875	23.83	23.44	23.00	22.52	19.38	14.73	8.32
17.000	24.68	24.27	23.81	23.32	20.07	15.26	8.61
17.125	25.52	25.10	24.63	24.12	20.76	15.78	8.91
17.250	26.36	25.93	25.45	24.92	21.46	16.31	9.20

13½%
Old Rate

Payment Adjustments
(As % of Old Payment)

NEW RATE (%)	YEARS REMAINING IN TERM						
	30	29	28	27	26	25	24
10.500	-20.14	-19.95	-19.74	-19.51	-19.27	-19.00	-18.71
10.625	-19.32	-19.14	-18.94	-18.72	-18.49	-18.23	-17.96
10.750	-18.50	-18.33	-18.14	-17.93	-17.71	-17.46	-17.20
10.875	-17.68	-17.51	-17.33	-17.14	-16.92	-16.69	-16.44
11.000	-16.86	-16.70	-16.53	-16.34	-16.14	-15.92	-15.68
11.125	-16.03	-15.88	-15.72	-15.54	-15.35	-15.14	-14.91
11.250	-15.20	-15.06	-14.91	-14.74	-14.56	-14.36	-14.15
11.375	-14.37	-14.24	-14.10	-13.94	-13.77	-13.58	-13.38
11.500	-13.54	-13.42	-13.28	-13.13	-12.97	-12.80	-12.61
11.625	-12.71	-12.59	-12.47	-12.33	-12.18	-12.01	-11.83
11.750	-11.87	-11.77	-11.65	-11.52	-11.38	-11.23	-11.06
11.875	-11.04	-10.94	-10.83	-10.71	-10.58	-10.44	-10.28
12.000	-10.20	-10.11	-10.00	-9.89	-9.77	-9.64	-9.50
12.125	-9.36	-9.27	-9.18	-9.08	-8.97	-8.85	-8.72
12.250	-8.51	-8.44	-8.35	-8.26	-8.16	-8.06	-7.94
12.375	-7.67	-7.60	-7.53	-7.44	-7.36	-7.26	-7.15
12.500	-6.82	-6.76	-6.70	-6.62	-6.55	-6.46	-6.37
12.625	-5.98	-5.92	-5.87	-5.80	-5.73	-5.66	-5.58
12.750	-5.13	-5.08	-5.03	-4.98	-4.92	-4.85	-4.78
12.875	-4.28	-4.24	-4.20	-4.15	-4.10	-4.05	-3.99
13.000	-3.42	-3.39	-3.36	-3.33	-3.29	-3.24	-3.20
13.125	-2.57	-2.55	-2.52	-2.50	-2.47	-2.44	-2.40
13.250	-1.71	-1.70	-1.68	-1.67	-1.65	-1.63	-1.60
13.375	-0.86	-0.85	-0.84	-0.83	-0.82	-0.81	-0.80
13.500	0.00	0.00	0.00	0.00	0.00	0.00	0.00
13.625	0.86	0.85	0.84	0.84	0.83	0.82	0.80
13.750	1.72	1.71	1.69	1.67	1.65	1.63	1.61
13.875	2.58	2.56	2.54	2.51	2.48	2.45	2.42
14.000	3.45	3.42	3.38	3.35	3.31	3.27	3.22
14.125	4.31	4.27	4.23	4.19	4.14	4.09	4.03
14.250	5.17	5.13	5.09	5.03	4.98	4.91	4.85
14.375	6.04	5.99	5.94	5.88	5.81	5.74	5.66
14.500	6.91	6.85	6.79	6.72	6.65	6.56	6.47
14.625	7.78	7.72	7.65	7.57	7.48	7.39	7.29
14.750	8.65	8.58	8.50	8.42	8.32	8.22	8.11
14.875	9.52	9.44	9.36	9.27	9.16	9.05	8.93
15.000	10.39	10.31	10.22	10.12	10.00	9.88	9.75
15.125	11.27	11.18	11.08	10.97	10.85	10.71	10.57
15.250	12.14	12.04	11.94	11.82	11.69	11.55	11.39
15.375	13.01	12.91	12.80	12.67	12.54	12.38	12.22
15.500	13.89	13.78	13.66	13.53	13.38	13.22	13.04
15.625	14.77	14.65	14.53	14.39	14.23	14.06	13.87
15.750	15.65	15.52	15.39	15.24	15.08	14.90	14.70
15.875	16.52	16.40	16.26	16.10	15.93	15.74	15.53
16.000	17.40	17.27	17.12	16.96	16.78	16.58	16.36
16.125	18.28	18.15	17.99	17.82	17.63	17.42	17.19
16.250	19.17	19.02	18.86	18.68	18.48	18.26	18.02
16.375	20.05	19.90	19.73	19.54	19.34	19.11	18.86
16.500	20.93	20.77	20.60	20.41	20.19	19.95	19.69
16.625	21.81	21.65	21.47	21.27	21.05	20.80	20.53
16.750	22.70	22.53	22.34	22.14	21.90	21.65	21.37
16.875	23.58	23.41	23.22	23.00	22.76	22.50	22.21
17.000	24.47	24.29	24.09	23.87	23.62	23.35	23.04
17.125	25.35	25.17	24.96	24.74	24.48	24.20	23.89
17.250	26.24	26.05	25.84	25.60	25.34	25.05	24.73
17.375	27.13	26.93	26.72	26.47	26.20	25.90	25.57
17.500	28.02	27.82	27.59	27.34	27.07	26.76	26.41

Payment Adjustments
(As % of Old Payment)

13½% Old Rate

NEW RATE (%)	23	22	21	20	15	10	5
			YEARS REMAINING IN TERM				
10.500	-18.40	-18.06	-17.70	-17.31	-14.86	-11.39	-6.59
10.625	-17.66	-17.34	-16.99	-16.61	-14.26	-10.93	-6.32
10.750	-16.91	-16.61	-16.27	-15.91	-13.66	-10.46	-6.05
10.875	-16.17	-15.87	-15.56	-15.21	-13.06	-10.00	-5.78
11.000	-15.42	-15.14	-14.84	-14.51	-12.46	-9.54	-5.51
11.125	-14.67	-14.40	-14.11	-13.80	-11.85	-9.07	-5.24
11.250	-13.91	-13.66	-13.39	-13.10	-11.24	-8.61	-4.96
11.375	-13.16	-12.92	-12.66	-12.39	-10.63	-8.14	-4.69
11.500	-12.40	-12.18	-11.94	-11.67	-10.02	-7.67	-4.42
11.625	-11.64	-11.43	-11.20	-10.96	-9.41	-7.20	-4.15
11.750	-10.88	-10.68	-10.47	-10.24	-8.79	-6.73	-3.87
11.875	-10.11	-9.93	-9.74	-9.52	-8.18	-6.25	-3.60
12.000	-9.35	-9.18	-9.00	-8.80	-7.56	-5.78	-3.33
12.125	-8.58	-8.43	-8.26	-8.08	-6.94	-5.31	-3.05
12.250	-7.81	-7.67	-7.52	-7.36	-6.32	-4.83	-2.78
12.375	-7.04	-6.91	-6.78	-6.63	-5.69	-4.35	-2.50
12.500	-6.26	-6.15	-6.03	-5.90	-5.07	-3.87	-2.22
12.625	-5.49	-5.39	-5.28	-5.17	-4.44	-3.39	-1.95
12.750	-4.71	-4.62	-4.53	-4.44	-3.81	-2.91	-1.67
12.875	-3.93	-3.86	-3.78	-3.70	-3.18	-2.43	-1.39
13.000	-3.15	-3.09	-3.03	-2.96	-2.55	-1.95	-1.12
13.125	-2.36	-2.32	-2.28	-2.23	-1.91	-1.46	-0.84
13.250	-1.58	-1.55	-1.52	-1.49	-1.28	-0.98	-0.56
13.375	-0.79	-0.78	-0.76	-0.74	-0.64	-0.49	-0.28
13.500	0.00	0.00	0.00	0.00	0.00	0.00	0.00
13.625	0.79	0.78	0.76	0.75	0.64	0.49	0.28
13.750	1.58	1.56	1.53	1.49	1.28	0.98	0.56
13.875	2.38	2.34	2.29	2.24	1.93	1.47	0.84
14.000	3.17	3.12	3.06	2.99	2.57	1.97	1.12
14.125	3.97	3.90	3.83	3.75	3.22	2.46	1.41
14.250	4.77	4.69	4.60	4.50	3.87	2.95	1.69
14.375	5.57	5.48	5.37	5.26	4.52	3.45	1.97
14.500	6.37	6.26	6.15	6.02	5.17	3.95	2.25
14.625	7.18	7.05	6.92	6.77	5.83	4.45	2.54
14.750	7.98	7.85	7.70	7.54	6.48	4.95	2.82
14.875	8.79	8.64	8.48	8.30	7.14	5.45	3.11
15.000	9.60	9.44	9.26	9.06	7.80	5.95	3.39
15.125	10.41	10.23	10.04	9.83	8.46	6.45	3.68
15.250	11.22	11.03	10.82	10.60	9.12	6.96	3.96
15.375	12.03	11.83	11.61	11.36	9.79	7.46	4.25
15.500	12.85	12.63	12.39	12.13	10.45	7.97	4.53
15.625	13.66	13.43	13.18	12.91	11.12	8.48	4.82
15.750	14.48	14.24	13.97	13.68	11.78	8.99	5.11
15.875	15.29	15.04	14.76	14.45	12.45	9.50	5.40
16.000	16.11	15.85	15.55	15.23	13.12	10.01	5.69
16.125	16.93	16.65	16.35	16.01	13.80	10.52	5.97
16.250	17.76	17.46	17.14	16.79	14.47	11.03	6.26
16.375	18.58	18.27	17.94	17.57	15.14	11.55	6.55
16.500	19.40	19.08	18.73	18.35	15.82	12.06	6.84
16.625	20.23	19.90	19.53	19.13	16.50	12.58	7.13
16.750	21.05	20.71	20.33	19.91	17.18	13.10	7.43
16.875	21.88	21.52	21.13	20.70	17.86	13.62	7.72
17.000	22.71	22.34	21.93	21.49	18.54	14.13	8.01
17.125	23.54	23.16	22.74	22.27	19.22	14.66	8.30
17.250	24.37	23.98	23.54	23.06	19.91	15.18	8.59
17.375	25.20	24.80	24.35	23.85	20.59	15.70	8.89
17.500	26.04	25.62	25.15	24.65	21.28	16.22	9.18

13¾%
Old Rate

Payment Adjustments
(As % of Old Payment)

NEW RATE (%)	YEARS REMAINING IN TERM						
	30	29	28	27	26	25	24
10.750	-19.88	-19.70	-19.50	-19.28	-19.04	-18.79	-18.51
10.875	-19.07	-18.90	-18.71	-18.50	-18.27	-18.03	-17.76
11.000	-18.26	-18.10	-17.91	-17.72	-17.50	-17.27	-17.01
11.125	-17.45	-17.29	-17.12	-16.93	-16.73	-16.50	-16.26
11.250	-16.64	-16.49	-16.32	-16.14	-15.95	-15.74	-15.51
11.375	-15.82	-15.68	-15.52	-15.35	-15.17	-14.97	-14.75
11.500	-15.00	-14.87	-14.72	-14.56	-14.39	-14.20	-13.99
11.625	-14.19	-14.06	-13.92	-13.77	-13.60	-13.43	-13.23
11.750	-13.36	-13.24	-13.12	-12.97	-12.82	-12.65	-12.47
11.875	-12.54	-12.43	-12.31	-12.18	-12.03	-11.87	-11.70
12.000	-11.72	-11.61	-11.50	-11.38	-11.24	-11.10	-10.94
12.125	-10.89	-10.79	-10.69	-10.58	-10.45	-10.31	-10.17
12.250	-10.06	-9.97	-9.88	-9.77	-9.66	-9.53	-9.40
12.375	-9.23	-9.15	-9.06	-8.97	-8.86	-8.75	-8.62
12.500	-8.40	-8.33	-8.25	-8.16	-8.06	-7.96	-7.85
12.625	-7.57	-7.50	-7.43	-7.35	-7.27	-7.17	-7.07
12.750	-6.73	-6.67	-6.61	-6.54	-6.47	-6.38	-6.29
12.875	-5.89	-5.84	-5.79	-5.73	-5.66	-5.59	-5.51
13.000	-5.06	-5.01	-4.97	-4.92	-4.86	-4.80	-4.73
13.125	-4.22	-4.18	-4.14	-4.10	-4.05	-4.00	-3.95
13.250	-3.38	-3.35	-3.32	-3.28	-3.25	-3.20	-3.16
13.375	-2.53	-2.51	-2.49	-2.46	-2.44	-2.41	-2.37
13.500	-1.69	-1.68	-1.66	-1.64	-1.63	-1.61	-1.58
13.625	-0.85	-0.84	-0.83	-0.82	-0.81	-0.80	-0.79
13.750	0.00	0.00	0.00	0.00	0.00	0.00	0.00
13.875	0.85	0.84	0.83	0.82	0.82	0.81	0.79
14.000	1.70	1.68	1.67	1.65	1.63	1.61	1.59
14.125	2.55	2.53	2.50	2.48	2.45	2.42	2.39
14.250	3.40	3.37	3.34	3.31	3.27	3.23	3.19
14.375	4.25	4.21	4.18	4.14	4.09	4.04	3.99
14.500	5.10	5.06	5.02	4.97	4.91	4.85	4.79
14.625	5.96	5.91	5.86	5.80	5.74	5.67	5.59
14.750	6.81	6.76	6.70	6.63	6.56	6.48	6.40
14.875	7.67	7.61	7.54	7.47	7.39	7.30	7.20
15.000	8.53	8.46	8.39	8.31	8.22	8.12	8.01
15.125	9.38	9.31	9.23	9.14	9.04	8.94	8.82
15.250	10.24	10.16	10.08	9.98	9.87	9.76	9.63
15.375	11.10	11.02	10.93	10.82	10.71	10.58	10.44
15.500	11.96	11.87	11.77	11.66	11.54	11.40	11.25
15.625	12.83	12.73	12.62	12.50	12.37	12.23	12.07
15.750	13.69	13.59	13.47	13.35	13.21	13.05	12.88
15.875	14.55	14.45	14.32	14.19	14.04	13.88	13.70
16.000	15.42	15.30	15.18	15.04	14.88	14.71	14.52
16.125	16.28	16.16	16.03	15.88	15.72	15.54	15.33
16.250	17.15	17.02	16.88	16.73	16.56	16.37	16.15
16.375	18.02	17.89	17.74	17.58	17.40	17.20	16.97
16.500	18.89	18.75	18.60	18.43	18.24	18.03	17.80
16.625	19.75	19.61	19.45	19.28	19.08	18.86	18.62
16.750	20.62	20.48	20.31	20.13	19.92	19.70	19.44
16.875	21.49	21.34	21.17	20.98	20.77	20.53	20.27
17.000	22.36	22.20	22.03	21.83	21.61	21.37	21.10
17.125	23.23	23.07	22.89	22.68	22.46	22.20	21.92
17.250	24.11	23.94	23.75	23.54	23.30	23.04	22.75
17.375	24.98	24.81	24.61	24.39	24.15	23.88	23.58
17.500	25.85	25.67	25.47	25.25	25.00	24.72	24.41
17.625	26.73	26.54	26.34	26.10	25.85	25.56	25.24
17.750	27.60	27.41	27.20	26.96	26.70	26.40	26.08

Payment Adjustments 13¾%
(As % of Old Payment)   Old Rate

NEW RATE (%)	YEARS REMAINING IN TERM						
	23	22	21	20	15	10	5
10.750	-18.21	-17.88	-17.53	-17.15	-14.76	-11.33	-6.57
10.875	-17.47	-17.16	-16.83	-16.46	-14.16	-10.88	-6.30
11.000	-16.74	-16.44	-16.12	-15.77	-13.57	-10.42	-6.04
11.125	-16.00	-15.71	-15.41	-15.07	-12.97	-9.96	-5.77
11.250	-15.26	-14.99	-14.69	-14.37	-12.37	-9.49	-5.50
11.375	-14.51	-14.26	-13.98	-13.68	-11.77	-9.03	-5.23
11.500	-13.77	-13.52	-13.26	-12.97	-11.16	-8.57	-4.95
11.625	-13.02	-12.79	-12.54	-12.27	-10.56	-8.10	-4.68
11.750	-12.27	-12.05	-11.82	-11.56	-9.95	-7.63	-4.41
11.875	-11.52	-11.31	-11.09	-10.86	-9.34	-7.17	-4.14
12.000	-10.76	-10.57	-10.37	-10.15	-8.73	-6.70	-3.87
12.125	-10.01	-9.83	-9.64	-9.43	-8.12	-6.23	-3.59
12.250	-9.25	-9.09	-8.91	-8.72	-7.51	-5.75	-3.32
12.375	-8.49	-8.34	-8.18	-8.00	-6.89	-5.28	-3.05
12.500	-7.72	-7.59	-7.44	-7.28	-6.27	-4.81	-2.77
12.625	-6.96	-6.84	-6.71	-6.56	-5.65	-4.33	-2.49
12.750	-6.19	-6.09	-5.97	-5.84	-5.03	-3.85	-2.22
12.875	-5.43	-5.33	-5.23	-5.12	-4.41	-3.38	-1.94
13.000	-4.66	-4.58	-4.49	-4.39	-3.78	-2.90	-1.67
13.125	-3.88	-3.82	-3.74	-3.67	-3.16	-2.42	-1.39
13.250	-3.11	-3.06	-3.00	-2.94	-2.53	-1.94	-1.11
13.375	-2.34	-2.30	-2.25	-2.20	-1.90	-1.45	-0.84
13.500	-1.56	-1.53	-1.50	-1.47	-1.27	-0.97	-0.56
13.625	-0.78	-0.77	-0.75	-0.74	-0.63	-0.49	-0.28
13.750	0.00	0.00	0.00	0.00	0.00	0.00	0.00
13.875	0.78	0.77	0.75	0.74	0.64	0.49	0.28
14.000	1.57	1.54	1.51	1.48	1.27	0.98	0.56
14.125	2.35	2.31	2.27	2.22	1.91	1.46	0.84
14.250	3.14	3.08	3.03	2.96	2.55	1.95	1.12
14.375	3.93	3.86	3.79	3.71	3.20	2.45	1.40
14.500	4.72	4.64	4.55	4.45	3.84	2.94	1.68
14.625	5.51	5.41	5.31	5.20	4.49	3.43	1.96
14.750	6.30	6.19	6.08	5.95	5.13	3.93	2.25
14.875	7.09	6.98	6.85	6.70	5.78	4.42	2.53
15.000	7.89	7.76	7.61	7.46	6.43	4.92	2.81
15.125	8.69	8.54	8.38	8.21	7.09	5.42	3.10
15.250	9.48	9.33	9.16	8.97	7.74	5.92	3.38
15.375	10.28	10.12	9.93	9.73	8.39	6.42	3.67
15.500	11.09	10.90	10.70	10.48	9.05	6.92	3.95
15.625	11.89	11.69	11.48	11.24	9.71	7.42	4.24
15.750	12.69	12.48	12.26	12.01	10.37	7.93	4.52
15.875	13.50	13.28	13.04	12.77	11.03	8.43	4.81
16.000	14.30	14.07	13.82	13.53	11.69	8.94	5.10
16.125	15.11	14.87	14.60	14.30	12.35	9.45	5.38
16.250	15.92	15.66	15.38	15.07	13.02	9.95	5.67
16.375	16.73	16.46	16.16	15.84	13.68	10.46	5.96
16.500	17.54	17.26	16.95	16.61	14.35	10.97	6.25
16.625	18.35	18.06	17.73	17.38	15.02	11.49	6.54
16.750	19.17	18.86	18.52	18.15	15.69	12.00	6.83
16.875	19.98	19.66	19.31	18.92	16.36	12.51	7.12
17.000	20.80	20.47	20.10	19.70	17.04	13.03	7.41
17.125	21.61	21.27	20.89	20.48	17.71	13.54	7.70
17.250	22.43	22.08	21.68	21.25	18.39	14.06	7.99
17.375	23.25	22.88	22.48	22.03	19.06	14.58	8.28
17.500	24.07	23.69	23.27	22.81	19.74	15.10	8.57
17.625	24.89	24.50	24.07	23.59	20.42	15.61	8.86
17.750	25.71	25.31	24.87	24.37	21.10	16.14	9.16

Payment Adjustments
(As % of Old Payment)

NEW RATE (%)	YEARS REMAINING IN TERM						
	30	29	28	27	26	25	24
11.000	-19.63	-19.45	-19.26	-19.05	-18.83	-18.58	-18.31
11.125	-18.83	-18.66	-18.48	-18.28	-18.06	-17.83	-17.57
11.250	-18.03	-17.87	-17.69	-17.50	-17.30	-17.07	-16.83
11.375	-17.23	-17.07	-16.91	-16.73	-16.53	-16.32	-16.08
11.500	-16.42	-16.28	-16.12	-15.95	-15.76	-15.56	-15.34
11.625	-15.62	-15.48	-15.33	-15.17	-14.99	-14.80	-14.59
11.750	-14.81	-14.68	-14.54	-14.39	-14.22	-14.04	-13.84
11.875	-14.00	-13.88	-13.75	-13.60	-13.44	-13.27	-13.08
12.000	-13.19	-13.07	-12.95	-12.82	-12.67	-12.51	-12.33
12.125	-12.37	-12.27	-12.15	-12.03	-11.89	-11.74	-11.57
12.250	-11.56	-11.46	-11.35	-11.24	-11.11	-10.97	-10.81
12.375	-10.74	-10.65	-10.55	-10.44	-10.33	-10.20	-10.05
12.500	-9.93	-9.84	-9.75	-9.65	-9.54	-9.42	-9.29
12.625	-9.11	-9.03	-8.95	-8.86	-8.76	-8.65	-8.53
12.750	-8.29	-8.22	-8.14	-8.06	-7.97	-7.87	-7.76
12.875	-7.46	-7.40	-7.33	-7.26	-7.18	-7.09	-6.99
13.000	-6.64	-6.59	-6.53	-6.46	-6.39	-6.31	-6.22
13.125	-5.81	-5.77	-5.71	-5.66	-5.59	-5.52	-5.45
13.250	-4.99	-4.95	-4.90	-4.85	-4.80	-4.74	-4.68
13.375	-4.16	-4.13	-4.09	-4.05	-4.00	-3.95	-3.90
13.500	-3.33	-3.30	-3.27	-3.24	-3.21	-3.17	-3.12
13.625	-2.50	-2.48	-2.46	-2.43	-2.41	-2.38	-2.34
13.750	-1.67	-1.65	-1.64	-1.62	-1.61	-1.59	-1.56
13.875	-0.83	-0.83	-0.82	-0.81	-0.80	-0.79	-0.78
14.000	0.00	0.00	0.00	0.00	0.00	0.00	0.00
14.125	0.84	0.83	0.82	0.81	0.81	0.80	0.78
14.250	1.67	1.66	1.64	1.63	1.61	1.59	1.57
14.375	2.51	2.49	2.47	2.45	2.42	2.39	2.36
14.500	3.35	3.32	3.29	3.26	3.23	3.19	3.15
14.625	4.19	4.16	4.12	4.08	4.04	3.99	3.94
14.750	5.03	4.99	4.95	4.90	4.85	4.79	4.73
14.875	5.87	5.83	5.78	5.72	5.66	5.60	5.52
15.000	6.72	6.67	6.61	6.55	6.48	6.40	6.32
15.125	7.56	7.50	7.44	7.37	7.29	7.21	7.11
15.250	8.40	8.34	8.27	8.20	8.11	8.02	7.91
15.375	9.25	9.18	9.11	9.02	8.93	8.83	8.71
15.500	10.10	10.02	9.94	9.85	9.75	9.64	9.51
15.625	10.95	10.87	10.78	10.68	10.57	10.45	10.31
15.750	11.79	11.71	11.61	11.51	11.39	11.26	11.11
15.875	12.64	12.55	12.45	12.34	12.21	12.07	11.92
16.000	13.49	13.40	13.29	13.17	13.03	12.89	12.72
16.125	14.34	14.24	14.13	14.00	13.86	13.70	13.53
16.250	15.20	15.09	14.97	14.83	14.68	14.52	14.34
16.375	16.05	15.94	15.81	15.67	15.51	15.34	15.14
16.500	16.90	16.78	16.65	16.50	16.34	16.16	15.95
16.625	17.76	17.63	17.49	17.34	17.17	16.98	16.76
16.750	18.61	18.48	18.34	18.18	18.00	17.80	17.58
16.875	19.47	19.33	19.18	19.01	18.83	18.62	18.39
17.000	20.32	20.18	20.03	19.85	19.66	19.44	19.20
17.125	21.18	21.03	20.87	20.69	20.49	20.27	20.02
17.250	22.04	21.89	21.72	21.53	21.32	21.09	20.83
17.375	22.90	22.74	22.57	22.37	22.16	21.92	21.65
17.500	23.75	23.59	23.42	23.21	22.99	22.74	22.47
17.625	24.61	24.45	24.26	24.06	23.83	23.57	23.28
17.750	25.47	25.30	25.11	24.90	24.66	24.40	24.10
17.875	26.33	26.16	25.96	25.74	25.50	25.23	24.92
18.000	27.19	27.01	26.81	26.59	26.34	26.06	25.74

Payment Adjustments
(As % of Old Payment)
14% Old Rate

NEW RATE (%)	23	22	21	20	15	10	5
				YEARS REMAINING IN TERM			
11.000	-18.02	-17.71	-17.36	-16.99	-14.65	-11.28	-6.56
11.125	-17.29	-16.99	-16.66	-16.31	-14.06	-10.83	-6.29
11.250	-16.56	-16.27	-15.96	-15.62	-13.47	-10.37	-6.02
11.375	-15.83	-15.56	-15.26	-14.93	-12.88	-9.91	-5.75
11.500	-15.10	-14.83	-14.55	-14.24	-12.28	-9.45	-5.48
11.625	-14.36	-14.11	-13.84	-13.55	-11.68	-8.99	-5.21
11.750	-13.62	-13.38	-13.13	-12.85	-11.08	-8.52	-4.94
11.875	-12.88	-12.66	-12.42	-12.15	-10.48	-8.06	-4.67
12.000	-12.14	-11.93	-11.70	-11.45	-9.88	-7.60	-4.40
12.125	-11.39	-11.20	-10.98	-10.75	-9.28	-7.13	-4.13
12.250	-10.65	-10.46	-10.26	-10.05	-8.67	-6.66	-3.86
12.375	-9.90	-9.73	-9.54	-9.34	-8.06	-6.20	-3.58
12.500	-9.15	-8.99	-8.82	-8.64	-7.45	-5.73	-3.31
12.625	-8.39	-8.25	-8.10	-7.93	-6.84	-5.25	-3.04
12.750	-7.64	-7.51	-7.37	-7.21	-6.23	-4.78	-2.76
12.875	-6.88	-6.77	-6.64	-6.50	-5.61	-4.31	-2.49
13.000	-6.13	-6.02	-5.91	-5.79	-4.99	-3.84	-2.21
13.125	-5.37	-5.28	-5.18	-5.07	-4.37	-3.36	-1.94
13.250	-4.60	-4.53	-4.44	-4.35	-3.75	-2.88	-1.66
13.375	-3.84	-3.78	-3.71	-3.63	-3.13	-2.41	-1.39
13.500	-3.08	-3.02	-2.97	-2.91	-2.51	-1.93	-1.11
13.625	-2.31	-2.27	-2.23	-2.18	-1.88	-1.45	-0.83
13.750	-1.54	-1.52	-1.49	-1.46	-1.26	-0.97	-0.56
13.875	-0.77	-0.76	-0.74	-0.73	-0.63	-0.48	-0.28
14.000	0.00	0.00	0.00	0.00	0.00	0.00	0.00
14.125	0.77	0.76	0.75	0.73	0.63	0.48	0.28
14.250	1.55	1.52	1.49	1.46	1.26	0.97	0.56
14.375	2.32	2.29	2.24	2.20	1.90	1.46	0.84
14.500	3.10	3.05	2.99	2.93	2.54	1.95	1.12
14.625	3.88	3.82	3.75	3.67	3.17	2.43	1.40
14.750	4.66	4.58	4.50	4.41	3.81	2.92	1.68
14.875	5.44	5.35	5.26	5.15	4.45	3.42	1.96
15.000	6.23	6.13	6.01	5.89	5.09	3.91	2.24
15.125	7.01	6.90	6.77	6.64	5.74	4.40	2.52
15.250	7.80	7.67	7.53	7.38	6.38	4.90	2.81
15.375	8.59	8.45	8.29	8.13	7.03	5.39	3.09
15.500	9.37	9.22	9.06	8.87	7.68	5.89	3.37
15.625	10.16	10.00	9.82	9.62	8.33	6.39	3.66
15.750	10.96	10.78	10.59	10.37	8.98	6.89	3.94
15.875	11.75	11.56	11.35	11.13	9.63	7.39	4.23
16.000	12.54	12.34	12.12	11.88	10.28	7.89	4.51
16.125	13.34	13.13	12.89	12.64	10.94	8.39	4.80
16.250	14.13	13.91	13.66	13.39	11.60	8.89	5.08
16.375	14.93	14.70	14.43	14.15	12.25	9.40	5.37
16.500	15.73	15.48	15.21	14.91	12.91	9.90	5.66
16.625	16.53	16.27	15.98	15.67	13.57	10.41	5.94
16.750	17.33	17.06	16.76	16.43	14.24	10.92	6.23
16.875	18.13	17.85	17.54	17.19	14.90	11.43	6.52
17.000	18.94	18.64	18.31	17.96	15.56	11.93	6.81
17.125	19.74	19.43	19.09	18.72	16.23	12.45	7.10
17.250	20.54	20.23	19.87	19.49	16.90	12.96	7.39
17.375	21.35	21.02	20.66	20.25	17.56	13.47	7.68
17.500	22.16	21.82	21.44	21.02	18.23	13.98	7.97
17.625	22.97	22.61	22.22	21.79	18.91	14.50	8.26
17.750	23.78	23.41	23.01	22.56	19.58	15.01	8.55
17.875	24.59	24.21	23.79	23.34	20.25	15.53	8.84
18.000	25.40	25.01	24.58	24.11	20.93	16.05	9.13

14¼%
Old Rate

Payment Adjustments
(As % of Old Payment)

NEW RATE (%)	YEARS REMAINING IN TERM						
	30	29	28	27	26	25	24
11.250	-19.38	-19.21	-19.03	-18.83	-18.61	-18.37	-18.11
11.375	-18.59	-18.43	-18.25	-18.06	-17.86	-17.63	-17.38
11.500	-17.80	-17.64	-17.48	-17.30	-17.10	-16.88	-16.65
11.625	-17.00	-16.86	-16.70	-16.53	-16.34	-16.13	-15.91
11.750	-16.21	-16.07	-15.92	-15.76	-15.58	-15.38	-15.17
11.875	-15.41	-15.28	-15.14	-14.99	-14.82	-14.63	-14.43
12.000	-14.62	-14.49	-14.36	-14.21	-14.05	-13.88	-13.69
12.125	-13.82	-13.70	-13.58	-13.44	-13.29	-13.12	-12.94
12.250	-13.02	-12.91	-12.79	-12.66	-12.52	-12.36	-12.19
12.375	-12.21	-12.11	-12.00	-11.88	-11.75	-11.60	-11.44
12.500	-11.41	-11.31	-11.21	-11.10	-10.98	-10.84	-10.69
12.625	-10.60	-10.52	-10.42	-10.32	-10.20	-10.08	-9.94
12.750	-9.79	-9.72	-9.63	-9.53	-9.43	-9.31	-9.19
12.875	-8.99	-8.91	-8.83	-8.75	-8.65	-8.54	-8.43
13.000	-8.18	-8.11	-8.04	-7.96	-7.87	-7.78	-7.67
13.125	-7.36	-7.30	-7.24	-7.17	-7.09	-7.01	-6.91
13.250	-6.55	-6.50	-6.44	-6.38	-6.31	-6.23	-6.15
13.375	-5.74	-5.69	-5.64	-5.59	-5.53	-5.46	-5.39
13.500	-4.92	-4.88	-4.84	-4.79	-4.74	-4.68	-4.62
13.625	-4.10	-4.07	-4.04	-4.00	-3.95	-3.91	-3.86
13.750	-3.28	-3.26	-3.23	-3.20	-3.17	-3.13	-3.09
13.875	-2.47	-2.45	-2.43	-2.40	-2.38	-2.35	-2.32
14.000	-1.64	-1.63	-1.62	-1.60	-1.59	-1.57	-1.55
14.125	-0.82	-0.82	-0.81	-0.80	-0.79	-0.78	-0.77
14.250	0.00	0.00	0.00	0.00	0.00	0.00	0.00
14.375	0.82	0.82	0.81	0.80	0.80	0.79	0.78
14.500	1.65	1.64	1.62	1.61	1.59	1.57	1.55
14.625	2.48	2.46	2.44	2.41	2.39	2.36	2.33
14.750	3.30	3.28	3.25	3.22	3.19	3.15	3.11
14.875	4.13	4.10	4.07	4.03	3.99	3.94	3.89
15.000	4.96	4.92	4.88	4.84	4.79	4.73	4.67
15.125	5.79	5.75	5.70	5.65	5.59	5.53	5.46
15.250	6.62	6.57	6.52	6.46	6.40	6.32	6.24
15.375	7.45	7.40	7.34	7.27	7.20	7.12	7.03
15.500	8.29	8.23	8.16	8.09	8.01	7.92	7.82
15.625	9.12	9.06	8.98	8.90	8.81	8.72	8.61
15.750	9.96	9.88	9.81	9.72	9.62	9.52	9.40
15.875	10.79	10.72	10.63	10.54	10.43	10.32	10.19
16.000	11.63	11.55	11.46	11.35	11.24	11.12	10.98
16.125	12.46	12.38	12.28	12.17	12.05	11.92	11.77
16.250	13.30	13.21	13.11	12.99	12.87	12.72	12.57
16.375	14.14	14.04	13.94	13.81	13.68	13.53	13.36
16.500	14.98	14.88	14.76	14.64	14.49	14.34	14.16
16.625	15.82	15.71	15.59	15.46	15.31	15.14	14.96
16.750	16.66	16.55	16.42	16.28	16.13	15.95	15.76
16.875	17.50	17.38	17.25	17.11	16.94	16.76	16.56
17.000	18.34	18.22	18.08	17.93	17.76	17.57	17.36
17.125	19.19	19.06	18.92	18.76	18.58	18.38	18.16
17.250	20.03	19.90	19.75	19.58	19.40	19.19	18.96
17.375	20.87	20.74	20.58	20.41	20.22	20.01	19.77
17.500	21.72	21.58	21.42	21.24	21.04	20.82	20.57
17.625	22.56	22.42	22.25	22.07	21.86	21.63	21.38
17.750	23.41	23.26	23.09	22.90	22.69	22.45	22.18
17.875	24.26	24.10	23.92	23.73	23.51	23.26	22.99
18.000	25.10	24.94	24.76	24.56	24.33	24.08	23.80
18.125	25.95	25.78	25.60	25.39	25.16	24.90	24.61
18.250	26.80	26.63	26.44	26.22	25.99	25.72	25.42

Payment Adjustments 14¼%
(As % of Old Payment)
Old Rate

NEW RATE (%)	YEARS REMAINING IN TERM						
	23	22	21	20	15	10	5
11.250	-17.83	-17.53	-17.20	-16.84	-14.55	-11.23	-6.54
11.375	-17.11	-16.82	-16.50	-16.16	-13.96	-10.77	-6.27
11.500	-16.39	-16.11	-15.81	-15.48	-13.38	-10.32	-6.01
11.625	-15.66	-15.40	-15.11	-14.79	-12.79	-9.86	-5.74
11.750	-14.94	-14.68	-14.41	-14.11	-12.19	-9.40	-5.47
11.875	-14.21	-13.97	-13.71	-13.42	-11.60	-8.94	-5.20
12.000	-13.48	-13.25	-13.00	-12.73	-11.00	-8.48	-4.93
12.125	-12.74	-12.53	-12.29	-12.04	-10.41	-8.02	-4.66
12.250	-12.01	-11.81	-11.59	-11.35	-9.81	-7.56	-4.39
12.375	-11.27	-11.08	-10.87	-10.65	-9.21	-7.10	-4.12
12.500	-10.53	-10.35	-10.16	-9.95	-8.61	-6.63	-3.85
12.625	-9.79	-9.63	-9.45	-9.25	-8.00	-6.17	-3.57
12.750	-9.05	-8.90	-8.73	-8.55	-7.40	-5.70	-3.30
12.875	-8.30	-8.16	-8.01	-7.85	-6.79	-5.23	-3.03
13.000	-7.56	-7.43	-7.29	-7.14	-6.18	-4.76	-2.76
13.125	-6.81	-6.70	-6.57	-6.44	-5.57	-4.29	-2.48
13.250	-6.06	-5.96	-5.85	-5.73	-4.96	-3.82	-2.21
13.375	-5.31	-5.22	-5.12	-5.02	-4.34	-3.34	-1.93
13.500	-4.55	-4.48	-4.40	-4.31	-3.73	-2.87	-1.66
13.625	-3.80	-3.74	-3.67	-3.67	-3.11	-2.39	-1.38
13.750	-3.04	-2.99	-2.94	-2.88	-2.49	-1.92	-1.11
13.875	-2.28	-2.25	-2.21	-2.16	-1.87	-1.44	-0.83
14.000	-1.52	-1.50	-1.47	-1.44	-1.25	-0.96	-0.55
14.125	-0.76	-0.75	-0.74	-0.72	-0.62	-0.48	-0.28
14.250	0.00	0.00	0.00	0.00	0.00	0.00	0.00
14.375	0.76	0.75	0.74	0.72	0.63	0.48	0.28
14.500	1.53	1.51	1.48	1.45	1.25	0.97	0.56
14.625	2.30	2.26	2.22	2.18	1.88	1.45	0.84
14.750	3.07	3.02	2.96	2.90	2.52	1.94	1.12
14.875	3.84	3.77	3.71	3.63	3.15	2.42	1.39
15.000	4.61	4.53	4.45	4.36	3.78	2.91	1.67
15.125	5.38	5.29	5.20	5.10	4.42	3.40	1.96
15.250	6.15	6.06	5.95	5.83	5.06	3.89	2.24
15.375	6.93	6.82	6.70	6.57	5.69	4.38	2.52
15.500	7.71	7.59	7.45	7.30	6.33	4.87	2.80
15.625	8.49	8.35	8.20	8.04	6.97	5.36	3.08
15.750	9.26	9.12	8.96	8.78	7.62	5.86	3.37
15.875	10.05	9.89	9.71	9.52	8.26	6.35	3.65
16.000	10.83	10.66	10.47	10.27	8.91	6.85	3.93
16.125	11.61	11.43	11.23	11.01	9.55	7.35	4.22
16.250	12.39	12.20	11.99	11.76	10.20	7.85	4.50
16.375	13.18	12.98	12.75	12.50	10.85	8.35	4.79
16.500	13.97	13.75	13.51	13.25	11.50	8.85	5.07
16.625	14.75	14.53	14.28	14.00	12.16	9.35	5.36
16.750	15.54	15.30	15.04	14.75	12.81	9.85	5.64
16.875	16.33	16.08	15.81	15.50	13.46	10.35	5.93
17.000	17.12	16.86	16.57	16.25	14.12	10.86	6.22
17.125	17.91	17.64	17.34	17.01	14.78	11.37	6.50
17.250	18.71	18.42	18.11	17.76	15.44	11.87	6.79
17.375	19.50	19.21	18.88	18.52	16.10	12.38	7.08
17.500	20.30	19.99	19.65	19.28	16.76	12.89	7.37
17.625	21.09	20.78	20.42	20.04	17.42	13.40	7.66
17.750	21.89	21.56	21.20	20.80	18.09	13.91	7.95
17.875	22.69	22.35	21.97	21.56	18.75	14.42	8.24
18.000	23.49	23.14	22.75	22.32	19.42	14.93	8.53
18.125	24.29	23.92	23.52	23.08	20.08	15.45	8.82
18.250	25.09	24.71	24.30	23.85	20.75	15.96	9.11

14½%
Old Rate

Payment Adjustments
(As % of Old Payment)

NEW RATE (%)	YEARS REMAINING IN TERM						
	30	29	28	27	26	25	24
11.500	-19.13	-18.97	-18.80	-18.61	-18.40	-18.17	-17.92
11.625	-18.35	-18.20	-18.03	-17.85	-17.65	-17.43	-17.19
11.750	-17.57	-17.42	-17.27	-17.09	-16.90	-16.69	-16.47
11.875	-16.79	-16.65	-16.50	-16.33	-16.15	-15.95	-15.74
12.000	-16.00	-15.87	-15.73	-15.57	-15.40	-15.21	-15.00
12.125	-15.21	-15.09	-14.96	-14.81	-14.64	-14.47	-14.27
12.250	-14.43	-14.31	-14.18	-14.04	-13.89	-13.72	-13.54
12.375	-13.64	-13.53	-13.41	-13.28	-13.13	-12.97	-12.80
12.500	-12.85	-12.74	-12.63	-12.51	-12.37	-12.22	-12.06
12.625	-12.05	-11.96	-11.85	-11.74	-11.61	-11.47	-11.32
12.750	-11.26	-11.17	-11.07	-10.96	-10.85	-10.72	-10.57
12.875	-10.46	-10.38	-10.29	-10.19	-10.08	-9.96	-9.83
13.000	-9.67	-9.59	-9.51	-9.42	-9.31	-9.20	-9.08
13.125	-8.87	-8.80	-8.72	-8.64	-8.55	-8.45	-8.33
13.250	-8.07	-8.00	-7.94	-7.86	-7.78	-7.69	-7.58
13.375	-7.27	-7.21	-7.15	-7.08	-7.01	-6.92	-6.83
13.500	-6.46	-6.41	-6.36	-6.30	-6.23	-6.16	-6.08
13.625	-5.66	-5.62	-5.57	-5.52	-5.46	-5.40	-5.33
13.750	-4.85	-4.82	-4.78	-4.73	-4.68	-4.63	-4.57
13.875	-4.05	-4.02	-3.98	-3.95	-3.91	-3.86	-3.81
14.000	-3.24	-3.22	-3.19	-3.16	-3.13	-3.09	-3.05
14.125	-2.43	-2.41	-2.39	-2.37	-2.35	-2.32	-2.29
14.250	-1.62	-1.61	-1.60	-1.58	-1.57	-1.55	-1.53
14.375	-0.81	-0.81	-0.80	-0.79	-0.78	-0.78	-0.77
14.500	0.00	0.00	0.00	0.00	0.00	0.00	0.00
14.625	0.81	0.81	0.80	0.79	0.79	0.78	0.77
14.750	1.63	1.61	1.60	1.59	1.57	1.55	1.53
14.875	2.44	2.42	2.40	2.38	2.36	2.33	2.30
15.000	3.26	3.23	3.21	3.18	3.15	3.11	3.07
15.125	4.07	4.05	4.01	3.98	3.94	3.89	3.85
15.250	4.89	4.86	4.82	4.78	4.73	4.68	4.62
15.375	5.71	5.67	5.63	5.58	5.52	5.46	5.39
15.500	6.53	6.48	6.43	6.38	6.32	6.25	6.17
15.625	7.35	7.30	7.24	7.18	7.11	7.03	6.95
15.750	8.17	8.12	8.05	7.98	7.91	7.82	7.72
15.875	8.99	8.93	8.86	8.79	8.70	8.61	8.50
16.000	9.82	9.75	9.67	9.59	9.50	9.40	9.28
16.125	10.64	10.57	10.49	10.40	10.30	10.19	10.06
16.250	11.46	11.39	11.30	11.20	11.10	10.98	10.85
16.375	12.29	12.21	12.12	12.01	11.90	11.77	11.63
16.500	13.11	13.03	12.93	12.82	12.70	12.57	12.42
16.625	13.94	13.85	13.75	13.63	13.50	13.36	13.20
16.750	14.77	14.67	14.56	14.44	14.31	14.16	13.99
16.875	15.60	15.49	15.38	15.25	15.11	14.95	14.78
17.000	16.42	16.32	16.20	16.06	15.92	15.75	15.56
17.125	17.25	17.14	17.02	16.88	16.72	16.55	16.35
17.250	18.08	17.97	17.84	17.69	17.53	17.35	17.14
17.375	18.91	18.79	18.66	18.51	18.34	18.15	17.94
17.500	19.74	19.62	19.48	19.32	19.14	18.95	18.73
17.625	20.57	20.45	20.30	20.14	19.95	19.75	19.52
17.750	21.41	21.27	21.12	20.95	20.76	20.55	20.32
17.875	22.24	22.10	21.95	21.77	21.58	21.36	21.11
18.000	23.07	22.93	22.77	22.59	22.39	22.16	21.91
18.125	23.91	23.76	23.59	23.41	23.20	22.97	22.70
18.250	24.74	24.59	24.42	24.23	24.01	23.77	23.50
18.375	25.57	25.42	25.24	25.05	24.83	24.58	24.30
18.500	26.41	26.25	26.07	25.87	25.64	25.38	25.10

Payment Adjustments
(As % of Old Payment)

14½% Old Rate

NEW RATE (%)	YEARS REMAINING IN TERM						
	23	22	21	20	15	10	5
11.500	-17.65	-17.35	-17.03	-16.69	-14.45	-11.18	-6.53
11.625	-16.94	-16.65	-16.35	-16.01	-13.87	-10.72	-6.26
11.750	-16.22	-15.95	-15.65	-15.34	-13.28	-10.27	-5.99
11.875	-15.50	-15.24	-14.96	-14.66	-12.70	-9.82	-5.72
12.000	-14.78	-14.54	-14.27	-13.98	-12.11	-9.36	-5.46
12.125	-14.06	-13.83	-13.57	-13.30	-11.52	-8.90	-5.19
12.250	-13.33	-13.11	-12.87	-12.61	-10.93	-8.44	-4.92
12.375	-12.61	-12.40	-12.17	-11.93	-10.33	-7.99	-4.65
12.500	-11.88	-11.68	-11.47	-11.24	-9.74	-7.52	-4.38
12.625	-11.15	-10.97	-10.77	-10.55	-9.14	-7.06	-4.11
12.750	-10.42	-10.25	-10.06	-9.86	-8.54	-6.60	-3.84
12.875	-9.68	-9.53	-9.35	-9.17	-7.94	-6.14	-3.57
13.000	-8.95	-8.80	-8.64	-8.47	-7.34	-5.67	-3.30
13.125	-8.21	-8.08	-7.93	-7.77	-6.74	-5.20	-3.02
13.250	-7.47	-7.35	-7.22	-7.08	-6.13	-4.74	-2.75
13.375	-6.73	-6.62	-6.51	-6.38	-5.53	-4.27	-2.48
13.500	-5.99	-5.90	-5.79	-5.67	-4.92	-3.80	-2.20
13.625	-5.25	-5.16	-5.07	-4.97	-4.31	-3.33	-1.93
13.750	-4.50	-4.43	-4.35	-4.26	-3.70	-2.86	-1.65
13.875	-3.76	-3.70	-3.63	-3.56	-3.09	-2.38	-1.38
14.000	-3.01	-2.96	-2.91	-2.85	-2.47	-1.91	-1.11
14.125	-2.26	-2.22	-2.18	-2.14	-1.86	-1.43	-0.83
14.250	-1.51	-1.48	-1.46	-1.43	-1.24	-0.96	-0.55
14.375	-0.75	-0.74	-0.73	-0.71	-0.62	-0.48	-0.28
14.500	0.00	0.00	0.00	0.00	0.00	0.00	0.00
14.625	0.76	0.74	0.73	0.72	0.62	0.48	0.28
14.750	1.51	1.49	1.46	1.43	1.25	0.96	0.56
14.875	2.27	2.24	2.20	2.15	1.87	1.44	0.83
15.000	3.03	2.98	2.93	2.87	2.50	1.93	1.11
15.125	3.79	3.73	3.67	3.60	3.12	2.41	1.39
15.250	4.55	4.48	4.41	4.32	3.75	2.89	1.67
15.375	5.32	5.24	5.15	5.05	4.38	3.38	1.95
15.500	6.08	5.99	5.89	5.77	5.02	3.87	2.23
15.625	6.85	6.74	6.63	6.50	5.65	4.36	2.51
15.750	7.62	7.50	7.37	7.23	6.28	4.85	2.79
15.875	8.39	8.26	8.12	7.96	6.92	5.34	3.07
16.000	9.16	9.02	8.86	8.69	7.56	5.83	3.36
16.125	9.93	9.78	9.61	9.43	8.20	6.32	3.64
16.250	10.70	10.54	10.36	10.16	8.84	6.81	3.92
16.375	11.47	11.30	11.11	10.90	9.48	7.31	4.20
16.500	12.25	12.06	11.86	11.63	10.12	7.81	4.49
16.625	13.02	12.83	12.61	12.37	10.77	8.30	4.77
16.750	13.80	13.59	13.36	13.11	11.41	8.80	5.06
16.875	14.58	14.36	14.12	13.85	12.06	9.30	5.34
17.000	15.36	15.13	14.87	14.59	12.71	9.80	5.63
17.125	16.14	15.90	15.63	15.34	13.36	10.30	5.91
17.250	16.92	16.67	16.39	16.08	14.01	10.80	6.20
17.375	17.70	17.44	17.15	16.83	14.66	11.30	6.49
17.500	18.48	18.21	17.91	17.57	15.31	11.81	6.77
17.625	19.27	18.98	18.67	18.32	15.97	12.31	7.06
17.750	20.05	19.76	19.43	19.07	16.62	12.82	7.35
17.875	20.84	20.53	20.20	19.82	17.28	13.33	7.64
18.000	21.62	21.31	20.96	20.57	17.94	13.83	7.93
18.125	22.41	22.09	21.73	21.32	18.60	14.34	8.22
18.250	23.20	22.86	22.49	22.08	19.26	14.85	8.51
18.375	23.99	23.64	23.26	22.83	19.92	15.36	8.80
18.500	24.78	24.42	24.03	23.59	20.58	15.88	9.09

14¾%
Old Rate

Payment Adjustments
(As % of Old Payment)

NEW RATE (%)	YEARS REMAINING IN TERM						
	30	29	28	27	26	25	24
11.750	-18.89	-18.74	-18.57	-18.39	-18.19	-17.97	-17.73
11.875	-18.12	-17.97	-17.81	-17.64	-17.45	-17.24	-17.01
12.000	-17.35	-17.21	-17.06	-16.89	-16.71	-16.51	-16.29
12.125	-16.57	-16.44	-16.30	-16.14	-15.96	-15.77	-15.57
12.250	-15.80	-15.67	-15.54	-15.39	-15.22	-15.04	-14.84
12.375	-15.02	-14.90	-14.77	-14.63	-14.47	-14.30	-14.12
12.500	-14.24	-14.13	-14.01	-13.87	-13.73	-13.56	-13.39
12.625	-13.46	-13.36	-13.24	-13.12	-12.98	-12.82	-12.66
12.750	-12.68	-12.58	-12.47	-12.36	-12.23	-12.08	-11.93
12.875	-11.90	-11.80	-11.70	-11.59	-11.47	-11.34	-11.19
13.000	-11.11	-11.03	-10.93	-10.83	-10.72	-10.59	-10.46
13.125	-10.33	-10.25	-10.16	-10.07	-9.96	-9.85	-9.72
13.250	-9.54	-9.47	-9.39	-9.30	-9.20	-9.10	-8.98
13.375	-8.75	-8.68	-8.61	-8.53	-8.44	-8.35	-8.24
13.500	-7.96	-7.90	-7.84	-7.76	-7.68	-7.60	-7.50
13.625	-7.17	-7.12	-7.06	-6.99	-6.92	-6.84	-6.76
13.750	-6.38	-6.33	-6.28	-6.22	-6.16	-6.09	-6.01
13.875	-5.58	-5.54	-5.50	-5.45	-5.39	-5.33	-5.26
14.000	-4.79	-4.75	-4.72	-4.67	-4.63	-4.57	-4.52
14.125	-3.99	-3.97	-3.93	-3.90	-3.86	-3.82	-3.77
14.250	-3.20	-3.17	-3.15	-3.12	-3.09	-3.06	-3.02
14.375	-2.40	-2.38	-2.36	-2.34	-2.32	-2.29	-2.26
14.500	-1.60	-1.59	-1.58	-1.56	-1.55	-1.53	-1.51
14.625	-0.80	-0.80	-0.79	-0.78	-0.77	-0.77	-0.76
14.750	0.00	0.00	0.00	0.00	0.00	0.00	0.00
14.875	0.80	0.80	0.79	0.78	0.78	0.77	0.76
15.000	1.60	1.59	1.58	1.57	1.55	1.54	1.52
15.125	2.41	2.39	2.37	2.35	2.33	2.30	2.28
15.250	3.21	3.19	3.17	3.14	3.11	3.08	3.04
15.375	4.02	3.99	3.96	3.93	3.89	3.85	3.80
15.500	4.82	4.79	4.76	4.72	4.67	4.62	4.56
15.625	5.63	5.59	5.55	5.50	5.45	5.39	5.33
15.750	6.44	6.40	6.35	6.30	6.24	6.17	6.10
15.875	7.25	7.20	7.15	7.09	7.02	6.95	6.86
16.000	8.06	8.01	7.95	7.88	7.81	7.72	7.63
16.125	8.87	8.81	8.75	8.67	8.59	8.50	8.40
16.250	9.68	9.62	9.55	9.47	9.38	9.28	9.17
16.375	10.49	10.42	10.35	10.26	10.17	10.06	9.94
16.500	11.30	11.23	11.15	11.06	10.96	10.84	10.72
16.625	12.12	12.04	11.95	11.86	11.75	11.63	11.49
16.750	12.93	12.85	12.76	12.65	12.54	12.41	12.27
16.875	13.75	13.66	13.56	13.45	13.33	13.19	13.04
17.000	14.56	14.47	14.37	14.25	14.12	13.98	13.82
17.125	15.38	15.28	15.17	15.05	14.92	14.76	14.60
17.250	16.19	16.09	15.98	15.85	15.71	15.55	15.37
17.375	17.01	16.90	16.79	16.65	16.51	16.34	16.15
17.500	17.83	17.72	17.59	17.46	17.30	17.13	16.93
17.625	18.64	18.53	18.40	18.26	18.10	17.92	17.72
17.750	19.46	19.35	19.21	19.06	18.90	18.71	18.50
17.875	20.28	20.16	20.02	19.87	19.69	19.50	19.28
18.000	21.10	20.98	20.83	20.67	20.49	20.29	20.06
18.125	21.92	21.79	21.64	21.48	21.29	21.08	20.85
18.250	22.74	22.61	22.46	22.29	22.09	21.88	21.64
18.375	23.56	23.43	23.27	23.09	22.89	22.67	22.42
18.500	24.39	24.24	24.08	23.90	23.70	23.47	23.21
18.625	25.21	25.06	24.90	24.71	24.50	24.26	24.00
18.750	26.03	25.88	25.71	25.52	25.30	25.06	24.79

Payment Adjustments 14¾%
(As % of Old Payment)
Old Rate

NEW RATE (%)	YEARS REMAINING IN TERM						
	23	22	21	20	15	10	5
11.750	-17.47	-17.18	-16.87	-16.53	-14.35	-11.12	-6.51
11.875	-16.76	-16.49	-16.19	-15.86	-13.77	-10.67	-6.24
12.000	-16.05	-15.79	-15.50	-15.19	-13.19	-10.22	-5.98
12.125	-15.34	-15.09	-14.82	-14.52	-12.61	-9.77	-5.71
12.250	-14.63	-14.39	-14.13	-13.85	-12.02	-9.32	-5.44
12.375	-13.91	-13.69	-13.44	-13.17	-11.44	-8.86	-5.18
12.500	-13.19	-12.98	-12.75	-12.49	-10.85	-8.40	-4.91
12.625	-12.47	-12.27	-12.05	-11.81	-10.26	-7.95	-4.64
12.750	-11.75	-11.56	-11.36	-11.13	-9.67	-7.49	-4.37
12.875	-11.03	-10.85	-10.66	-10.45	-9.08	-7.03	-4.10
13.000	-10.31	-10.14	-9.96	-9.76	-8.48	-6.57	-3.83
13.125	-9.58	-9.43	-9.26	-9.08	-7.89	-6.11	-3.56
13.250	-8.85	-8.71	-8.56	-8.39	-7.29	-5.64	-3.29
13.375	-8.12	-7.99	-7.85	-7.70	-6.69	-5.18	-3.02
13.500	-7.39	-7.28	-7.15	-7.01	-6.09	-4.71	-2.74
13.625	-6.66	-6.56	-6.44	-6.31	-5.49	-4.25	-2.47
13.750	-5.93	-5.83	-5.73	-5.62	-4.88	-3.78	-2.20
13.875	-5.19	-5.11	-5.02	-4.92	-4.28	-3.31	-1.92
14.000	-4.45	-4.38	-4.31	-4.22	-3.67	-2.84	-1.65
14.125	-3.71	-3.66	-3.59	-3.52	-3.06	-2.37	-1.38
14.250	-2.97	-2.93	-2.88	-2.82	-2.45	-1.90	-1.10
14.375	-2.23	-2.20	-2.16	-2.12	-1.84	-1.43	-0.83
14.500	-1.49	-1.47	-1.44	-1.41	-1.23	-0.95	-0.55
14.625	-0.75	-0.73	-0.72	-0.71	-0.62	-0.48	-0.28
14.750	0.00	0.00	0.00	0.00	0.00	0.00	0.00
14.875	0.75	0.74	0.72	0.71	0.62	0.48	0.28
15.000	1.50	1.47	1.45	1.42	1.24	0.96	0.55
15.125	2.25	2.21	2.17	2.13	1.86	1.44	0 83
15.250	3.00	2.95	2.90	2.85	2.48	1.92	1.11
15.375	3.75	3.69	3.63	3.56	3.10	2.40	1.39
15.500	4.50	4.43	4.36	4.28	3.72	2.88	1.67
15.625	5.26	5.18	5.09	4.99	4.35	3.36	1.95
15.750	6.01	5.92	5.82	5.71	4.98	3.85	2.23
15.875	6.77	6.67	6.56	6.43	5.61	4.34	2.51
16.000	7.53	7.42	7.29	7.16	6.23	4.82	2.79
16.125	8.29	8.17	8.03	7.88	6.87	5.31	3.07
16.250	9.05	8.92	8.77	8.60	7.50	5.80	3.35
16.375	9.81	9.67	9.51	9.33	8.13	6.29	3.63
16.500	10.58	10.42	10.25	10.05	8.77	6.78	3.91
16.625	11.34	11.17	10.99	10.78	9.40	7.27	4.19
16.750	12.11	11.93	11.73	11.51	10.04	7.77	4.48
16.875	12.87	12.68	12.47	12.24	10.68	8.26	4.76
17.000	13.64	13.44	13.22	12.97	11.32	8.75	5.04
17.125	14.41	14.20	13.96	13.71	11.96	9.25	5.33
17.250	15.18	14.96	14.71	14.44	12.60	9.75	5.61
17.375	15.95	15.72	15.46	15.18	13.25	10.25	5.90
17.500	16.72	16.48	16.21	15.91	13.89	10.74	6.18
17.625	17.49	17.24	16.96	16.65	14.54	11.24	6.47
17.750	18.26	18.00	17.71	17.39	15.19	11.75	6.76
17.875	19.04	18.77	18.46	18.13	15.84	12.25	7.04
18.000	19.81	19.53	19.22	18.87	16.49	12.75	7.33
18.125	20.59	20.30	19.97	19.61	17.14	13.26	7.62
18.250	21.36	21.06	20.73	20.35	17.79	13.76	7.91
18.375	22.14	21.83	21.48	21.09	18.44	14.27	8.20
18.500	22.92	22.60	22.24	21.84	19.10	14.77	8.48
18.625	23.70	23.37	23.00	22.58	19.75	15.28	8.77
18.750	24.48	24.14	23.76	23.33	20.41	15.79	9.06

15%
Old Rate

Payment Adjustments
(As % of Old Payment)

NEW RATE (%)	YEARS REMAINING IN TERM						
	30	29	28	27	26	25	24
12.000	-18.65	-18.51	-18.35	-18.17	-17.98	-17.77	-17.54
12.125	-17.89	-17.75	-17.60	-17.43	-17.25	-17.05	-16.83
12.250	-17.13	-16.99	-16.85	-16.69	-16.52	-16.32	-16.11
12.375	-16.36	-16.24	-16.10	-15.95	-15.78	-15.60	-15.40
12.500	-15.59	-15.48	-15.35	-15.20	-15.04	-14.87	-14.68
12.625	-14.83	-14.72	-14.59	-14.46	-14.31	-14.14	-13.96
12.750	-14.06	-13.95	-13.84	-13.71	-13.57	-13.41	-13.24
12.875	-13.29	-13.19	-13.08	-12.96	-12.83	-12.68	-12.52
13.000	-12.51	-12.42	-12.32	-12.21	-12.08	-11.95	-11.79
13.125	-11.74	-11.66	-11.56	-11.45	-11.34	-11.21	-11.07
13.250	-10.97	-10.89	-10.80	-10.70	-10.59	-10.47	-10.34
13.375	-10.19	-10.12	-10.03	-9.94	-9.84	-9.73	-9.61
13.500	-9.41	-9.35	-9.27	-9.19	-9.09	-8.99	-8.88
13.625	-8.64	-8.57	-8.50	-8.43	-8.34	-8.25	-8.15
13.750	-7.86	-7.80	-7.74	-7.67	-7.59	-7.51	-7.41
13.875	-7.07	-7.02	-6.97	-6.91	-6.84	-6.76	-6.68
14.000	-6.29	-6.25	-6.20	-6.14	-6.08	-6.02	-5.94
14.125	-5.51	-5.47	-5.43	-5.38	-5.33	-5.27	-5.21
14.250	-4.73	-4.69	-4.66	-4.62	-4.57	-4.52	-4.47
14.375	-3.94	-3.91	-3.88	-3.85	-3.81	-3.77	-3.72
14.500	-3.15	-3.13	-3.11	-3.08	-3.05	-3.02	-2.98
14.625	-2.37	-2.35	-2.33	-2.31	-2.29	-2.27	-2.24
14.750	-1.58	-1.57	-1.56	-1.54	-1.53	-1.51	-1.49
14.875	-0.79	-0.78	-0.78	-0.77	-0.76	-0.76	-0.75
15.000	0.00	0.00	0.00	0.00	0.00	0.00	0.00
15.125	0.79	0.79	0.78	0.77	0.77	0.76	0.75
15.250	1.58	1.57	1.56	1.55	1.53	1.52	1.50
15.375	2.38	2.36	2.34	2.32	2.30	2.28	2.25
15.500	3.17	3.15	3.13	3.10	3.07	3.04	3.00
15.625	3.96	3.94	3.91	3.88	3.84	3.80	3.76
15.750	4.76	4.73	4.69	4.66	4.61	4.56	4.51
15.875	5.55	5.52	5.48	5.43	5.38	5.33	5.27
16.000	6.35	6.31	6.27	6.21	6.16	6.09	6.02
16.125	7.15	7.10	7.05	7.00	6.93	6.86	6.78
16.250	7.95	7.90	7.84	7.78	7.71	7.63	7.54
16.375	8.75	8.69	8.63	8.56	8.48	8.40	8.30
16.500	9.55	9.49	9.42	9.34	9.26	9.17	9.06
16.625	10.35	10.28	10.21	10.13	10.04	9.94	9.82
16.750	11.15	11.08	11.00	10.91	10.82	10.71	10.59
16.875	11.95	11.88	11.79	11.70	11.60	11.48	11.35
17.000	12.75	12.67	12.59	12.49	12.38	12.26	12.12
17.125	13.55	13.47	13.38	13.28	13.16	13.03	12.88
17.250	14.36	14.27	14.17	14.06	13.94	13.80	13.65
17.375	15.16	15.07	14.97	14.85	14.72	14.58	14.42
17.500	15.97	15.87	15.76	15.64	15.51	15.36	15.19
17.625	16.77	16.67	16.56	16.43	16.29	16.13	15.96
17.750	17.58	17.47	17.36	17.23	17.08	16.91	16.73
17.875	18.38	18.28	18.15	18.02	17.86	17.69	17.50
18.000	19.19	19.08	18.95	18.81	18.65	18.47	18.27
18.125	20.00	19.88	19.75	19.60	19.44	19.25	19.04
18.250	20.80	20.69	20.55	20.40	20.23	20.03	19.82
18.375	21.61	21.49	21.35	21.19	21.02	20.82	20.59
18.500	22.42	22.29	22.15	21.99	21.81	21.60	21.37
18.625	23.23	23.10	22.95	22.78	22.60	22.38	22.14
18.750	24.04	23.90	23.75	23.58	23.39	23.17	22.92
18.875	24.85	24.71	24.55	24.38	24.18	23.95	23.70
19.000	25.66	25.52	25.36	25.17	24.97	24.74	24.48

Payment Adjustments
(As % of Old Payment)

15% Old Rate

NEW RATE (%)	23	22	21	20	15	10	5
			YEARS REMAINING IN TERM				
12.000	-17.29	-17.01	-16.71	-16.38	-14.25	-11.07	-6.50
12.125	-16.59	-16.32	-16.03	-15.72	-13.67	-10.62	-6.23
12.250	-15.88	-15.63	-15.35	-15.05	-13.10	-10.17	-5.96
12.375	-15.18	-14.94	-14.67	-14.39	-12.52	-9.72	-5.70
12.500	-14.47	-14.24	-13.99	-13.72	-11.94	-9.27	-5.43
12.625	-13.76	-13.55	-13.31	-13.05	-11.35	-8.82	-5.16
12.750	-13.05	-12.85	-12.62	-12.38	-10.77	-8.36	-4.90
12.875	-12.34	-12.15	-11.94	-11.70	-10.19	-7.91	-4.63
13.000	-11.63	-11.45	-11.25	-11.03	-9.60	-7.45	-4.36
13.125	-10.91	-10.74	-10.56	-10.35	-9.01	-7.00	-4.09
13.250	-10.20	-10.04	-9.86	-9.67	-8.42	-6.54	-3.82
13.375	-9.48	-9.33	-9.17	-8.99	-7.83	-6.08	-3.55
13.500	-8.76	-8.62	-8.47	-8.31	-7.24	-5.62	-3.28
13.625	-8.04	-7.91	-7.78	-7.63	-6.64	-5.15	-3.01
13.750	-7.31	-7.20	-7.08	-6.94	-6.04	-4.69	-2.74
13.875	-6.59	-6.49	-6.37	-6.25	-5.45	-4.23	-2.46
14.000	-5.86	-5.77	-5.67	-5.56	-4.85	-3.76	-2.19
14.125	-5.13	-5.06	-4.97	-4.87	-4.25	-3.29	-1.92
14.250	-4.40	-4.34	-4.26	-4.18	-3.64	-2.83	-1.65
14.375	-3.67	-3.62	-3.56	-3.49	-3.04	-2.36	-1.37
14.500	-2.94	-2.90	-2.85	-2.79	-2.44	-1.89	-1.10
14.625	-2.21	-2.18	-2.14	-2.10	-1.83	-1.42	-0.83
14.750	-1.47	-1.45	-1.43	-1.40	-1.22	-0.95	-0.55
14.875	-0.74	-0.73	-0.71	-0.70	-0.61	-0.47	-0.28
15.000	0.00	0.00	0.00	0.00	0.00	0.00	0.00
15.125	0.74	0.73	0.72	0.70	0.61	0.48	0.28
15.250	1.48	1.46	1.43	1.41	1.23	0.95	0.55
15.375	2.22	2.19	2.15	2.11	1.84	1.43	0.83
15.500	2.96	2.92	2.87	2.82	2.46	1.91	1.11
15.625	3.71	3.65	3.59	3.52	3.08	2.39	1.38
15.750	4.45	4.39	4.31	4.23	3.70	2.87	1.66
15.875	5.20	5.12	5.04	4.94	4.32	3.35	1.94
16.000	5.95	5.86	5.76	5.66	4.94	3.83	2.22
16.125	6.69	6.60	6.49	6.37	5.56	4.31	2.50
16.250	7.44	7.34	7.22	7.08	6.19	4.80	2.78
16.375	8.19	8.08	7.94	7.80	6.81	5.28	3.06
16.500	8.95	8.82	8.67	8.51	7.44	5.77	3.34
16.625	9.70	9.56	9.40	9.23	8.07	6.26	3.62
16.750	10.45	10.30	10.14	9.95	8.70	6.75	3.90
16.875	11.21	11.05	10.87	10.67	9.33	7.23	4.18
17.000	11.96	11.79	11.60	11.39	9.96	7.72	4.47
17.125	12.72	12.54	12.34	12.11	10.60	8.22	4.75
17.250	13.48	13.29	13.07	12.84	11.23	8.71	5.03
17.375	14.24	14.04	13.81	13.56	11.87	9.20	5.32
17.500	15.00	14.79	14.55	14.29	12.50	9.70	5.60
17.625	15.76	15.54	15.29	15.02	13.14	10.19	5.88
17.750	16.52	16.29	16.03	15.74	13.78	10.69	6.17
17.875	17.28	17.04	16.77	16.47	14.42	11.19	6.46
18.000	18.05	17.80	17.51	17.20	15.06	11.68	6.74
18.125	18.81	18.55	18.26	17.93	15.71	12.18	7.03
18.250	19.58	19.31	19.00	18.67	16.35	12.68	7.31
18.375	20.34	20.06	19.75	19.40	17.00	13.18	7.60
18.500	21.11	20.82	20.49	20.13	17.64	13.69	7.89
18.625	21.88	21.58	21.24	20.87	18.29	14.19	8.17
18.750	22.65	22.34	21.99	21.60	18.94	14.69	8.46
18.875	23.41	23.10	22.74	22.34	19.59	15.20	8.75
19.000	24.18	23.86	23.49	23.08	20.24	15.70	9.04

Table 3
Borrower's Worst-Case APR

     The annual percentage rate (APR) is the effective interest rate on the loan. It is the result of combining discount points (and certain other loan charges) spread over time with the face (or stated) interest rate. Each discount point is a fee of 1 percent of the loan amount that is charged to the borrower at origination of the loan. Discount points are a onetime charge, so the longer the loan is outstanding, the less effect the points have on the annual percentage rate. Conversely, the more quickly the loan is retired, the greater the effect of discount points on the APR. The body of Table 3 shows a worst-case APR when interest rates rise, assuming that the loan is held to maturity. See Table 5 for the APR with discount points for a loan that is retired after one year.

     Table 3 is used to do worst-case projections for ARMs with annual adjustment caps of 2 percentage points, lifetime caps of both 5 and 6 percentage points, and 30-year terms. The projection assumes that the interest rate on the ARM is adjusted upward each year to the maximum allowed under the caps. The far left-hand column shows original interest rates ranging from 2 percent to 14 percent. The other columns indicate the effective interest rate on the ARM held to maturity for discount points ranging in number from zero to six. The annual percentage rate is the actual yield to the lender (and paid by the borrower) when the loan is held to maturity.

Example

A 30-year adjustable-rate loan is originated at a 5 percent interest rate with three discount points and 2/5 caps. Interest rates rise sharply such that the maximum interest rate is reached every year as follows:

Year 1	5%
Year 2	7%
Year 3	9%
Years 4–30	10%

The APR is 9.42 percent, which is a combination of the annual interest rate shown above on a loan offered with three discount points. To find this, go to page 260 of Table 3, showing a 30-year term and 2 percent annual and 5 percent lifetime caps. Go down the column for three discount points to the row for 5.00 percent initial rate. The APR shown in 9.42 percent.

Borrower's Worst-Case APR

INITIAL RATE (%)	DISCOUNT POINTS CHARGED						
	0	1	2	3	4	5	6
2.00	6.22	6.31	6.40	6.49	6.59	6.68	6.78
2.25	6.46	6.55	6.65	6.74	6.84	6.93	7.03
2.50	6.70	6.79	6.88	6.98	7.08	7.18	7.28
2.75	6.94	7.03	7.13	7.23	7.32	7.43	7.53
3.00	7.18	7.27	7.37	7.47	7.57	7.67	7.78
3.25	7.42	7.51	7.61	7.71	7.82	7.92	8.03
3.50	7.66	7.76	7.85	7.96	8.06	8.17	8.27
3.75	7.90	7.99	8.10	8.20	8.31	8.41	8.52
4.00	8.14	8.24	8.34	8.45	8.55	8.66	8.77
4.25	8.37	8.48	8.58	8.69	8.79	8.90	9.02
4.50	8.61	8.72	8.83	8.93	9.04	9.15	9.26
4.75	8.86	8.96	9.07	9.17	9.29	9.40	9.51
5.00	9.09	9.20	9.31	9.42	9.53	9.65	9.77
5.25	9.33	9.44	9.55	9.66	9.78	9.89	10.01
5.50	9.57	9.68	9.79	9.91	10.02	10.14	10.26
5.75	9.81	9.92	10.03	10.15	10.27	10.39	10.51
6.00	10.05	10.16	10.28	10.39	10.51	10.63	10.75
6.25	10.28	10.40	10.52	10.64	10.76	10.88	11.00
6.50	10.52	10.64	10.76	10.88	11.00	11.13	11.25
6.75	10.76	10.88	11.00	11.12	11.25	11.38	11.50
7.00	11.00	11.12	11.24	11.36	11.49	11.62	11.75
7.25	11.24	11.36	11.48	11.61	11.74	11.86	12.00
7.50	11.47	11.60	11.72	11.85	11.98	12.11	12.25
7.75	11.71	11.84	11.97	12.10	12.22	12.36	12.50
8.00	11.95	12.08	12.21	12.34	12.47	12.61	12.74
8.25	12.19	12.32	12.45	12.58	12.72	12.85	12.99
8.50	12.43	12.55	12.69	12.82	12.96	13.10	13.24
8.75	12.66	12.80	12.93	13.07	13.21	13.35	13.49
9.00	12.90	13.04	13.17	13.31	13.45	13.60	13.74
9.25	13.14	13.27	13.41	13.56	13.70	13.84	13.99
9.50	13.38	13.51	13.65	13.80	13.94	14.09	14.24
9.75	13.62	13.76	13.90	14.04	14.18	14.34	14.49
10.00	13.85	13.99	14.14	14.28	14.43	14.59	14.74
10.25	14.09	14.23	14.38	14.53	14.68	14.83	14.99
10.50	14.32	14.47	14.62	14.77	14.92	15.08	15.24
10.75	14.56	14.71	14.86	15.01	15.17	15.33	15.48
11.00	14.80	14.95	15.10	15.26	15.41	15.58	15.73
11.25	15.04	15.19	15.34	15.50	15.65	15.82	15.98
11.50	15.28	15.43	15.58	15.74	15.91	16.07	16.23
11.75	15.51	15.67	15.83	15.98	16.15	16.31	16.48
12.00	15.75	15.91	16.06	16.23	16.39	16.56	16.74
12.25	15.98	16.14	16.31	16.47	16.64	16.81	16.99
12.50	16.22	16.38	16.55	16.72	16.88	17.06	17.24
12.75	16.46	16.63	16.79	16.95	17.13	17.30	17.49
13.00	16.70	16.86	17.03	17.20	17.38	17.55	17.73
13.25	16.94	17.10	17.27	17.44	17.62	17.80	17.98
13.50	17.17	17.34	17.51	17.69	17.86	18.05	18.23
13.75	17.41	17.58	17.75	17.93	18.11	18.30	18.48
14.00	17.64	17.82	17.99	18.18	18.36	18.54	18.73

Borrower's Worst-Case APR

INITIAL RATE (%)	DISCOUNT POINTS CHARGED						
	0	**1**	**2**	**3**	**4**	**5**	**6**
2.00	6.93	7.02	7.12	7.21	7.31	7.41	7.51
2.25	7.16	7.26	7.35	7.45	7.55	7.65	7.76
2.50	7.40	7.50	7.59	7.70	7.79	7.90	8.00
2.75	7.64	7.74	7.84	7.93	8.04	8.14	8.25
3.00	7.87	7.97	8.07	8.17	8.28	8.39	8.49
3.25	8.11	8.21	8.31	8.42	8.52	8.62	8.73
3.50	8.35	8.45	8.55	8.65	8.76	8.87	8.98
3.75	8.58	8.68	8.79	8.90	9.00	9.11	9.22
4.00	8.82	8.92	9.03	9.14	9.25	9.36	9.47
4.25	9.06	9.16	9.27	9.37	9.48	9.60	9.72
4.50	9.29	9.40	9.51	9.62	9.73	9.84	9.96
4.75	9.53	9.64	9.75	9.86	9.97	10.09	10.20
5.00	9.77	9.87	9.98	10.09	10.21	10.33	10.45
5.25	10.00	10.11	10.22	10.34	10.45	10.57	10.69
5.50	10.23	10.34	10.46	10.58	10.69	10.81	10.94
5.75	10.47	10.58	10.70	10.81	10.94	11.06	11.18
6.00	10.70	10.82	10.94	11.06	11.18	11.30	11.43
6.25	10.94	11.05	11.17	11.30	11.42	11.55	11.68
6.50	11.17	11.29	11.41	11.54	11.66	11.79	11.92
6.75	11.41	11.53	11.65	11.77	11.90	12.03	12.16
7.00	11.64	11.77	11.89	12.02	12.15	12.27	12.41
7.25	11.88	12.00	12.13	12.26	12.38	12.52	12.65
7.50	12.11	12.24	12.37	12.49	12.63	12.76	12.90
7.75	12.35	12.47	12.60	12.73	12.87	13.01	13.15
8.00	12.58	12.71	12.84	12.98	13.11	13.25	13.39
8.25	12.81	12.94	13.08	13.21	13.35	13.49	13.63
8.50	13.05	13.18	13.32	13.45	13.59	13.73	13.88
8.75	13.28	13.41	13.56	13.69	13.84	13.98	14.12
9.00	13.51	13.65	13.79	13.93	14.07	14.22	14.37
9.25	13.75	13.88	14.03	14.17	14.32	14.46	14.62
9.50	13.98	14.12	14.26	14.41	14.56	14.71	14.86
9.75	14.21	14.36	14.50	14.65	14.80	14.95	15.11
10.00	14.45	14.59	14.74	14.89	15.04	15.20	15.36
10.25	14.68	14.83	14.98	15.13	15.28	15.44	15.60
10.50	14.92	15.07	15.22	15.37	15.53	15.69	15.84
10.75	15.15	15.30	15.45	15.61	15.76	15.92	16.09
11.00	15.39	15.54	15.69	15.85	16.01	16.17	16.34
11.25	15.62	15.77	15.93	16.09	16.25	16.41	16.58
11.50	15.86	16.01	16.17	16.33	16.49	16.66	16.83
11.75	16.09	16.25	16.41	16.56	16.74	16.90	17.07
12.00	16.32	16.48	16.64	16.81	16.97	17.14	17.32
12.25	16.55	16.72	16.88	17.05	17.22	17.39	17.57
12.50	16.79	16.95	17.11	17.28	17.46	17.63	17.81
12.75	17.02	17.19	17.35	17.52	17.70	17.88	18.06
13.00	17.25	17.42	17.59	17.77	17.94	18.12	18.30
13.25	17.49	17.66	17.83	18.00	18.13	18.36	18.55
13.50	17.72	17.89	18.07	18.24	18.43	18.61	18.80
13.75	17.96	18.13	18.30	18.49	18.66	18.85	19.04
14.00	18.19	18.36	18.54	18.72	18.91	19.10	19.29

Table 4
Borrower's Worst-Case Monthly Payments

Table 4 is used to perform worst-case *payment* projections of ARMs. The assumptions and loan characteristics are the same as those used in Table 3. In addition, the ARM principal balance at origination is assumed to be $100,000.

The body of Table 4 shows the monthly payments for the first four years of the loan term (payments in the remaining years are the same as in the fourth year). The far left-hand column shows original interest rates of 2 percent to 14 percent. The other columns show monthly payments in dollars for years 1, 2, 3, and 4 of the term.

Payments are linear in proportion to the amount borrowed, so this table can be applied to any loan amount. Just compare the original loan to the $100,000 loan to derive a factor and multiply the factor by the payment for $100,000.

Example

A $100,000 adjustable-rate mortgage is originated at a 6 percent interest rate with a 30-year full amortization term. Caps are 2 percentage points (annual) and 5 percentage points (life of loan).

The initial mortgage payment is $599.55 (year 1). For year 2, interest rates spike to the maximum allowed, which is 8 percent. The payment rises to $730.86.* (This payment is read across the 6 percent initial rate line; see example for Table 2.) The third-year interest rate rises to 10 percent, so the payment becomes $869.06* (read across the 6 percent initial rate line). For years 4–30, the maximum interest rate of 11 percent is reached. The principal and interest payment can reach $939.87,* as shown at the intersection of the 6 percent initial rate line and the 4–30-year column for "Age of Loan." This figure was derived by these tables, which calculated the remaining balance of the loan for each interest rate.

As a check, use Table 2 for the percentage increase:

Year	Old Payment	Old Rate	New Rate	Table 2 increase	Remaining Term	New Payment*
1	$599.55	6%	8%	21.90%	29 years	$730.85
2	$730.85	8%	10%	18.91%	28 years	$869.05
3	$869.05	10%	11%	8.15%	27 years	$939.88
4–30	$939.88					

* Truncation or rounding may affect payments by a cent or two.

Borrower's Worst-Case Monthly Payments
For a $100,000 ARM with Annual Adjustments

INITIAL RATE (%)	AGE OF LOAN (YEARS)			
	1	2	3	4–30
2.00	369.62	474.03	588.81	649.04
2.25	382.25	488.56	605.06	666.08
2.50	395.12	503.32	621.50	683.29
2.75	408.24	518.29	638.13	700.68
3.00	421.60	533.48	654.95	718.23
3.25	435.21	548.89	671.94	735.95
3.50	449.04	564.50	689.10	753.82
3.75	463.12	580.31	706.43	771.84
4.00	477.42	596.32	723.92	790.00
4.25	491.94	612.51	741.57	808.30
4.50	506.69	628.90	759.37	826.74
4.75	521.65	645.47	777.32	845.30
5.00	536.82	662.21	795.41	863.99
5.25	552.20	679.13	813.63	882.79
5.50	567.79	696.21	831.98	901.71
5.75	583.57	713.46	850.46	920.74
6.00	599.55	730.86	869.05	939.87
6.25	615.72	748.41	887.77	959.09
6.50	632.07	766.11	906.59	978.42
6.75	648.60	783.95	925.52	997.83
7.00	665.30	801.93	944.55	1017.33
7.25	682.18	820.04	963.68	1036.90
7.50	699.21	838.27	982.90	1056.56
7.75	716.41	856.63	1002.21	1076.29
8.00	733.76	875.11	1021.61	1096.09
8.25	751.27	893.69	1041.08	1115.95
8.50	768.91	912.39	1060.63	1135.88
8.75	786.70	931.19	1080.26	1155.86
9.00	804.62	950.09	1099.95	1175.90
9.25	822.68	969.09	1119.71	1196.00
9.50	840.85	988.18	1139.53	1216.14
9.75	859.15	1007.36	1159.42	1236.33
10.00	877.57	1026.62	1179.36	1256.57
10.25	896.10	1045.96	1199.35	1276.85
10.50	914.74	1065.38	1219.39	1297.16
10.75	933.48	1084.87	1239.49	1317.52
11.00	952.32	1104.44	1259.62	1337.90
11.25	971.26	1124.07	1279.80	1358.32
11.50	990.29	1143.76	1300.02	1378.77
11.75	1009.41	1163.52	1320.28	1399.25
12.00	1028.61	1183.33	1340.58	1419.76
12.25	1047.90	1203.20	1360.91	1440.29
12.50	1067.26	1223.12	1381.27	1460.84
12.75	1086.69	1243.09	1401.66	1481.42
13.00	1106.20	1263.11	1422.08	1502.02
13.25	1125.77	1283.17	1442.53	1522.63
13.50	1145.41	1303.28	1463.00	1543.26
13.75	1165.11	1323.42	1483.50	1563.91
14.00	1184.87	1343.61	1504.02	1584.58

Borrower's Worst-Case Monthly Payments

For a $100,000 ARM with Annual Adjustments

**30-YEAR TERM
2% Annual Cap
6% Lifetime Cap**

INITIAL RATE (%)	AGE OF LOAN (YEARS)			
	1	2	3	4–30
2.00	369.62	474.03	588.81	711.76
2.25	382.25	488.56	605.06	729.53
2.50	395.12	503.32	621.50	747.47
2.75	408.24	518.29	638.13	765.55
3.00	421.60	533.48	654.95	783.79
3.25	435.21	548.89	671.94	802.17
3.50	449.04	564.50	689.10	820.69
3.75	463.12	580.31	706.43	839.34
4.00	477.42	596.32	723.92	858.12
4.25	491.94	612.51	741.57	877.01
4.50	506.69	628.90	759.37	896.03
4.75	521.65	645.47	777.32	915.16
5.00	536.82	662.21	795.41	934.39
5.25	552.20	679.13	813.63	953.72
5.50	567.79	696.21	831.98	973.15
5.75	583.57	713.46	850.46	992.67
6.00	599.55	730.86	869.05	1012.28
6.25	615.72	748.41	887.77	1031.97
6.50	632.07	766.11	906.59	1051.74
6.75	648.60	783.95	925.52	1071.58
7.00	665.30	801.93	944.55	1091.49
7.25	682.18	820.04	963.68	1111.47
7.50	699.21	838.27	982.90	1131.51
7.75	716.41	856.63	1002.21	1151.62
8.00	733.76	875.11	1021.61	1171.77
8.25	751.27	893.69	1041.08	1191.98
8.50	768.91	912.39	1060.63	1212.24
8.75	786.70	931.19	1080.26	1232.54
9.00	804.62	950.09	1099.95	1252.89
9.25	822.68	969.09	1119.71	1273.28
9.50	840.85	988.18	1139.53	1293.70
9.75	859.15	1007.36	1159.42	1314.17
10.00	877.57	1026.62	1179.36	1334.66
10.25	896.10	1045.96	1199.35	1355.18
10.50	914.74	1065.38	1219.39	1375.74
10.75	933.48	1084.87	1239.49	1396.32
11.00	952.32	1104.44	1259.62	1416.92
11.25	971.26	1124.07	1279.80	1437.55
11.50	990.29	1143.76	1300.02	1458.20
11.75	1009.41	1163.52	1320.28	1478.87
12.00	1028.61	1183.33	1340.58	1499.56
12.25	1047.90	1203.20	1360.91	1520.27
12.50	1067.26	1223.12	1381.27	1540.99
12.75	1086.69	1243.09	1401.66	1561.72
13.00	1106.20	1263.11	1422.08	1582.47
13.25	1125.77	1283.17	1442.53	1603.23
13.50	1145.41	1303.28	1463.00	1624.00
13.75	1165.11	1323.42	1483.50	1644.78
14.00	1184.87	1343.61	1504.02	1665.57

Table 5
APR for First Year

The body of Table 5 shows the annual percentage rate (APR) on the ARM for the first year of its term, including the full effect of discount points taken in the first year.

Table 3 assumes that discount points are spread over the full amortization term (and Table 3 also assumes maximum interest rate increases over the life of the loan). By contrast, Table 5 provides the APR assuming that the loan is paid off at the end of the first year. Thus, for the first year, each discount point is equivalent to an interest rate increase of slightly more than 1 percent.

Example

A 30-year adjustable-rate mortgage is originated at a 6 percent initial interest rate, plus three discount points. Monthly payments are made for 12 months, and then the outstanding balance is paid in full. The three discount points reduce the amount actually borrowed (from $100,000 face to $97,000), yet the full face amount must be repaid, with interest at 6 percent. Thus, the annual percentage rate will be greater than 9 percent (6 percent interest plus three points in one year on a $97,000 loan). It is 9.17 percent, as shown in Table 5. Find this figure at the intersection of 6 percent initial rate and three discount points charged.

APR for First Year

INITIAL RATE (%)	DISCOUNT POINTS CHARGED						
	0	1	2	3	4	5	6
2.00	2.00	3.03	4.07	5.12	6.18	7.26	8.34
2.25	2.25	3.28	4.32	5.37	6.43	7.51	8.60
2.50	2.50	3.53	4.57	5.63	6.69	7.77	8.86
2.75	2.75	3.78	4.82	5.88	6.95	8.02	9.11
3.00	3.00	4.03	5.08	6.13	7.20	8.28	9.37
3.25	3.25	4.28	5.33	6.38	7.45	8.53	9.62
3.50	3.50	4.53	5.58	6.63	7.71	8.79	9.88
3.75	3.75	4.78	5.83	6.89	7.96	9.04	10.14
4.00	4.00	5.03	6.08	7.14	8.21	9.30	10.39
4.25	4.25	5.29	6.33	7.40	8.46	9.55	10.65
4.50	4.50	5.54	6.59	7.65	8.72	9.81	10.91
4.75	4.75	5.79	6.84	7.90	8.98	10.06	11.16
5.00	5.00	6.04	7.09	8.15	9.23	10.32	11.42
5.25	5.25	6.29	7.34	8.41	9.48	10.58	11.68
5.50	5.50	6.54	7.60	8.66	9.74	10.83	11.93
5.75	5.75	6.79	7.85	8.92	10.00	11.08	12.19
6.00	6.00	7.04	8.10	9.17	10.25	11.34	12.44
6.25	6.25	7.29	8.36	9.42	10.50	11.60	12.71
6.50	6.50	7.55	8.61	9.67	10.76	11.85	12.96
6.75	6.75	7.80	8.86	9.93	11.01	12.11	13.22
7.00	7.00	8.05	9.11	10.18	11.27	12.37	13.48
7.25	7.25	8.30	9.36	10.44	11.52	12.62	13.73
7.50	7.50	8.55	9.61	10.69	11.78	12.88	13.99
7.75	7.75	8.80	9.87	10.94	12.03	13.13	14.25
8.00	8.00	9.05	10.12	11.20	12.29	13.39	14.51
8.25	8.25	9.31	10.37	11.45	12.54	13.65	14.76
8.50	8.50	9.56	10.63	11.71	12.80	13.90	15.02
8.75	8.75	9.81	10.88	11.96	13.05	14.16	15.28
9.00	9.00	10.06	11.13	12.21	13.31	14.42	15.54
9.25	9.25	10.31	11.38	12.46	13.56	14.67	15.80
9.50	9.50	10.56	11.63	12.72	13.82	14.93	16.05
9.75	9.75	10.81	11.89	12.98	14.07	15.18	16.31
10.00	10.00	11.07	12.14	13.23	14.33	15.44	16.57
10.25	10.25	11.32	12.39	13.48	14.58	15.70	16.83
10.50	10.50	11.57	12.65	13.73	14.84	15.95	17.08
10.75	10.75	11.82	12.90	13.99	15.09	16.21	17.34
11.00	11.00	12.07	13.15	14.24	15.35	16.47	17.60
11.25	11.25	12.32	13.40	14.50	15.61	16.72	17.86
11.50	11.50	12.57	13.65	14.75	15.86	16.98	18.11
11.75	11.75	12.82	13.91	15.00	16.11	17.24	18.38
12.00	12.00	13.07	14.16	15.26	16.37	17.49	18.63
12.25	12.25	13.32	14.41	15.51	16.63	17.75	18.89
12.50	12.50	13.57	14.67	15.76	16.88	18.01	19.15
12.75	12.75	13.83	14.92	16.02	17.14	18.27	19.41
13.00	13.00	14.08	15.17	16.28	17.39	18.52	19.66
13.25	13.25	14.33	15.42	16.53	17.65	18.78	19.93
13.50	13.50	14.58	15.68	16.78	17.90	19.04	20.18
13.75	13.75	14.83	15.93	17.04	18.16	19.29	20.44
14.00	14.00	15.09	16.18	17.29	18.41	19.55	20.70

Table 6
Value of Below-Market Initial Rate

Table 6 is used to evaluate below-market initial rates on ARMs, commonly referred to as "teaser" rates. Each page covers a range of initial interest rates. Overall, initial rates of 2 percent to 11.75 percent are covered. Each page is divided into two sections: the upper part is used for ARMs with one-year adjustment periods; the lower part is for ARMs with two-year adjustment periods. The far left-hand column shows the built-in increase in the interest rate after the initial period, when the teaser rate expires. Each column covers a different initial interest rate applied to the ARM. The numbers in the body of the table indicate the value of the teaser rate as a percentage of the original principal.

Example

An adjustable-rate mortgage is originated at 6 percent interest with a 30-year amortization term. At origination the fully indexed interest rate for this type of loan was 7 percent. Adjustments are annual. By offering a 6 percent rate for the first year instead of the fully indexed rate of 7 percent, the lender is providing an inducement known as a "teaser" rate.

The body of these tables shows that the benefit to the borrower is 0.96 percent (almost 1 percent) of the loan. To determine this, find the page with a one-year renewal term (top) and initial interest rate of 6 percent.

Because the fully indexed rate is 1 percent higher, the built-in rate increase is 1 percent. Find the intersection of 1.00 percent Rate Increase and 6.00 percent Initial Rate to derive the answer: 0.96 (the teaser is worth almost 1 percent of the loan value).

Given the above example, but assuming that the initial adjustment period is two years, the value of the initial rate reduction is 1.84 percent.

Value of
Below-Market Initial Rate

One-Year Renewal Term
INITIAL RATE (%)

RATE INCR (%)	2.00	2.25	2.50	2.75	3.00	3.25	3.50	3.75
0.00%	0.00	0.00	0.00	0.00	0.00	0.00	0.00	0.00
0.25%	0.24	0.24	0.24	0.24	0.24	0.24	0.24	0.24
0.50%	0.49	0.49	0.49	0.49	0.49	0.49	0.49	0.48
0.75%	0.73	0.73	0.73	0.73	0.73	0.73	0.73	0.73
1.00%	0.97	0.97	0.97	0.97	0.97	0.97	0.97	0.97
1.25%	1.21	1.21	1.21	1.21	1.21	1.21	1.21	1.21
1.50%	1.46	1.45	1.45	1.45	1.45	1.45	1.45	1.45
1.75%	1.70	1.69	1.69	1.69	1.69	1.69	1.69	1.68
2.00%	1.94	1.93	1.93	1.93	1.93	1.93	1.92	1.92
2.25%	2.17	2.17	2.17	2.17	2.17	2.16	2.16	2.16
2.50%	2.41	2.41	2.41	2.41	2.40	2.40	2.40	2.40
2.75%	2.65	2.65	2.65	2.64	2.64	2.64	2.64	2.63
3.00%	2.89	2.89	2.88	2.88	2.88	2.87	2.87	2.87
3.25%	3.12	3.12	3.12	3.12	3.11	3.11	3.11	3.10
3.50%	3.36	3.36	3.35	3.35	3.35	3.34	3.34	3.34
3.75%	3.60	3.59	3.59	3.59	3.58	3.58	3.58	3.57
4.00%	3.83	3.83	3.82	3.82	3.82	3.81	3.81	3.81
4.25%	4.06	4.06	4.06	4.05	4.05	4.05	4.04	4.04
4.50%	4.30	4.29	4.29	4.29	4.28	4.28	4.27	4.27
4.75%	4.53	4.53	4.52	4.52	4.51	4.51	4.51	4.50
5.00%	4.76	4.76	4.75	4.75	4.74	4.74	4.74	4.73
5.25%	4.99	4.99	4.98	4.98	4.98	4.97	4.97	4.96
5.50%	5.22	5.22	5.22	5.21	5.21	5.20	5.20	5.19
5.75%	5.45	5.45	5.45	5.44	5.44	5.43	5.42	5.42
6.00%	5.68	5.68	5.67	5.67	5.66	5.66	5.65	5.65

Two-Year Renewal Term
INITIAL RATE (%)

RATE INCR (%)	2.00	2.25	2.50	2.75	3.00	3.25	3.50	3.75
0.00%	0.00	0.00	0.00	0.00	0.00	0.00	0.00	0.00
0.25%	0.48	0.48	0.48	0.47	0.47	0.47	0.47	0.47
0.50%	0.95	0.95	0.95	0.95	0.95	0.94	0.94	0.94
0.75%	1.42	1.42	1.42	1.42	1.41	1.41	1.41	1.41
1.00%	1.89	1.89	1.89	1.88	1.88	1.88	1.87	1.87
1.25%	2.36	2.36	2.35	2.35	2.35	2.34	2.34	2.33
1.50%	2.83	2.82	2.82	2.81	2.81	2.80	2.80	2.79
1.75%	3.29	3.28	3.28	3.27	3.27	3.26	3.26	3.25
2.00%	3.75	3.74	3.74	3.73	3.72	3.72	3.71	3.70
2.25%	4.21	4.20	4.19	4.19	4.18	4.17	4.16	4.16
2.50%	4.66	4.65	4.65	4.64	4.63	4.62	4.62	4.61
2.75%	5.12	5.11	5.10	5.09	5.08	5.07	5.06	5.06
3.00%	5.57	5.56	5.55	5.54	5.53	5.52	5.51	5.50
3.25%	6.01	6.01	6.00	5.99	5.98	5.97	5.95	5.94
3.50%	6.46	6.45	6.44	6.43	6.42	6.41	6.40	6.39
3.75%	6.91	6.89	6.88	6.87	6.86	6.85	6.84	6.82
4.00%	7.35	7.34	7.32	7.31	7.30	7.29	7.27	7.26
4.25%	7.79	7.77	7.76	7.75	7.74	7.72	7.71	7.70
4.50%	8.22	8.21	8.20	8.18	8.17	8.16	8.14	8.13
4.75%	8.66	8.65	8.63	8.62	8.60	8.59	8.57	8.56
5.00%	9.09	9.08	9.06	9.05	9.03	9.02	9.00	8.99
5.25%	9.52	9.51	9.49	9.48	9.46	9.44	9.43	9.41
5.50%	9.95	9.94	9.92	9.90	9.89	9.87	9.85	9.84
5.75%	10.38	10.36	10.34	10.33	10.31	10.29	10.28	10.26
6.00%	10.80	10.78	10.77	10.75	10.73	10.71	10.70	10.68

Value of Below-Market Initial Rate

One-Year Renewal Term

RATE INCR (%)	INITIAL RATE (%)							
	4.00	4.25	4.50	4.75	5.00	5.25	5.50	5.75
0.00	0.00	0.00	0.00	0.00	0.00	0.00	0.00	0.00
0.25	0.24	0.24	0.24	0.24	0.24	0.24	0.24	0.24
0.50	0.48	0.48	0.48	0.48	0.48	0.48	0.48	0.48
0.75	0.73	0.72	0.72	0.72	0.72	0.72	0.72	0.72
1.00	0.97	0.96	0.96	0.96	0.96	0.96	0.96	0.96
1.25	1.20	1.20	1.20	1.20	1.20	1.20	1.20	1.20
1.50	1.44	1.44	1.44	1.44	1.44	1.44	1.44	1.43
1.75	1.68	1.68	1.68	1.68	1.68	1.67	1.67	1.67
2.00	1.92	1.92	1.92	1.92	1.91	1.91	1.91	1.91
2.25	2.16	2.16	2.15	2.15	2.15	2.15	2.15	2.14
2.50	2.40	2.39	2.39	2.39	2.39	2.38	2.38	2.38
2.75	2.63	2.63	2.63	2.62	2.62	2.62	2.62	2.61
3.00	2.87	2.86	2.86	2.86	2.85	2.85	2.85	2.85
3.25	3.10	3.10	3.10	3.09	3.09	3.09	3.08	3.08
3.50	3.34	3.33	3.33	3.33	3.32	3.32	3.32	3.31
3.75	3.57	3.57	3.56	3.56	3.55	3.55	3.55	3.54
4.00	3.80	3.80	3.79	3.79	3.79	3.78	3.78	3.77
4.25	4.03	4.03	4.03	4.02	4.02	4.01	4.01	4.01
4.50	4.27	4.26	4.26	4.25	4.25	4.24	4.24	4.24
4.75	4.50	4.49	4.49	4.48	4.48	4.47	4.47	4.46
5.00	4.73	4.72	4.72	4.71	4.71	4.70	4.70	4.69
5.25	4.96	4.95	4.95	4.94	4.94	4.93	4.93	4.92
5.50	5.19	5.18	5.18	5.17	5.17	5.16	5.15	5.15
5.75	5.41	5.41	5.40	5.40	5.39	5.39	5.38	5.38
6.00	5.64	5.64	5.63	5.63	5.62	5.61	5.61	5.60

Two-Year Renewal Term

RATE INCR (%)	INITIAL RATE (%)							
	4.00	4.25	4.50	4.75	5.00	5.25	5.50	5.75
0.00	0.00	0.00	0.00	0.00	0.00	0.00	0.00	0.00
0.25	0.47	0.47	0.47	0.47	0.47	0.47	0.47	0.46
0.50	0.94	0.94	0.94	0.93	0.93	0.93	0.93	0.93
0.75	1.40	1.40	1.40	1.40	1.39	1.39	1.39	1.39
1.00	1.87	1.86	1.86	1.86	1.85	1.85	1.85	1.84
1.25	2.33	2.32	2.32	2.32	2.31	2.31	2.30	2.30
1.50	2.79	2.78	2.78	2.77	2.77	2.76	2.76	2.75
1.75	3.24	3.24	3.23	3.23	3.22	3.21	3.21	3.20
2.00	3.70	3.69	3.68	3.68	3.67	3.66	3.66	3.65
2.25	4.15	4.14	4.13	4.13	4.12	4.11	4.10	4.10
2.50	4.60	4.59	4.58	4.57	4.57	4.56	4.55	4.54
2.75	5.05	5.04	5.03	5.02	5.01	5.00	4.99	4.98
3.00	5.49	5.48	5.47	5.46	5.45	5.44	5.43	5.42
3.25	5.93	5.92	5.91	5.90	5.89	5.88	5.87	5.86
3.50	6.37	6.36	6.35	6.34	6.33	6.32	6.30	6.29
3.75	6.81	6.80	6.79	6.78	6.76	6.75	6.74	6.72
4.00	7.25	7.24	7.22	7.21	7.20	7.18	7.17	7.15
4.25	7.68	7.67	7.65	7.64	7.63	7.61	7.60	7.58
4.50	8.11	8.10	8.08	8.07	8.05	8.04	8.02	8.01
4.75	8.54	8.53	8.51	8.50	8.48	8.47	8.45	8.43
5.00	8.97	8.95	8.94	8.92	8.91	8.89	8.87	8.85
5.25	9.40	9.38	9.36	9.34	9.33	9.31	9.29	9.27
5.50	9.82	9.80	9.78	9.77	9.75	9.73	9.71	9.69
5.75	10.24	10.22	10.20	10.18	10.17	10.15	10.13	10.11
6.00	10.66	10.64	10.62	10.60	10.58	10.56	10.54	10.52

Value of Below-Market Initial Rate

One-Year Renewal Term
INITIAL RATE (%)

RATE INCR (%)	6.00	6.25	6.50	6.75	7.00	7.25	7.50	7.75
0.00	0.00	0.00	0.00	0.00	0.00	0.00	0.00	0.00
0.25	0.24	0.24	0.24	0.24	0.24	0.24	0.24	0.24
0.50	0.48	0.48	0.48	0.48	0.48	0.48	0.48	0.48
0.75	0.72	0.72	0.72	0.72	0.72	0.72	0.71	0.71
1.00	0.96	0.96	0.96	0.95	0.95	0.95	0.95	0.95
1.25	1.20	1.19	1.19	1.19	1.19	1.19	1.19	1.19
1.50	1.43	1.43	1.43	1.43	1.43	1.43	1.42	1.42
1.75	1.67	1.67	1.67	1.66	1.66	1.66	1.66	1.66
2.00	1.91	1.90	1.90	1.90	1.90	1.90	1.89	1.89
2.25	2.14	2.14	2.14	2.13	2.13	2.13	2.13	2.12
2.50	2.38	2.37	2.37	2.37	2.37	2.36	2.36	2.36
2.75	2.61	2.61	2.60	2.60	2.60	2.60	2.59	2.59
3.00	2.84	2.84	2.84	2.83	2.83	2.83	2.82	2.82
3.25	3.08	3.07	3.07	3.07	3.06	3.06	3.06	3.05
3.50	3.31	3.30	3.30	3.30	3.29	3.29	3.29	3.28
3.75	3.54	3.54	3.53	3.53	3.52	3.52	3.52	3.51
4.00	3.77	3.77	3.76	3.76	3.75	3.75	3.75	3.74
4.25	4.00	4.00	3.99	3.99	3.98	3.98	3.98	3.97
4.50	4.23	4.23	4.22	4.22	4.21	4.21	4.20	4.20
4.75	4.46	4.46	4.45	4.45	4.44	4.44	4.43	4.43
5.00	4.69	4.68	4.68	4.67	4.67	4.66	4.66	4.65
5.25	4.92	4.91	4.91	4.90	4.90	4.89	4.88	4.88
5.50	5.14	5.14	5.13	5.13	5.12	5.12	5.11	5.10
5.75	5.37	5.37	5.36	5.35	5.35	5.34	5.34	5.33
6.00	5.60	5.59	5.58	5.58	5.57	5.57	5.56	5.55

Two-Year Renewal Term
INITIAL RATE (%)

RATE INCR (%)	6.00	6.25	6.50	6.75	7.00	7.25	7.50	7.75
0.00	0.00	0.00	0.00	0.00	0.00	0.00	0.00	0.00
0.25	0.46	0.46	0.46	0.46	0.46	0.46	0.46	0.46
0.50	0.92	0.92	0.92	0.92	0.92	0.92	0.91	0.91
0.75	1.38	1.38	1.38	1.37	1.37	1.37	1.37	1.36
1.00	1.84	1.84	1.83	1.83	1.82	1.82	1.82	1.81
1.25	2.29	2.29	2.28	2.28	2.28	2.27	2.27	2.26
1.50	2.75	2.74	2.73	2.73	2.72	2.72	2.71	2.71
1.75	3.20	3.19	3.18	3.18	3.17	3.16	3.16	3.15
2.00	3.64	3.64	3.63	3.62	3.61	3.61	3.60	3.59
2.25	4.09	4.08	4.07	4.06	4.05	4.05	4.04	4.03
2.50	4.53	4.52	4.51	4.50	4.49	4.49	4.48	4.47
2.75	4.97	4.96	4.95	4.94	4.93	4.92	4.91	4.90
3.00	5.41	5.40	5.39	5.38	5.37	5.36	5.34	5.33
3.25	5.85	5.83	5.82	5.81	5.80	5.79	5.78	5.76
3.50	6.28	6.27	6.25	6.24	6.23	6.22	6.20	6.19
3.75	6.71	6.70	6.68	6.67	6.66	6.64	6.63	6.62
4.00	7.14	7.13	7.11	7.10	7.08	7.07	7.06	7.04
4.25	7.57	7.55	7.54	7.52	7.51	7.49	7.48	7.46
4.50	7.99	7.98	7.96	7.95	7.93	7.91	7.90	7.88
4.75	8.42	8.40	8.38	8.37	8.35	8.33	8.32	8.30
5.00	8.84	8.82	8.80	8.79	8.77	8.75	8.73	8.71
5.25	9.26	9.24	9.22	9.20	9.18	9.17	9.15	9.13
5.50	9.67	9.65	9.64	9.62	9.60	9.58	9.56	9.54
5.75	10.09	10.07	10.05	10.03	10.01	9.99	9.97	9.95
6.00	10.50	10.48	10.46	10.44	10.42	10.40	10.38	10.35

Value of Below-Market Initial Rate

One-Year Renewal Term
INITIAL RATE (%)

RATE INCR (%)	8.00	8.25	8.50	8.75	9.00	9.25	9.50	9.75
0.00	0.00	0.00	0.00	0.00	0.00	0.00	0.00	0.00
0.25	0.24	0.24	0.24	0.24	0.24	0.24	0.24	0.24
0.50	0.48	0.48	0.47	0.47	0.47	0.47	0.47	0.47
0.75	0.71	0.71	0.71	0.71	0.71	0.71	0.71	0.71
1.00	0.95	0.95	0.95	0.95	0.95	0.94	0.94	0.94
1.25	1.19	1.18	1.18	1.18	1.18	1.18	1.18	1.18
1.50	1.42	1.42	1.42	1.42	1.41	1.41	1.41	1.41
1.75	1.65	1.65	1.65	1.65	1.65	1.65	1.64	1.64
2.00	1.89	1.89	1.88	1.88	1.88	1.88	1.88	1.87
2.25	2.12	2.12	2.12	2.11	2.11	2.11	2.11	2.10
2.50	2.35	2.35	2.35	2.35	2.34	2.34	2.34	2.34
2.75	2.59	2.58	2.58	2.58	2.57	2.57	2.57	2.57
3.00	2.82	2.81	2.81	2.81	2.81	2.80	2.80	2.80
3.25	3.05	3.05	3.04	3.04	3.04	3.03	3.03	3.02
3.50	3.28	3.28	3.27	3.27	3.26	3.26	3.26	3.25
3.75	3.51	3.50	3.50	3.50	3.49	3.49	3.48	3.48
4.00	3.74	3.73	3.73	3.73	3.72	3.72	3.71	3.71
4.25	3.97	3.96	3.96	3.95	3.95	3.94	3.94	3.93
4.50	4.19	4.19	4.18	4.18	4.17	4.17	4.17	4.16
4.75	4.42	4.42	4.41	4.41	4.40	4.40	4.39	4.39
5.00	4.65	4.64	4.64	4.63	4.63	4.62	4.62	4.61
5.25	4.87	4.87	4.86	4.86	4.85	4.85	4.84	4.83
5.50	5.10	5.09	5.09	5.08	5.08	5.07	5.06	5.06
5.75	5.32	5.32	5.31	5.31	5.30	5.29	5.29	5.28
6.00	5.55	5.54	5.54	5.53	5.52	5.52	5.51	5.50

Two-Year Renewal Term
INITIAL RATE (%)

RATE INCR (%)	8.00	8.25	8.50	8.75	9.00	9.25	9.50	9.75
0.00	0.00	0.00	0.00	0.00	0.00	0.00	0.00	0.00
0.25	0.46	0.45	0.45	0.45	0.45	0.45	0.45	0.45
0.50	0.91	0.91	0.91	0.90	0.90	0.90	0.90	0.90
0.75	1.36	1.36	1.35	1.35	1.35	1.35	1.34	1.34
1.00	1.81	1.81	1.80	1.80	1.79	1.79	1.79	1.78
1.25	2.26	2.25	2.25	2.24	2.24	2.23	2.23	2.22
1.50	2.70	2.70	2.69	2.68	2.68	2.67	2.67	2.66
1.75	3.14	3.14	3.13	3.12	3.12	3.11	3.10	3.10
2.00	3.58	3.58	3.57	3.56	3.55	3.55	3.54	3.53
2.25	4.02	4.01	4.00	4.00	3.99	3.98	3.97	3.96
2.50	4.46	4.45	4.44	4.43	4.42	4.41	4.40	4.39
2.75	4.89	4.88	4.87	4.86	4.85	4.84	4.83	4.82
3.00	5.32	5.31	5.30	5.29	5.28	5.27	5.25	5.24
3.25	5.75	5.74	5.73	5.71	5.70	5.69	5.68	5.67
3.50	6.18	6.17	6.15	6.14	6.13	6.11	6.10	6.09
3.75	6.60	6.59	6.58	6.56	6.55	6.53	6.52	6.51
4.00	7.03	7.01	7.00	6.98	6.97	6.95	6.94	6.92
4.25	7.45	7.43	7.42	7.40	7.38	7.37	7.35	7.34
4.50	7.87	7.85	7.83	7.82	7.80	7.78	7.77	7.75
4.75	8.28	8.26	8.25	8.23	8.21	8.19	8.18	8.16
5.00	8.70	8.68	8.66	8.64	8.62	8.61	8.59	8.57
5.25	9.11	9.09	9.07	9.05	9.03	9.01	8.99	8.97
5.50	9.52	9.50	9.48	9.46	9.44	9.42	9.40	9.38
5.75	9.93	9.91	9.89	9.87	9.84	9.82	9.80	9.78
6.00	10.33	10.31	10.29	10.27	10.25	10.23	10.20	10.18

Value of
Below-Market Initial Rate

One-Year Renewal Term
INITIAL RATE (%)

RATE INCR (%)	10.00	10.25	10.50	10.75	11.00	11.25	11.50	11.75
0.00	0.00	0.00	0.00	0.00	0.00	0.00	0.00	0.00
0.25	0.24	0.24	0.24	0.24	0.23	0.23	0.23	0.23
0.50	0.47	0.47	0.47	0.47	0.47	0.47	0.47	0.47
0.75	0.71	0.71	0.70	0.70	0.70	0.70	0.70	0.70
1.00	0.94	0.94	0.94	0.94	0.94	0.93	0.93	0.93
1.25	1.17	1.17	1.17	1.17	1.17	1.17	1.17	1.16
1.50	1.41	1.41	1.40	1.40	1.40	1.40	1.40	1.40
1.75	1.64	1.64	1.64	1.63	1.63	1.63	1.63	1.63
2.00	1.87	1.87	1.87	1.86	1.86	1.86	1.86	1.86
2.25	2.10	2.10	2.10	2.09	2.09	2.09	2.09	2.08
2.50	2.33	2.33	2.33	2.32	2.32	2.32	2.32	2.31
2.75	2.56	2.56	2.56	2.55	2.55	2.55	2.54	2.54
3.00	2.79	2.79	2.79	2.78	2.78	2.78	2.77	2.77
3.25	3.02	3.02	3.01	3.01	3.01	3.00	3.00	3.00
3.50	3.25	3.25	3.24	3.24	3.23	3.23	3.23	3.22
3.75	3.48	3.47	3.47	3.46	3.46	3.46	3.45	3.45
4.00	3.70	3.70	3.69	3.69	3.69	3.68	3.68	3.67
4.25	3.93	3.93	3.92	3.92	3.91	3.91	3.90	3.90
4.50	4.16	4.15	4.15	4.14	4.14	4.13	4.13	4.12
4.75	4.38	4.38	4.37	4.37	4.36	4.35	4.35	4.34
5.00	4.61	4.60	4.59	4.59	4.58	4.58	4.57	4.57
5.25	4.83	4.82	4.82	4.81	4.81	4.80	4.79	4.79
5.50	5.05	5.05	5.04	5.03	5.03	5.02	5.02	5.01
5.75	5.28	5.27	5.26	5.26	5.25	5.24	5.24	5.23
6.00	5.50	5.49	5.48	5.48	5.47	5.46	5.46	5.45

Two-Year Renewal Term
INITIAL RATE (%)

RATE INCR (%)	10.00	10.25	10.50	10.75	11.00	11.25	11.50	11.75
0.00	0.00	0.00	0.00	0.00	0.00	0.00	0.00	0.00
0.25	0.45	0.45	0.45	0.45	0.44	0.44	0.44	0.44
0.50	0.89	0.89	0.89	0.89	0.89	0.88	0.88	0.88
0.75	1.34	1.33	1.33	1.33	1.33	1.32	1.32	1.32
1.00	1.78	1.77	1.77	1.77	1.76	1.76	1.75	1.75
1.25	2.22	2.21	2.21	2.20	2.20	2.19	2.19	2.18
1.50	2.65	2.65	2.64	2.64	2.63	2.63	2.62	2.61
1.75	3.09	3.08	3.08	3.07	3.06	3.06	3.05	3.04
2.00	3.52	3.51	3.51	3.50	3.49	3.48	3.48	3.47
2.25	3.95	3.94	3.94	3.93	3.92	3.91	3.90	3.89
2.50	4.38	4.37	4.36	4.35	4.34	4.33	4.32	4.31
2.75	4.81	4.80	4.79	4.78	4.76	4.75	4.74	4.73
3.00	5.23	5.22	5.21	5.20	5.19	5.17	5.16	5.15
3.25	5.65	5.64	5.63	5.62	5.60	5.59	5.58	5.57
3.50	6.07	6.06	6.05	6.03	6.02	6.01	5.99	5.98
3.75	6.49	6.48	6.46	6.45	6.43	6.42	6.41	6.39
4.00	6.91	6.89	6.88	6.86	6.85	6.83	6.82	6.80
4.25	7.32	7.30	7.29	7.27	7.26	7.24	7.22	7.21
4.50	7.73	7.72	7.70	7.68	7.66	7.65	7.63	7.61
4.75	8.14	8.12	8.11	8.09	8.07	8.05	8.03	8.02
5.00	8.55	8.53	8.51	8.49	8.47	8.46	8.44	8.42
5.25	8.95	8.94	8.92	8.90	8.88	8.86	8.84	8.82
5.50	9.36	9.34	9.32	9.30	9.28	9.26	9.24	9.22
5.75	9.76	9.74	9.72	9.70	9.67	9.65	9.63	9.61
6.00	10.16	10.14	10.12	10.09	10.07	10.05	10.03	10.00

Table 7
Annual Loan
Balance Remaining

The body of Table 7 offers the remaining balance of a fixed-rate self-amortizing loan after a period of time. The remaining balance is expressed in dollars per hundred borrowed, or a percentage of the original loan.

Tables are provided for original loan terms of 15 and 30 years and interest rates from 2 percent to 15 percent, in $1/4$ percent increments. Balances at every year of age are offered for 15-year original terms. For 30-year original terms, balances are offered for the first 10 years of age, then by 5-year increments.

Example 1

A loan with a 6 percent initial rate and 30-year-term is originated for $100,000. After one year, the principal balance is 98.77 percent of the initial loan, which is approximately $98,770. The factor of 98.77 is found at the intersection of 6 percent under "Interest Rate (%)" and 29 "Years Remaining in Term."

After 20 years, 54 percent of the initial principal remains. The factor of 54.00 is at the intersection of 6 percent interest and 10 years remaining in term. Therefore, the remaining balance after 20 years will be $54,000. (The loan had a 30-year full amortization term, so after 20 years, 10 years remain.)

Example 2

Table 7 can also be used for adjustable-rate loans. Loans of different interest rates amortize at different speeds. Table 7 may therefore easily be used for the initial fixed-rate period of an ARM. Remaining balances of ARM loans require a new calculation for each period.

For example, assume the following loan:

- Original principal: $100,000
- Original term: 30 years
- Initial interest rate: 6 percent for the first year
- Adjusted interest rate: 8 percent for the second year

What is the balance after two years?
Solution:

1. Find the balance remaining after one year: 98.77% = $98,770
2. To find the amount of an 8 percent rate loan reduced during the second year, divide the 28-year factor by the 29-year factor:

$$\text{28-year factor at 8\%} \quad \frac{98.26}{99.16} = 0.9909$$
$$\text{29-year factor at 8\%}$$

3. Multiply the result by 98.77 to derive the remaining balance:

$$98.77 \times 0.9909 = 97.871$$
$$97.871 \times \$100,000 = \$97,871$$

Percentage of Original Loan Amount

30-YEAR TERM
Fixed Interest Rate

INTEREST RATE (%)	YEARS REMAINING IN TERM						
	29	28	27	26	25	24	23
2.00	97.54	95.03	92.48	89.87	87.20	84.49	81.72
2.25	97.64	95.22	92.75	90.23	87.64	85.00	82.30
2.50	97.73	95.41	93.02	90.58	88.08	85.51	82.87
2.75	97.82	95.59	93.29	90.92	88.50	86.00	83.43
3.00	97.91	95.76	93.54	91.26	88.91	86.48	83.98
3.25	98.00	95.93	93.79	91.59	89.31	86.95	84.52
3.50	98.08	96.09	94.04	91.90	89.70	87.41	85.04
3.75	98.16	96.25	94.27	92.21	90.08	87.86	85.56
4.00	98.24	96.41	94.50	92.51	90.45	88.30	86.06
4.25	98.31	96.56	94.72	92.81	90.81	88.72	86.55
4.50	98.39	96.70	94.93	93.09	91.16	89.14	87.03
4.75	98.46	96.84	95.14	93.36	91.50	89.54	87.49
5.00	98.52	96.97	95.34	93.63	91.83	89.94	87.95
5.25	98.59	97.10	95.54	93.89	92.15	90.32	88.39
5.50	98.65	97.23	95.73	94.14	92.46	90.69	88.82
5.75	98.71	97.35	95.91	94.38	92.76	91.05	89.23
6.00	98.77	97.47	96.08	94.61	93.05	91.40	89.64
6.25	98.83	97.58	96.25	94.84	93.34	91.74	90.03
6.50	98.88	97.69	96.42	95.06	93.61	92.07	90.42
6.75	98.93	97.79	96.57	95.27	93.88	92.38	90.79
7.00	98.98	97.89	96.73	95.47	94.13	92.69	91.15
7.25	99.03	97.99	96.87	95.67	94.38	92.99	91.50
7.50	99.08	98.08	97.01	95.86	94.62	93.28	91.83
7.75	99.12	98.17	97.15	96.04	94.85	93.56	92.16
8.00	99.16	98.26	97.28	96.22	95.07	93.83	92.48
8.25	99.21	98.34	97.41	96.39	95.28	94.09	92.78
8.50	99.24	98.42	97.53	96.55	95.49	94.34	93.08
8.75	99.28	98.50	97.64	96.71	95.69	94.58	93.36
9.00	99.32	98.57	97.75	96.86	95.88	94.81	93.64
9.25	99.35	98.64	97.86	97.00	96.06	95.04	93.91
9.50	99.38	98.71	97.96	97.14	96.24	95.25	94.16
9.75	99.41	98.77	98.06	97.27	96.41	95.46	94.41
10.00	99.44	98.83	98.15	97.40	96.57	95.66	94.65
10.25	99.47	98.89	98.24	97.52	96.73	95.85	94.88
10.50	99.50	98.94	98.33	97.64	96.88	96.04	95.10
10.75	99.53	99.00	98.41	97.75	97.03	96.22	95.31
11.00	99.55	99.05	98.49	97.86	97.16	96.39	95.52
11.25	99.57	99.10	98.56	97.97	97.30	96.55	95.72
11.50	99.60	99.14	98.63	98.06	97.42	96.71	95.90
11.75	99.62	99.19	98.70	98.16	97.55	96.86	96.09
12.00	99.64	99.23	98.77	98.25	97.66	97.00	96.26
12.25	99.66	99.27	98.83	98.33	97.77	97.14	96.43
12.50	99.67	99.31	98.89	98.42	97.88	97.28	96.59
12.75	99.69	99.34	98.95	98.50	97.98	97.40	96.74
13.00	99.71	99.38	99.00	98.57	98.08	97.53	96.89
13.25	99.72	99.41	99.05	98.64	98.18	97.64	97.03
13.50	99.74	99.44	99.10	98.71	98.26	97.75	97.17
13.75	99.75	99.47	99.15	98.78	98.35	97.86	97.30
14.00	99.77	99.50	99.19	98.84	98.43	97.96	97.43
14.25	99.78	99.53	99.23	98.90	98.51	98.06	97.55
14.50	99.79	99.55	99.27	98.95	98.58	98.15	97.66
14.75	99.80	99.58	99.31	99.01	98.65	98.24	97.77
15.00	99.81	99.60	99.35	99.06	98.72	98.33	97.87

Percentage of Original Loan Amount

INTEREST RATE (%)	YEARS REMAINING IN TERM					
	22	21	20	15	10	5
2.00	78.89	76.01	73.06	57.44	40.17	21.09
2.25	79.54	76.71	73.82	58.35	41.04	21.67
2.50	80.17	77.40	74.56	59.26	41.91	22.26
2.75	80.80	78.08	75.30	60.16	42.79	22.86
3.00	81.41	78.75	76.02	61.05	43.66	23.46
3.25	82.01	79.41	76.73	61.94	44.54	24.07
3.50	82.59	80.06	77.43	62.81	45.41	24.68
3.75	83.17	80.69	78.11	63.68	46.28	25.30
4.00	83.73	81.31	78.78	64.54	47.15	25.92
4.25	84.28	81.91	79.44	65.39	48.02	26.55
4.50	84.82	82.51	80.09	66.23	48.89	27.18
4.75	85.34	83.09	80.72	67.06	49.75	27.81
5.00	85.85	83.65	81.34	67.88	50.61	28.45
5.25	86.35	84.21	81.95	68.69	51.47	29.08
5.50	86.84	84.75	82.54	69.49	52.32	29.73
5.75	87.31	85.28	83.12	70.28	53.16	30.37
6.00	87.77	85.79	83.69	71.05	54.00	31.01
6.25	88.22	86.29	84.24	71.81	54.84	31.66
6.50	88.66	86.78	84.78	72.56	55.67	32.30
6.75	89.08	87.25	85.30	73.30	56.49	32.95
7.00	89.49	87.72	85.81	74.02	57.30	33.60
7.25	89.89	88.17	86.31	74.73	58.11	34.25
7.50	90.28	88.60	86.79	75.43	58.91	34.89
7.75	90.65	89.03	87.27	76.11	59.70	35.54
8.00	91.02	89.44	87.72	76.78	60.48	36.19
8.25	91.37	89.84	88.17	77.44	61.25	36.83
8.50	91.71	90.22	88.60	78.08	62.02	37.48
8.75	92.04	90.60	89.02	78.71	62.77	38.12
9.00	92.36	90.96	89.43	79.33	63.52	38.76
9.25	92.67	91.31	89.82	79.93	64.26	39.40
9.50	92.97	91.65	90.21	80.52	64.98	40.04
9.75	93.26	91.98	90.58	81.10	65.70	40.67
10.00	93.53	92.30	90.94	81.66	66.41	41.30
10.25	93.80	92.61	91.29	82.21	67.10	41.93
10.50	94.06	92.90	91.62	82.75	67.79	42.56
10.75	94.31	93.19	91.95	83.28	68.47	43.18
11.00	94.55	93.47	92.26	83.79	69.13	43.80
11.25	94.78	93.74	92.57	84.29	69.79	44.42
11.50	95.00	93.99	92.86	84.77	70.44	45.03
11.75	95.22	94.24	93.14	85.24	71.07	45.64
12.00	95.42	94.48	93.42	85.71	71.69	46.24
12.25	95.62	94.71	93.68	86.15	72.31	46.84
12.50	95.81	94.93	93.94	86.59	72.91	47.44
12.75	96.00	95.15	94.18	87.02	73.50	48.03
13.00	96.17	95.35	94.42	87.43	74.09	48.62
13.25	96.34	95.55	94.65	87.83	74.66	49.20
13.50	96.50	95.74	94.87	88.22	75.22	49.78
13.75	96.66	95.92	95.08	88.60	75.77	50.35
14.00	96.81	96.10	95.28	88.97	76.31	50.92
14.25	96.95	96.27	95.48	89.33	76.84	51.49
14.50	97.09	96.43	95.67	89.68	77.36	52.05
14.75	97.22	96.59	95.85	90.02	77.87	52.60
15.00	97.35	96.74	96.02	90.34	78.37	53.15

Percentage of
Original Loan Amount

INTEREST RATE (%)	YEARS REMAINING IN TERM						
	14	13	12	11	10	9	8
2.00	94.23	88.33	82.32	76.19	69.94	63.55	57.04
2.25	94.33	88.53	82.60	76.54	70.34	63.99	57.50
2.50	94.44	88.73	82.88	76.88	70.73	64.43	57.96
2.75	94.54	88.92	83.15	77.22	71.13	64.86	58.42
3.00	94.64	89.12	83.43	77.56	71.52	65.29	58.88
3.25	94.74	89.31	83.69	77.90	71.91	65.72	59.33
3.50	94.84	89.49	83.96	78.23	72.29	66.15	59.78
3.75	94.94	89.68	84.22	78.56	72.68	66.57	60.23
4.00	95.03	89.86	84.48	78.89	73.06	66.99	60.68
4.25	95.13	90.05	84.74	79.21	73.44	67.42	61.13
4.50	95.22	90.23	85.00	79.53	73.81	67.83	61.58
4.75	95.31	90.40	85.25	79.85	74.19	68.25	62.02
5.00	95.41	90.58	85.50	80.17	74.56	68.66	62.46
5.25	95.50	90.75	85.75	80.48	74.92	69.07	62.90
5.50	95.58	90.92	85.99	80.79	75.29	69.48	63.34
5.75	95.67	91.09	86.23	81.09	75.65	69.89	63.78
6.00	95.76	91.26	86.47	81.40	76.01	70.29	64.21
6.25	95.84	91.42	86.71	81.70	76.36	70.69	64.65
6.50	95.93	91.58	86.94	82.00	76.72	71.08	65.07
6.75	96.01	91.74	87.17	82.29	77.07	71.48	65.50
7.00	96.09	91.90	87.40	82.58	77.41	71.87	65.93
7.25	96.17	92.05	87.63	82.87	77.76	72.26	66.35
7.50	96.25	92.21	87.85	83.15	78.10	72.64	66.77
7.75	96.33	92.36	88.07	83.44	78.43	73.03	67.19
8.00	96.40	92.51	88.29	83.72	78.77	73.41	67.60
8.25	96.48	92.65	88.50	83.99	79.10	73.78	68.01
8.50	96.55	92.80	88.71	84.26	79.42	74.16	68.42
8.75	96.62	92.94	88.92	84.53	79.75	74.53	68.83
9.00	96.69	93.08	89.12	84.80	80.07	74.89	69.23
9.25	96.76	93.22	89.33	85.06	80.39	75.26	69.63
9.50	96.83	93.35	89.53	85.32	80.70	75.62	70.03
9.75	96.90	93.49	89.72	85.58	81.01	75.97	70.43
10.00	96.97	93.62	89.92	85.83	81.32	76.33	70.82
10.25	97.03	93.75	90.11	86.08	81.62	76.68	71.21
10.50	97.10	93.88	90.30	86.33	81.92	77.03	71.59
10.75	97.16	94.00	90.49	86.57	82.22	77.37	71.98
11.00	97.22	94.13	90.67	86.81	82.51	77.71	72.36
11.25	97.28	94.25	90.85	87.05	82.80	78.05	72.73
11.50	97.34	94.37	91.03	87.29	83.09	78.38	73.11
11.75	97.40	94.49	91.20	87.52	83.37	78.71	73.48
12.00	97.46	94.60	91.38	87.75	83.65	79.04	73.84
12.25	97.52	94.71	91.55	87.97	83.93	79.36	74.21
12.50	97.57	94.83	91.72	88.19	84.20	79.68	74.57
12.75	97.63	94.94	91.88	88.41	84.47	80.00	74.93
13.00	97.68	95.04	92.04	88.63	84.74	80.31	75.28
13.25	97.73	95.15	92.20	88.84	85.00	80.62	75.63
13.50	97.79	95.26	92.36	89.05	85.26	80.93	75.98
13.75	97.84	95.36	92.51	89.26	85.52	81.23	76.32
14.00	97.89	95.46	92.67	89.46	85.77	81.53	76.66
14.25	97.94	95.56	92.82	89.66	86.02	81.83	77.00
14.50	97.98	95.65	92.96	89.86	86.27	82.12	77.33
14.75	98.03	95.75	93.11	90.05	86.51	82.41	77.66
15.00	98.08	95.84	93.25	90.24	86.75	82.70	77.99

Percentage of Original Loan Amount

INTEREST RATE (%)	YEARS REMAINING IN TERM						
	7	6	5	4	3	2	1
2.00	50.40	43.63	36.71	29.66	22.47	15.13	7.64
2.25	50.87	44.08	37.14	30.04	22.78	15.36	7.77
2.50	51.33	44.54	37.57	30.43	23.10	15.59	7.89
2.75	51.80	45.00	38.00	30.81	23.42	15.83	8.02
3.00	52.26	45.45	38.43	31.20	23.75	16.07	8.15
3.25	52.73	45.91	38.86	31.59	24.07	16.31	8.29
3.50	53.19	46.37	39.30	31.98	24.40	16.55	8.42
3.75	53.65	46.82	39.73	32.37	24.72	16.79	8.55
4.00	54.12	47.28	40.16	32.76	25.05	17.03	8.69
4.25	54.58	47.74	40.60	33.15	25.38	17.28	8.82
4.50	55.03	48.19	41.03	33.55	25.72	17.53	8.96
4.75	55.49	48.65	41.47	33.94	26.05	17.78	9.10
5.00	55.95	49.10	41.90	34.34	26.39	18.03	9.24
5.25	56.41	49.56	42.34	34.74	26.72	18.28	9.38
5.50	56.86	50.01	42.78	35.13	27.06	18.53	9.52
5.75	57.31	50.47	43.21	35.53	27.40	18.78	9.66
6.00	57.76	50.92	43.65	35.93	27.74	19.04	9.80
6.25	58.21	51.37	44.09	36.33	28.08	19.30	9.95
6.50	58.66	51.82	44.52	36.73	28.42	19.56	10.09
6.75	59.11	52.27	44.96	37.13	28.77	19.81	10.24
7.00	59.55	52.72	45.39	37.54	29.11	20.08	10.39
7.25	60.00	53.17	45.83	37.94	29.46	20.34	10.54
7.50	60.44	53.62	46.26	38.34	29.80	20.60	10.69
7.75	60.88	54.06	46.70	38.74	30.15	20.86	10.84
8.00	61.31	54.51	47.13	39.15	30.50	21.13	10.99
8.25	61.75	54.95	47.56	39.55	30.85	21.40	11.14
8.50	62.18	55.39	48.00	39.95	31.19	21.66	11.29
8.75	62.61	55.83	48.43	40.35	31.54	21.93	11.44
9.00	63.04	56.27	48.86	40.76	31.90	22.20	11.60
9.25	63.47	56.71	49.29	41.16	32.25	22.47	11.75
9.50	63.89	57.14	49.72	41.56	32.60	22.74	11.91
9.75	64.31	57.57	50.15	41.97	32.95	23.01	12.07
10.00	64.73	58.01	50.58	42.37	33.30	23.29	12.22
10.25	65.15	58.44	51.00	42.77	33.66	23.56	12.38
10.50	65.56	58.86	51.43	43.17	34.01	23.84	12.54
10.75	65.97	59.29	51.85	43.58	34.36	24.11	12.70
11.00	66.38	59.71	52.28	43.98	34.72	24.39	12.86
11.25	66.79	60.14	52.70	44.38	35.07	24.66	13.02
11.50	67.19	60.56	53.12	44.78	35.43	24.94	13.18
11.75	67.59	60.97	53.54	45.18	35.78	25.22	13.35
12.00	67.99	61.39	53.95	45.58	36.13	25.50	13.51
12.25	68.38	61.80	54.37	45.97	36.49	25.77	13.67
12.50	68.77	62.21	54.78	46.37	36.84	26.05	13.84
12.75	69.16	62.62	55.20	46.77	37.20	26.33	14.00
13.00	69.55	63.03	55.61	47.16	37.55	26.61	14.17
13.25	69.93	63.43	56.02	47.56	37.90	26.89	14.33
13.50	70.31	63.83	56.42	47.95	38.26	27.17	14.50
13.75	70.69	64.23	56.83	48.34	38.61	27.46	14.66
14.00	71.06	64.63	57.23	48.73	38.97	27.74	14.83
14.25	71.44	65.02	57.64	49.12	39.32	28.02	15.00
14.50	71.80	65.42	58.04	49.51	39.67	28.30	15.17
14.75	72.17	65.80	58.43	49.90	40.02	28.58	15.34
15.00	72.53	66.19	58.83	50.29	40.37	28.87	15.51

BARRON'S BUSINESS KEYS

Each "key" explains approximately 50 concepts and provides a glossary and index. Each book: Paperback, approx. 160 pp., 4³⁄₁₆" x 7", $5.95 – $7.95 Can., $8.50 – $11.50.

Keys to Buying Foreclosed and Bargain Homes, 2nd Edition *(1294-5)

Keys to Incorporating, 3rd Edition *(1300-3)

Keys to Investing in Common Stocks, 4th Edition *(2447-1)

Keys to Investing in Options and Futures, 3rd Edition *(1303-8)

Keys to Investing in Real Estate, 3rd Edition *(1295-3)

Keys to Investing in Your 401(K), 2nd Edition *(1298-8) *(1296-1)

Keys to Personal Financial Planning, 3rd Edition *(2099-9)

Keys to Purchasing a Condo or a Co-op, 2nd Edition *(1305-4)

Keys to Reading an Annual Report, 3rd Edition *(1306-2)

Keys to Risks and Rewards of Penny Stocks (4300-6)

Keys to Starting a Small Business (4487-8)

Keys to Understanding the Financial News, 3rd Edition *(1308-9)

Available at bookstores, or by mail from Barron's. Enclose check or money order for full amount plus sales tax where applicable and 18% for postage & handling (minimum charge $5.95). NY State and California residents add sales tax. Prices subject to change without notice. $ = U.S. dollars • Can. $ = Canadian dollars • Barron's ISBN Prefix, 0-8120, *indicates 0-7641

Barron's Educational Series, Inc.
250 Wireless Boulevard • Hauppauge, NY 11788
In Canada: Georgetown Book Warehouse
34 Armstrong Avenue, Georgetown, Ont. L7G 4R9
www.barronseduc.com

(#10) R 4/04

More selected BARRON'S titles:

BARRON'S ACCOUNTING HANDBOOK, 3rd ED.
Joel G. Siegel and Jae K. Shim
Provides accounting rules, guidelines, formulas and techniques, etc., to help students and business professionals work out accounting problems.
Hardcover, $35.00, Canada $48.95/ISBN 0-7641-5282-3, 880 pages

REAL ESTATE HANDBOOK, 5th ED.
Jack P. Friedman and Jack C. Harris
A dictionary/reference for everyone in real estate. Defines approximately 2000 legal, financial, and architectural terms.
Hardcover, $35.00, Canada $49.00/ ISBN 0-7641-5263-7, approx. 780 pages

HOW TO PREPARE FOR THE REAL ESTATE LICENSING EXAMS: SALESPERSON, BROKER, APPRAISER, 6th ED.
Bruce Lindeman and Jack P. Friedman
Reviews current exam topics and features updated model exams and supplemental exams, all with explained answers.
Paperback, $14.95, Canada $21.00/ISBN 0-7641-0773-9, 340 pages

BARRON'S FINANCE AND INVESTMENT HANDBOOK, 6th ED.
John Downes and Jordan Elliot Goodman
This hard-working handbook of essential information defines more than 3000 key terms, and explores 30 basic investment opportunities. The investment information is thoroughly up-to-date.
Hardcover, $39.95, Canada $55.95/ISBN 0-7641-5554-7, 1408 pages

FINANCIAL TABLES FOR MONEY MANAGEMENT
Stephen S. Solomon, Dr. Clifford Marshall, Martin Pepper, Jack P. Friedman, and Jack C. Harris
Pocket-sized handbooks of interest and investment rate tables used easily by average investors and mortgage holders.
Each book: Paperback.
Adjustable Rate Mortgages, 2nd Ed., $8.95, Canada $11.50/0-8120-1529-0, 288 pp.
Canadian Mortgage Payments, 3rd Ed., Canada $8.95/0-7641-2374-2, 336 pp.
Mortgage Payments, 3rd Ed., $7.95, Canada $11.50/0-7641-1801-3, 336 pp.
Real Estate Loans, 3rd Ed., $7.95, Canada $11.50/0-7641-1800-5, 350 pp.

Books may be purchased at your bookstore or by mail from Barron's. Enclose check or money order for total amount plus sales tax where applicable and 18% for postage and handling (minimum charge $5.95). NY State and California residents add sales tax. Prices subject to change without notice.

Barron's Educational Series, Inc.
250 Wireless Blvd., Hauppauge, NY 11788
In Canada: Georgetown Book Warehouse
34 Armstrong Ave., Georgetown, Ontario L7G 4R9
www.barronseduc.com

(#11) R4/04

More selected BARRON'S titles:

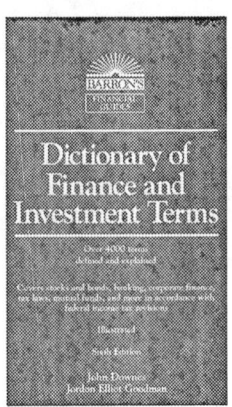

(#12) R 5/04